Sharī^{c}ah – Islamic Law

Sharīᶜah

Islamic Law

by

ʿAbd ar-Raḥmān I. Doi

revised and expanded by

ʿAbdaṣṣamad Clarke

Ta-Ha Publishers Ltd

www.taha.co.uk

Second Revised Edition

Published by: Ta-Ha Publishers Ltd.
Unit 4, The Windsor Centre
Windsor Grove
London
SE27 9NT

Website: www.taha.co.uk

E-mail: sales@taha.co.uk

First edition by: Abdur Rahman I. Doi

Second Edition by: Abdur Rahman I. Doi and Abdassamad Clarke

General Editor: Dr. Abia Afsar-Siddiqui

Typeset in Koufra by: Abdassamad Clarke

A catalogue record of this book is available from the British Library.

ISBN-13: 978 1 842000 85 3 (paperback)

ISBN-13: 978 1 842000 87 8 (hardback)

Printed and bound by: Mega Printing, Turkey

E-mail: msu@mega.com.tr

Web-site: http://www.mega.com.t

بسم الله الرحمن الرحيم

In the name of Allah, the All-Merciful, the Most Merciful.
May Allah bless Muḥammad and his family and companions
and grant them perfect peace.

Contents

Tables

Preface

THIS BOOK BY THE LATE ᶜABD AR-RAḤMĀN I. DOI, may Allah be merciful to him, has long been essential in English. Ta-Ha Publishers felt that it was, however, long overdue a new edition.

Apart from editing it, my work has principally been as follows:

1. To use throughout the translation of Qur'ān by Abdalhaqq and Aisha Bewley, *The Noble Qur'ān: a rendition of its meanings in English.* This is not only because of the excellence of its English but also because of its scholarship and its drawing on the corpus of traditional commentaries on the Qur'ān, so that it is the most reliable and orthodox translation, as well as the most readable.

2. To locate and ascertain all the hadith used and to translate them with reference to the standard commentaries.

3. I have used Ibn Juzayy al-Kalbī's *Taqrīb al-wuṣūl ilā ᶜilm al-uṣūl* for some of the passages on the *uṣūl al-fiqh,* his *al-Qawānīn al-fiqhiyyah* for many of the passages of *fiqh,* particularly because of his presenting the positions of the four *madhhabs* in the context of the agreement (*ijmāᶜ*) of the scholars, and his *Kitāb at-tashīl li ᶜulūm at-tanzīl* as one of the most reliable *tafsīr* works on the Qur'ān, all in my own translation.

There are quite a few other sources drawn upon, such as the *tafsīr* of al-Qurṭubī, the *Ḥāshiyah* of ad-Dasūqī on the *Sharḥ al-kabīr* of ad-Dardīr, *al-Waraqāt* of al-Juwaynī and a number of other sources, and where possible I give them in my own translations from the Arabic.

4. I have also used Aisha Bewley's unpublished translation of the *Risālah* of Ibn Abī Zayd al-Qayrawānī which is generously available from her website. This is because the author drew on the *Risālah* a great deal, and not only in the places where he acknowledged it, but in many other passages of the work, presumably because of his close acquaintance with it in Nigeria.

The original intention was simply to revise and typeset the book, but as work progressed it became clear that this would not be sufficient, and Ta-Ha Publishers came to feel that so much new work had been done that it warranted the addition of my name as co-author. Certainly, I did not wish to ascribe to the author opinions that were not his, and wanted as much as possible to remain true to his intent and approach in this book. I hope I have been somewhat successful in that, but it has undoubtedly not been completely possible.

The book is a significant one, working, as it does, through the *muᶜāmalāt* or 'ordinary transactions' of the *Sharīᶜah*, sometimes giving the judgements of the four schools and the major *ᶜulamā'*, which is very necessary for us in this day if only to have a good general knowledge of the *dīn*, but also so that we can show the correct respect for the judgements of the four schools and courtesy towards each other. This is, however, in no sense to encourage the kind of mix-and-match, do-it-yourself *Sharīᶜah* that has been prevalent in recent decades.

The book clearly does not contain the entire *Sharīᶜah* because it does not include the acts of worship since they have been so thoroughly treated elsewhere. Moreover, this book cannot be regarded as an exhaustive treatment of the subject matter in the sense that might be expected of a 'manual'. It is, however, a serious introduction to something the committed student would have to pursue with properly qualified teachers, preferably in a traditional setting, and in the medium of the Arabic language.

It would have been impossible to complete this book without the help of a number of other people, first of all the publishers, Mr Afsar Siddiqui and his daughter Dr Abia Afsar-Siddiqui whose support throughout the project and determination to see it completed to the highest possible standards was indispensable. Then I would like to mention the help of my wife Suád Østergaard whose careful reading and editing of the first draft was vital. Shaykh Ali Laraki al-Husseini gave great help in the most difficult passages in the book on the subject of inheritance, and I am grateful to Hajj Uthman Ibrahim-Morisson for advice that helped to shape the final form of the book.

Introduction

WHAT, WE MIGHT ASK, is the significance of the publication of a weighty tome such as this on the *Sharīᶜah* of Islam at this time, in this language and in these countries? We assume the reader's understanding that the legal systems built up by Europeans over centuries incorporating basic liberties such as habeas corpus have been dismantled and are being replaced increasingly by the most totalitarian structures, which informed commentators see as perilously close to fascism. It was perhaps inevitable that something built on the frail foundations of human thought could be thus perverted, but was nonetheless terribly shocking to those who saw the accelerated process during their own lifetimes and recognised it for what it was.

It seems there is no going back. Once the framework of liberties has been demolished, there would appear to be no way to restore it. Its demolition had long preceded the more draconian manifestations. The classically trained Conservative MP Enoch Powell recognised that apparently minor legislation such as speeding fines had in essence abolished the whole basis of British law, for common law (also the basis of US law), depended on someone reporting an offence to an officer of the law who took statements and gathered evidence, later to be presented before a judge and twelve peers of the accused in a jury, the accused being represented by defence counsel and able to challenge the evidence or bring evidence of his own. Then the jury, having considered the case for the prosecution and the case for the defence, passed judgement, and the judge, weighing the case and the judgement carefully, passed sentence. However, in speeding and parking fines a single person sums up in his person the arresting officer, prosecution – the counsel for the defence having been abolished – judge, jury, and executioner of the sentence, thus effectively ending a legal system that had endured from before the time of King John and which had been erected on the basis of foundations such as the Magna Carta. We have not even begun to talk about the legislation for the 'terrorist threat'.

Now, the world simultaneously slips into a lawless chaos, in which unbridled corporate greed is paralleled by organised crime, street thugs and hoodlums, both unchecked in any effective sense by government and police, along with the rise of a totalitarian control of the citizenry unparalleled in world history and of such dimensions as neither Hitler nor Stalin could have aspired to. The two poles of political motion, a conservatism that protected the aristocratic and arguably benign rule of monarchy and a socialism that campaigned for the rights of the poor and the workers, have been replaced by 'centrist' parties which, without exception, kow-tow to banking and financial powers, leaving democratic voters with no alternative whatsoever. This is the end of the European-inspired dream of a just order based on rational thought and the will of the people, all of them. This totalitarian order now extends from the Amazonian jungles to the mountains of Afghanistan, and is close to realisation of its most cherished aim: a world state.

Lest anyone think that the world state will be our salvation, let them reflect on the fact that our European and American states, which feel themselves so civilised, and are so smug about the apparent peace and lack of warfare on home soil, in reality grew out of horrendous civil wars, after which they resolved never again to fight on their own turf, achieving this by the simple expedient of being continually involved in wars elsewhere. The English civil war led rapidly to the Glorious Revolution, establishment of the Bank of England and the birth of the British Empire out of the barrel of the gun trained on the hapless Chinese, Indians and Africans et al. The US civil war equally led to the century and more in which the

US was continuously at war somewhere on the earth, that country's economy largely based also on weapons manufacture, leading to the remark of Lewis Lapham, editor of Harper's, to the effect that most recent US wars have been advertising, because the economy largely depends on arms exports.

Thus, human aggression has not been tamed in Judaeo-Christian society but merely unleashed elsewhere in the world in series of genocidal wars against the poorer peoples of the earth. The world state will not be a placid and peaceful middle class suburb, but something akin to the dystopic visions of our artists and thinkers: a high-tech élite in highly policed towers surrounded by disenfranchised and criminalised underclasses of almost sub-humans. The war will no longer be 'out there' but increasingly, as we witness today, right in the cities: permanent civil war, although it will never be identified as such. "Only a god can save us now," in the words of the great German philosopher Martin Heidegger in his one and only newspaper interview.

Only a god can save us now, since it is precisely the lack of belief in a god that drives the nihilism of the age. But Heidegger deliberately chose the indefinite form 'a god', since there is no hope that the Judaeo-Christian God will do so, his demise having been seen so clearsightedly by Nietzshe.

When in the meeting a group of us had with former Home Secretary Charles Clarke we suggested that the key to terrorism is nihilism we overestimated his education. If he had understood Dostoyevsky he would have known that the origins of the all-too-obvious nihilism of the anarchist suicide bombers lay in their parents' middle-class, middle-aged atheist materialism and failure of moral courage, and he would have seen that the young suicide bombers who so terrified him were the children of a society with no belief left in anything except living for the moment, that 'living' being a suicidal rush to extinction with the aid of every single unhygienic sexual practice and toxic substance available.

Only a god can save us and it is only the *Sharīᶜah* that can replace the monstrous distortion that is modern law, yet the suggestion that the *Sharīᶜah* as 'a system' can save us is utterly fatuous, for indeed in the hands of a totalitarian state, even the *Sharīᶜah,* which is an embodiment of mercy, can be turned into a tool of tyranny and oppression.

To understand this, we must understand something of the term 'guidance', which has two aspects: first, explaining and making clear what is right and what is wrong. In that sense, this book is a manifestation of that first type of guidance, since it is an explanation of what is right and wrong as shown by the last revelation of the Divine to all mankind by means of the Messenger Muḥammad ﷺ. However, the second guidance is precisely the one that is needed at this point, and without it the *Sharīᶜah* will be ineffective.

It is good to point out to the alcoholic that his addiction is killing him, but it is often superfluous since he is exactly the person who knows it better than anyone else. The wisdom and the guidance lies in showing him how to disengage from his suicidal habit. For this a deep knowledge of the human self is required. Unfortunately modern man is burdened with a ghastly materialistic view of the human self that inevitably traps him in an addiction that is so extreme that it amounts to an addiction to his own destruction. How else to explain the apparently unstoppable devastation of the biosphere and of every form of human conviviality that we experience almost daily?

For this benign science of the human self there is a precondition, which is that the human being wants it and asks for it, and only a god can help us, but since the God of the Judaeo-Christian age is dead, that anthropomorphic deity, whose theological contradictions weighed him down, not only must we turn to a god, but to One Who is beyond our existing conceptions of Him, and we must ask for the wisdom that will allow us not to hurtle to our own destruction, and will allow us to benefit from this first guidance, this clear manifestation of what is right and what is wrong that is the *Sharīᶜah* of Islam.

And because things don't just fall down from heaven but have their pathways in this world and on this earth, we must ask to meet the people who have this guidance, who embody it and who can pass it on, having received it in transmission over the generations from the best of mankind, the last Messenger from the Lord of the Worlds, Muḥammad, may Allah bless him and grant him peace.

Chapter 1

Dīn and Society

CONTEXT IS ALMOST EVERYTHING. One of the Companions was asked in a gathering whether a homicide could be forgiven, and he replied that no, a killer cannot be forgiven, and that to kill a *mu'min* dooms the person to Hell forever. On another occasion, a man asked the same question, and the Companion answered, yes, no one must ever despair of the mercy of Allah, and Allah can forgive everything to the one who turns to Him sincerely. When the man had gone, his companions asked why on these two occasions he had given such utterly contradictory answers? He replied that the first man was on his way to kill someone and he had to prevent the murder. The second man had actually killed someone and was full of regret over it, and so he had not wanted to cut him off from hoping in Allah and turning in *tawbah* to Him.

This profound story is about much more than adapting the knowledge of the *dīn* in a pragmatic way to circumstances, since it has almost everything that you might need to know for the real application of *Sharīᶜah*. It is, of course, understood that the story only refers to the rights of Allah. As to the deceased person's rights and those of his relative, they have to be dealt with by a competent *qāḍī*.

The first matters that concern us are: what manner of individual is it who will live by *Sharīᶜah* and, equally importantly, apply it in his role as *amīr*, *qāḍī* or *muftī*, and what type of society is it in which it will be put into effect?

To answer the second question first, it can only be the case that the *Sharīᶜah* will be put into effect in exactly this society we have today, for if we are to wait for the ideal society, we will be utopians and dreamers. Thus, if it is this society, then it is vital that we understand it. If we entertain our own fantasies about how it is or how it ought to be, then that will impede us in our work. Indeed, if we also give way to fantasy about what Islam is and what the *Sharīᶜah* is, we will be doubly incapacitated.

First, we must understand that in both east and west today there is only one society, and that the old categories of Muslim and non-Muslim societies no longer apply. I do not mean that as a legal judgement, but as a historical understanding. Today's world is the world of global capitalism, but please do not automatically understand that term in a Marxist sense. In the world of capitalism the various religions are allowed temple-space. This is the old Roman form.

Christian society was doomed, once it had made its compact with Rome in the early centuries, to perpetuate the Roman secular form. It was not that Rome was christianised, but that Christianity was romanised. The secular world is the Roman state transmitted to us over the centuries by Christianity. The Romans, faced with multifarious tribes and cultures, simply destroyed them and granted the survivors permission to become Roman citizens and to maintain temples to their gods. The modern age is one in which the global order permits religions the status of cults and the right to maintain temples, as long as the religions adhere to the basic order of the 'Empire'. This is as much true in the hills of Afghanistan today as on the streets of New York.

This must be known with clarity before embarking on any action, and it is the reason why, almost without exception, the fighters have failed. Any analysis that pits East against West, or Islam against the West is simply not grappling with reality. The guns and bombs must be put away, not in order to become moderate Muslims as opposed to fundamentalists, but because otherwise we have not understood the real nature of the fight that is being waged in today's world, and make no mistake, war is raging as never before.

We say, and Allah knows best, that it is vital for people concerned about the *Sharī^{c}ah* to be knowledgeable about the nature of our society today, and there is probably no way to that knowledge without some understanding of European history; the Renaissance, the agricultural and industrial revolutions, the French revolution, etc., the history and philosophy of science, and the history of banking and finance, among other things. Moreover, there is no way to understand those things in the predigested form they are fed to us today by the media and the academic world which, with honourable exceptions, have both become shameless propagandists for the global secular order. Thus, the scholar is going to have to extend his scope beyond the already considerable work involved in understanding the *Sharī^{c}ah*.

Sharī^{c}ah derives from the same root as the ordinary modern Arabic word for a road: *shāri^c*. The nature of a road, as opposed to a path (*ṭarīq*), is of a broad way in between two edges, and thus the *Sharī^{c}ah* is a broad way whose parameters are what is obligatory and what is forbidden, and that if someone is in between these two then they are on the road. It is the failure of literalist understandings that everything is reduced to a text, and the discrimination that is vital between what is *ḥarām* and what is disliked but not *ḥarām* has been lost, as has the difference between what is obligatory and what is recommended. The blurring of these distinctions has been catastrophic for the Muslims.

The Islamic *Sharī^{c}ah* is a broad and generous way whose obligations and prohibitions are minimal and easily understandable. Advancing onwards to the embodiment of what is recommended and the abandonment of what is disliked has always been the way of the right-acting Muslims in their spiritual progress, but they have taken it as a discipline on themselves without imposing it on others, just as the great *awliyā'* have then abandoned much that is *ḥalāl* in their desire that nothing come between them and their Lord, without considering for a second that they should require that of other people. So we have a glimpse here of the individuals who will embody the *Sharīᶜah*. However, we are going to defer its further exploration to a later point; for the moment we need to understand more about *Sharīᶜah*.

For a linguistic understanding we resort to Lane's *Arabic-English Lexicon*, which is simply a translation into English of the classic Arabic-Arabic lexicons, and thus an accurate reflection of how the Muslims understand the Arabic language: "*Sharīᶜah: ... a watering place; a resort of drinkers...* signifies *a place of descent to water.*" Thus, we have a sense of nourishment and a 'way' with a purpose and a goal.

Approaching it from another perspective, we are faced with the now commonplace reference to the *Sharīᶜah* as 'Islamic law' or '*Sharīᶜah* law'.

Surprisingly, we use the word 'law' in two distinct ways:

First, as a description of a process in nature that appears to be invariable and often has expression in a regular way, usually expressed mathematically, i.e. a physical law. The *Oxford Dictionary* has:

> a regularity in natural occurrences, esp. as formulated or propounded in particular instances (the laws of nature; the law of gravity; Parkinson's law).

Second, law as the rules governing a society. Again from the *Oxford Dictionary*:

> a. a rule enacted or customary in a community and recognized as enjoining or prohibiting certain actions and enforced by the imposition of penalties.
>
> b. a body of such rules (the law of the land; forbidden under Scots law).

Although the growth of these two forms has been side by side, it is surprising to find that they do not impinge on each other, for the implication of the former is that there is simply nothing accidental at all in the world, and that every single thing is interconnected with every other single thing. This would imply that gathering a few democratic 'representatives' to thrash out legislation on the basis of their opinions, and more importantly, the opinions of whoever funded their election campaigns, is unlikely to produce a law that is meaningful in the scientific sense. So there is a clash between these two foundational aspects of the society of which, whether we like it or not, we are members.

Islamic law is *revealed,* i.e. it emerges from a seeing into how things are, granted by the Real, the True. Within this *Sharīcah* there is the legislation of limits, punishments and penalties, compensatory payments for homicide and physical injury, etc., that are in harmony with how things are and which, when honoured, preserve human society and preserve: *dīn,* life, sanity, property, lineage, and honour.[1]

Once there are more than a few people there is a society, and of necessity there must be governance. Few people in history have found a way around this. Contrary to the abhorrent Hobbsian perspective, we do not take a cynical pragmatic view that simply permits the construction of a state that coerces people or deceives them. It behoves the modern Muslim to understand the history of the modern idea of the 'state'. Its birth in the throes of Catholic-Protestant civil war, and its adoption of the Roman secular view of separation between church and state, is one aspect we must know about, for Islamic governance is there in order to see *Sharīcah* put into effect, and may not maintain an Olympian detachment from these matters.

In addition, the conception of the world and the human being in terms of physical causality necessarily led to their being pictured as machines, with the inevitable consequence that human institutions, such as education, medicine and the state itself, took on a mechanical character, with the citizen merely being processed as opposed to governed. The inner logic of technology means that states must evolve into super-states and ultimately the world-state. It is thus doubly futile for Muslims to aspire to nation-state entities or even super-states, whether Islamic or not, first, because the machine is a profoundly inhuman and anti-human conception of governance, and second, because the nation-state has already been superceded and the super-state is about to be. Apart from that, it is futile since we have already a perfectly legitimate organic form of governance that endured throughout a millennium and a half and is perfectly fit for our future.[2]

Finally, we must tackle the individual who will live by this *Sharīʿah* and who will in some cases apply it in his role as *amīr*, *qāḍī* or *muftī*. That person must necessarily be sane, an adult and a Muslim, and for that latter we turn to the definition of the Messenger of Allah ﷺ in the famous hadith of Jibrīl in Imām an-Nawawī's collection of *Forty Hadith*.

عُمَرُ بنُ الخَطَّابِ، قال: بَيْنا نَحنُ عِنْدَ رسولِ اللهِ صلى الله عليه وسلم ذاتَ يومٍ، إذْ طَلَعَ

عَلَيْنا رَجُلٌ شَدِيدُ بَياضِ الثِّيابِ، شَدِيدُ سَوادِ الشَّعرِ، لا يُرى عَلَيهِ أَثَرُ السَّفَرِ، ولا يَعرِفُهُ

مِنّا أَحَدٌ، حتّى جَلَسَ إلى النبيِّ صلى الله عليه وسلم. فَأَسْنَدَ رُكبَتَيهِ إلى رُكبَتَيهِ، ووَضَعَ

كَفَّيهِ على فَخِذَيهِ، وقال: يا محمَّدُ! أَخْبِرْني عنِ الإسلامِ. فقالَ رسولُ اللهِ صلى الله عليه

وسلم: ﴿الإسلامُ أَنْ تَشهَدَ أَنْ لا إلهَ إلّا اللهُ وأَنَّ محمَّدًا رسولُ اللهِ صلى الله عليه وسلم،

وتُقِيمَ الصَّلاةَ، وتُؤْتِيَ الزَّكاةَ، وتَصومَ رمضانَ، وتَحُجَّ البَيتَ، إنِ استَطَعْتَ إليهِ سَبيلًا﴾ قال:

صَدَقْتَ. قال فعَجِبْنا لهُ، يَسأَلُهُ ويُصَدِّقُهُ. قال: فأَخْبِرْني عنِ الإيمانِ. قال: ﴿أَنْ تُؤْمِنَ باللهِ،

ومَلائِكَتِهِ، وكُتُبِهِ، ورُسُلِهِ، واليومِ الآخِرِ، وتُؤْمِنَ بالقَدَرِ خَيرِهِ وشَرِّهِ﴾ قال: صَدَقْتَ. قال:

فأَخْبِرْني عنِ الإحسانِ؟ . قال: ﴿أَنْ تَعبُدَ اللهَ كأَنَّكَ تَراهُ. فإِنْ لم تَكُنْ تَراهُ، فإِنَّهُ يَراكَ﴾ .

قال: فأَخْبِرْني عنِ السّاعةِ. قال: ﴿ما المَسؤُولُ عنها بأَعلَمَ مِنَ السّائِلِ﴾ قال: فأَخْبِرْني عن

أَماراتِها . قال: ﴿أَنْ تَلِدَ الأَمةُ رَبَّتَها . وأَنْ تَرى الحُفاةَ العُراةَ، العالةَ، رِعاءَ الشّاءِ، يَتَطاوَلونَ في

البُنيانِ﴾ . قال ثم انطَلَقَ . فلَبِثْتُ مَلِيًّا . ثم قال لي: ﴿يا عُمَرُ! أَتَدري مَنِ السّائِلُ؟﴾ قُلْتُ:

اللهُ ورسولُهُ أَعلَمُ. قال: ﴿فإِنَّهُ جِبريلُ. أَتاكُم يُعَلِّمُكُم دِينَكُم﴾ .

From ʿUmar ﷺ there is that he said, "While we were sitting with the Messenger of Allah ﷺ one day a man came up to us whose

> clothes were extremely white, whose hair was extremely black, upon whom no trace of travel could be seen, and whom none of us knew, until he sat down close to the Prophet ﷺ so that he rested his knees upon his knees and placed his two hands upon his thighs and said, 'Muhammad, tell me about Islam.' The Messenger of Allah ﷺ said, 'Islam is that you witness that there is no god but Allah and that Muhammad is the Messenger of Allah, and you establish the prayer, and you give the *Zakāh*, and you fast Ramaḍān, and you perform the Ḥajj of the House if you are able to take a way to it.' He said, 'You have told the truth,' and we were amazed at him asking him and [then] telling him that he told the truth. He said, 'Tell me about *Īmān*.' He said, 'That you believe in Allah, His angels, His books, His messengers, and the Last Day, and that you affirm the Decree, the good of it and the bad of it.' He said, 'You have told the truth.' He said, 'Tell me about *Iḥsān*.' He said, 'That you worship Allah as if you see Him, for if you don't see Him then truly He sees you.' He said, 'Tell me about the Hour.' He said, 'The one asked about it knows no more than the one asking.' He said, 'Then tell me about its signs.' He said, 'That the female slave should give birth to her mistress, and you see poor, naked, barefoot shepherds of sheep and goats competing in raising buildings.' He went away, and I remained some time. Then he said, 'ᶜUmar, do you know who the questioner was?' I said, 'Allah and His Messenger know best.' He said, 'He was Jibrīl who came to you to teach you your *dīn*'."
> (An-Nawawī, *al-Arbaᶜūn*, published in English translation as *The Complete Forty*, Ta-Ha Publishers, London, UK, 1998. Hadith number two. It is narrated in *Ṣaḥīḥ Muslim*.)[3]

Imām an-Nawawī ؓ remarks in his commentary:

> In his statement ﷺ, "This was Jibrīl who came to teach you your *dīn*" there is proof that Īmān, Islām and Iḥsān are together called '*dīn*'.

Thus the person who will embody and put into effect the *Sharīᶜah* will be described by these three dimensions of *dīn* that are qualitatively quite different from each other and not merely hierarchical layers. Outwardly, while performing the actions named Islam, the person will inwardly be characterised by having a trust in the unseen matters, and will be working towards the perfection of these two outward and inward realms in the process that is called *iḥsān* and defined as worshipping Allah, exalted is He, as if you see Him, for if you do not see Him, He sees you.

Islam corresponds to the zone of outward action, and whereas the *dīn* comprises these three dimensions, yet the word Islam is ordinarily understood to stand as a sufficient name for the entire *dīn* because of the priority that outward behaviour, action and deeds have. This priority of Islam over its other two dimensions is expressed in the *āyah*:

إِنَّ الدِّينَ عِندَ اللَّهِ الْإِسْلَامُ

The dīn with Allah is Islam. (Sūrah Āl cImrān: 19)

Outward actions comprise two sorts: *cibādah*, acts of worship, and *mucāmalah*, ordinary transactions such as those detailed in this book, including marriage, divorce, buying, selling, renting and hiring, etc. Both *cibādah* and *mucāmalah* are comprised in *Sharīcah*, although since a great deal of attention has already been lavished on *cibādah* in English, this book will concentrate almost exclusively on *mucāmalah*.

The threefold schema of Shaykh cAbd al-Wāḥid ibn cĀshir comes to our aid in delineating the three dimensions of Islam in another fashion. He says:

وَحُكْمُنَا الْعَقْلِيُّ قَضِيَّةٌ بِلَا

وَقْفٍ عَلَى عَادَةٍ أَوْ وَضْعٍ جَلَا

Our intellectual judgement is a matter without

dependence on experience or a revealed text which makes clear.[4]

In this the Shaykh refers to *kalām*/*caqīdah*, the intellectual articulation of what may be said about the Creator, as being a science that does not rest on scientific observation and experiment but equally not on revelation, for in fact, our acceptance of the revelation depends on a prior sound *caqīdah*. The knowledge of what is necessarily true about Him, what is inconceivable for Him and what is conceivable, is a science that relies on the intellect, with the proviso that the Qur'ānic understanding of intellect is that it is the faculty of the heart. What is necessarily true, what is inconceivable and conceivable have those things that are immediately obvious and those things that are obvious after reflection, making it a six-fold elaboration. This is the science that is in the zone of axiomatic truth. Thus, the Shaykh outlines the threefold nature of sciences:

1. Purely intellectual sciences, the most familiar example of which is mathematics, which do not depend on experience, experiment or revelation. For our purposes here it is *ᶜaqīdah,* i.e. knowing what may rationally be said about Allah and His Messengers. This knowledge, the Shaykh says, is the first obligation on those who are charged with responsibility.
2. Sciences that derive purely from revelation, such as the *Sharīᶜah*. Thus the knowledge of the Last Day, the Garden and the Fire we accept on trust from the Messenger ﷺ. And the fact that the prayer of *Maghrib* is three *rakᶜahs* in the first two of which the Qur'ān is recited aloud and in the third of which the Fātiḥah is recited silently is neither a purely rational process nor one based on experience and experiment.
3. Observational sciences based on experience and experiment such as the science of medicine or chemistry. It is my view that this is represented in our tripartite picture of the sciences of the *dīn* by the science of *iḥsān* the beginning of which comprises purification of the heart from negative qualities such as greed, envy, malice, spite, anger, etc., and its adornment with noble qualities such as generosity, bravery, forbearance, abstinence, etc., for this is a science which, while firmly rooted in the *āyāt* of the Qur'ān and the Sunnah of the Messenger of Allah ﷺ,[5] is reliant on experience and is transmitted by those who have experience of it and who have attained its fruits.

So, the above is the context within which *Sharī^cah* must be seen. These are the knowledges that must illuminate the man or woman of the *Sharī^cah.*

With few honourable exceptions, the Newtonian adherent of physical causality will, as surely as day follows night, go on to create the native reservations, the Guantanamo Bays, the gulags and the concentration camps of this world.

It is only the submitted person, aware of his or her Lord, worshipping Allah in the day and the night, longing for knowledge of Him, seeing generosity and mercy as means to that all-consuming end, who will make the law the key to the just society that it undoubtedly is.

Allah alone grants success.

Notes

[1] *See* ash-Shāṭibī in his *al-Muwāfaqāt* in which he elaborated an understanding of the purposes (*maqāṣid*) of the *Sharīᶜah* as preserving: *dīn*, life, wealth, lineage, sanity, and, some add, honour. This is a fascinating insight but, if improperly understood, a dangerous one, in that it may allow people to imagine that the *Sharīᶜah* stands purely on these 'principles' and can thus be redesigned according to them. But, since *Sharīᶜah* is revealed it must be transmitted as it is and not tampered with, although understanding its purposes help the *muftī* and the *qāḍī* when struggling to reach a judgement on a new issue.

[2] *See* Clarke, Abdassamad, *The Falsity of the Concept of the Islamic State,* http://www.bogvaerker.dk/state.html

[3] *See* Bewley, Abdalhaqq, *Islam: basic practices and beliefs*, Ta-Ha Publishers, London, UK, 2008, for a very full exposition of the meanings of this profound hadith.

[4] Ibn ᶜĀshir, ᶜAbd al-Wāḥid, *al-Murshid al-muᶜīn fī aḍ-ḍarūri min ᶜulūm ad-dīn.*

[5] *See:* Laraki, Ali, *A General Introduction to the Science of Taṣawwuf* (unpublished); and Shaykh ᶜAbd al-Qādir ᶜĪsā, *Ḥaqā'iq ᶜan at-taṣawwuf.*

Part I
Principles (*uṣūl*) of the *Sharīᶜah* and the *Madhhabs*

Chapter 2

What is *Sharīᶜah*?

Allah is the Lawgiver

SHARĪᶜAH is an Arabic word meaning the road to be followed. Literally it means 'the way to a watering place'. It is the path not only leading to Allah, exalted is He, but the path shown by Allah, the Creator Himself, through His Messenger, the Prophet Muḥammad ﷺ. In Islam, Allah alone is the Sovereign and it is He Who has the right to ordain a path for the guidance of mankind. Thus it is only *Sharīᶜah* that liberates man from servitude to other than Allah. This is the only reason why Muslims are obliged to strive for the implementation of this path, and no other path.

ثُمَّ جَعَلْنَاكَ عَلَى شَرِيعَةٍ مِنَ الْأَمْرِ فَاتَّبِعْهَا وَلَا تَتَّبِعْ أَهْوَاءَ الَّذِينَ لَا يَعْلَمُونَ

> *Then We placed you on the right road (sharīᶜah) of Our Command, so follow it. Do not follow the whims and desires of those who do not know.*
> (Sūrat al-Jāthiyah 45: 18)

The absolute knowledge which is required to lay down a path for human life is not possessed by any group of people.

The Injunctions on Justice in the Divine Revelations

There are a number of Qur'ānic injunctions commanding Muslims to do justice. Right from the beginning, Allah sent with His Messengers three gifts which aim at rendering justice and guiding the entire human society to the path of peace. In Sūrat al-Ḥadīd, Allah says:

لَقَدْ أَرْسَلْنَا رُسُلَنَا بِالْبَيِّنَاتِ وَأَنْزَلْنَا مَعَهُمُ الْكِتَابَ وَالْمِيزَانَ لِيَقُومَ النَّاسُ بِالْقِسْطِ وَأَنْزَلْنَا الْحَدِيدَ فِيهِ

بَأْسٌ شَدِيدٌ وَمَنَافِعُ لِلنَّاسِ

We sent Our Messengers with the Clear Signs and sent down the Book and the Balance with them so that mankind might establish justice. And We sent down iron in which there lies great force and which has many uses for mankind. (Sūrat al-Ḥadīd 57: 24)

Three things are mentioned as gifts of Allah. They are the Book, the Balance and iron, which stand as emblems of three things which hold society together, *viz*: revelation, which commands good and forbids evil; justice, which gives to each person his due; and the strong force of the law, which maintains sanctions against evildoers.

Justice is a command of Allah, and whosoever violates it faces grievous punishment:

إِنَّ اللهَ يَأْمُرُ بِالْعَدْلِ وَالْإِحْسَانِ وَإِيتَاءِ ذِي الْقُرْبَى وَيَنْهَى عَنِ الْفَحْشَاءِ وَالْمُنْكَرِ وَالْبَغْيِ يَعِظُكُمْ

لَعَلَّكُمْ تَذَكَّرُونَ

Allah commands justice and doing good and giving to relatives. And He forbids indecency and doing wrong and tyranny. He warns you so that hopefully you will pay heed. (Sūrat an-Naḥl 16: 90)

Justice is a comprehensive term, and may include all the virtues of good behaviour. But Islam asks for something warmer and more human, namely the doing of good deeds even where perhaps they are not strictly demanded by justice, such as returning good for ill, or obliging those who "have no claim" on you; and of course the fulfilling of the claims of those whose claims are recognised in social life. Similarly, the opposites are to be avoided: everything that is recognised as shameful, and everything that is really unjust, and any inward rebellion against Allah's law or our own conscience in its most sensitive form.

The Prophet of Allah ﷺ is asked to tell people to behave justly as the Creator, the Nourisher and the Cherisher of all has commanded it:

قُلْ أَمَرَ رَبِّي بِالْقِسْطِ

Say: "My Lord has commanded justice." (Sūrat al-A'rāf 7: 28)

The command is repeated in Sūrat an-Nisā':

إِنَّ اللهَ يَأْمُرُكُمْ أَن تُؤَدُّوا الْأَمَانَاتِ إِلَى أَهْلِهَا وَإِذَا حَكَمْتُم بَيْنَ النَّاسِ أَن تَحْكُمُوا بِالْعَدْلِ

Allah commands you to return to their owners the things you hold on trust and, when you judge between people, to judge with justice. (Sūrat an-Nisā' 4: 57)

The Prophet ﷺ is asked to administer justice according to the *Kitāb Allāh* (Book of Allah):

إِنَّا أَنزَلْنَا إِلَيْكَ الْكِتَابَ بِالْحَقِّ لِتَحْكُمَ بَيْنَ النَّاسِ بِمَا أَرَاكَ اللهُ وَلَا تَكُن لِّلْخَائِنِينَ خَصِيماً

We have sent down the Book to you with the truth so that you can judge between people according to what Allah has shown to you. But do not be an advocate for the treacherous. (Sūrat an-Nisā' 4: 104)

The commentators explain this passage with reference to the case of Ṭa'imah ibn Ubayriq, who was nominally a Muslim, but in reality was a hypocrite and given to all sorts of wicked deeds. He was suspected of having stolen a set of armour, and when the trail was hot, he planted the stolen property in the house of a Jew, where it was found. The Jew denied the charge and accused Ṭa'imah, but the sympathies of the Muslim community were with Ṭa'imah on account of his nominal profession of Islam. The case was brought to the Messenger ﷺ, who acquitted the Jew according to the strict principles of justice, as "guided by Allah". Attempts were made to prejudice him and deceive him into using his authority to favour Ṭa'imah.

The general lesson is that the right-acting man is faced with all sorts of subtle wiles: the wicked will feign any honourable motives to appeal to his highest sympathies and to deceive him and use him as an instrument for defeating justice. He should be careful and cautious, and seek the help of Allah for protection against deception and for firmness in dealing the strictest justice without fear or favour. To do otherwise is to betray a sacred trust;

the trustee must defeat all attempts made to mislead him.

Justice must be done equally and to all and sundry even if it is to be done against oneself, or one's parents or relatives. There must be no differences between rich and poor with respect to the execution of justice. All are slaves of Allah, and must be judged according to the Book of Allah.

يَا أَيُّهَا الَّذِينَ آمَنُوا كُونُوا قَوَّامِينَ بِالْقِسْطِ شُهَدَاءَ لِلَّهِ وَلَوْ عَلَى أَنفُسِكُمْ أَوِ الْوَالِدَيْنِ وَالْأَقْرَبِينَ إِن يَكُنْ
غَنِيًّا أَوْ فَقِيرًا فَاللَّهُ أَوْلَى بِهِمَا فَلَا تَتَّبِعُوا الْهَوَى أَن تَعْدِلُوا وَإِن تَلْوُوا أَوْ تُعْرِضُوا فَإِنَّ اللَّهَ كَانَ بِمَا
تَعْمَلُونَ خَبِيرًا

> *You who have īmān! Be upholders of justice, bearing witness for Allah alone, even against yourselves or your parents and relatives. Whether they are rich or poor, Allah is well able to look after them. Do not follow your own desires and deviate from the truth. If you twist or turn away, Allah is aware of what you do.* (Sūrat an-Nisā' 4: 135)

Justice is Allah's attribute, and to stand firm for justice, even if it is detrimental to our own interests as we conceive them, or the interests of those who are near and dear to us, is to be a witness to Allah. According to the Latin saying, "Let justice be done though heaven should fall."

However, Islamic justice is something higher than the formal justice of Roman law or any other human law. It is even more penetrating than the subtler justice found in the speculations of the Greek philosophers. It searches out the innermost motives, because we are to act as in the presence of Allah to Whom all things, acts and motives are known.

Some people may be inclined to favour the rich, because they expect something from them. Some people may be inclined to favour the poor because they are generally helpless. Partiality in either case is wrong. We are asked to be just, without fear or favour. Both the rich and the poor are under Allah's protection as far as their legitimate interests are concerned, but they cannot expect to be favoured at the expense of others. Allah can protect the interests of all, far better than can any person.

In the *Sharīᶜah,* therefore, there is explicit emphasis on the fact that Allah is the Lawgiver, and the whole *Ummah,* the nation of Islam, is merely His trustee. It is because of this principle that the *Ummah* enjoys a derivative rule-making power and not an absolute law-creating prerogative. The Islamic *dawlah* (governance and the governed), like the whole of what one might call Islamic political psychology, views the *Dār al-Islām* (Abode of Islam) as one vast homogeneous commonwealth of people who have a common goal and a common destiny and who are guided by a common ideology in all matters both spiritual and temporal. The entire Muslim *Ummah* lives under the *Sharīᶜah* to which every member has to submit, with sovereignty belonging to Allah alone.[1]

Every Muslim who is capable and qualified to give a sound opinion on matters of *Sharīᶜah,* is entitled to interpret the law of Allah when such interpretation becomes necessary. In this sense Islamic policy is a democracy. But where an explicit command of Allah or His Prophet ﷺ already exists, no Muslim leader or legislature, or any religious scholar can form an independent judgement; not even all the Muslims of the world together can have any right to make the least alteration in it.

The executive function, therefore, under the *Sharīᶜah* is vested solely in the just ruler, who appoints his delegates, and who is responsible only to Allah and to the *Sharīᶜah* as represented by the *ᶜulamā'* and *fuqahā'* in whom the legislative function of deriving rulings from the Book of Allah and the Sunnah is vested. New rulings according to the needs of the time and circumstances are only made by these people learned in the guiding principles of law.[2]

The fundamental principle on which rests the Islamic legal system is that the laws of Islam are not passed in a heated assembly by men who ardently desire the legislation in their interest, against men who ardently oppose it in their interest. The judgements of Islam are firmly based upon the *Sharīᶜah* and are, therefore in the interest of the people as a whole. They are not the work of warring politicians, but of sober jurists.[3]

The reason why there is a greater degree of stability in the *Sharīᶜah* compared to any other man-made legislation in the world is due to its Divine origin.

The difference between other legal systems and the *Sharīᶜah* is that the fountainhead of the *Sharīᶜah* is the Qur'ān and the Sunnah, i.e. *al-waḥy al-jalī* (the revelation per se) and *al-waḥy al-khafī* (the hidden revelation). The Qur'ān and the Sunnah are gifts given to the entire *Ummah*. Therefore the *Ummah* as a whole is collectively responsible for the administration of justice. This is the reason why no legislative or consultative assembly in any Muslim land has any power to encroach on any legal right of the members of the *Ummah* and those who live with them in peaceful co-existence.

The other important point in this regard is that in the *Sharīᶜah*, justice is administered in the name of Allah, one of Whose names is *al-ᶜAdl* – The Just One and the Giver of Justice. Any injustice or any tribal or racial consideration is a grave wrong action and disobedience to Allah. "To judge justly" is, therefore, a religious duty and a devotional act. Neither a king, nor a caliph or a sultan can ever claim his words are law as was done by tyrannical rulers from Pharoah to Louis XIV. They are not the fountainhead of justice even though some wrong-headed Muslim rulers might have arrogated such authority to themselves. With this in mind, we shall proceed to examine briefly the sources and the aims of the *Sharīᶜah*.

The Aims of the *Sharīᶜah*

The *Sharīᶜah* originated from the direct commands of Allah; but there is the provision or power given to man in order to interpret and expand the Divine commands by means of analogical deduction and through other processes.[4] Unlike Roman law, which developed from action, or English Common Law, which developed from writs[5], the very first source of the *Sharīᶜah* is the Noble Qur'ān. The second source is the Sunnah or the practice of the Prophet Muḥammad ﷺ who explained:

> I leave two things among you. You will never go astray while holding them firmly: the Book of Allah and the Sunnah of His

Prophet. (Mālik in *al-Muwaṭṭa'*, Book 46, Number 46.1.3; al-Ḥākim in *al-Mustadrak*)

The third source is the *ijmāᶜ* (consensus) of the *ᶜulamā'*, and the fourth is *qiyās* (analogical deduction), and these two provide detailed understanding derived from the Qur'ān and the Sunnah, covering the myriad problems that arise in the course of life. As a matter of fact, the ideal code of conduct or pure way of life which is the *Sharīᶜah* has much wider scope and purpose than an ordinary legal system in the western sense of the term.[6] The *Sharīᶜah,* through this process, aims at regulating the relationship of human beings with Allah and with each other. This is the reason why *Sharīᶜah* law cannot be separated from Islamic ethics. The process of revelation of various rulings (*aḥkām*) of the Qur'ān shows that the revelation came down when some social, moral or religious necessity arose, or when some Companions consulted the Prophet ﷺ concerning some significant problems which had repercussions on the lives of Muslims.

The Qur'ān, therefore, is the best commentary (*tafsīr*) on the Qur'ān and the main source of the *Sharīᶜah.*

The scholars of the Qur'ān have enumerated varying numbers of verses of legal rulings, which are generally considered to be approximately 500.[7] They deal with marriage, polygyny, dower, maintenance, rights and obligations of the spouses, divorce and various modes of dissolution of marriage, the period of retreat after divorce (*ᶜiddah*), fosterage, contracts, loans, deposits, weights and measures, removal of injury, oaths and vows, punishments for crimes, wills, inheritance, equity, fraternity, liberty, justice to all, principles of governance, fundamental human rights, laws of war and peace, judicial administration, etc.[8]

The Qur'ānic injunctions, from which are derived the *Sharīᶜah,* are further explained and translated into practice by the Sunnah of the Prophet ﷺ. Sunnah literally means a way, a practice, and a rule of life; and refers to the exemplary conduct or the model behaviour of the Prophet ﷺ in what he did, said or approved. Thus it became a very important source of the *Sharīᶜah* only second in authority to the Noble Qur'ān.

Besides the Qur'ān and the Sunnah, the consensus of the learned men and jurists, known in *Sharī^c^ah* terminology as *ijmā^c^*, plays an important role in Islamic law. *Qiyās* or analogical deduction is also recognised as a legitimate source of the Islamic legal system since it provides an instrument to cope with the growing needs and requirements of society. But such analogical deduction is based on very strict, logical and systematic principles and is not to be misconstrued merely as people's fancies and imaginings. Alongside these four sources, the *Sharī^c^ah* takes into consideration *istiḥsān* or juristic preference or equity, as against *qiyās*, which helps in providing elasticity and adaptability to the entire Islamic legal system. The concept of *al-maṣlaḥah al-mursalah* (matters which are in the public interest and which are not specifically defined in the *Sharī^c^ah*)was enunciated by Imām Mālik ibn Anas (d. 173 AH/795 CE) and has also become a part of the *Sharī^c^ah*.

Justice as Respect for People

The central notion of justice in the *Sharī^c^ah* is based on mutual respect of one human being for another. The just society in Islam means the society that secures and maintains respect for persons through various social arrangements that are in the common interests of all members. A person as a *khalīfah* of Allah (vicegerent of Allah) on earth must be treated as an end in himself and never merely as a means since he is the cream of creation and hence the central theme of the Qur'ān. What is required is the equal integrity of each person in the society and his loyalty which in turn will make it the duty of society to provide equally for each person's pursuit of happiness. This is the reason why things which are unlawful (*ḥarām*) for Muslims but lawful for non-Muslims will not be forbidden them in Muslim society.

Politically, respect for persons was the motivating thought behind the *kalimah ash-shahādah*, the creed of confession of Islam, which rejected any other deity other than Allah Who created all human beings as equal irrespective of their tribes or clans. It was this teaching which made Quraysh, the Prophet Muḥammad's ﷺ

tribesmen, angry when he helped to liberate slaves and destitutes like Bilāl, Zayd and many others in the early days of Islam. It is a fact of history that all of Khadījah's wealth was spent after freeing the slaves; and before her death she ﷺ, along with the Prophet ﷺ, could hardly get a square meal a day. It was the same principle which guided Madīnah, the first Muslim city, as shown in its charter, which guaranteed individual rights irrespective of religious beliefs to the communities living in Madīnah.

Respect for persons in the *Sharīᶜah* is rooted in the Divine injunctions of the Qur'ān and the precepts of the Prophet ﷺ. The Bill of Rights, Suffrage, Civil Rights and the slogans for political equality we know today are of a very recent origin and seem to be mere echoes of what the *Sharīᶜah* taught 1400 years ago. The treatment accorded by the *Sharīᶜah* endorsed the aristocracies of birth, race, wealth – features that vary from person to person – but made a higher criterion of respect: *taqwā*, the fear of Allah.

إِنَّ أَكْرَمَكُمْ عِندَ اللَّهِ أَتْقَاكُمْ

The noblest among you in Allah's sight is the one with the most taqwā. (Sūrat al-Ḥujurāt 49: 13)

The *Sharīᶜah*, it should be noted, gives priority to human welfare over human liberty. Muslims as well as non-Muslims living under Muslim governance are duty bound not to exploit common resources to their own advantage, destroy good productive land, and ruin a potential harvest or encroach upon a neighbour's land. Since a man in Islam is not merely an economic animal, each person's equal right to life and to a decent standard of living, has priority over so-called economic liberty.

Behind every legal, social or political institution of Islam, there is a divine sanction which every believer is expected to reverence no matter where he lives. He cannot change his own whims into laws. There are the limits of Allah (*ḥudūdu'llāh*) which are imposed in order to curtail man's ambitions and devices. *Ḥalāl* (permissible) and *ḥarām* (prohibited) are clearly mentioned and these are the boundaries which every Muslim as well as non-

Muslim living with them must respect. If one transgresses any of these limits, he is doing wrong or committing a crime. Even between these two boundaries of 'permissible' and 'prohibited', there exist things which are doubtful (*mushtabihāt*), which must be refrained from in order to avoid excesses. In the ḥadīth the Prophet ﷺ says:

> The *ḥalāl* is clear and the *ḥarām* is clear and in between them are ambivalent matters which many people do not know. Whoever guards himself against ambivalent matters has secured his *dīn* and his honour. Whoever falls into ambivalent matters will fall into the *ḥarām*, like the shepherd who shepherds [his flock] around forbidden pasturage, he is certain to pasture [his flock] in it. Certainly, every king has his forbidden pasturage. Certainly, Allah's forbidden pasturage is the things he has forbidden. Certainly in the body there is a lump of flesh which when it is sound the whole body is sound and when it is corrupt the whole body is corrupt. Certainly it is the heart. (Al-Bukhari, *kitāb al-īmān, bāb faḍl man istabra'a li dīnihi;* and Muslim, *kitāb al-musāqāh, bāb akhdh al-ḥalāl wa tark ash-shubuhāt*)

In reality, these limits provide safeguards for the rights of people and nations and give people a sense of responsibility to Allah and hence to all mankind. These limits stop him from being inhuman, and make him respect the lives and property of others, and give equality of treatment to all individuals, male and female, before the law. In commercial dealings, these limits provide for respect for contractual dealings and pledged words and the prohibition of usury and gambling. In the case of individual conduct, these limits provide for the prohibition of intoxicants, the prevention of injustice towards servants, the giving of charity to poor relations and the strict observation of the laws governing inheritance. In the dealings with nations, these limits provide for respect for treaties, and give a strict code of conduct for one's dealings with one's fellow men by not destroying the enemies' means of sustenance, and by showing mercy to an enemy who has surrendered and respect for non-combatants. In short, in every action of a man's dealings with fellow men there are limits (*ḥudūd*) imposed by Allah which are nothing but the sanctions of the Divine *Sharīᶜah*.

Judicial power, according to the *Sharīᶜah,* must always operate in conformity with equity, even to the benefit of an enemy or to the detriment of a relative. The *Sharīᶜah* does not allow the slightest modification to its application of perfect justice, or any form of arbitrary procedure to replace it. It firmly establishes the rule of law, eliminating all differences between high and low.

The Qur'ān asserts that all mankind, born of the same father and mother, form one single family, that the God of men is Unique, that the Creator has ordered men according to nations and tribes so that they may know, and assist one another, for the good of all.

In the administration of justice, therefore, a judge must be upright, sober, calm and cool. Nothing should act on his mind so that he deviates from the path of rectitude. If he does wrong, he is not only responsible to the people but also to Allah. The noble Prophet ﷺ advised: "No judge shall pass a judgement between two men while he is angry" (Aḥmad; al-Bukhārī, *kitāb al-aḥkām, bāb hal yaqḍī al-qāḍī aw yuftī wa huwa ghaḍbān;* Muslim, *kitāb al-aqḍiyah, bāb karāhah qaḍā' al-qāḍī wa huwa ghaḍbān*; Abū Dāwūd and Ibn Mājah also narrated it). He must not let feelings of kindness prevent him from executing the ordained sentences for the prescribed crimes. In the Qur'ān Allah says: *"and do not let compassion for either of them possess you where Allah's dīn is concerned, if you have īmān in Allah and the Last Day. A number of mu'minūn should witness their punishment"* (Sūrat an-Nūr 24: 2). He must decide disputes with as much speed and promptness as possible, for delayed justice produces no appreciable good. He must not accept any present or bribery from the parties concerned. He must strive hard to arrive at a just conclusion. The Prophet ﷺ said: "Allah is with a judge so long as he is not unjust. When he is (intentionally) unjust, he leaves him and shayṭān sticks to him" (At-Tirmidhī, *abwāb al-aḥkām ᶜan rasūl Allāh* ﷺ, *bāb mā jā'a fī al-imām al-ᶜādil*). To a judge, all are equal in the eyes of the law. As Allah dispenses justice among His subjects, so a judge should judge without any distinction whatsoever. The Prophet ﷺ said: "The previous nations were destroyed because they let off persons of high rank and punished the poor and the helpless." In the *Sharīᶜah,* a judge is a judge for every matter – civil, criminal and military. There is no separate judiciary for separate civil, criminal and military jurisdictions.

The basic principles of the *Sharīᶜah,* therefore, can be summed up as follows:

a. The larger interests of society take precedence over the interests of the individual.
b. Although 'relieving hardship' and 'promoting benefit' are both among the prime objectives of the *Sharīᶜah,* the former takes precedence over the latter.
c. A bigger loss cannot be inflicted to relieve a smaller loss or a bigger benefit cannot be sacrificed for a smaller one. Conversely, a smaller harm can be inflicted to avoid a bigger harm or a smaller benefit can be sacrificed for a larger benefit.

The *Qāḍī* (Judge) and His Responsibilities Under the Sharīᶜah

QUALIFICATION OF A *QĀḌĪ*:

As we have seen, Islam gives great importance to justice which must be done at all costs. Those who perform the function of *qāḍīs* (judges) or *Qāḍī al-Quḍāt* (Chief Justice) must not only be men of deep insight and profound knowledge of the *Sharīᶜah,* but they must also have integrity and be God-fearing, forthright and honest. The Messenger of Allah ﷺ is narrated to have said:

> *Qāḍīs* are of three types. One type will go to the Garden and the remaining two will end up in the Fire. The one who will go to the Garden is the one who understands the truth and judges accordingly. One who judges unjustly after understanding the truth, will go to the Fire. Likewise a *qāḍī* who judges out of ignorance will also go to the Fire. (Abū Dāwūd, *awwal kitāb al-aqḍiyah, bāb fi al-qāḍī yukhṭi'u;* and Ibn Mājah, *kitāb al-aḥkām, bāb al-ḥākim yajtahidu fayuṣīb al-ḥaqq*)

The above ḥadīth shows how delicate and responsible the position of *qāḍī* is in Islam. His knowledge of the Qur'ān and *Sharīᶜah* must be very deep and it is vital that he judge justly. Otherwise, it can ruin his spiritual future in the next world. The life of this world is only for a limited period while the life of the next world is forever. So why would one undertake to be a judge if one does not have the required qualifications and character for the post? In another ḥadīth:

مَن جُعِلَ قاضِياً فقَضَى بينَ النّاسِ فقَدْ ذُبِحَ بغَيْرِ سِكِّين.

It is reported by Abū Hurayrah ﷺ that the Messenger of Allah ﷺ said, "Someone who is made a *qāḍī* and passes judgement between people has been slaughtered without a knife." (Aḥmad, Abū Dāwūd, *awwal kitāb al-aqḍiyah, bāb fī ṭalab al-qaḍā'*; Ibn Mājah, *kitāb al-aḥkām, bāb dhikr al-quḍāt;* and al-Ḥākim)

Naturally, a man who is appointed as a *qāḍī* does not have an easy job to perform. If he becomes slightly irresponsible and unjust, he will be caught on the Day of Judgement. On the other hand, when he is just and administers justice according to the Book of Allah and the Sunnah of the Prophet ﷺ, he is taken to be an enemy by highly influential people in society. The responsibility of a *qāḍī* is like a double-edged sword, and one has to be extraordinarily careful in the discharge of it. The following is the guidance from the Sunnah of the Prophet ﷺ which every judge must follow in their task of administering justice:

1. *Equality of all litigants*: While treating people with the courtesy due to their rank and standing, the Muslim judge must treat all litigants equally whether they are kings or their pages, masters or their servants, rich or poor, relatives or strangers and friends or foe:

عَنْ عُبادَةَ بنِ الصّامت: قالَ: قالَ رَسُولُ الله صلى الله عليه وسلم: أَقِيمُوا حُدُودَ الله في القَرِيبِ والبَعِيدِ. ولا تَأْخُذْكُم في الله لَومةُ لائِمٍ.

It is reported by ᶜUbādah ibn aṣ-Ṣāmit that the Messenger of Allah ﷺ said: "Let the *ḥudūd* of Allah be applied equally to your relatives and to total strangers. You should not care for the reproach of any critic whatsoever." (Ibn Mājah, *kitāb al-ḥudūd, bāb iqāmat al-ḥudūd;* and *Mishkāt, bāb al-ḥudūd*)

The Prophet ﷺ also said:

عَنْ عَائِشَةَ قَالَتْ : قَالَ رَسُولُ اللَّهِ ﷺ : أَقِيلُوا ذَوِي الْهَيْئَاتِ عَثَرَاتِهِمْ إِلَّا الْحُدُودَ .

It is reported by ᶜĀ'ishah ﵂ that the Messenger of Allah ﷺ said: "Forgive the shortcomings of highly respected people except for [transgressions of] the *ḥadd* limits." (Abū Dāwūd, *awwal kitāb al-ḥudūd, bāb fī al-ḥadd yushfaᶜu;* and *Mishkāt, bāb al-ḥudūd*)

2. *Defendant and litigant must appear before the qāḍī*: Even though one is a highly placed person or a king or an emperor or a high ranking government administrator, he must not be exempted from appearing before the judge to answer the charges levelled against him:

It is reported by ᶜAbdullāh ibn az-Zubayr ﵁ that the Messenger of Allah ﷺ said: "Both parties to a dispute must he brought before the judge." (Aḥmad and Abū Dāwūd, *awwal kitāb al-aqḍiyah, bāb kayta yajlisu al-khaṣmān bayna yadayyi al-qāḍī; Mishkāt, bāb al-aqḍiyah*)

3. *The defendant should be given the right to take an oath:* The human being, being what he is, will keep on grumbling and blaming others for his own faults or hide his faults in order to escape punishment. If everyone's claims were taken seriously, there would be a proliferation of claimants to people's lives and property. The remedy is suggested by the Prophet ﷺ as follows:

عَنِ ابْنِ عَبَّاسٍ ﵄ ، أَنَّ رَسُولَ اللَّهِ ﷺ ، قَالَ : لَوْ يُعْطَى النَّاسُ بِدَعْوَاهُمْ ، لَادَّعَى رِجَالٌ أَمْوَالَ قَوْمٍ وَدِمَاءَهُمْ ، لَكِنِ الْبَيِّنَةُ عَلَى الْمُدَّعِي وَالْيَمِينُ عَلَى مَنْ أَنْكَرَ .

It is reported by ᶜAbdullāh ibn ᶜAbbās ﵁ that the Messenger of Allah ﷺ said: "If people were to be given according to what they claim, men would claim people's property and blood, but clear evidence is required of a claimant and an oath is required of someone who denies [the claim]." (Muslim, *kitāb al-aqḍiyah, bāb al-yamīn ᶜalā al-muddaᶜā ᶜalayhi;* some of it is in al-Bukhārī.)

The above guidance of the Prophet provides defendants with an opportunity to be acquitted of calumny against them.

4. *The judge must be careful in awarding ḥadd punishments*: The ḥadd punishment is meant to be a deterrent so that people may

not become complacent and so commit crimes simply because they find the punishment to be nominal. But while awarding *ḥadd* punishments the judge must make sure that the crime has definitely been committed. If there is a slight doubt in establishing the crime, he should refrain from awarding a *ḥadd* punishment.

> It is reported by ᶜĀ'ishah ﵂ that the Messenger of Allah ﷺ said: "As far as possible, refrain from awarding *ḥadd* punishments to a Muslim. If there is found any excuse (or doubt), leave him alone because it is better for the judge to err in acquitting the accused rather than erring in awarding him punishment." (At-Tirmidhī, *abwāb al-ḥudūd ᶜan rasūl Allāh ﷺ, bāb mā jā'a fī dar' al-ḥudūd*)

From the above ḥadīth, it is also clear that the judge must endeavour to the best of his ability to find the crime committed by the accused. To keep the accused in unlawful custody without due process of law is also unjust.

Is the Responsibility that Comes with the Position of Judge best Avoided?

Although the responsibility of a *qāḍī* is very great, it is essential that learned jurists must accept the position of judge in order to administer justice and save humanity from chaos, anarchy and the law of the jungle. The Messenger of Allah ﷺ said to ᶜAmr ibn al-ᶜĀṣ:

> If a judge passes judgement and so exercises *ijtihād*, and arrives at the correct decision he is doubly rewarded, and if he passes judgement and so exercises *ijtihād* and arrives at a wrong decision, he is still rewarded singly. (Muslim, *kitāb al-aqḍiyah, bāb bayān ajr al-ḥākim idhā ijtahada fa aṣāba aw akhṭa'a*; al-Bukhārī, *kitāb al-itiṣām bi al-kitāb wa as-sunnah, bāb ajr al-ḥākim idhā ijtahada fa aṣāba aw akhṭa'a*; Abū Dāwūd and at-Tirmidhī also transmitted it.)

The best instrument in the hands of a *qāḍī* are the Book of Allah, the Sunnah of the Prophet ﷺ, the decisions of the Companions, the Followers, and the Followers of the Followers, particularly that on which they were unanimously agree, and, above all, *taqwā* (fear of Allah). With these, if he administers justice and makes a mistake, Allah will forgive him and reward him. Some people erroneously put forward the case of Imām Abū Ḥanīfah who refused to accept the position of judge on account of his personal piety. But they forget that although Imām Abū Ḥanīfah ﷺ himself refused to be a judge, he did not stop his companion and disciple Abū Yūsuf from rendering the same services to the *Ummah*. The Prophet ﷺ once said:

> I am but a man to whom you bring your disputes. Perhaps one of you is more eloquent in his proof than the other, so I give judgement according to what I have heard from him. Whatever I decide for him which is part of the right of his brother, he must not take any of it, for I am granting him a portion of the Fire. (Mālik in the *Muwaṭṭa'*, Book 36, Number 36.1 (Stimulation of Desire to Judge Correctly).1; Aḥmad, al-Bukhārī, *kitāb al-maẓālim, bāb ithm man khāṣama fī bāṭil wa huwa yaᶜlamuhu*; and Muslim, *kitāb al-aqḍiyah, bāb al-ḥukm bi aẓ-ẓāhir wa al-laḥn bi al-ḥujjah*; and the Four.)

When this could happen to the rightly guided Messenger of Allah ﷺ, what about an ordinary member of his *Ummah*?

The Caliph ᶜUmar's ﷺ Guidance for Judges

Judges were appointed for the administration of justice by the Prophet ﷺ himself. He sent Muᶜādh ibn Jabal ﷺ to Yemen as a judge. Likewise, he had entrusted judicial tasks to ᶜAlī ibn Abī Ṭālib ﷺ and Ibn Yasār. The *Khulafā' ar-Rāshidūn* ﷺ continued with the same practice and sent judges to different parts of the Muslim world. Sayyidunā ᶜUmar appointed Abu'd-Dardā' ﷺ to help him as a *qāḍī* in Madīnah. Shurayḥ was appointed judge in Baṣra, and Abū Mūsā al-Ashᶜarī ﷺ in Kūfa in Iraq.

The memorable letter of Sayyidunā ᶜUmar ﷺ written to Abū Mūsā al-Ashᶜarī ﷺ on the eve of his appointment as *qāḍī* outlines the functions and responsibilities of a Muslim judge and is equally relevant even today. Among other things he said in the letter:

> Try to understand the depositions that are made before you because it will be useless to consider a plea that is not valid. Consider all before you in the court equal and (consider them equal) in giving your attention to them so that highly placed people may not expect you to be partial and the humble may not

despair of justice from you. The claimant must produce evidence. An oath must be taken from the defendant. It is permissible to have compromise among Muslims but not an agreement through which the *ḥarām* (prohibited) would be turned into the *ḥalāl* (permissible) and vice versa.

If you have given a judgement yesterday and today you arrive at a correct opinion upon re-thinking, you must not feel prevented from retracting your first judgement, because justice is primary, and it is better to retract than to continue in error. Use your own individual judgement about matters that perplex and about which an answer is neither to be found in the Qur'ān or in the Sunnah. Know the similitude and weigh the issues accordingly (here Abū Mūsā is asked to use his personal judgement and arrive at a logical conclusion through the use of *qiyās* and *ijtihād*).[9] If someone brings a claim, which he may or may not be able to prove, decide a time-limit for him. If he produces evidence within the time-limit set (by you), you should allow his claim, otherwise you are at liberty to give judgement against him. This is the best way to forestall or clear any possible doubt. All Muslims are acceptable as witnesses against each other, except those who have received an (earlier) punishment provided by the *Sharīᶜah,* and those who are proved to have given false witness, and those who are suspected partially on the ground of client status or relationship because Allah praised be His name, forgives one because of taking oaths and postpones punishment in the face of the evidence. Avoid showing weariness, fatigue and annoyance at litigants. Allah will grant you a great reward and give you a good reputation for establishing justice in the courts of justice. Good bye.

Shūrā: Mutual Consultation in the Sharīᶜah

Since the *Ummah's* first allegiance is to Allah, all the affairs of the Muslims should be guided by the Book of Allah. Human inspiration, intellect and judgement in running their affairs should be based on the authority, power and wisdom of Allah. Unlike human power, this power is good and merciful. Unlike human wisdom, this wisdom is necessarily complete and indisputable.

Whatever Allah has given us is merely for the convenience of this life, but we should always be mindful of the fact that whatever is with Allah is better and more lasting.[10] Therefore our efforts should be directed not only to making this life better but to securing the life hereafter. Believers should put their trust in Allah while executing all their affairs, should avoid crimes and shameful deeds and should forgive even when they are angry.[11] After making us aware of our responsibility, in Sūrat ash-Shūrā, Allah says:

وَالَّذِينَ اسْتَجَابُوا لِرَبِّهِمْ وَأَقَامُوا الصَّلَاةَ وَأَمْرُهُمْ شُورَى بَيْنَهُمْ وَمِمَّا رَزَقْنَاهُمْ يُنْفِقُونَ

...those who respond to their Lord and establish ṣalāt, and manage their affairs by mutual consultation and give of what We have provided for them. (Sūrat ash-Shūrā 42: 38)

Muslim jurists have said that when mutual consultation was made incumbent upon the Prophet himself ﷺ, it really becomes incumbent upon his followers to resort to *shūrā* in all activities whether individual, social or political. *Shūrā* is for those matters outside of the rulings of Allah, such as in warfare and other similar affairs. The Messenger of Allah ﷺ used to receive revelation from Allah, hence, he was not seemingly in need of advice but Allah still asked him to do so. It is on this basis that Ibn Taymiyyah has said that, "The leader has no other option but to resort to *shūrā* since Allah had commanded His Prophet ﷺ to do so. Everyone else, therefore, has a special need for consultation."[12] The Prophet ﷺ has said in a *ḥadīth*: "If I were to make anyone a caliph without consultation, I would have named ʿAbdullāh ibn Masʿūd."[13]

Likewise, the Caliph ʿUmar ؓ also said that caliphate can never function without mutual consultation.

عَنْ عُمَرَ أَنَّهُ قَالَ: لَا خِلَافَةَ إِلَّا عَنْ مَشُورَةٍ.

It is narrated from ʿUmar that he said, "There is no caliphate without consultation."[14]

Before the Battle of Uḥud, the Companions of the Prophet ﷺ had recommended that it would be better to defend themselves against the enemy coming from Makkah by staying in Madīnah. But Ḥamzah, the uncle of the Prophet ؓ and other young men were of the opinion that they should go bravely out of Madīnah and fight the enemy. After reviewing their opinions the Prophet ﷺ decided (*ᶜazm*) to go out of Madīnah and fight. Later the older companions persuaded the young men to withdraw their suggestion. The young men went to the Prophet ﷺ and regretfully withdrew their opinion, but the Prophet ﷺ said that now, after weighing the viewpoints in the consultation process, he had made his resolve and it would be contrary to the prophetic mission to go back on the final resolution.[15]

The other fine example to show how the right-acting caliphs depended on mutual consultation with the public is that of Caliph ᶜUmar ؓ who was of the opinion that after the conquest of Iraq and Syria the land should not be divided among the warriors as booty but should be made a *waqf*[16] so that through its produce and income the essential works of public welfare could be carried out. But some Companions opposed the view of the Caliph. When they could not find any solution through mutual consultation, the Caliph called a public meeting in the Prophet's mosque for general consultation and addressed the public in the following words: "I have not just gathered you here and troubled you for nothing. The reason for inviting you is that you should also participate in the trust of the caliphate which has been entrusted to me by you. Undoubtedly, I am an ordinary human being like you. I want that those who have opposed my point of view and those who have favoured it should declare it openly. I do not wish that you should follow my point of view, because you all possess the Book of Allah (from which you may derive guidance to resolve the issue)." Finally, after this process he did decide to make the lands of Iraq and Syria into a *waqf* for the benefit of the Muslims.

Mutual consultation is, therefore, one of the great qualities that the Muslim has to cultivate. It is commanded by Allah in Sūrah Āl ᶜImrān:

فَبِمَا رَحْمَةٍ مِنَ اللَّهِ لِنْتَ لَهُمْ وَلَوْ كُنْتَ فَظًّا غَلِيظَ الْقَلْبِ لَانْفَضُّوا مِنْ حَوْلِكَ فَاعْفُ عَنْهُمْ
وَاسْتَغْفِرْ لَهُمْ وَشَاوِرْهُمْ فِي الْأَمْرِ فَإِذَا عَزَمْتَ فَتَوَكَّلْ عَلَى اللَّهِ إِنَّ اللَّهَ يُحِبُّ الْمُتَوَكِّلِينَ

> *It is a mercy from Allah that you were gentle with them. If you had been rough or hard of heart, they would have scattered from around you. So pardon them and ask forgiveness for them, and consult with them about the matter. Then when you have reached a firm decision, put your trust in Allah. Allah loves those who put their trust in Him.* (Sūrah Āl ᶜImrān: 159)

For this reason, consultation among Muslims is an important part of the beautiful and elaborate building of the Islamic way of life. To do any collective work without prior mutual consultation is not only the way of ignorant people but is also clear defiance of the rule laid down by Allah. The great importance given to the whole process of consultation is based upon three reasons:

First, it is unjust to decide a matter concerning two or more people by oneself. In collective matters nobody has the right to do according to their own sweet will. The people concerned with a matter should be consulted, and if it concerns a large number of persons then people who represent them[17] should be sounded out for their considered opinion.

Second, if a man tries to act autocratically or arbitrarily, he either wants to usurp the rights of others or he considers himself superior and holds them in contempt. From the moral point of view both these attitudes are reprehensible. However, even a trace of these wrong attitudes cannot be found in the believer (*mu'min*), who is neither so selfish as to take unfair advantage of others, nor so proud and self-conceited as to believe himself a paragon of intelligence and knowledge.

Third, it is a great responsibility to take decisions on matters relating to the rights and interests of others. Anyone, who is conscious of Allah and His inevitable judgement, would not dare to assume the burden of such a responsibility alone. Such reckless acts are only done by those people who are devoid of fear of Allah and without care for the hereafter. In coming to a decision on a line of action concerning a collective matter, Allah-fearing people with awareness of the Day of Judgement will necessarily try to consult all the people or their trusted representatives so that a just and impartial decision is made, and so that, if a mistake is ever made, the burden of responsibility does not fall on one person alone.

These are the three reasons which, if one ponders them, one can understand why mutual consultation is a necessary requirement of the type of values taught by Islam. The Islamic way of life requires that the principle of consultation should be applicable to every minor or major collective affair. In the affairs of the household, husband and wife should consult each other before doing anything, and when the children attain the age of puberty their opinion should also be taken into account. If the affairs of the whole family are being dealt with, then counsel should be sought from every sane adult family member.

If the affairs are those of relatives, a clan, a tribe, a whole village, or an entire town or city and it is not possible to take counsel with everybody, then decisions should be reached in consultation with a gathering or gatherings of selected, trusted representatives of the people. If the affairs belong to a whole people then the leader can be appointed after consultation.[18] He in turn should run their affairs with the help of such counsellors he and the people trust.

The rule of *"and [who] manage their affairs by mutual consultation"* by its very nature demands five things for its fulfilment.

First, those people, whose rights and interests are involved, have full freedom of expression and should also be kept informed about how their affairs are being run. They have the duty to courteously remind those in authority if they see any deficiency, negligence or error in the proper discharge of the duties of leadership pertaining to their affairs or the affairs of the *dīn*.

Second, the person responsible for shouldering the management of collective affairs should be appointed according to one of the methods endorsed by the practice of the Companions or accepted by the people of knowledge. This includes his election by the people of standing in knowledge and *dīn*, his appointment after consultation by the previous Caliph, and his election by a group chosen by the previous Caliph to do so. It is also accepted by the *fuqahā'* that if someone does seize power by force, it is obligatory to obey him *if* he establishes the *dīn* and is obviously not a *kāfir*.

Third, his counsellors are not a fixed body of people and are chosen for a variety of considerations in different circumstances. They are chosen for their knowledge, experience, wisdom and expertise in their domains.

Fourth, his counsellors should advise him honestly but courteously. This falls under the traditional understanding of *al-amr bi'l-maᶜrūf wa'n-nahy ᶜani'l-munkar* – commanding the good and forbidding the wrong.

Fifth, the ruler is not bound to accept their advice even though he ought to seek it. That is because when Allah, exalted is He, says, *"Then when you have reached a firm decision, put your trust in Allah"* using the second person singular, i.e. the "you" addressed is a single man. So the ruler alone must make his decision and is not required to follow the majority verdict or even the unanimous agreement of his advisers.

With the above explanation of the Islamic principle of consultation (*shūrā*) the basic fact should also be kept in full view that *shūrā* is not the last word, nor the absolute authority in running the affairs of Muslims, but it is definitely limited within the confines of the *Dīn* of Islam, the Islamic code of life which has been revealed by Allah himself. It is dependent upon the fundamental principle that in whatever matter there is difference of opinion between the Muslims they should refer it to His Book, the Noble Qur'ān, and the Sunnah of the Prophet ﷺ. According to this basic principle Muslims can consult each other about matters in the *Sharīᶜah* regarding the correct meaning of a particular clause and correct observance of it in order to fulfil its purposes; but they cannot confer together with the purpose of replacing or altering in any manner the ruling or decision of Allah and His Messenger ﷺ by their own conclusions.

This is a vast topic, whose outlines have only been sketched.

Notes

[1] Kumo Sulaiman, *The Rule of Law and Independence of Judiciary under the Sharīᶜah*. C.I.L.S. Publications, Zaria.
[2] Cf. Pickthal, Marmaduke Muḥammad, *Cultural Sides of Islam*, Lahore, 1976, p.181.
[3] *Ibid.*, p.181.
[4] Hamidullah Muḥammad, *Muslim Conduct of State*, Lahore, 1973, p.12.
[5] Coulson, N.J., *A History of Islamic Law*, Edinburgh, p.8.
[6] *Ibid.*, p.83.
[7] As-Suyūṭī, Jalāl ad-Dīn, *al-Itqān fī ᶜulūm al-Qur'ān*.
[8] ᶜAbd al-Wahhāb ibn Khallāf has classified these verses in the following order: seventy verses on family law, seventy verses on civil law, thirty verses on penal law, thirteen verses on jurisdiction and procedures, ten verses on constitutional law, twenty-five verses on international law, twenty verses on economic and financial order, and fifty verses on sources of law in general. Cf. *Uṣūl al-fiqh*, Cairo, 1956, pp.34-35.
[9] The words in brackets are the author's.
[10] Sūrat ash-Shūrā 42: 36.
[11] Sūrat ash-Shūrā 42: 38.
[12] *As-Siyāsat ash-sharᶜiyyah* p.75.
[13] *Mustadrak* of al-Ḥākim.
[14] *Kanz al-ᶜummāl* from Ibn Abī Shaybah, and from Ibn al-Anbārī in *al-Maṣāḥif.*
[15] *Fatḥ al-bārī*, Vol.7, see the Battle of Uḥud.
[16] See Chapter 18, C. *Waqf.*
[17] The representatives can be in the capacity of people having expert

knowledge such as on military strategy, the ins-and-outs of the market, women knowledgeable in matters pertaining to women in particular, etc. They do not have to be representatives elected by democratic processes, but must be persons known, trusted and respected in the community at large.

[18] Appointment of a *khalīfah* by mutual consultation among people chosen for the task is one of the acceptable methods of appointment of a leader since it was that adopted by ʿUmar ☸ to appoint his successor. He himself chose seven people to choose a Caliph from among six of them. Other methods include his appointment by the leading members of the community as in the case of Abū Bakr ☸ and Alī ibn Abī Ṭālib ☸ or his appointment by the previous ruler as in the case of Abū Bakr's ☸ appointment of ʿUmar ☸ after consultation with the leading Companions. The *fuqahā'* also agree that if someone not worthy of the caliphate seizes it and then does not adhere to or propagate a false *ʿaqīdah*, and does establish the prayer, collect and distribute the *zakāh* and see to the *jihād*, that it is obligatory to obey him even though he is not necessarily the best man for the job.

Chapter 3

The Noble Qur'ān

The First Textual Source of *Sharīᶜah*

The Book of Allah

THE QUR'ĀN IS THE BOOK OF ALLAH (*Kitāb Allāh*)[1] revealed through the last of the Prophets, Muhammad ﷺ. It contains the knowledge (*ᶜilm*)[2] imparted by Allah and the guidance (*hudā*) for men who are right-acting for all time to come. It is a declaration (*bayān*)[3] of the truth and a light (*nūr*)[4] to show the right path. It is the Wise (*al-Ḥakīm*),[5] the complete exhortation (*mawᶜiẓah*)[6] and the clear message (*al-Balāgh*).[7] It is the rope of Allah (*Ḥabl-Allāh*)[8] by holding to which individuals and nations can achieve success. It is the remedy (*ash-Shifā'*)[9] for all the spiritual ailments of men. It is a constant reminder (*adh-Dhikr*)[10] for all of us that prophets will no longer come for our guidance. It acts as the criterion (*al-Furqān*)[11] to choose between truth and falsehood.

As the final revelation (*tanzīl*)[12] from Allah, it is the embodiment of the fairest statements (*aḥsan al-ḥadīth*)[13] and Divine words of wisdom (*ḥikmah*).[14]

The Qur'ān provides a code of conduct for every believer and is the command (*amr*)[15] and a warrant (*tadhkirah*)[16] for him. Its injunctions are manifest (*mubīn*),[17] sublime (*ᶜālī*)[18] and blessed (*mubārak*).[19]

Early religious books were either short or very long, but the Qur'ān falls in between them and is of medium size.

The revelation's transcription and final compilation in the deserts of Arabia was a remarkable feat considering the fact that very little writing had taken place before the Qur'ān.[20]

The Qur'ān is divided into 114 chapters and contains 86,430 words and 323,760 letters of the alphabet. The total number of verses is 6,666. In order to facilitate its reading the Qur'ān is divided into thirty convenient *juz'* sections (*ajzā'*), sixty *ḥizb* sub-sections (*aḥzāb*), 540 *rukū*^c divisions and seven *manāzil*. There are fourteen (according to some fifteen, and according to the People of Madīnah eleven) places in the Qur'ān where the words used are so commanding that the reciter must prostrate in awe to glorify Allah.

The Qur'ān was revealed piecemeal over a period of twenty-two years, two months and twenty-two days according to the needs of time and to provide solutions to the problems which came before the Prophet ﷺ.

The first revelation of the Qur'ān began on the fifteenth night of the month of Ramaḍān in the forty-first year of the Prophet's life ﷺ. Its first sūrah was revealed in the Cave of Hirā' when the verse, *"Recite: In the Name of your Lord who created, created man from clots of blood. Recite: And your Lord is the Most Generous...,"* (Sūrat al-^cAlaq 96: 1-3) was revealed.

The last verse of the Qur'ān, *"Today I have perfected your dīn for you and completed My blessing upon you and I am pleased with Islam as a dīn for you,"* (Sūrat al-Mā'idah 5: 3) was revealed on the ninth Dhu'l-Ḥijjah in the tenth Year of Hijrah when the Prophet ﷺ was in the sixty-third year of his life.

Tafsīr of the Noble Qur'ān (Exegesis):

The Companions (*Ṣaḥābah*) of the Prophet ﷺ saw the Qur'ān as a rich source of divine wisdom and spent their lives in search of the treasures lying buried in it. Their labour brought out those pearls of wisdom which illuminate our thought patterns even today.

The first of the intellectual activity of the *Ummah,* therefore, was the *tafsīr* or exegesis of the Qur'ān which, in a way, helped in explaining the norms of *Sharī^cah* contained in the Qur'ān.

The word *tafsīr* is derived from the Arabic word *fasara* which means 'to make clear', 'to show the objective', or 'to lift the curtain'. *Tafsīr,* therefore, would mean the science through which the Book of Allah can be understood. According to ^cAllāmah Shāh ^cAbd al-ᶜAzīz ad-Dihlawī, an exegete should keep in mind the following three conditions when he seeks to interpret the Qur'ān:

1. Every word should be explained with its real meaning so that it shows the reality of its objective. In order to achieve this, the scholar has to employ linguistic knowledge and grammar.
2. Everything should be explained with reference to the context of the main theme of the revelation.
3. The interpretation should not be contrary to the sayings of the Companions, who witnessed the coming of the revelations to the Messenger of Allah ﷺ.

Tafsīr, therefore, means the science which clarifies the meaning of the Qur'ānic injunctions and the causes of their revelation.

Qur'ān is the best *tafsīr* of the Qur'ān

The first and foremost *tafsīr* or commentary on the Qur'ān is the Qur'ān itself[21], one part of which helps to elucidate another. This can be seen throughout the Qur'ān, for example, when we pray in Sūrat al-Fātiḥah: *"Guide us on the Straight Path (aṣ-ṣirāṭ al-mustaqīm)."*[22] We would like to know what that straight path is. The entire Qur'ān is full of examples to show us that path, as if the Noble Qur'ān is the answer to that prayer and yearning of the believers. Likewise, in the same Sūrah, we read: *"the Path of those whom You have blessed"*[23] and so we ask ourselves, 'who are these blessed and fortunate people?' The Noble Qur'ān gives us the categories of these Prophets and utterly truthful people, martyrs and right-acting people[24] through the examples of His Prophets and Messengers as well as other true believers. Various ambivalent (*mujmal*) Qur'ānic statements are elucidated in the light of specific (*mubayyan*) ones. To take a concrete example, Allah ﷻ says: *"All livestock animals are ḥalāl for you, except those that are recited to you now"*. (Sūrat al-Anᶜām 6: 1) The purpose of this statement becomes comprehensible in the light of another verse of the same chapter: *"Ḥarām for you are carrion, blood and pork…"*. (Sūrat al-Anᶜām 6: 3) Similarly, explaining the absolute (*muṭlaq*) by the restricted (*muqayyad*) and the general (*ᶜāmm*) by the particular (*khāṣṣ*) is a part of the method of explaining parts of the Qur'ān in the light of other related parts of the Qur'ān.[25] By applying this method Muslim scholars also try to obviate problems posed by verses which seem to be mutually contradictory.

The work of Muqātil ibn Sulaymān (d. 150 AH/767 CE), *Mutashābih fī al-Qur'ān,* is a good example of a relatively early grappling with this problem. The clarification of the meaning of the Qur'ānic verses was one of the main functions of the prophetic office. Ibn Khaldūn said: "The Prophet ﷺ used to clarify the ambivalent (*mujmal*) and to distinguish between the abrogating verses and the abrogated ones, and to make this clear to his Companions".[26] "We learn from ḥadīth that the Prophet ﷺ at times used to explain some verses. For example, he explained that the words, *'those with anger on them'* (occurring in Sūrat al-Fātiḥah) allude to the Jews. Again, he explained: *'nor of the misguided'* (in the same chapter) as alluding to the Christians."[27] There are numerous other instances of the same nature in ḥadīth works which illustrate this point.

When the Messenger of Allah ﷺ was asked about some verses, the answers he gave were authoritative explanations of those verses. For instance when *"Those who have īmān and do not mix up their īmān with any wrongdoing, they are the ones who are safe"* (Sūrat al-Anᶜām 6: 82) was revealed, people found it difficult to comprehend its import, and hence asked the Prophet ﷺ as to who of them did not commit wrong against himself. The Prophet ﷺ made it clear that here is meant *'Shirk,* associating others with Allah' which has been characterised elsewhere in the Qur'ān (Sūrah Luqmān 31: 13) as a *'mighty wrong.'*[28] There were occasions when the Companions consulted the Prophet ﷺ, and his silence or corrections were themselves considered a kind of commentary. When the verse *"And eat and drink until you can clearly discern the white thread from the black thread of the dawn"* (Sūrat al-Baqarah 2:187) was revealed, ᶜAdī ibn Ḥātim took two ropes, one white and the other black, and looked at them, but failed to distinguish one from the other. Then he went to the Prophet ﷺ in the morning and told him about what had happened. The Prophet ﷺ explained that what was meant by it was the black of night and the white of day.[29] This Prophetic Commentary (*tafsīr nabawī*) is to be found in the collections of traditions made by al-Bukhārī, Muslim, at-Tirmidhī, and others.

The birth of the science of *tafsīr*

The Noble Qur'ān has given rise to so voluminous a literature in languages in the last century – Urdu, Swahili and Hausa – that a single man could not even peruse the whole of it in his lifetime. Apart from these languages, a lot of Qur'ānic literature has come into existence in many European, African and Asian languages spoken in the Muslim world – Arabic, Persian and Turkish – in our present time. It has been rightly remarked: "There is no book in whose service so much talent, so much labour, so much time and money have been expended as has been the case with the Qur'ān."[30] If one looks at *al-Itqān fī ᶜulūm al-Qur'ān* by Imām Jalāl ad-Dīn as-Suyūṭī (d. 911 AH/1533 CE) one can realise the encyclopaedic nature of the Qur'ānic sciences. During the lifetime of the Prophet ﷺ, the Companions used to ask him questions relating to the interpretation of the Noble Qur'ān and the different aspects of injunctions (*aḥkām*) contained in it. The Messenger of Allah ﷺ used to explain to them matters concerning all the Qur'ānic verses.

The result of these exercises was that the Companions came to know all about the causes of revelation (*asbāb an-nuzūl*) of different verses. They were also able to distinguish between the *nāsikh* (abrogating) and *mansūkh* (abrogated) verses.

The Prophet ﷺ undertook to explain and interpret the verses of the Noble Qur'ān to the Companions as was directed by Allah. This fact is evident in the Qur'ānic verse which reads:

وَأَنزَلْنَا إِلَيْكَ الذِّكْرَ لِتُبَيِّنَ لِلنَّاسِ مَا نُزِّلَ إِلَيْهِمْ وَلَعَلَّهُمْ يَتَفَكَّرُونَ

> *And We have sent down the Reminder to you so that you can make clear to mankind what has been sent down to them so that hopefully they will reflect.* (Sūrat an-Naḥl 16: 44)

All things he had said in explanation or to which he had given silent approval were committed to memory by the Companions. Those who embraced Islam or were born after the death of the Prophet ﷺ used to inquire from the Companions about the Prophet's explanations of the various verses of the Noble Qur'ān. The Companions on their own part used to tell their Followers (*tābiᶜūn*) not only the Prophet's explanations of the various verses, but also of other interpretations to which the Prophet ﷺ had given his silent approval.

Most of the Companions were men of great learning. A majority of them had committed the whole of the Qur'ān to memory. Almost all of them had emerged as great Qur'ān reciters right from the time of the Messenger of Allah ﷺ.

In fact, it would be fair to say that the Companions were tutored by the Prophet ﷺ himself and they knew the Qur'ān better than all the major scholars of our time. The Companions, as has been noted above, transmitted the Sunnah of the Prophet ﷺ to the Followers (*tābiᶜūn*) and the Followers in their turn transmitted it to their own followers (*tābiᶜu't-tābiᶜīn*).

The Follower Abū ᶜAbd ar-Raḥmān as-Sulamī (d. 82 AH/701 CE) said: "Those who recited Qur'ān to us, like ᶜUthmān ibn ᶜAffān and ᶜAbdullāh ibn Masᶜūd and others, said that when they learnt ten verses from the Prophet ﷺ, they did not go beyond that unless they thoroughly understood them and put them into practice."[31] Thus the Companions used to spend years learning the surāhs of the Qur'ān. Imām Mālik says in his *Muwaṭṭa'* that ᶜAbdullāh ibn ᶜUmar spent eight years memorising Sūrat al-Baqarah.[32]

The four *Khulafā' ar-rāshidūn* ؓ – the Caliphs who took the right way – were undoubtedly pre-eminent early *tafsīr* scholars (commentators) of the Qur'ān since they witnessed the coming of the revelations (*waḥy*) and learnt their inner meanings directly from the Prophet ﷺ. Other recognised scholars of the Qur'ān in the time of the Prophet ﷺ, who may aptly be described as scholars of *tafsīr* were:

1. ᶜAbdullāh ibn ᶜAbbās (d. 68 AH/687 CE)
2. ᶜAbdullāh ibn Masᶜūd (d. 32 AH/653 CE)
3. Ubayy ibn Kaᶜb (d. 20 AH/640 CE)

4. Zayd ibn Thābit (d. 45 AH/665 CE)
5. Abū Mūsā al-Ashʿarī (d. 44 AH/664 CE) and
6. ʿAbdullāh ibn az-Zubayr (d. 73 AH/692 CE)[33]

The leading narrators of *tafsīr,* taken in order of the amount they related, were: Ibn ʿAbbās, Ibn Masʿūd, ʿAlī, and Ubayy ibn Kaʿb. Ibn ʿAbbās was called the learned man of the community (*ḥibr al-ummah*), the interpreter of the Qur'ān (*tarjumān al-Qur'ān*), and the ocean (*baḥr*). It was related that Jibril told the Prophet ﷺ that Ibn ʿAbbās was the best (*khayr*) of the community.[34] Ibn ʿAbbās, as some scholars observe, was the father of *tafsīr.* His wide knowledge in many fields assisted him in this arduous task. His knowledge of the Arabic language and literature was also very extensive, which is illustrated by the following incident. Nāfiʿ ibn al-Azraq once asked him a large number of questions relating to the Qur'ān, requiring him to provide corroborative evidence from Arabic poetry. Ibn ʿAbbās gave the meanings of two hundred words citing a verse of pre-Islamic poetry for each in proof of his contentions.[35]

Many Companions of the Prophet ﷺ were proud of Ibn ʿAbbās and praised him. Among them was Sayyidunā ʿAlī, the fourth Caliph of Islam, who said of his *tafsīr*: "It is as if he were looking at the unseen through a thin veil." Ibn ʿUmar said: "Ibn ʿAbbās is the most knowledgeable person of the community of Muḥammad about what was revealed to him ﷺ."[36] His being the forefather of the Abbasids may have played some part in the attribution of a large number of traditions to him.

The other great scholar of the Qur'ān in the early days was ʿAbdullāh ibn Masʿūd. He spent his time in understanding the deeper meaning of the Qur'ān. The recognition of his depth of knowledge is given even by ʿAlī ibn Abī Ṭālib. Once he was asked about ʿAbdullāh ibn Masʿūd and his scholarship, and he replied as follows: "He knows the Qur'ān and the Sunnah, and his knowledge is the best."[37] His *qirā'ah* (method of recitation) is well known to scholars of *tafsīr,* and his opinions relating to *tafsīr* in the books of ḥadīth and *tafsīr* are considered highly authentic. After Ibn Masʿūd comes ʿAlī followed by Ubayy ibn

Kaᶜb. Ubayy is a great authority in Qur'ānic Commentary. Ḥajjī Khalīfah states: "There is a major copy [of a *tafsīr*] which Abū Jaᶜfar ar-Rāzī related from ar-Rabīᶜ ibn Anas from Abu'l-ᶜĀliyah from Ubayy ibn Kaᶜb."[38] Nothing is known of what happened to this copy but his explanatory opinions are found in the books of *tafsīr* and ḥadīth. Those four were the greatest of the Companions in the field of *tafsīr* and much more is related from them than from others. There are some Companions who related traditions relevant to questions of *tafsīr* such as ᶜĀ'ishah (d. 58 AH/678 CE), Abū Hurayrah (d. 59 AH/679 CE), ᶜAbdullāh ibn ᶜAmr ibn al-ᶜĀṣ (d. 63 AH/683 CE), ᶜAbdullāh ibn ᶜUmar ibn al-Khaṭṭāb (d. 73 AH/692 CE), Jābir ibn ᶜAbdullāh al-Anṣārī (d. 74 AH/693 CE), and Anas ibn Mālik (d. 91 AH/709 CE).[39]

The great Companions who had learnt the Qur'ān and its *tafsīr* directly from the Prophet himself ﷺ passed away one by one. The task of developing the science of *tafsīr*, therefore, rested on the Followers (the *tābiᶜūn*, the successors of the *ṣaḥābah*) who were tutored by the noble Companions of the Prophet ﷺ.

There were three main schools of Qur'ānic Commentary which had developed by the end of the first half of the first century.

The first was that of Makkah whose master was ᶜAbdullāh ibn ᶜAbbās (d. 68 AH/688 CE) and whose students were Saᶜīd ibn Jubayr (d. 94 AH/712 CE or 95 AH/713 CE), Mujāhid ibn Jabr al-Makkī (d. 104 AH/722 CE), ᶜIkrimah, the *mawlā* of Ibn ᶜAbbās (d. 105 AH/723 CE), Ṭāwūs ibn Kaysān al-Yamanī (d. 106 AH/724 CE) and ᶜAṭā' ibn Abī Rabāḥ (d. 114 AH/732 CE).[40]

The second school was that of Iraq which recognised Ibn Masᶜūd as its master (and also some other Companions, but the school accepted him as its main authority). Its students were ᶜAlqamah ibn Qays (d. 102 AH/720 CE), al-Aswad ibn Yazīd (d. 75 AH/694 CE), Masrūq ibn al-Ajdaᶜ (d. 63 AH/682 CE), Mara al-Hamdānī (d. 76 AH/695 CE), ᶜĀmir ash-Shaᶜbī (d. 105 AH/723 CE), al-Ḥasan al-Baṣrī (d. 121 AH/738 CE), Qatādah as-Sadūsī, (d. 117 AH/735 CE), and Ibrāhīm an-Nakhaᶜī (d. 195 AH/713 CE).[41]

Finally, there was the school of Madīnah which, as the first capital of Islam, was full of Companions and Muslim scholars, the most famous being Ubayy ibn Kaᶜb. His students were Abu'l-ᶜĀliyah (d. 90 AH/708 CE), Muḥammad ibn Kaᶜb al-Qarẓī (d. 117 AH/735 CE), and Zayd ibn Aslam (d. 130 AH/747 CE) under whom his son ᶜAbd ar-Raḥmān ibn Zayd and Mālik ibn Anas studied.[42]

The works of *tafsīr* at this stage included commentary on more verses than before, and the Followers began to compose their commentaries as well. Although some of them transmitted the opinion of Companions outside their school, most of their material was attributed to the founder of their own school. In the immediate period following, we find the following prominent scholars in the field of *tafsīr*: Ismāᶜīl as-Suddī (d. 128 AH/745 CE), aḍ-Ḍaḥḥāk ibn Muzāḥim (d. 105 AH/723 CE), al-Kalbī (d. 146 AH/763 CE), Muqātil ibn Ḥayyān (d. before 150 AH/767 CE) and Muqātil ibn Sulaymān (d. 150 AH/767 CE).

Since *tafsīr*-writing began in the lifetime of the Prophet Muhammad ﷺ, it is not possible to pinpoint and say that such and such a *tafsīr* is the oldest extant. It is likely that there were many works of *tafsīr*, but some of them have not survived to the present. It is, however, generally believed that the oldest extant work on *tafsīr* is that of aṭ-Ṭabarī who died in 310 AH/922 CE as believed by classical scholars like Muḥammad adh-Dhahabī[43] in his famous work at-*Tafsīr wa'l-mufassirūn* and modern scholars like Aḥmad Amīn.[44]

Having said this however, it is a fact that the earlier *tafsīrs* of Mujāhid ibn Jabr al-Makkī, Zayd ibn ᶜAlī (d. 122 AH/740 CE), ᶜAṭā' al-Khurasānī (d. 133/755 CE), Muhammad ibn as-Sā'ib al-Kalbī (d. 146 AH/763 CE) and Muqātil ibn Sulaymān al-Khurasānī (d. 150 AH/767 CE) are still extant and available.[45] The process of *tafsīr*-writing has continued right up to our day and will continue.

After these famous people came the four great Imāms, (Imām Mālik, Imām Abū Ḥanīfah, Imām ash-Shāfiᶜī, Imām Aḥmad ibn Ḥanbal) who established the principles of the science of Islamic jurisprudence. Due to their efforts a scientific form of study, collection and compilation of the Sunnah and ḥadīth evolved. Rules were established by different scholars for the determination of the authenticity of any ḥadīth ascribed to the Prophet ﷺ and for the detection of weakness in it, either on the ground of doubt in the character of one of the narrators or on the ground of the unsoundness of the text.

One of those who so formulated these rules was Muḥammad aṭ-Ṭabarī who was a contemporary of al-Bukhārī, the great collector of ḥadīth. He was the first man to write on Qur'ānic exegesis explaining it side-by-side with the Sunnah. He was, indeed, the first scholar to make the study of the exegesis a distinct discipline. In his thirty-volume book[46] he gave *tafsīr* of the Qur'ān on the basis of what had been explained by the Companions.

In later years, commentators and Qur'ānic scientists formulated various rules of interpretation, which enabled both the Arab as well as the non-Arab Muslim scholar to write works of *tafsīr* in Arabic and other languages.

Some of these rules related to *i^c^rāb* – syntactic inflection or the science of the various inflections of words, literal or virtual, by reason of the various governing words – and *balāghah* – eloquence. They were collected in the form of books. The most famous of such books is az-Zamakhsharī's *al-Kashshāf*[47] which literally means "the book that unveils". Az-Zamakhsharī was an eminent Mu^c^tazilite, a rationalist and a philosopher. Therefore, many scholars of Qur'ānic exegesis have criticised his work as consisting mostly of mu^c^tazilite thought. However, despite this criticism, his book remains one of the most authoritative works on the subject, particularly in respect of the meanings of Arabic words.

The period of the ^c^Abbasid Caliphate was a period of intellectual renaissance (*an-Nahdah Islamiyyah*) in which the Muslim world was exposed to different foreign ideas. The knowledge gained in this manner was woven into the fabric of Islamic thought and culture. Consequently, scholastic theology (*^c^ilm al-kalām*) emerged wherein the articles of Islamic faith and the attributes of Allah were discussed to establish the unity (*tawḥīd*) of Allah. The most celebrated work on the subject of *^c^ilm al-kalām* is Sayyid Sharīf Jurjānī's *Sharḥ al-Mawāqif*, his commentary on the famous work *al-Mawāqif*. *^c^Ilm al-kalām* was also significant in the development of some schools of Sufism. Imām Fakhr ad-Dīn ar-Rāzī, author of a voluminous *Tafsīr* and of *Mafātīḥ al-Ghayb,* was the most outstanding example of the convergence of Sufism and *ᶜilm al-kalām.*

Isrā'īliyyāt in *Tafsīr*

In later centuries, Muslims used to seek information from Jews newly converted to Islam about the stories of the ancient civilisations mentioned in the Noble Qur'ān. The narration and explanations of ancient events by these *Ahl al-Kitāb* (People of the Book) used to be taken as authentic and final by the Arabs for they did not know anything about them. One such narrator was Kaᶜb al-Aḥbār, a learned Jew who converted to Islam and who was one of the Followers. But the Arabs later discovered their mistakes as many of these explanations and narrations were proved to be false. These false explanations and narrations are called *Isrā'īliyyāt*[48] and some of them can still be found in the works of *tafsīr.*[49] The reason for the acceptance of the explanations and narrations of these stories from the newly converted Jews was the following tradition:

> Convey from me even if it is one single verse and narrate from the Israelites and there is no harm. Whosoever attributes a lie to me intentionally, should prepare his residence in the Fire. (Al-Bukhārī, *kitāb al-anbiyā', bāb mā dhukira ᶜan Banī Isrā'īl*)

There is a limit to what one can accept from the People of the Book. Some commentators have differed in giving the names of the *Aṣḥāb al-Kahf*[50] (People of the Cave), the colour of their dog and their actual number. Allah says: *"Say: 'My Lord knows best their number. Those who know about them are very few.' So do not enter into any argument concerning them, except in relation to what is clearly known."* (Sūrat al-Kahf 18: 22) There are also differences about the name of the boy killed by Aliser, the names of the birds enlivened for Ibrāhīm ﷺ by Allah, and the type of wood of the staff of Mūsā ﷺ, etc.[51]

Some scholars held the opinion that wherever the texts of the Qur'ān and the ḥadīth are silent on a particular story, the direction contained in the aforesaid ḥadīth would suffice, and a Muslim is allowed to accept the explanations or narrations given by the People of the Book. They further expiated on their stand and said that such explanations and narration should be classified into the following categories:

1. Those which our texts approve; we must accept all of them.
2. Those which our texts reject; we must reject all of them.
3. Those about which our texts are silent; we have the freedom to explore.

Two Kinds of *Tafsīr*

1. *At-tafsīr bi'l-ma'thūr* – *tafsīr* according to what is narrated

The first books of this class of *tafsīr* are:

a. The *tafsīr* attributed to Ibn cAbbās
b. The *tafsīr* of Ibn cUtaybah
c. The *tafsīr* of Ibn Abī Khātim
d. The *tafsīr* of Abu'sh-Shaykh Ibn Ḥabbān
e. The *tafsīr* of Ibn cAṭiyyah
f. *Ad-Durr al-manthūr fi't-tafsīr bi'l-ma'thūr* by Imām as-Suyūṭī
g. The *tafsīr* of Abu'l-Layth as-Samarqandī called *Baḥr al-culūm*
h. The *tafsīr* of Abū Isḥāq called *al-Kashf wa'l-bayān can tafsīr al-Qur'ān*
i. *Jāmic al-bayān tafsīr al-Qur'ān* by Ibn Jarīr aṭ-Ṭabarī
j. The *tafsīr* of Ibn Abī Shaybah
k. The *tafsīr* of al-Baghawī called *Macālim at-tanzīl*
l. The *tafsīr* by Ibn Kathir called *Tafsīr al-Qur'ān al-cAẓīm*
m. The *tafsīr* of ash-Shawkānī called *Fatḥ al-Qadīr*

2. *At-Tafsīr bi'l-Macqūl wa bi'd-Dirāyah* – *Tafsīr* according to intellectual understanding:

In this kind of *tafsīr*, the commentator relies much on his own reasoning and initiative to interpret the verses of the Noble Qur'ān. It subsequently led to the development of exegesis in the light of linguistic and mystical interpretations of the Qur'ān and took the following forms:

A. *At-tafsīr al-lughawī* (linguistic *tafsīr)*

This is linguistic interpretation of the Noble Qur'ān. Notable works in this class are:

i. *Tafsīr al-Kashshāf* by Maḥmūd ibn cUmar az-Zamakhsharī, the Muctazilite scholar. Az-Zamakhsharī has described the beauty of language and style of the Noble Qur'ān, and shown that the Book is a great miracle (*mucjizah*).
ii. *Tafsīr al-Baḥr al-Muḥīṭ* by Abū Ḥayyān al-Andalūsī.

B. *At-Ta'wīl, Falsafā wa't-Taṣawwuf* (Philosophical or Sufic Interpretations)

This is a purely philosophical and spiritual exposition of the Noble Qur'ān. The most famous works of this kind are:

i. *Mafātīḥ al-ghayb* by Imām Fakhr ad-Dīn ar-Rāzī.
ii. *Al-Lubāb fi macānī at-tanzīl* by al-Khāzin.

C. *Isrā'īliyyāt*

These works are based on the explanations and narrations received from Jews newly converted to Islam regarding the stories mentioned in the Noble Qur'ān. The works in this category are:

i. *Tafsīr Ibn Ḥayyān* by Ibn Ḥayyān.
ii. *Al-Jāmic li aḥkām al-Qur'ān* by al-Qurṭubī. It sorts out the authentic transmissions from among the various explanations. However, this *tafsīr* is much greater than simply being confined to *Isrā'īliyyāt* and is truly encyclopaedic in scope covering linguistic, *Sharīcah* and other domains of *tafsīr*.

D. *Tafsīr āyāt al-aḥkām* – Commentary on the Verses of Injunctions

These works contain explanations of the verses of injunctions (*āyāt al-aḥkām*) in the Noble Qur'ān. Outstanding works in this class are:

a. *Aḥkām al-Qur'ān* by Ibn al-ᶜArabī al-Mālikī.
b. *Al-Jāmiᶜ li aḥkām al-Qur'ān* by al-Qurṭubī.
c. *Aḥkām al-Qur'ān* by al-Jaṣṣāṣ al-Ḥanafī.

E. *Tafsīr ar-riwāyah wa'd-dirāyah* – Commentary through narration and understanding

These works have taken into consideration both the narrations (*riwāyah*) and the understanding (*dirāyah*) concerning the verses of the Noble Qur'ān. The outstanding works in this category are:

a. *Tafsīr al-Qur'ān al-ᶜAẓīm* of Ibn Kathīr.
b. *Fatḥ al-Qadīr* by ash-Shawkānī.

Other works of *tafsīr* that can be listed in the category of *tafsīr bi'r-ra'y* (*tafsīr* through theoretical reflection) are the following:

a. The *tafsīr* of ᶜAbd ar-Raḥmān ibn Kaysān al-Aṣamm.
b. The *tafsīr* of Abū al-Jabā'ī.
c. The *tafsīr* of ᶜAbd al-Jabbār.
d. The *tafsīr* of an-Nasafī called *Madārik at-tanzīl wa ḥaqā'iq at-ta'wīl*.
e. The *tafsīr* of al-Bayḍawī called *Anwār al-tanzīl wa asrār at-ta'wīl*.
f. The *Tafsīr al-Jalālayn* by Jalāl ad-Dīn al-Maḥallī and Jalāl ad-Dīn as-Suyūṭī.

The *Tafsīr* in Use in This Book

One of the most concise *tafsīrs* is that of Muḥammad ibn Aḥmad ibn Juzayy al-Kalbī, *Kiṭāb at-tashīl li ᶜulūm at-tanzīl*. Ibn Juzayy, who was born in 693 AH/1294 CE and died in the battle of Ṭarīfah 741 AH/1340 CE, was from Granada, Spain. He transmitted the traditional commentaries' material in a very clear and uncluttered form, showing the varying interpretations made by commentators – occasionally refuting discredited views, and the differing *fiqh* judgements derived from the *āyāt*. The work is particularly useful for its introduction, which summarises the sciences necessary for *tafsīr*, and a dictionary of words used in the Noble Qur'ān.

Risk in Imaginary *Tafsīr*

It is very risky to undertake the interpretation of the Noble Qur'ān on the basis of personal opinion without reference to the authorities stated above. The Prophet ﷺ warned:

وَمَنْ قَالَ فِي الْقُرْآنِ بِرَأْيِهِ فَلْيَتَبَوَّأْ مَقْعَدَهُ مِنَ النَّارِ

> Whoever speaks about the Qur'ān by his own opinion, let him take his seat in the Fire. (At-Tirmidhī, *abwāb tafsīr al-Qur'ān ᶜan rasūl Allāh* ﷺ, *bāb mā jā'a fī alladhī yufassiru al-Qur'ān bi ra'yihi;* an-Nasā'ī and Abū Dāwūd also narrate it. This is the version of at-Tirmidhī)

Some Companions were very careful and remained silent and would not comment on the Qur'ān. It is narrated about the Follower Saᶜīd ibn al-Musayyab that:

> Whenever he was asked about the *tafsīr* of any verse from the Qur'ān, he said: "We do not say anything on the matter of the Qur'ān." (Narrated by Imām Mālik in the *Muwaṭṭa'*)[52]

The risk involved in embarking on personal interpretation of the Noble Qur'ān can best be understood by considering the example of the explanation of the following verse:

وَاللَّاتِي يَأْتِينَ الْفَاحِشَةَ مِن نِّسَائِكُمْ فَاسْتَشْهِدُوا عَلَيْهِنَّ أَرْبَعَةً مِّنكُمْ فَإِن شَهِدُوا فَأَمْسِكُوهُنَّ فِي الْبُيُوتِ حَتَّىٰ يَتَوَفَّاهُنَّ الْمَوْتُ أَوْ يَجْعَلَ اللَّهُ لَهُنَّ سَبِيلًا

> *If any of your women commit fornication, four of you must be witnesses against them. If they bear witness, detain them in their homes until death releases them or Allah ordains another procedure for their case.* (Sūrat an-Nisā' 4: 15)

Some of the commentators maintain that this verse relates to women committing fornication among themselves. However, other commentators argue that it applies to those women who commit adultery with men or women. So far so good, but a major difference among the commentators has arisen on the question as to whether this particular verse has been abrogated by another verse on the same subect, or whether it has been given a permanent place in the Noble Qur'ān.

الزَّانِيَةُ وَالزَّانِي فَاجْلِدُوا كُلَّ وَاحِدٍ مِنْهُمَا مِئَةَ جَلْدَةٍ وَلَا تَأْخُذْكُم بِهِمَا رَأْفَةٌ فِي دِينِ اللَّهِ إِن كُنتُمْ

تُؤْمِنُونَ بِاللَّهِ وَالْيَوْمِ الْآخِرِ وَلْيَشْهَدْ عَذَابَهُمَا طَائِفَةٌ مِنَ الْمُؤْمِنِينَ

*A woman and a man who commit fornication: flog both of them with
one hundred lashes and do not let compassion for either of them possess
you where Allah's dīn is concerned, if you have īmān in Allah and the
Last Day. A number of mu'minūn should witness their punishment.*
(Sūrat an-Nūr 24: 2)

A majority of the commentators agree that the former verse has
been abrogated by the latter, but there are other commentators who
say that it has not been abrogated. They include Ibn al-‘Arabī. He has
advanced the argument that this is a verse setting a limit for its own
operation and application: women who fornicate should be kept in
their houses until death has overtaken them or until Allah in His
mercy ordains another procedure. According to him if the latter
situation takes place, the first part of the injunction will still apply.
The latter verse does not abrogate it since it does not contradict the
first part of the injunction from Allah, namely, taking the evidence
of four reliable witnesses. However, commenting on the *āyah* from
Sūrat an-Nisā' cited above and the *āyah* that follows it: "*If two
men commit a like abomination, punish them. If they make tawbah and
reform, leave them alone. Allah is Ever-Returning, Most Merciful*" (Sūrat
an-Nisā' 4: 16), Ibn ‘Abbās ⬡ said:

كَانَتِ الْمَرْأَةُ إِذَا زَنَتْ حُبِسَتْ فِي الْبَيْتِ حَتَّى تَمُوتَ وَالرَّجُلُ أُوذِيَ بِالتَّعْزِيرِ وَالضَّرْبِ بِالنِّعَالِ ،

فَنَزَلَتْ ﴿ الزَّانِيَةُ وَالزَّانِي فَاجْلِدُوا كُلَّ وَاحِدٍ مِنْهُمَا مِئَةَ جَلْدَةٍ ﴾ وَإِن كَانُوا مُحْصَنِينَ رَجْمًا بِسُنَّةِ

رَسُولِ اللَّهِ ﷺ فَهُوَ سَبِيلُهُمَا

When a woman fornicated, she would be confined in the
house until she died and a man would be punished through
discretionary punishment (*ta‘zīr*) and beating with shoes. Then
was revealed the following verse: "*A woman and a man who commit
fornication: flog both of them with one hundred lashes*" (Sūrat an-
Nūr 24: 2). If they were both married or had been married and
consummated their marriage (*muḥṣan*), they should be stoned

to death according to the Sunnah of the Prophet ﷺ since that is the path for them.

The Qur'ānic *āyāt* of 'clear judgements' and those 'open to interpretation'

According to the Qur'ān, it has two systems of meanings: the clear judgements (*muḥkam*) and those open to interpretation (*mutashābih*):

هُوَ الَّذِي أَنْزَلَ عَلَيْكَ الْكِتَابَ مِنْهُ آيَاتٌ مُحْكَمَاتٌ هُنَّ أُمُّ الْكِتَابِ وَأُخَرُ مُتَشَابِهَاتٌ فَأَمَّا الَّذِينَ فِي قُلُوبِهِمْ زَيْغٌ فَيَتَّبِعُونَ مَا تَشَابَهَ مِنْهُ ابْتِغَاءَ الْفِتْنَةِ وَابْتِغَاءَ تَأْوِيلِهِ وَمَا يَعْلَمُ تَأْوِيلَهُ إِلَّا اللَّهُ وَالرَّاسِخُونَ فِي الْعِلْمِ يَقُولُونَ آمَنَّا بِهِ كُلٌّ مِنْ عِنْدِ رَبِّنَا وَمَا يَذَّكَّرُ إِلَّا أُولُوا الْأَلْبَابِ

It is He who sent down the Book to you from Him: āyāt containing clear judgements – they are the core of the Book – and others which are open to interpretation. Those with deviation in their hearts follow what is open to interpretation in it, desiring conflict, seeking its inner meaning. No one knows its inner meaning but Allah. Those firmly rooted in knowledge say, "We have īmān in it. All of it is from our Lord." But only people of intelligence pay heed. (Sūrah Āl ᶜImrān 3: 7)

This verse gives us an important clue to the interpretation of the Noble Qur'ān.

Broadly speaking the Qur'ān may be divided into two portions, not arranged separately but intermingled, *viz*:

1. The portion of 'clear judgements' which is the nucleus or foundation of the Book: 'the core of the Book' or literally 'the mother of the Book'.
2. The portion which is figurative, metaphorical, allegorical or 'open to interpretation'.

It is fascinating for people to take up the latter portion and exercise their ingenuity about their inner meaning; but they refer to such profound matters that human language is inadequate to deal with them and no human being can be sure about their meanings, which are known to Allah alone. On the other hand, the verses of 'clear judgement' (*muḥkam*) refer to the *āyāt* on *tawḥīd*, the categorical orders of the *Sharīᶜah* (the law), and the statements on human behaviour and character which are plain to human understanding. In other words, the verses which are 'the mother of the Book' include those which form the very foundations on which rests the essence of Allah's message, and in this respect they are distinguishable from the various illustrative parables and allegories contained in the other type of verses.

It is worth noting that in a sense the whole of the Qur'ān has both 'clear judgements' and 'allegorical meaning'.[53] In this sense the division between *muḥkam* and *mutashābih* would not be between the words of the verses but between the meanings to be attached to them. Each verse is a sign or a symbol. What it represents is something which is both immediately applicable, and yet eternal and independent of time and space. The wise man will understand that every verse possesses an 'essence' and as well, carries an illustrative clothing given to that essence. So he would try to understand the essence as best he can, but not waste his energy or time in hairsplitting about the illustrative clothing.

The Prophet ﷺ has, for his own part, transmitted every word and letter of the Noble Qur'ān to humanity and explained all of them with clear details to preclude every possibility of confusion or change in their form, content and meaning. He did it with such vigour and assiduity that Allah even had to say:

فَلَعَلَّكَ بَاخِعٌ نَّفْسَكَ عَلَىٰٓ ءَاثَٰرِهِمْ إِن لَّمْ يُؤْمِنُوا۟ بِهَٰذَا ٱلْحَدِيثِ أَسَفًا

> *Perhaps you may destroy yourself with grief, chasing after them, if they do not have īmān in these words.* (Sūrat al-Kahf 18: 6)

The requisites for *tafsīr* writing

Tafsīr writing is a very serious matter because it is so intimately concerned with every Muslim's reliance on their belief (*īmān*). Explaining the Qur'ān on the basis of its translations or on the basis of one's own personal opinions and reasoning cannot be regarded as *tafsīr*. Those who indulge in interpreting the Qur'ān with the help of their fertile brains and unbridled whims would do well to remember the following warning of the Prophet ﷺ: "Whoever spoke about the Qur'ān by his own opinion, let him take his seat in the Fire." (At-Tirmidhī, an-Nasā'ī and Abū Dāwūd. This is the version of at-Tirmidhī)

Before a person takes up *tafsīr* writing he should:

1. Possess a sound and thorough knowledge of the Arabic language because, as Mujāhid has said: "*Tafsīr* is not permissible for someone who is not an *ᶜālim* (knowledgeable scholar) in the Arabic language";
2. Be well grounded in *ᶜilm al-maᶜānī* (knowledge of rhetoric);
3. Have a sound and thorough knowledge of the ḥadīth literature and the science of ḥadīth;
4. Have an ability through the knowledge of the ḥadīth, to recognise that which is ambiguous (*mubham*) and to elaborate on that which is abbreviated or abridged (*mujmal*);
5. Have a sound knowledge from ḥadīth of the causes of the revelation (*asbāb an-nuzūl*) of different verses;
6. Have a thorough knowledge of the abrogating and abrogated verses (*nāsikh wa mansūkh*);
7. Possess good knowledge of the principles of Islamic jurisprudence (*uṣūl al-fiqh*);
8. Possess knowledge of the science of recitation of the Qur'ān (*ᶜilm al-tajwīd*); and
9. Be a man of *taqwā* (fear of Allah).
10. Ibn Juzayy al-Kalbī includes knowledge of the science of *taṣawwuf* as necessary for the commentator.

Besides the above requirements there are also others that a person should possess before he can be qualified as a *mufassir* (commentator).

When a man whose Islamic knowledge is inadequate and superficial resorts to 'interpreting' the *āyāt* of the Qur'ān he seeks refuge in the figments of his own imagination in order to conceal his ignorance of the subect and in this process uses the Noble Qur'ān as an object of his logic and reason. So it was that

the Caliph ᶜUmar ❀ branded such commentators of the Qur'an
as *aᶜdā as-Sunnah* or 'enemies of the Sunnah'. He said:

> There will be people who will dispute with you by producing
> the Qur'ān as their proof. You should apprehend them with
> the *ḥadīth* because the companions of the Sunnah have the best
> knowledge of the Book of Allah.

In the light of the above discussion, the following emerge as
the qualities of a *mufassir*:

1. He should never entertain any doubts as to the principles
and injunctions contained in the verses of the Qur'ān, for
Allah says:

$$ذَلِكَ الْكِتَابُ لَا رَيْبَ فِيهِ$$

That is the Book, without any doubt. (Sūrat al-Baqarah 2: 1)

2. He must be a right-acting man, a person of *taqwā* (*muttaqī*)'
as the Qur'ān gives guidance to those who are God fearing.

$$هُدًى لِلْمُتَّقِينَ$$

It contains guidance for those who have taqwā. (Sūrat al-Baqarah 2: 1)

3. He should believe in Allah and the unseen and must not be
an atheist or a deviant in his faith.

$$الَّذِينَ يُؤْمِنُونَ بِالْغَيْبِ$$

[In it is guidance for] those who have iman in the Unseen. (Sūrat al-Baqarah 2: 2)

4. He must be regular in his five daily prayers for the Qur'ān
says:

$$وَيُقِيمُونَ الصَّلَاةَ$$

And who establish ṣalāh. (Sūrat al-Baqarah 2: 2)

$$إِنَّ الصَّلَاةَ تَنْهَى عَنِ الْفَحْشَاءِ وَالْمُنْكَرِ$$

Ṣalāh precludes indecency and wrongdoing. (Sūrat al-ᶜAnkabūt 29: 45)

5. He must be charitable:

وَمِمَّا رَزَقْنَاهُمْ يُنفِقُونَ

And (in it is guidance for those who) give of what We have provided for them. (Sūrat al-Baqarah 2: 2)

The legal injunctions of the Qur'ān (*āyāt al-aḥkām*)

The importance of *āyāt al-aḥkām*

The *aḥkām* (injunctions) of the Qur'ān are of primary importance in the life of Muslims. They form the sources of the *Sharīᶜah.* They are contained in the *āyāt al-aḥkām.* According to Imām as-Suyūṭī[54] there are 500 verses with legal connotations in the Qur'ān. However, there are other scholars who feel that the number of verses of *aḥkām* is more than this number and yet others consider their number to be less than 500. Whatever the case may be, these *āyāt al-aḥkām* form the code of conduct for every Muslim from birth to death. They provide the touchstone to distinguish true from false, good from bad and *ḥalāl* (lawful) from *ḥarām* (unlawful) in every sphere of life. This is the reason why the Noble Qur'ān is also called *al-Furqān,* the Criterion. The Qur'ān, unlike purely man-made laws, is not amendable. Therefore, the Qur'ānic *aḥkām* have remained the same for the last 1400 years. With these preliminary remarks, we may proceed to some of these *āyāt al-aḥkām.*

General Classification of the verses of the Qur'ān

The verses of the Noble Qur'ān can be classified into four categories as follows:

1. Those which teach mankind through the remembrance of the gifts of Allah – *ᶜilm at-tadhkīr bi ālā' Allah* – علم التذكير بآلاء الله

There are numerous gifts of Allah like water, air, the sun, moon, day, night, the heavens, earth, children, vegetation, and animals etc., which point out the existence of Allah, His Divine Lordship and His Oneness, etc.

إِنَّ فِي ذَٰلِكَ لَآيَاتٍ لِّقَوْمٍ يَتَفَكَّرُونَ

There are Signs in that for people who reflect. (Sūrat ar-Racd 13: 3)[55]

فَبِأَيِّ آلَاءِ رَبِّكُمَا تُكَذِّبَانِ

So which of your Lord's blessings do you both then deny? (Sūrat ar-Raḥmān 55: 13)[56]

2. Those which teach mankind by reminding about various happenings, incidents, etc., – *cilm at-tadhkīr bi ayyām Allāh* – علم التّذكير بأيّام الله

A number of events show how Allah had helped His prophets and other right-acting people, and how He had punished wrongdoers. The examples of Allah's help to the prophets Ibrāhīm ﷺ, Ismācīl ﷺ, Mūsā ﷺ, Hārūn ﷺ, cĪsā ﷺ and Muḥammad ﷺ can be seen throughout the pages of the Qur'ān.

The examples of Allah's punishment of the wrongdoers can also be observed in the Qur'ān, for example in the cases of Fircawn (Pharaoh), Nimrud, Qārūn, Abū Lahab and the communities of cĀd and Thamūd.

3. Those which teach mankind through reminding about death and events after it – *cilm at-tadhkīr bi'l-mawt wa mā bacd al-mawt* – علم التّذكير بالموت و ما بعد الموت

Death and all the events which follow it are mentioned in the Noble Qur'ān:

a. Questioning in the grave by Munkar and Nakīr
b. The *Barzakh*, i.e. the intermediate state after death until the Day of Rising
c. The *Qiyāmah* – the Day of Rising from the dead
d. The Day of Judgement
e. The rewards and punishments
f. The Garden and the Fire
g. The Beatific Vision – gazing on the Face of Allah

4. Those which teach mankind the injunctions of the Qur'ān – *cilm at-tadhkīr bi āyāt al-aḥkām* – علم التّذكير بآيات الأحكام

Many verses contain the commands or injunctions of Allah for governing the conduct of every Muslim from birth to death whose observance will bring him his eternal happiness. These verses are called *āyāt al-aḥkām*. They may be grouped in four categories:

i. Comprehensive injunctions: أحكام المجمل

These are the comprehensive commands contained in the Noble Qur'ān, about which it does not give details. For example, the injunctions concerning purification (*ṭahārah*), prayers (*ṣalāh*), fasting (*ṣawm*), *zakāh*, and Ḥajj etc., are all mentioned in the Qur'ān, but detailed rules about these are to be found in the Sunnah and in the ḥadīth of the Prophet ﷺ.

ii. Comprehensive and detailed injunctions – أحكام المجمل والمفصّل

The comprehensive and detailed injunctions are those which are contained in verses some of which mention the commands in brief but others in detail and others again leave the details to the Sunnah and the ḥadīth, as for example, injunctions on war, peace, *jihād*, prisoners of war, booty and relations with non-Muslims. These details are not merely left to the Sunnah and the ḥadīth alone, but *ijtihād* can also be a method to find suitable solutions to the problems for which there are no texts.

iii. Detailed injunctions – أحكام المفصل

These injunctions are contained in the verses of the Qur'ān with complete details of the commands. Therefore, there is no room for *ijtihād*, e.g. the *ḥadd* punishments, rules governing retaliation (*qiṣāṣ*), equitable relations, unintentional homicide, murder, theft (*saraqah*), robbery (*ḥirābah*), fornication and adultery (*zinā*), and defamation (*qadhf*).

iv. Fundamental principles of guidance derived from injunctions:

The Noble Qur'ān also mentions certain fundamental principles for the guidance of Muslims in acting according to other injunctions.

However, these principles have no clear-cut definitions either in the Qur'ān or the Sunnah except basic norms. They are to be provided through the strict process of *ijtihād*. They are:

a. the principle of freedom
b. the principle of justice (*ᶜadl*)
c. the principle of consultation (*shūrā*)
d. the principles of public interest (*maṣlaḥah mursalah*)
e. the principle of equity

It is the consensus among interpreters of the Qur'ān and among Muslim *fuqahā'* that any Muslim who legislatively innovates or enacts laws contrary to what Allah has revealed, enforcing his own laws while renouncing the revealed ones – unless he believes that his innovated or self-imposed laws are a correct interpretation of Allah's revelation or is forced to do it by some overwhelming necessity – would be classified under one of the categories of *mufsidūn, fāsiqūn, ẓālimūn,* or *kāfirūn*. For example, if a ruler does not apply the Islamic penalties for theft or slander or adultery because he does not believe in them and prefers the judgements of man-made law, such a ruler is definitely considered an unbeliever. If a ruler fails to apply Islamic jurisprudence for reasons other than disbelief, he is considered a wrongdoer (*ẓālim*), and if, as a result of neglecting Islamic jurisprudence, he violates people's rights or overlooks the principles of justice and equality, he is considered a rebel.[57]

Notes

[1] Sūrat al-Baqarah 2: 1-2.
[2] Sūrat al-Baqarah 2: 145.
[3] Sūrah Āl ᶜImrān 3: 138.
[4] Sūrat an-Nisā' 4: 4.
[5] Sūrah Yūnus 10: 1.
[6] Sūrah Yūnus 10: 57.
[7] Sūrah Ibrāhīm 14: 52.
[8] Sūrah Āl ᶜImrān 3: 103.
[9] Sūrat al-Isrā' 17: 82.
[10] Sūrat al-Anbiyā' 21: 50.
[11] Sūrat al-Furqān 25: 1.
[12] Sūrat az-Zumar 39: 23.
[13] Sūrat al-Qamar 54: 5.
[14] Sūrat aṭ-Ṭalaq 65: 6.
[15] Sūrat al-Ḥāqqah 69: 58.
[16] Sūrat az-Zukhruf 43: 1-2.
[17] Sūrat az-Zukhruf 43: 4.
[18] Sūrat al-Burūj 85: 21.
[19] Sūrat al-Anbiyā' 21: 50. For detailed discussion of the subject see al-Qaṭṭān, Mannāᶜ, *Mabāḥith fī ᶜulūm al-Qur'ān*, Riyadh, 1976. pp. 21-23.
[20] For details of the contents of the Qur'ān see Doi, A. Rahman I., *Introduction to the Qur'ān*, Lagos, 1972, pp. 34-37.
[21] See for details on this subject, az-Zarakhshī, Badr ad-Dīn, *al-Burhān fī ᶜulūm al-Qur'ān*, edited by M. Ibrahim, 2 volumes, Cairo 1957-58.
[22] Sūrat al-Fātiḥah 1: 5.
[23] Sūrat al-Fātiḥah 1: 6.

[24] Sūrat an-Nisā' 4: 69. *"Whoever obeys Allah and the Messenger will be with those whom Allah has blessed: the Prophets and the ṣiddīqūn, the martyrs and the ṣāliḥūn."*
[25] For details see adh-Dhahabī, Muḥammad, *at-Tafsīr wa'l-mufassirūn*, Cairo 1961, vol.1, pp. 38-39.
[26] Ibn Khaldun, *al-Muqaddimah*, Cairo (undated). p. 382.
[27] At-Tirmidhī, Muḥammad ibn cĪsā, *aṣ-Ṣaḥīḥ*, Bulaq, 1875, p. 48.
[28] Adh-Dhahabī, *Op. Cit.*, vol.1 p.46.
[29] Al-Jaṣṣāṣ, Aḥmad ibn cAlī ar-Rāzī, *Aḥkām al-Qur'ān*, Istanbul, 1916, vol. 1, p. 288.
[30] cAlī, A. Yūsuf, *The Holy Quran – text, translation and commentary*, Dar al-Arabiyyah, Beirut, undated, p. ix.
[31] Al-Qaṭṭān, Mannāc, *Mabāḥith fī culūm al-Qur'ān*, Riyadh, 1976, p. 347.
[32] *Ibid.*
[33] As-Suyūṭī, *al-Itqān*, *Op. Cit.*, p. 968.
[34] *Ibid.*, p. 909.
[35] As-Suyūṭī, *al-Itqān*, *Op. Cit.*, pp. 282-309.
[36] Adh-Dhahabī, Muḥammad, *at-Tafsīr wa'l-mufassirūn*, *Op. Cit.*, vol. 1, p. 69.
[37] Adh-Dhahabī, *Op. Cit.*, vol. 1, p. 86.
[38] Ḥājjī Khalīfah, *Kashf aẓ-Ẓunūn*, Istanbul, 1941, vol. 1, p. 429.
[39] *Ibid.*, vol. 2, p. 430.
[40] Adh-Dhahabī, *Op. Cit.*, vol. 1, p. 101.
[41] *Ibid.*, vol. 1, p. 118.
[42] *Ibid.*, vol. 1, p. 114.
[43] Adh-Dhahabī, Muḥammad, *at-Tafsīr wa'l-mufassirūn*, *Op. Cit.*, vol. 1, p. 209.
[44] Aḥmad Amīn, *Fajr al-Islam*, Cairo, 1928, p. 274.
[45] *See* as-Sawwāf, Mujāhid Muḥammad, *Early Tafsīr – A Survey of Qur'ānic Commentary up to 150 AH*, an article in *Islamic Perspective*, ed. Khurshid Aḥmad and Z. Anṣārī, Leicester, 1979, pp. 135-45.
[46] Aṭ-Ṭabarī, Ibn Jarīr.
[47] Az-Zamakhsharī.
[48] For details of *Isrā'īliyyāt*, cf. Abū Shahbā, Muḥammad, *al-Isrā'īliyyāt wa'l-mawḍūcāt fī kutub at-tafsīr.*

[49] As examples may be cited: the stories of Ādam and Ḥawwā' (Eve), Hārūt and Mārūt, Yūsuf ﷺ, the building of the Kaᶜbah, the killing of Jālūt by the prophet Dāwūd ﷺ, the Ark of Nūḥ ﷺ, the corruption of the Israelites, the Companions of the Cave (*Aṣḥāb al-Kahf*), Dhu'l-Qarnayn, Yājūj and Mājūj (Gog and Magog), the Queen of Saba' (Sheba) Bilqīs, etc.

[50] *See* Sūrat al-Kahf.

[51] For further details on *Isrā'īliyyāt* see al-Qaṭṭān, Mannā', *Mabāḥith fī ᶜulūm al-Qur'ān, Op. Cit.*, pp. 349-59.

[52] It is not to be found in the copy of the *Muwaṭṭa'* of Yaḥyā, but perhaps it is in other narrations. The author also cites al-Qaṭṭān, Mannā', *Mabāḥith, Op. Cit.*, p.352.

[53] Sūrah Hūd 11: 1, Sūrat az-Zumar 39: 23.

[54] As-Suyūṭī, *al-Itqān fī ᶜulūm al-Qur'ān*.

[55] Also, cf. Sūrat an-Naḥl 16: 11, Sūrat an-Naḥl 16: 69, Sūrat ar-Rūm 30: 21, Sūrat az-Zumar 39: 42, Sūrat al-Jāthiyah 45: 13.

[56] In Sūrat ar-Raḥmān it is repeated 31 times.

[57] Naturally it cannot be left to those who are unqualified to pass judgement on rulers for this only leads to civil strife, as we see today with the emergence of radicalised groups of Muslims who pass judgement carelessly on all Muslim rulers in this manner, and then extend the judgement to their subjects considering it legitimate to kill Muslims who live under rulers they have judged to be outside the pale of Islam. Such a result is clearly a modern *Khawārij* phenomenon and is not the intention of the authors of this book.

Chapter 4

The Sunnah
Second Textual Source of the *Sharīᶜah*

The Sunnah as the exegesis of the Qur'ān

THE NOBLE QUR'ĀN WAS REVEALED to the Prophet Muhammad ﷺ who never spoke from his own imagination, but only told what Allah had revealed to him. The Noble Qur'ān bears witness to this:

مَا ضَلَّ صَاحِبُكُمْ وَمَا غَوَىٰ وَمَا يَنطِقُ عَنِ الْهَوَىٰ إِنْ هُوَ إِلَّا وَحْيٌ يُوحَىٰ

Your companion is not misguided or misled, nor does he speak from whim. It is nothing but Revelation revealed. (Sūrat an-Najm 53: 2-4)

These verses were revealed to counter three false charges Quraysh levelled against the Prophet ﷺ:

1. That he was going astray either through a defect in intelligence or through carelessness;
2. That he was being misled or deceived by evil spirits (*jinn*) and so was *majnūn* (possessed by a *jinn*);
or
3. That he was speaking whimsically or impulsively, or from a selfish desire to impress with his own personality.

These verses confirmed that the Prophet ﷺ received revelation from Allah which guided all his thoughts and actions. The real import of the above verses is that they show the importance of the Sunnah in the interpretation of the entire message of the Qur'ān and in the formation of the Islamic way of life.

It is for this reason that after the Qur'ān, which is the speech of Allah and the first textual source of Islamic *Sharīᶜah*, the Sunnah stands in second place as the 'hidden revelation' (*waḥy khafī*). The Qur'ānic verse lends support to this when Allah says:

وَأَنْزَلْنَا إِلَيْكَ الذِّكْرَ لِتُبَيِّنَ لِلنَّاسِ مَا نُزِّلَ إِلَيْهِمْ وَلَعَلَّهُمْ يَتَفَكَّرُونَ

And We have sent down the Reminder to you so that you can make clear to mankind what has been sent down to them so that hopefully they will reflect. (Sūrat an-Naḥl 16: 44)

In addition to the above Qur'ānic proof there is yet another from a ḥadīth confirming that the Sunnah is no less important in interpreting the Qur'ān:

أَلَا وَإِنِّي قَدْ أُوتِيتُ الْكِتَابَ وَمِثْلَهُ مَعَهُ

Certainly, I have been given the Book and the like of it along with it. (Aḥmad in his *Musnad* and Abū Dāwūd, *awwal kitāb as-sunnah, bāb fī luzūm as-sunnah*)

But in cases where the Sunnah is silent as to the interpretation of the Qur'ānic verses, recourse may be had to the way the Companions of the Prophet ﷺ had interpreted them. This is underscored by a saying of Ibn Masᶜūd ؓ:

كَانَ الرَّجُلُ مِنَّا إِذَا تَعَلَّمَ عَشَرَ آيَاتٍ لَمْ يُجَاوِزْهُنَّ حَتَّى يَعْرِفَ مَعَانِيَهُنَّ وَالْعَمَلَ بِهِنَّ ، فَتَعَلَّمْنَا الْقُرْآنَ وَالْعَمَلَ جَمِيعاً

When any man of us learnt ten *āyāt* he would not go beyond them until he knew their meanings and how to practise them. So we learnt the Qur'ān and the practice (*ᶜamal*) together. (The same sense is transmitted of Ibn Masᶜūd ؓ in *Kanz al-ᶜummāl*)

This statement shows that the Companions were well versed in the interpretation of the Qur'ān. In the absence of any guidance from the Noble Qur'ān and the Sunnah of the Prophet ﷺ the interpretation of the verses of the Noble Qur'ān by the Companions is binding on us.

The following example shows how the Companions used to interpret the verses of the Noble Qur'ān.

A woman came to ᶜAbdullāh ibn Masᶜūd ؓ and said:

"I have learnt that you teach certain things, and you say that those who tattoo and have themselves tattooed have been cursed by Allah, exalted is He, whereas I have read the Qur'ān from cover to cover and did not find therein what you are saying."

Ibn Masᶜūd said, "Go and read the Qur'ān again."

After doing so, she presented herself again and said, "Even now I have not discovered in the Qur'ān what you say."

Ibn Masᶜūd replied:

أَمَا قَرَأْتَ ﴿وَمَا آتَاكُمُ الرَّسُولُ فَخُذُوهُ وَمَا نَهَاكُمْ عَنْهُ فَانْتَهُوا﴾ ؟

"Have you not recited, '*Whatever the Messenger gives you, you should accept and whatever He forbids you, you should forgo*'?" (Sūrat al-Ḥashr 59: 7)

When she said yes, ᶜAbdullāh ibn Masᶜūd said:

فَهُوَ ذَاكَ

"So it is that," i.e. it is what I have said.

In other words, whatever is in the Sunnah is covered by the *āyah* of the Qur'ān mentioned by Ibn Masᶜūd.

In reality, the entire life of the Prophet ﷺ, whatever he did or said, was according to the teachings of the Qur'ān and hence, if all the events of his life and his teachings are taken together with all the authentic ḥadīth, we get a complete *tafsīr* of the Qur'ān put into practice by the Messenger of Allah ﷺ himself, the bearer of the Divine Revelation.

The causes of revelation (*asbāb an-nuzūl*) and other explanations of the Qur'ān that we find in the collections of ḥadīth of Imām al-Bukhārī, Imām Muslim, Imām at-Tirmidhī et al., which form the *tafsīr an-nabawī*, are not complete, although they have been arranged according to the *sūrahs* of the Qur'ān by these great scholars of ḥadīth. There might be traditions of the Prophet ﷺ relevant to three or four *āyāt* of a *sūrah* while there is nothing relating to its remaining verses. There are scholars, however, who believe that the Prophet ﷺ commented on the whole Qur'ān, and one of these is Ibn Taymiyyah.[1] What seems more plausible is the statement of ᶜĀ'ishah ﵂: "The Prophet ﷺ commented only on some *āyāt* of the Book of Allah (and his commentary consisted of) what Jibrīl had taught him."[2]

As a youth, ᶜAbdullāh ibn ᶜAbbās ﵄ used to comment on the Qur'ān even in the presence of the other Companions. ᶜUmar ibn al-Khaṭṭāb ﵁ used to give precedence to Ibn ᶜAbbās amongst the Companions, so they complained to him about that. ᶜUmar called Ibn ᶜAbbās and then asked the Companions about the explanation of Sūrat an-Naṣr, *"When Allah's help and victory have arrived"*. The Companions said various things. Ibn ᶜAbbās said that it referred to the time of the death of the Messenger of Allah ﷺ. ᶜUmar ﵁ endorsed that view and thereby justified his preference for the young Ibn ᶜAbbās.[3]

It is significant that there is no explicit mention in the *sūrah* of the time of death of the Prophet ﷺ. What the statement of Ibn ᶜAbbās implies is that when victory comes everything is completed, meaning that the Prophet ﷺ had completed his task. Hence, nothing lay in store for him except to return to the mercy of Allah.

The primary sources of the *dīn* of Islam are the Qur'ān and the Sunnah. The Qur'ān is the Speech of Allah. The Prophet ﷺ did not have anything to do with its words; it was revealed to him as it is now read. Whilst the Qur'ān gives the Muslims a primary rule of life, there are many matters where guidance for practical living is necessary but about which the Qur'ān says nothing. In such things the obvious thing is to follow the custom or usage of the Prophet ﷺ (Sunnah). There were ancient customs which could be acceptable in some cases, but on matters pertaining to the *dīn* of Islam there was the custom or practice of the earliest believers who had been the contemporaries and Companions of the Prophet ﷺ himself. Eventually there came into existence traditions which gave formal statement to what the Sunnah of the earliest Muslims was on a variety of matters. Sunnah literally means a way, rule, manner of acting or mode of life. In consequence of this, there arose in Islam a class of students who made it their business to investigate and hand down the minutest details concerning the life of the Prophet ﷺ.

Before long, attention came to be concentrated on the Prophet ﷺ and his manner of life, because in their eyes he was the ideal Muslim, to be imitated by his followers. In other words, the Sunnah of the Prophet ﷺ established a model of behaviour which every Muslim should aspire to reach. Certainly, who else could be a better guide for Muslims than the Prophet ﷺ himself? His words and deeds, therefore, became a source of inspiration for Muslims in all times to come.

During his life and after his death, reports of the wonderful sayings of the Prophet ﷺ began to circulate. The collections of these sayings continued to increase as they were gathered from the Companions of the Prophet ﷺ. Then they were subjected to standardisation and selection.

This represented the practice, words and confirmation – sometimes silent – of the Prophet ﷺ or the words and deeds of his companions, and it became a supplement to the Book of Allah. The Sunnah, in other words, is the second pillar after the Qur'ān upon which every Muslim rests the fabric of his faith and life. The body of traditions circulated orally for some time, as indicated by the word *ḥadīth*, commonly used for 'tradition' but which literally means 'a saying conveyed to a man either through hearing or through witnessing an event'. It is also used to denote 'conversation', i.e. the telling of something 'new' (*ḥadīth* literally means 'new'). The records of the practice, words and confirmation of other people's words and deeds, therefore, were called *ḥadīth*. But the name for the practice is Sunnah (custom or usage), whose plural is *Sunan*.

Ḥadīth,[4] in short, are one of the essential storerooms of the Sunnah of the Prophet ﷺ,[5] serving an essential need of the Muslims as communities and individuals. *Ḥadīth* arose in three ways:

1. Verbal teaching done by the Prophet ﷺ himself, which it was his custom to repeat three times respecting important things.[6] Then he used to listen to the Companions to make

sure that they had learnt them correctly.[7] Even when delegations arrived in Madīnah, the Prophet ﷺ had charged the Madīnans not only to accommodate them but to teach them the message of Islam and its practices through the Qur'ān and the Sunnah. The Prophet ﷺ used to ask them questions to find out how much they had learnt.[8]

2. Teaching by means of writing was done by the Prophet ﷺ through various letters that he wrote to kings, rulers, chieftains and Muslim governors. These letters contain invitations to enter Islam, and instructions concerning *zakāh*, forms of worship, etc.[9]
3. Teaching done by the Prophet ﷺ through practical demonstration such as the way to perform *wuḍū'* (ritual ablution), *ṣalāh* (prayers), Ḥajj and fasting. His instruction in respect of the *ṣalāh* in particular was:

صَلُّوا كَمَا رَأَيْتُمُونِي أُصَلِّي

Pray as you have seen me pray. (Al-Bukhārī, *kitāb al-adhān, bāb al-adhān li al-musāfir idhā kānū jamāᶜah wa al-iqāmah wa kadhālika bi ᶜArafah wa Jamᶜ wa qawl al-mu'adhdhin aṣ-ṣalātu fī ar-riḥāl fī al-laylah al-bāridah aw al-muṭīrah*)

Importance of *ḥadīth* for the *dīn* and the law in Islam

As we have seen earlier, the Qur'ān supplements the Qur'ān as a source of Islamic law. Muslims turn to both sources for answers to every problem, whether connected to acts of worship or ordinary transactions. The importance of the *ḥadīth* in this regard can be realised when one considers the zeal and enthusiasm with which every group of Muslims, every party, and every movement supplied itself with *ḥadīth* which gave prophetic authority for its particular point of view.

After the death of the Prophet ﷺ, every case that came up for decision had either to be referred to the Noble Qur'ān or to some judgement or saying of the Prophet ﷺ, and hence these obtained a high reputation. There are numerous cases on record in which a right was claimed on the basis of a judgement or saying of the

Prophet ﷺ, and evidence was demanded for the authenticity of that saying.

For instance, Fāṭimah ؓ, the daughter of the Prophet ﷺ, claimed that she was entitled to an inheritance from the Prophet ﷺ. However, according to a *ḥadīth* the Prophet ﷺ had said, "We [prophets] are not inherited from; what we leave is *ṣadaqah*" (Al-Bukhārī, *kitāb al-farā'iḍ, bāb qawl an-nabiyyi* ﷺ *lā nūrathu, mā taraknā ṣadaqah*). Abū Bakr cited this *ḥadīth* to Fāṭimah, and no one disputed its truth, and so Fāṭimah's claim was not accepted. Incidents of this sort happened almost daily in the early days of that first community and became the occasion for verifying the authenticity of many sayings of the Prophet ﷺ.

Not only was the trustworthiness of particular *ḥadīth* established beyond all doubt, but *ḥadīth* in general obtained wide circulation, and from being known only to certain individuals here and there, became commonly known to many. The *ḥadīth* literature, as we now have it, provides us with precepts and lived examples from the Messenger of Allah ﷺ covering all the duties of mankind; it is foundational to that system of law, theology and spiritual path which is Islam. Muslim law is so very comprehensive that all the minute acts of a Muslim are guarded by it. A Muslim, in reality, is told by this code not only what is required of him and what he is prohibited, but also what is recommended, what is disliked, and what is simply permissible, with illustrations from the lives and actions of the Messenger of Allah ﷺ and his Companions. The highest intention in all of this rises above the thought of reward or punishment to the sublime level of seeking to please Allah, exalted is He.

In *Sharīᶜah*, therefore, actions are divided into five classes, as follows:

1. *Farḍ* or *wājib*: an obligatory duty for the performance of which there is a Divine reward and for the omission of which there is punishment, both legal and Divine.
2. *Mandūb* or *mustaḥabb*: a recommended desirable act for which there is a Divine reward but for whose omission there is no legal or Divine punishment.

3. *Jā'iz* or *mubāḥ*: a permissible action, which is legally indifferent. Nevertheless, this action may be raised to the level of an act of worship which is *mustaḥabb* if by it obedience to Allah is intended, such as eating food in order to have the strength to performs acts of worship.
4. *Makrūh*: a disapproved act for the commission of which there is no legal or Divine punishment, but for the abandonment of which there is a Divine reward.
5. *Ḥarām*: a forbidden act which is punishable both legally in this world and by Allah, and for the abandonment of which there is Divine reward.

(This subject will be treated in greater detail in Chapter 8)

After understanding the above framework of Muslim law, it is understandable that it was essential to receive guidance from the life history of the Prophet ﷺ himself. For this reason, all the records of the manners and customs of the Prophet ﷺ, of the little details of his life and his conversations were collected.

Thus, traditions were important in the development of the Islamic legal system and jurisprudence. The *Muwaṭṭa'* of Imām Mālik ibn Anas (d. 179 AH/795 CE) shows, for example, how the law can be drawn from these usages and traditions of the Prophet ﷺ. This book, the first of its kind, helped to build up a system of law based partly on traditions as well as upon, in the case of Mālikī *fiqh*, the established practice of the People of Madīnah of the first right-acting generations. It was followed later by many books, but in particular the *Musnad* of Imām Aḥmad ibn Ḥanbal (d. 241 AH/855 CE). In short, after the Noble Qur'ān the Sunnah is the primary source of Islamic law, and the *ḥadīth* serve an important function in determining the Sunnah.

Growth and development of the science of *ḥadīth*

Islam spread throughout the world with astonishing speed. Within a century the names of Allah and His Prophet, Muḥammad ﷺ, were cried out in the words of the *mu'adhdhin* from the minarets of mosques throughout a great part of the world. It is very interesting to note that Islam was taught by the Prophet Muḥammad ﷺ both as a set of acts of worship (*ᶜibādāt*) and as the ordinary transactions (*muᶜāmalāt*) of life, both comprising what is often called a way of life or life transaction. Therefore, the Noble Qur'ān contains the revelations from Allah pertaining to all aspects of life both in mundane existence and the life hereafter. It contains a number of laws, for example, rules in regard to marriage, inheritance and the care of orphans, etc. However, the Qur'ān is not meant to be a book of law or a book of history or sociology. It is a book of guidance in which Allah speaks to His creatures in such a way as to guide them to lead better and more decent lives. The Qur'ān does not settle the questions arising from diverse categories, such as systematic and moral theology, rites, civil and military law, although it is the source for guidance in all these domains.

The Noble Qur'ān, even with its wealth of detail, needs the additional element of *fatwā* (legal judgement) and tradition, and the *ḥadīth* were collected to fulfil this need. As far as eastern religions are concerned, their followers built gorgeous temples for their deities, but the Muslims wrote systematic works on sciences such as the *asmā' ar-rijāl*, the science of verifying the narrators of the *ḥadīth*; who reported and from whom, and what the characters of the narrators were, both in public and private. This tremendous accomplishment was one amongst several to which the early Muslims devoted their lives in study, including the sciences of *kalām*, the exegesis of the Qur'ān and the compilation of the *ḥadīth*, etc.

Al-Bukhārī, the noted traditionist, whose compilation of the ḥadīth is known among Muslims as one of the most correct, recalls a ḥadīth from the Messenger of Allah, Muḥammad ﷺ as reported by ᶜAbdullāh ibn Masᶜūd ﷺ that the best *ḥadīth*, i.e. discourse, is the Book of Allah.[10] The word *ḥadīth* is a noun derived from the verb *ḥadatha* which means, in a broad sense, to recount a tale or make verbal communication of any kind. The Noble Qur'ān is as it was revealed to the Prophet Muḥammad ﷺ and as it was heard on the tongue of the Prophet Muḥammad

ﷺ, since he led his life according to the teachings of the Qur'ān and his whole life was inspired by Allah, exalted is He.

The *ḥadīth* of the Prophet ﷺ are a key source for the Sunnah or the "Way of Life", the custom and practice of the early Muslim community. They were invoked to prove that certain acts were performed by the Prophet ﷺ and are therefore to be imitated by all faithful Muslims. It is from this point of view that some scholars use *ḥadīth* and *Sunnah* interchangeably, although others insist on retaining *Sunnah* for 'custom and practice' and *ḥadīth* for 'accounts and narrations'.

During the lifetime of the Prophet ﷺ, the Muslims did not need any other guide in the matters of either a spiritual or a secular nature. After his death, the early right-acting Muslims imitated him and strictly followed his example. Therefore, they always referred to the words and deeds of Muḥammad ﷺ. The work of collecting *ḥadīth* was later to become a separate matter from the study of the law but was originally very much connected to it. They began to compile everything that he had said and done, what he had refrained from doing, and what he had given tacit approval to by his silence. Above all, a record was being gathered of all the cases he had judged and of his decisions; of all the answers he had given to formal questions on the acts of worship and the ordinary transactions of daily life, and on the true nature of the Divine, the angelic realm and the next life, etc.

At first, each Companion had his own collection in memory or in writing. Then these collections were transmitted on to others. This is how the chain of transmission came about. In time a tradition evolved which consisted formally of two essential parts: the text (*matn*) as it was handed down, and the chain of transmission (*isnād*), being those people over whose lips it had passed, for example, "X said, 'Y narrated that, "Z said that W said… – until it came to the last link after which there followed the *matn*, 'The Messenger of Allah ﷺ said, "Seeking knowledge is obligatory upon every Muslim man and woman."''''" The writing down of the traditions aided the memory to retain that which had already been learned.

Asmā' ar-rijāl – The Names of the Narrators

In order to know the lives, careers and characters of the persons who constituted the links in the chains of the different *isnāds*, there developed the science of the *asmā' ar-rijāl*, which means literally "the names of the men" i.e. narrators. In fact, it is the biographies of the narrators of *ḥadīth* and any aspects of their lives which may be helpful in determining their identity, veracity and reliability.

The earliest formal collections of traditions, which include the *Muwaṭṭa'* of Imām Mālik and possibly the *Kitāb al-āthār* of Imām Abū Ḥanīfah were grouped according to juristic subject matter. However, there quickly grew a literature of *ḥadīth* works which were generally in the form known as *Musnad*. These are arranged according to the final narrator in the chain, the Companion who is the original narrator from the Messenger of Allah ﷺ. Each *ḥadīth* which gave the saying or described the action of the Prophet ﷺ was preceded by its *isnād*, or chain of transmitters. This took it back to the Companion of the Prophet ﷺ who had himself heard the statement or witnessed the event given in the *matn* or text of the *ḥadīth*, as authority for the Sunnah of the Prophet ﷺ. These were then listed under the name of the final link in the *isnād* as we have mentioned above.

The following example will show clearly how this was done.

According to al-Bukhārī (*kitāb aṣ-ṣawm, bāb aṣ-ṣā'im idhā akala aw shariba nāsiyan*), "^{c}Abdān narrated to us, "Yazīd ibn Zuray^{c} informed us, 'Hishām narrated to us, "Ibn Sīrīn narrated to us from Abū Hurayrah ؓ from the Prophet ﷺ who said, 'If he forgets and then eats and drinks, he should complete his fast, because it was only Allah Who fed him and gave him to drink.'""'"

From these examples it will be observed that the narrations are generally done in direct speech thus, "*A* told me, saying that, '*B* said, "*C* informed me saying, '*D* mentioned that he heard *E* narrate, "I heard *F* ask the Messenger of Allah ﷺ…"'"'"

A more practical arrangement was by subject matter since at an early period the working jurists needed collections of traditions which they might use in rendering decisions in practical cases. There grew up the practice on the basis of the *Muwaṭṭa'*, etc. of arranging collections under the rubrics suggested by the needs of the jurists in the matters of inheritance, debts, and acts of worship, etc. Thus, al-Bukhārī groups together a number of *ḥadīth* concerning fasting. Some of these include *ḥadīth* "on the necessity of the fast of Ramaḍān", "on the fasting person who eats and drinks from forgetfulness", etc.

The later *ḥadīth* scholars who followed this procedure in the method of arranging their collections did so about the middle of the third century AH when *ḥadīth* had attained major importance as a means of determining the practices and beliefs of the community. The primary aims of the narrators was to establish unerring authority for laws and customs. Thus, although the collectors (or narrators) devoted scrupulous attention to the *isnād*, so far as the arrangement of the traditions was concerned the *isnād* was subordinate to the *musnad*, i.e. the subject-matter of the tradition. Traditions were recorded according to their subjects which were arranged under the subject headings of the law books. Such books were *muṣannafāt*.

Gradually six such collections, made in the latter part of the third century of Islam, succeeded in gaining such general approval that later generations tacitly accepted them as the six canonical collections (*aṣ-Ṣiḥāḥ as-sittah*). However, it was some considerable time before they achieved this status, and many other works have very high standing with *ḥadīth* scholars. The six works we refer to are:

1. The *Ṣaḥīḥ* of al-Bukhārī (d. 256 AH/870 CE)
2. The *Ṣaḥīḥ* of Muslim (d. 261 AH/875 CE)
3. The *Sunan* of Ibn Mājah (d. 273 AH/887 CE)
4. The *Sunan* of Abū Dāwūd (d. 275 AH/888 CE)
5. The *Jāmiᶜ* of at-Tirmidhī (d. 279 AH/892 CE)
6. The *Sunan* of an-Nasā'ī (d. 303 AH/915 CE)

In preparing their collections these traditionists obviously used a critical technique of selection to decide what to include and exclude. Al-Bukhārī, for example, examined and memorised 600,000 traditions of which he chose to include in his *Ṣaḥīḥ* only 7,397. Their purpose was to assemble a body of traditions which would serve as a rule of life for practising Muslims. So their primary interest was in selecting such traditions as would give clear guidance concerning what Muslim belief and practice should be, what things were permissible and approved, and what things were not permissible or were disapproved of.

In their attempt to set up tests of authenticity which would exclude inauthentic or doubtful material, these traditionists picked on the *isnād* as the measure. They worked out an elaborate system for testing the trustworthiness of these 'chains' and of the individuals who formed the links therein, so that an *isnād* could be labelled 'excellent', 'good', 'fair', 'weak', etc., and the tradition itself rated accordingly.

Therefore, the *isnād* is almost as important an element in a *ḥadīth* as the *matn* itself. As traditionists began to write their commentaries on the *ḥadīth* literature, general principles of criticism emerged and there came into existence the criticism of the *ḥadīth* relating to the *isnād* and that relating to the *matn*.

However, it must be borne in mind that some of these principles represent a later, post Imām ash-Shāfi^cī, development, with both of the two most ancient *madhhabs*, those of Imām Abū Ḥanīfah and Imām Mālik representing the schools of Kūfa and Madīnah respectively, holding to the use of *ḥadīth* that later scholars effectively disavowed: *mursal* (ascribed directly to the Prophet ﷺ by one of the Followers or Followers of the Followers without mention of the Companion or Companions, or the Follower or Followers from whom he heard the *ḥadīth*), *mawqūf* (a statement of a Companion) and *balāghāt* (in which the narrator merely says, "It has reached me that the Prophet ﷺ...".

The following is a summary of the principles of criticism of the *isnād*.

1. All the traditions must be traced back to its original reporter through an unbroken line of transmitters. These transmitters must be of excellent character, be truthful, must have good retentive memories, and have high qualities of intellect and heart. If the *isnād* is broken, the *ḥadīth* may yet still be used but will be of a lesser

standing than one with an unbroken *isnād*. However, this later view neglected many traditions which had been narrated by the earliest generations and accepted by them as authoritative.

2. Every tradition which reported an event or happening that occurred frequently in the presence of a large number of people, must have been originally reported by several narrators.

On the basis of these strict principles, many traditions narrated by a single Companion (*ṣaḥābī*) were rejected or downgraded. As for example, a *ḥadīth* was said to have been reported by Sayyidunā Abū Bakr ﷺ alone, in which he said that at the time of the call to prayer (*adhān*), the Muslims kissed their thumbs when the name of the Messenger of Allah ﷺ was recited. Since this event would have had to have taken place in the presence of a large number of Muslims, five times a day without fail, it should have been reported by a large number of narrators. Since it is only reported by one Companion, the ḥadīth is regarded as less weighty than others.

As far as the *matn* is concerned, the following principles of *ḥadīth* criticism are laid down:

1. The text should not be contrary to the text or the teachings of the Qur'ān or the agreed upon basic principles of Islam.
2. *Ḥadīth* should not be against the dictates of reason or the laws of nature or common sense.
3. *Ḥadīth* should not be contrary to other *ḥadīth* already accepted by the authorities of this science as reliable and authentic according to the proper criteria.
4. *Ḥadīth* which sing lavish praise of the excellence of any tribe, place or persons should generally be regarded as suspect.
5. *Ḥadīth* that contain dates and minute details of future events should be regarded as suspect.
6. *Ḥadīth* that contain some remarks attributed to the Prophet ﷺ that are not in keeping with the Islamic belief

about the nature of prophethood and the position of the Prophet ﷺ or which contain expressions that are not suitable or appropriate for him, should also be regarded as suspect.

Such strict principles of *ḥadīth* criticism are extremely necessary since the *ḥadīth* of the Prophet ﷺ are of great importance, but are of course subordinate to the Qur'ān. This is the reason why all the important Muslim jurists belonging to the first three generations of the Muslim era preferred *ḥadīth* to *qiyās* (analogical deduction). In some cases, some of them refused to express their individual opinions on legal matters in cases in which the ḥadīth was known to them. Jurists such as Imām Mālik and Imām Abū Ḥanīfah also accepted the practice of the Companions as an important legal authority since it was modelled closely on the practice of the Prophet ﷺ, and Mālik, as is well known, held the practice of the People of Madīnah as an authoritative proof. The Companions followed the footsteps of their master scrupulously.

The Noble Qur'ān advocates the acceptance of the Sunnah as a source of the Islamic legal system. Allah says, "*Whatever the Messenger gives you, you should accept and whatever He forbids you, you should forgo.*" (Sūrat al-Ḥashr 59: 7)

QUALIFICATIONS OF A TRANSMITTER OF *ḤADĪTH*

It is agreed by all the scholars of *ḥadīth* as well as the jurists of Islam that a transmitter of *ḥadīth* should possess certain qualifications to be acceptable. He must be of firm faith, truthful, mature in age and a person of great integrity. He must be conversant with the names, careers and characters of the early narrators of traditions. In short, Imām ash-Shāfiᶜī has summed up the qualifications of a transmitter of traditions in the following words in his *Risālah*:

> He must be of firm faith and well known for his truthfulness in whatever he narrates. He should understand its contents and should know well how the change in expression affects the ideas expressed therein. He should report verbatim what he learnt from his teacher, and not narrate in his own words the sense of what he had learnt. He must possess a retentive memory and

if he has reported from a book, he should remember the book well. He should refrain from making a report on the authority of those whom he met but from whom he did not learn anything. His report must be in agreement with what has been reported by those who are recognised to have good memories, if they have also transmitted these reports.

Classification of *Ḥadīth*

Scholars of *ḥadīth* literature have divided traditions into three main categories according to the degree of their reliability, with a number of sub-categories. This classification is based on:

1. The perfection or imperfection of the chain of transmitters
2. The freedom of the text from any concealed defects
3. Acceptance or rejection of any *ḥadīth* by the Companions, their Followers (*tābiᶜūn*), or their Followers' Followers (*tābiᶜu't-tābiᶜīn*). Ḥadīth can be classified as *mutawātir* (transmitted with several or numerous chains of transmission), *mashhūr* (transmitted with two chains of transmission), *āḥād* or *khabar al-wāḥid* (transmitted by a single individual) or *mursal* (ascribed directly to the Prophet ﷺ by one of the Followers or Followers of the Followers without mention of the Companion or Companions, or the Follower or Followers from whom he heard the *ḥadīth*). The three categories of ḥadīth according to their quality are:

a. The *ṣaḥīḥ*: these are the authentic ḥadīth which are declared thus after applying all tests.

b. The *ḥasan*: these are fair traditions, although inferior in the matter of authenticity to the *ṣaḥīḥ*.

c. The *ḍaᶜīf*: these are weak traditions which are not very reliable.

Ḍaᶜīf or weak traditions are sub-divided further as follows, taking into consideration the degree of the defects in their narrators (*ruwāt*) or in the texts (*matn*) of the reports:

a. *Muᶜallaq* traditions: these are traditions in which one or two transmitters are omitted in the beginning of the *isnād*.

b. *Maqṭū^{c}* traditions: these are traditions which are narrated by a Follower, a man of second category, from the Prophet ﷺ.
c. *Munqaṭi^{c}* traditions: these are broken traditions in the middle of whose *isnād* someone is omitted.
d. *Mursal* traditions: incomplete traditions from the *isnād* of which a Companion is omitted, e.g. a Follower said, "The Prophet ﷺ said …" This, however, is a matter of disagreement among the scholars, since both of the earliest schools, the Ḥanafī and Mālikī, agree in regarding the *mursal* traditions of many of the early narrators as being authoritative.
e. *Muṣaḥḥaf* traditions: traditions which have a mistake in the words or letters of the *isnād* or the *matn*, e.g. *Ḥasan* is written as *Ḥashan*.
f. *Shādhdh*: irregular traditions with reliable chains of narrators but whose meanings are contrary to other similarly attested traditions narrated by the majority of contemporary transmitters.
g. *Mawḍū^{c}* traditions: fabricated and untrue traditions.

Ḥadīth Qudsī

Ḥadīth qudsī are a special type of *ḥadīth* which, according to the majority of jurists, are worded, unlike the Qur'ān, by the Prophet ﷺ, although the meaning or content is inspired by Allah. They are the words of Allah reported by the Prophet ﷺ in his own wording. The normal type of *ḥadīth*, on the other hand, consist of the statements of the Prophet ﷺ himself on his own initiative, and they augment the revelation (*waḥy*). An example of *ḥadīth qudsī* narrated in *Ṣaḥīḥ Muslim* is: "My slaves, I have forbidden injustice to Myself and have forbidden it between you, so do not wrong each other…" *Ḥadīth qudsī* usually begin in a slightly different manner, e.g.:

قَالَ رَسُولُ اللَّهِ ﷺ فِيمَا يَرْوِيهِ عَنْ رَبِّهِ عَزَّ وَجَلَّ ...

The Messenger of Allah ﷺ said, in that which he narrated from his Lord ﷻ …

Therefore, in *ḥadīth qudsī*, since the wording is that of the Messenger of Allah ﷺ while its meaning and contents are from Allah, it is *waḥy* in meaning but not in its wording (*waḥy bi'l-maᶜnā bi dūn al-lafẓ*).[11] It is unlike Qur'ān which is recited in prayers (*ṣalāh*) and whose recitation is a devotion (*ᶜibādah*) because there is a well known *ḥadīth* that anyone who recites a letter from the Book of Allah will be rewarded the like of ten good deeds.[12] On the other hand, the *ḥadīth qudsī* is not to be recited in prayers nor has it this kind of reward for its recitation.

Āḥād: Narrations of single narrators

The *āḥād* or *khabar al-wāḥid* are narrations of single narrators. The bulk of traditions fall into this category. Jurists differ on what qualifies an *āḥād* tradition for acceptance. Mālik insisted that it should not contravene the practice of the People of Madīnah. Ash-Shāfiᶜī demanded authenticity, i.e. that it be *ṣaḥīḥ*, that the chain of transmission be uninterrupted and that the narrators be renowned for their honesty and ability to comprehend and quote accurately. Aḥmad ibn Ḥanbal agreed with ash-Shāfiᶜī on the importance of it being uninterrupted in its chain of transmission, while the Ḥanafīs accepted the *āḥād* transmissions provided the narrator was trustworthy and the narration made good sense. An example of such an *āḥād* tradition is, "There should be no bequest in favour of an heir."[13]

The four periods of *ḥadīth* scholars

The following is a list of great scholars of *ḥadīth* who have contributed a great deal to the science of *ḥadīth*, right from the time of the Prophet ﷺ to the end of the first century of the *Hijrah*. This is the first period of *ḥadīth* scholars.

First Period

The Companions of the Prophet ﷺ

Those who have narrated more than 1000 *Ḥadīth*

	Name	Year of death	Age at death	Number of narrations of hadith	Number of pupils
1.	Abū Hurayrah	59 AH/679 CE	78	5374	800
2.	ᶜAbdullāh ibn ᶜAbbās	68 AH/688 CE	71	2660	
3.	ᶜĀ'ishah, Umm al-mu'minīn	58 AH/678 CE	67	2210	
4.	ᶜAbdullāh ibn ᶜUmar	78 AH/697 CE	94	1560	
5.	Anas ibn Mālik	93 AH/712 CE	103	1286	
6.	Abū Saᶜīd al-Khudrī	74 AH/693 CE	84	1170	

THOSE WHO HAVE NARRATED BETWEEN 500 AND 1000 *Ḥadīth*

7.	ᶜAbdullāh ibn ᶜAmr ibn al-ᶜĀṣ	63 AH/683 CE			
8.	Sayyidunā ᶜUmar	23 AH/644 CE			
9.	Sayyidunā ᶜAlī	40 AH/660 CE			

THOSE WHO HAVE NARRATED MORE THAN 100 AND LESS THAN 500 *Ḥadīth*

10.	Sayyidunā Abū Bakr	13 AH/634 CE			
11.	Sayyidunā ᶜUthmān	36 AH/656 CE			

12.	Umm Salamah	59 AH/679 CE			
13.	Abū Mūsā al-Ashᶜarī	52 AH/672 CE			
14.	Abū Dharr al-Ghifārī	32 AH/653 CE			
15.	Abū Ayyūb al-Anṣārī	51 AH/671 CE			
16.	Ubayy ibn Kaᶜb	19 AH/640 CE			
17.	Muᶜādh ibn Jabal	18 AH/639 CE			

Famous *Tābiᶜūn* (Followers of the Companions)

The following are famous *tābiᶜūn* who rendered great services to the sciences of *ḥadīth:*

1. Saᶜīd ibn al-Musayyab: born in the second year of Sayyidunā ᶜUmar's caliphate and died in 105 AH/723 CE.
2. ᶜUrwah ibn az-Zubayr: died in 94 AH/713 CE.
3. Sālim ibn ᶜAbdullāh ibn ᶜUmar: died in 106 AH/724 CE.
4. Nāfiᶜ the *mawlā* of ᶜAbdullāh ibn ᶜUmar: died in 117 AH/ 735 CE.

The great *ḥadīth* scholars of the second period

The second period of the development of the sciences of ḥadīth ends roughly at the middle of the second century of the Hijrah calendar. A group of the Followers of the Followers rendered a great service to this cause; they are as follows:

1. Muḥammad Ibn Shihāb az-Zuhrī: died in 124 AH/742 CE in Makkah.
2. ᶜAbd al-Malik ibn Jurayj: died in 150 AH/767 CE in Makkah.
3. Imām al-Awzāᶜī in Syria: died in 157 AH/774 CE.
4. Maᶜmar ibn Rashīd in Yemen: died in 153 AH/770 CE.
5. Sufyān ath-Thawrī in Kūfa: died in 161 AH/778 CE.
6. Ḥammād ibn Salamah in Baṣra: died in 167 AH/784 CE.
7. ᶜAbdullāh ibn al-Mubārak in Khurāsān: died in 181 AH/797 CE.

8. Imām Mālik ibn Anas in Madīnah: died in 179 AH/795 CE.

THE GREAT SCHOLARS OF ḤADĪTH OF THE THIRD PERIOD

In the third period of *ḥadīth* studies, scholars tried to separate the *ḥadīth* of the Prophet ﷺ from the words and deeds of the Companions (*āthār aṣ-ṣaḥābah*) and the verdicts of the Followers (*aqwāl at-tābiᶜīn*). This was a period of valuable research which yielded the following *ḥadīth* sciences for the protection of the *ḥadīth* literature:

1. The science of the asmā' ar-rijāl

It was through this science that the study of the life histories of 500,000 narrators has been preserved for posterity. In no other *dīn* has so much care been taken over such detailed studies, and this is the reason why the lives of these remarkable personalities are not shrouded in mystery. The most famous works compiled many centuries later, such as *Tahdhīb al-kamāl* by Imām Yūsuf al-Mizzī (d. 742 AH/ 1341 CE), *Tahdhīb at-tahdhīb* by Ḥāfiẓ Ibn Ḥajar (d. 852 AH/ 1448 CE) and *Tadhkirat al-ḥuffāẓ* by adh-Dhahabī (d. 748 AH/1347 CE) are treasures in this field of study.

2. The science of the muṣṭalaḥ al-ḥadīth

It was through this science that the classification of *ḥadīth* as authentic or weak and their criteria are studied. In this field the famous work is that of Abū ᶜAmr ᶜUthmān ibn aṣ-Ṣalāḥ (d. 577 AH/1181 CE) named *ᶜUlūm al-ḥadīth* and known as *Muqaddimah Ibn aṣ-Ṣalāḥ*.

3. The science of gharīb al-ḥadīth

It was through this science that the difficult and unusual words of *ḥadīth* were studied and research made on their linguistic origins. The famous work of az-Zamakhsharī (d. 538 AH/1144 CE) in this field is *al-Fā'iq* and that of Ibn al-Athīr (d. 606 AH1210 CE) is his *an-Nihāyah fī gharīb al-ḥadīth*.

4. The science of fiqh al-ḥadīth

It was through this science that research was carried out into the *ḥadīth* concerned with the legal injunctions of the Qur'ān. Books such as *Iclām al-muwaqqicīn* by Ḥāfiẓ Ibn Qayyim (d. 751 AH/1350 CE) and *Ḥujjat Allāh al-bālighah* of Shāh Walī Allāh ad-Dihlawī (d. 1176 AH/1763 CE) are well known in this field.

5. The science of al-aḥādīth al-mawḍūcah (fabricated ḥadīth)

It was through this science that the authentic *ḥadīth* were separated from fabricated narrations. *Al-Fawā'id al-majmūcah* of Imām ash-Shawkānī (d. 1255 AH/1839 CE) and *al-Li'ālī al-masmūcah* of Jalāl ad-Dīn as-Suyūṭī (d. 911 AH/1505 CE) are the famous works on this subject.

6. The science of the beginnings of the ḥadīth (aṭrāf al-ḥadīth)

It is through this science that one knows which narration will be found where and who is actually its narrator. If one has only a small fraction of a *ḥadīth,* the rest of it, including its chains of narration, can be found through this science. Famous works such as *Tuḥfat al-ashrāf* of Ḥāfiẓ al-Mizzī (d. 742 AH/1341 CE) give full indexes of the *Ṣiḥāḥ as-sittah* (the six *ṣaḥīḥ* collections of *ḥadīth*). This great scholar took twenty-six years to complete this book. Orientalists have used such works and, with a few additions here and there, have then claimed 'originality' for their works on the *ḥadīth,* which have come to be considered original even by the world's Muslims simply because knowledge of the sciences of the *dīn* declined after Muslim lands fell into the hands of the imperialists. Orientalists, as well as Muslim scholars who study in the West, refer mostly to plagiarised works of orientalism rather than the originals of Muslim savants, and thus criticise the *ḥadīth* literature unduly.

This list can be very lengthy since there are about one hundred sciences on which *ḥadīth* scholars have worked. These sciences helped tremendously in the growth and development of Islamic jurisprudence and became one of the foundations of the *Sharīcah.*

THE SCHOLARS OF HADĪTH OF THE THIRD PERIOD AND THEIR WORKS ARE AS FOLLOWS:

Name	Work
1. Imām Aḥmad ibn Ḥanbal (d. 241. AH/855 CE)	*Musnad Aḥmad*
2. Imām Muslim ibn Ḥajjāj al-Qushayrī (d. 261 AH/875 CE)	*Ṣaḥīḥ Muslim*
3. Imām Muḥammad ibn Ismāᶜīl al-Bukhārī (d. 256 AH/870 CE)	*Ṣaḥīḥ al-Bukhārī*
4. Imām Abū Dāwūd Ashᶜath as-Sijistānī (d. 275. AH/888 CE)	*Sunan Abū Dāwūd*
5. Imām Abū Ismāᶜīl at-Tirmidhī (d. 279 AH/892 CE)	*Jāmiᶜ at-Tirmidhī*
6. Imām Aḥmad ibn Shuᶜayb an-Nasā'ī (d. 303 AH/916 CE)	*As-Sunan al-Mujtabā*
7. Imām Muḥammad ibn Yazīd ibn Mājah al-Qazwīnī (d. 273 AH/886 CE)	*Sunan Ibn Mājah*

THE FOURTH PERIOD OF ḤADĪTH SCHOLARS

The fourth period begins from the fifth century of the *Hijrah* and continues until today. In this period, mostly selections of *ḥadīth* from the earlier works or commentaries (*sharḥ*) on the earlier works have been written, and some scholars are busy explaining points arising out of these works even today. The famous works of early writers of the fourth period are as follows:

Name	Work
1. Walī ad-Dīn al-Khaṭīb (d. 749 AH/1347 CE)	*Mishkāt al-maṣābīḥ*
2. Abū Zakariyā Yaḥyā ibn Sharaf an-Nawawī (d. 676 AH/1277 CE)	*Riyāḍ aṣ-ṣāliḥīn*
3. Abu'l-Barakāt ᶜAbd as-Salām ibn Taymiyyah (d. 652 AH/1254 CE), the grandfather of Taqī ad-Dīn Aḥmad ibn Taymiyyah (d. 728 AH/1328 CE). Imām ash-Shawkānī wrote *Nayl al-awṭār* in 8 volumes in commentary on this work.	*Muntaqā al-akhbār*
4. Ḥāfiẓ Ibn Ḥajar (d. 752 AH/1351 CE)	*Bulūgh al-marām*
5. Muḥammad ibn Ismāᶜīl (d. 1182 AH/1726 CE)	*Subul as-Salām*

There are many other commentaries written in different languages of the Muslims from all over the world. The work continues.

Notes

[1] As-Suyūṭī, Jalāl ad-Dīn, *al-Itqān fī ᶜulūm al-Qur'ān*. Calcutta, 1856, p.822; see also adh-Dhahabī, *at-Tafsīr wa'l-mufassirūn Op. Cit.*, vol. 1, p.4919.

[2] Ibn ᶜAṭiyah, ᶜAbd-al-Ḥaqq al-Gharnāṭī, ed. Jeffery, Arthur; *Muqaddimatān fī ᶜulūm al-Qur'ān*, (Two introductions to the Qur'ānic Sciences: The introduction to the *Kitab al-Mabānī* and the introduction of Ibn ᶜAṭiyah to his *tafsīr*), *Muqaddimat Kitāb al-Mabānī*, Maktabat al-Khaniji, Cairo, 1954, p. 182; Ibn Khaldūn, *al-Muqaddimah*, p. 263.

[3] As-Sayis, Muḥammad ᶜAlī, *Tafsīr āyāt al-aḥkām*, Cairo, 1953, vol. 4, p.128.

[4] See M. M. Aᶜẓamī, *Studies in Ḥadīth Methodology and Literature*, Indianapolis, 1977, pp. 9-31.

[5] Other sources for the Sunnah include the *ᶜamal* or practice of the people of Madīnah of the earliest generations.

[6] *Ṣaḥīḥ al-Bukhārī*, Chapter on Islam, p.30.

[7] *Ibid.*, Chapter on *Wuḍū'*, p. 75.

[8] Aḥmad ibn Ḥanbal, *Musnad*, Cairo, 1313 AH, p.206.

[9] Ḥamidullāh, Dr. Muḥammad, *al-Wathā'iq as-siyāsiyyah*, Beirut, 1968.

[10] al-Bukhārī, Abū ᶜAbdullāh Muḥammad ibn Ismāᶜīl, (194-256 AH/870 CE) *al-Jāmiᶜ aṣ-Ṣaḥīḥ*, Edited by Ludolf Krehl and Th. W. Juynboll, 4 vols., Leiden: E.J. Brill, 1862-1908, *bāb iᶜtiṣām*, iv. p.240.

[11] Al-Qaṭṭān, Mannāᶜ, *Mabāḥith fī ᶜulūm al-Qur'ān*, Riyadh, 1976, p. 26.

[12] Narrated by at-Tirmidhī from Ibn Masᶜūd ﷺ.

[13] The heir receives a fixed share of the inheritance.

Chapter 5

Ijmā^c
The Third Textual Source of *Sharī^{c}ah*

THE FIRST TWO TEXTUAL SOURCES of *Sharī^{c}ah* are the Qur'ān and the Sunnah. The third textual source is *ijmā^c*. Among the intellectual sources are *qiyās* and *ijtihād* – which are derived from the legal injunctions of the Noble Qur'ān and the Sunnah of the Prophet ﷺ, which is the embodiment of the revelation of the Qur'ān. Hence, the final sanction for all intellectual activities in respect of the development of the *Sharī^{c}ah* comes from nowhere else but the Qur'ān. Therefore, a *ḥadīth* which is contrary to the Qur'ān may not be authentic. We shall later examine in detail the intellectual sources of the *Sharī^{c}ah* and their Qur'ānic sanctions.

Ijmā^c: Consensus

Ijmā^c is the consensus of juristic opinions of the learned *^{c}ulamā'* of the *Ummah* after the death of the Messenger of Allah ﷺ and can be defined as the consensus of the Companions of the Prophet ﷺ and the unanimous agreement reached on the decisions taken by subsequent learned *muftīs* and jurists on various matters.

Allah, exalted is He, encourages seeking the views of others on matters of the *dīn,* as He said in the Noble Qur'ān:

فَبِمَا رَحْمَةٍ مِّنَ اللَّهِ لِنتَ لَهُمْ وَلَوْ كُنتَ فَظًّا غَلِيظَ الْقَلْبِ لَانفَضُّوا مِنْ حَوْلِكَ فَاعْفُ عَنْهُمْ
وَاسْتَغْفِرْ لَهُمْ وَشَاوِرْهُمْ فِي الْأَمْرِ فَإِذَا عَزَمْتَ فَتَوَكَّلْ عَلَى اللَّهِ إِنَّ اللَّهَ يُحِبُّ الْمُتَوَكِّلِينَ

It is a mercy from Allah that you were gentle with them. If you had been rough or hard of heart, they would have scattered from around you. So pardon them and ask forgiveness for them, and consult with them about the matter. Then when you have reached a firm decision, put your trust in Allah. Allah loves those who put their trust in Him. (Sūrah Āl ᶜImrān 3: 159)

Allah, exalted is He, has also said:

وَالَّذِينَ اسْتَجَابُوا لِرَبِّهِمْ وَأَقَامُوا الصَّلَاةَ وَأَمْرُهُمْ شُورَى بَيْنَهُمْ وَمِمَّا رَزَقْنَاهُمْ يُنفِقُونَ

...those who respond to their Lord and establish ṣalāh, and manage their affairs by mutual consultation and give of what We have provided for them. (Sūrat ash-Shūrā 42: 38)

The Prophet Muhammad ﷺ also supported the process of *ijmāᶜ* when he said:

لَا تَجْتَمِعُ أُمَّتِي عَلَى ضَلَالَةٍ

My *Ummah* will not unite on an error. (Ibn Abī ᶜĀṣīm, *as-Sunnah,* from Anas.)[1]

The practice of *ijmāᶜ* can be traced back to the days of the Companions of the Prophet ﷺ as can be seen from the following example. Allah, exalted is He, does not state the punishment for someone who drinks alcohol. However, agreement was reached by the consensus of the Companions when Sayyidunā ᶜAlī ibn Abī Ṭālib ؓ said: "He who drinks, becomes drunk; he who becomes drunk, raves; he who raves, accuses people falsely [of sexual indecency] and should be given eighty strokes of the cane according to the injunction of the Noble Qur'ān. Allah, exalted is He, said:

وَالَّذِينَ يَرْمُونَ الْمُحْصَنَاتِ ثُمَّ لَمْ يَأْتُوا بِأَرْبَعَةِ شُهَدَاءَ فَاجْلِدُوهُمْ ثَمَانِينَ جَلْدَةً وَلَا تَقْبَلُوا لَهُمْ شَهَادَةً أَبَداً وَأُوْلَئِكَ هُمُ الْفَاسِقُونَ

But those who make accusations against chaste women and then do not produce four witnesses: flog them with eighty lashes and never again accept them as witnesses. Such people are deviators." (Sūrat an-Nūr 24: 4)

Ijmāᶜ owes its origins to the following Qur'ānic verses in Sūrat an-Nisā':

وَمَن يُشَاقِقِ الرَّسُولَ مِن بَعْدِ مَا تَبَيَّنَ لَهُ الْهُدَى وَيَتَّبِعْ غَيْرَ سَبِيلِ الْمُؤْمِنِينَ نُوَلِّهِ مَا تَوَلَّى وَنُصْلِهِ جَهَنَّمَ وَسَاءَتْ مَصِيراً

But if anyone opposes the Messenger after the guidance has become clear to him, and follows other than the path of the muminun, We will hand him over to whatever he has turned to, and We will roast him in Hell. What an evil destination! (Sūrat an-Nisā' 4: 115)

يَا أَيُّهَا الَّذِينَ آمَنُواْ أَطِيعُواْ اللّهَ وَأَطِيعُواْ الرَّسُولَ وَأُوْلِي الأَمْرِ مِنكُمْ فَإِن تَنَازَعْتُمْ فِي شَيْءٍ فَرُدُّوهُ إِلَى اللّهِ وَالرَّسُولِ إِن كُنتُمْ تُؤْمِنُونَ بِاللّهِ وَالْيَوْمِ الآخِرِ

You who have īmān! obey Allah and obey the Messenger and those in command among you. If you have a dispute about something, refer it back to Allah and the Messenger, if you have īmān in Allah and the Last Day. (Sūrat an-Nisā' 4: 59)

Consultation (*shūrā*) with knowledgeable people and the use of juristic reason (*ijtihād*) were normal preliminaries for arriving at a binding *ijmāᶜ* in the early history when the core of the Muslim community was collected in one place. The Caliphs who took the right way (*al-Khulafā' ar-Rāshidūn* ﷺ) always consulted the Companions whenever a novel issue arose. The Caliphate of Abū Bakr ﷺ was based and run on this process of the *ijmāᶜ* of the Companions. Later *ijmāᶜ*, however, documents the fact of complete agreement of the *ᶜulamā'* of that period on a matter, whether they were congregated in one place or widely dispersed, whether they had met each other and discussed the matter or not.

The following few practical examples are based on *ijmāᶜ*. The invalidity of a contract for the purchase of goods yet to be manufactured (*ᶜaqd al-istiṣnāᶜ*) is an *ijmāᶜ*. The normal rule is that the sale of non-existent goods is not valid because of uncertainty (*gharar*).

Juristic consensus is aimed at providing a practical solution. In the field of inheritance, for example, it is agreed that if a person is predeceased by his father, then the grandfather – taking the share of the father – participates in the inheritance of the estate with the son.

It is also agreed that a grandmother is entitled to a sixth of the estate. The *ijmā*ᶜ on this issue is based on a decision attributed by al-Mughīrah ibn Shuᶜbah ﷺ (d. 50 AH/ 670 CE) to the Prophet ﷺ. This is an example of a consensus upon a Sunnah, for indeed consensus is not valid where it contravenes the Book or the Sunnah.

In the field of family law it is agreed that since the Qur'ān proscribes marriages with mothers and daughters then, by the same token, grandmothers and granddaughters, however far removed, fall within the prohibited degrees.

The minimum period of gestation is six months according to all schools of *fiqh*, but an example of lack of *ijmā*ᶜ is the disagreement over the maximum period of gestation, which is set differently by the *madhhabs,* in some of them it being accepted that it can be two, three or even more years. The consequence of this view is that divorced or widowed women who come with children after some considerable time may not even have their cases raised before the *qāḍī* for judgement.

The consensus of the *ᶜulamā'* must be based on the Book of Allah, the Sunnah of the Prophet ﷺ, his verdicts (*qawl ar-Rasūl*), his actions and his example (*fiᶜl ar-Rasūl*), remembering that some actions of the Prophet ﷺ can be of a very special nature which cannot be applicable to ordinary people. Lastly, the consensus should be based on what the Prophet ﷺ confirmed whether by his affirmation or his silence (*taqrīrāt ar-Rasūl*).

*Ijmā*ᶜ can be divided into three broad categories: *ijmā*ᶜ *al-qawl* (consensus verbally articulated), *ijmā*ᶜ *al-fiᶜl* (consensus expressed by deed) and *ijmā*ᶜ *as-sukūt* (consensus expressed by silence over an issue, i.e. by not expressing disagreement with or opposition to it).

*Ijmā*ᶜ can also be subdivided into two broad categories: *ijmā*ᶜ *al-ᶜazīmah* (regular consensus) and *ijmā*ᶜ *ar-rukhṣah* (irregular consensus).

As regards consensus that is verbally articulated, if an issue is raised and all the jurists assent to it by voicing their approval, the consensus of opinion is regular, but if it is raised and none of them says anything whether in contradiction or in affirmation, the consensus of opinion is irregular. Nonetheless both of them are valid in Islamic Law.

As regards *ijmā^{c}* expressed by deed, if a jurist does something and none of the other jurists challenge him, the *ijmā^{c}* is regular; but if a jurist does something, and one or more jurists question him, the *ijmā^{c} al-fi^{c}l* is irregular. Nonetheless, both of them is valid as far as Islamic Law is concerned. During the time of Imām Mālik and Abū Ḥanīfah, the eligibility of jurists who could sanction *ijmā^{c}* became a matter of controversy. According to some jurists, such as Aḥmad ibn Ḥanbal ؓ, it is only the Companions of the Prophet ﷺ who were in a position to sanction *ijmā^{c}*. According to the Shi'ites[2], however, the *ijmā^{c}* can only be sanctioned by the *Ahl al-Bayt* (the people of the house of the Prophet ﷺ), that is – in their interpretation[3] – the descendants of ^{c}Alī ؓ and Fāṭimah ؓ, the daughter of the Prophet ﷺ.

According to Imām Mālik, the *ijmā^{c}* of the People of Madīnah of his time and preceding times had an unequalled standing in the transmission of the Sunnah, a standing greater than many of the *ḥadīth*. Mālikīs also see the later *ijmā^{c}* of the *^{c}ulamā'* much as do the other schools. However, as far as the Ḥanafī school of thought is concerned, the *ijmā^{c}* can be sanctioned by any qualified jurists irrespective of abode or *madhhab*. The jurists also disagree among themselves as to the number of jurists who can ratify *ijmā^{c}*. According to Imām Mālik and Imām Abū Ḥanīfah, the number need not necessarily be very great. Some jurists put the number as three jurists while some others say that two will suffice for the purpose.[4] The jurists also say that *ijmā^{c}* of the Companions of the Prophet ﷺ could only have been repealed by the jurists, i.e. the Companions, who lived at that period. It is the same with a consensus reached on any issue by the jurists of a particular age: it is unacceptable for later jurists to oppose it.

The jurists say that any *ijmā^{c}* that has to do with some marginal issue on *^{c}ibādah* (religious worship), must be ratified by all. Al-Bājī said that the consensus on every issue which is obligatory both for ordinary people and scholars is only established by the agreement of both. If an ordinary Muslim does not agree with a matter, it must be accepted as invalid. On the other hand, if the *ijmā^c* has anything to do with those ordinary transactions (*mu^cāmalāt*) which not every Muslim has to know about and which need thorough reasoning, the ordinary Muslim's point of view need not be considered.

Some people think that the Mālikī *madhhab* considers that the established practice of the people of Madīnah (*^camal ahl al-Madīnah*) of the first generations of the Companions, the Followers, and the Followers of the Followers, provides a valid *ijmā^c*, but that other schools disagreed on this point. However, the Mālikīs consider the established practice of the people of Madīnah not as an *ijmā^c* but as an authentic transmission of the Sunnah equivalent to a *mutawātir ḥadīth* transmitted by a large number of people in every generation to large numbers in the subsequent generations.

Some Ḥanbalīs (as well as some other jurists) accept the only binding *ijmā^c* to be the agreement of the four *Khulafā' ar-Rāshidūn* ﷺ.

Similarly, other jurists consider the *fatwās* (juridical opinions and decisions) of the Companions[5] as *ijmā^c* binding upon the *Ummah*. Some Ḥanbalī scholars are of the view that *ijmā^c* is not binding if reached more than one generation after the death of the Messenger of Allah ﷺ, because it is nearly impossible to obtain the express agreement of every single qualified jurist after that stage of the spread of Islam.

Most jurists agree that only an express *ijmā^c* is binding. However, Ḥanafī jurists consider the silence of the jurists with regard to the vocal expression of a particular opinion as an effective implied agreement provided that; (a) there is evidence that the silent jurists were really well acquainted with the issue and (b) a reasonable period of time elapsed after the view was expressed to enable other jurists to devote sufficient time for research and analysis. If both conditions are met, say Ḥanafī jurists, the silence of jurists amounts to approval.

No matter how high the rank of the *ᶜulamā'* and how thorough their deliberations, no amount of *ijmāᶜ* can abrogate a text (*naṣṣ*) i.e., a provision laid down in the Qur'ān or the Sunnah of the Prophet ﷺ. It should also be remembered that no *ijmāᶜ* was reached or could have been reached except after the death of the Prophet ﷺ, that is, after all the text was revealed or stated, for *ijmāᶜ* is based always on the interpretation of the Qur'ān and Sunnah.

If any *ijmāᶜ* is soundly founded on the texts of the Qur'ān and the Sunnah it cannot be repealed by any subsequent consensus; but if the *ijmāᶜ* is simply based on public interest (*al-maṣāliḥ al-mursalah*), it may be repealed if public welfare so requires. In short, *ijmāᶜ* is a proof for all the four schools of Islamic jurisprudence.

Imām ash-Shāfiᶜī has fully discussed *ijmāᶜ* as one of the sources of *Sharīᶜah* in his famous *Risālah*.[6] The following discourse of ash-Shāfiᶜī throws enough light on *ijmāᶜ*:

> Someone said to me, "I have understood your school respecting the rulings of Allah and then the rulings of His Messenger, and that whoever accepts from the Messenger of Allah has accepted from Allah, because Allah has made obedience to His Messenger obligatory, and the proof is established by what you have said that it is not *ḥalāl* for a Muslim who knows the Book and the Sunnah to say anything contrary to either one of them. And I know that this is the obligation of Allah. But what is your proof for your following that which people are agreed on unanimously of those things for which there is no textual source that it is the ruling of Allah, and which they do not cite from the Prophet ﷺ? Do you claim, what others say, that their *ijmāᶜ* will only be on the basis of a reliable Sunnah, even if they did not cite it?"
>
> "As to that which the *ᶜulamā'* do not relate [from the Prophet ﷺ], which they may or may not relate as a tradition from the Prophet ﷺ, we cannot consider it as related on the authority of the Prophet ﷺ because one may relate only what he has heard, for no one is permitted to relate [on the authority of the Prophet ﷺ] information which may or may not be true. So we accept the decision of the *ᶜulamā'* because we have to obey their authority, and we know that wherever there are Sunnahs of the Prophet ﷺ, the *ᶜulamā'* cannot be ignorant of them, although it is possible that some of them are, and we know that *ᶜulamā'* can neither

agree on anything contrary to the Sunnah of the Prophet ﷺ nor on an error."

Someone may ask: "Is there any evidence in support of what you hold?"

Then it is said, "Sufyān informed us from ᶜAbd al-Malik ibn ᶜUmayr from ᶜAbd ar-Raḥmān ibn ᶜAbdullāh ibn Masᶜūd from his father that the Messenger of Allah ﷺ said, 'May Allah give victory to a slave [who hears my words, remembers them, guards them, and hands them on. Many a transmitter of law is no lawyer himself, and many may transmit law to others who are more versed in law than they.' (Aḥmad, Ibn Mājah)]

Sufyān (also) told us from ᶜAbdullāh ibn ᶜAlī Sulaymān ibn Yasār from his father, who said: 'ᶜUmar ibn al-Khaṭṭāb delivered a *khuṭbah* at al-Jābiyah in which he said: "The Messenger of Allah stood among us by an order from Allah, as I am now standing among you, and said:

'Honour my Companions, then those who follow them [the Followers], and then those who follow them [the Followers of the Followers]; then lying will appear, so much so that a man will swear an oath without being required to do so, and he will testify without being asked to do so. Whoever would be pleased with being established in the middle and best part of the Garden should cling to the group (*jamāᶜah*) because shayṭān is with the individual, and he is further away from two. A man must not be isolated alone with a [marriageable] woman, because shayṭān is the third of them. Whoever is made happy by his good actions and grieved by his bad actions is a *mu'min*.'[7]

He asked: "What is the meaning of the Prophet's order to cling closely to the group?"

Imām ash-Shāfiᶜī replied: "There is but one meaning for it."

He asked: "How is it possible that there is only one meaning?"

Imam ash-Shāfiᶜī replied: "When their group divided up in the lands, nobody was able to cling to a group of people who were physically widely dispersed and who had been found to comprise, as a society, Muslims and disbelievers, people of *taqwā* and dissolute people. So to cling to [the group] physically was meaningless because it was not possible and because collecting together physically does nothing, so that clinging to their group was meaningless except in the sense of what the group adhered to of reckoning some things *ḥalāl* and some *ḥarām,* in [their] obedience in respect of those two.

"And whoever passes the same verdict as the united group (*jamāᶜah*) of the Muslims has certainly clung to their group. But whoever contradicts and opposes that which the united group of the Muslims give as a verdict has opposed their group which he was commanded to cling to. Forgetfulness only occurs in the small sect, but as for in the large group it is not possible in it entirely, for there to be neglect of the Book nor of the Sunnah nor of analogical deduction, inshā'Allāh."

Notes

[1] At-Tirmidhī has a *hadith* of Ibn ᶜUmar, "Allah, exalted is He, will never unite my *Ummah*" – or he said, "the *Ummah* of Muḥammad on error."(*abwāb al-fitan an rasūl Allāh* ﷺ, *bāb fī luzūm al-jamāᶜah*)

[2] Ordinary shi'ites of the 'Twelvers' are considered to be outside the fold of the *Ahl as-Sunnah wa'l-Jamāᶜah* but not necessarily outside the fold of Islam. The author mentions their position here for completeness.

[3] The *Ahl al-Bayt* comprise the wives of the Messenger of Allah ﷺ and his relatives through his uncles such as al-ᶜAbbās and Abū Ṭālib, and his descendants through his daughter Fāṭimah and son-in-law and cousin ᶜAlī ibn Abī Ṭālib, may Allah be pleased with all of them.

[4] The author means that if a small number of prominent *ᶜulamā'* report that 'all the *ᶜulamā'*' are united this establishes the existence of consensus. He does not mean that the agreement of two or three *ᶜulamā'* is itself consensus.

[5] In the case where none of the other Companions or great *fuqahā'* of the Followers disagreed with their *fatwās* so that their silence is regarded as proof of consensus.

[6] Ash-Shāfiᶜī, *ar-Risālah,* translated by ᶜAbdaṣṣamad Clarke.

[7] In the year 638 CE the Caliph ᶜUmar went to al-Jābiyah, a village on the outskirts of Damascus, where he met with several leading Companions. For the rest of the tradition see ash-Shāfiᶜī, *Musnad,* Vol. 2, p. 187; and Ibn Ḥanbal, Vol. 1, pp.112, 176-81.

Chapter 6

The Intellectual Principles of *Sharī^c^ah*

Qiyās: Analogical deduction

AMONG THE INTELLECTUAL PRINCIPLES are *qiyās* and *ijtihād*. *Qiyās* could be defined, in Islamic parlance, as analogy, or analogical deduction. In other words, *qiyās* is the legal principle introduced in order to arrive at logical legal conclusions on certain matters pertaining to the welfare of the Muslims. In exercising this, however, it must be based on Qur'ān, Sunnah and *ijmā^c^*.

Although this legal principle was in use among the earlier generations, it was made famous by Imām Abū Ḥanīfah, the founder of the Ḥanafī school, in Iraq, with which it subsequently became widely associated. The reasons for his reliance upon it were not unconnected with the need to curb speculative thinking and people's tendency to digress from Islamic legal reasoning.

During the period of the Abbasids, people engaged in reading various texts on logic, philosophy, etymology, linguistics, the literatures of various places, and foreign works, which to some extent tended to corrupt their thought processes and lead them astray. They wanted to apply what they had studied in these foreign texts to Islamic jurisprudence. Many new Muslims in far away lands had brought with them their philosophical outlooks, their cultures and even some of their religious and legal notions into the fold of Islam. Abū Ḥanīfah used a disciplined *qiyās* as a measure to curb their untrained thinking and to keep them in check.

There are some people who are against this legal principle. In this regard, there are scholars and jurists who may be termed as anti-*qiyās* and others pro-*qiyās*. Each and every one of them produced evidence to support his stand.

Those who are against *qiyās* have said that Allah, exalted is He, revealed the Noble Qur'ān to us for our guidance, no more, no less. A Muslim must look for the solution to his problems in the Qur'ān. Allah, exalted is He, has said:

مَا فَرَّطْنَا فِي الْكِتَابِ مِنْ شَيْءٍ ثُمَّ إِلَىٰ رَبِّهِمْ يُحْشَرُونَ

We have not omitted anything from the Book – then they will be gathered to their Lord. (Sūrat al-Anᶜām 6: 38)

They also supported their argument by *ḥadīth* of the Prophet ﷺ. Above all, they doubted the proper functionality of *qiyās* from the Islamic legal point of view.

The pro-*qiyās* group also supported their stand with Qur'ānic *āyāt*, traditions of the Prophet Muhammad ﷺ and statements of his Companions.

Allah, exalted is He, said:

فَاعْتَبِرُوا يَا أُولِي الْأَبْصَارِ

People of insight, take note! (Sūrat al-Ḥashr 59: 3)

The use of the verb *iᶜtabirū*, *'take note!'*, is understood to refer to using the intellect in this fashion, of deducing analogically from apparent cases to solve cases that are not apparent.

The pro-*qiyās* group say that the people of understanding referred to in this verse must use their common sense to deduce Islamic law. They support their argument by quoting the *ḥadīth* of the Prophet ﷺ.

Some of the companions of Muᶜādh ibn Jabal narrated that when the Messenger of Allah ﷺ wanted to send Muᶜādh to the Yemen he said, "How will you pass judgement if a case comes to you?" He answered, "I will pass judgement by the Book of Allah." He said, "If you do not find it in the Book of Allah?" He said, "Then by the Sunnah of the Messenger of Allah ﷺ." He said, "If you do not find it in the Sunnah of the Messenger of Allah ﷺ nor in the Book of Allah?" He said, "I will exert my intellect and I will not fall short." The Messenger of Allah ﷺ struck him on the chest and said, "Praise belongs to Allah Who guided the messenger of the Messenger of Allah ﷺ to agree with that which pleases the Messenger of Allah." (Abū Dāwūd, *awwal kitāb al-aqḍiyah, bāb ijtihād ar-ra'y fī al-qaḍā'*)

It is narrated also that during his lifetime the Prophet ﷺ sent Abū Mūsā al-Ashᶜarī ؓ to the Yemen, and told him to judge on the basis of the Qur'ān, and that if he did not find a solution in the Qur'ān, he should make use of the Sunnah of the Prophet, and that if he did not find the solution in the Sunnah of the Prophet ﷺ, he should use his own judgement.

During the lifetime of the Companions of the Prophet ﷺ, the Companions arrived at various decisions by analogical deduction, for example on the punishment that should be given to a drunkard, as we saw before when we cited it as an example of a consensus that they reached. Sayyidunā ᶜAlī ؓ said: "He who drinks, becomes drunk; he who becomes drunk raves; he who raves accuses people falsely [of sexual indecency] and he who accuses people falsely should be given eighty lashes." So he deduced by analogy that the drunkard should be given eighty lashes. And the Companions agreed unanimously on his verdict which became the *ijmāᶜ* of the *Ummah*.

From all that has been said so far, we can deduce that there is nothing wrong in using *qiyās* in deriving a logical conclusion in Islamic law in-as-much as that conclusion does not go against the injunctions of the Noble Qur'ān or the Sunnah of the Prophet ﷺ.

Similarly, there arose a problem about the appointment of a Caliph after the death of the Prophet ﷺ. The Prophet's choice of Abū Bakr ؓ as spiritual leader to act as *imām* in congregational prayers was the basis for the selection of Abū Bakr ؓ as political leader. The Companions agreed unanimously and reached *ijmāᶜ* on this decision and thus on this use of analogical deduction.

Another interesting example of analogical deduction is that of the *qiyās* and *ijtihād* by Sayyidunā ᶜUmar ؓ, the second Caliph. He asked the Prophet ﷺ whether a kiss during the fast invalidates the fast even though no orgasm is reached. The Prophet ﷺ posed a question: "Does rinsing one's mouth invalidate the fast?" 'Umar ؓ replied: "No, it is alright to do so." So the Prophet ﷺ indicated that similarly the fast is not invalidated by a kiss if it is not accompanied by orgasm.

Note: when a Muslim intentionally breaks his fast during the month of Ramaḍān, he is obliged to expiate it (*kaffārah*) in the following manner:

a. By freeing a slave;
b. Or he ought to fast for two month consecutively in lieu of that;
c. Or, if his health will not stand two months' fasting, then he must feed sixty destitute people.

Imām Mālik also gave a verdict based on *qiyās* about the remarriage of a wife of a missing person after the *qāḍī* has issued a decree deeming him dead, although he subsequently reappears. He compared it with the remarriage of a divorced wife who has been reaccepted by her husband into the matrimonial bond but who had in the meantime remarried because the return was not communicated to her. In both cases the wife observed a waiting period: the *'iddah* of the widow in the first case, and the *'iddah* of *ṭalāq* [divorce] in the second case. In both cases the women entered into the second marriage in good faith. The Caliph 'Umar had given a *fatwā* that in the case of a woman who was not made aware that her husband had taken her back becomes the lawful wife of the new husband. Imām Mālik said that the same applies in the case of the former wife of the missing person as she becomes the legal wife of the new husband.

The Prophet ﷺ was asked by a woman whether she could perform the Ḥajj on behalf of her aged father. The Prophet ﷺ replied that she could, just as she may discharge a debt on his behalf.

Imām ash-Shāfiʿī was asked a question about *qiyās* or analogical deduction as one of the sources of *Sharīʿah*, and the Imām replied to this question in his *Risālah*:

> He said, "So for what reason do you say, 'One gives verdict by *qiyās* concerning that for which there is nothing [in the] Book

nor [in the] Sunnah nor [in the] *ijmāᶜ*.' So is *qiyās* the text of an obligatory transmission of information?"

I said, "If *qiyās* had been the text of the Book or the Sunnah one would have said with respect to everything that is the text of the Book, 'This is the judgement of Allah,' and with respect to everything that is the text of the Sunnah, 'This is the judgement of the Messenger of Allah ﷺ,' and we would not say about it that it is *qiyās*."

He said, "So what is *qiyās*? Is it *ijtihād* or are they two distinct matters?"

I said, "They are two terms for a single meaning."

He said, "What is their common basis?"

I said, "Everything that happens to a Muslim has a binding ruling or on the path of the truth for it there exists an indication, and he must follow it if there is a ruling specifically for it, and if there is nothing specifically for it, the indication for the right way in it has to be sought by *ijtihād*, and *ijtihād* is *qiyās*."

He was asked: "If scholars apply *qiyās* correctly, will they arrive at the right answer in the eyes of Allah and will it be permissible for them to disagree in their answer through *qiyās*? Have they been ordered to seek one or different *qiyās*? Have they been ordered to seek one or different answers for each question? What is the proof of the position that they should apply *qiyās* on the basis of the literal rather than the implicit meaning of a precedent, and that it is permissible for them to disagree in their answers? Should (*qiyās*) in matters concerning scholars themselves be applied differently from the way it is applied in matters concerning others? Who is the person qualified to exercise *ijtihād* through *qiyās* in matters concerning himself, not others, and who is the person who can apply it in matters concerning himself as well as others?"

Imām ash-Shāfiᶜī replied: "[Legal] knowledge is of various kinds. The first consists of the right decision in the literal and implied senses; the other, of the right answer in the literal sense only. The right decisions (in the literal and implied senses) are those based (either) on Allah's command or on a Sunnah of the Messenger of Allah ﷺ related by the public from an (earlier) public.

"So these [Allah's commands and the Sunnah] are the two routes which testify concerning that which is *ḥalāl* that it is *ḥalāl* and concerning that which is *ḥarām* that it is *ḥarām*. And this is the one which it is not permitted to anyone, in our view, to be ignorant of and about which there is no doubt.

"Secondly, (Legal) knowledge of the specialist type consists of traditions related by a few and known only to scholars, but others are under no obligation to be familiar with it. Such knowledge may either be found among all or a few of the scholars, related to a reliable transmitter from the Prophet. This is the (kind of) knowledge which is binding on scholars to accept and it constitutes the right decision in the literal sense such as we accept the validity of the testimony of two witnesses. This is right (only) in the literal sense, because it is possible that evidence of the two witnesses might be false.

"Thirdly, there is legal knowledge derived from *ijmāᶜ* (consensus).

"Finally, there is legal knowledge derived from *ijtihād* (personal reasoning) through *qiyās*, by virtue of which right decisions are sought. Such decisions are right in the literal sense to the person who applies analogy; not to the majority of scholars, for nobody knows what is hidden except Allah."

He asked: "If (legal) knowledge is derived through *qiyās* provided it is rightly applied – should (the scholars) who apply analogy agree on most (of the decisions), although we might find them disagreeing on some?

Imam ash-Shāfiᶜī replied: "*Qiyās* is of two kinds: the first, if the case in question is similar to the original meaning [of the precedent], no disagreement on this kind [is permitted]. The second, if the case in question is similar to several precedents, *qiyās* must be applied to the precedent nearest in resemblance and most appropriate. But those who apply *qiyās* are likely to disagree [in their answers]."

He asked: "Will you give examples known to me explaining that [legal] knowledge is of two kinds, the one consisting of the right decision in literal and implicit senses, and the other of the right decisions in the literall, not the implicit, sense?"

Imam ash-Shāfiᶜī replied: "if we were in the sacred mosque and the Kaᶜbah is in sight, do you not agree that we should face it (in prayer) with certainty?"

He said: "That is right."

Imam ash-Shāfiᶜī asked: "(since) the duties of prayer, the payment of Zakat, performance of pilgrimage and the like have been compulsory on us, are we not under obligation to perform them in the right ways?"

He replied: "That is right."

Imam ash-Shāfiᶜī asked: "Since the duty imposed on us to punish the fornicator with a hundred stripes, to scourge him who casts an imputation (of adultery) with eighty, to put to death him who apostatises, and to cut off (the hand of) him who steals, are we not under obligation to do so (only) to him who steals, are we not under obligation to do so (only) to him whose offence is established with certainty on (the basis of) his admission?"

He replied: "That is right."

Imam ash-Shāfiᶜī asked: "Should not (the decisions) be the same whether we were obligated to take them against our selves or others although we realise that we know about our selves what others do not know, and we do not know about others but outward observation what we know about ourselves inwardly?"

He replied: "That is right."

Imam ash-Shāfiᶜī then asked: "Are we not under obligation to face the Sacred House (in prayer) where we may be?"

He replied: "That is right."

Imam ash-Shāfiᶜī asked: "Do you hold that we (could always) face the Sacred house correctly?"

He replied: "No, not always as correctly as when you were able to see (the Sacred House); however the duty imposed on you was fulfilled. "

Imam ash-Shāfiᶜī asked: "Are we not obligated to accept the just character of a man on the basis of his outward behaviour, and establish marital and inheritance relationship with him on (the basis of) his outward acceptance of Islam?"

He replied: "That is right."

Imam ash-Shāfiᶜī said: "Yet he may not be just in character inwardly."

He replied: "That is quite possible; but you are under no obligation to accept save what is explicit."

Imam ash-Shāfiᶜī asked: "So it is not lawful for us to establish marital inheritance relationship with him, and to accept his testimony, and is it unlawful for us to kill him on the basis of (our) explicit (knowledge) of him? But if others should discover him to be an unbeliever, would it not be lawful for them to kill him and to repudiate marital and inheritance relationship or whatever else he had been permitted to do?"

He replied: "That is right."

Imam ash-Shāfiᶜī then asked: "Thus the obligation imposed on us toward the same person differs in accordance with the degree of our understanding of it and others' understanding of it?"

He replied: "Yes, for each one fulfils his obligation on the basis of his own understanding."

Imam ash-Shāfiᶜī said: "Thus we hold concerning matters on which there is no binding explicit text that these should be sought by *ijtihād* – through *qiyās* because we are under obligation to arrive at the right answers according to us."

He asked: "Are you not seeking the answer to one question through different means?"

Imam ash-Shāfiᶜī replied: "Yes, whenever the grounds are different."

He asked: "Give me an example."

Imam ash-Shāfiᶜī replied: "If a man admits an obligation on his part to Allah or to another person, I should take a decision against him on the strength of his admission; if he does not admit, I should take the decision on the evidence against him,; if no evidence can be established against him, I should take the decision on the basis of an oath taken by him which might acquit him; if he refuses (to take the oath), I should ask the other party to take an oath and I should make the decision against him on the basis of the oath of the other party, it is understood that (one's own) admission against himself owing to (one's natural) covetousness and greed is more certain than the evidence of others, since they might make a mistake or tell a lie against another. The evidence of witnesses of just character against a person should be regarded as nearer the truth) than (the accused) refusal to take an oath, or (nearer to the truth) than the oath taken by the other party (against him), since the latter might not be just in character. Thus the decision is taken on several grounds, some of them stronger than others."

He said: "That is all right, but if he refuses to take an oath, we (the Ḥanafī school) will take the decision (against him) on the ground of his refusal."

Imam ash-Shāfiᶜī said: "But you will have taken a decision on an evidence weaker than ours."

He said: "Yes, however, I disagree with you on the source of evidence (on the strength of which you have taken the decision)."

Imam ash-Shāfiᶜī said: "The stronger evidence for your decision was his admission, although one is liable to make an unfounded or erroneous admission (on the strength of which) a decision might be taken against a person."

He said: "That is correct; for you are under no other obligation than that."

Imam ash-Shāfiᶜī asked: "Do you not agree that we are under an obligation to take the right decision by one of two means; either by certainty based on literal, not implicit meanings?"

He replied: "Yes, but is there any explicit text in the Book or the Sunnah in support (of your opinion)."

Imam ash-Shāfiᶜī said: "Yes, in such examples as I have (already) discussed concerning the determination of the Qiblah for myself and others. For Allah said:

'But they cannot grasp any of His knowledge save what He wills.' (Sūrat al-Baqarah 2: 256)" (Ash-Shāfiᶜī, *ar-Risālah,* translated by Majid Khadduri, Baltimore 1961, pp.288-293.)

Having considered the pros and cons of *qiyās*, Imām ash-Shāfiᶜī, who had initially been antagonistic towards it, agreed that *qiyās* can also be accepted as one of the principles of Islamic law provided it is strict *qiyās*. What he means by strict *qiyās* is that it must be based on the Qur'ān, the Sunnah and the *ijmāᶜ* (the consensus of opinion of the Companions or the jurists).

Jurists have laid down the conditions under which *qiyās* can be accepted, among which are:

a. that *qiyās* be resorted to only when there is no solution to the matter in the Qur'ān or in the Sunnah.
b. that *qiyās* not go against the principles of Islam.
c. that *qiyās* not go against the context of the Qur'ān, nor be in conflict with the Sunnah of the Prophet ﷺ.
d. that it be a strict *qiyās* based either on the Qur'ān, the Sunnah or the *ijmāᶜ*.

There are two types of *qiyās*: i. *qiyās jalī* (open or clearly visible *qiyās;* and ii. *qiyās khafī* (hidden *qiyās*).

With regards to *qiyās jalī,* all alcohol is forbidden on the grounds of its being an intoxicant as is wine, which is specially prohibited textually, whereas there is no text that refers to beer, for example.

As regards *qiyās khafī,* Allah, exalted is He, ordered us to give out *zakāh*. It was the Prophet Muhammad ﷺ who explained how it should be given. He said among other things, that one sheep or goat must be give as *zakāh* on every forty sheep or goats. Giving some poor men a goat might be of little or no use to him. Therefore, in the Ḥanafī *madhhab,* we are allowed to sell that goat and give him the money. He would perhaps appreciate money more than a goat. It is well to bear in mind though that the idea of the *ṣadaqah* of the goat is that a goat may give milk every day whereas money is only spent once. The things that are given in *zakāh* are inherently fruitful, including gold and silver which are potentially capital, whereas money is spent once only and then it is gone.

There are some who oppose the use of *qiyās*. Muᶜtazilites like Ibrāhīm ibn Sayyār, and scholars of the Ẓāhirī school, including Ibn Ḥazm of Andalusia, also opposed the use of *qiyās*.

Shi'ite sects such as the *Ithnā ᶜAshariyyah* (the Twelvers), *Uṣūlis* and the Ibadites (a Kharijite sect) employ the terms *ᶜaql* (intellect) and *ra'y* (theoretical considerations) for the concept of *qiyās*.

Ijtihād

The Arabic word for *ijtihād* literally means an effort or an exercise of one's intellect to arrive at one's own judgement. Ibn Juzayy al-Kalbī said, "It is incumbent according to Mālik and the dominant majority of the *ʿulamā'*... There is no disagreement over the permissibility of *ijtihād* after the death of the Messenger of Allah ﷺ." (Ibn Juzayy al-Kalbī, *Taqrīb al-wuṣūl ilā ʿilm al-uṣūl, al-fann al-khāmis fī ʿilm al-uṣūl, al-bāb al-awwal fī al-ijtihād*. Translated by Abdassamad Clarke.)

In its widest sense, it means the use of human reason in the elaboration and explanation of the *Sharīʿah*. It covers a variety of processes, ranging from the interpretation of the text of the Qur'ān and the assessment of the authenticity of *ḥadīth*. *Qiyās* or analogical reasoning, then, is a particular form of *ijtihād*, the method by which the principles established by the Qur'ān, Sunnah and *ijmāʿ* are to be extended and applied to the solution of new problems not expressly dealt with before.

Ijtihād, therefore, is exercise of reasoning by a jurist to arrive at a logical conclusion to a legal issue, and to deduce the conclusion as to the effectiveness of a legal precept in Islam. Imām Muḥammad ibn Idrīs ash-Shāfiʿī supported the idea of *ijtihād* by quoting a verse of the Qur'ān in substantiation. Allah, exalted is He, has said:

وَمِنْ حَيْثُ خَرَجْتَ فَوَلِّ وَجْهَكَ شَطْرَ الْمَسْجِدِ الْحَرَامِ وَحَيْثُ مَا كُنتُمْ فَوَلُّوا وُجُوهَكُمْ شَطْرَهُ

> *Wherever you come from, turn your face to the Masjid al-Ḥarām. Wherever you are, turn your faces towards it.* (Sūrat al-Baqarah 2: 144)

Imām ash-Shāfiʿī maintained that, in certain cases, if someone does not exercise his intellect, he will not be able to know in what direction the Masjid al-Ḥarām is. Therefore, Allah Himself indirectly encourages us to exercise our reasoning. To be able to derive logical conclusions on certain matters is a great gift to mankind.

Ibn Juzayy al-Kalbī, the famed scholar and Qur'ānic commentator of Granada, Spain said:

> The preconditions for the exercise of *ijtihād* are that the person:
>
> 1. Be *mukallaf* (i.e. legally responsible before Allah).

2. Have *ᶜadālah* (i.e. be a person of probity whose standing in knowledge and unblemished good character would allow him to be appointed as a witness for legal and official purposes).

3. Be possessed of an excellent memory and understanding.

4. Be possessed of knowledge of the sciences fundamentally important for *ijtihād*, which are five in number:

a. The Book of Allah, exalted is He, which he must necessarily memorise and recite excellently well (with *tajwīd*) even if only according to one of the seven modes recognised and accepted by the entire *Ummah*, the understanding its meanings, in particular the *āyāt* on legal rulings (*aḥkām*), having knowledge of which *āyāt* were revealed in Makkah and which in Madīnah, and knowledge of those which are decisive and those which abrogate and those which are abrogated (*nāsikh wa mansūkh*) and other sciences.

Some of those who study the sciences of the principles (*uṣūl*) of *fiqh* said that it is not a precondition that he memorise the Qur'ān, not even the *āyāt* on legal rulings, but rather that he know where they are so that he can investigate them when in need of that, but this is wrong for two reasons:

Firstly, because rulings are derived from other *āyāt* than those which are well known for them, so that one is forced to have memorised the whole.

Secondly, because someone who does without memorising the Book of Allah ought not to be an *imām* in the *dīn* of Allah, when the Messenger of Allah ﷺ has said, "The Book of Allah is the strong rope of Allah and His straight path. In it is information about those who preceded you, and news about those who will succeed you, and the rulings on what occurs between you. Whatever tyrant abandons it, Allah will break him. Whoever seeks guidance from something other than it, Allah will send astray." Surely, this is sufficient as a warning for whoever abandons it and seeks guidance from anything other than it.

b. Memorisation of the *ḥadīth* of the Messenger of Allah ﷺ and the *ḥadīth* of his Companions, memorising of their chains of transmission and knowledge of the men who narrated them, because the *imāms* of the *ḥadīth* scholars, may Allah be pleased with them and reward them with the best, had undertaken the job of recognising the transmitters, invalidating some of them and validating others, distinguishing the *ṣaḥīḥ ḥadīth* from

> others, recording them in their compilations, so much so, that it sufficed for those who came after them in the difficult task of recognising the chains of transmission and the narrators, and so that becomes an attribute of the perfection of the *mujtahid*.
>
> Some people said that it is not stipulated that the *mujtahid* must memorise *ḥadīth*, and this also is mistaken since most of the rulings are stated textually in the *ḥadīth*, so that if one does not know the *ḥadīth* one will give *fatwā* according to analogical reasoning or another weak form of evidence and thus contradict prophetic texts.
>
> c. Knowledge of *fiqh*, and memorisation of the *madhhab*s of the *ᶜulamā'* in *Sharīᶜah* rulings so that in the positions he takes he will model himself on the right-acting first generations and so that he will choose from their verdicts those which are most sound and weightiest, and so that he will not entirely deviate from their judgements and thus vitiate the consensus. Mālik, even considering the dignity of his position, used to model himself on preceding *ᶜulamā'* and follow the ways that they had taken (*madhhab*s).
>
> d. Knowledge of the principles (*uṣūl*) of *fiqh* because it is the instrument by which one arrives at *ijtihād*.
>
> e. Knowledge of what one needs of the sciences of the Arabic language, such as grammar and idiomatic usages, so that by means of that he will understand the Qur'ān and the *ḥadīth* since they are both in the Arabic language.
>
> As for his knowledge of sciences other than those we have mentioned, they are not a precondition for *ijtihād* in *Sharīᶜah* rulings, but an attribute of perfection, and whoever wants to exercise *ijtihād* in any art must necessarily know it and know its tools. (Ibn Juzayy al-Kalbī, *Taqrīb al-wuṣūl ilā ᶜilm al-uṣūl, al-fann al-khāmis fī ᶜilm al-uṣūl, al-bāb ath-thāmin fī shurūṭ al-ijtihād*. Translated by Abdassamad Clarke.)

Therefore, before one can be a *mujtahid*, one has to be knowledgeable about the *dīn* of Islam, the Sunnah, *fiqh* and *uṣūl al-fiqh*. He should know:

a. *Asbāb an-nuzūl* (causes of the revelation): he must be so well versed in the study of Qur'ān, that he knows the reason why the verses and chapters of the Qur'ān were revealed and the occasion when each one of them was revealed.

b. *Nāsikh wa mansūkh* (abrogating and abrogated verses): he must know which verses abrogate others and which are abrogated.
c. *Ḥadīth*: the traditions of the Prophet Muḥammad ﷺ, that is, he must know the distinction between ḥadīth which are *ṣaḥīḥ* (authentic), *mawḍūᶜ* (fabricated), *ḥasan* (good), *ḍaᶜīf* (weak) and so on.
d. *Nāsikh wa mansūkh ḥadīth* (abrogating and abrogated *ḥadīth*): he must know which *ḥadīth* are abrogated by *āyāt* of Qur'ān or by other *ḥadīth* and which *ḥadīth* abrogated other *ḥadīth*.
e. He must know the principles of *ijmāᶜ* well, and the matters which are agreed upon by the *ᶜulamā'* of the *Ummah*.
f. He must know the rules of *qiyās* and the conditions that surround it.
g. He must be knowledgeable of the Arabic language, since this is the instrument for understanding the above-mentioned *uṣūl*.

This is only a small part of the list of *uṣūl* (principles) which the *mujtahid* must know. When we look at the different types of *mujtahid* we will see other requirements, e.g. the *mujtahid fi'l-masā'il* must be knowledgeable about the cases that have already occasioned an *ijtihād*. Different *madhhab*s have different *uṣūl* (principles) that the *mujtahid* must know.

Apart from academic excellence a *mujtahid* must possess good character. Among the qualities he must possess are *ᶜadālah* i.e. being someone whose testimony would be acceptable in a court of law:

a. He must genuinely be a Muslim, that is, not a nominal Muslim; rather, he must be a practising one, because omitting any of the obligations of Islam is a matter about which there is difference of opinion, some scholars considering it *kufr* and others simply a major wrong action, but sometimes a capital offence.
b. He must have *taqwā* and abide by all the injunctions of the Noble Qur'ān and the Sunnah.

c. He must not be affected by heretical tendencies.
d. He must be just, reliable, trustworthy and free from iniquitous practices.

Mujtahids can be classified into three broad categories:

i. *Mujtahid fi'sh-sharīᶜah* (*mujtahid* in the *Sharīᶜah*) or *mujtahid muṭlaq* (an absolute *mujtahid*): those who did *ijtihād* in the matter of *Sharīᶜah,* working directly from the Book of Allah, the Sunnah and the *ijmāᶜ*. These were the Companions of the Prophet ﷺ and their Followers and the Followers of the Followers up until the third century of Islam and they include the Imāms of the *madhhab*s.
ii. *Mujtahid fi'l-madhhab*: those who do *ijtihād* on the basis of the principles of the Imāms who founded the schools of jurisprudence.
iii. *Mujtahid fi'l-masā'il*: *mujtahids* who give *fatwās* or juristic opinions on matters of the *dīn* according to the legacy of cases and *fatwās* already delivered within the *madhhab*s.

Most forms of *ijtihād* must have their starting points in a principle of the Qur'ān, Sunnah or consensus. However, the schools of Imām Mālik and Imām Aḥmad ibn Ḥanbal consider *al-maṣāliḥ al-mursalah* (considerations of public interest) a valid part of the *uṣūl*. *Ijtihād* cannot be used to achieve a result which contradicts a ruling established by any of the three fundamental sources.

Whenever a new case presents itself, reasoning analogically (by *qiyās*) on the basis of an original case covered by the Qur'ān, the Sunnah or *ijmāᶜ* is possible provided the effective cause (*ᶜillah*) is common to both cases. For example, wine is prohibited textually, and the effective cause (*ᶜillah*) for this prohibition is its causing intoxication. Therefore, other intoxicants like spirits and beer, and drugs like heroin, cocaine and marijuana are prohibited by analogical reasoning because they also lead to intoxication and loss of one's senses. In this way the prohibition is extended by analogical deduction. The majority of Muslims, including the four major schools, accept *qiyās* and *ijtihād* to determine the juristic basis for reasoning on an issue. Analogical reasoning has the following elements:

a. An original subject (*aṣl*)
b. An object of the analogy, being a new subject (*farᶜ*)
c. An effective cause (*ᶜillah*) common to both subjects
d. A ruling arrived at by analogical reasoning (*ḥukm*)

In the case of the prohibition of an intoxicant like gin, the following four points exist:

i. Wine is the original subject (*aṣl*)
ii. Gin is the new subject under investigation (*farᶜ*)
iii. Intoxication is the cause common (*ᶜillah*) to both subjects
iv. The prohibition of gin is the resultant ruling (*ḥukm*)

The following are some other examples of arriving at a ruling through the use of analogical deduction:

1. In Sūrat al-Jumuᶜah in the Qur'ān, Allah prohibits selling after the last call to Jumuᶜah prayer. The rule is extended by analogical reasoning to other kinds of transactions and engagements that distract Muslims from attending the Jumuᶜah prayer.
2. In the Sunnah of the Prophet ﷺ a killer may not inherit one of the fixed shares (*farā'iḍ*) from his victim if he is a relative. This rule is extended to the law of bequests (*waṣiyyah*) as well.

Much controversy has unnecessarily been aroused around subjects such as the so-called 'closure of the door of *ijtihād*.' However, this only refers to one type of *ijtihād*, that known as *muṭlaq* 'absolute', which is the *ijtihād* of those who derive rulings directly from the primary sources: the Qur'ān, Sunnah and *ijmāᶜ*. Muslim scholars agree that this door has been closed. However, other types of *ijtihād* still exist, such as *ijtihād fi'l-madhhab*, i.e. within the *madhhab* according to the principles of the Imāms of the *madhhab*s, and *ijtihād* on the basis of an existing body of *fatwās* within a school.

In recent times, Muslim scholars like Jamāl ad-Dīn al-Afghānī and his disciple Muḥammad ᶜAbduh wrote and talked about 're-opening the door of *ijtihād*', a door which, as we have seen, has not been closed. They were a part of a movement that claimed to be *salafī*, i.e. adhering firmly to the right-acting first generations, but which used this as a lever to disempower the legal rulings of the *^culamā'* and the *madhhabs*, particularly in the realm of trade and commerce. Thus, Muḥammad ^cAbduh is rightly notorious for his *fatwā* justifying the acceptance and payment of interest, and for his denial that interest is usury. Today, these two men and their adherents are increasingly regarded as suspect.

Thus, the door of *ijtihād* has never been closed, and the *Sharī^cah* retains the flexibility that *ijtihād* has always given it. To my mind, Shaykh al-Afghānī and Muḥammad ^cAbduh simply over-played their hand.

Istiḥsān or Juridical Preference

Ibn Juzayy said:

> This is a valid argument according to Abū Ḥanīfah contrary to others, indeed so much so that ash-Shāfi^cī said, "Whoever uses juridical preference (*istiḥsān*) has laid down *Sharī^cah*."
>
> Then people differed about what it means. Al-Bājī [the Mālikī] said, "It is to pass verdict according to the strongest of two proofs." On this basis it is unanimously agreed to be a valid proof.
>
> Some said that it is a ruling without any evidence in favour of it, and on this basis it is unanimously agreed to be *ḥarām*, since that is to follow one's whims and desires.
>
> Some said that it is an evidence which is produced within the *mujtahid*'s self which does not help him to express it. And the best statement is that it is that which the *mujtahid* regards as preferable because of his reflection and consideration. (*Ibid.*)

Istiḥsān has been mentioned indirectly in the Noble Qur'ān in the following verse:

الَّذِينَ يَسْتَمِعُونَ الْقَوْلَ فَيَتَّبِعُونَ أَحْسَنَهُ أُولَٰئِكَ الَّذِينَ هَدَاهُمُ اللَّهُ وَأُولَٰئِكَ هُمْ أُولُوا الْأَلْبَابِ

> *Those who listen well to what is said and follow the best of it, they are the ones whom Allah has guided, they are the people of intelligence.* (Sūrat az-Zumar 39: 18)

The commentators (*mufassirūn*) have interpreted this verse in two ways. If *'what is said'* in this verse is taken as any word, the clause would mean that people with *taqwā* should listen to all that is said and choose the best of it for general good – as long as that word is according to the spirit of the divine message. However, if *'what is said'* is taken here to mean the Word of Allah, it would mean that they should listen reverently to it, and where permissible alternative courses are allowed for those who are not strong enough to follow the higher course, those *'people of intelligence'* should prefer to attempt the higher course of conduct. For example, it is permitted within limits to punish those who wrong us, but the nobler course is to repel evil with good.[1] We should try to follow the nobler course.

Maṣāliḥ al-Mursalah: Public Interest

Public interest is also regarded in *Sharīᶜah* as a basis of law. The jurists of different schools have used different Arabic terms to describe it. Ḥanafīs regard *istiḥsān* – meaning equitable preference to find a just solution – as being the same as it. Imām Mālik called it *al-maṣāliḥ al-mursalah,* that is, public benefit or public welfare. The Arabic word *maṣāliḥ* means welfare and *mursal* literally means to set loose i.e. from the text. Imām Aḥmad ibn Ḥanbal used the term *istiṣlāḥ* – seeking the best solution for the general interest. The Ḥanbalī scholar Ibn Qudāmah as well as the Mālikī jurist Ibn Rushd occasionally used the term *istiḥsān*. The only school which does not recognise *istiḥsān* as a source is the Shāfiᶜī school. According to Imām ash-Shāfiᶜī, if it were allowed, it would open the door to the unrestricted use of fallible human opinion since public interest, will vary from place to place and time to time.

It should be noted that the concept of public welfare and general interest can really be very helpful particularly in cases which are not regulated by any authoritative text of the Book of Allah, the Sunnah or *ijmāᶜ*. In that case, equitable consideration may override the results of strict *qiyās,* taking public interest into consideration. Shāfiᶜī jurists have employed *istidlāl* to achieve similar results by avoiding merely the application of strict *qiyās*. *Istidlāl* is the process of seeking guidance, basis and proof from the sources although its dictionary meaning is merely argumentation. With this brief introduction, we shall examine some examples.

1. The *bayᶜ bi'l-wafā'* or sale subject to future redemption was allowed because of the practical need for such transactions in the interest of public welfare.
2. *Sitr al-ᶜawrah* – covering the private parts. Only a woman's husband may see her naked, but where necessary, a male physician may be allowed to examine and diagnose a woman.
3. Divorce pronounced during a terminal sickness (*maraḍ al-mawt*), even if effected as irrevocable *ṭalāq*, will not deprive the divorced wife of her share of the inheritance. The husband in reality is seeking to deprive her of her rights and avoid his obligations. Some Shāfiᶜī and Ẓāhirī jurists disagree with the majority of *ᶜulamā'* on this issue. Ḥanafī jurists maintain that the entitlement of the divorced wife lasts during her *ᶜiddah* period while Ḥanbalīs take the view that she will be entitled to participate as long as she has not remarried. Mālikīs however, accord her the right to participate in the inheritance even if she has remarried, provided the deceased did not recover in between the terminal illness and his ultimate death.
4. The *ḥadd* punishment of amputation of the hand for theft will not be applied even if all the evidence proved that it was really committed, if it occurred during a period of famine when no food was available and arguably the person was forced to steal. Imām ash-Shāfiᶜī said that he would apply this rule simply because Sayyidunā ᶜUmar decided a case in this way. He did not think that it was done on the principle of *istiḥsān*.
5. The eating of meat which has not been slaughtered according to Islamic rite (*dhabīḥah*) is permissible where no other lawful food is available. This comes under the

rule of pressing necessity (*ḍarūrah*). The *fuqahā'* have a saying:

$$الضَّرُورَاتُ تُبِيحُ الْمَحْظُورَاتِ$$

Pressing necessities make forbidden things permissible.

Of course, pressing necessities have their proper definition in the *Sharīʿah* and this permission cannot be used frivolously, i.e. it often refers to life-threatening emergencies.

6. Destruction of lawful food-stuff is not ordinarily allowed, but ʿUmar 🙵 ordered the spilling of milk that had been mixed with water as a punishment to prevent dishonest persons engaged in the sale of adulterated milk.

7. The second call to prayer (*adhān*) for Jumuʿah prayer was not a practice in the time of the Prophet 🙵 and the first two caliphs. Sayyidunā ʿUthmān ibn ʿAffān 🙵, the third caliph, initiated it as a reminder for the public benefit.

Imām Mālik ibn Anas gave several juristic decisions (*fatwā*) based on *maṣāliḥ al-mursalah* (public interest). Some of them are as follows:

a. The Muslim ruler may ask for additional taxes from wealthy citizens in a period of emergency.

b. A caliph or a ruler does not have to be the most meritorious claimant, otherwise strife would be inevitable, i.e. as Ibn Juzayy said when enumerating the requirements of a ruler:

If people agree [on pledging allegiance] to one who does not meet all of the conditions then it is permitted, from fear of causing dissension and sedition. (Ibn Juzayy, *al-fātiḥah fīmā yajibu fī al-itiqādāt min uṣūl ad-diyānāt, al-Qawānīn al-fiqhiyyah, al-bāb ath-thāmin fī al-imāmah*. Translated by Abdassamad Clarke.)

c. Imām Mālik as well as Imām Aḥmad ibn Ḥanbal prohibited the sale of grapes, the sale of which is otherwise legal, to a wine merchant because he will use them to ferment wine which is unlawful.

d. The sale of arms during a civil disturbance is prohibited as it may intensify the struggle.

Most of these rules could fit into Ḥanafī *istiḥsān* or Shāfiᶜī *qiyās*.

Istiṣḥāb: Legal Presumption

Istiṣḥāb is a rule of evidence that provides for a legal presumption of continuance of conditions (*al-ḥāl*). In other words, it is the presumption in the law that a state of affairs known to exist in the past continues to exist until the contrary is proved. *Istiṣḥāb* is accepted by all schools of Islamic jurisprudence as a subsidiary source of the *Sharīᶜah*. There is a presumption of innocence until guilt is established. This presumption is based on *istiṣḥāb*. According to one view there will be a similar presumption of a matter being *ḥalāl* in the absence of a specific prohibition, although the contrary view is that things are assumed to be *ḥarām* in the absence of a specific declaration that they are *ḥalāl*. The *fuqahā'* who held the former view have a saying:

الأَصْلُ فِي الأَشْيَاءِ الإِبَاحَةُ

The basic situation in matters is that they are permissible.[2]

A marriage is presumed to subsist until its dissolution (*ṭalāq*) becomes known. In the case of *ᶜibādah*, mere doubt does not vitiate the validity of rites. Supposing a man after *wuḍū'* entertains a doubt as to whether he still has his *wuḍū'* to perform the prayers, then a presumption of purity (*ṭuhr*) is made. Similarly, if he genuinely thinks that he has performed the correct number of prostrations (*sajdah*), a mere doubt will not affect this genuine belief. In the case of an ownership title, a judge will presume ownership from valid title deeds until the contrary is proved. If a man is missing (*mafqūd*), his wife remains his legal wife until the court, after due enquiries issues a decree to the contrary, based upon the legal presumption that he is dead.

***Sadd adh-dharā'iᶜ*: blocking the means of access**

Sadd adh-dharā'iᶜ serves to block the means of access where an act is permissible in itself but leads to something *ḥarām,* then it becomes *ḥarām.* An example is that embracing women other than one's wives or relatives is in itself permissible but since it can lead to sexual relations it becomes *ḥarām.*

***ᶜUrf* and *ᶜĀdāt* (custom)**

ᶜUrf "known practice" and *ᶜādāt* "customs" are recognised as a subsidiary sources by all schools of jurisprudence. The Mālikī school attaches more importance to custom than other schools. However, customary rules remain valid only so long as there is no provision on the matter in the Qur'ān and the Sunnah. If any custom contradicts any other rule of *Sharīᶜah,* they will be considered outside the pale of Islamic law.

Notes

[1] *See* Sūrat al-Aḥzāb 33: 96.

[2] *See* Chapter 8, "The Categories of Fiqh" for a more in-depth discussion of this matter.

Chapter 7

The Four Schools of Fiqh and Their Imāms

THE *SHARĪ^cAH,* as we have shown before, is from Allah, embodying the Creator's justice and mercy. The main tasks of the Prophet ﷺ in the *Sharī^cah* were to correctly convey the divine revelation and interpret it and establish justice (*^cadl*). The Qur'ān and the Sunnah were put into practice by the Prophet ﷺ and his Companions, who studied the life-giving laws contained in the book of Allah and the Sunnah of the Messenger of Allah ﷺ. Imām ash-Shāfi^cī ranked the study of *Sharī^cah,* which is based on these sources, as higher than supererogatory prayers (*nawāfil*). *Sharī^cah* is undoubtedly the backbone of the *dīn* of Islam. The *^culamā'* took to this study right from the time of the Companions.

Differences of opinion (*ikhtilāf*) are a mercy (*raḥmah*)

Imāms Abū Ḥanīfah, Mālik, ash-Shāfi^cī and Aḥmad ibn Ḥanbal, the founders of the four Sunnī schools of law, have rendered a great service to the cause of Islamic jurisprudence. Neither did they want to alter the spirit or letter of the Qur'ān, nor the Sunnah of the Prophet ﷺ as is contended by some non-Muslims as well as by some recent scholars of Islam. If one closely examines the *fiqh* of the four schools, one will never come across substantial difference in the basic matters. The differences mainly centre around the derivative legal rulings (*furū^c*) and principles of *fiqh* (*uṣūl al-fiqh*) rather than the fundamental principles of the *dīn*. It is about such differences that the Messenger of Allah has said: "My *Ummah's* differences of opinion (*ikhtilāf*) are a blessing." (*Al-Jāmiᶜ aṣ-ṣaghīr,* Jalāl ad-Dīn as-Suyūṭī).[1] It is through this blessing that Muslims today have inherited such a comprehensive *corpus juris* which provides guidance in every walk of life. Imām Abū Ḥanīfah (80-150 AH/699-767 CE) and Imām Mālik ibn Anas (93-179 AH/712-795 CE) were the two jurists who, properly speaking, inherited the legacy of the special 'knowledge' of the Followers with both their agreements and disagreements. They adopted a similar attitude to that of their predecessors by relying on the Qur'ān, the Sunnah and the verdicts of the Companions, especially their consensus, consensus being one of the three main sources of Islamic law. These were followed by reliance on their *ijtihād*, although Imām Mālik placed more reliance on the verdicts of his teachers than did Abū Ḥanīfah. Nevertheless, in cases where there was an irreconcilable conflict or difference of opinion among the Companions, both the Iraqi and Hijazi jurists followed what was narrated and practised by their predecessors.

The two leaders, as well as their main students, came closer after the travels made by Imām Abū Ḥanīfah and his companions Imām Abū Yūsuf and Imām Muḥammad ibn al-Ḥasan ash-Shaybānī to Makkah and Madīnah, where Imām Abū Ḥanīfah met Imām Mālik and the companions of ᶜAbdullāh ibn ᶜAbbās ﷺ, where Muḥammad ibn al-Ḥasan studied the *Muwaṭṭa'* of Imām Mālik with the author himself, and where Abū Yūsuf learnt it from a pupil of Mālik.

The famous jurist and scholar of Egypt, al-Layth ibn Saᶜd (d. 175 AH/791 CE), as with other scholars elsewhere, was engaged in discussions on *fiqh*. Imām Mālik sent a brotherly message to him objecting to his passing judgements contrary to the practice (*ᶜamal*) of the People of Madīnah. In the correspondence between them, al-Layth's reply and its acknowledgement of the importance of the practice of the People of Madīnah is very famous.

Muḥammad ibn al-Ḥasan ash-Shaybānī, the disciple of Imām Abū Ḥanīfah, later wrote a book on jurisprudence dealing with these matters. Imām ash-Shāfiᶜī (150-204 AH/767-820 CE) thought to bridge the widening gap between the *fiqh* of Iraq and that of Madīnah by visiting Iraq and acquainting himself with the differences between the Hijazis and Iraqis, and he wrote the *Risālah* pointing out the defects and weaknesses in the legal thinking of contemporary jurists and emphasising the importance of adhering to the Qur'ān, the Sunnah, the conclusive *ijmāᶜ* of the Muslim jurists, and using the appropriate *qiyās* – as the main sources of law – excluding arbitrary judgements (in his view *istiḥsān*), local and partial agreements, inauthentic narrations and unfounded practices. The *Risālah* of ash-Shāfiᶜī, by taking the jurist from the area of details (*furūᶜ*) to the subject of fundamental principles, formulated what had previously been understood implicitly: the science of *uṣūl al-fiqh* – the principles or sources of jurisprudence – upon which the *Sharīᶜah* subsequently safely and systematically developed. Thus it was the joint efforts of the three Imāms which brought about a healthy development. However, the three *madhhabs* were never reconciled on the issue of the *ᶜamal* and each made use of the science of *uṣūl* to ground its own rulings properly. Ironically, rather than uniting the two older *madhhabs* as he had intended, Imām ash-Shāfiᶜī instead became regarded as the founder of a third *madhhab* which his students ascribed to him after his death ﷺ.

The effort made by ash-Shāfiᶜī to formulate a systematic jurisprudence was parallelled by another type of specialist research, namely the collection of all the traditions from the different provinces, sifting acceptable narrations from the unacceptable. Imām Aḥmad ibn Ḥanbal, the fourth Imām and jurist (164-241 AH), wrote the *Musnad*, a comprehensive book on *ḥadīth*. In his *fiqh*, he relied mostly on the Qur'ān, the *ḥadīth*, the verdicts of the Companions and the Followers – irrespective of their home towns – and the process of *ijtihād*.

The love and respect of these jurists for each others was so great that some of them visited and studied with others who were contemporary with them. They disagreed on certain matters but remained very close. Imām Abū Ḥanīfah, thirteen years older than Imām Mālik, sat in on the lessons of Imām Mālik who welcomed him respectfully and made him sit next to him.

Imām Muḥammad ibn al-Ḥasan, the famous disciple of Imām Abū Ḥanīfah, went to Madīnah and learnt the *Muwaṭṭa'* from Imām Mālik for three years after the death of his teacher, Abū Ḥanīfah. Imām Mālik and Imām Abū Ḥanīfah both learnt *ḥadīth* from Imām Muḥammad ibn Shihāb az-Zuhrī, a teacher who did not feel it below his dignity to learn from Imām Mālik who was his own pupil. Imām Jaᶜfar aṣ-Ṣādiq (d. 198 AH/814 CE) was the teacher of both Imām Abū Ḥanīfah and Imām Mālik. Likewise, both Imāms also learnt from a famous scholar of the Followers, Muḥammad ibn al-Munkadir al-Madanī (d.131 AH/749 CE). Imām ash-Shāfiᶜī also became a student of *ḥadīth* and *fiqh* under the guidance of Imām Mālik, and he said, "If it had not been for Mālik and Sufyān ibn ᶜUyaynah, the science of *ḥadīth* would not have existed in the Ḥijāz." About the *Muwaṭṭa'* of Imām Mālik, Imām ash-Shāfiᶜī said: "There has not appeared on Earth a book that is closer to the Qur'ān than the book of Mālik."

Imām ash-Shāfiᶜī said about the Ḥanafī Imām, Muḥammad ibn al-Ḥasan, the disciple of Abū Ḥanīfah, that when he used to discuss any juristic point, it seemed as if a revelation were descending. He used to write down his lectures.[2] Imām Muḥammad also had great respect for Imām ash-Shāfiᶜī. Once he was going to the court of Hārūn ar-Rashīd and met Imām ash-Shāfiᶜī on the way. Imām Muḥammad got down from his horse and asked his servant to go and inform the Caliph that he would not be present at court that day. Imām ash-Shāfiᶜī insisted that he should go to the court and that he would see him another day, to which Imām Muḥammad replied that it was not essential for him to go to the Caliph's court.[3] Imām ash-Shāfiᶜī and Imām Muḥammad used to have discussions (*munāẓarāt*), and used to agree and disagree on many points, a sign of healthy academic enquiry, which was a common practice in Iraq in those days, although unknown in the Madīnah of the first generations.

Likewise, Imām Aḥmad ibn Ḥanbal learnt *ḥadīth* from Yaḥyā ibn Saᶜīd al-Qaṭṭān, the famous disciple of Imām Abū Ḥanīfah.

It is said that while asking questions, out of respect for the teacher, Imām Aḥmad would stand from the time of the *ᶜAṣr* prayer to the *Maghrib* (sunset) prayer.[4] Imām Aḥmad used to say about his teacher that he had never seen anyone like him.[5] Imām Aḥmad ibn Ḥanbal also used to say about ᶜAbdullāh ibn al-Mubārak, another pupil of Imām Abū Ḥanīfah, that during the life of this scholar, no-one else had ever tried to exert as much effort in acquiring the knowledge of *ḥadīth* as he had. Al-Khaṭīb al-Baghdādī, the famous historian, narrates the statement of Imām Aḥmad ibn Ḥanbal that, "When I first wanted to learn the science of *ḥadīth*, I first went to Imām Abū Yūsuf," another disciple of Imām Abū Ḥanīfah, from whom he narrated many *ḥadīth*.[6] The above examples show that the Imāms were teachers and pupils of each other, all working for a common goal: that is to serve the Muslims in enhancing their knowledge of the *Sharīᶜah*. The treasures of knowledge that they have left behind guide the *Ummah* even today and will do so for all time to come. Let us now examine the lives and works of the four leaders of *fiqh*.

The founders of the schools of *fiqh*

1. Imām Abū Ḥanīfah

The Ḥanafī school of *fiqh* in Kūfa in Iraq was the first to be founded. The one who did that was Nuᶜmān ibn Thābit ibn Nuᶜmān ibn al-Mirzabān ibn Zūṭā ibn Māh (d. 150 AH/767 CE), a non-Arab scholar of Persian descent who is well know by his *kunyah* Abū Ḥanīfah. Kūfa during this period had become well known as a seat of learning. The teaching of ᶜAbdullāh ibn Masᶜūd (d. 32 AH/653 CE), the Companion and a great scholar of the Qur'ān and the Sunnah, had flourished in Kūfa where he taught from the time that the Caliph ᶜUmar sent him there as a *qāḍī* and teacher.

His early life

Imām Nuᶜmān ibn Thābit Abū Ḥanīfah belonged to that luminous period of the Followers, the successors of the *Ṣaḥābah* (the Companions of the Prophet ﷺ). Al-Khaṭīb of Baghdad said that Abū Ḥanīfah was born in the year 80 AH/699 CE. His father Thābit called upon the Caliph ᶜAlī ؓ to pray for him and his family. Al-Khaṭīb said: "I believe that his prayer bore fruit".[7] Abū Ḥanīfah was a *tābiᶜ* (Follower), since, in his early youth, he had the good fortune of witnessing the period in which some Companions still lived. The notable names of Companions still alive at that time in Kūfa include Anas ibn Mālik (d. 93 AH/712 CE) the personal servant of the Prophet ﷺ, Sahl ibn Saᶜd (d. 91 AH/710 CE) and Abū Ṭufayl ᶜĀmir ibn Wāthilah (d. 100 AH/719 CE) who died when Abū Ḥanīfah was twenty years old. ᶜAynī, the commentator of the *Hidāyah,* said that Abū Ḥanīfah even heard *ḥadīth* from the Companions.

Abū Ḥanīfah was first brought up as a trader like his ancestors, but he soon started taking a deep interest in knowledge. During this period Islamic learning was being spread by great scholars and imams of the Followers like al-Awzāᶜī in Syria and al-Layth in Egypt.[8]

His education

One day when Abū Ḥanīfah was passing by the house of Imām ash-Shaᶜbī, a learned scholar of Kūfa, ash-Shaᶜbī mistook him for a student and asked: "Where are you going young man?" Abū Ḥanīfah named a merchant whom he was going to see. "I meant to ask," said ash-Shaᶜbī, "whose classes do you attend?" "Nobody's sir." Ash-Shaᶜbī said: "I see signs of intelligence in you. You ought to sit in the company of learned men." As if it had sparked a new light in Abū Ḥanīfah's heart, he embarked on study and became a great imam in the field of *fiqh* and *ḥadīth.*

He attended the classes of Ḥammād in *fiqh* and then became his student in *ḥadīth.* Abū'l-Maḥāsin ash-Shāfiᶜī gives a list of the *ḥadīth* teachers of Abū Ḥanīfah, ninety-three of whom were Followers who belonged to Kūfa.[9]

The scholars from whom he learnt in Kūfa were ash-Shaᶜbī, Salamah ibn Kuhayl, Muḥārib ibn Dithār, Abū Isḥāq as-Sabīᶜī, ᶜAwn ibn ᶜAbdullāh, ᶜAmr ibn Murrah, al-Aᶜmash, Ḥabīb ibn Thābit al-Anṣārī, Simāk ibn Ḥarb and many others. In Baṣra, he learnt from Qatādah and Shu^cbah, famous scholars who had studied *ḥadīth* under Companions of the Prophet ﷺ. Sufyān ath-Thawrī called Shu^cbah 'Amīr al-Mu'minīn in *ḥadīth*', the Commander of the Believers in *ḥadīth*. Shu^cbah was so impressed by and attached to Abū Ḥanīfah that he once said of him: "Just as I know that the sun is bright, I know for certain that learning and Abū Ḥanīfah are doubles of each other."[10] Shu^cbah had permitted Imām Abū Ḥanīfah to teach *ḥadīth* and narration. Someone asked Yaḥyā ibn Ma^cīn, one of the teachers of Imām al-Bukhārī, about Abū Ḥanīfah. He replied: "It is enough for me to know that Shu^cbah had permitted him to teach *ḥadīth* and narration. Shu^cbah after all was Shu^cbah."[11]

After his education in Kūfa and Basra, Imām Abū Ḥanīfah went to Makkah and Madīnah, the fountainheads of learning, and became a student of the famous scholar ^cAṭā' ibn Abī Rabāḥ. ^cAbdullāh ibn ^cUmar, the son of the Caliph ^cUmar ﷺ, recognising the merits of ^cAṭā' ibn Abī Rabāḥ said, "Why do people come to me when ^cAṭā' ibn Abī Rabāḥ is there for them to go to?"[12] During the Ḥajj, there used to be issued a general proclamation prohibiting anybody but ^cAṭā' ibn Abī Rabāḥ from giving *fatwā* (a juristic decision).[13] Great scholars like al-Awzā^cī, az-Zuhrī and ^cAmr ibn Dīnār were alumni of his school.[14] ^cAṭā' ibn Abī Rabāḥ questioned him about his beliefs while considering him for admission to his circle. Abū Ḥanīfah replied: "Sir, I do not speak ill of the people of earlier generations (*aslāf*), I do not call wrongdoers *kāfirūn* and I believe in the Decree (*qaḍā* and *qadar*)". On hearing this ^cAṭā' was pleased and permitted him to be his student.[15] Until ^cAṭā's death in 115 AH, Abū Ḥanīfah always visited him whenever he visited Makkah and respectfully sat in his circles. While in Makkah, he also attended the classes of ^cIkrimah, the freed slave and disciple of the famous scholar ^cAbdullāh ibn ^cAbbās, and who had the good fortune of learning *ḥadīth* and *fiqh* from Jābir, Abū Hurayrah, ^cAbdullāh ibn ^cUmar, ^cUqbah ibn ^cĀmir, Ṣafwān, and Abū Qatādah apart from his master ^cAbdullāh ibn ^cAbbās. It is said of ^cIkrimah that he taught at least seventy Followers. Sa^cīd ibn Jubayr was once asked if he knew anyone more learned than him among his contemporaries? He replied that it was ᶜIkrimah. ᶜIkrimah taught Imām Abū Ḥanīfah with great care and personal attention, making him so very proficient that he allowed Abū Ḥanīfah to exercise personal judgement and give rulings in his lifetime.[16]

His encounter with Imām al-Bāqir

Imām Abū Ḥanīfah's fame as a great scholar and the repute of his intellectual gifts and originality spread far and wide. However, along with his fame there spread adverse remarks by some superficial observers saying that he was a *qayyās*, someone who made analogical deductions. On his second visit to Madīnah, he met Imām al-Bāqir. When he was introduced to Imām al-Bāqir, the latter said:

> "So it is you who contradicts the traditions of my grandfather [the Prophet ﷺ] on the basis of *qiyās*".
>
> Abū Ḥanīfah said: "May Allah forbid. Who dares contradict the *ḥadīth*? After you sit down, Sir, I shall explain my position".
>
> The following conversation took place between the two great men and it shows how attached Imām Abū Ḥanīfah was to the fundamental principles of Islam:
>
> Abū Ḥanīfah: "Who is the weaker, man or woman?"
>
> Imām al-Bāqir: "Woman."
>
> Abū Ḥanīfah: "Which of them is entitled to the larger share of the inheritance?"
>
> Imām al-Bāqir: "The man."
>
> Abū Ḥanīfah: "Now, if I had been making deduction more through analogy, I should have said that women should get the larger share, because on the face of it, the weaker one is entitled to more consideration. But I have not said so."
>
> "To take up another subject, which do you think is the higher duty, prayer (*ṣalāh*) or fasting (*ṣawm*)?"
>
> Imām al-Bāqir: "Prayer."
>
> Abū Ḥanīfah: "That being the case, it should be permissible for a

woman during the period of her menstruation (*ḥayḍ*) to postpone her prayers but not her fast (which is less important than the prayer). But the ruling I give (following in the footsteps of the Messenger of Allah ﷺ) is that she must postpone her fasting and not her prayers."

Imām al-Bāqir was so impressed by this dialogue and the firmness of Imām Abū Ḥanīfah's faith and his love for the Prophet ﷺ that he immediately got up and kissed Imām Abū Ḥanīfah's forehead".[17]

His humility

Imām Abū Ḥanīfah later studied for some time with Imām al-Bāqir and Imām Jaᶜfar aṣ-Ṣādiq. As a keen scholar Imām Abū Ḥanīfah never felt it below his dignity to learn from anyone. Imām Mālik was thirteen years his junior, but he often attended his lectures and learned *ḥadīth* from him. Imām Mālik used to receive him with great respect and used to make him sit beside him. Imām Abū Ḥanīfah is particularly famous for having had innumerable teachers. Abū Hafṣ said that Abū Ḥanīfah learnt *ḥadīth* from at least four thousand scholars. One of the main reasons why Imām Abū Ḥanīfah attached himself to so many teachers and attended so many teaching circles was that he wanted to acquaint himself with the different principles and methods in vogue so that by a comparative study of them he could arrive at some system of his own.[18] Although his merit was recognised by his teacher Ḥammād, and he had become a full *mujtahid,* due to his sincerity he refrained from establishing a school of his own even though he was forty years of age. As long as Ḥammād lived, out of respect for his teacher, he never extended his feet towards his house. When Ḥammād died in 120 AH/738 CE, he was offered his position and accepted, although reluctantly. At this juncture he dreamt that he was digging up the Prophet's grave ﷺ. He was very frightened and wanted to give up the chair. Ibn Sīrīn comforted him and interpreted the dream as an indication that he was reviving the dead branches of learning in Islam. It was then that Abū Ḥanīfah settled down to teach. He became so famous that everywhere he travelled, people gathered round him to meet him, and for discussions and debates with him. His students came from all over the Muslim world. He was visited by a large number of people who came to listen to his discourses, so much so that be began to be suspected of complicity in every upheaval that took place in the country.

Imām Abū Ḥanīfah's rejection of the post of qāḍī

In 132 AH/750 CE the Umayyad dynasty was overthrown by the Abbasids. The first Abbasid caliph died after only ruling for four years, and was succeeded by his brother al-Manṣūr. Apart from the extermination of the Umayyads, al-Manṣūr started fighting against the *Ahl al-bayt*. In 145 AH/762 CE the followers of Muḥammad an-Nafs az-Zakiyyah, supporting him in his laying claim to the caliphate, took up arms against al-Manṣūr. Muḥammad an-Nafs az-Zakiyyah died fighting against al-Manṣūr's forces, and his brother Ibrāhīm also laid claim to the caliphate and continued the fight after him. Imām Abū Ḥanīfah had supported Ibrāhīm, because he considered him worthy of the caliphate. Later in 146 AH/763 CE when Ibrāhīm was overpowered by the Caliph, he began to arrest the supporters of Ibrāhīm, one of whom was Imām Abū Ḥanīfah. However, when he was brought to the court, his courtiers recognised him and respectfully presented him to the Caliph, saying: "This man is the greatest living *^c^ālim* (learned man)." When al-Manṣūr listened to the Imām and realised how learned he was, he offered him the post of chief *qāḍī* (judge). Imām Abū Ḥanīfah declined the offer, saying that he was not fit for the post. Al-Manṣūr became angry and shouted: "You are a liar." He immediately retorted, "If I am a liar, then my statement that I am not fit for the post of *qāḍī* is true since a liar cannot be appointed judge."

Al-Manṣūr, in anger, took the vow that he would make Abū Ḥanīfah accept the post, but the Imām too vowed not to accept it. The Caliph ordered that he should be imprisoned, but his reputation as a scholar and teacher made the Caliph allow him to teach even in prison. Imām Muḥammad ibn al-Ḥasan, the famous disciple of Imām Abū Ḥanīfah, was tutored by him while in prison. When more and more people visited the prison to listen to the Imām, al-Manṣūr saw another danger to his authority, and allegedly decided to poison the Imām.

His death

In the month of Rajab 150 AH/767 CE, the Imām died while saying his prayers. The funeral prayer was performed six times, and each time fifty thousand people took part in the prayer. Even after his burial, people kept on coming from different places and saying funeral prayers for about twenty days.

In 459 AH/1067 CE, a mausoleum was built on his tomb by the Seljuq ruler Alp Arslan, who also built a large madrasah nearby.

Disciples of Imām Abū Ḥanīfah

Imām Abū Ḥanīfah left a large number of disciples behind him. Abū'l-Maḥāsin ash-Shāfiᶜī listed the names of nine hundred and eighteen disciples, but the most well known of them are the following:

1. Qāḍī Abū Yūsuf

He was born in 113 AH/731 CE as the son of a poor labourer. Imām Abū Ḥanīfah helped financially to relieve his problems. After Imām Abū Ḥanīfah's death, he was appointed *qāḍī* in the year 166 AH/783 CE by the Caliph Mahdī. Hārūn ar-Rashīd appointed him *Qāḍī al-quḍāt,* the Grand Qāḍī or Chief Justice. As a versatile scholar, apart from his mastery over *fiqh,* he was very well versed in *ḥadīth.* He wrote many books which are quoted by Ibn an-Nadīm in his famous work *Kitāb al-fihrist,* but the most well known is his *Kitāb al-kharāj* which is a collection of judicial views on the *kharāj* (tribute)[19] and *jizyah* (poll tax) that are levied on People of the Book living under the *dhimmah* contract, and on the classification of lands according to its productivity, etc. He also fearlessly admonished the Caliph in this book. He died in 182 AH.

2. Muḥammad ibn al-Ḥasan ash-Shaybānī

Imām Muḥammad was born in 135 AH near Damascus. He came to Kūfa for his studies. He learnt from Imām Abū Ḥanīfah while he was in prison, and after his death he completed his education under Imām Abū Yūsuf. Then he went to Madīnah, where he learnt *ḥadīth* from Imām Mālik. In turn Imām ash-Shāfiᶜī was one of his most eminent pupils. Imām ash-Shāfiᶜī said: "Whenever Imām Muḥammad expounds a point of law, it seemed as if the angel of revelation had descended upon him." According to an-Nawawī, the famous *ḥadīth* scholar, Imām ash-Shāfiᶜī once said: "I took a camel load of learning from Imām Muḥammad." Imām Aḥmad ibn Ḥanbal was once asked as to where he had learnt all the subtle points of law, he replied: "From the books of Muḥammad ibn al-Ḥasan." His famous works are the *Mabsūṭ*, originally written by Abū Yūsuf but revised and edited by him. Other works are *al-Jāmiᶜ aṣ-ṣaghīr, al-Jāmiᶜ al-kabīr, az-Ziyādāt, Kitāb al-ḥujaj* and *as-Siyar aṣ-ṣaghīr wa'l-kabīr*, the *Kitāb al-āthār* which was his edited transmission of the *ḥadīth* of Imām Abū Ḥanīfah and his *Muwaṭṭa'* which was his transmission of the *ḥadīth* he learnt from Imām Mālik. He died in 189 AH/805 CE.

3. *Imām Zufar*

He was born in 110 AH/728 CE, and was a great scholar of *ḥadīth* and very well versed in analogical deduction (*qiyās*). Imām Abū Ḥanīfah used to call him the greatest of his companions in the field of analogical deduction. He died in 158 AH/775 CE.

The followers of the Ḥanafī school have spread throughout the world particularly in Asia and the Middle East.

2. IMĀM MĀLIK IBN ANAS

The period of the Companions of the Prophet ﷺ had just come to an end when Imām Mālik ibn Anas was born in Madīnah, the City of the Messenger (*Madīnah ar-Rasūl*) and 'the city' par-excellence. Madīnah was the centre of Islamic learning during that period of the Followers (*tābiᶜūn*), the disciples or pupils of the Companions, where the recognised masters of Islamic learning lived who attracted scholars from different parts of the Muslim world.

His early life

Imām Mālik was born in 93 AH/712 CE as mentioned by as-Samᶜānī in his famous work on genealogy *Kitāb al-ansāb* and adh-Dhahabī in his *Tadhkirat al-ḥuffāẓ*.[20] Some scholars, such as Ibn Khallikān, have recorded that the Imām was born in 95 AH/714 CE and Yāfiᶜī has said 94 AH/713 CE.[21]

The Imām belonged to a royal Arab family of Ḥimyar from Yemen which had settled in Madīnah after the advent of Islam. Just as the family of Imām Mālik was famous before Islam for their hospitality and other fine qualities, they became equally well known after they had accepted Islam but in a different way altogether. Their services to the cause of Islam are well known.

The genealogy of Imām Mālik is: Mālik, the son of Anas, the son of Mālik, the son of Abū ᶜĀmir, the son of ᶜAmr, the son of al-Ḥarth, the son of Ghaymān, the son of Khuthayl (but some say Juthayl), the son of ᶜAmr, the son of al-Ḥarth who was also well know as Dhū Aṣbaḥ.

It was Abū ᶜĀmir who accepted Islam and was one of the Companions of the Messenger of Allah ﷺ being present at all of the major events except for Badr. The Imām's grandfather was one of the four men who carried the body of ᶜUthmān ibn ᶜAffān to the grave. Imām Mālik's honorific (*kunyah*) was Abū ᶜAbdullāh. When he became very famous as a great scholar in Madīnah, people referred to him as Imām Dār al-Hijrah (the Imām of the Abode of the Emigration) meaning the leader in knowledge in Madīnah.

His birth took place during the period of the Umayyad caliphate in the reign of Caliph Wālid ibn ᶜAbd al-Malik, the third ruler of that dynasty, whose territories had expanded as far as Spain in Europe, Morocco (the *Maghrib*) in Africa and India in Asia. Although the Umayyads had shifted their capital from Madīnah to Damascus in Syria, the importance of the city of the Prophet had continued since every Muslim able to do so would visit the city even if he had to travel a long distance. Even if Madīnah was no longer the political capital of Islam, it continued its spiritual and educational role as was the case in the lifetime of the Prophet

ﷺ. Since then, however, Islam had spread far and wide, and enthusiastic Muslim scholars, Arabs and non-Arabs alike, came and lived in Madīnah to sit at the feet of famous scholars, many making the journey purely for the purpose of learning from Imām Mālik ibn Anas.

His Education

The family of Imām Mālik, during his early childhood, had already become well known as scholars and teachers in Islamic learning. The Imām's grandfather, also called Mālik, was a famous scholar of *ḥadīth* and is considered to be one of the narrators of *ṣaḥīḥ ḥadīth*. He was alive until Imām Mālik reached the age of ten. By that time Imām Mālik had started his schooling. His uncle Abū Suhayl was a recognised scholar of *ḥadīth* and a teacher of Imām az-Zuhrī, a very famous contemporary of Imām Mālik. The Imām's father Anas and another uncle Rabīc were also scholars of *ḥadīth* as they narrated *ḥadīth* from their father Mālik, Imām Mālik's grandfather. Imām Mālik was such a keen scholar right from childhood that once, while his teacher was lecturing the students, a snake fell into Mālik's lap from the ceiling. All the students ran away while he remained seated, undisturbed as if nothing had happened at all. He was so engrossed in his studies, that even a snake could not distract him.

MĀLIK'S TEACHERS

1. Abū Radīm Nāfic ibn cAbd ar-Raḥmān

In the field of Qur'ān studies, the Imām learnt how to read and recite the Noble Qur'ān according to the established principles of *tajwīd*[22] from the famous scholar Abū Radīm Nāfic ibn cAbd ar-Raḥmān who is well known in this field throughout the Muslim world even today, and who is the transmitter of the narration of the Qur'ān of the People of Madīnah. His narration is widely recited in North and West Africa. Abū Radīm died in the year 169 AH/786 CE.

2. *Nāfi^c the mawlā of Ibn ^cUmar*

Nāfi^c was a great scholar of *ḥadīth* during the early years of Imām Mālik's life. He learnt from his famous master ^cAbdullāh ibn ^cUmar since Nāfi^c was his freed slave who had served him for thirty years of his life. Those who knew the place of ^cAbdullāh ibn ^cUmar in *ḥadīth* literature would realise what a great opportunity it was for Nāfi^c to learn from such a great scholar who was always surrounded by pupils. ^cAbdullāh ibn ^cUmar was the son of ^cUmar ibn al-Khaṭṭāb, the second caliph of Islam, and one of the closest Companions of the Prophet ﷺ.

Apart from learning *ḥadīth* from ^cAbdullāh ibn ^cUmar, Nāfi^c had also the good fortune of serving other Companions and scholars in the field of *ḥadīth*: ^cĀ'ishah, Umm Salamah, Abū Hurayrah, the famous narrator of *ḥadīth*, and Abū Sa^cīd al-Khudrī and many others. His pupils include not only Mālik but other luminaries of that period whose names are famous in Islamic learning, like Ibn Jurayj, az-Zuhrī, Imām al-Awzā^cī and Ayyūb as-Sakhtiyānī. Imām Mālik was in the habit of asking juristic opinions of his great teacher with the phrase: "What did Ibn ^cUmar say about these issues?" Who could be a greater authority on the juristic decisions and opinions of ^cAbdullāh ibn ^cUmar than his closest pupils such as Nāfi^c? Although the Imām had a large number of teachers, he respected Nāfi^c to such an extent that he often used to say, "Whenever I have heard a *ḥadīth* of Nāfi^c from Ibn ^cUmar I do not care if I do not hear it from anyone else."

This is the reason why the *Muwaṭṭa'* is full of *ḥadīth* which are narrated by Imām Mālik on the authority of Nāfi^c who heard them from ^cAbdullāh ibn ^cUmar, and following him in his high esteem for this chain of transmission the *^culamā'* called such *ḥadīth* from Mālik from Nāfi^c from ^cAbdullāh ibn ^cUmar, the golden *silsilah* (chain of transmission) because of the high standing of each one of the narrators.

The Caliph ^cUmar ibn ^cAbd al-^cAzīz, who was himself a great scholar, chose Nāfi^c as a teacher for the Egyptians and sent him there. It is only in Islam that a freed slave, through his *taqwā*, devotion and scholarship, can be raised to such high authority that *ḥadīth* narrated by him are considered amongst the most authentic, and he was respected as a great scholar by the ruling caliphs. He died in 117 AH/735 CE but some say 120 AH/738 CE.

3. Jaᶜfar aṣ-Ṣādiq

Imām Jaᶜfar aṣ-Ṣādiq was also one of the teachers of Imām Mālik. Apart from being a great scholar, he belonged to the family of the Prophet ﷺ. He was a great grandson of al-Ḥusayn, the grandson of the Prophet. His father, Muḥammad al-Bāqir, was also a great scholar. The chains of his narration of *ḥadīth* goes back through his father Imām Muḥammad al-Bāqir, ᶜUrwah ibn az-Zubayr, Muḥammad ibn al-Munkadir and ᶜAṭā'.[23] Apart from Imām Mālik, his pupils included Sufyān ath-Thawrī, Shuᶜbah, Abū ᶜĀṣim Yaḥyā al-Anṣārī, Imām Abū Ḥanīfah and Sufyān ibn ᶜUyaynah. Imām Jaᶜfar aṣ-Ṣādiq died in 198 AH/814 CE.

4. Muḥammad ibn Yaḥyā al-Anṣārī

Muḥammad ibn Yaḥyā was another teacher of Imām Mālik. He was also a Follower. He used to teach in the Masjid an-Nabawī, the Prophet's mosque in Madīnah. Muḥammad ibn Yaḥyā died in 121 AH/739 CE at the age of 74 years.

5. Abū Ḥāzim Salamah ibn Dīnār

Abū Ḥāzim was another scholar of the Followers and a teacher of Imām Mālik. He used to teach in the Prophet's mosque and he died in 140 AH/757 CE.

6. Yaḥyā ibn Saᶜīd

Yaḥyā ibn Saᶜīd was also a scholar of the Followers and pupil of ᶜAlī Zayn al-ᶜĀbidīn ibn al-Ḥusayn, ᶜAdī ibn Thābit and Anas ibn Mālik. Apart from Imām Mālik, Ḥammād, Shuᶜbah and Sufyān ath-Thawrī were his pupils. He died in 143 AH/760.

7. Hishām ibn ᶜUrwah

Hishām ibn ᶜUrwah, a venerable and well known Follower, was also a teacher of Imām Mālik. He had heard traditions from many Companions and was the teacher of several other great scholars of *ḥadīth*, such as Sufyān ath-Thawrī and Sufyān ibn ᶜUyaynah.

Later, he went to Kūfa in the period of the Caliph Abū Ja^c^far al-Manṣūr, the Abbasid, and people flocked round him to listen to his teachings on *tafsīr* and *ḥadīth*. The Caliph al-Manṣūr greatly respected him and led the funeral prayer when Hishām died. According to Ibn Sa^c^d, he was reliable in the science of *ḥadīth* and knew large numbers of them. Abū Ḥātim has described him as the Imām in the science of *ḥadīth*.

8. Ibn Shihāb az-Zuhrī

Perhaps one of the greatest of the teachers of Imām Mālik was Ibn Shihāb az-Zuhrī. He died in 124 AH/742 CE. One of the greatest *^c^ulamā'* of Madīnah in his time, and he is counted as one of the first to record *ḥadīth* and *fiqh*.

9. Rabī^c^ah ar-Ra'y

Rabī^c^ah ibn ^c^Abd ar-Raḥmān ar-Ra'y was one of the most famous of Mālik's teachers and Mālik attended his circle for many years. He was given the honorific name *ar-Ra'y*, meaning theoretical reflection. He died in 136 AH/754 CE. Mālik said when he died, "The sweetness of *fiqh* has gone since Rabī^c^ah died."

10. Ibn Hurmuz

Mālik spent seven or eight years devoted to Abū Bakr ^c^Abdullāh ibn Yazīd, better known as Ibn Hurmuz, often studying the entire day alone with him. Otherwise, we know almost nothing at all about Ibn Hurmuz. He died in 148 AH/765 CE.

Famous pupils of Imām Mālik and authentic transmitters of the Muwaṭṭa'

Imām Mālik's fame spread far and wide and contemporary scholars from different parts of the Muslim world of that period considered it to be a great privilege to sit in the circle of the Imām and listen to his lessons on *ḥadīth* and rulings on various juristic and legal issues. Many of them took down full notes and memorised and copied the text of the *Muwaṭṭa'*, the famous collection of *ḥadīth*, traditions, transmission of the practice of Madīnah, legal rulings and explanatory material by Mālik. This activity helped a great deal since these scholars returned to their countries with an authentic copy of the *Muwaṭṭa'* which they had also memorised and on which they based their teachings of the *ḥadīth* and jurisprudence of Imām Mālik. Almost 1300 scholars came to learn from him. We shall give a brief biographical sketch of the most prominent of these scholars which will also help us to see why their copies of the *Muwaṭṭa'* are the most authentic.

1. Yaḥyā ibn Yaḥyā al-Maṣmūdī (d. 234 AH/849 CE)

He belonged to the Berber tribe Maṣmūdah and came from Spain. He travelled twice to Madīnah, the first time to learn from Imām Mālik, and then returned to his country to teach the science of *ḥadīth* and jurisprudence. Yaḥyā first went to Madīnah in the last year of Imām Mālik's life and learnt from him all of the *Muwaṭṭa'*. However, he had already learnt the *Muwaṭṭa'* from Ziyād ibn ᶜAbd ar-Raḥmān who was the first to teach the *madhhab* of Mālik in Andalusia. When he came to narrate the *Muwaṭṭa'* himself he was not absolutely sure that he had heard the three chapters from the book of *iᶜtikāf* directly from Imām Mālik, so out of scrupulousness, he narrated them from Ziyād. Mālik died later that year 179 AH/795 CE. Yaḥyā was present at his funeral prayer and burial. Yaḥyā also learnt from other pupils and contemporaries of Imām Mālik such as ᶜAbdullāh ibn Wahb, al-Layth ibn Saᶜd al-Miṣrī, Sufyān ibn ᶜUyaynah, and Ibn al-Qāsim the source for *al-Mudawwanah*. On his return to Andalusia the Amīr of Cordoba asked him to accept appointment as *qāḍī* of Cordoba, but he declined. He was a man of *taqwā*.

It is through his narration that the *Muwaṭṭa'* became well known in North Africa and Andalusia, and when people, both scholars and the masses, speak about THE *Muwaṭṭa'* it is the narration of Yaḥyā that they mean. He died in 234 AH/849 CE.

2. Ibn Wahb Abū Muḥammad ᶜAbdullāh ibn Salamah al-Fihrī al-Miṣrī.

His famous works include *al-Jāmiᶜ al-ḥadīth, Kitāb al-manāsik, Kitāb al-maghāzī* and *Kitāb at-tafsīr, al-Muwaṭṭa'*. He died in 199 AH/815 CE.

3. Abū ᶜAbdullāh ᶜAbd ar-Raḥmān ibn al-Qāsim ibn Khālid al-ᶜUtaqī

Perhaps the most illustrious and important pupil of Imām Mālik keeping his company for nineteen years until his death. He used to recite the Qur'ān twice a day. Apart from narrating a version of the *Muwaṭṭa'*, his most important contribution was to be the main source for the *Mudawwanah* which in many ways is the second pillar of the *madhhab.* He died in Egypt in 191 AH/807 CE.

Other pupils

Abū ᶜAbd ar-Raḥmān ᶜAbdullāh ibn Maslamah al-Ḥārithī well known as al-Qaᶜnabī. (d. 221 AH/836 CE)
ᶜAbdullāh ibn Yūsuf ad-Dimashqī well known as at-Tinnīsī.
Abū Yaḥyā Maᶜn ibn ᶜĪsā ibn Dīnār al-Madanī (d. 198 AH/814 CE)
Saᶜīd ibn Kathīr ibn ᶜUfayr ibn Muslim al-Anṣārī (d. 226 AH/841 CE)
Yaḥyā ibn Yaḥyā ibn Bukayr al-Miṣrī (d. 231 AH/846 CE)
Abū Muṣᶜab az-Zuhrī, Qāḍī of Madīnah (d. 242 AH/856 CE)
Muṣᶜab az-Zubayrī (d. 236 AH/851 CE)
Muḥammad ibn Mubārak aṣ-Ṣūrī (d. 215 AH/830 CE)
Sulaymān ibn Burd ibn Najīḥ at-Tujībī (d. 210 AH/825 CE)
Suwayd ibn Saᶜīd al-Harawī (d. 240 AH/854 CE)
Muḥammad ibn al-Ḥasan ash-Shaybānī the pupil of Abū Ḥanīfah and Imām of the Ḥanafī *madhhab.*
Dhu'n-Nūn al-Miṣrī (d. 245AH/859 CE), who is better known as a Ṣūfī, learnt from Mālik and memorised the *Muwaṭṭa'* from him.

All the above scholars have left the most authentic copies of the *Muwaṭṭa'* which they learnt from Imām Mālik. Those who benefited from the study circle of Imām Mālik included Abbasid Caliphs such as Abū Jaᶜfar al-Manṣūr, who was the one who ordered Mālik to compose the *Muwaṭṭa'* and gave him instructions in how to proceed in that work, and al-Mahdī, Hārūn ar-Rashīd and his sons Amīn and Ma'mūn, as well as learned jurists like Abū Ḥanīfah, ash-Shāfiᶜī, Muḥammad ibn al-Ḥasan ash-Shaybānī and Qāḍī Abū Yūsuf.

Imām Mālik as a teacher

According to adh-Dhahabī in his famous work *Tadhkirat al-ḥuffāẓ*, even Abū Ḥanīfah used to sit in the presence of Mālik with the respect with which one sits in the presence of one's teacher. Although it reflects great humility on the part of the older scholar Abū Ḥanīfah and his fine *adab*, it also shows the great respect which Imām Abū Ḥanīfah had for Imām Mālik ibn Anas.

Imām Mālik's method of teaching his pupils was unique in his time, and it is the same system which is followed in the traditional Qur'ānic schools and in mosque teachings in West Africa till today. Imām Mālik liked his pupils to read aloud (*ᶜarḍ*) while he himself listened – as it was what he had learnt from his teachers in Madīnah – rather than himself reading out to his pupils while they listened (*samāᶜ*).[24] Some people objected to this system, Yaḥyā ibn Sālim did not like this method and left the school simply on this ground.

Imām Mālik, the teacher would sit on a high seat with the Book of Allah and his collections of *ḥadīth* by his side and the students sitting around him, and they would jot down notes of the Imām's lectures. If the number of pupils grew very large, one of the best pupils with a strong memory would stand up and repeat the teacher's words without altering the theme and substance of the master's words and thus conveying them to those further away from the centre of the gathering. The person chosen by Imām Mālik to do this job was Ibn ᶜUlayyah and the Imām's contemporary, Shuᶜbah, had chosen Ādam ibn Abī Iyās for the same function.

Imām Mālik's contemporaries were luminaries in the field of Islamic scholarship and particularly Islamic jurisprudence. Among the scholars who where alive at that time were Imām al-Awzāᶜī in Syria, Ḥammād in Baṣra, Imām Abū Ḥanīfah in Kūfa, Sufyān ath-Thawrī in Kūfa and al-Layth ibn Saᶜd in Egypt.

Imām Mālik as a muḥaddith and a jurist:

As a great *muḥaddith*, that is a scholar and authority on the science of *ḥadīth*, he scrutinised all kinds of transmissions, *khuṭbahs* of the Prophet ﷺ, expositions on Qur'ānic matters, stories and biographical narrations about the excellent qualities of the Companions of the Prophet and the explanations of Qur'ān and *ḥadīth* by the Companions and their traditions. After careful consideration, he then compiled about a thousand *ḥadīth* in his *Muwaṭṭa'*, although many narrations show that it was originally much larger and that he trimmed it until it became its present size.

All his legal theories and its codification is based on the Book of Allah and the Sunnah of the Prophet ﷺ very often judging the *ᶜamal* or practice, down to his own time, of the People of Madīnah as the very best evidence of the Sunnah. Weakness in quoting traditions and giving a legal judgement based on them would always create problems for later generations. This is the reason why the once strong *madhhab* of al-Awzāᶜī, a recognised *mujtahid* and a great scholar and contemporary of Imām Mālik in Syria, would ultimately not endure. This is further confirmed when someone asked Imām Aḥmad ibn Ḥanbal his opinion of al-Awzāᶜī. He replied: "He is weak in *ḥadīth* and weak in judgement." Some of the *ᶜulamā'* said: "Al-Awzāᶜī is an imām in *fiqh* but not in the Sunnah. Ath-Thawrī is an imām in the Sunnah but not in the *fiqh*. Mālik is an imām in both."

Although Imām Mālik is a famous *muḥaddith* (*ḥadīth* scholar) his legal rulings required the use of *ijtihād*. Ibn Qutaybah (d. 276 AH/889 CE) the famous traditionist, therefore enumerated him as one of the *Ahl ar-Ra'y* (people of theoretical considerations) in a chapter of the same name in his *Kitāb al-maᶜārif*.

During the period of Imām Mālik, the *ᶜulamā'* were concerned with recording the Sunnah and the judgements that had been made based on the Sunnah. In Madīnah that was recognised to comprise knowledge of the practice of the People of Madīnah and of the *ḥadīth*. In subsequent times, and particularly after the appearance of ash-Shāfiᶜī, a group concerned themselves with collecting *ḥadīth* and *riwāyāt* (narrations). The collection of *ḥadīth* was a marathon task, and it required travelling from place to place even to record one *ḥadīth* and establish its chain of narrators.

Other groups of scholars collected and examined the *ḥadīth* with a view to deducing rulings from them.

Imām Mālik was so very careful in selecting the *ḥadīth* while compiling his famous work *Muwaṭṭa'* that he even did not include the narrations made by his father Anas and his uncle Rabīᶜ on the authority of his grandfather.

As a jurist he fearlessly gave his *fatwās* (juristic decisions) even if the ruling Caliph disliked it. Once he was asked not to issue a *fatwā* about divorce pronounced under duress. Other imams said that it would be considered a divorce even if given under duress, but Imām Mālik said that there would be no divorce. Jaᶜfar ibn Sulaymān, the governor of Madīnah and a cousin of the Caliph al-Manṣūr, ordered Imām Mālik not to give such a *fatwā*, but the Imām publicly gave his opinion and was flogged because of it, yet he continued to give the *fatwā* until the governor relented. The point at issue here is that anything to which people are coerced, including pledging allegiance to the Caliph, is not binding.

Imām Mālik used to refrain from giving *fatwā* even if asked by people who had travelled from afar. Once a man came after travelling for about six months, and sought Imām Mālik's legal opinion. The Imām replied: "Please tell your people that Imām Mālik has said that he cannot answer that question." Ibn Abī Uways said that once Imām Mālik told him that sometimes such questions are posed to him that out of anxiety he could not eat or drink. If someone knowledgeable corrected him in any juristic opinion, the Imām used to accept it immediately.[25]

Imām Mālik has narrated few *ḥadīth* or opinions from the great scholars of Iraq. Shuᶜayb ibn Ḥarb once asked Imām Mālik: "Why have you not narrated anything from the people of Iraq?" He replied: "Our elders (*aslāf*) have not narrated anything from their elders, hence our youngsters have also not narrated anything from their youngsters." He made clear on many occasions that he did not accept most of the scholars of Iraq. However, one of his great *shuyūkh* (teachers) was Ayyūb as-Sakhtiyānī, a well known Follower who came from Baṣra. Many of his renowned pupils also came from Iraq.

Madīnan fiqh

The greatest contribution that Imām Mālik made was recording the practice of the People of Madīnah, their *fiqh* and their *ḥadīth*, providing illustrations from the Prophet ﷺ and his Companions, their Followers, whom he met, and the Followers of the Followers of his own generation. Madīnah was the centre where all branches of Islamic learning were taught by great scholars and dedicated people who had learnt the sciences of the Qur'ān, the Sunnah, the *ḥadīth* and the principles of jurisprudence from the Prophet ﷺ and his Companions. Although all of the Companions had departed this life, famous scholars amongst the Followers and the sons and grandsons of the Companions were still living in Madīnah in great numbers in the time of Imām Mālik. Among them there were seven outstanding Followers who became central figures in *fiqh* and *ḥadīth*, and all questions of law were generally referred to them: the seven *fuqahā'* of Madīnah among whom, for example, figured Sulaymān ibn Yasār and Sālim ibn ᶜAbdullāh. Sulaymān was a slave of Maymūnah, the Mother of the Muslims and wife of the Prophet ﷺ and Sālim was the grandson of ᶜUmar and was taught by his father ᶜAbdullāh ibn ᶜUmar. These seven Followers constituted a consultative body to which all *Sharīᶜah* questions were referred.[26] The Madīnan *fiqh* that Imām Mālik transmitted was the outcome of the efforts of these knowledgeable and right-acting Followers based on the authority of the verdicts of the Companions and the Sunnah of the Prophet ﷺ.

Imām Mālik died on the 11th Rabīᶜ al-Awwal, in 179 AH/795 CE at the age of 86, and was buried in Jannat al-Baqīᶜ in Madīnah.

An assessment of the Muwaṭṭa' of Imām Mālik

Professor N. J. Coulson, in his book *A History of Islamic Law*, has said:

> In the jurisprudence of the years 770-800 the reasoning of individual scholars, local consensus and the reported precedent (Sunnah) of Muḥammad, lay in uneasy juxtaposition. This stage of legal development is mirrored in the first written compendium

> produced in Islam - the *Muwaṭṭa'* of the Madīnan scholar Mālik ibn Anas (d. 796 CE).[27]

Those who are well versed in *fiqh* and *uṣūl al-fiqh* as well as the science of *ḥadīth* know that this is far from the truth. The *Muwaṭṭa'* of Imām Mālik does not "mirror" in any sense "the uneasy juxtaposition of the reasoning of individual scholars, local consensus and the reported precedents of the Prophet," but it is the most authentic[28] compilation of *ḥadīth*, traditions of the Companions and Followers, and some of the Companions and the Followers' interpretations of all the important aspects of a Muslim's way of life. Hence the *Muwaṭṭa'* begins with the *ṣalāh* (five daily prayers), goes on to deal with the other pillars of Islam, and then various legal aspects as taught through the precepts of the Prophet ﷺ and understood and practised by the Companions and the Followers.

The style of the *Muwaṭṭa'* followed by Imām Mālik is such that it helps a reader to understand, first of all, what the Prophet ﷺ had to say on the subject. Since the final authority in *Sharīᶜah* is to be derived from the Qur'ān and the Sunnah, any *ḥadīth* conflicting with the teachings and the spirit of the Qur'ān is not to be regarded as a *ḥadīth* but as a mere fabrication. However, such evaluations are subject to very demanding rules and not just anyone can make a proper determination. The invariable practice of Mālik, that of opening his discussion of a topic with quotations from relevant *ḥadīth* or similarly authoritative precedents of the Companions, lend the *Muwaṭṭa'* great authenticity. Hence, Imām Muḥammad ibn Idrīs ash-Shāfiᶜī has rightly said, "There has not appeared on the earth any book after the Book of Allah, more authentic (*ṣaḥīḥ*) than the book of Mālik." In another narration Imām ash-Shāfiᶜī is reported to have said:

> There is nothing more correct on the earth after the Book of Allah than the *Muwaṭṭa'* of Mālik.

مَا وُضِعَ عَلَى الْأَرْضِ كِتَابٌ هُوَ أَقْرَبُ إِلَى الْقُرْءَانِ مِنْ كِتَابِ مَالِكَ

> There has not been placed on the earth a book which is closer to the Qur'ān than the book of Mālik.

In yet another narration, Imām ash-Shāfiᶜī said, "There is nothing more useful after the Book of Allah than the *Muwaṭṭa'* of Mālik."

Imām ash-Shāfiᶜī's authority is unquestionable, as he is also the imam of a school of Islamic theology and jurisprudence. Imām Aḥmad ibn Ḥanbal has said the following about Imām ash-Shāfiᶜī's mastery of the *Muwaṭṭa'*:

كُنتُ سَمِعتُ الموطّأ من بضعة عشر رجلًا من حفّاظ أصحاب مالك فأعدته على الشافعيّ لأنّي وجدته أقومهم

> I studied the *Muwaṭṭa'* under ten or so of Mālik's students who used to memorise it. Finally I checked my memorisation by reading it to ash-Shāfiᶜī because I found him to be the most correct of them.[29]

Now, whose opinion are we going to consider more reliable: the western orientalist or Imām ash-Shāfiᶜī? Naturally, every Muslim the world over, will accept the judgement of the latter. The western scholar's view about the *Muwaṭṭa'* is as follows:

> Mālik's chosen method of composing his treatise (*Muwaṭṭa'*) was first to report such precedents as were known, and then to consider them, interpret them, and accept them or otherwise in the light of his own reasoning and the legal tradition of Madīnah. His supreme criterion was the local consensus of opinion, and there was nothing so sacrosanct about traditions (*hadith*) from the Prophet or other precedents that enabled them to override his authority in cases of conflict. The *Muwaṭṭa'* is essentially a manual of the doctrine currently endorsed by the establishment of Madīnah.[30]

This creates the impression that Imām Mālik sought only to report the precedents which were known in Madīnan circles with a view to then subjecting them to his own personally concocted process of evaluation, and that his real achievement was to create out of Madīnan consensus a mechanism for the circumvention of *ḥadīth,* since he did not hold traditions from the Prophet ﷺ or other precedents from the Companions and Followers to be beyond contradiction. This is an egregious misinterpretation of Imām Mālik's position on *ᶜamal,* the practice of the people of Madīnah, which Mālik considered to be like a kind of living *ḥadīth* transmission of the Sunnah. Since large numbers of people in Madīnah had held to the same practice, he considered this the same as the strongest possible *ḥadīth* transmitted by numerous chains of transmission (*mutawātir*). Imām Mālik's intention, as can be understood from the following incident narrated by aṭ-Ṭabarī, was to record the authentic *ḥadīth* and the exact practice of the time of the Companions and the Followers in the heartland of Islam and in the city of the Prophet ﷺ, 'the city' par excellence. This was the reason why he actually wrote his book.

It is narrated by Muḥammad ibn ᶜUmar who said that he heard from Imām Mālik ibn Anas the following:

> When the Abbasid caliph Abū Jaᶜfar al-Manṣūr performed his pilgrimage (and came to Madīnah) he called me. When I met him, I narrated *hadith*. He asked me some questions and I replied. Then he said: "I desire that I may make copies of your book *Muwaṭṭa'* and then send them to all the Muslim lands and order people to act upon them and not to cross the limits". He (Imām Mālik) replied: "Amīr al-Mu'minīn, do not do so."[31]

Imām Mālik was a great imam who wished to revive the practice of the Sunnah of the Messenger of Allah ﷺ and he spent his life collecting *ḥadīth* and he chose the most authentic ones to be included in his *Muwaṭṭa'*. To say that Imām Mālik held nothing sacrosanct about the *ḥadīth* of the Prophet, is to level the very grave charge against him that he lacked respect and love for the Prophet ﷺ. The *Muwaṭṭa'* is not merely a manual of doctrines but it is the foremost collection of *ḥadīth* and the authentic guide to the *Sharīᶜah* of Islam.

The same orientalist, while discussing the genesis of *Sharīᶜah* law, further confuses the prevailing situation in Imām Mālik's time. He says:

> It should finally be stressed that there was no suggestion, at this stage, that the Prophet was other than a human interpreter of the divine revelation; his authority lay in the fact that he was closest, in time and spirit, to the Qur'ān and as such was the ultimate starting point of the Islamic Sunnah.[32]

This is a widespread misunderstanding among non-Muslim scholars of Islam who write books on Islam without any respect for the *īmān* (belief) of Muslims. At the time of Imām Mālik, and before him and after him up until our day and until the end of time, every Muslim, through the commitment to the *shahādah*, believes that the Prophet Muḥammad ﷺ is not merely 'a human interpreter of the divine revelation', but the Messenger of Allah (*Rasūlu'llāh*). His authority did not lie merely 'in the fact that he was closest, in time and spirit, to the Qur'ān', and as such was the ultimate starting point of the Islamic Sunnah, but that he was the person to whom the Qur'ān was revealed for the guidance of mankind, and hence, he was the best interpreter of the Qur'ān.

The orientalists have greatly confused this important matter of the relationship between the *ᶜamal* (practice) of the People of Madīnah and the *ḥadīth* of the Messenger of Allah ﷺ in the *Muwaṭṭa'* of Imām Mālik.[33]

3. Imām Muḥammad ibn Idrīs ash-Shāfiᶜī

Abū Muḥammad ᶜAbd ar-Raḥmān ibn Abī Ḥātim ar-Rāzī who died in 327 AH/938 CE is the earliest and most accurate biographer of Imām ash-Shāfiᶜī. He says that Imām Muḥammad ibn Idrīs ash-Shāfiᶜī was born at Gaza, a small town on the Mediterranean Sea. Some other biographers say he was born at Ascalon (ᶜAsqalān) which is not far from Gaza in the year 150 AH/767 CE, the very year in which Imām Abū Ḥanīfah died. He belonged to the tribe of Quraysh and was thus a relative of the Prophet Muḥammad ﷺ. After his father's death, his mother took him to Palestine and lived with a Yemeni tribe to which her ancestors belonged. Later she travelled to Makkah with ash-Shāfiᶜī when he was ten years old.[34] From his early childhood he displayed a sharp intelligence and was excellent in memorisation. He was eloquent in speech and was very good in poetry and Arabic language, as well as in his legal studies.

His early life

As a child ash-Shāfiᶜī was very intelligent and bright, always keen to learn the traditional Islamic sciences. Like every Muslim child in those days, he began his studies with learning the Qur'ān, which he memorised at the early age of seven years. During that time Imām Mālik's famous work *Muwaṭṭa'* was a well known book on *ḥadīth* and *fiqh* in the Ḥijāz and other parts of the Muslim world, since it was among the very first works to be composed in Islam. We are told that ash-Shāfiᶜī memorised the complete *Muwaṭṭa'* at the age of fifteen.[35] He studied Islamic jurisprudence under the well known scholar Muslim ibn Khālid az-Zanjī, the *muftī* of Makkah (d. 180 AH/796 CE) and Sufyān ibn ᶜUyaynah (d. 198 AH/796 CE).[36]

He left Makkah for Madīnah to study at the feet of Imām Mālik ibn Anas. Imām ash-Shāfiᶜī was then twenty years of age, and continued his study with Imām Mālik until the latter's death in the year 179 AH/796 CE. By the time of Imām Mālik's death, ash-Shāfiᶜī had already gained a reputation as a famous jurist in Ḥijāz and other places.[37]

Ash-Shāfiᶜī in Iraq

When the governor of Yemen visited Madīnah, he was so impressed by the great learning of ash-Shāfiᶜī that he persuaded him to take up a government position as an administrator, which ash-Shāfiᶜī accepted for a short while. We were told that ash-Shāfiᶜī's frankness brought him into conflict with government officials and he was deported to Iraq in chains in 187 AH/803 CE. Various unfounded allegations, including that of conspiracy, were levelled against him. This happened during the caliphate of Hārūn ar-Rashīd of the Abbasid dynasty.

Ash-Shāfiᶜī was presented to the Caliph along with other conspirators but he was pardoned by the Caliph when the eloquent ash-Shāfiᶜī successfully defended himself. In the court of Hārūn ar-Rashīd, it is said, he discussed with the Caliph every conceivable branch of knowledge including Greek medicine and philosophy in their original languages.[38] Fortunately for him Imām Muḥammad ibn al-Ḥasan ash-Shaybānī (d. 189 AH/805 CE) the famous Ḥanafī jurist was present in the court of Hārūn. He helped him by confirming that ash-Shāfiᶜī was a famous scholar of *fiqh* and that his life ought to be spared. Ash-Shāfiᶜī's discussion with Hārūn so much delighted the Caliph that he became his patron.[39] Ash-Shāfiᶜī found peace of heart and mind in Baghdad and devoted his time to serious studies with Imām ash-Shaybānī.

His study of the Ḥanafī and Mālikī Schools

With his bitter experience of past government service, he vowed not to take up any government job again, although he was patronised by the Caliph.

Ash-Shāfiᶜī's in-depth studies with Imām Mālik had made him an expert on the Mālikī school of thought, but now, in Baghdad, he had a new opportunity to go deep into the Ḥanafī school of Islamic jurisprudence. He lived with Ḥanafī jurists and discussed various legal issues with them, defending the position of his master Imām Mālik[40] and he became reputed as an upholder of *ḥadīth*. Thus, ash-Shāfiᶜī had the privilege of studying in depth both the Mālikī and Ḥanafī systems.

Ash-Shāfiᶜī then moved to Egypt in the year 188 AH/804 CE via Ḥarīrān, Syria and Makkah. Because of his earlier stay in Makkah, as well as his growing fame as an eminent jurist, he was well received in Makkah where he delivered lectures in the Ḥaram ash-Sharīf. During the course of his lectures, ash-Shāfiᶜī, who was now an expert on both the Mālikī and Ḥanafī school of thought, expressed various differences of opinion with and departures from the legal positions of Imām Abū Ḥanīfah and Imām Mālik. Many of his supporters, who followed the Mālikī school, were disappointed on listening to his discourses, but he still had an impact on some scholars, one of whom was Imām Aḥmad ibn Ḥanbal, who was then studying in Makkah. In spite of his difference of opinion with Imām Mālik, Imām ash-Shāfiᶜī respected Imām Mālik and his *Muwaṭṭa'* as we have seen.[41]

Later, he returned to Baghdad to spend a short period of three or four years there in 194 AH/810 CE. While he was in Baghdad, the Caliph al-Ma'mūn (d. 218AH/833 CE) invited him to occupy the position of *qāḍī* (judge), but ash-Shāfiᶜī refused. In the meantime, he was invited to come to Egypt by ᶜAbdullāh ibn

Mūsā. He left Baghdad finally in the year 198 AH/814 CE at the age of fifty. Some of his biographers say that since ash-Shāfiᶜī vehemently opposed the Muᶜtazilī doctrine, which the ruling Caliph supported, he decided to leave Baghdad as quickly as possible.[42]

Ash-Shāfiᶜī in Egypt

Ash-Shāfiᶜī found himself in a congenial atmosphere in Egypt. It was here that most of his mature work was written. He was always surrounded by large numbers of scholars from different parts of the world who came to learn *fiqh* and *uṣūl al-fiqh* from him. His leading disciples, such as Rabīᶜ ibn Sulaymān al-Murādī (d. 270 AH/880 CE), Abū Yaᶜqūb al-Buwayṭī (d. 231 AH/845 CE), Abū Ibrāhīm ibn Yaḥyā al-Muzanī (d. 274 AH/877 CE) and many others, listened keenly to his discourses and recorded every word that the great master uttered. It was the practice of Imām ash-Shāfiᶜī that whatever was written down by his disciples was read aloud to him and he would correct the text.[43] This is the reason why the discourses of Imām ash-Shāfiᶜī have been preserved extremely accurately for us. The well-known works of ash-Shāfiᶜī like *Kitāb al-Umm* and *ar-Risālah* are some of the most famous contributions in the field of Islamic legal studies.

Imām ash-Shāfiᶜī was a man of impressive personality and was well known for his straight-forwardness and *taqwā*. He lived his life with meagre resources, but he was still very generous to the poor and the needy. His biographer ar-Rāzī says that he was in the habit of giving everything that he could lay his hands on to the poor.

His death

It is said that a man called Fityān, a follower of Imām Mālik in Egypt, was defeated in argument by ash-Shāfiᶜī during his lectures and discourses, and that as a result Fityān's followers attacked ash-Shāfiᶜī after one of his lectures, and badly injured him. A few days later ash-Shāfiᶜī died.[44] There is another view, that Imām ash-Shāfiᶜī suffered from a serious intestinal illness which made him very weak during the last years of his life, and he died as a natural result of the illness on the last day of Rajab in 204 AH/20th January 820 CE in Old Cairo. He was buried near Mount al-Muqattam. About four centuries after his death a large domed Mausoleum was built over his grave by the Ayyubid sultan, al-Mālik al-Kāmil in the year 608 AH/1212 CE.

Ash-Shāfiᶜī's most famous work

Amongst the works of Imām ash-Shāfiᶜī, the *Kitāb ar-risalāh fī uṣūl al-fiqh,* commonly known as *ar-Risālah,* is one of the most famous books of Islamic jurisprudence. Imām ash-Shāfiᶜī himself refers to *ar-Risālah* very often as 'our book' or 'my book', showing the importance he himself attached to it.

Perhaps there were two books of the same name. The old *Risālah* and the new *Risālah.* In the old *Risālah,* ash-Shāfiᶜī set forth the system of the Qur'ān, including those general and particular rules, abrogating and abrogated communications and the Sunnah, as the authoritative sources of the *Sharīᶜah.* It also included discourses on *ijmāᶜ* and *qiyās.* Unfortunately, the text of the old *Risālah* has not reached us except for a few passages which are reproduced by other scholars in their books. The new *Risālah,* which has been transmitted to us, has had a great impact on Islamic jurisprudence. It gained him the title of the father of Islamic jurisprudence.

The *Risālah* was composed in Egypt after ash-Shāfiᶜī had settled there. Therefore it reflects the mature legal opinions of Imām ash-Shāfiᶜī while he was at the zenith of his career as a learned man in the field of jurisprudence. In the *Risālah* Imām ash-Shāfiᶜī not only emphasised the Sunnah as the source of the *Sharīᶜah* but also drew heavily on the Sunnah in the formulation of the rules of law. In reality the *Risālah* was written mainly to defend the viewpoints of traditionalists concerning the overriding authority of the Sunnah. His greatest authorities on Sunnah were Imām Mālik and Sufyān ibn ᶜUyaynah, whom he quotes time and time again.

On the other hand, a key formative experience was derived from the intense debates that he had with Ḥanafī jurists during his stay in Baghdad. His discussions with the Ḥanafīs had a great influence on his legal thinking, particularly during his stay with Imām Muḥammad ibn al-Ḥasan ash-Shaybānī. In his other famous book, *Kitāb al-Umm*, Imām ash-Shāfiᶜī has devoted a whole section of the book to his discussion with eminent jurists of his time like Imāms Mālik, al-Awzāᶜī, Abū Ḥanīfah, Abū Yūsuf and Muḥammad ash-Shaybānī. That he had studied the works of these eminent jurists with such care and profundity shows how great a scholar Imām ash-Shāfiᶜī was.

Imām ash-Shāfiᶜī was undoubtedly a great jurist and an eminent scholar of *ḥadīth* who will be remembered by people for all time to come. Ash-Shāfiᶜī has had such an impact on people in the field of Islamic jurisprudence that the Shāfiᶜī school is named after him and millions of Muslims today follow his footsteps in various juristic judgements that he left behind for their guidance. His followers are mainly found in Yemen, Egypt, Syria, in countries of south east Asia like Malaysia and Indonesia, in East Africa and to some extent scattered in other parts of the Muslim world.

4. Imām Aḥmad ibn Muḥammad ibn Ḥanbal

Imām Aḥmad ibn Muḥammad ibn Ḥanbal was born in Marw on the 20th of Rabīᶜ al-Awwal in the year 164 AH/780 CE. His father, Muḥammad, was a reputed warrior (*mujāhid*) and lived in Baṣra in Iraq. It is said that when his father went to Marw as a fighter, Imām Aḥmad was born during his sojourn there. While still an infant he was brought to Baghdad where his father died at the early age of thirty. The entire responsibility of his upbringing was thus thrown on the shoulders of his mother Ṣafiyyah bint Maymūnah bint Mālik ash-Shaybānī.

His early life

Imām Aḥmad was very inquisitive and intelligent as a child, keenly interested in furthering his education. He began his early study of *ḥadīth* literature in the year 179 AH/795 CE, when he was only sixteen years old. It is said that he became such a great scholar of *ḥadīth* and that he remembered almost a million *ḥadīth*.

After Qur'ān, therefore, he based his juristic opinions almost entirely on *ḥadīth* and became an eminent jurist of his time as well as famed for all time to come.

Imām Aḥmad's teachers

The following were some of the teachers of Imām Aḥmad ibn Ḥanbal: Imām Muḥammad ash-Shāfiʿī, Bishr ibn al-Mufaḍḍal, Ismāʿīl ibn ʿUlayyah, Jarīr ibn ʿAbd al-Ḥamīd, Yaḥyā ibn Saʿīd ibn al-Qaṭṭān, ʿAbdullāh ibn Namīr, Sufyān ibn ʿUyaynah and Wakīʿ ibn al-Jarrāḥ. Some of his teachers, such as Abū Dāwūd, Aswal ibn Amīr, Imām ash-Shāfiʿī, Yaḥyā ibn Ādam, Imām al-Bukhārī, Imām Muslim and Yazīd ibn Hārūn, narrated *ḥadīth* from their illustrious pupil.[45]

His most famous pupils include Abū Bakr al-Athram, Ḥanbal ibn Isḥāq, Abū'l-Qāsim al-Baghawī and many others, and his son ʿAbdullāh ibn Aḥmad ibn Ḥanbal was one of the main transmitters from him.

The Relationship between Imām Aḥmad and Imām ash-Shāfiʿī

The famous scholar Abū Bakr al-Bayhaqī has mentioned that ash-Shāfiʿī was the most important of Imām Aḥmad's teachers. It is true that Imām Aḥmad had a special attachment to Imām ash-Shāfiʿī as is seen in the special importance his narrations have in his famous book *Musnad Aḥmad*. Imām ash-Shāfiʿī also had great respect for Imām Aḥmad because of his sincerity of purpose and outstanding scholarship. Once, when Imām ash-Shāfiʿī met Imām Aḥmad in Baghdad in 199 AH, he asked Imām Aḥmad to acquaint him with any *ḥadīth* that he had traced as correct whether from Ḥijāz, Syria or Iraq, which he would like to put into practice. He added that he was not like the scholars of Ḥijāz who did not like to accept *ḥadīth* which had spread in other parts of the Muslim world, branding them as untrue or saying, "We do not consider them true or untrue", but as far as he was concerned he acted on true *ḥadīth* no matter where he found them.

Imām ash-Shāfiʿī, in spite of his being one of the most learned of his time, used to refer to Imām Aḥmad whenever he had any difficulty about *ḥadīth*.[46] Imām ash-Shāfiᶜī described Imām Aḥmad as the "most learned in matters of *ḥadīth*."

Imām Aḥmad's taqwā

Imām Aḥmad was a scholar with great *taqwā* who devoted his life to the service of *ḥadīth* and *fiqh*. Once, when the Abbasid Caliph Hārūn ar-Rashīd told Imām ash-Shāfiᶜī that he needed a *qāḍī* to be sent to the Yemen, Imām ash-Shāfiᶜī spoke to Aḥmad ibn Ḥanbal who was then only thirty years of age and a student in the circle of ash-Shāfiᶜī. Imām Aḥmad refused bluntly saying, "I came to your place in search of knowledge and not for you to thrust upon me the delicate position of a *qāḍī*." Ash-Shāfiᶜī remained silent.

Imām Aḥmad was so scrupulous that he did not even like to pray behind his son or uncle nor did he go to their houses to eat because both of them had accepted government positions under the caliph. It is said that once he was very hungry for three days, and he did not have anything in the house. His wife borrowed a little flour from a neighbour and wanted to make bread as quickly as possible. She rushed to her son's house to bake the bread. Imām Aḥmad did not like it and from that day onwards asked that the door leading to his son's house be closed. He did so because his son was an employee of the caliph.

Once the Caliph al-Ma'mūn distributed some gold as *ṣadaqah* among the scholars of *ḥadīth*. While all the traditionists accepted, Aḥmad refused. When Imām Aḥmad was in the Yemen, his financial condition was very bad. His teacher, Shaykh ᶜAbd ar-Razzāq, the famous *ḥadīth* scholar and author of the *Muṣannaf*, came to know about it, and took a handful of gold dinars and presented them to Imām Aḥmad. Aḥmad said: "I do not need them." His condition at this time was such that his clothes were almost worn out and he had no others to put on. He tried to hide himself in his house and locked the doors. People came in search of him and came to know the reason for his hiding. They tried to offer a little money but the Imām only accepted one dinar out of it on condition that he would repay it by rendering some service such as writing or copying a book.

The famous *ḥadīth* scholar Abū Dāwūd said about Imām Aḥmad

that to sit in his company was a matter of gaining great reward in the next world (*ākhirah*). He never quarrelled with anyone in all his life. The scholar al-Bayhaqī has reported from Imām Aḥmad that when someone asked him a definition of a *mutawakkil* (someone who relies on Allah), Imām Aḥmad said that it is someone who does not pin hope on anyone but Allah.

His inquisition

Imām Aḥmad ibn Ḥanbal in later years came to be seen as a challenge to the caliph and his religious authority. As a result, he was imprisoned for a long time and was treated harshly by a number of rulers. But as a man of conscience, he never surrendered to the wrong-headed views of the authorities.

There exists a lot of material on his inquisition. The suffering of Imām Aḥmad really started when he came into conflict with the Muᶜtazilīs and their philosophy. The Muᶜtazilīs were rationalists and were unfortunately patronised by the Caliphs al-Ma'mūn, al-Muᶜtaṣim Billāh and al-Wāthiq, who had accepted the Muᶜtazilī viewpoint and made it the official creed and imposed it on the Muslims. Imām Aḥmad and other traditionists flatly refused the Muᶜtazilī doctrine and asserted the uncreated nature of the Qur'ān, which was contradicted by the ruling Abbasid caliphs. It was for this reason that he was brought from Baghdad to Tarsus in chains to appear before al-Ma'mūn's inquisition. This trial continued after the death of al-Ma'mūn in 218 AH/833 CE.

It was during the reign of the Caliph al-Muᶜtaṣim Billāh in particular, that he patiently suffered corporal punishment and imprisonment.

The Caliph, recognising the learning and piety of Imām Aḥmad, went to him from time to time to request him to accept the creed of the Muᶜtazilīs, in which case the Caliph himself would free him from the chains and would become his follower and he would become the most favoured courtier. But Imām Aḥmad refused to surrender to the confused Muᶜtazilī ideology. In anger, Caliph al-Muᶜtaṣim ordered his servants to trample him under their feet and many of his joints were dislocated as a result of this cruelty.

The Imām was kept in chains. He was thrown into prison in Baghdad where he spent nearly thirty months. There was no light in his cell, and he was not given a lamp at night. When the Imām insisted on his traditional belief and did not agree with the Muctazilī doctrine put forward by cAbd ar-Raḥmān al-Muctāzilī and Isḥāq ibn Ibrāhīm, a large group of executioners were brought, his hands were tied and he was whipped until he fell unconscious. In spite of all these atrocities, and the flogging that caused his blood to flow, the Imām kept on saying that the Qur'ān is uncreated, it is the knowledge of Allah (*cilm'Allāh*) and anyone who said that the knowledge of Allah is created has committed the wrong of disbelief (*kufr*). The Caliph al-Muctaṣim became apprehensive about his future in this world and the next, and on the 25th of Ramadan in the year 221 AH/836 CE ordered the punishment stopped and the chains removed. When the wounds began to heal, al-Muctaṣim made sure that his deputies came and enquired about the health of the Imām. He repented of his actions, but it was not until the reign of al-Mutawakkil, after the death of al-Muctaṣim and his successor al-Wāthiq, that the heresy came to an end and the Imām was restored to honour.

Imām Aḥmad forgave everyone except those who had committed a great wrong against the Book of Allah. Imām al-Bukhārī says that when news of the Imām's suffering reached Baṣra, Abū'l-Walīd aṭ-Ṭayālisī said: "If Imām Aḥmad had been born among the Israelites, perhaps he would have been a prophet of Allah".

His work

Imām Aḥmad wrote many books, the most important of which are *Kitāb al-camal, Kitāb at-tafsīr, Kitāb an-nāsikh wa'l-mansūkh, Kitāb az-zuhd, Kitāb al-masā'il, Kitāb al-faḍā'il, Kitāb al-manāsik* and *Kitāb al-īmān*. The best known work of Imām Aḥmad is his *Musnad* in which he narrated 28,000-29,000 of the *ḥadīth* that he had collected. Imām Aḥmad died in 241 AH/856 CE. The people of Baghdad turned out for his funeral prayer in huge numbers.

The Four Schools

By the end of the ninth century CE, the four major Sunnī schools had come to agree on a common ground, namely that the primary sources of Islamic law are:

1. The Qur'ān
2. The Sunnah
3. *Ijmā*[c] (juristic consensus) and
4. *Qiyās* (reasoning by analogy)

Notes

[1] Jalāl ad-Dīn as-Suyūṭī said, "Naṣr al-Maqdisī [narrated it] in *al-Ḥujjah,* and al-Bayhaqī in *ar-Risālah al-Ash*[c]*ariyyah* without an *isnād,* and al-Ḥalīmī, Qāḍī Ḥusayn and the Imām al-Ḥaramayn and others, and probably its origins are in some of the books of the *Ḥuffāẓ* which have not reached us." (*Al-Jāmi*[c] *aṣ-ṣaghīr*)

[2] See *Tazyīn al-Mālik,* reported by Abū Nu[c]aym, pp 13-16.

[3] Ibn Ḥajar, *Tawālī at-ta'sīs,* Cairo, p 69.

[4] *Ibid.*

[5] *Fatḥ al-mughīth.*

[6] Adh-Dhahabī, *Mīzān al-i*[c]*tidāl,* see introduction.

[7] Al-Khaṭīb, *Tārīkh Baghdād.*

[8] Ibn Jazlah, *Mukhtaṣar tārīkh al-Khaṭīb al-Baghdādī,* see notes on Imām Abū Ḥanīfah.

[9] Abū'l-Qāsim ibn Ka's, *Manāqib an-Nu*[c]*mān.*

[10] See Afandi, Muḥammad Kāmil (*qāḍī* of Baghdad), *Manāqib al-Imām al-A*[c]*ẓam,* 1136 AH (in Turkish).

[11] Ad-Dimashqī, Muḥammad ibn Yūsuf ibn [c]Alī, [c]*Uqūd al-jummān fī manāqib an-Nu*[c]*mān, Op. Cit.,* chapter 10.

[12] *Ibid.*

[13] Shiblī Nu[c]mānī, *Sīrat an-Nu*[c]*mān* (Urdu) translated into English by Hadi Husain, Lahore 1977 p. 25.

[14] *Ibid.*

[15] *Ibid.*

[16] Cf. Ibn Jazālah, *Mukhtaṣar tārīkh al-Khaṭīb al-Baghdādī, Op. Cit.*

[17] Shiblī Nu[c]mānī, *Sīrat an-Nu*[c]*mān, Op. Cit.,* pp 25-26.

[18] Ad-Dimashqī, [c]*Uqūd al-jummān fī manāqib an-Nu*[c]*mān, Op. Cit.,* see chapter 16.

[19] *Kharāj* came about because rather than the *mujāhidūn* taking the land won in *jihād* as spoils it was left to its owners who instead paid a tribute according to the amount of land and its quality. Ed.
[20] Adh-Dhahabī, *Tadhkirat al-ḥuffāẓ*, vol.1, p.175-190. Also *cf.* as-Samᶜānī *Kitāb al-ansāb*.
[21] Al-Yāfiᶜī, *Ṭabaqāt al-fuqahā'*.
[22] *Tajwīd*: the correct recitation of Qur'ān giving each letters its proper pronunciation. Ed.
[23] Al-Yāfiᶜī, *Ṭabaqāt al-fuqahā'*.
[24] Ibn Khallikān, Abū'l-ᶜAbbās Shams ad-Dīn, *Wafayāt al-aᶜyān*, ed. Muḥammad Muḥyī ad-Dīn, Cairo 1948. See notes on Imām Mālik.
[25] *Fatḥ al-mughīth*, pp. 238-9.
[26] Az-Zawāwī, *Manāqib Mālik*, p. 131.
[27] Coulson, N. J., *A History of Islamic Law*, Edinburgh 1964, p. 43.
[28] "The absolute truth is that the *Muwaṭṭa'* is *ṣaḥīḥ* with nothing being excluded from that." The introduction to the *Isᶜāf al-mubaṭṭa'* of as-Suyūṭī.
[29] *Cf.* ᶜAbd al-Bāqī, Muḥammad Fu'ād, (edited by), *al-Muwaṭṭa'*, Kitāb ash-Shaᶜb, Cairo (undated), p. 1.
[30] Coulson, N. J., *A History of Islamic Law, Op. Cit.*, p. 46-47.
[31] Aṭ-Ṭabarī, *Dhayl al-mudhayl*, p. 107.
[32] Coulson, N. J., *A History of Islamic Law, Op. Cit.*
[33] For a more thorough exposition of this matter see Dutton, Yasin, *The Origins of Islamic Law: The Qur'ān, the Muwaṭṭa', and Madīnan ᶜAmal*, Curzon Press, Surrey, 1999.
[34] Ar-Rāzī, Ibn Abī Ḥātim, *Kitāb adab ash-Shāfiᶜī wa manāqibuh*, ed. Muḥammad Zāhid al-Kawtharī, Cairo 1953.
[35] Al-Khaṭīb, *Tārīkh Baghdād*, Cairo 1931, vol. 2, p. 59.
[36] Ibn ᶜAbd al-Barr, *al-Intiqā'*, Cairo 1932, p. 71.
[37] Ibn Ḥajar, *Tawālī at-ta'sīs li maᶜālī Ibn Idrīs*, Cairo 1301 AH, pp. 79-82.
[38] Have been unable to find a source for this text, nor any confirmation that ash-Shāfiᶜī knew Greek. Ed.
[39] Abū Nuᶜaym al-Aṣfahānī, *Kitāb ḥilyat al-awliyā'*, Cairo 1938, vol. 9, p. 29.
[40] Ibn ᶜAbd al-Barr, *Op. Cit.*, pp. 94-98.

[41] Al-Baghdādī, Khaṭīb, *Op. Cit.*, vol. 2, p. 68.
[42] Ibn Ḥajar, *Tawālī at-ta'sīs, Op. Cit.*, p. 84.
[43] Abū Zahra, *ash-Shāfi^c^ī*, Cairo, 1948, p. 28.
[44] Yaqūt, *Mu^c^jam al-udabā'*, ed. Margolioth, London, 1931, vol. 4, pp. 394-395.
[45] Adh-Dhahabī, *Tadhkirat al-ḥuffāẓ*. See also Ibn Abī Ya^c^lā, *aṭ-Ṭabaqāt.*
[46] Adh-Dhahabī, *Tadhkirat al-ḥuffāẓ*. See also Ibn Abī Ya^c^lā, *aṭ-Ṭabaqāt.*

Part II
The Categories of Fiqh

Chapter 8

The Categories of Fiqh in the *Sharīᶜah*

THE *SHARĪᶜAH* presents clear guidance on the five categories of *fiqh*: the obligatory, recommended, permissible, disliked and forbidden, based on the teachings of the Qur'ān and the Sunnah. Allah decides what is obligatory, recommended, permissible, disliked and forbidden, together with the Prophet ﷺ through what He revealed to him. What is *ḥalāl* is declared through Qur'ānic injunctions, and likewise, nobody but Allah and His Messenger ﷺ has authority to declare any food, drink, dress or trade and business *ḥarām* or unlawful. Al-Miqdām ibn Maᶜdīkarib narrated that the Messenger of Allah ﷺ said:

> And what the Messenger of Allah declares *ḥarām* is like what Allah declares *ḥarām*. (At-Tirmidhī, *bāb mā nuhiya ᶜanhu annahu yuqālu ᶜinda ḥadīth rasūli'llāh ṣalla'llāhu alayhi wa sallam*)

Ibn Juzayy said in his *Taqrīb al-wuṣūl ilā ᶜilm al-uṣūl*:

> Concerning the categories of rulings, and they are fivefold: *wājib* (obligatory), *mandūb* (recommended), *ḥarām* (forbidden), *makrūh* (disliked) and *mubāḥ* (permissible).
>
> The obligatory is that which the *Sharīᶜah* demands with binding force that it be done.
>
> The recommended is that which the *Sharīᶜah* demands that it be done but not with binding force.
>
> The forbidden is that which the *Sharīᶜah* demands with binding force that it be abandoned.
>
> The disliked is that which the *Sharīᶜah* demands be abandoned but not with binding force.

The permissible is that which the *Sharī^c^ah* neither demands that it be done nor abandoned.

These definitions are more authentic than their definition in terms of reward and punishment, such as when they say that the obligatory is that in the doing of which there is reward and in the abandonment of which there is punishment, for two reasons:

First, that neither the reward and punishment are essential attributes of the rulings, but are both recompenses for them, so that it is not valid to use them as the definition for them.

Second, that the punishment may be voided if Allah pardons, and the reward may be voided if the intention is void.

One similarly repudiates those who say that the obligatory is that for the abandonment of which one is blamed, and the forbidden is that for the doing of which one is blamed.

As to the *ḥalāl* and the *ḥarām*, in the Qur'ān, Allah says:

قُلْ مَنْ حَرَّمَ زِينَةَ اللَّهِ الَّتِي أَخْرَجَ لِعِبَادِهِ وَالطَّيِّبَاتِ مِنَ الرِّزْقِ قُلْ هِيَ لِلَّذِينَ آمَنُوا فِي الْحَيَاةِ الدُّنْيَا خَالِصَةً يَوْمَ الْقِيَامَةِ كَذَلِكَ نُفَصِّلُ الْآيَاتِ لِقَوْمٍ يَعْلَمُونَ قُلْ إِنَّمَا حَرَّمَ رَبِّيَ الْفَوَاحِشَ مَا ظَهَرَ مِنْهَا وَمَا بَطَنَ وَالْإِثْمَ وَالْبَغْيَ بِغَيْرِ الْحَقِّ وَأَنْ تُشْرِكُوا بِاللَّهِ مَا لَمْ يُنَزِّلْ بِهِ سُلْطَانًا وَأَنْ تَقُولُوا عَلَى اللَّهِ مَا لَا تَعْلَمُونَ

Say: 'Who has forbidden the fine clothing Allah has produced for His slaves and the good kinds of provision?' Say: 'On the Day of Rising such things will be exclusively for those who had īmān during their life in the dunyā.' In this way We make the Signs clear for people who know. Say: 'My Lord has forbidden indecency, both open and hidden, and wrong action, and unrightful tyranny, and associating anything with Allah for which He has sent down no authority, and saying things about Allah you do not know.' (Sūrat al-A^c^rāf 7: 32-33)

According to some people the basic principle in the matter of all restrictive ordinances is that a thing which is not disallowed is deemed to be lawful, as the well-known juridical dictum has it:

الْأَصْلُ فِي الْأَشْيَاءِ الْإِبَاحَةُ

The original situation with respect to things is that they are lawful.

In other words, everything is presumed to be lawful, unless it is definitely prohibited by law. This position is based on an interpretation of the following verse of the Noble Qur'ān:

هُوَ الَّذِي خَلَقَ لَكُم مَّا فِي الْأَرْضِ جَمِيعاً ثُمَّ اسْتَوَى إِلَى السَّمَاءِ فَسَوَّاهُنَّ سَبْعَ سَمَاوَاتٍ وَهُوَ بِكُلِّ شَيْءٍ عَلِيمٌ

It is He who created everything on the earth for you and then directed His attention up to heaven and arranged it into seven regular heavens. He has knowledge of all things. (Sūrat al-Baqarah 2: 29)

In which Allah says that He *"created everything on the earth for you"*. He, exalted is He, further says:

أَلَمْ تَرَوْا أَنَّ اللَّهَ سَخَّرَ لَكُم مَّا فِي السَّمَاوَاتِ وَمَا فِي الْأَرْضِ وَأَسْبَغَ عَلَيْكُمْ نِعَمَهُ ظَاهِرَةً وَبَاطِنَةً وَمِنَ النَّاسِ مَن يُجَادِلُ فِي اللَّهِ بِغَيْرِ عِلْمٍ وَلَا هُدًى وَلَا كِتَابٍ مُّنِيرٍ

Do you not see that Allah has subjected to you everything in the heavens and earth and has showered His blessings upon you, both outwardly and inwardly? Yet there are people who argue about Allah without knowledge or guidance or any illuminating Book. (Sūrah Luqmān 31: 20)

The position of the Muslims is, however, more complex than this. Imām al-Juwaynī, known as Imām al-Ḥaramayn, said in *al-Waraqāt,* his classic work on *uṣūl al-fiqh* (the principles of *fiqh*):

As for prohibition and permission, some people say that things are prohibited except for that which the *Sharīᶜah* permits, so that if there is nothing in the *Sharīᶜah* found to show permissibility one holds to the original situation which is prohibition. Some people say the opposite, which is that the basic situation is that things are permitted except for that which the *Sharīᶜah* prohibits.

Ibn Juzayy al-Kalbī said in *Taqrīb al-wuṣūl ilā ᶜilm al-uṣūl*:

According to al-Ashᶜarī there is that the *Sharīᶜah* is that which brings about [knowledge of] the good [*ḥalāl*] or the bad [*ḥarām*] in everything, and that no judgement is reliably established before the transmission of *Sharīᶜah* laws.

And al-Abhurī said that things, before the transmission of *Sharīᶜah*, are assumed to be prohibited, and Abu'l-Faraj said that they are assumed to be permitted, and everyone else hesitated over it.

Of all these bounties of Allah, the lawful and the unlawful are clearly shown, as the Prophet ﷺ is narrated to have said:

عَنْ أَبِي الدَّرْدَاءِ قَالَ: قَالَ رَسُولُ اللَّهِ ﷺ : ﴿مَا أَحَلَّ اللهُ فِي كِتَابِهِ فَهُوَ حَلَالٌ وَمَا حَرَّمَ هُوَ حَرَامٌ وَمَا سَكَتَ عَنْهُ فَهُوَ عَفْوٌ فَاقْبَلُوا مِنَ اللهِ عَافِيَتَهُ فَإِنَّ اللهَ لَمْ يَكُنْ لِيَنْسَى شَيْئًا﴾ ثُمَّ تَلَا ﴿وَمَا كَانَ رَبُّكَ نَسِيًّا﴾ .

From Abu'd-Dardā' there is that he said: The Messenger of Allah ﷺ said, "That which Allah declares *ḥalāl* in His Book is *ḥalāl*, and that which He declares *ḥarām* is *ḥarām*, and that about which He was silent then it is pardoned (*ᶜafw*), so accept from Allah His security, for Allah would not forget anything," and then he recited, "*Your Lord does not forget*. (Sūrah Maryam 19: 64)" (Al-Bazzār, and aṭ-Ṭabarānī in *al-Kabīr* as reported by al-Haythamī in *Majmaᶜ az-zawāʾid*)

Those things which are made unlawful are enumerated in detail in the Noble Qur'ān:

وَقَدْ فَصَّلَ لَكُمْ مَا حَرَّمَ عَلَيْكُمْ

He has made clear to you what He has made ḥarām for you. (Sūrat al-Anᶜām 6: 118)

Allah has fixed limits in respect of everything, and through the guidance of His Messenger ﷺ given in the Sunnah, and its transmission and explication by his Companions and their Followers, every aspect is fully explained to us. We are told not to enter into unnecessary discussion about those things which are not mentioned in detail. The Prophet ﷺ is narrated to have said:

إِنَّ اللَّهَ تَعَالَى حَدَّ حُدُودًا فَلَا تَعْتَدُوهَا ، وَفَرَضَ فَرَائِضَ فَلَا تُضَيِّعُوهَا ، وَحَرَّمَ أَشْيَاءَ فَلَا تَنْتَهِكُوهَا ، وَتَرَكَ أَشْيَاءَ مِنْ غَيْرِ نِسْيَانٍ مِنْ رَبِّكُمْ وَلَكِنْ رَحْمَةً مِنْهُ لَكُمْ فَاقْبَلُوهَا وَلَا تَبْحَثُوا عَنْهَا .

> Allah, exalted is He, has defined limits so do not transgress them, and has made obligations obligatory so do not waste them, and has made things *ḥarām* so do not violate them, and left some things, not out of forgetfulness on the part of your Lord, but rather as a mercy from Him to you, so accept them and do not investigate them. (Al-Ḥākim in *al-Mustadrak* from Abū Thaᶜlabah)

Banī Isrā'īl, according to the Noble Qur'ān, tried to find excuses in order to render lawful things that are unlawful. We should not invent pretexts to make lawful what is declared unlawful. It would be an act of *kufr* to do so since what is declared unlawful by Allah and His Messenger ﷺ will remain unlawful till the Last Day.

What is unlawful for a pauper is equally unlawful for a caliph, king, emperor, or ruler. What is unlawful for an imām is also unlawful for his follower. There is no double-standard in the *Sharīᶜah* of Islam. Arabs and non-Arabs are equal before the law, and that which is *ḥarām* for one will always remain *ḥarām* for others.

Not only does the *Sharīᶜah* declare it unlawful to steal from Muslims, it is equally unlawful to steal from non-Muslims. Stolen property, whether taken from a Muslim or non-Muslim, remains unlawful, whoever the taker. This is contrary to the deviation that happened among Banī Isrā'īl, about which Allah tells us:

ذَلِكَ بِأَنَّهُمْ قَالُوا لَيْسَ عَلَيْنَا فِي الْأُمِّيِّينَ سَبِيلٌ وَيَقُولُونَ عَلَى اللَّهِ الْكَذِبَ وَهُمْ يَعْلَمُونَ

> *That is because they say, 'We are under no obligation where the gentiles are concerned.' They tell a lie against Allah and they know it.* (Sūrah Āl ᶜImrān 3: 75)

Banī Isrā'īl were told not to catch fish on the Sabbath, then they tried to change what was *ḥarām* but they were only deceiving themselves. They used to dig ditches on Friday so that fish might accumulate in them and then they could collect them on Sunday. To fabricate devices and tricks (*ḥiyal*) is unlawful in the *Sharīᶜah* of Islam.

It is unfortunate that some among the Muslims have begun to follow in the footsteps of the Jews by finding flimsy excuses to make lawful what is already declared unlawful in the Book and the Sunnah. The two most attractive things for such people in modern times are alcohol and usury. With respect to alcohol, they have found attractive names for various drinks and taken up drinking. Thus the prophecy of the Messenger of Allah ﷺ is confirmed in modern times:

عَنْ عُبَادَةَ بْنِ الصَّامِتِ قَالَ: قَالَ رَسُولُ اللَّهِ ﷺ : ﴿لَيَسْتَحِلَّنَّ طَائِفَةٌ مِنْ أُمَّتِي الْخَمْرَ بِاسْمٍ يُسَمُّونَهَا إِيَّاهُ﴾ .

From ᶜUbādah ibn aṣ-Ṣāmit there is that he said: The Messenger of Allah ﷺ said, "A party of my *Ummah* will try to make wine *ḥalāl* by means of a name with which they name it." (Aḥmad in his *Musnad)*

Likewise, he has said about usury something that has come true today:

يَأْتِي عَلَى النَّاسِ زَمَانٌ يَسْتَحِلُّونَ الرِّبَا بِاسْمِ الْبَيْعِ

There will come a time when people will declare usury lawful under the name of trade. (*Ighāthan al-Lahfan,* vol. 1, p. 352 10)

And this is echoed in the *āyah* in which He, exalted is He, says:

ذَلِكَ بِأَنَّهُمْ قَالُوا إِنَّمَا الْبَيْعُ مِثْلُ الرِّبَا

That is because they say, 'Trade is the same as ribā.' (Sūrat al-Baqarah 2: 274)

No matter how well-intentioned one might think oneself to be, changing the name does not transform an unlawful act into a lawful one, or vice-versa.

Similarly the means leading to something *ḥarām* is also itself *ḥarām* in Islam. Anything that facilitates or leads to an act of adultery, theft, brigandage or murder, is also *ḥarām*. One who brews, sells and distributes wine is committing as *ḥarām* an act as the person who drinks the alcohol, and in fact he is more wrongdoing since his act leads more than one person to do something *ḥarām*, whereas the solitary drinker only destroys himself. A witness to a usurious contract, an agent, the lender and borrower of money on usurious terms are also committing unlawful acts.

Between the categories of clearly lawful and unlawful, there are things which are of doubtful nature. As a matter of *taqwā* and scrupulousness (*waraᶜ*) one should keep away from them. The Prophet ﷺ advised:

عَنِ النُّعْمَانِ بْنِ بَشِيرٍ قَالَ: سَمِعْتُهُ يَقُولُ سَمِعْتُ رَسُولَ اللَّهِ ﷺ يَقُولُ: ﴿إِنَّ الْحَلالَ بَيِّنٌ وَإِنَّ الْحَرَامَ بَيِّنٌ وَبَيْنَهُمَا مُشْتَبِهَاتٌ لا يَعْلَمُهُنَّ كَثِيرٌ مِنَ النَّاسِ، فَمَنِ اتَّقَى الشُّبُهَاتِ اسْتَبْرَأَ لِدِينِهِ وَعِرْضِهِ، وَمَنْ وَقَعَ فِي الشُّبُهَاتِ وَقَعَ فِي الْحَرَامِ، كَالرَّاعِي يَرْعَى حَوْلَ الْحِمَى، يُوشِكُ أَنْ يَرْتَعَ فِيهِ، أَلَا وَإِنَّ لِكُلِّ مَلِكٍ حِمًى، أَلَا وَإِنَّ حِمَى اللَّهِ مَحَارِمُهُ﴾.

From Abū ᶜAbdullāh an-Nuᶜmān ibn Bashīr ؓ, there is that he said: I heard the Messenger of Allah ﷺ saying, "The *ḥalāl* is clear and the *ḥarām* is clear and in between them are ambivalent matters which many people do not know. Whoever guards himself against ambivalent matters has secured his *dīn* and his honour. Whoever falls into ambivalent matters will fall into the *ḥarām*, just as the shepherd who shepherds [his flock] around forbidden pasturage is certain to pasture [his flock] in it. Certainly, every king has his forbidden pasturage. Certainly, Allah's forbidden pasturage is the things he has forbidden." (Al-Bukhārī, *bāb faḍl man istabra'a li dīnihi,* and Muslim, *bāb akhdh al-ḥalāl wa tark ash-shubuhāt*)

There are moments in a man's life when he finds himself at the very limit of his resources. He may be so very destitute that he may not be able to get lawful bread. In spite of all his efforts, he might not find a job. Surely, in such circumstances, it is his Muslim neighbours and the entire Muslim society which has really failed him in spite of the *zakāh* and *ṣadaqah* in Islam. How is it possible for someone to remain hungry in an Islamic society? In case, someone finds himself in an utterly helpless situation and his wife and children are facing starvation, he may, out of necessity, partake of what is clearly declared unlawful (*ḥarām*). This is more evident in the case where someone may be travelling far from civilisation in waste lands or deserts and finds nothing *ḥalāl* to eat and is in danger of starving to death. This rule applies to other human necessities as well:

فَمَنِ اضْطُرَّ غَيْرَ بَاغٍ وَلَا عَادٍ فَلَا إِثْمَ عَلَيْهِ إِنَّ اللَّهَ غَفُورٌ رَحِيمٌ

But anyone who is forced to eat it – without desiring it or going to excess in it – commits no crime. Allah is Ever-Forgiving, Most Merciful. (Sūrat al-Baqarah 2: 173)

Injunctions in Respect of *Ḥalāl* and *Ḥarām* Food

A *mu'min,* that is, a believer, is someone who willingly accepts Allah as his Creator and accepts obedience to Allah and His Messenger ﷺ as his mode of life, striving to seek His pleasure in all his actions in this world. A *mu'min* also believes that another life is coming after the present mundane existence. He also believes in the Day of Judgement and that whoever has a pure *tawḥīd* and obeys the commands of Allah and His Prophet ﷺ is sure to have a good life in the hereafter and that whoever is a *kāfir* and violates these commands will bear eternal punishment, and that those who, while having pure *tawḥīd,* still do serious wrong actions will finally enter the Garden either forgiven by Allah for their misdeeds or purified by the terrible punishment of the Fire.

A believer is not left without guidance. The Qur'ān and the Sunnah have values and norms for all actions, even eating and drinking. In the Noble Qur'ān Allah says that one should: *"eat what is good and lawful on the earth."*

أَيُّهَا النَّاسُ كُلُوا مِمَّا فِي الْأَرْضِ حَلَالًا طَيِّبًا وَلَا تَتَّبِعُوا خُطُوَاتِ الشَّيْطَانِ إِنَّهُ لَكُمْ عَدُوٌّ مُبِينٌ

Mankind! eat what is good and lawful on the earth. And do not follow in the footsteps of Shaytan. He truly is an outright enemy to you. (Sūrat al-Baqarah 2: 168)

In this verse, there is a general instruction given to all mankind concerning food and drink irrespective of whether they are Muslims, people of the Book (Jews and Christians), pagans, Buddhists, humanists or atheists. The Creator tells all creatures to follow His command and eat what is pure, clean, wholesome, nourishing and pleasing to the taste. All these qualities are beautifully summed up in the word *tayyib* in the above verse of the Qur'ān. The injunction contained in this verse is that the *jāhiliyyah* practices dating from before the dawn of Islam must be rejected. All restrictions they had wrongly imposed upon themselves should be broken since they are based on superstition. Whatever they have made lawful or unlawful is from their own imagination, and is the handiwork of shayṭān.

The pagan Arab custom of eating congealed blood is an example of such a custom. It was the blood of a sacrificed animal that they used to smear on the walls of the Kaᶜbah and which they used to eat fried as a delicacy.

Injustice

It must be noted, however, that of more importance in this argument is the exercise of justice and mercy, for it is very easy for the matter of *ḥalāl* and *ḥarām* to take on a religious and ritualistic quality as is the case with the kosher requirements of the Jews. In the slaughter of animals it is the Islamic method outlined below that is a mercy to the animal and a just way to take its life.

Food that is acquired through some injustice to other people is equally as *ḥarām* as meat that has been slaughtered contrary to the *Sharīᶜah*. It means that food is *ḥarām* or deeply abhorrent which is bought with proceeds taken from people against their will, as in the case of taxes taken from an unwilling population,[1] or property that has been expropriated by the state or anyone else such as banks illegally, and anything earned in a usurious transaction, since this latter is also an unjust way of acquiring wealth.

Emphasis on eating of the good things (*ṭayyib*) is given in verse 172 of Sūrat al-Baqarah:

يَا أَيُّهَا الَّذِينَ آمَنُوا كُلُوا مِن طَيِّبَاتِ مَا رَزَقْنَاكُمْ وَاشْكُرُوا لِلَّهِ إِن كُنتُمْ إِيَّاهُ تَعْبُدُونَ

> *You who have īmān! eat of the good things We have provided for you and give thanks to Allah if you worship Him alone.* (Sūrat al-Baqarah 2: 172)

The above verse is particularly addressed to the believers who have faith in Allah and His Messenger ﷺ. We are told to eat of the good things and be grateful to Him, since gratitude for Allah's gifts is a high form of worship (*ᶜibādah*). Those who have faith have been told that if by accepting Islam, they have accepted the Divine law just as they claimed, then they should shun all the superstitious beliefs and the restrictions on certain foods of the days of the *jāhiliyyah* period. These were not ordained by Allah but by the Qurashī pagan priests, Jewish rabbis and monks. The Prophet's hadith ﷺ on the same subject:

عَنْ أَنَسِ بْنِ مَالِكٍ قَالَ: قَالَ رَسُولُ اللَّهِ صَلَّى اللَّهُ عَلَيْهِ وَسَلَّمَ مَنْ صَلَّى صَلَاتَنَا وَاسْتَقْبَلَ قِبْلَتَنَا

وَأَكَلَ ذَبِيحَتَنَا فَذَلِكَ الْمُسْلِمُ الَّذِي لَهُ ذِمَّةُ اللَّهِ وَذِمَّةُ رَسُولِهِ فَلَا تُخْفِرُوا اللَّهَ فِي ذِمَّتِهِ

> It is narrated from Anas ibn Mālik ؓ who said: The Messenger of Allah ﷺ said, "Whoever prays our prayer and faces our *qiblah* and eats our slaughtered meat, that is the Muslim who has the covenant of Allah and the covenant of His Messenger, so do not be treacherous towards Allah in respect of His covenant." (al-Bukhārī, *bāb faḍl istiqbāl al-qiblah)*

We can deduce from the above *ḥadīth* that a man who prays and faces the *qiblah* does not absorb himself completely in the *Ummah* of Islam until he leaves *jāhiliyyah* practices concerning food and drink and is free from the superstitions of his forefathers. If he continues with past practices in spite of the fact that he prays facing the Kaᶜbah he is not a complete Muslim.

The following Qur'ānic injunctions explain clearly the foods which are unwholesome physically, morally and spiritually:

إِنَّمَا حَرَّمَ عَلَيْكُمُ الْمَيْتَةَ وَالدَّمَ وَلَحْمَ الْخِنزِيرِ وَمَا أُهِلَّ بِهِ لِغَيْرِ اللَّهِ فَمَنِ اضْطُرَّ غَيْرَ بَاغٍ وَلَا عَادٍ فَلَا إِثْمَ عَلَيْهِ إِنَّ اللَّهَ غَفُورٌ رَحِيمٌ

He has only forbidden you carrion, blood and pork and what has been consecrated to other than Allah. But anyone who is forced to eat it – without desiring it or going to excess in it – commits no crime. Allah is Ever-Forgiving, Most Merciful. (Sūrat al-Baqarah 2: 173)

When one is forced by necessity and eats unlawful food without wilful disobedience to the injunctions of Allah concerning foods and drinks, then he is guiltless. Howver, in this verse, the permission for the use of unlawful things is given conditionally. The following three conditions should be kept in mind:

1. The man who ventures to eat the unlawful must really be in a helpless state and driven by utter necessity to save his life and that of his dependants, for example, on account of hunger or thirst his life is in danger and there is nothing available except unlawful food, or due to illness, there was no way of saving his life except eating that food as a remedy.
2. There is absolutely no intention to break the law of Allah in eating unlawful food but he is driven by necessity.
3. Even if one has to eat unlawful food out of utter necessity, more of it than is ncessary should not be taken. It is said by the *fuqahā'* that the man in the desert forced to eat carrion, must eat and eat well and take some with him for his journey, in order to get back to where there is *ḥalāl* food. However, if a few morsels of *ḥarām* food or a little drink of some *ḥarām* fluid can save one's life, more than that quantity of it should not be consumed.

حُرِّمَتْ عَلَيْكُمُ الْمَيْتَةُ وَالدَّمُ وَلَحْمُ الْخِنزِيرِ وَمَا أُهِلَّ لِغَيْرِ اللَّهِ بِهِ وَالْمُنْخَنِقَةُ وَالْمَوْقُوذَةُ وَالْمُتَرَدِّيَةُ وَالنَّطِيحَةُ وَمَا أَكَلَ السَّبُعُ إِلَّا مَا ذَكَّيْتُمْ وَمَا ذُبِحَ عَلَى النُّصُبِ وَأَن تَسْتَقْسِمُوا بِالْأَزْلَامِ ذَٰلِكُمْ فِسْقٌ

Ḥarām for you are carrion, blood and pork, and what has been consecrated to other than Allah, and animals which have been strangled, and animals which have been killed by a blow, and animals which have fallen to their death, and animals which have been gored, and animals which wild beasts have eaten – except those you are able to slaughter properly – and animals which have been sacrificed on altars, and deciding things by means of divining arrows – that is deviance. (Sūrat al-Mā'idah 5: 3)

In Sūrat al-Anᶜām, the foods which are declared unlawful are mentioned in the following verses:

وَلَا تَأْكُلُوا مِمَّا لَمْ يُذْكَرِ اسْمُ اللَّهِ عَلَيْهِ وَإِنَّهُ لَفِسْقٌ وَإِنَّ الشَّيَاطِينَ لَيُوحُونَ إِلَى أَوْلِيَائِهِمْ لِيُجَادِلُوكُمْ وَإِنْ أَطَعْتُمُوهُمْ إِنَّكُمْ لَمُشْرِكُونَ

Do not eat anything over which the name of Allah has not been mentioned. To do so is sheer deviance. The shayṭāns inspire their friends to dispute with you. If you obeyed them you would then be mushrikūn. (Sūrat al-Anᶜām 6: 121)

قُلْ لَا أَجِدُ فِي مَا أُوحِيَ إِلَيَّ مُحَرَّمًا عَلَى طَاعِمٍ يَطْعَمُهُ إِلَّا أَنْ يَكُونَ مَيْتَةً أَوْ دَمًا مَسْفُوحًا أَوْ لَحْمَ خِنْزِيرٍ فَإِنَّهُ رِجْسٌ أَوْ فِسْقًا أُهِلَّ لِغَيْرِ اللَّهِ بِهِ فَمَنِ اضْطُرَّ غَيْرَ بَاغٍ وَلَا عَادٍ فَإِنَّ رَبَّكَ غَفُورٌ رَحِيمٌ

Say: 'I do not find, in what has been revealed to me, any food it is ḥarām to eat except for carrion, flowing blood, and pork – for that is unclean – or some deviance consecrated to other than Allah. But if anyone is forced to eat it, without desiring to or going to excess in it, your Lord is Ever-Forgiving, Most Merciful.' (Sūrat al-Anᶜām 6: 145)

And speaking about some of the people who were given the Book before the Muslims and their *Sharīᶜah*, Allah, exalted is He, says:

وَعَلَى الَّذِينَ هَادُوا حَرَّمْنَا كُلَّ ذِي ظُفُرٍ وَمِنَ الْبَقَرِ وَالْغَنَمِ حَرَّمْنَا عَلَيْهِمْ شُحُومَهُمَا إِلَّا مَا حَمَلَتْ ظُهُورُهُمَا أَوِ الْحَوَايَا أَوْ مَا اخْتَلَطَ بِعَظْمٍ ذَلِكَ جَزَيْنَاهُمْ بِبَغْيِهِمْ وَإِنَّا لَصَادِقُونَ

We made ḥarām for the Jews every animal with an undivided hoof, and in respect of cattle and sheep, We made their fat ḥarām for them, except what is attached to their backs or guts or mixed up with bone. That is how We repaid them for their insolence. And We certainly speak the truth. (Sūrat al-Anᶜām 6: 146)

From the above Qur'ānic injunctions it is clear that a Muslim must abstain from eating the following kinds of foods:

1. PORK

The pig is an animal whose habits – such as eating excrement and, on occasion, its own young – are well known. When one sees them in those conditions, it makes their flesh repulsive. Moreover, eating the flesh of swine can become a cause of various medical conditions. The ancient Egyptians and Phoenicians as well as the Jews regarded swine as unclean as is mentioned by Hastings in his *Dictionary of the Bible* (Vol. iv. p. 633).

The Bible's abhorrence of swine is clear no matter what may be the practice of the modern 'Christian' world. The flesh and blood of swine are characteristically described as repulsive. "And the swine ... he is unclean to you." 'And the swine ... It is unclean to you; ye shall not eat of their flesh, nor touch their dead carcase." (Deuteronomy: 14: 8) There are similar references in Mark: 11-12 and Matthew: 7-6.

The Noble Qur'ān refers to swine as *khinzīr* which when applied to anything other than the animal itself is a term of contempt just as is true in English of the word 'swine' as applied to 'a low, greedy or vicious person' (*New Standard Dictionary of English Language*, New York). The *Shorter Oxford Dictionary* describes 'swine' as "applied opprobriously to a sexual, degraded or coarse person; also (in mod. use) as a mere term of contempt or abuse," and 'swinish' is explained as 'coarse, gross or degraded in nature'. (*Shorter Oxford Dictionary*, 3rd edition, with corrections 1969) The word 'pig' is applied to a person who is selfish, mean, unclean and degenerate.

For a believer (*mu'min*) all the above explanations are unnecessary since he firmly believes in the commands of the

Qur'ān which categorically forbid the eating of the flesh of swine (pork, bacon, or ham).

2. *MAYTAH* – CARRION

For a Muslim, eating the carcase of anything that has died a natural death or been killed in some way that is contrary to the *Sharīᶜah* method of slaughter is forbidden. The Noble Qur'ān describes this in the word *maytah.*

3. BLOOD POURED FROM AN ANIMAL BY FORCE

Eating and drinking blood is also forbidden. Some people like to collect blood and boil it and turn it into a cake looking like liver and then eat it. In Britain this is called 'black pudding'. This is forbidden.

4. THE FLESH OF A STRANGLED ANIMAL

The flesh of any animal that is strangled to death is forbidden for a Muslim.

5. THE FLESH OF AN ANIMAL BEATEN TO DEATH

The flesh of an animal beaten to death is also forbidden.

6. THE FLESH OF AN ANIMAL THAT DIES IN A FALL.

If an animal dies through falling from a height, its flesh is forbidden for a Muslim.

7. THE FLESH OF AN ANIMAL THAT IS GORED TO DEATH

If an animal is gored to death during a fight with another animal, its flesh is forbidden for a Muslim.

8. THE FLESH OF AN ANIMAL A PART OF WHICH IS EATEN BY A WILD BEAST

If a part of the flesh of an animal is eaten by a wild animal it is forbidden for a Muslim. This is also highly unhygienic.

9. The flesh of an animal that dies a natural death

If an animal dies through sickness or otherwise, its flesh is also forbidden for a Muslim.

10. The flesh of an animal slaughtered for worship of an idol.

Islam is purely the *dīn* of *tawḥīd* and any form of *shirk* is considered as the greatest of wrong actions. The Noble Qur'ān says that an animal which is slaughtered in the name of any idol or in the name of anything other than Allah is forbidden for a Muslim. This means that the animal is slaughtered for the worship of an entity whose name is recited while slaughtering it.

According to the Sunnah of the Prophet ﷺ, a Muslim should say *Bismilllāh Allāhu Akbar* "In the name of Allah, Allah is greater" while slaughtering an animal.

With the exception of fish and locusts, no animals are lawful unless they are slaughtered according to the Islamic law namely by drawing the knife across the throat and cutting the jugular vein and wind-pipe, repeating at the same time the phrase mentioned above. *Dhabḥ* (sacrifice) is of two kinds:

Dhabḥ ikhtiyārī: This is the intentional slaughter of an animal reciting the name of Allah while drawing the knife across its throat.

Dhabḥ iḍtirārī: This is the slaughter through necessity affected by wounds as in the shooting of birds and animals. In this case the phrase *Bismilllāh Allāhu Akbar* must be said at the time of the discharge of the arrow from its bow, the bullet from the gun or the release of a hunting dog or falcon.

11. Beasts of Prey with Canine Teeth

Abū Thaclabah said:

عَنْ أَبِي ثَعْلَبَةَ رَضِيَ اللّٰهُ عَنْهُ أَنَّ رَسُولَ اللّٰهِ صَلَّى اللّٰهُ عَلَيْهِ وَسَلَّمَ نَهَى عَنْ أَكْلِ كُلِّ ذِي نَابٍ مِنَ السِّبَاعِ

> From Abū Thaᶜlabah ﷺ there is that the Messenger of Allah ﷺ forbade the eating of wild animals possessing canine teeth. (Al-Bukhārī, *bāb akl kulli dhī nāb min as-sibāᶜ*)

According to many other *ḥadīth,* birds of prey with claws or talons are also included in the above, for example:

عَنْ عَلِيٍّ قَالَ: ﴿ نَهَى رَسُولُ اللَّهِ ﷺ عَنْ كُلِّ ذِي نَابٍ مِنَ السِّبَاعِ وَعَنْ كُلِّ ذِي مِخْلَبٍ مِنَ الطَّيْرِ ﴾ .

> From ᶜAlī there is that he said: "The Messenger of Allah ﷺ forbade every fanged wild animal and every taloned bird." (Aḥmad, Abū Yaᶜlā and aṭ-Ṭaḥāwī, as cited in *Kanz al-ᶜummāl*)

Animals like the domestic donkey are also forbidden according to *ḥadīth.*

According to *al-Hidāyah,* all quadrupeds which seize their prey with their teeth and all birds that seize it with their talons are unlawful for Muslims in normal circumstances.

It is lawful to make use of the wool and hair of a dead animal. Similarly, it is lawful to make use of that which is removed from animals while they are alive. But what is considered better in the Mālikī view, is for such things to be washed first, before they are used.

It is not lawful to make use of the feathers of a dead bird, its beak, its nails and teeth. It is reprehensible to use the tusks of the elephant, but, there are conflicting views with regards to this.

If a mouse falls into a quantity of butter, or oil or honey, all of which are in liquid form, and dies in it; it must be thrown away, and must not be eaten. However, there is no harm in using the oil, or something of that sort in which a mouse dies, for example, as fuel for a lamp but only in places other than mosques. Mosques must be free from anything mixed with something unclean.

If however, the butter, the oil or honey, were in a solid state, the dead mouse and the butter, oil or honey around it should be thrown away, and the remainder may be used for food. Ṣaḥnūn, one of the most famous Mālikī jurists, is of the opinion that, if the dead mouse, had been in the foodstuff for a long time, it must be thrown away.[2]

Hunting for the purpose of sport alone is detestable in the eyes of *Sharīᶜah,* but hunting for a purpose other than sport is lawful. If a trained dog or a trained falcon, is set upon any kind of game, animal or bird, whose flesh is lawful, the game is lawful as food for consumption.

It is lawful to eat the flesh of the game your falcon or dog has brought you, the prey being already dead, without your having been able to slaughter it in the normal Islamic way.

Any game you are able to bring down, whether by bullet, arrow or spear, you are free to eat its flesh. If you are able to take hold of it before it is dead, you can then slaughter it in the normal way. However, if it dies before you are able to slaughter it, you can nevertheless eat its meat if it has indeed been killed by your bullet, arrow or spear. If the hunter finds the game already dead, his arrow having hit a vital spot, there is no harm in eating the flesh of such game.[3]

If one slaughters an animal for the purpose of sacrifice or another purpose and forgets to pronounce the formula: *Bismilllāh Allāhu Akbar* "In the name of Allah, Allah is greater", it is permissible for such an animal to be eaten. However, if one omits to pronounce it deliberately, the animal thus slaughtered must not be eaten.

Similarly, the hunter who forgets to pronounce the *Bismilllāh Allāhu Akbar* at the time he lets loose the falcon or dog after the game, the flesh of such game can be eaten by Muslims. If, however, he deliberately omits to pronounce the formula, the flesh of the game thus killed is not wholesome.

An animal killed sacrificially on the occasion of *ᶜĪd al-Kabīr,* or for the purpose of making expiation for an error in the rites of *Hajj,* or slaughtered on the occasion of naming a child, must not have any part of it sold.

A man is permitted to eat the flesh of the animal he has slaughtered as a sacrifice on the occasion of *ᶜĪd al-Kabīr,* but it is better for him to give away part of it as *ṣadaqah,* though this is not obligatory.

A pilgrim must not eat the flesh of an animal he slaughters for the purpose of making a sacrifice to atone for an error he committed in the *Hajj* rites, nor does he eat of the flesh of the animal he slaughters to compensate for game he has killed while in a state of *iḥrām*. Neither should he eat the flesh of an animal he has vowed to slaughter for the sake of the poor.[4]

Notes

[1] The *ṣāliḥūn* and *ᶜulamā'* used to avoid funds that came from the ruler lest they may have been taken, wittingly or unwittingly from people against their will, or may have come from the *zakāh* and been diverted from its proper purpose, or derived from illegal extra taxation above and beyond the *zakāh*.
[2] Ibn Abī Zayd al-Qayrawānī, *Risālah, Op. Cit.* Ch. 29
[3] Ibn Abī Zayd al-Qayrawānī, *Risālah*, Zaria, 1976, see Chapter 29 *Bāb fi'l-ḍaḥāyā wa'dh-dhabā'iḥ*. pp. 78-83 22. *Ibid*
[4] *Ibid.*

Part III
Family Relations

Chapter 9

Az-Zawāj: Marriage

The purpose of marriage

ALLAH CREATED MEN AND WOMEN FOR THEM to provide company for one another, love one another, procreate and live in peace and tranquillity obeying the commands of Allah and the direction of his Messenger ﷺ. In the Qur'ān, Allah, exalted is He, says:

وَمِنْ آيَاتِهِ أَنْ خَلَقَ لَكُم مِّنْ أَنفُسِكُمْ أَزْوَاجاً لِّتَسْكُنُوا إِلَيْهَا وَجَعَلَ بَيْنَكُم مَّوَدَّةً وَرَحْمَةً إِنَّ فِي ذَلِكَ لَآيَاتٍ لِّقَوْمٍ يَتَفَكَّرُونَ

Among His Signs is that He created spouses for you of your own kind so that you might find tranquility in them. And He has placed affection and compassion between you. There are certainly Signs in that for people who reflect. (Sūrat ar-Rūm 30: 21)

In the Qur'ān Allah further says:

وَاللَّهُ جَعَلَ لَكُم مِّنْ أَنفُسِكُمْ أَزْوَاجاً وَجَعَلَ لَكُم مِّنْ أَزْوَاجِكُم بَنِينَ وَحَفَدَةً وَرَزَقَكُم مِّنَ الطَّيِّبَاتِ

Allah has given you wives from among yourselves, and given you children and grandchildren from your wives, and provided good things for you. (Sūrat an-Naḥl 16: 72)

Apart from the Book of Allah, there are many traditions of the Prophet Muhammad ﷺ which further explain the Islamic institution of marriage. The traditional saying, 'There is no monasticism in Islam' can perhaps be interpreted to the contrary in the light of the numerous *ḥadīth* of the Prophet ﷺ in which he defined the monasticism of Islam as *ribāṭ* or *jihād*, as for example when he said to ᶜUthmān ibn Maẓᶜūn:

يَا عُثْمَانُ هَلْ تَدْرِي مَا رَهْبَانِيَّةُ الإِسْلامِ؟ الْجِهَادُ فِي سَبِيلِ اللَّهِ

ᶜUthmān! Do you know what the monasticism of Islam is? It is *jihād* in the way of Allah. (Al-Bayhaqī in *Shuᶜab al-īmān*, ch. 70, *fī aṣ-ṣabr ᶜalā al-maṣā'ib wa ᶜammā tanziᶜu ilayhi an-nafs min laddhatin ma shahwah*)

Celibacy is not considered a virtue in Islam or taken as a means of getting closer to Allah as is done in other religions like Christianity, Buddhism and Jainism, etc. The Prophet ﷺ advised:

يَا مَعْشَرَ الشَّبَابِ! مَنِ اسْتَطَاعَ مِنكُمُ الْبَاءَةَ فَلْيَتَزَوَّجْ، فَإِنَّهُ أَغَضُّ لِلْبَصَرِ وَأَحْصَنُ لِلْفَرْجِ

Young men! whoever of you is able to marry, should marry, for that will help him to lower his gaze and guard his private parts. (Al-Bukhārī, *bāb qawl an-nabiyyi ṣalla'llāhu ᶜalayhi wa sallama man istaṭāᶜa minkum fa'lyatazawwaj*)

It means it will help him to be modest and the Prophet ﷺ referred to modesty as a 'part of *īmān*:'

الْحَيَاءُ مِنَ الإِيمَانِ

Modesty is part of *īmān*. (Al-Bukhārī, *bāb al-ḥayā'*)

In order to achieve modesty and complete one's *īmān*, marriage is prescribed by the Messenger of Allah ﷺ:

النِّكَاحُ سُنَّتِي فَمَنْ لَمْ يَعْمَلْ بِسُنَّتِي فَلَيْسَ مِنِّي

Marriage is my Sunnah; so whoever does not practice my Sunnah is not of me. (Ibn Mājah from ᶜĀ'ishah ؓ, *bāb mā jā'a bi faḍl an-nikāḥ*)

With these Qur'ānic injunctions and the guidance of the Prophet ﷺ in mind, we shall examine the institution of marriage in *Sharīᶜah*.

The word *zawj* is used in the Qur'ān for one of a pair, a spouse or a mate; in common usage it connotes a married person. Another usage is for species:

أَوَلَمْ يَرَوْا إِلَى الْأَرْضِ كَمْ أَنبَتْنَا فِيهَا مِن كُلِّ زَوْجٍ كَرِيمٍ

Have they not looked at the earth and seen how We have made every sort of beneficial species grow in it? (Sūrat ash-Shuʿarāʾ 26: 7)

Allah informs us in the Qurʾān that even in the Garden we shall have mates.

وَلَهُمْ فِيهَا أَزْوَاجٌ مُطَهَّرَةٌ

They will have there spouses of perfect purity. (Sūrat al-Baqarah 2: 24)

Allah created humans from one self, Adam (the first male), from which He created Eve (Ḥawā the first female). However, the story of creating Eve from a rib of Adam is not mentioned in the Qurʾān although there are references to that in some *ḥadīth*.

يَا أَيُّهَا النَّاسُ اتَّقُوا رَبَّكُمُ الَّذِي خَلَقَكُم مِّن نَّفْسٍ وَاحِدَةٍ وَخَلَقَ مِنْهَا زَوْجَهَا وَبَثَّ مِنْهُمَا رِجَالًا كَثِيرًا وَنِسَاءً

O mankind! have taqwā of your Lord who created you from a single self and created its mate from it and then disseminated many men and women from the two of them. (Sūrat an-Nisāʾ 4: 1)

The Prophet ﷺ ordered Muslims to marry as soon as they are able. The family is a key element of Islamic society, and marriage is the way in Islam to bring about such an institution. Extra-marital relations are categorically prohibited except for a man's relations with his slave women.

وَلَا تَقْرَبُوا الزِّنَى إِنَّهُ كَانَ فَاحِشَةً وَسَاءَ سَبِيلًا

And do not go near to fornication. It is an indecent act, an evil way. (Sūrat al-Isrāʾ 17: 32)

It is only logical that in Islam it is Allah Who sets up rules to regulate the functioning of the family whereby both spouses can find peace, love, security and intimacy. These elements are necessary for accomplishing the greatest purpose of marriage: the worship of Allah (*ᶜibādah*). Just as marriage does not merely mean having sex with your spouse, so worship does not only mean the performance of rituals but also essentially implies right action in all transactional behaviour. The concept of *ᶜibādah* is very wide. Every good deed, every service to humanity, every useful productive effort, every good word, and even a Muslim couple's love-making is a part of true worship of the Creator if one intends it thus. If both husband and wife observe this main purpose, this cardinal purpose of their union, they will easily learn how to help each other achieve this goal – a goal greater than and beyond themselves. They would learn how to tolerate each other, how to overcome their difficulties and their shortcomings and how to love one another for the sake of Allah.

The second purpose of marriage is to respond to the basic biological instinct of procreation. Children are the realisation of motherhood and fatherhood. Muslims are particular in providing the most wholesome atmosphere possible for bringing up offspring. To give birth to children and neglect them is a crime toward society, towards the children, and even towards the parents themselves. A child who is deprived of the ample love of his or her parents, and not properly enfolded in an Islamic way of life at an early age, and left to baby-sitters and nurseries may never find their identity which they should have developed in a consistent manner during their childhood. Without a family life governed by Islam, how can we expect a child to have a Muslim conscience, Islamic values and right action?

The *Sharīᶜah* has prescribed clear rights and obligations on parents and their offspring. Parents are legally responsible for the education and maintenance of their children. These in turn, are legally responsible for accommodating and maintaining their parents, if they so require, in their old age. Both parents and children inherit from each other according to the law of *mīrāth* (inheritance) specified in the Qur'ān and elaborated in considerable detail in the Sunnah and the works of *fiqh*. Neither of them is permitted to deprive the other of their respective shares in the legacy.

This is only one part of the large family code of Islam. What is of importance here is the husband-wife relationship – their roles within the context of the understanding of the pivotal verses from Sūrat ar-Rūm cited above.

Apart from the importance of the values of rest, peace, love, and mercy, Islam does not stop there. Its original concept of the family is bolstered by recognising the roles of men and women as being that each acts in accordance with his or her biological condition. The man, with his strength and aggression, attends to what are called the 'instrumental' functions: maintenance, protection, dealings with matters of the world outside the home and leadership within the family. The woman attends to caring for and rearing the children, organising the home, and creating its loving atmosphere. Wives may not be forced by their husbands to work for money, but work and trade are not prohibited to women in *Sharīᶜah* provided they do so with modesty and with the permission of their husbands. They are not recommended to undertake such activities unless there is a justification for them to go to work and it should be done without prejudice to their husbands' rights. Once a woman marries, she is bound by the Islamic ruling on the functioning of the family. If she has her own property or fortune, and if she opts to use or invest such wealth she is entitled to do so without her husband's permission, provided this does not impinge upon her marital obligations, and her responsibilities to her children. Therefore, marriage in Islam broadly speaking is:

a. a means of emotional and sexual gratification
b. a mechanism for reducing tension
c. a means of legitimate procreation
d. social placement
e. an approach to inter-family alliance and group solidarity
f. an act of *taqwā*

g. a form of *^cibādah*, i.e. worship of Allah and obedience to His Messenger ﷺ.

The above definitions and purposes are quite elaborate and comprise many views about functions in the family. Nevertheless, there is an intricate cause and effect relationship between the family and society.

Islam is an integral whole and Muslims are supposed to adopt it in its entirety.

أَفَتُؤْمِنُونَ بِبَعْضِ الْكِتَابِ وَتَكْفُرُونَ بِبَعْضٍ فَمَا جَزَاءُ مَنْ يَفْعَلُ ذَلِكَ مِنْكُمْ إِلَّا خِزْيٌ فِي الْحَيَاةِ الدُّنْيَا وَيَوْمَ الْقِيَامَةِ يُرَدُّونَ إِلَى أَشَدِّ الْعَذَابِ

Do you, then, believe in one part of the Book and reject the other? What repayment will there be for any of you who do that except disgrace in the dunyā? And on the Day of Rising, they will be returned to the harshest of punishments. (Sūrat al-Baqarah 2: 85)

From the foregoing discussion it becomes clear that in the *Sharī^cah* celibacy is not recommended and that it is enjoined upon Muslims to marry. The purpose of marriage in Islam, as we have seen, is not mere carnal pleasure but the establishment of an institution wherein men and women procreate in order to preserve the human race and satisfy normal sexual urges in security, comfort and happiness, and whereby they may guard themselves against lewdness and indecency.

Is marriage obligatory?

According to Imams Abū Ḥanīfah, Aḥmad ibn Ḥanbal and Mālik ibn Anas although marriage in its origin may be deemed to be recommended, for certain individuals it becomes obligatory (*wājib*).[1]

However, Imam ash-Shāfi^cī considered marriage to be permissible (*mubāḥ*).[2]

Ibn Juzayy al-Kalbī summed up the *fiqh* succinctly in the following:

> In general terms marriage is recommended, but the Ẓāhiriyyah considered it obligatory. In detail, it divides up into five cases:

1. Obligatory, and this is in the case where someone is capable of it in terms of wealth, and fears illicit sexual relations for himself.

2. Recommended, and this is in the case of someone who is capable of it in terms of wealth, but has no fear of illicit sexual relations for himself.

3. Forbidden, and this is in the case of the person who is incapable [of it in terms of wealth] and has no fear [of illicit sexual relations].

4. Disapproved, and this is in the case of someone who does not fear illicit sexual relations but has a fear that he will not be able to fulfil its rights.

5. Permitted, and this is every other case apart from the above.[3]

According to the Mālikī school, it is obligatory (*farḍ*) for a Muslim to marry even though he may not be in a position to earn his living, on the following three conditions:[4]

1. If he fears that by not marrying he will commit fornication (*zinā*).
2. If he is unable to fast to control his passion or if he can fast but his fasting does not help him to refrain from fornication.
3. He does not have a woman slave.

Some *fuqahā'* disagree on this point, and suggest that if he cannot produce a lawful livelihood, he must not marry, and that if he marries without any hope of obtaining a lawful income, he would commit theft. Thus, in order to avoid one evil, he would become a victim of another.[5]

The Ḥanafī school considers marriage obligatory subject to the following four conditions:

1. If a man is sure that he will commit *zinā* if he does not marry.
2. If he cannot fast, or even if he can fast, it does not help him to control his passion. If fasting helps him, he must fast rather than marry.
3. If he does not have or cannot buy a woman slave.
4. If he is able to pay the dower (*mahr*) and is capable of

earning lawful livelihood. If he is not capable of earning his livelihood lawfully, it is not obligatory for him to marry.[6]

Marriage is forbidden (*ḥarām*) to a man if he does not possess the means to maintain his wife and children or if he suffers from an illness serious enough to affect his wife and his progeny.

It is disapproved (*makrūh*) for a man who possesses no sexual desire at all or who has no love for children, or who is sure to slacken in his religious obligations as a result of marriage.[7]

The Prophet ﷺ enjoined upon his followers to contract marriage because he had a definite object in view for them. There is a *ḥadīth* in which he ﷺ said:

عَنْ أَنَسٍ : قَالَ رَسُولُ اللَّهِ ﷺ ﴿إِذَا تَزَوَّجَ الْعَبْدُ فَقَدِ اسْتَكْمَلَ نِصْفَ الدِّينِ ، فَلْيَتَّقِ اللَّهَ فِي النِّصْفِ الْبَاقِي﴾

It is narrated by Anas ◈ that the Messenger of Allah ﷺ said: "When a man marries, he has fulfilled half of his *dīn*, so let him have *taqwā* of Allah regarding the remaining half." (Aḥmad in his *Musnad* from Anas)

The Prophet ﷺ considered marriage for a Muslim as 'a half of his *dīn*.' Perhaps this is because it may shield him from promiscuity, adultery, fornication and sexual deviance which could ultimately lead to many other crimes including slander, violent quarrelling, homicide, loss of property and finally the disintegration of the family on which so much emphasis has been placed by the Prophet ﷺ.

According to the Prophet ﷺ the remaining half of the *dīn* which is complementary to the first half, can be attained by *taqwā* (abandonment of what is forbidden and undertaking what is commanded).

In yet another *ḥadīth*, the Prophet ﷺ mentioned the best thing that a Muslim can aspire to have after *taqwā* is a good and obedient wife.

عَنْ أَبِي أُمَامَةَ عَنِ النَّبِيِّ ﷺ أَنَّهُ قَالَ : ﴿مَا اسْتَفَادَ الْمُؤْمِنُ بَعْدَ تَقْوَى اللَّهِ خَيْرًا لَهُ مِنْ زَوْجَةٍ

صَالِحَة ، إِنْ أَمَرَهَا أَطَاعَتْهُ، وَإِنْ نَظَرَ إِلَيْهَا سَرَّتْهُ، وَإِنْ أَقْسَمَ عَلَيْهَا أَبَرَّتْهُ، وَإِنْ غَابَ عَنْهَا نَصَحَتْهُ فِي نَفْسِهَا وَمَالِهِ ﴾

> Abū Umāmah said that the Prophet ﷺ said: "After *taqwā* of Allah, a believer benefits by nothing better for himself than a right-acting wife who obeys him if he gives her a command, pleases him if he looks at her, and if he adjures her to do something [that is not *ḥarām*] she fulfils it, and is true to him regarding her person and his property whenever he is absent from her." (Ibn Mājah, *bāb afḍal an-nisā'*)

The Prophet ﷺ laid great stress on right action, *taqwā* and trueness as the main criteria in the choice of life partners. "Whoever marries a woman" said the Prophet ﷺ, "for her power and position, then Allah will only increase him in humiliation; and whoever marries her for her wealth, then Allah, exalted is He, will only increase him in poverty; and whoever marries her for her beauty, then Allah will only increase him in ignobility; and whoever marries a woman in order to lower his eyes and to render his private parts chaste and to keep good relations with his kin, then he will have that, and he will be blessed in her and Allah will bless her in him." (Narrated by Ibn an-Najjār from Anas)

Thus, *taqwā* and right action must be uppermost in the motives for marriage.

The Prophet ﷺ also said:

ثَلاثَةٌ حَقٌّ عَلَى اللهِ عَوْنُهُمْ، الْمُجَاهِدُ فِي سَبِيلِ اللهِ، وَالْمُكَاتَبُ الَّذِي يُرِيدُ الأَدَاءَ، وَالنَّاكِحُ الَّذِي يُرِيدُ العَفَافَ.

> There are three persons whom Allah ﷻ Himself has undertaken to help: first, the person who wages *jihād* in the way of Allah, the slave who writes a contract to buy his freedom intending to fulfil it; and someone who marries with a view to securing his chastity." (from Abū Hurayrah, Aḥmad in his *Musnad* at-Tirmidhī *bāb mā jā'a fī al-mujāhid wa an-nākiḥ wa al-mukātab wa ᶜawn Allāh iyyāhum*, an-Nasā'ī *bāb maᶜūnat Allāh an-nākiḥ alladhī*

yurīdu al-ᶜafāf, Ibn Mājah *bāb al-mukātab,* and al-Ḥākim in *al-Mustadrak*)

Celibacy: a non-Islamic practice

Islam does not subscribe to the view that the exercise of the natural instinct for sex is incompatible with the highest degree of dignity or the cultivation of the noblest values. Natural instincts, just like mental faculties and physical prowess, are a gift from Allah. They are not evil in themselves; if they are properly used, they become good, if improperly used, they become evil.

Therefore, if we define celibacy as abstaining from marriage and sexual relations for religious reasons, it is a violation of human nature. This is the reason why Allah does not permit celibacy or monasticism as a way of life. In the Qur'ān Allah says:

> *They invented monasticism – We did not prescribe it for them – purely out of desire to gain the pleasure of Allah, but even so they did not observe it as it should have been observed.* (Sūrat al-Ḥadīd 57: 27)

We are also told that we should not run after the pleasures of the world or make the amassing of wealth the pursuit of our lives; but in this verse above we are reminded that we should not go to the other extreme. Celibacy is disapproved in Islam except under unusual circumstances. We are thus required to keep the balance between the material and spiritual sides of life.

Men invented the doctrine of 'original sin.' "Behold", says the psalmist, "I was shapened in iniquity, and in sin did my mother conceive me." (Psalms 51: 5) It is entirely possible that it is the Christian translation of this text that inserts into it the Christian doctrine of original sin, i.e. that human beings are intrinsically sinful when they are born. The doctrine of original sin is entirely against Islam in which the offices of father and mother are held in the highest veneration. Every child is born pure. Celibacy is not seen as a virtue, and may even be a vice.

This attitude of Islam towards marriage contrasts with the teaching of Christianity that virginity is best but that for those who find this impossible, marriage is permissible. "It is better to marry than to burn," as St. Paul straightforwardly puts it

(Corinthians 7: 9). "To the unmarried and the widows I say it is well for them to remain single as I do," he said. St. Paul further explains: "I want you to be free from anxieties. The unmarried man is anxious about the affairs of the Lord, how to please the Lord; but the married man is anxious about worldly affairs, how to please his wife; and his interests are divided. And the unmarried women or girl is anxious about the affairs of the Lord, how to be holy in body and spirit; but the married woman is anxious about worldly affairs, how to please her husband. I say this for your own good, not to lay any restraint upon you, but to promote good and order and to secure your undivided devotion to the Lord." (*Ibid.*, 7: 8)

The Messenger of Allah ﷺ said: "Marriage is my Sunnah, so whoever does not practise my Sunnah is not of me." (Ibn Mājah narrated it from ᶜĀ'ishah, *bāb mā jā'a bi faḍl an-nikāḥ*). Islam considers parenthood to be the duty of every human being capable of it. In the civilised world of today many people refuse to take on the responsibility of parenthood, offering as an excuse the insufficiency of their means to support a family. The Qur'ān disposes of this flimsy excuse in these simple words, *"If they are poor, Allah will enrich them from His bounty."* (Sūrat an-Nūr 24: 32)

Selection of a spouse

The Prophet ﷺ recommended that in the selection of a bride, a man should see the intended bride before proposing lest a blunder in choice or an error in judgement should deflect the very purpose of marriage. However, a man should not gaze passionately on the would-be bride but only have a look at her face and hands to gain some idea about her personality and beauty.[8]

If a man so desires he may appoint a woman to go, see, and interview the would-be bride, so that she might fully describe the type of woman she is.[9]

Since believing men and women are referred to equally in the Noble Qur'ān, a woman also has the right to look at her would-be husband.[10]

The special permission to have a glance at the prospective wife or husband does not contravene the following code of conduct for believing men and women given in the Generous Qur'ān:

قُل لِّلْمُؤْمِنِينَ يَغُضُّوا مِنْ أَبْصَارِهِمْ وَيَحْفَظُوا فُرُوجَهُمْ ذَٰلِكَ أَزْكَىٰ لَهُمْ إِنَّ اللَّهَ خَبِيرٌ بِمَا يَصْنَعُونَ

Say to the mu'minūn that they should lower their eyes and guard their private parts. That is purer for them. Allah is aware of what they do. (Sūrat an-Nūr 24: 30)

وَقُل لِّلْمُؤْمِنَاتِ يَغْضُضْنَ مِنْ أَبْصَارِهِنَّ وَيَحْفَظْنَ فُرُوجَهُنَّ وَلَا يُبْدِينَ زِينَتَهُنَّ إِلَّا مَا ظَهَرَ مِنْهَا
وَلْيَضْرِبْنَ بِخُمُرِهِنَّ عَلَىٰ جُيُوبِهِنَّ وَلَا يُبْدِينَ زِينَتَهُنَّ إِلَّا لِبُعُولَتِهِنَّ أَوْ آبَائِهِنَّ أَوْ آبَاءِ بُعُولَتِهِنَّ أَوْ أَبْنَائِهِنَّ
أَوْ أَبْنَاءِ بُعُولَتِهِنَّ أَوْ إِخْوَانِهِنَّ أَوْ بَنِي إِخْوَانِهِنَّ أَوْ بَنِي أَخَوَاتِهِنَّ أَوْ نِسَائِهِنَّ أَوْ مَا مَلَكَتْ أَيْمَانُهُنَّ أَوِ
التَّابِعِينَ غَيْرِ أُولِي الْإِرْبَةِ مِنَ الرِّجَالِ أَوِ الطِّفْلِ الَّذِينَ لَمْ يَظْهَرُوا عَلَىٰ عَوْرَاتِ النِّسَاءِ وَلَا يَضْرِبْنَ
بِأَرْجُلِهِنَّ لِيُعْلَمَ مَا يُخْفِينَ مِن زِينَتِهِنَّ وَتُوبُوا إِلَى اللَّهِ جَمِيعًا أَيُّهَ الْمُؤْمِنُونَ لَعَلَّكُمْ تُفْلِحُونَ

Say to the mu'min women that they should lower their eyes and guard their private parts and not display their adornments – except for what normally shows – and draw their head-coverings across their breasts. They should only display their adornments to their husbands or their fathers or their husbands' fathers, or their sons or their husbands' sons or their brothers or their brothers' sons or their sisters' sons or other women or those they own as slaves or their male attendants who have no sexual desire or children who still have no awareness of women's private parts. Nor should they stamp their feet so that their hidden ornaments are known. Turn to Allah every one of you, mu'minūn, so that hopefully you will have success. (Sūrat an-Nūr 24: 31)

The choice of partner and the power of compulsion (*ijbār*)

A. The suitor and the would-be bride are not allowed to remain alone together, because the Prophet ﷺ said that whenever you leave a man and a woman alone there is always a third present and that is Shayṭān. There is no notion of courtship in Islam where a man and a girl date each other for some time in the belief that they will come to know each other better. Neither is there the concept of simply moving in with each other as 'partners' and living as man and wife, and then after some years and the birth of children, perhaps deciding to actually marry. In spite of all this intimacy, couples often fail to understand each other and relationships break up, and if they do marry they often find that the elongated period of courtship or living together has not helped to yield any better understanding between them. The present alarming rate of divorce in the world today proves this point.

It is reported that when al-Mughīrah ibn Shuᶜbah made a proposal of marriage to a woman the Prophet asked him if he had ever seen her and on his replying in the negative, he enjoined him to see her, because "it was likely to bring about greater love and concord between them." The jurists almost all agree upon the *istiḥbāb* (approval) of looking at the woman whom one intends to marry. And since the contract is effected by the consent of two parties, the man and the woman, and one of them is expressly told to satisfy himself about the other by looking at her, it would be that the woman has the same right to satisfy herself before giving her assent. The consent of both the man and the woman is an essential of marriage, and the Noble Qur'ān lays down expressly that the two must agree:

> *...do not prevent them from marrying their husbands if they have mutually agreed to it.* (Sūrat al-Baqarah 2: 232)[11]

B. The choice of partner by a Muslim girl is subject to the overriding power of compulsion (*ijbār*) granted to her father in the Mālikī school.

This is a safety measure in the interest of the girl herself. If the father or the guardian of the girl finds that in her immaturity or over-zealousness she is going to marry a man possessing a bad character or lacking the proper means of livelihood, he may stop her from marrying that man and find a more suitable person to whom to give her in marriage.

Free consent of the parties

Marriage in reality is a covenant (*mīthāq*)[12] meaning a solemn agreement between husband and wife, which must be recorded in writing.[13] They should agree subject to the *Sharīᶜah.*[14] As there can be no agreement unless both parties give their consent to it, marriage in Islam can only be contracted with the free consent of the two parties. The Prophet ﷺ said: "A previously married woman is not to be married until she is consulted, and the virgin is not to be married until her permission is sought." (Al-Bukhārī, *bāb fi an-nikāḥ*) One of al-Bukhārī's chapters is entitled thus: 'The marriage of someone who is coerced is not valid'[15] and a *ḥadīth* is quoted showing that the Prophet ﷺ repudiated such a marriage. A virgin girl came to the Prophet and said that her father had her married against her wishes, and the Prophet gave her the right to repudiate the marriage.[16] The Mālikī school, however, in accordance with the practice of the People of Madīnah gives power of compulsion to the father.

With regard to divorced women, in the Qur'ān Allah says: "*When you divorce women and they reach the end of their ᶜiddah, do not prevent them from marrying their first husbands if they have mutually agreed to it with correctness and courtesy.*" (Sūrat al-Baqarah 2: 232)

With regard to widows Allah, exalted is He, says; "*Those of you who die leaving wives behind should make a bequest to their wives of maintenance for a year without them having to leave their homes. But if they do leave you are not to blame for anything they do with themselves with correctness and courtesy,*" (Sūrat al-Baqarah 2: 238) for instance, by remarrying, in which case they forego their claim to additional maintenance during the reminder of the year.

Prohibited degrees of marriage

The laws of marriage have been so framed by the *Sharīᶜah* that they may help to establish the *Ummah*. To this end the Qur'ān and the Sunnah have prescribed the prohibited degrees in marriage, which can be divided into two categories:

1. The permanently prohibited degrees
2. The temporarily prohibited degrees

THE PERMANENT PROHIBITIONS

The permanently prohibited degrees are contained in Sūrat an-Nisā'.

وَلَا تَنكِحُوا۟ مَا نَكَحَ آبَاؤُكُم مِّنَ النِّسَاءِ إِلَّا مَا قَدْ سَلَفَ إِنَّهُ كَانَ فَاحِشَةً وَمَقْتًا وَسَاءَ سَبِيلًا
حُرِّمَتْ عَلَيْكُمْ أُمَّهَاتُكُمْ وَبَنَاتُكُمْ وَأَخَوَاتُكُمْ وَعَمَّاتُكُمْ وَخَالَاتُكُمْ وَبَنَاتُ الْأَخِ وَبَنَاتُ الْأُخْتِ
وَأُمَّهَاتُكُمُ اللَّاتِي أَرْضَعْنَكُمْ وَأَخَوَاتُكُم مِّنَ الرَّضَاعَةِ وَأُمَّهَاتُ نِسَائِكُمْ وَرَبَائِبُكُمُ اللَّاتِي فِي
حُجُورِكُم مِّن نِّسَائِكُمُ اللَّاتِي دَخَلْتُم بِهِنَّ فَإِن لَّمْ تَكُونُوا۟ دَخَلْتُم بِهِنَّ فَلَا جُنَاحَ عَلَيْكُمْ وَحَلَائِلُ
أَبْنَائِكُمُ الَّذِينَ مِنْ أَصْلَابِكُمْ وَأَن تَجْمَعُوا۟ بَيْنَ الْأُخْتَيْنِ إِلَّا مَا قَدْ سَلَفَ إِنَّ اللَّهَ كَانَ غَفُورًا رَّحِيمًا

Do not marry any women your fathers married – except for what may have already taken place. That is an indecent act, a loathsome thing and an evil path. Ḥarām for you are: your mothers and your daughters and your sisters, your maternal aunts and your paternal aunts, your brothers' daughters and your sisters' daughters, your foster mothers who have suckled you, your foster sisters by suckling, your wives' mothers, your stepdaughters who are under your protection: the daughters of your wives whom you have had sexual relations with (though if you have not had sexual relations with them there is nothing blameworthy for you in it then), the wives of your sons whom you have fathered, and marrying two sisters at the same time – except for what may have already taken place. Allah is Ever-Forgiving, Most Merciful. (Sūrat an-Nisā' 4: 22-24)

From the above verses it is clear that a Muslim must not marry the following:

1. His mother.
2. His stepmother(s). In the *Jāhiliyyah* period a stepson or brother inherited his father's widow(s). Similar practices continue in Yorubaland in Nigeria, where, in some cases, the eldest son inherits the youngest wife of his father.
3. His grandmother(s). Grandmothers include fathers' and mothers' mothers however remote.
4. His daughter(s). Daughters include granddaughters i.e. sons' or daughters' daughters however remote.

5. His sister(s), including full or consanguine and uterine sisters.
6. His fathers' sister(s), including the grandfathers' sister(s).
7. His mothers' sister(s), including the grandmothers' sister(s).
8. His brothers' daughter(s).
9. His foster mother.
10. His foster mother's sister(s).
11. His sisters' daughter(s).
12. His foster sister(s).
13. His wife's mother.
14. His stepdaughter(s) born to his wife with whom he has consummated his relationship. If the marriage was not consummated there is no prohibition.
15. His sons' wives: this will not include wives of persons whom one treats as adopted.

Temporary prohibitions

Temporary prohibitions are those which can be removed by a change of circumstances. They are as follows:

1. A man must not marry two sisters in marriage at one and the same time. The temporary prohibition here is removed as soon as his wife dies and he may take her sister in marriage. This provision also applies to his wife's aunt as well as niece.
2. A man must not marry a married woman. However, the impediment is removed immediately on the dissolution of her marriage either by the death of her former husband or divorce followed by completion of the period of *ᶜiddah*, i.e. the waiting period that widows undergo on the death of their husbands of four months and ten days, or in the case of divorced women, a period of three menstrual cycles.
3. A man must not have more than four wives at a time. However, the impediment is removed as soon as one of the wives dies or is divorced.

4. A man must not marry a woman during her *ᶜiddah*. However, the impediment is removed as soon as the period of *ᶜiddah* expires.

In the Qur'ān, Allah, exalted is He, says:

وَلَكِن لَّا تُوَاعِدُوهُنَّ سِرًّا إِلَّآ أَن تَقُولُوا قَوْلاً مَّعْرُوفاً وَلَا تَعْزِمُوا عُقْدَةَ النِّكَاحِ حَتَّى يَبْلُغَ الْكِتَابُ أَجَلَهُ

But do not make secret arrangements with them, rather only speak with correctness and courtesy. Do not finally decide on the marriage contract until the prescribed period has come to its end. (Sūrat al-Baqarah 2: 235)

This means that a man must not make a specific proposal to a woman in *ᶜiddah*. However, one can send implied words like the following to a woman whose husband dies or who has been irrevocably or finally divorced: "I wish to find a woman of good character."

However, if a woman is within the *ᶜiddah* of a divorce in which the husband's taking her back (*rajᶜah*) is still possible, a man should not send her even implied words for she is still considered as the legal wife of the ex-husband. By doing so, one could become instrumental in breaking up a family in which there are still chances of reconciliation.

THE CASE OF TWO SUITORS FOR THE SAME WOMAN

The Prophet ﷺ disapproved of two suitors vying with one another for marriage to the same woman. This is so because such a situation is likely to create enmity between two Muslim brothers. The Prophet ﷺ is narrated to have said:

لَا يَحِلُّ لِإِمْرِئٍ مُسْلِمٍ أَنْ يَخْطُبَ عَلَى خِطْبَةِ أَخِيهِ حَتَّى يَتْرُكَ وَلَا يَبِيعَ عَلَى بَيْعِ أَخِيهِ حَتَّى يَتْرُكْ

It is not lawful for a Muslim to propose marriage on top of his brother's proposal until he withdraws [the proposal] nor to offer for sale on top of his brother's offer to sell until he withdraws [the offer]. (Aḥmad narrated it in the *Musnad* from ᶜUqbah ibn ᶜĀmir)

However, the father's right of compulsion stands at a different level. If he finds that his daughter is going to marry a man who is of bad character or a man who is not in a position to take on a family he may stop his daughter from going ahead with the proposal.[17]

Some people regard this as only a moral obligation whereas others view it as a moral as well as legal obligation. However, to reduce the efficacy of the above tradition to the level where the second suitor would not be compelled to opt out of his proposal would be tantamount to paying less attention to the Qur'ānic injunction:

وَمَا آتَاكُمُ الرَّسُولُ فَخُذُوهُ وَمَا نَهَاكُمْ عَنْهُ فَانْتَهُوا

Whatever the Messenger gives you, you should accept and whatever He forbids you, you should forgo. (Sūrat al-Ḥashr 59: 7)

The only person given the power to make proposals on top of the proposal of a suitor is the father, who has been vested with the power of compulsion where he foresees some detrimental effects resulting from the marriage.

Imam Abū Ḥanīfah, Imām ash-Shāfiᶜī and Imām Mālik held the view that it is a wrong action to make a proposal on top of the proposal of a brother, but that if the second suitor is successful it will suffice that he seek the forgiveness of the first suitor and seek the forgiveness of Allah.[18] However, the Ẓāhirīs consider such a marriage void. I submit that the former view appears more rational and sound in comparison to the latter which may create more problems than it seeks to solve.

Notes

[1] *Ḥāshiyat ad-Dasūqī* on the *Sharḥ al-kabīr,* vol. II, p. 9: 215
[2] See Abū Zahra, *Aḥwāl Shakhṣiyyah* p. 9. 24.
[3] Ibn Juzayy al-Kalbī, *al-Qawānīn al-fiqhiyyah,* p. 199. Dar al-Kitab al-Arabi, Beirut, Lebanon.
[4] Al-Jazīrī, ᶜAbd ar-Raḥmān, *al-Fiqh ᶜalā al-madhāhib al-arbiᶜah* vol. IV, pp 4, Cairo 1970.
[5] *Ibid* p. 5.
[6] *Ibid* p. 6.
[7] *Ibid*
[8] *cf, Ḥāshiyat ad-Dasūqī,* vol. 2, p. 215
[9] *Mawāhib al-Jalīl,* vol. III, p. 405
[10] *Ḥāshiyat ad-Dasūqī,* vol. II, p. 215
[11] Although the *āyah* refers to the case of women being divorced and wishing to remarry an earlier husband, it crucially refers to their having "mutually agreed to it."
[12] Sūrat an-Nisā' 4: 21
[13] Sūrat al-Baqarah 2: 282
[14] Sūrat al-Baqarah 2: 232
[15] Al-Bukhārī, *bāb lā yajūzu nikāḥu al-mukrah*
[16] Abū Dāwūd, *bāb fi al-bikr yuzawwijuhā abūhā wa lā yasta'miruhā*
[17] *Mawāhib al-Jalīl* vol. III. The case of Abū Jahm ibn Ḥudhayfah and Muᶜāwiyah ibn Abī Ṣufyān is instructive here. They proposed marriage to Fāṭimah bint Qays. The Prophet ﷺ advised Fāṭimah not to marry any of them on the ground that Muᶜāwiyah was then a pauper and Abū Jahm was harsh and so she married Usāmah. However, it is not in fact the exercise of compulsion but a case of friendly good counsel, since the Prophet ﷺ was not Fāṭimah's father or guardian

and she was not a virgin but someone remarrying after a divorce.
[18] *cf.* Ibn ᶜAsākir in his book *Kitāb ashal al-madārik* vol. II, p. 68

Chapter 10

The Marital Relationship in Islam

MUSLIMS WANT TO BUILD COMMUNITY. This is why they give maximum attention to family affairs. If the foundation of the family is strong, the foundation of community is strong. Every family member has his rightful place and is charged to carry out his responsibilities with *taqwā*. Allah says about the beauty of the relationship between man and wife:

وَمِنْ آيَاتِهِ أَنْ خَلَقَ لَكُم مِّنْ أَنفُسِكُمْ أَزْوَاجاً لِّتَسْكُنُوا إِلَيْهَا وَجَعَلَ بَيْنَكُم مَّوَدَّةً وَرَحْمَةً إِنَّ فِي ذَلِكَ لَآيَاتٍ لِّقَوْمٍ يَتَفَكَّرُونَ

Among His Signs is that He created spouses for you of your own kind so that you might find tranquillity in them. And He has placed affection and compassion between you. There are certainly Signs in that for people who reflect. (Sūrat ar-Rūm : 21)

In this *āyah* Allah describes the affection He has put between man and woman that is the basis of married life. In another extraordinary image that emphasises the nature of the assistance man and woman give each other within marriage, He says:

هُنَّ لِبَاسٌ لَّكُمْ وَأَنتُمْ لِبَاسٌ لَّهُنَّ

They are clothing for you and you for them. (Sūrat al-Baqarah 2: 187)

In the Generous Qur'ān Allah ﷻ says, describing further the roles of men within marriage, and what ought to happen when things begin to break down in the marriage:

الرِّجَالُ قَوَّامُونَ عَلَى النِّسَاءِ بِمَا فَضَّلَ اللهُ بَعْضَهُمْ عَلَى بَعْضٍ وَبِمَا أَنْفَقُوا مِنْ أَمْوَالِهِمْ فَالصَّالِحَاتُ

قَانِتَاتٌ حَافِظَاتٌ لِلْغَيْبِ بِمَا حَفِظَ اللهُ وَاللَّاتِي تَخَافُونَ نُشُوزَهُنَّ فَعِظُوهُنَّ وَاهْجُرُوهُنَّ فِي

الْمَضَاجِعِ وَاضْرِبُوهُنَّ فَإِنْ أَطَعْنَكُمْ فَلَا تَبْغُوا عَلَيْهِنَّ سَبِيلًا

Men have charge of (qawwāmūn) women because Allah has preferred
the one above the other and because they spend their wealth on them.
Right-acting women are obedient, safeguarding their husband's interests
in his absence as Allah has guarded them. If there are women whose
disobedience you fear, you may admonish them, refuse to sleep with
them, and then beat them. But if they obey you, do not look for a way
to punish them. (Sūrat an-Nisā' 4: 34)

Allah informs us in this verse that men are *qawwāmūn* i.e. protectors and maintainers of women. The word *qawwāmūn* signifies a person who takes the responsibility of safeguarding the interest of another person.

This position comes to men as opposed to women not only because, generally speaking, they have more physical strength and greater capacity for hard work, but also because it is extremely important that in every family, there should be a head who is looked to as an authority to settle things between the members of the family. It is for this reason that the family are asked to obey the husband. Allah has described the obedient wife as the most right-acting.

However, it should be borne in mind that a wife should not obey her husband if what is asked of her is against Allah's orders, because obedience is first to Allah, just as is the case with a ruler who asks people to do something that is clearly *harām*; no one is obliged to obey in this case.

It is human nature that some squabbles and misunderstandings may arise in the family. Therefore each member of the family has been asked to have *taqwā* of Allah, to be steadfast and to exercise self-restraint. In the context of the verse we have quoted, it must be understood that in quarrels between men and women it is all too common for men to resort to violence. In our age, in the UK for example, the statistics on wife-beating and domestic violence make depressing reading. The verse on the matter must be seen as entering into an existing situation and legislating two steps prior to beating which will take the heat and temper out of the quarrel, and thus hopefully there is almost no need for any kind of beating, for most domestic violence takes place in the heat of the moment. Allah does not legislate the beating of women, but in the context of the fact that men sometimes do beat their wives, Allah legislates on the matter.

The foregoing verse prescribes certain measures which should be taken in settling disputes between couples. They are:

1. Admonition

Before taking any other measure which may be to the detriment of the couple, the wife should be admonished in a reasonable manner. And if this proves effective, there is no need to resort to any harsher measure.

2. Severing conjugal relations

If admonition by the husband fails to correct his wife, the husband may refuse to share his bed with her. This, however, must be confined to a reasonable period of time and should not be continued indefinitely.

3. Light beating

Wife-beating is discouraged by the Messenger of Allah ﷺ and by Muslim jurists. However, if the wife's behaviour is against the injunctions of Allah and the Sunnah of the Prophet ﷺ, beating her in a light manner may become necessary. However, the Prophet ﷺ has enjoined that she must not be beaten on the face or in such a way as may leave a mark on her body.

4. Arbitration

Islam discourages, as much as possible, taking family disputes to courts of law. A verse of Qur'ān says that if there is a dispute between the wife and the husband, one arbiter from each family should be appointed to resolve it. (Sūrat an-Nisā' 4: 35)

Finally, the Qur'ān warns men that if women obey and correct their ways, they should not be nagged and the men should not find fault with them in order to annoy them. The relationship between husband and wife in the Qur'ān is described as we have seen already: *"They are clothing for you and you for them."* (Sūrat al-Baqarah 2: 187)

The marriage of husband and wife is for mutual support, comfort and protection, fitting each other as a garment fits the body. Clothing is both for show and concealment. The question of sex is always delicate to handle. Here we are told that even in such matters a clear, open and honest course is better than fraud or self-deception. A husband and wife who are bound together by the love and tenderness that Allah has put between them are indeed clothing for each other. The Noble Qur'ān says, *"but the garment of taqwā – that is best!"* (Sūrat al-Aᶜrāf 7: 26) so that husband and wife should be such garments for each other.

> *Women possess rights similar to those held over them to be honoured with fairness; but men have a degree above them. Allah is Almighty, All-Wise.* (Sūrat al-Baqarah 2: 228)

The statement that men are a degree above them simply shows that authority to run the house belongs either to the husband or the wife, and it is here given to the husband, as it is the duty of the men to maintain the women.

> *Men have charge of women because Allah has preferred the one above the other and because they spend their wealth on them.* (Sūrat al-Baqarah 2: 34)

ᶜĀ'ishah narrated that the Prophet ﷺ said, "The best of you is he who treats his family best and I am the one who treats his family best." (At-Tirmidhī, *bāb faḍl azwāj an-nabiyyi ṣalla'llāhu ᶜalayhi wa sallam*). He was himself always most careful and considerate in respect of all that concerned women. On one occasion he was on a journey when women were also in the party. At a certain stage in the journey, the camel drivers fearing that they were late began to drive the camels fast. The Messenger of Allah ﷺ told them, "Mind the crystals. Mind the crystals!" (Abū Nuᶜaym in *al-Ḥilyah* and ᶜAbd ar-Razzāq from Anas) meaning that they should pay due regard to the comfort of the women. The term 'crystal' with respect to women implies that they are precious. On another occasion Abū Hurayrah narrated that he explained that a woman by her nature is like a rib, "such that if you try to straighten it you break it, and if you leave it, it remains crooked." (Al-Bukhārī, *bāb qawl Allāh ta*c*ālā: wa idh qāla rabbuka li al-malā'kati innī jā*c*ilun fī al-arḍi khalīfah*, Muslim, *bāb al-waṣiyyah bi an-nisā'*)

In short, it is the husband's right that his wife obey him willingly in everything which is not forbidden; she should not obey him if he asks her to do that which is against the command of Allah and the guidance of His Messenger ﷺ. She must try to keep herself as pleasing as possible for her husband and must not display anger towards him. cĀ'ishah said:

سَأَلْتُ رَسُولَ اللَّهِ ﷺ: أَيُّ النَّاسِ أَعْظَمُ حَقّاً عَلَى الْمَرْأَةِ؟ قَالَ ﴿زَوْجُهَا﴾ قَالَتْ: فَأَيُّ النَّاسِ أَعْظَمُ حَقّاً عَلَى الرَّجُلِ؟ قَالَ ﴿أُمُّهُ﴾

> She asked the Messenger of Allah: "Who has greater right over a woman?" He (the Prophet ﷺ) replied: "Her husband." She asked: "Then who has greater right over a man?" He replied: "His mother." (Al-Ḥākim, *al-Mustadrak*)

The Prophet ﷺ further said:

لَوْ أَمَرْتُ أَحَداً أَنْ يَسْجُدَ لِأَحَدٍ لَأَمَرْتُ الْمَرْأَةَ أَنْ تَسْجُدَ لِزَوْجِهَا مِنْ عِظَمِ حَقِّهِ

> If I had ordered anyone to prostrate before anyone, I would have ordered a woman to prostrate before her husband, taking into consideration the great right he has over her. (Abū Dāwūd, *bāb fī ḥaqq az-zawj* c*alā al-mar'ah*; at-Tirmidhī, *bāb mā jā'a fī ḥaqq az-zawj* c*alā al-mar'ah*; Ibn Mājah, *bāb ḥaqq az-zawj* c*alā al-mar'ah;* and Ibn Ḥibbān)

However, the *dīn* of Islam teaches uncompromising *tawḥīd*, and no one must prostrate before anyone except the Creator. The above *ḥadīth* of the Prophet indicates a husband's rights over his wife and her rights over him.

To safeguard women is here a noble task laid on men's shoulders for them to raise them up to the place in the creation Allah has appointed for them. It is not the old style of paternal family values but it is a nourishing form of behaviour, and the man's looking out for the best for all family members: parents, wives and children.

The Noble Qur'ān lays the greatest possible stress on kindly and good treatment of wives. The Noble Qur'ān asks men to *"treat them kindly"*.[1] Kindness is even recommended when a man dislikes his wife, for *"If you dislike them, it may well be that you dislike something in which Allah has placed a lot of good."* (Sūrat an-Nisā' 4: 19) The Prophet ﷺ laid great stress upon good treatment of wives. He said: "Accept my counsel in the matter of [doing good to] women."(Al-Bukhārī, *bāb qawl Allāh taᶜālā: wa idh qāla rabbuka li'l-malā'kati innī jāᶜilun fī al-arḍi khalīfah*)[2] In his famous address at the farewell pilgrimage, he again laid particular stress on the good treatment of women: "So have *taqwā* of Allah with respect to women, for you have taken them by the protection of Allah[3]... and they have the right over you that you provide for them and clothe them with kindness." (Muslim, *bāb ḥajjat an-nabiyyi ṣalla'llāhu ᶜalayhi wa sallam*)

In the main, womankind's special gift is bringing up children. She has been created in such a way that the quality of love is predominant in her, and she is devoid of the overriding sternness of men; she therefore inclines to one side sooner than men do, and on account of this quality, she is compared to a rib in a *ḥadīth* of the Prophet ﷺ. (Al-Bukhārī, *bāb al-waṣāh bi an-nisā'*) Her being curved like a rib is adduced as an argument for being tolerant towards her instead of trying to force her to change.

Marriage with a person who associates partners with Allah (*mushrikah*)

While marriage with the 'People of the Book' is permitted to Muslim men, it is completely forbidden to marry a person who associates partners with Allah in any form, whether she happens to be an idol-worshipper or someone who has given up Islam (*murtaddah*) and reverted to worship of other-than-Allah, or a worshipper of cows or other animals, trees, or stones. The Qur'ān commands in the following words:

وَلَا تَنكِحُوا الْمُشْرِكَاتِ حَتَّىٰ يُؤْمِنَّ وَلَأَمَةٌ مُّؤْمِنَةٌ خَيْرٌ مِّن مُّشْرِكَةٍ وَلَوْ أَعْجَبَتْكُمْ وَلَا تُنكِحُوا الْمُشْرِكِينَ حَتَّىٰ يُؤْمِنُوا وَلَعَبْدٌ مُّؤْمِنٌ خَيْرٌ مِّن مُّشْرِكٍ وَلَوْ أَعْجَبَكُمْ أُولَٰئِكَ يَدْعُونَ إِلَى النَّارِ وَاللَّهُ يَدْعُو إِلَى الْجَنَّةِ وَالْمَغْفِرَةِ بِإِذْنِهِ وَيُبَيِّنُ آيَاتِهِ لِلنَّاسِ لَعَلَّهُمْ يَتَذَكَّرُونَ

> *Do not marry women of the mushrikūn until they have īmān. A slavegirl who is one of the muminūn is better for you than a woman of the mushrikūn, even though she may attract you. And do not marry men of the mushrikūn until they have īmān. A slave who is one of the muminun is better for you than a man of the mushrikūn, even though he may attract you. Such people call you to the Fire whereas Allah calls you, with His permission, to the Garden and forgiveness. He makes His Signs clear to people so that hopefully they will pay heed.* (Sūrat al-Baqarah 2: 221)

The cause of revelation of this verse was the story of Kannāz ibn Ḥuṣayn al-Ghanawī whom the Messenger of Allah ﷺ had sent to Makkah on a mission. He knew a woman called ᶜAnāq in Makkah with whom he was greatly in love in the days of *jāhiliyyah*. She came to him and he told her that Islam has forbidden whatever used to happen in the *jāhiliyyah* period. She replied, "In that case marry me". Kannāz said, "Not before I ask for the Prophet's permission." When he sought the Prophet's advice, he said that Kannāz could not marry her since he was a Muslim while she was one who associated partners with Allah. (*Al-Jāmiᶜ li aḥkām al-Qur'ān* of al-Qurṭubī, in commentary on *wa lā tunkiḥū...* (Sūrat al-Baqarah 2: 221))

There is yet another cause of revelation mentioned by ᶜAbdullāh ibn ᶜAbbās in respect of ᶜAbdullāh ibn Rawāḥah, a Companion of the Prophet who had a black slave girl. He once became angry with her. When the Prophet ﷺ came to know about it, he asked ᶜAbdullāh ibn Rawāḥah in the following words:

> "What is the matter, ᶜAbdullāh?
>
> ᶜAbdullāh replied: "Messenger of Allah, she fasts, prays and does *wuḍū'* properly and believes in Allah, that there is no god but Allah and that you are the Messenger of Allah."

> The Prophet ﷺ said: "ᶜAbdullāh, she is a believer."
>
> ᶜAbdullāh said, "Then, by Allah Who has sent you with the truth, I will free her and marry her."
>
> When ᶜAbdullāh married her, many Muslims taunted him that he had married a slave girl, since they liked to marry free women, even if they associated partners with Allah, but were of good lineage. It was on this occasion that the above verse was revealed. (*Ibid.*)

If a Muslim woman renounces Islam, she does not remain legally married, just as if her husband renounces Islam, then the marriage is dissolved. Such marriages become null and void automatically.

We have been prohibited from marrying idolatrous spouses because they *"call you to the Fire."* (Sūrat al-Baqarah 2: 221)

This means that such a marriage might mislead Muslims into the ways of *shirk*, because the relations between husband and wife are not merely sexual but spiritual and cultural as well. It is possible that the Muslim spouse might influence their non-Muslim spouse, their children and her (or his) family in favour of the Islamic way of life. By the same token, it is equally possible that the spouse who associates partners with Allah might imbue their Muslim spouse, his (or her) family or their offspring, with the spirit and ways of *shirk*. Most probably as a result of such a marriage, a mixture of Islam and non-Islam will be bred in such a family. A non-Muslim might approve of this, but a Muslim cannot afford to do so. One who sincerely believes in Allah can never take such a risk. He would not do anything that might mislead him or his progeny into disbelief, blasphemy and *shirk*.

Marriage with the 'people of the book' (*Ahl al-Kitāb*)

The 'People of the book' are the Jews and the Christians, those who believe in books of Allah such as the Tawrāh and Injīl that were revealed to the prophets Mūsā and ᶜĪsā respectively, peace be upon both of them. Marriage with women of the People of the Book is permitted in Islam according to the following injunction in the Qur'ān:

اليومَ أُحِلَّ لَكُمُ الطَّيِّبَاتُ وَطَعَامُ الَّذِينَ أُوتُوا الْكِتَابَ حِلٌّ لَكُمْ وَطَعَامُكُمْ حِلٌّ لَهُمْ وَالْمُحْصَنَاتُ مِنَ

الْمُؤْمِنَاتِ وَالْمُحْصَنَاتُ مِنَ الَّذِينَ أُوتُوا الْكِتَابَ مِن قَبْلِكُمْ إِذَا آتَيْتُمُوهُنَّ أُجُورَهُنَّ مُحْصِنِينَ غَيْرَ

مُسَافِحِينَ وَلَا مُتَّخِذِي أَخْدَانٍ

Today all good things have been made ḥalāl for you. And the food of those given the Book is also ḥalāl for you and your food is ḥalāl for them. So are chaste women from among the muminun and chaste women of those given the Book before you, once you have given them their dowries in marriage, not in fornication or taking them as lovers.
(Sūrat al-Mā'idah 5: 5)

There is a consensus of the ʿulamā' of the Ahl as-Sunnah wa'l-Jamāʿah that marriage with Jewish and Christian women is permitted as it was the practice of the Companions (Ṣaḥābah) of the Prophet ﷺ like ʿUthmān, Ṭalḥah, Ibn ʿAbbās, Ḥudhayfah and the Followers (Tābiʿūn) such as Saʿīd ibn al-Musayyab, Saʿīd ibn Jubayr, al-Ḥasan, Mujāhid, Ṭāwus, ʿIkrimah and others.

Nevertheless, ʿAbdullāh ibn ʿUmar was of the opinion that one should not marry a Jewish or Christian woman. He used to say, "Allah has forbidden marriage with those who associate partners with Allah, and I can only understand it as major *shirk* when a woman says that her Lord is ʿĪsā who is one of the slaves of Allah." (*cf.* Sayyid Sabiq, *Fiqh as-Sunnah*, p. 208-209)

Although there are examples of the Companions (Ṣaḥābah) and the Followers (Tābiʿūn) who married *kitābiyyāt* (women of the people of the Book), one has to be cautious before contracting such a marriage. The Companions had exemplary characters and their lives were full of right-action and *taqwā*. They knew how to behave so that their children were not over influenced by their mothers in terms of their *dīn*. There is not a single example of the Ṣaḥābah or the Tābiʿūn whose children transgressed the limits of Allah or changed over to their mother's religion. Therefore, marriage with such women is permitted but is generally discouraged and considered abhorrent (*makrūh*). This was the position of Imām Mālik.

> Mālik said: "I disapprove of marrying Jewish and Christian women of the people of the *dhimmah*[4]." He said, "I do not declare it *ḥarām*. It is because she eats pork and drinks wine and he sleeps with her and kisses her while that is in her mouth, and she bears him children and will raise the child on her *dīn* and feed it the *ḥarām* and give it wine to drink." (Ṣaḥnūn, *al-Mudawwanat al-kubrā, kitāb an-nikāḥ as-sādis, fī nikāḥ nisā' ahl al-kitāb wa imā'ihim*)

Since there are a good number of marriageable Muslim women it would be considered unlawful, according to the *ijtihād* of certain *ᶜulamā'*, to marry *kitābiyyāt* women, and this is based on a judgement of ᶜUmar ibn al-Khaṭṭāb ﷺ. Since Muslim women cannot marry the men of the People of the Book, who will marry them in those circumstances? It is better then that Muslim men marry Muslim women.

The jurists of the four schools of Islamic jurisprudence have discussed marriage with *kitābiyyāt* women and given their juristic views. According to the Ḥanafī school it is unlawful to marry a woman of the People of the Book if she is in a country which happens to be in the 'abode of war' (*Dār al-Ḥarb*[5]), because that can open up a door to mischief since her children would be more inclined towards her ways.[5] The Mālikī school, on the other hand, has two views. The first is that marriage with a woman of the People of the Book is completely disapproved (*makrūh*) whether she is a *dhimmī*, i.e. living by the contract of the *dhimmah* under Muslim governance, or one living in the abode of war. The dislike of marriage to women of the latter category is greater. The second opinion is that there is no complete disapproval in marrying one of the People of the Book because the Qur'ānic words have given explicit approval. They show disapproval of such a marriage in the abode of Islam because it is not forbidden for her to drink wine or eat pork or go to the church, and her husband may not prevent her doing these things, and this affects her children's religious beliefs and behaviour, and, as Imām Mālik said, the husband will kiss her on the mouth.

It is not essential for a woman of the People of the Book that both her parent are *Ahl al-Kitāb*; her marriage will be valid even if her father is a *kitābī* and her mother is an idol worshipper. The Shāfiᶜī and Ḥanbalī schools believe that both her parents must be *Ahl al-Kitāb* in order to have a valid marriage and that if her father is a *kitābī* and her mother is an idol worshipper the marriage is unlawful even though she has reached the age of puberty and has accepted the religion of her father.[7]

Marriage with Ṣābi'ūn and Majūs

The Noble Qur'ān mentions the Jews, the Ṣābi'ūn, and the Christians in the following words:

إِنَّ الَّذِينَ آمَنُوا وَالَّذِينَ هَادُوا وَالصَّابِئُونَ وَالنَّصَارَى مَنْ آمَنَ بِاللَّهِ وَالْيَوْمِ الْآخِرِ وَعَمِلَ صَالِحًا فَلَا
خَوْفٌ عَلَيْهِمْ وَلَا هُمْ يَحْزَنُونَ

> *Those who have īmān and those who are Jews and the Sabaeans and the Christians, all who have īmān in Allah and the Last Day and act rightly will feel no fear and will know no sorrow.* (Sūrat al-Mā'idah 5: 69)

The same theme is repeated in Sūrat al-Baqarah, verse 62. Ibn Kathīr sums up concerning the Ṣābi'ūn thus:

> As for the Ṣābi'ūn they differ about them. Mujāhid said, "The Ṣābi'ūn are a people, in between the Jews and Christians, who have no *dīn*."
>
> Abu'l-ᶜĀliyah and aḍ-Ḍaḥḥāk said, "Ṣābi'ūn are a sect of the People of the Book who recite the Zabūr [thought to be the originals of the Psalms]." For this reason Abū Ḥanīfah and Isḥāq [ibn Rāhwayh] said, "There is no harm in the meat they slaughter." Abū Jaᶜfar ar-Rāzī said, "It has reached me that the Ṣābi'ūn are a people who worship angels and recite the Zabūr and pray towards the *qiblah*."
>
> Wahb ibn Munabbih was asked about the Ṣābi'ūn and said, "Someone who knows Allah alone and has no *Sharīᶜah* by which he acts, but has not innovated *kufr*."
>
> ᶜAbd ar-Raḥmān ibn Zayd said, "The Ṣābi'ūn were a people of one of the *dīns* in the Jazīrah of Mosul, who said, *'lā ilāha illa'llāh* – There is no god but Allah' but who had no actions, no book and no prophet, only the saying, *'lā ilāha illa'llāh* – There is no god but Allah.'" He said, "They did not have the gift of a messenger and

so because of that the idolaters used to say about the Prophet ﷺ and his Companions:

$$\langle\!\langle \text{هؤُلَاءِ الصَّابِئُونَ} \rangle\!\rangle \ , \ \text{يُشَبِّهُونَهُم بِهِم يَعْنِي فِي قَوْلِ لَا إِلَه إِلَّا اللَّه}$$

'These are Ṣābi'ūn'; they likened them (the Companions) to them (the Ṣābi'ūn) in saying *Lā ilāha illa'llāh*".

Al-Khalīl said, "They are a people whose *dīn* resembles the *dīn* of the Christians except that their *qiblah* is towards the direction of the south, claiming that they are on the *dīn* of Nūḥ ﷺ."...

The most obvious of the statements – and Allah knows best – is the verdict of Mujāhid and those who adhered to him and Wahb ibn Munabbih that they were a people who were not on the *dīn* of the Jews, nor that of the Christians or the Majūs nor were they idolaters. They were only people who remained in their condition of *fiṭrah* and they had no established *dīn* which they followed. For this reason the idolaters used to dismiss those who accepted Islam as Ṣābi'ūn, i.e. people who had left all other religions of the people of the earth by doing that. Some of the *ʿulamāʾ* said, "The Ṣābi'ūn are those people whom the *daʿwah* of the Prophet ﷺ has not reached," and Allah knows best. (Ibn Kathīr, *Tafsīr al-Qur'ān al-ʿAẓīm*)

ʿAllāmah Yūsuf ʿAlī, quoting the *Encyclopaedia Britannica* considers them a people who played an important part in the history of Arabia whose inscriptions were like those of the Phoenicians and Babylonians, and who had a flourishing kingdom in Yemen in South Arabia about 800-700 BCE. They worshipped the planets, and, he further conjectures, the Queen of Sheba of the Bible, who is Bilqīs of the Qur'ān, was connected with them.[8] In the time of the Caliph al-Ma'mūn in 830 CE, a group of people in Harran in Syria claimed the privileges of the People of the Book. They wore a peculiar dress and had long hair, worshipped stars and had Hellenic tendencies like the Jews contemporary with ʿĪsā (Jesus).[9]

I do not agree with Yūsuf ʿAlī when he extends the term Ṣābi'ūn to cover followers of Buddha, Confucius or of the Vedas. Marriage with such people definitely comes under the category of marriage to idolaters.

As far as the Majūs or Zoroastrians are concerned they are not *Ahl al-Kitāb* as they have no book, nor do they believe in prophethood but rather they worship fire. Imam ash-Shāfiʿī narrated that Sayyidunā ʿUmar once mentioned the Majūs and said, "I do not know how to treat the Majūs." ʿAbd ar-Raḥmān ibn ʿAwf, a famous Companion of the Prophet ﷺ replied to him:

سمعت رسول الله ﷺ يقول ﴿سنوا بهم سنة أهل الكتاب﴾

"I heard the Messenger of Allah saying, 'Treat them in the same way as *Ahl al-Kitāb*." (Ibn Abī Shaybah, *al-Muṣannaf*)

However, this ruling has limits: it is not permitted to marry their women nor to eat their meat.

After understanding whom a Muslim man is allowed to marry, it is important to note that in no circumstances is a Muslim woman permitted to marry a non-Muslim, whether he happens to be People of the Book or otherwise.

The injunction is contained in the following verse of the Noble Qur'ān:

يا أيها الذين آمنوا إذا جاءكم المؤمنات مهاجرات فامتحنوهن الله أعلم بإيمانهن فإن علمتموهن مؤمنات فلا ترجعوهن إلى الكفار لا هن حلٌّ لهم ولا هم يحلون لهن

You who have īmān! when women who have īmān come to you as emigrants, submit them to a test. Allah has best knowledge of their īmān. If you know they are mu'minūn, do not return them to the kuffār. They are not ḥalāl for the kuffār nor are the kuffār ḥalāl for them. (Sūrat al-Mumtaḥanah 60: 10)

In this verse Allah has ordered the believers that when emigrant women come to them, and once they have ascertained that they are indeed believers, they must in no circumstances be sent back to the disbelievers. Once they have left their original places due to their belief in Islam and love for Allah and his Prophet, they must not be allowed to suffer at the hands of disbelievers, even those to whom they were originally married.

وَلَن يَجْعَلَ اللَّهُ لِلْكَافِرِينَ عَلَى الْمُؤْمِنِينَ سَبِيلاً

Allah will not give the kuffār any way against the mu'minūn. (Sūrat an-Nisā' 4: 141)

Solemnising marriage according to the Sunnah

There are two special elements of the Muslim marriage. They are: *ījāb* and *qabūl* or proposal and acceptance.

According to the Mālikīs, there are five requirements of a marriage: 1. The guardian, without whom there is no legal marriage; 2. The dower; 3. The bridegroom; 4. A bride who is neither in *ᶜiddah* nor in the state of *iḥrām*, and; 5. The *ṣīghah*, the form the marriage rite takes, which means *ījāb* and *qabūl*, i.e. proposal and acceptance.

The Shāfiᶜīs have enumerated the following five conditions: the husband, wife, guardian, two witnesses and the *ṣīghah* (*ījāb* and *qabūl*).

The Ḥanafī school lays emphasis on the *ṣīghah*. Definite and clear words must be uttered in the *ījāb* and *qabūl*, and the acceptance must be made in the gathering where *ījāb* is uttered (*fī majlis al-ījāb*).

It is *mustaḥabb* (a commendable act) to give a small homily (*khuṭbah*) before the marriage rites are performed. This may provide a forum for informing and advising the bride and bridegroom of their marital responsibilities in Islam.

It may be long as occasion demands, but the shortest recommended form is just to say:

الْحَمْدُ لِلَّهِ وَالصَّلاةُ وَالسَّلامُ عَلَى رَسُولِ اللَّهِ

Praise be to Allah and blessings and peace be on the Messenger of Allah.

After the above words of praise for Allah and the blessings and peace on the Messenger of Allah, it is a Sunnah of the Prophet ﷺ to recite the following three verses of the Qur'ān which are appropriate to this occasion:

يَا أَيُّهَا الَّذِينَ آمَنُوا اتَّقُوا اللَّهَ حَقَّ تُقَاتِهِ وَلَا تَمُوتُنَّ إِلَّا وَأَنتُم مُّسْلِمُونَ

*You who have īmān! have taqwā of Allah with the taqwā due to Him
and do not die except as Muslims.* (Sūrah Āl ʿImrān 3: 102)

يَا أَيُّهَا النَّاسُ اتَّقُوا رَبَّكُمُ الَّذِي خَلَقَكُم مِّن نَّفْسٍ وَاحِدَةٍ وَخَلَقَ مِنْهَا زَوْجَهَا وَبَثَّ مِنْهُمَا رِجَالًا

كَثِيرًا وَنِسَاءً وَاتَّقُوا اللَّهَ الَّذِي تَسَاءَلُونَ بِهِ وَالْأَرْحَامَ إِنَّ اللَّهَ كَانَ عَلَيْكُمْ رَقِيبًا

*O mankind! have taqwā of your Lord who created you from a single
self and created its mate from it and then disseminated many men and
women from the two of them. Have taqwā of Allah in whose name you
make demands on one another and also in respect of your families. Allah
watches over you continually.* (Sūrat an-Nisāʾ 4: 1)

يَا أَيُّهَا الَّذِينَ آمَنُوا اتَّقُوا اللَّهَ وَقُولُوا قَوْلًا سَدِيدًا يُصْلِحْ لَكُمْ أَعْمَالَكُمْ وَيَغْفِرْ لَكُمْ ذُنُوبَكُمْ وَمَن يُطِعِ

اللَّهَ وَرَسُولَهُ فَقَدْ فَازَ فَوْزًا عَظِيمًا

*You who have īmān! have taqwā of Allah and speak words which hit
the mark. He will put your actions right for you and forgive you your
wrong deeds. All who obey Allah and His Messenger have won a mighty
victory.* (Sūrat al-Aḥzāb 33: 70-71)

I   n   ᶜ   Ī   ᵭe   v

prayers or occasional homilies, if they do not contain *tashahhud*,
it is incomplete, as the following *hadīth* suggests:

عَنْ أَبِي هُرَيْرَةَ أَنَّ النَّبِيَّ ﷺ قَالَ ﴿كُلُّ خُطْبَةٍ لَيْسَ فِيهَا تَشَهُّدٌ فَهِيَ كَالْيَدِ الْجَذْمَاءِ﴾

It is reported by Abū Hurayrah that the Prophet ﷺ said: "Every
khuṭbah that does not have *tashahhud* in it, is like a leprous hand."
(Abū Dāwūd, *bāb fī al-khuṭbah*; and at-Tirmidhī, *bāb mā jāʾa fī
khuṭbah an-nikāḥ*)

It is also recommended (*mustaḥabb*) that a short prayer (*duʿā*)
be said. The shortest prayer as a sunnah of the Prophet ﷺ is as
follows:

بَارَكَ اللَّهُ لَكَ وَعَلَيْكَ وَجَمَعَ بَيْنَكُمَا فِي خَيْرٍ

May Allah bless you, and may blessing be upon you and may He unite you in good. (Saᶜīd ibn Manṣūr)

There is no harm in saying longer prayers after this.

Likewise, a *walīmah* (marriage feast) according to all the *ᶜulamā'* of all the schools of law is *sunnah mu'akkadah*. There does not need to be any extravagance or show in the feast. It can even be bread and meat or just a small goat slaughtered and feasted upon, or according to the wealth and standing of the groom. This was an example set by the Prophet ﷺ while giving Fāṭimah in marriage to ᶜAlī:

لَا بُدَّ لِلْعُرُوسِ مِنْ وَلِيمَةٍ

The Messenger of Allah said: "The bridegroom has to give a *walīmah*. (Aḥmad, *Musnad* from Buraydah, Ibn ᶜAsākir, aṭ-Ṭabarānī, *al-Muᶜjam al-kabīr, Buraydah ibn al-Ḥaṣīb al-Aslami yukannā Abā ᶜAbdillāh*)

The role of guardians in valid Muslim marriages

The jurists of the Shāfiᶜī and Mālikī schools consider the approval of the guardian for someone to marry his ward as one of the essential conditions of a valid Muslim marriage, but the Ḥanafī and Ḥanbalī schools consider the consent of the guardian merely an ingredient. The latter two schools put greater emphasis on the proposal and acceptance. All four schools derived their views from *ḥadīth* of the Prophet ﷺ. The Shāfiᶜī and Mālikī schools have based their view on the following *ḥadīth*:

النَّبِيُّ ﷺ قَالَ ﴿أَيُّمَا امْرَأَةٍ نَكَحَتْ بِغَيْرِ إِذْنِ وَلِيِّهَا فَنِكَاحُهَا بَاطِلٌ﴾

The Prophet ﷺ said: "Any woman who married without the permission of her guardian, her marriage is null and void." (Aṭ-Ṭabarānī from Ibn ᶜAmr، Abū Dāwūd, *bāb fi al-walī;* at-Tirmidhī, *bāb mā jā'a lā nikāḥ illā bi walī;* Ibn Mājah, *bāb lā nikāḥ illā bi walī;* al-Ḥākim in *al-Mustadrak* and Aḥmad in the *Musnad* all from ᶜĀ'ishah)

The *ḥadīth* of the Prophet further clarifies as to who can play the role of a guardian:

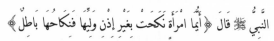

لَا تُزَوِّجُ الْمَرْأَةُ الْمَرْأَةَ، وَلَا تُزَوِّجُ الْمَرْأَةُ نَفْسَهَا

A woman cannot give a woman away in marriage and a woman cannot give herself away in marriage. (Ibn Mājah in the *Sunan* from Abū Hurayrah, *bāb lā nikāḥ illā bi walī*)

In the absence of a father or near relative, the king, amir or ruler can be a guardian. There is the case of a woman who came to the Prophet ﷺ and offered herself to him in marriage, but the Messenger of Allah ﷺ did not wish to marry her, so he married her then and there to a person who could not even settle any dowry on her due to his poverty. There was no natural guardian (father or near relative) present at the time. (Al-Bukhārī, *bāb as-sulṭān walī*)

In certain verses of the Qur'ān there is no mention at all of a guardian in express words. As for example, "*When you divorce women and they reach the end of their ʿiddah, do not prevent them from marrying their first husbands if they have mutually agreed to it with correctness and courtesy.*" (Sūrat al-Baqarah 2: 232) However, there is another verse which speaks of the need of a guardian and his careful decision. As for example, in the case of a *thayyib* (a woman who has had a husband), the Qur'ān says: "*And do not marry [believing women to] men of the idolaters until they have īmān.*" (Sūrat al-Baqarah 2: 221) This verse is addressed to women's guardians, who therefore have no right to give consent in such cases, but whose authority is implicitly understood.

As we have seen before, a divorced woman is not to be prevented from marrying in a lawful manner. (Sūrat al-Baqarah 2: 232) In the case of a widow, the Qur'ān says, "*But if they do leave you are not to blame for anything they do with themselves with correctness and courtesy.*" (Sūrat al-Baqarah 2: 240) This verse recognises the widow's right to marry someone herself. These two verses clearly recognise the right of the *thayyib* (a divorced woman or widow) to give herself in marriage, and prohibit the guardian from interference when the woman herself is satisfied. This is quite in accordance with a *ḥadīth* quoted by Abū Dāwūd that the widow and the divorced woman have greater right to dispose of themselves (in marriage) than their guardians. (Abū Dāwūd, *bāb fī ath-thayyib*)

Although Imām Abū Ḥanīfah gives freedom to the virgin who has reached the age of puberty to marry according to her choice, the consent of the guardian is still one of the conditions of marriage. He argues that a woman who has attained the age of majority can dispose of her property without reference to a guardian, so she is also entitled to dispose of her person. At the same time it cannot be denied that there is a natural bashfulness about the virgin, and moreover, she has not the same experience of men and affairs as have a widow or a divorced woman and it is therefore in the order of things that her choice of a husband should be subject to the approval of a father or other guardian, who would also settle the terms, and guard her against being misled by unscrupulous people. However, as the guardian is in fact only needed to protect her, her will must ultimately prevail according to the Ḥanafī school.

The Prophet ﷺ has said: "The widow and the divorced woman must not be married until their command is sought, and the virgin must not be married until her consent is obtained." (Al-Bukhārī, *bāb lā yunkiḥu al-ab wa ghayruhu al-bikr wa ath-thayyib illā bi riḍāhā*) Besides, "When a man gives his daughter in marriage and she dislikes it, the marriage will be repudiated."[10] There is already a case in which the Prophet ﷺ once repudiated such a marriage.

Guardianship and marriage of a minor

According to the Ḥanafī school, the marriage contract of a minor boy or girl is lawful, whether the minor girl is a virgin or a *thayyib*, provided the guardian is one of the *ᶜaṣabah* (male relations on the father's side). Imam Mālik also recognises such a marriage but only when the guardian is the father. Imam ash-Shāfiᶜī recognises such a marriage only when the guardian is the father or grandfather. The Ḥanafī view is that if the minor has been given in marriage by a guardian who is not the father or grandfather, the minor has the option on attaining majority of repudiating the marriage. However, as a *ḥadīth* already quoted shows, even if the father gives away his daughter in marriage against her wishes, and she is of age, the marriage can be repudiated if the girl so desires. If on coming of age, a girl, who was married off when a minor, finds the match unsuitable, then the marriage can be repudiated. (Abū Dāwūd, *bāb fī al-bikr yuzawwijuhā abūhā wa lā yasta'miruhā*)

The Last *Khuṭbah*

The last *khuṭbah* of the Prophet ﷺ at ᶜArafah is very significant for us, since it was delivered when the Prophet ﷺ knew that he had not much longer to live, and so it contains some of his last advice for the Muslims. He has put the marital relationship in memorable words:

> Now! Accept my counsel to you to treat women well, for they are just like captives with you, and you possess nothing of them other than this [counsel to treat them well] unless they do something patently indecent. If they do that then forsake them in their beds, and strike them lightly but not such that leaves a mark. Then if they obey you, do not seek any way against them. Now! You have a right over women, and women have a right over you. As for your right over women, they should not seat those [men or women] you dislike on your couch, and they should not give those you dislike permission to enter your houses. Now! Their right over you is that you should treat them well in dressing them and feeding them. (Ibn Mājah, *bāb ḥaqq al-mar'ah ᶜalā zawjihā;* and at-Tirmidhī, *bāb mā jā'a fī ḥaqq al-mar'ah ᶜalā zawjihā)*

Notes

[1] *cf.* Sūrat al-Baqarah 2: 229, 231 and Sūrat an-Nisā' 4: 19

[2] *istawṣū* has a variety of possible meanings including "counsel each other among yourselves to treat them well," and "accept my counsel about them and act by it and be gentle with them and keep good company with them."

[3] "In this there is the exhortation to safeguard the rights of women and there is counsel respecting them and keeping their company in a kind manner. And many *ṣaḥīḥ ḥadīth* are narrated giving counsel about them and explaining their rights and warning against falling short in that, which I have collected, or the greater part of them, in *Riyāḍ aṣ-ṣāliḥīn*." Imām an-Nawawī in his commentary on *Ṣaḥīḥ Muslim*.

[4] i.e. women living in communities of people of the Book who have accepted to live under Muslim governance.

[5] *Dār al-Ḥarb* traditionally referred to all lands in which the *Sharīᶜah* does not rule, as opposed to *Dār al-Islām* where the *Sharīᶜah* is in place. It has been suggested that *Dār al-Ḥarb* might better be known as *Dār ad-Daᶜwah* 'the abode of invitation [to Islam].'

[6] *Al-Fiqh ᶜalā al-madhāhib al-arbiᶜah Op. Cit.*, vol. 4, p. 76.

[7] *Ibid* p. 77

[8] Yūsuf ᶜAlī, The Holy Qur'ān – see note 76

[9] *Ibid.*

[10] This is the chapter heading from *Ṣaḥīḥ al-Bukhārī* in which Imām al-Bukhārī narrates the *ḥadīth* proving this point.

Chapter 11

Ta^caddud az-Zawjāt: Polygyny

POLYGYNY[1] OR MARRYING MORE THAN ONE WIFE is not new. It has existed from time immemorial among different peoples in various parts of the world. The Arabians were polygynous even before the advent of Islam and so were many other people in most parts of the world at that time. The *jāhiliyyah* Arabs used to marry a large number of women and considered them as chattels. In much of Africa there was the practice of limitless polygyny as was also the case with some of the prophets, the revelation to the final Messenger ﷺ limiting it rather than instituting it. In many cases there had been nothing even like marriage, as women could be bought and sold at will.

The institution of polygyny was recognised among the Medes, Babylonians, Abyssinians and Persians. When one goes through the Jewish and Christian religious scriptures, one finds that polygyny was an accepted part of life. Mūsā (Moses) ﷺ allowed polygyny among his people. All the Prophets mentioned in the Tawrāh, the old Testament and the Qur'ān were polygynous with the exception of the Prophet ᶜĪsā (Jesus) ﷺ who did not marry at all.

It was practised by the Greeks among whom it was already prevalent that a wife was not only transferrable but also marketable (something we do not condone). It was customary in the tribes of Africa, Australia and later in modern times with the Mormons of America. Even the Hindu law of India does not restrict polygyny.[2] The laws of Manu laid down specific conditions for celebrating subsequent marriages; it said: "A barren wife may be superseded in the eighth year; she whose children (all) die, in the tenth; she who bears only daughters, in the eleventh; but she who is quarrelsome, without delay." (Manu 9: 81)

Qur'ānic verses and *ḥadīth* on polygyny

With the advent of Islam, far from innovating polygyny as a new practice, the revelation limited the existing institution to a maximum of four wives at any one time and that too with a number of rules attached to it which we will study here. The only Qur'ānic verses that refer to polygyny are as follows:

وَإِنْ خِفْتُمْ أَلَّا تُقْسِطُوا فِي الْيَتَامَى فَانكِحُوا مَا طَابَ لَكُم مِّنَ النِّسَاءِ مَثْنَى وَثُلَاثَ وَرُبَاعَ فَإِنْ خِفْتُمْ أَلَّا تَعْدِلُوا فَوَاحِدَةً أَوْ مَا مَلَكَتْ أَيْمَانُكُمْ

If you are afraid of not behaving justly towards orphans, then marry other permissible women, two, three or four. But if you are afraid of not treating them equally, then only one, or those you own as slaves. (Sūrat an-Nisā' 4: 3)

The above rule on polygyny refers to justice being done to orphans. It was revealed immediately after the battle of Uḥud when the Muslim communities were left with many orphans and widows and some captives of war. The governing principle is that of treating orphans and widows with great humanity and equity. As Yūsuf Ali says, the occasion is past but the principle remains, and we might add that it is a situation that recurs in many guises throughout history in all cultures. Marry orphans if you are quite sure that you will protect their interests and their property and that you will do them and your other dependants justice. The verse is not merely limited to orphans but has a general application about marriage in Islam. Muslim jurists, therefore, have laid down the following conditions if someone wants to take more than one wife:

1. He should have enough financial capacity to look after the needs of the additional wives he has undertaken.
2. He must do equal justice to them all. Each wife should

be treated equally in fulfilling their conjugal and other rights.

If a man feels that he will not be able to treat them equally and with justice or he does not have the means to support them equally and with justice he should restrict himself to marrying only one wife.

Imam Mālik says in the *Muwaṭṭa'* that Ghaylān ibn Salamah accepted Islam and he had ten wives. The Messenger of Allah ﷺ said:

أَمْسِكْ مِنْهُنَّ أَرْبَعاً وَفَارِقْ سَائِرَهُنَّ

> Keep four of them and separate from the others. (Mālik, *al-Muwaṭṭa', bāb jāmiᶜ aṭ-ṭalāq*)

Similarly Abū Dāwūd mentions from al-Ḥārith bin Qays:

قَالَ : أَسْلَمْتُ وَعِنْدِي ثَمَانِي نِسْوَةٍ ، فَذَكَرْتُ ذَلِكَ لِلنَّبِيِّ ﷺ فَقَالَ: ﴿اخْتَرْ مِنْهُنَّ أَرْبَعاً﴾

> I accepted Islam and I had eight wives. I mentioned it to the Prophet ﷺ. He said: "Choose four out of them". (Abū Dāwūd, *bāb man aslama wa ᶜindahu nisā' akthar min arbaᶜ aw ukhtān*)

Marrying more than one wife makes it absolutely essential for one to be as just as is humanly possible to each of them. The very object of marriage in Islam is to have a healthy family where a man and his wife or wives and children live in peace, love and harmony as is required in the injunctions of the Qur'ān.

> *Among His Signs is that He created spouses for you of your own kind so that you might find tranquillity in them. And He has placed affection and compassion between you.* (Sūrat ar-Rūm 30: 20)

Thus man as the father and woman as the mother of the children dwell together and bring up a family in unity. Different people have different temperaments but if kindness, love, tenderness and tranquillity can be maintained, such a family unit is successful. If this is not possible then one must limit oneself to what one can easily manage, that is, one wife.

In essence polygyny is a part of the noble Sunnah of the Messenger of Allah ﷺ himself. There is simply no need to apologise for or justify polygyny as it is a positive and natural practice in itself. In addition in the following situations polygyny is often the best solution:

1. When a wife is suffering from a serious disease like paralysis, epilepsy or a contagious disease. In this circumstance it will be better if there is another wife to look after the needs of the husband and children. Her presence will also help the sick wife.
2. When a wife is proved barren and after medical examination experts have given their opinion that she is not capable of bearing a child. The husband then may marry a second wife so that he may have children since a child is a joyous event in life.
3. When she is of unsound mind. In that case the husband and the children would suffer a great deal, and a second wife might be a solution.
4. When a woman has reached old age and has become weak and infirm and cannot look after the house and the property of her husband.
5. When the husband finds out that she has bad character and cannot be reformed, and yet he does not divorce her. He should then have another wife.
6. When she has moved away from the husband's house and has become disobedient and the husband finds it difficult to reform her. He should then take another wife.
7. During a period of war when men are killed and women are left behind in very large numbers, polygyny can provide the best solution.
8. Apart from the above circumstances, if a man feels that he cannot do without a second wife and when he has the means to support her, he should take another wife.

Only limited polygyny is allowed

With the advent of Islam a limit was put on the previously limitless polygyny practised in the *jāhiliyyah* society of Arabs and non-Arabs. It was a fashion with chiefs and with tribal rulers to keep big harems. Even some Muslim rulers became victims of passion and seemed to practise limitless polygyny in the later periods of Islamic history, but this is a misunderstanding, as there is no limit to the number of slave women a man may own and with whom he may have sexual relations. However, limitless polygyny has no place in Islam. A Muslim can marry up to four wives and not more at any given time. It was only lawful for the Prophet ﷺ to marry more than four wives at a given time.

Some of the Ẓāhirī school maintained that the Qur'ānic words, *mathnā*, mean 'in twos'; *thulātha*, 'in threes'; and *rubā^c^* 'in fours', and thus the number permitted swells to eighteen in number. There are some who think erroneously that *'mathnā wa thulātha wa rubā^c^'* put together comes to nine and thus up to nine wives are allowed in Islam. These are, in reality, wrong interpretations of the Qur'ānic injunction and contrary to what is the agreement of the people of knowledge. The Prophetic interpretation of this verse is contained in the following *ḥadīth*:

عَنِ ابْنِ شِهَابٍ، أَنَّهُ قَالَ : بَلَغَنِي أَنَّ رَسُولَ اللَّهِ ﷺ قَالَ لِرَجُلٍ مِنْ ثَقِيفٍ أَسْلَمَ، وَعِنْدَهُ عَشْرُ نِسْوَةٍ حِينَ أَسْلَمَ الثَّقَفِيُّ : أَمْسِكْ مِنْهُنَّ أَرْبَعًا ، وَفَارِقْ سَائِرَهُنَّ

It is narrated from Ibn Shihāb that he said, "It has reached me that the Messenger of Allah ﷺ said to a man from Thaqīf[3] who accepted Islam, and he had ten wives when the Thaqafī accepted Islam, 'Retain four of them and separate from the rest of them.'" (Mālik, *al-Muwaṭṭa', bāb jāmi^c^ aṭ-ṭalāq*)

Once a Muslim marries more than one wife, it is essential for him to treat them equally in matters of food, residence, clothing and even in fulfilling their sexual rights. If he cannot do that, he must not take more wives. If he feels able to fulfil his responsibilities to only one, he should not marry two. Secondly, if he can do justice to two but no more, he should not marry three. The final limit is four wives.

فَإِنْ خِفْتُمْ أَلَّا تَعْدِلُوا فَوَاحِدَةً أَوْ مَا مَلَكَتْ أَيْمَانُكُمْ

But if you are afraid of not treating them equally, then only one, or those you own as slaves. (Sūrat an-Nisā' 4: 3)

The justice referred to in this verse only relates to what is humanly achievable in terms of equitable treatment.

The Qur'ān refers to human weakness in the following words:

وَلَن تَسْتَطِيعُوا أَن تَعْدِلُوا بَيْنَ النِّسَاءِ وَلَوْ حَرَصْتُمْ فَلَا تَمِيلُوا كُلَّ الْمَيْلِ فَتَذَرُوهَا كَالْمُعَلَّقَةِ

You will not be able to be completely fair between your wives, however hard you try. But do not be completely partial so as to leave a wife, as it were, suspended in mid-air. (Sūrat an-Nisā' 4: 129)

Muḥammad ibn Sīrīn in explaining this verse said that this inability referred to in the Qur'ān is in respect of love and sexual intercourse. Qāḍī Abū Bakr ibn al-ᶜArabī said: "No one can control his heart since it is entirely in the hands of Allah." The same is the case in cohabitation when one may satisfy one wife better than another. Since this was not the intention of the man, it is not his fault and hence he will not be held responsible. The mother of the *mu'minūn*, ᶜĀ'ishah, narrated thus about the Prophet ﷺ:

عَنْ عَائِشَةَ : أَنَّ النَّبِيَّ ﷺ كَانَ يَقْسِمُ بَيْنَ نِسَائِهِ فَيَعْدِلُ وَيَقُولُ: ﴿ اللَّهُمَّ هَذِهِ قِسْمَتِي فِيمَا أَمْلِكُ،
فَلَا تَلُمْنِي فِيمَا تَمْلِكُ وَلَا أَمْلِكُ ﴾

The Prophet ﷺ apportioned and was fair, and used to say, "O Allah, this is my distribution in respect of that which I control, but do not hold me responsible for what is in Your control and I have no control over." (At-Tirmidhī, *bāb mā jā'a fī at-taswiyah bayna aḍ-ḍarā'ir*)

Here the reference is to the heart and matters connected with the heart when the *ḥadīth* speaks of the things under Allah's control as Abū Dāwūd explains in his *Sunan*.[4] After understanding the aspect of equal justice to one's wives, the following *ḥadīth* of the Prophet must be kept in mind to avoid excess.

The Prophet ﷺ said: "A man who marries more than one woman and then does not deal justly with them, will be resurrected with half his faculties paralysed."

Preservation of the higher values and promotion of right-action must be the constant objective. Permission to marry more than one woman is necessary for the preservation of high social values and for safeguarding society from promiscuity. At this point it becomes relevant to quote the American Christian evangelist Billy Graham on polygyny:

> Christianity cannot do so, it is to its detriment. Islam has permitted polygamy as a solution to social ills and has allowed a certain degree of latitude to human nature, but only strictly within the framework of the law. Christian countries make a great show of monogamy, but actually they practise polygamy. No one is unaware of the part mistresses play in society. In this respect, Islam is a fundamentally honest religion and permits a Muslim to marry a second wife if he MUST, but strictly forbids all clandestine amatory associations in order to safeguard the moral probity of the community.

The Modernist approach to polygyny.

There is a growing tendency to consider some Islamic institutions outmoded when they do not conform to the western pattern of life. This is particularly true in the case of polygyny which some scholars vehemently oppose. They even tried to misinterpret certain verses of the Qur'ān saying that polygyny is not allowed in Islam. The two verses of the Qur'ān which they have referred to in strengthening their argument are verses 3 and 129 of Sūrat an-Nisā' (chapter 4 of the Qur'ān). Verse 3 reads: *"If you are afraid of not behaving justly towards orphans, then marry other permissible women, two, three or four. But if you are afraid of not treating them equally, then only one…."* Verse 129 reads: *"You will not be able to be completely fair between your wives, however hard you try."*

The argument usually advanced in respect of the above two verses is that Islam has allowed marrying more than one wife on the condition that the man be perfectly fair and just to all his wives. However, this condition is, to all intents and purposes, impossible to fulfil, as is mentioned in verse 129 quoted above. Hence, they argue that polygyny is not allowed in Islam because a man who marries more than one wife puts himself in an impossible position. They say that when someone fears injustice, they must not marry more than one wife.

The modernists consider verse 129 a clause and a legal condition attached to polygynous unions. They say that since impartial treatment cannot be attained, one must restrict oneself to monogamy. But 'impartial treatment' in the matter of residence, food and clothing is a relative term which will differ from person to person and country to country according to the economic standards of the society.

The impact of the colonial era on Muslim countries was so great that the law of personal status imposed restrictions on a husband marrying more than one wife. The first attempt of this kind was made in Syria in 1953. Syrian law on personal status (Decree No. 59) of 1953 stated: "The judge is empowered to refuse permission to a married man to marry another woman if it is established that he is not in a position to support two wives..." (Art. 17). Here it is stipulated that one must not take an additional wife unless one is capable of supporting them.[5] In this case the Syrian jurists, trained in western countries, maintained that the Qur'ānic provision in verse three of Sūrat an-Nisā' should be regarded as a positive legal precondition to the exercise of polygyny and enforced as such by the courts on the principle that those avenues that lead to abuse must be closed (*sadd adh-dharā'iᶜ*).

They made it essential for a prospective husband to seek the permission of the court to marry. It was required by Article 17 of the law that the *qāḍī* may withhold permission to a man who is already married to marry a second wife, where it is established that he is not in a position to support both. Those who contravene this are considered to be liable to penalties and the court would not recognise the marriage although, in spite of the penalty clause, they did not go as far as declaring the marriage invalid.

In Tunisia, polygyny was prohibited outright by the law of personal status in 1957. The Tunisian Code of Personal Status, 1957 says: "Polygamy is forbidden. Any person who, having entered into a bond of marriage, contracts another marriage before the dissolution of the preceding one, is liable to one year's imprisonment and a fine..." (Art. 18). Here too, modern jurists, influenced by the western pattern of life, declared that the Qur'ānic verse of Sūrat an-Nisā' would not be construed strictly as a moral exhortation but as a legal condition for polygyny, and therefore, no second marriage should be permissible unless and until adequate evidence was forthcoming that the wives would be treated impartially. They reasoned that in modern social and economic conditions such impartial treatment was practically an impossibility. Hence, they maintained that the essential condition of polygyny was impossible to fulfil. In other words, the Tunisian jurists went a step further than the Syrians and completely prohibited polygyny, contrary to explicit Qur'ānic provision.

The Moroccan code of 1958 took a middle course and prohibited polygyny conditionally when there existed any apprehension of unequal treatment. The Moroccan Code of Personal Status, 1958 says: "Polygyny is prohibited where it is likely to involve injustice towards the wives..." (Art. 30). The marriage contract concerning the second wife is not to be drawn up until she has been informed that her prospective spouse is already married. The courts were only allowed to intervene by granting divorce on the grounds of unequal treatment, which is not that much of a departure from the Mālikī school of jurisprudence practised in Morocco and which allows a co-wife to claim divorce if she is not maintained properly.

Similarly in Iraq, the law of personal status of 1959 did not declare polygyny prohibited but imposed restrictions on the institution. The Iraqi Code of Personal Status, 1959 reads: "It is not permissible to marry more than one woman without authorisation from the judge. The granting of permission is conditional upon the sufficiency of the husband's financial status for the support of the wives, and that it be for a genuine benefit" (Art. 3). One could not marry a second wife without the permission of the *qāḍī* who would not grant permission unless he was satisfied that there was no fear of any unequal treatment of the wives.

In Pakistan, a restriction was placed on polygynous marriages by the Muslim Family Law Ordinance of 1961 which required that written permission from the Arbitration Council be obtained before one could marry a second wife. Pakistan's Family Law Ordinance, provided: "No man, during the subsistence of an existing marriage, shall, except with the previous permission in writing of the Arbitration Council contract another marriage..." (Sec. 6). The permission would only be granted if the Arbitration Council was satisfied that the proposed marriage was necessary and just. In this case the consent of the existing wife was required except in cases of insanity, physical infirmity or sterility. However, it was essential to obtain the Council's permission before contracting a second marriage, whatever the case. The person who contravened this was liable to be imprisoned for up to a year or had to pay a fine of up to 5000 rupees, or both. If the *mahr* was deferred, he was required to pay it forthwith and the existing wife had the right of divorce. In spite of all these restrictions, if a second marriage was contracted without the Council's permission it would not be considered legally invalid.

The above examples lead us naturally to a consideration of the conflict between the Qur'ānic injunctions and the so-called reforms in respect of polygyny in some Muslim countries. There are countries, such as Saudi Arabia, most countries in East and West Africa, and in Asia, where the *Sharīᶜah* law of polygyny has not been tampered with by modernist forces. Then, there are countries like Syria and Tunisia where polygyny, obviously allowed in the Qur'ān and the Sunnah, has been made prohibited by law. Then, there are other countries where serious restrictions have been imposed by law on contracting a second marriage, but where the marriage, if it takes place, is not rendered invalid.

It is interesting to note that these law reforms in Muslim countries are of recent origin, since they were first introduced in Syria in 1953 and some other Muslim countries later followed suit. It is my candid view that the countries which have prohibited polygyny by law have gone against the injunctions of the Qur'ān and the Sunnah of the Prophet ﷺ and the practice of the

Companions, the Followers and the Followers of the Followers, i.e. the right-acting first generations (*salaf*).

It should be borne in mind that the role of the Prophet ﷺ did not end with one announcement of the Sunnah or the way of life to the world at large. He was to guide the people who followed him, explaining to them the implications of all the approved actions, the moral code, the divine injunctions and the form of law that sustained the whole. If polygyny were not allowed, he would have stopped people from practising it in his lifetime. There are a number of *ḥadīth* in which cases from polygynous families were brought to him. Solutions were found and justice was done, and in some cases marriages were dissolved. However, there is not a single *ḥadīth* that suggests that polygyny was forbidden by the Prophet ﷺ or the caliphs who took the right way after him or Muslim rulers of the Umayyad and the Abbasid dynasties.

There is the important question of the role of the *ᶜulamā'* and *fuqahā'* of Islam, the great learned men and jurists, who have tried to guide the *Ummah* after the death of the Prophet ﷺ. The great imams and the founders and leaders of the four schools of Islamic jurisprudence and their students have left behind volumes of works. They too have tried to find a solution to the problems arising out of polygynous unions, but have never prohibited polygyny outright. What has been discovered since 1953 that the great *ᶜulamā'* over the last 1400 years, had they been aware of it, would have persuaded them to prohibit polygyny? By declaring prohibition, the so-called modernist reformers have refused to accept the Qur'ānic injunction and have directly rejected the Sunnah of the Prophet ﷺ declaring it unworkable and have also disregarded the opinions of the great *ᶜulamā'*.

Since Tunisia in 1957 polygyny was banned in some Muslim countries. Much has been written in appreciation of these reformers by European scholars. The existence of such reforms are cited as a factor which makes people more cautious in contracting a second marriage, or else moves them to be more reckless in marrying more wives. If one takes statistics of polygynous marriages before and after the restrictions in

Syria and Tunisia, one would find few cases where people have refrained from contracting a second marriage. At the same time it has heightened tensions in the minds of those who are capable, both economically and physically of marrying more wives. A few have married contrary to the law and undergone penalties, but many have taken the shortcut of secretly entering into extra-marital relations following the life-style of the western world.

There is a dearth of empirical evidence which might enable us to answer the crucial questions: "Has the prohibition of polygyny served as a deterrent?" or "Has Muslim society prospered better as a result of the prohibition?" Quite naturally, the empirical evidence in this field will remain extremely scarce.

It is commonplace to say that the imaginary fear of the misuse of polygyny is widespread and enduring in the minds of Western-trained Muslim elites. The question is whether such fear, even if justified to some extent knowing how unpredictable human nature is, will remain uppermost when we think of the alternative of importing the moral vices of the contemporary world, where human nature has proved that marriage, divorce, commerce and all other aspects of the law are bound to be misused.

Those Muslims countries that have imposed heavy fines and imprisonment (or both) on someone who does not first obtain the permission of the Arbitration Council, as in Pakistan, or an authorisation from the judge, as in Morocco, are obviously in violation of the *Sharīᶜah* provision on polygyny. The permission will only be granted if the existing wife gives her consent except in cases of insanity, physical infirmity or sterility. Thus, obliging a man to justify his intention by giving convincing reasons would give the arbitration councils or courts far more power in restraining necessary polygynous marriages.

Some women tend to be very jealous by nature, and in spite of the fact that the husband needs a second wife on reasonable grounds, she will not understand her husband's needs, nor would the court easily understand the man's need since, "one would have a great difficulty in explaining, biologically, such a sudden change of heart." (Ingells, N. W., *Biology of Sex*, quoted by

Khalid Rashid *Op. Cit.* p. 72) If his legitimate biological desires are suppressed, it could give rise to adultery, concubinage and prostitution. The best course open for Muslims, therefore is to strive to follow the Qur'ānic advice:

وَمَا آتَاكُمُ الرَّسُولُ فَخُذُوهُ وَمَا نَهَاكُمْ عَنْهُ فَانْتَهُوا

Whatever the Messenger gives you, you should accept and whatever He forbids you, you should forgo. (Sūrat al-Ḥashr 59: 7)

The *Ummah* has survived successfully for over fourteen hundred years without these reforms and it will, inshā'Allāh, continue to do so into the future.[6]

Notes

[1] Polygyny refers to a man marrying more than one wife; polyandry refers to a woman marrying more than one husband, and polygamy covers all cases of multiple partners whether husbands or wives. Thus polygyny is the correct term to use here.
[2] *cf.* Rashid, Khalid, *Muslim Law*, Lucknow 1979, p. 73
[3] Ghaylān ibn Salamah as mentioned in the *ḥadīth* above.
[4] Abū Dāwūd, *bāb fī al-qism bayn an-nisā'*
[5] *cf.* Coulson, *A History of Islamic Law*, Edinburgh, 1971, p. 208
[6] The author has no vested interests because he has only one wife.

Chapter 12

Unlawful Forms of Marriage

Mut^c^ah: Temporary marriage

MUT^C^AH IS A FORBIDDEN FORM OF MARRIAGE which is contracted for a short period in exchange for a fixed remuneration. It was a pre-Islamic contract which was allowed in the early formative period of Islam before the *Sharī^c^ah* of Islam reached its completion. The reason it was allowed was that new Muslims were passing through a transitional period from *jāhiliyyah* to Islam. In the *jāhiliyyah* period sexual liaisons were so common that they were not considered wrong. Just as the injunctions concerning usury (*ribā*) and wine (*khamr*) were revealed only gradually, since people were so used to them, *mut^c^ah* was only allowed in the early days for people going on *jihād* or military expeditions (*ghazawāt*). Those whose faith was still weak were prone to sexual liaisons while away on *jihād*. Those who had strong *īmān*, however, even expressed the desire to be castrated in order to curb their passion. ^c^Abdullāh ibn Mas^c^ūd ﷺ said:

> We used to go on military expeditions with the Messenger of Allah ﷺ and we did not take our women with us. We asked the Prophet if we could have ourselves castrated. The Messenger of Allah ﷺ refused us to do so and allowed us to marry by giving a woman clothing for a certain period. (Ibn Jarīr aṭ-Ṭabarī, *Tahdhīb al-āthār* as cited in *Kanz al-^c^ummāl*)

It is also narrated that Sayyidunā ^c^Alī ﷺ said to Ibn ^c^Abbās:

إنَّ النَّبيَّ ﷺ نَهى عَنِ المُتْعَةِ وعَنْ لُحُومِ الحُمُرِ الأَهْلِيَّةِ زَمَنَ خَيبَرَ

The Prophet forbade temporary marriage and the eating of the flesh of the domestic donkey at the time of Khaybar. (Al-Bukhārī, *bāb nahā rasūl Allāh* ﷺ *ᶜan nikāḥ al-mutᶜah ākhiran*)

After the *Sharīᶜah* of Islam had almost reached its completion, it was again made unlawful (*ḥarām*). The temporary permission granted due to force of circumstances was revoked immediately after the Opening of Makkah to Islam.

According to a narration, the Prophet ﷺ declared:

فَإِنَّ اللهَ تَعالَى قَدْ حَرَّمَهَا عَلَيْكُمْ إِلَى يَوْمِ القِيَامَةِ.

For Allah, exalted is He, has made it unlawful for you until the Day of Rising. (ᶜAbd ar-Razzāq, *Muṣannaf*)

Muslims want to build a healthy society but *mutᶜah* marriage is basically equivalent to prostitution. There is consensus of the *ᶜulamā'* that it is unlawful. The only opinion contrary to this view was that of ᶜAbdullāh ibn ᶜAbbās, but he quickly realised the gravity of the situation and the misuse people made of this form of marriage, which had only been allowed in circumstances of warfare, and he ceased to consider it lawful. (Al-Bukhārī, also *cf. Zād al-maᶜād* vol. 4, p. 7)

Some *shīᶜah* consider it lawful even today, although it is seldom practised and it is a deeply unfortunate effect of the impact of *shīᶜism* on Islam that some Muslims now consider it permissible.

Shighār

In pre-Islamic Arabia, *shighār* was a recognised form of marriage which was forbidden by the Prophet Muhammad ﷺ after the advent of Islam because this form of marriage deprives the woman of her rights.[1]

Shighār is an Arabic term which means a dog lifting a leg while it is passing water, or a woman lifting her leg for sexual intercourse. *Shighār* marriage is that someone, *"gave him in marriage a woman on the condition of his giving him in marriage another, without dowry [for either]."* (Lane's *Arabic-English Lexicon*) The women are deprived of their dowries and so the word has been applied to this undesirable form of marriage since there is a resemblance to picking up women. *Mahr* (dowry) is the right of women and a means of their security not a bride-price to be enjoyed by her parents. It is forbidden to give one's daughter or sister in marriage in exchange for taking in marriage another man's daughter, sister or ward without paying a dowry.

Marriage with foster relations

Marriage is prohibited with a person having a foster relationship corresponding to a blood relationship. Allah says, "*Ḥarām for you are: ... your foster mothers who have suckled you, your foster sisters by suckling...*" (Sūrat an-Nisā' 4: 23)

The Prophet ﷺ said:

نعم، إن الرضاعة تحرم ما يحرم من الولادة

> Yes, breast-feeding makes all those things unlawful which are unlawful through corresponding birth relations. (Al-Bukhārī, *bāb ash-shahādah ᶜalā al-ansāb wa ar-raḍāᶜ al-mustafīḍ wa al-mawt al-qadīm*)

It renders marriage unlawful to the person related through suckling.

Marriage of a woman with a man who marries her paternal or maternal aunt

It is narrated:

نهى رسول الله ﷺ أن تنكح المرأة على عمتها أو خالتها

> Jābir said, "The Messenger of Allah ﷺ forbade that a woman should be married to a man who has married her paternal or maternal aunt." (Al-Bukhārī, *bāb lā tunkaḥu al-mar'atu ᶜalā ᶜammatihā*)

Notes

[1] In European history the dowry was paid by the bride to the bridegroom, but in Islam it is paid by the bridegroom to the bride. Dowry (*mahr*) is more fully discussed in Chapter 13.

Chapter 13

Mahr (Dowry)

No marriage without *Mahr*

MAHR (DOWRY[1]) IS THE MARRIAGE GIFT that the bridegroom gives his bride upon marriage. It has been mentioned in the Noble Qur'ān: *"Give women their dowry (ṣaduqāt) as an outright gift."* (Sūrat an-Nisā' 4: 4) It is an essential part of a Muslim marriage. It is given by the bridegroom to his bride in accordance with their mutual agreement and that of her guardian. It may be of a value from a quarter of a dinar to a thousand dinars or however much is agreed upon. *Mahr* is not like the African custom of giving a bride-price since marriage in Islam is not the sale of a girl or woman to her husband. It also differs from the old European system of dowry in which the father used to give his daughter a heavy dowry at the time of her marriage which became the property of the husband, as an inducement for him to marry the girl. Christians and Hindus in Kerala and other parts of India had the same practice. Fathers were required to pay very heavy dowries to find suitable husbands for their daughters. In the *jāhiliyyah* society of the Arabs, the *mahr* was also considered the property of the bride's guardian.

The amount of dowry varies in the *Sharīcah* according to the educational qualifications, professional standing, wealth and social status of the bridegroom and according to the negotiations undertaken by the bride's guardian on her behalf. It is a marriage gift from the bridegroom to his bride and becomes her exclusive property and the husband has no right to it whatsoever. The advent of Islam elevated the status of women; dowry is given as a mark of respect. Even if the marriage ends in divorce (*ṭalāq*), the dowry remains the wife's property and the husband has no right to take it back, except in the case of a *khul*^c divorce in which the divorce takes place at the request of the wife in consideration of some payment, for example, the return of the whole or part of the dowry paid to her.

In other words, dowry is a sum of money or other property promised by the bridegroom to be paid or delivered to the bride in consideration of the marriage.

Another word used for *mahr* in the Noble Qur'ān is *ajr* meaning reward, and is a gift given to the bride. In fact, *ajr* is that in which there is gain but no loss. The word *ṣaduqah* (pl. *ṣaduqāt*) is also used in the Noble Qur'ān[2] to signify the nuptial gift, and in *ḥadīth* it is sometimes called *ṣadāq* which derives from the same root. Another word used in the Noble Qur'ān is *farīḍah,*[3] literally: what has been made obligatory or an appointed portion. The word *mahr* is also used in *ḥadīth* to signify the dowry or nuptial gift. According to the Qur'ān, the dowry is given as a free gift by the bridegroom to the bride, at the time of contracting the marriage: *"Give women their dowry (ṣaduqah) as an outright gift."* (Sūrat an-Nisā' : 4)

The payment of the dowry on the part of the bridegroom is an admission of the independence of the bride, for she becomes the owner of property immediately on her marriage, though before it she may not have owned anything.

The settling of a dowry on the woman upon marriage is obligatory: *"Apart from that He has made all other women ḥalāl for you provided you seek them with your wealth in marriage and not in fornication. When you consummate your marriage with them give them their prescribed dowry."* (Sūrat an-Nisā' 4: 24)

In the case of a Muslim marrying a Christian or a Jewish woman, the Qur'ānic injunction is: *"So are chaste women from among the mu'minūn [ḥalāl for you] and chaste women of those given the Book before you, once you have given them their dowries in marriage, not in fornication or taking them as lovers."* (Sūrat al-

Mā'idah 5: 5) It would appear from this that the Noble Qur'ān renders the payment of dowry necessary for a valid marriage. The *ḥadīth* of the Prophet ﷺ also leads to the same conclusion.

Sayyidunā ᶜUmar ؓ the second caliph and Qāḍī Shurayḥ determined that if a wife remits the whole of the dowry or part of it but later on demands it, the husband shall be compelled to pay it because the very fact that she demands it is a clear proof that she did not remit it of her own free will.

When is the dowry to be paid?

The payment of the dowry is necessary even though it might be a very small sum.[4] In exceptional cases, a marriage is legal even if the amount of *mahr* has not been specified; but nevertheless it is obligatory and must be paid afterwards. Thus the Noble Qur'ān says, speaking of divorce: *"There is nothing wrong in your divorcing women before you have touched them or allotted a dowry to them."* (Sūrat al-Baqarah 2: 236) This shows that marriage is not valid without specifying a dowry. In *ḥadīth* the Messenger of Allah ﷺ also spoke of the validity of a marriage, even though dowry has not been named.[5] However, the dowry most be paid, either at the time of consummation of marriage or afterwards. The amount of the dowry in this case would depend upon the circumstances of the husband and the position of the wife. The Noble Qur'ān makes this clear by requiring the provision for the wife to depend upon the circumstances of the husband, *"But give them a gift – he who is wealthy according to his means and he who is less well off according to his means – a gift to be given with correctness and courtesy: a duty for all good-doers."* (Sūrat al-Baqarah 2: 236)

In a *ḥadīth* it is related that the case of a woman whose husband died before fixing a dowry and consummating the marriage, was referred to ᶜAbdullāh ibn Masᶜūd, who decided that she should be paid a dowry according to the dowry of a woman of like status with herself, and this decision was afterwards found to be in accordance with the decision of the Prophet ﷺ in a similar case.[6] In *fiqh*, it is called *mahr mithl* (lit. the dowry of those like her, or her equals) or the customary dowry. It is determined by the dowry of her sisters and paternal aunts and uncles' daughters, that is to say, with reference to the social position of her father's family. Therefore even if the dowry has not been specified upon marriage, it is to be determined and paid afterwards, and if it remains unpaid in the husband's lifetime, it is a charge on his property after his death. The words of the Noble Qur'ān require its payment upon marriage, barring exceptional circumstances when it may be determined or paid afterwards. The Mālikī school follows this rule and renders payment necessary upon marriage, while the Ḥanafī school treats it more or less as a debt owed by the husband.

Let us examine the injunction in the Noble Qur'ān about dowry:

وَآتُوا النِّسَاءَ صَدُقَاتِهِنَّ نِحْلَةً فَإِن طِبْنَ لَكُمْ عَن شَيْءٍ مِّنْهُ نَفْسًا فَكُلُوهُ هَنِيئًا مَّرِيئًا

Give women their dowry as an outright gift. But if they are happy to give you some of it, make use of it with pleasure and goodwill. (Sūrat an-Nisā' 4: 4)

These words make it obligatory upon a Muslim to give a dowry to a woman whom he takes as a wife. In Qur'ān Allah also exhorts Muslims to marry women with the permission of their (women's) guardians and to pay their dowers, even in the following case where they marry women who are slaves:

فَانكِحُوهُنَّ بِإِذْنِ أَهْلِهِنَّ وَآتُوهُنَّ أُجُورَهُنَّ بِالْمَعْرُوفِ

Marry them with their owners' permission and give them their dowries correctly and courteously. (Sūrat an-Nisā' 4: 25)

The dowry must be specified. If it is unspecified the bride and groom can deputise one of them or someone else to make a decision about it before consummation of the marriage. This is called *tafwīḍ* marriage. The specified dowry is the amount settled by the parties at the time of marriage or after the marriage is solemnised before consummation. In the case of a bridegroom who is a minor, his father would settle the amount of the dowry. The specified dowry can be either prompt (*muᶜajjal* or *naqd*) or deferred (*mu'ajjal* or *kāli'*) to a period less than the lifespans of the couple, and some have said that the longest term possible is forty years. If people accept a deferred dowry it is preferable that at least a quarter of a dīnār of it be paid before consummation of the marriage. When the dowry is prompt it is payable on demand. An unspecified dowry is the one which is not settled at the time of marriage or immediately after the marriage and then must be fixed according to the social position of the wife's family (*mahr mithl*).

What is a reasonable amount of dowry will depend on the relative position in life and social status of both parties to the marriage and will differ from place to place, period to period and country to country. The Prophet ﷺ also said:

لَا يَحِلُّ نِكَاحٌ إِلَّا بِوَلِيٍّ وَصَدَاقٍ وَشَاهِدَيْ عَدْلٍ.

"And no marriage is *ḥalāl* except with the guardian, the dowry and two reliable[7] witnesses." (Al-Bayhaqī from al-Ḥasan as a *mursal ḥadīth*)[8]

Thus it is clear that the dowry is an essential ingredient of Islamic marriage without which the contract is not complete. An *āyah* refers to the dowry as *ṣaduqah*. It has its own significance. Since the word is related to *ṣadaqah* which means charity, it is implied that the dowry is to be given as a free gift which becomes the property of the wife. Therefore she has full authority to retain her dowry for herself or give any portion of it to her husband or guardian or whoever else she wishes.

In another verse in the Noble Qur'ān Allah, exalted is He, declared:

وَإِنْ أَرَدْتُمُ اسْتِبْدَالَ زَوْجٍ مَكَانَ زَوْجٍ وَآتَيْتُمْ إِحْدَاهُنَّ قِنطَارًا فَلَا تَأْخُذُوا مِنْهُ شَيْئًا أَتَأْخُذُونَهُ بُهْتَانًا وَإِثْمًا مُبِينًا

If you desire to exchange one wife for another and have given your original wife a large amount, do not take any of it. Would you take it by means of slander and outright crime? (Sūrat an-Nisā' 4: 20)

This verse makes it clear that when a woman is divorced the dowry belongs to her, whatever its value. The husband is not entitled to take it by force, or by putting her under duress or subjecting her to slander. The husband should fear Allah and have *taqwā* and refrain from usurping the rights of his former wife. Allah further emphasises in the Qur'ān:

وَكَيْفَ تَأْخُذُونَهُ وَقَدْ أَفْضَى بَعْضُكُمْ إِلَى بَعْضٍ وَأَخَذْنَ مِنكُم مِّيثَاقاً غَلِيظاً

How could you take it when you have been intimate with one another and they have made a binding contract with you? (Sūrat an-Nisā' 4: 21)

It shows again that the dowry belongs to the woman and not her former husband. So if he tries to get it back through foul means such as slandering her, he earns the disapproval of Allah, exalted is He. In another verse in the Noble Qur'ān we find:

وَالْمُحْصَنَاتُ مِنَ النِّسَاءِ إِلاَّ مَا مَلَكَتْ أَيْمَانُكُمْ كِتَابَ اللَّهِ عَلَيْكُمْ وَأُحِلَّ لَكُم مَّا وَرَاءَ ذَلِكُمْ أَن
تَبْتَغُوا بِأَمْوَالِكُم مُّحْصِنِينَ غَيْرَ مُسَافِحِينَ فَمَا اسْتَمْتَعْتُم بِهِ مِنْهُنَّ فَآتُوهُنَّ أُجُورَهُنَّ فَرِيضَةً

And also married women, except for those you have taken in war as slaves. This is what Allah has prescribed for you. Apart from that He has made all other women ḥalāl for you provided you seek them with your wealth in marriage and not in fornication. When you consummate your marriage with them give them their prescribed dowry. (Sūrat an-Nisā' 4: 24)

The dowry is obligatory and without it no Muslim marriage can take place. When a man takes a woman in marriage, she surrenders her person to him, so a man should also surrender some of his property to her. Women retain the right to change the amount after reaching a mutual understanding with the husband.

The Qur'ān makes payment of the dowry obligatory not only in marriage between Muslims but also in marriage of a Muslim to a woman of the People of the Book i.e. the Jews and Christians.

وَالْمُحْصَنَاتُ مِنَ الْمُؤْمِنَاتِ وَالْمُحْصَنَاتُ مِنَ الَّذِينَ أُوتُوا الْكِتَابَ مِن قَبْلِكُمْ إِذَا آتَيْتُمُوهُنَّ أُجُورَهُنَّ

مُحْصِنِينَ غَيْرَ مُسَافِحِينَ وَلَا مُتَّخِذِي أَخْدَانٍ

So are chaste women from among the mu'minūn [ḥalāl for you] and chaste women of those given the Book before you, once you have given them their dowries in marriage, not in fornication or taking them as lovers. (Sūrat al-Mā'idah 20: 5)

In the Noble Qur'ān, Allah ﷻ also says:

لَّا جُنَاحَ عَلَيْكُمْ إِن طَلَّقْتُمُ النِّسَاءَ مَا لَمْ تَمَسُّوهُنَّ أَوْ تَفْرِضُوا لَهُنَّ فَرِيضَةً وَمَتِّعُوهُنَّ عَلَى الْمُوسِعِ قَدَرُهُ وَعَلَى الْمُقْتِرِ قَدَرُهُ مَتَاعًا بِالْمَعْرُوفِ حَقًّا عَلَى الْمُحْسِنِينَ

There is nothing wrong in your divorcing women before you have touched them or allotted a dowry to them. But give them a gift – he who is wealthy according to his means and he who is less well off according to his means – a gift to be given with correctness and courtesy: a duty for all good-doers. (Sūrat al-Baqarah 2: 236)

It shows that if a Muslim divorces his wife before the marriage is consummated or before a dowry is fixed he is required to give a suitable amount to the divorced woman according to his own capacity. However, if the *ṣadāq* is fixed before marriage and divorce is pronounced before consummation of the marriage, he has to pay half of the fixed dowry to her. (Sūrat al-Baqarah 2: 237)

No fixed amount for the dowry

Looking at the *Sharīᶜah* governing the rules of the dowry, no definite amount or a thing of a definite value is fixed as dowry. The injunction of the Qur'ān is silent on this issue. It is narrated by ᶜĀmir ibn Rabīᶜah that a woman belonging to Banū Fazārah was married with a pair of shoes as her dowry.

The Messenger of Allah ﷺ asked her:

﴿أَرَضِيتِ مِنْ نَفْسِكِ وَمَالِكِ بِنَعْلَيْنِ؟﴾ قَالَتْ: نَعَمْ. قَالَ: فَأَجَازَهُ.

"Are you happy with yourself that your property be a pair of shoes?" She said "Yes." The Prophet ﷺ then permitted her to marry. (Aḥmad in his *Musnad* from ᶜĀmir ibn Rabīᶜah, and at-Tirmidhī, *bāb mā jā'a fi muhūr an-nisā'*)

Likewise, a woman came to the Prophet ﷺ and said: "O Messenger of Allah, I wish to give myself to you." Then she stood for a long time waiting for an answer. Then a man stood up and said: "Messenger of Allah, if you do not need her, marry her to me." The Prophet ﷺ then asked him:

هَلْ عِنْدَكَ مِنْ شَيْءٍ تُصْدِقُهَا

Do you possess something that you can give as *ṣadaqah*?

He replied that he had only the large cloth wrapped around the lower half of the body [*izār*], which if given to her, he would be without. He was asked to give even if he had only an iron ring. Since he had none the Prophet ﷺ asked:

أَمَعَكَ مِنَ الْقُرْآنِ شَيْءٌ

Do you have anything from the Noble Qur'ān?

Yes, he said, and enumerated the sūrahs that he remembered. The Prophet ﷺ said:

قَدْ زَوَّجْنَاكَهَا بِمَا مَعَكَ مِنَ الْقُرْآنِ

I marry you to her for what you possess of the Qur'ān. (Al-Bukhārī, *bāb as-sulṭān walī*)

In this case, the chapters or portions of the Qur'ān that the man remembered were considered his dowry. But the *ḥadīth* must be properly understood. It does not negate the minimum dowry fixed by Imam Abū Ḥanīfah or Imam Mālik. Ibn al-Qayyim has explained this *ḥadīth* as meaning that the dowry is the right of a woman, and the woman mentioned in the above *ḥadīth* was satisfied with a man who was at least knowledgeable in the Qur'ān.

As for giving a large dowry, there is absolutely no harm in that. Once while giving the *khuṭbah* the Caliph ᶜUmar ؓ declared that no one should give more than 400 dirhams as dowry. When he descended, a Qurashī woman asked him: "Have you not heard Allah's injunctions?"

ᶜUmar went back to the minbar and declared:

وَآتَيْتُمْ إِحْدَاهُنَّ قِنطَاراً

...and have given your original wife a large amount... (Sūrat an-Nisā' 4: 20)

He then added:

إِنِّي كُنتُ قَدْ نَهَيْتُكُمْ أَنْ تَزِيدُوا فِي صَدُقَاتِهِنَّ عَلَى أَرْبَعَمَائَةِ دِرْهَمٍ، فَمَنْ شَاءَ أَنْ يُعْطِيَ مِنْ مَالِهِ مَا أَحَبَّ

I had forbidden you to give more than 400 dirhams as dowry. Whosoever wishes may give as much property as he wishes to give. (Narrated by Sa^c^īd bin Manṣūr and Abū Ya^c^lā)

The husband however, has no right to demand back anything of the dowry given to the wife in consideration for the marriage or ornaments, clothes, etc., given to her as gifts since once given, they become her property. It is against the *Sharī^c^ah* of Islam to ask for the return of anything given to another as a present or gift (Sūrat al-Baqarah 2: 229) except that category of gift which is entered into as an explicit exchange. The Prophet ﷺ likens the behaviour of someone who takes back his *ṣadaqah* or *zakāh* to a dog licking up its own vomit. It is illegal on the part of the husband to keep back or demand, after the divorce, what he himself gave to his wife. As a matter of fact Islam even exhorts the husband to give her something as a gift in the case of divorce. (Sūrat al-Baqarah 2: 241). The core of this matter is ownership: a wife owns her own property and no one else, not even her husband, has a right to it without her permission. Once the husband has given her a gift or dowry it is hers alone to do with as she likes.

Other conditions in respect of the dowry

The payment of dowry should be in the form of something that has value whether it be little or much. According to the Ḥanafī school the smallest amount of the dowry is ten dirhams or a dīnār but according to the Mālikī school the least dowry is equivalent to three dirhams or a quarter of a dīnār. However there is no fixed minimum in the Shāfiᶜī and Ḥanbalī schools. If one marries with a dower set in terms of a quantity of wine or pigs or anything that is unlawful in Islam or which cannot be owned or bought or sold by a Muslim, the marriage is null and void. All the jurists of the four schools agree upon this view. The Mālikī school insists that at least a quarter of a dīnār of the dowry should be given on the spot for the consummation of a valid marriage. The balance of the dowry can be given promptly on marriage or can be postponed until after the marriage.

The Ḥanafīs' point of view is that the payment of the dowry can be delayed, either part of it or the whole of it, but it must not be forgotten completely nor should the proposal for giving the dowry be made in an uncertain way, saying: "I marry you for 100 dirhams to be paid when the clouds come, or when the sky gives rain, or a traveller arrives, etc."

The Mālikīs say that the dowry may be a definite thing like a specific animal, by looking at it or by describing it such as 'this horse' or 'a particular kind of horse like the Arabian horse', or it may be a definite amount of money as mentioned earlier. If the dowry is not prompt it must not be delayed through a flimsy promise such as 'to be postponed until death or until our separation.'

According to the Shāfiᶜī and Ḥanbalī schools it is lawful to pay the entire dowry later as long as it is not forgotten completely. Once the amount of dowry is fixed and it is ready to hand, the payment should not be delayed.

According to the Mālikīs it may be given to the wife on the day of marriage except when the woman herself wants to take it later. The dowry should not be postponed simply because of the sickness of the wife. The Mālikī school view is that if it is fixed that at least a quarter of a dīnār be paid promptly and the balance later with the specific words, 'I marry you with a quarter of a dīnār or three dirhams to be paid promptly and the remaining 97 dirhams (for example) to be paid later on' that it is necessary in this case to pay her the three dirhams before consummation of the marriage and the remaining 97 later.

According to the Shāfiᶜī school the wife can refuse consummation to the husband if a dowry has been agreed but not paid. If the husband does not pay the dowry or provide maintenance for his wife, the wife can take action to annul the marriage. Shāfiᶜī jurists say that if the husband is unable to pay the dowry as agreed, then it is up to the wife either to be patient or to take the matter to the *qāḍī* to annul the marriage.

No limits have been put on the amount of the dowry. The words used in the Noble Qur'ān show that any amount of dowry may be settled on the wife, as we have seen. Thus no maximum amount has been laid down in the *fiqh* although some of the legal schools defined minimums. The Prophet ﷺ paid varying amounts to his wives: in one case the Negus paid the amount to Umm Ḥabībah (Abū Sufyān's daughter), who was then in Abyssinia where the marriage contract took pace, it being 4,000 dirhams, while in the case of other wives it was generally 480 dirhams. (Abū Dāwūd, *kitāb an-nikāḥ, bāb aṣ-ṣadāq*) The dowry of his daughter Fāṭimah was 480 dirhams.

The lowest amount mentioned in *ḥadīth* is a ring of iron (Al-Bukhārī, *kitāb al-libās, bāb khātam al-ḥadīd*), and a man who could not procure even that, was told to teach the Noble Qur'ān to his wife. (*Ibid.*) In some *ḥadīth* two handful of meal or dates are also mentioned. (Cf. Abū Dāwūd, *kitāb an-nikāḥ, bāb qillat al-mahr*) Nevertheless, most of the scholars do not think that these *ḥadīth* accurately reflect the actual practice, but rather that they are exceptional and unusual cases. The amount of the dowry may be increased or decreased by the mutual consent of the husband and wife, at any time after marriage; and this is plainly laid down in the Noble Qur'ān: "*When you consummate your marriage with them give them their prescribed dowry. There is nothing wrong in any further agreement you might come to after the dowry has been given.*" (Sūrat an-Nisā' 4: 24) The wife is the owner of the dowry and hence she may remit the dower wholly or partially. The remission of the dowry in the terminology of *fiqh* is called *hibat al-mahr.*

In the Ḥanafī school however, if the dowry has been specified (*al-mahr al-musammā*) then the question arises whether it is to be given promptly (*muᶜajjal* or *naqd*) or it is to be deferred or delayed (*mu'ajjal*). *Muᶜajjal* or prompt payment of the dowry is to be done immediately after marriage if demanded by the wife. If it is agreed that it is *mu'ajjal,* delayed or deferred, it becomes payable on dissolution of the marriage or when some misfortune brings about the breakdown of the family. When *mahr* is fixed (*musammā*), it may be split into two equal parts and it may be stipulated that one part shall be paid on the death of the husband or divorce or on the occasion of some special event.

Ibn Juzayy al-Kalbī summed up in his *al-Qawānīn al-fiqhiyyah*:

> It is permissible for the *ṣadāq* to be [part] in cash and [part] deferred for a specific period, within the lifetimes of the spouses ordinarily, but some have said that the longest possible period is forty years. It is preferred to unite the cash and the deferred amount and to pay in advance a quarter of a *dīnār* before consummation. Some people regard deferment as prohibited, but al-Awzāᶜī regarded it as permissible [to defer payment] until death or separation. (Ibn Juzayy al-Kalbī, *al-Qawānīn al-fiqhiyyah, al-kitāb al-awwal fī an-nikāḥ, al-bāb ar-rābi fī aṣ-ṣadāq*)

Notes

[1] It is almost impossible to find a suitable translation for *mahr* since 'dowry' according to the *Concise Oxford Dictionary* is "property or money brought by a bride to her husband." Nevertheless, we will use the term, but in the sense of the marriage gift given by the bridegroom to the bride upon marriage.

[2] Sūrat an-Nisā' 4: 4

[3] Sūrat al-Baqarah 2: 236

[4] Al-Bukhārī, *bāb qawl Allāh ta^cālā "wa ātū an-nisā'a ṣaduqātihim niḥlah"* (Sūrat an-Nisā' 4: 4) *wa kathrah al-mahr wa adnā mā yajūzu min aṣ-ṣadāq*

[5] Abū Dāwūd, *bāb fī man tazawwaja wa lam yusammi ṣadāqan ḥattā māt*

[6] *Ibid.*

[7] *^cAdl* here translated as 'reliable' and sometimes more literally as 'just' is more than just an assessment of character, but includes knowledge of the *fiqh* of marriage in some detail. Ordinarily the witnesses are appointed by the *amīr* and not by the bride and groom.

[8] There are many *ḥadīth* which support it.

Chapter 14

Ṭalāq: Divorce in *Sharīᶜah*

THERE CAN BE TIMES when it becomes difficult to continue a cordial relationship with one's spouse, when good advice does not work. When marriage becomes impossible, it may be better to separate amicably rather than drag on indefinitely, making the family home intolerable because in such circumstances the children are the first victims. In Islam marriage is a contract and the contract should be made to work but not forced to work when it becomes impossible. In such unavoidable circumstances divorce is permitted in the *Sharīᶜah*. Even then, however, a man must still bear in mind that his wife has taken a solemn covenant (*mīthāq*) from him:

وَأَخَذْنَ مِنكُم مِّيثَاقًا غَلِيظًا

And they have made a binding contract with you. (Sūrat an-Nisā' 4: 21)

Ṭalāq literally means to set an animal free. It is used to denote the legal method whereby a marriage is brought to an end. Although Islam allows divorce if there are sufficient grounds for it, yet the right is to be exercised only under exceptional circumstances. The Prophet ﷺ is narrated to have said:

أَبْغَضُ الْحَلَالِ عِنْدَ اللَّهِ عَزَّ وَجَلَّ الطَّلَاقُ

To Allah, mighty is He and majestic, the most hateful of the *ḥalāl* is divorce. (Abū Dāwūd, *kitāb aṭ-ṭalāq, bāb fī karāhiyyat aṭ-ṭalāq,* also Ibn Mājah, *kitāb aṭ-ṭalāq, bāb ḥaddathanā Suwayd ibn Saᶜīd*)

These words will always act as a strong check on the hasty recourse to and wanton abuse of the permissibility of divorce.

An aim of the *Sharīᶜah* is to establish a healthy family unit through marriage, but if for various reasons this purpose fails, there is no need to linger on under false hopes as is the practice among the adherents of other religions for whom divorce is not permitted. Islam encourages reconciliation between spouses rather than severance of relations, but where good relations between spouses become distinctly impossible, Islam does not keep them tied to a painful situation. This is made clear in the Noble Qur'ān. As soon as differences between the couple take a serious turn such as is likely to endanger their contract, it is ordained that arbiters be appointed to sort out these differences and bring about reconciliation between them. Allah says:

وَإِنْ خِفْتُمْ شِقَاقَ بَيْنِهِمَا فَابْعَثُوا حَكَمًا مِنْ أَهْلِهِ وَحَكَمًا مِنْ أَهْلِهَا إِنْ يُرِيدَا إِصْلَاحًا يُوَفِّقِ اللَّهُ بَيْنَهُمَا إِنَّ اللَّهَ كَانَ عَلِيمًا خَبِيرًا

If you fear a breach between a couple, send an arbiter from his people and an arbiter from her people. If the couple desire to put things right, Allah will bring about a reconciliation between them. Allah is All-Knowing, All-Aware. (Sūrat an-Nisā' 4: 35)

In case the arbitrators fail to effect a rapprochement between them, the Qur'ān permits such spouses to part. Allah says:

وَإِنْ يَتَفَرَّقَا يُغْنِ اللَّهُ كُلًّا مِنْ سَعَتِهِ وَكَانَ اللَّهُ وَاسِعًا حَكِيمًا

If a couple do separate, Allah will enrich each of them from His boundless wealth. Allah is All-Encompassing, All-Wise. (Sūrat an-Nisā' 4: 130)

If the stage of parting has been reached, the Qur'ān enjoins upon husbands not to misuse or abuse their position of power and leave the wife hanging but rather to dispose of the matter one way or the other.

وَلَن تَسْتَطِيعُوا أَن تَعْدِلُوا بَيْنَ النِّسَاءِ وَلَوْ حَرَصْتُمْ فَلَا تَمِيلُوا كُلَّ الْمَيْلِ فَتَذَرُوهَا كَالْمُعَلَّقَةِ وَإِن تُصْلِحُوا وَتَتَّقُوا فَإِنَّ اللَّهَ كَانَ غَفُورًا رَّحِيمًا

You will not be able to be completely fair between your wives, however hard you try. But do not be completely partial so as to leave a wife, as it were, suspended in mid-air. And if you make amends and have taqwā, Allah is Ever-Forgiving, Most Merciful. (Sūrat an-Nisā' 4: 129)

In the above *"so as to leave a wife, as it were, suspended in mid-air"* means to leave her as if she is neither married nor divorced, according to Ibn Juzayy al-Kalbī in his *tafsīr*.

In order to put an end to all uncertainties, in the Qur'ān Allah has laid down:

لِّلَّذِينَ يُؤْلُونَ مِن نِّسَائِهِمْ تَرَبُّصُ أَرْبَعَةِ أَشْهُرٍ فَإِن فَاءُوا فَإِنَّ اللَّهَ غَفُورٌ رَّحِيمٌ ۝ وَإِنْ عَزَمُوا الطَّلَاقَ فَإِنَّ اللَّهَ سَمِيعٌ عَلِيمٌ

Those who swear to abstain from sexual relations with their wives can wait for a period of up to four months. If they then retract their oath, Allah is Ever-Forgiving, Most Merciful. If they are determined to divorce, Allah is All-Hearing, All-Knowing. (Sūrat al-Baqarah 2: 226-7)

The above *āyāt* refer to the oath taken to forgo sexual relations with a wife, which amounts to a form of divorce (known as *īlā'*) after four months.

On the basis of these Qur'ānic injunctions and the guidance from the Sunnah of the Prophet ﷺ, the jurists of the four schools of Islamic jurisprudence have given clarifications on divorce. The *Sharḥ al-kabīr* has given the following five categories of divorce:

Divorce becomes *wājib* (obligatory) in the case of *ṭalāq al-ḥakamayn* in *shiqāq*, i.e. when two arbiters are called in and they decide that the couple must divorce.

Divorce is *makrūh* (disapproved) when it is not essential, if there is no harm anticipated either to one's self or one's wife, and there is still some hope of reconciliation. This is based on the *ḥadīth*: "Of all things which have been permitted, divorce is the most hated by Allah."

It is *mubāḥ* (permissible) when there is a need for it, particularly when the wife's character is bad (*sū' khuluq al-mar'ah*) and thus some harm is expected through the marriage continuing.

It is *mandūb* (recommended) when the wife is not fulfilling the essential duties towards her husband that Allah has imposed on her, or if she is unfaithful.

It is *maḥẓūr* (prohibited) when it is pronounced during the days of her monthly periods or in the period of post-natal bleeding. (*Ash-Sharḥ al-kabīr,* vol. 8, p. 234)[1]

In *Mughnī al-muḥtāj,*[2] the first four of the above categories of divorce are mentioned, but the fifth category is *ḥarām* (unlawful), and it is an innovated divorce (*ṭalāq al-bidᶜah*). Imām an-Nawawī mentioned only four kinds of divorce – *ḥarām, makrūh, wājib* and *mandūb* – in his *Sharḥ* on *Ṣaḥīḥ Muslim.*[3] According to him, there is no divorce which can be called *mubāḥ*.

The Mālikī jurist ad-Dardīr also agrees with the above view in his famous commentary on the *Mukhtaṣar* of Khalīl.[4]

In some of the above the apparently different technical terms are in fact almost synonyms, e.g. *maḥẓūr* (prohibited) is almost synonymous with *ḥarām,* although both have proper technical definitions.

Faskh: Annulment or abrogation of marriage

Like divorce, annulment (*faskh*) also brings an end to marriage. It literarily means to annul a deed or rescind a sale. It is decreed by the *qāḍī* after the careful consideration of an application made to him by the wife. If the *qāḍī* is satisfied that the situation of the woman is prejudiced by the marriage, he will annul the marriage. The conditions governing *ṭalāq* (divorce) and *faskh* are given in detail by jurists of the four schools of Islamic law.

It is *ṭalāq* in the following cases according to the Ḥanafī school:[5]

a. Pronouncements of divorce by the husband
b. *Īlā* divorce in which the husband swears an oath to abstain from sexual intercourse with his wife, and does not return to her within four months.

c. *Khulᶜ* divorce obtained by the wife in consideration of compensation paid to the husband such as the return of part or all of her dowry.
d. *Liᶜān*: in which the husband swears four times to have witnessed his wife in an act of adultery and a fifth time that the curse of Allah be upon him if he is lying, and the wife averts capital punishment by swearing four times that his evidence is not true and the fifth time that the wrath of Allah be upon her if he is truthful.
e. Separation because of a sexual defect (*ᶜayb jinsī*) in the husband such as impotence
f. Separation due to refusal (*ibā*) of Islam by the husband when the wife becomes a Muslim

It is *faskh* (annulment) in the following cases according to the Ḥanafī school:

a. Separation due to the apostasy of the spouses
b. Separation due to spoiling (*fasād*) of the marriage
d. Separation due to inequality of status (*kafā'ah*) or lack of compatibility of the husband.

It is *ṭalāq* according to the Shāfiᶜī and Ḥanbalī schools if there is:[6]

a. Pronouncement of *ṭalāq* by the husband
b. *Khulᶜ*
c. Declaration of *ṭalāq* by the *qāḍī* on the husband's refusal to give a divorce in the case of *īlā*

It is *faskh* according to the Shāfiᶜī and Ḥanbalī schools if there is:

a. Separation due to a defect in one of the spouses
b. Separation due to the husband's difficulty (*isār*) in providing maintenance for his wife
c. Separation due to *liᶜān*
d. Separation due to apostasy of one of the spouses
e. Separation due to spoiling of the marriage
f. Separation due to the husband's inequality of status (*kafā'ah*)

It is *ṭalāq* according to the Mālikī school in the following cases:[7]

a. Pronouncement of *ṭalāq* by the husband
b. *Khulᶜ*
c. Separation due to a defect in one of the spouses
d. Separation due to difficulty (*isār*) of the husband in providing maintenance for his wife
e. Separation due to harm (*ḍarar*) caused by one of the spouses to the other
f. Separation due to *īlā*
g. Separation due to incompatibility or inequality of status (*kafā'ah*)

It is *faskh* according to Mālikī *fiqh* in the following cases:

a. Separation due to the process of *liᶜān*
b. Separation due to the spoiling (*fasād*) of the marriage
c. Separation due to the denial of Islam by one of the spouses

Shiqāq: Breach of marriage agreement

Thus the *shiqāq* or breach of marriage agreement may arise from the conduct of either party as we have already enumerated. If either of the marriage partners misconducts himself or herself, or either of them is consistently cruel to the other, or, as may sometimes happen, they cannot live together in a marital agreement, the *shiqāq* in these cases is more express, but will still depend upon whether the parties can pull together or not. Divorce must always follow when one of the parties finds it impossible to continue the marriage agreement and is compelled to break it off.

There may also arise cases in which the husband is imprisoned for life or for a long period, or if he is absent and no news is heard of him or he is maimed for life and is unable to provide maintenance for his wife. It will be a case of *shiqāq* if the wife wants a divorce, but if she does not, the marriage will remain. In the case where the husband is aggrieved in a similar manner, he has the option of taking a second wife.

If either one of the couple reneges on Islam, the marriage will be judicially dissolved by divorce. If a non-Muslim couple embraces Islam, their marriage will continue to subsist. However, if only one of them accepts Islam and they were not People of the Book such a marriage is dissolved without a divorce. If the wife embraces Islam, the marriage is subsequently dissolved, and she starts to observe the *ᶜiddah;* but if the husband follows suit during the *ᶜiddah,* he will have first claim on her. If the husband accepts Islam, while the woman remains a Jew or a Christian, he has permission to retain her. If the husband accepts Islam but the woman is a Magian who then accepts Islam after him, they can continue as husband and wife, but if she does not accept Islam immediately, they are separated.

Procedure of divorce

There is laid down a procedure for divorce in the *Sharīᶜah* whereby reconciliation is encouraged wherever possible. However, if all efforts to reconcile and establish good relations between the two fails, and the husband and wife consider it impossible to live together any longer, they cannot be forced into remaining together. They may separate in peace and each of them may seek fulfilment with somebody else in a new marriage. Marriage is thus to be understood simply as a contract and should be made to work as long as love and respect for each other last. The aim of the *Sharīᶜah* is to establish a healthy family unit through marriage, but if this purpose fails there is no need to linger under pretences as is the practice among adherents of some other religions where divorce is theoretically not permitted and a vow is taken in the marriage ceremony that they will not separate 'until death do us part.'

It is unacceptable to leave one's wife hanging in mid-air and if there remains no chance for reconciliation then divorce is the last resort.

The divorce of the Sunnah

The *Sharīᶜah* only permits one to divorce one's wife or wives under definite conditions. Muslims can only divorce their wives once and then there is the *ᶜiddah* consisting of three distinct and separate menstrual periods within which time they may endeavour to become reconciled; but should all attempts at reconciliation prove unsuccessful, then in the third menstrual period the final separation becomes effective.

Divorce may be given orally or in writing, and it does not need to take place in the presence of witnesses. However, we are told in the Qur'ān:

> *Then when they have reached the end of their ᶜiddah either retain them with correctness and courtesy or part from them with correctness and courtesy. Call two upright men from among yourselves as witnesses.* (Sūrat aṭ-Ṭalāq 65: 2)

This is taken by the dominant majority of the jurists to mean that if the husband decides not to go through with the divorce before the expiry of the *ᶜiddah* and to take his wife back he should do that with witnesses, which is recommended in the Mālikī and Ḥanafī *madhhabs*, but some Mālikīs consider it obligatory.

Whatever the actual words used for divorce, they must expressly convey the intention that the marriage tie is being dissolved. As to whether a divorce would be effective under certain circumstances, there are differences between the schools. Evidently intention is as necessary a factor in the dissolution of marriage as in the marriage itself, but while some recognise that divorce is ineffective if given under compulsion, or in a state of intoxication, or in anger or jest, or by mistake or inadvertently, others hold it to be ineffective in some of these cases and effective in others. The Ḥanafī school's view is that the divorce becomes effective whether the words are uttered in sport or jest or in a state of drunkenness and whether a person utters them willingly or under compulsion, but Imām ash-Shāfiᶜī, for example, says that divorce in such circumstances does not become effective.

When is *ṭalāq* valid?

If due to extreme circumstances, one has to pronounce divorce, the following conditions must be satisfied for a divorce to be valid:

a. He should be sane (*ᶜāqil*)
b. He should not be a minor (*bāligh*)
c. He should be of independent discretion (*mukhtār*)

If a divorce is pronounced by an insane person or a child, it will not be considered valid. Abū Hurayrah has narrated the following *ḥadīth* from the Prophet ﷺ:

كُلُّ طلاقٍ جائزٌ، إلاَّ طلاقَ المعتوهِ المغلوبِ على عقلِه

All divorce is lawful except the divorce given by a person deficient in intellect whose intellect is overpowered. (At-Tirmidhī, *bāb mā jā'a fī ṭalāq al-maᶜtūh*. Al-Bukhārī narrates it in *bāb aṭ-ṭalāq fī al-ighlāq wa al-kurh wa as-sakrān wa al-majnūn wa amrihimā wa al-ghalaṭ wa an-nisyān fī aṭ-ṭalāq wa ash-shirk wa ghayrihi* as a statement of ᶜAlī without the final "whose intellect is overpowered.")

If a divorce is pronounced under duress, it will not be valid according to Mālik, ash-Shāfiᶜī, Aḥmad ibn Ḥanbal, ᶜAbdullāh ibn ᶜAbbās and others, but Abū Ḥanīfah considered it valid if the coercion proceeded from the amir.

If divorce is pronounced by an intoxicated person, it is not valid according to all schools of Islamic law. If the *ṭalāq* is pronounced in anger it will be considered unintentional and therefore not valid, as narrated in a *ḥadīth* of Imām Aḥmad, Abū Dāwūd, Ibn Mājah and al-Ḥākim. Similarly, divorce pronounced by mistake is not binding, according to all jurists. There is no divorce before marriage. The triple divorce pronounced at one and the same time, or when a wife is menstruating or in a state of *nifās* after childbirth, are innovated divorces and are *ḥarām* (unlawful) according to all jurists, but nevertheless they take effect.

However, the person who divorces his wife in her period or in post-natal *nifās* is compelled to take his wife back and wait until she is purified and then if he wishes he may divorce her. The divorce pronounced on a pregnant woman is binding according to all jurists except the Ḥanafīs.

The best form of *ṭalāq*: a check on separation

Of the several forms of divorce recognised in *Sharīᶜah* the one that bears the impress of the Prophet's ﷺ sanction and approval is referred to as the divorce of the Sunnah. This form of repudiation involves the following conditions, each of which is really intended to prevent a permanent breach if possible:

a. The husband, in the first place, must pronounce only one *ṭalāq* (repudiation). The object of this limitation is that he may subsequently, when better sense prevails, revoke the repudiation particularly if he has pronounced divorce from caprice or in a moment of excitement. He may take his wife back within the period of her *ᶜiddah,* which begins after the pronouncement of divorce.
b. The *ṭalāq* is to be pronounced when the wife is in a state of purity (*ṭuhr*) and when there is no bar to sexual intercourse. It is unlawful to pronounce repudiation when she is in the menses, although it will still take effect.
c. The husband must abstain from intercourse with his wife after pronouncing *ṭalāq* for the entire period of her *ᶜiddah.*[8] If they have sexual intercourse during that time, it is construed as his taking his wife back.

There is a tradition of accepted authenticity that throws considerable light on the wisdom underlying the last two restrictions. ᶜAbdullāh ibn ᶜUmar divorced his wife while she was menstruating, and the matter was reported to the Messenger of Allah ﷺ who said:

> Tell him to take her back and then to retain her until she becomes pure then menstruates and then becomes pure again. Then if he wishes he should retain her and if he wishes he should divorce her before touching her. This is the period during which Allah has ordered that women be divorced. (Al-Bukhārī, *kitāb at-tafsīr, bāb tafsīr sūrat aṭ-ṭalāq*)

Some commentators observe in connection with this tradition that the purpose of this condition is to avoid rash and hasty actions on the part of the husband through aversion and to give him the opportunity to reconsider his decision, so that perhaps he might change his mind, and exercise the right of return before the expiry of the period of *ᶜiddah*.

During this period, the marriage between the parties subsists and the husband retains his marital authority over his wife. He may, therefore, have access to his wife even without her permission, and can treat her as his wife, but this would actually amount to his exercising the right of *rajᶜah* (taking her back). During the *ᶜiddah*, the husband is under obligation to lodge his wife in his house in a separate room, and maintain her. The injunctions of the Qur'ān are quite clear on this point:

> *O Prophet! When any of you divorce women, divorce them during their period of purity and calculate their ᶜiddah carefully. And have taqwā of Allah, your Lord. Do not evict them from their homes, nor should they leave, unless they commit an outright indecency.* (Sūrat aṭ-Ṭalāq 65: 2)

And:

> *Let them live where you live, according to your means. Do not put pressure on them, so as to harass them. If they are pregnant, maintain them until they give birth. If they are suckling for you, give them their wages and consult together with correctness and courtesy.* (Sūrat aṭ-Ṭalāq 65: 6)

If the husband has pronounced one or two *ṭalāqs* and if within the prescribed period he abstains from intercourse with his wife, and does not exercise the right of taking the divorced wife back (*rajᶜah*), he loses the power to do so upon the expiration of the term, and the complete cessation of marital rights and duties takes place. A fresh marriage would be necessary for them to re-unite. (Sūrat al-Baqarah 2: 232)

Jurists, however, differ over the interpretation of the strict definition of the *ᶜiddah* in the above quoted verses of *rajᶜah*. Ḥanafī jurists are of the opinion that the husband retains the right of re-union up to the time of the purification of the wife by a bath after the third monthly menstruation. The same is the opinion of Sayyidunā Abū Bakr, Sayyidunā ᶜAlī, ᶜAbdullāh ibn ᶜAbbās, Abū Mūsā al-Ashᶜarī, ᶜAbdullāh ibn Masᶜūd and some other Companions. The jurists of the Mālikī and Shāfiᶜī schools, however, are of the opinion that the husband forfeits the right of re-union as soon as the wife begins the third menstruation. This opinion is based on the views of Sayyidatunā ᶜĀ'ishah, ᶜAbdullāh ibn ᶜUmar and the companion Zayd ibn Thābit. It is the unanimous view of all jurists based on the Qur'ān that the husband retains the right to take his wife back only when he has pronounced one or two divorces, but he forfeits that right when he pronounces three divorces.

Furthermore, if the husband has divorced his wife three times, it will not be lawful for him to have relations with her unless she marries another husband and this second marriage is consummated and then she is divorced again. Such a triple divorce (i.e. three divorces pronounced at one and the same time) is regarded as a *ḥarām* innovation (*bidᶜah*) but it is binding.

In the Mālikī school, as we have seen, the husband has the right to take his wife back, as long as she has not yet entered the third menstruation in the course of the *ᶜiddah*: the third menstruation in the case of a free woman, and second menstruation in the case of a slave woman. (Al-Qayrawānī, *Risālah*, *Op. Cit.* ch 32: *Bāb fi'n-nikāḥ wa'ṭ-ṭalāq*, pp. 89-97)

Divorce of the Sunnah is of two types: *ṭalāq rajᶜī* "divorce in which the husband retains the right to take his wife back within the *ᶜiddah*" and *ṭalāq bā'in* "final [but not irrevocable] divorce". The first two pronouncements of divorce followed by *ᶜiddah* periods for the wife with whom marriage has been consummated are called *ṭalāq rajᶜī* in which return to the conjugal relationship is still possible. When the divorce is pronounced for the third time it becomes *ṭalāq bā'in*.

Ṭalāq rajᶜī is based on the following Qur'ānic injunction:

الطَّلَاقُ مَرَّتَانِ فَإِمْسَاكٌ بِمَعْرُوفٍ أَوْ تَسْرِيحٌ بِإِحْسَانٍ

Divorce can be pronounced two times; in which case wives may be retained with correctness and courtesy or released with good will. (Sūrat al-Baqarah 2: 229)

This is a safety measure in the matrimonial relationship. Where divorce for mutual incompatibility is allowed there always remains a danger that the parties might act hastily then regret it and reconcile, and then again wish to separate. To prevent repetition of such capricious actions, this limit is prescribed by the Generous Qur'ān. Divorce with the possibility of reconciliation is only allowed twice. After that the parties must definitely make up their minds either to dissolve their marriage permanently or to live honourably together in mutual love and forbearance; neither party worrying the other nor grudging nor evading the duties and responsibilities of marriage.

In the *ṭalāq rajᶜī* the spouses can still enjoy the usual benefits from each other short of sexual relations since the marital relationship has not disappeared, sexual relations being an act of his taking her back. If one of them dies, the other will inherit from him or her, as the case may be. Maintenance will still remain available to the wife and children, but on divorce the wife loses her maintenance whereas the children's maintenance is still a duty on the husband. The *rajᶜah* or return is the right of the husband. In the Qur'ān Allah says:

وَبُعُولَتُهُنَّ أَحَقُّ بِرَدِّهِنَّ فِي ذَٰلِكَ إِنْ أَرَادُوا إِصْلَاحًا

> *Their husbands have the right to take them back within that time, if they desire to be reconciled.* (Sūrat al-Baqarah 2: 228)

It will suffice just to utter words like "I take you back" or the return can be effected through an action like resuming sexual relations, or kissing each other. According to Imām ash-Shāfiᶜī the return is only possible by uttering specific words. According to Imām Mālik it is not permissible to be in private with the divorced wife or to have sexual relations with her without her permission; but there is no harm in eating with her.

Ṭalāq bā'in is, for example, divorce with three pronouncements or divorce pronounced before consummation of the marriage. There is no possibility of return to conjugal relations. There are two kinds of *ṭalāq bā'in*: minor (*baynūnah ṣughrā*) and major (*baynūnah kubrā*). The *baynūnah ṣughrā* decreases the conjugal rights of the husband. In the event of the death of one of the parties, the other will not inherit from him or her, as the case may be. While in *baynūnah kubrā* all the conjugal rights cease.

The former husband cannot even remarry the former wife unless she marries another man who then divorces her without any intention of doing so merely to make her valid for remarriage to her former husband.

A severe restriction on frequency of *ṭalāq*

One can understand that the very spirit of the prescribed form of *ṭalāq* is geared towards the possibility of a revocation (*rajᶜah*) of the divorce and reconciliation of the couple. If, however, the couple fail to take advantage of the prescribed interim measures, and are determined to break from each other, and if the couple have already undergone two divorces and two reconciliations, the husband may pronounce the *ṭalāq* for the third time and thus dissolve the marriage definitively. The divorced wife is forthwith rendered unlawful to him and he cannot remarry her unless she first marries another person with a valid and binding contract, is divorced by that person, after bona fide consummation of the marriage, and completes the period of *ᶜiddah* consequent upon that divorce. (Sūrat al-Baqarah 2: 230)

This severe condition has been the subject of much comment particularly by non-Muslim critics who forget that the very existence of such a condition demonstrates that the principles of Islam are entirely opposed to the alleged facility or ease in giving divorce. The object of laying down such a strict rule, is to prevent a definite dissolution of marriage, by appealing to people's sense of honour.

This rule restrains the frequency of divorce among Muslims and it renders separation more rare by imposing a check on its frequent practice.

***Ṭalāq ḥasan* according to the Ḥanafī *madhhab*:**

In this form, which is a form common in the Ḥanafī *madhhab*, *ṭalāq* is pronounced as follows:

a. Three successive pronouncements of divorce are made.
b. They are made during three consecutive periods of *ṭuhr* (purity)

c. There is no intercourse during any of the three periods of purity.
d. It remains revocable until the third, final pronouncement of divorce is made, on pronouncement of which final formula the divorce becomes irrevocable.

Ṭalāq al-Bidᶜah: innovated divorce

During the life of the Prophet ﷺ, a new form of divorce made its appearance as an innovation (*bidᶜah*). In this form, *ṭalāq* becomes irrevocable as soon as it is pronounced. It happens in a number of different ways: the husband utters the formula "I divorce you; I divorce you; I divorce you!" in one sitting, or conveys it to the wife in writing. Other forms of expression are tantamount to irrevocable divorce such as saying to the wife, "You are *ḥarām* for me!" These forms of divorce leave no room for reconsideration or a change of mind. This is usually done by ignorant Muslims to satisfy their selfish motives or in a fit of anger. When such Muslims pronounce divorce thrice at one and the same sitting they commit a serious wrong action against the precepts of the *Sharīᶜah*. The Messenger of Allah ﷺ has very severely denounced this practice and Sayyidunā ᶜUmar ﷺ used to whip husbands who pronounced divorce thrice at one go.

In the event of a final divorce, the *Sharīᶜah* laws are very particular in providing for the protection of the wife's property against the avarice of the husband. If the divorce is due to a cause imputable to the husband, he has to pay off the *mahr* that has been settled as her right of dowry. "The wife thus occupies", observes Syed Ameer Ali, "a decidedly more advantageous position than the husband" in the *Sharīᶜah*.

At this juncture, it will be appropriate to look at the method of divorce that existed before the advent of Islam in order to understand the extent of reforms introduced by the Book of Allah and the Sunnah of the Prophet ﷺ.

The method of divorce before the advent of Islam

Divorce was practised in the pre-Islamic world, but the form and method of divorce were inhumane. Whenever a man became angry, whether for valid reasons or just to show his dislike and hatred of the woman, she had no recourse to any legal procedure nor could she receive any alimony or maintenance or any other kind of right from him.

Even when the Greeks were at the height of their civilisation, their form of divorce was not guided by any rules and regulations or conditions and restrictions. Divorce had become a part of their matrimonial life, and even if the two parties vowed to a condition at the agreement of the marriage not to separate from each other, the judge would still grant them divorce if the matter was taken to court.

The ancient Romans, on the other hand, looked upon divorce as impossible after religious wedding rites were performed but the husband was given limitless rights over the wife, to the extent that in some cases after quarrelling with each other the husband use to murder his wife in order to get rid of her, since according to their law there was no recourse to any legal action to separate. Later on, divorce was introduced among the Romans.

Among the later Romans, divorce was recognised. The laws of the Twelve Tables admitted divorce. However, a Roman had the power of summarily putting his wife to death for acts like drinking, poisoning and substitution of a spurious child, but the wife had no right to sue for divorce and, if she solicited separation, her temerity made her liable to punishment. In the later Republic, the facility and frequency of divorce could not contribute to happiness and virtue; and in fact it tended to destroy all mutual confidence and to exaggerate every trifling dispute. Gibbon says:

> In three centuries of prosperity and corruption, this principle was enlarged to frequent practice and pernicious abuse. Passion, interest, or caprice, suggested daily motives for the dissolution of marriage; a word, a sign, a message, a letter, the mandate of a freedman, declared the separation; the most tender of human connections was degraded to a transient society of profit or pleasure. (Edward Gibbon: *The Decline and Fall of the Roman Empire*, Volume IV. Chapter XLIV : Idea of the Roman Jurisprudence)

Judaism improved upon existing horrible conditions and divorce was legal but still men had immense powers in divorce. The husband could easily divorce his wife by levelling the flimsy charge of irreligiosity at her. Besides, according to their law if a woman had not given birth to a child after ten years of marriage, it was essential for the husband to divorce her.

According to ancient Hebraic law, a husband could divorce his wife for any cause which made her disagreeable to him and there were few or no checks on the arbitrary and capricious use of his power. Women however, were not allowed to demand divorce from their husbands for any reason whatsoever under the law.

Christianity, as shown in its scriptures, has a unique system of divorce. It opposed Judaism and declared divorce unlawful, mainly attributing that to the teaching of Jesus عليه السلام. It went so far as to declare any subsequent marriages of either of the divorced parties to be unlawful.

It is said in Matthew:

> It hath been said, whosoever shall put away his wife, let him give her a writing of divorcement. But I say unto you, that whosoever shall put away his wife, saving for the cause of fornication, causeth her to commit adultery: and whosoever shall marry her that is divorced committeth adultery. (Matthew 5: 31-32)

Likewise it is reported in Mark as follows:

> And he saith unto them whosoever shall put away his wife, and marry another committeth adultery against her. And if a woman shall put away her husband, and be married to another, she committeth adultery. (Mark 10: 11-12)

The whole subject of making divorce an impossibility is also based on the following teachings of the Bible: "Whatsoever God has put together, let no man put asunder." (Matthew, 19:6) When one thinks about the Christian position on divorce, it is surprising that it was initially allowed in the case of adultery of either party; when God put them together, who then is separating them? When there are pressing circumstances where the two life partners cannot live together under one roof and finally get separated, it is also done by God Himself since He is the Creator of the two partners.

Roman Catholics interpret Matthew as not being grounds for divorce at all. They say that there is no divorce in Christianity. Adultery automatically nullifies marriage. So in such cases it becomes obligatory for the man to desert his wife. Protestants allowed divorce on the grounds of adultery only, but not on any other grounds, including cruelty, high-handedness and prolonged quarrels.

Since the first recognition of divorce, of course, the legislation on divorce has become entirely utilitarian and available from the state for simple reasons of incompatibility. The Orthodox Coptic Church of Egypt has made many amendments to the Biblical provision for divorce. They include the wife's barrenness for three years, contagious disease and prolonged quarrelling where there is no hope of settlement, but these amendments are social and man-made rather than being based on the commands of the Bible.

Ancient Hindu Doctrine considered marriage an indissoluble tie, enduring beyond the death of either party. This was the reason why widows were burned alive along with the dead body of the husband.

Among the Arabs also, the power of divorce possessed by the husband was unlimited. They recognised no rule of humanity or justice in the treatment of wives.

In the *jāhiliyyah* period before Islam, the Arabs used to divorce their wives at any time, for no reason whatsoever. They were also in the habit of revoking the divorce, and then divorcing again as many time as they liked. They could, if they were so inclined, swear by one of their idols that they would have no intercourse with their wives, though still living with them. They could arbitrarily accuse their wives of adultery, dismiss them and leave them with such notoriety as would deter other suitors, while they themselves would go exempt from any formal responsibility for maintenance or legal punishment. (Ibrahim Abdel Hamid, *Dissolution of Marriage,* an article in Islamic Quarterly, vol. 3)

Imām Mālik, in his *Muwaṭṭa'* has given the following two situations prevalent in the early days of Islam coming down from the *jāhiliyyah* period:

> It used to be that a man would divorce his wife and then return to her before her *ᶜiddah* was over, and that was alright, even if he divorced her a thousand times. The man went to his wife and then divorced her and when the end of her *ᶜiddah* was in sight, he took her back and then divorced her and said, "No! By Allah, I will not go to you and you will never be able to marry again." Allah, the Blessed, the Exalted, sent down, *"Divorce can be pronounced two times; in which case wives may be retained with correctness and courtesy or released with good will."* (Sūrat al-Baqarah 2: 227) People then saw divorce in a new light from that day, whether they were divorced or not divorced. (Mālik ibn Anas, *Muwaṭṭa'*, Book 29, Number 29.28.80. Translated by Aisha Bewley and Yaqoub Johnson, Madina Press.)

Again:

> Allah, the Blessed, the Exalted, sent down about a man who divorced his wife and then returned to her while he had no need of her and did not mean to keep her so as to make the *ᶜiddah* period long for her by that in order to do her harm, *"Do not retain them by force, to transgress. Whoever does that has wronged himself."* (Sūrat al-Baqarah 2: 231) Allah warns them by that *āyah*. (Mālik ibn Anas, *Muwaṭṭa'*, Book 29, Number 29.28.81)

ᶜĀ'ishah ﷺ has reported that men used to divorce their wives at will and take them back at will even though they were in *ᶜiddah*, even at times divorcing her a hundred times or more. It is on such an occasion that the revelation came:

الطَّلاقُ مَرَّتَانِ فَإِمْسَاكٌ بِمَعْرُوفٍ أَوْ تَسْرِيحٌ بِإِحْسَانٍ

Divorce can be pronounced two times; in which case wives may be retained with correctness and courtesy or released with good will. (Sūrat al-Baqarah 2: 227) (At-Tirmidhī, *kitāb aṭ-ṭalāq wa al-liᶜān, bāb*))

Taḥlīl or *ḥalālah*

Taḥlīl or *ḥalālah,* which means legalising or making a thing lawful, was also a pre-Islamic practice. When the wife was divorced irrevocably after three pronouncements of divorce, and the husband wanted to take her back, she had first to marry a third person on condition that he would divorce her after having sexual relations with her. This was called *ḥalālah*. It is a mistake to confound *ḥalālah* with marriage since *ḥalālah* is a kind of punishment for the woman who had to undergo sexual relations with another man, whereas marriage is a perpetual marital tie in which divorce may not occur. It is for this reason that the Prophet ﷺ cursed those who resorted to this practice. He said: "The curse of Allah be on the man who commits *ḥalālah* and the man for whom the *ḥalālah* is committed." (At-Tirmidhī 9:25, *bāb mā jā'a fī al-muḥallil wa al-muḥallal lahu*) Sayyidunā ᶜUmar ؓ is reported to have said that if two men were brought to him who had taken part in the practice of *ḥalālah*, he would treat them as adulterers.

In other words Qur'ān and the Sunnah of the Prophet ﷺ warn against any prearranged scheme that a certain man should marry a certain divorced woman with the understanding that after sexual relations he would divorce her again to enable the former husband to re-marry his divorced wife. This is an unlawful act and such a marriage is no marriage at all but adultery and the woman does not become the lawful wife of the first husband by such a prearranged scheme. Sayyidunā ᶜAlī, ᶜAbdullāh ibn Masᶜūd, Abū Hurayrah and ᶜUqbah ibn ᶜĀmir all relate *ḥadīth* to the effect that the Prophet ﷺ cursed all who utilised such devices.

Three separate divorces

Three divorces pronounced on separate occasions, as allowed in the Qur'ān, of which the third is irrevocable, were of very rare occurrence, as such divorce naturally occurred over long intervals. The case of Rukānah is mentioned in the reports; he first divorced his wife in the time of the Prophet ﷺ, then remarried her and divorced her a second time in the rule of ᶜUmar ؓ, and finally in the caliphate of ᶜUthmān ؓ.

The Qur'ānic verse specifies as follows:

فَإِن طَلَّقَهَا فَلَا تَحِلُّ لَهُ مِن بَعْدُ حَتَّىٰ تَنكِحَ زَوْجًا غَيْرَهُ فَإِن طَلَّقَهَا فَلَا جُنَاحَ عَلَيْهِمَا أَن يَتَرَاجَعَا إِن ظَنَّا أَن يُقِيمَا حُدُودَ اللَّهِ وَتِلْكَ حُدُودُ اللَّهِ يُبَيِّنُهَا لِقَوْمٍ يَعْلَمُونَ

But if a man divorces his wife a third time, she is not ḥalāl for him after that until she has married another husband. Then if he divorces her, there is nothing wrong in the original couple getting back together provided they think they will remain within Allah's limits. These are Allah's limits which he has made clear to people who know. (Sūrat al-Baqarah 2: 230)

Custody (*ḥaḍānah*)

The custody of children belongs to the mother after divorce, while the father has the duty of their maintenance. This condition remains in force until a boy becomes sexually mature, and until a girl is married and the marriage is consummated. If the mother dies or marries another husband, the right of custody passes into the hands of their maternal grandmother; after that comes the maternal aunt and so on. However, if there are none of the mother's maternal relations the custody passes into the hands of sisters and then paternal aunts. If there are none of these, the right passes into the hands of agnates. (Al-Qayrawānī, *Risālah*, ch 33: *Bāb fi'l-ᶜiddah wa'n-nafaqah*, pp. 98-101)

Differences of opinion of the four schools of Islamic jurisprudence in the matter of divorce

The Ḥanafī school is of the view that it is unlawful (*ḥarām*) to divorce one's wife as long as there is stability in the relations of the couple. Imām ash-Shāfiᶜī, however, does not consider it unlawful. Imām Abū Ḥanīfah and Imām Mālik considered the pronouncement of the triple divorce *ḥarām* and a *bidᶜah*, and for the one who gives it, it is a wrong action. Imām Aḥmad ibn Ḥanbal and Imām ash-Shāfiᶜī do not reckon the act *ḥarām*.

Sicknesses like leprosy (*baraṣ*)[9] cannot be grounds for divorce according to Imām Abū Ḥanīfah, but Imām ash-Shāfiᶜī and Imām Mālik say that this can be grounds for divorce. If a man pronounces divorce in the throes of death (*maraḍ al-mawt*), and he dies while she is still in *ᶜiddah*, the wife will still be entitled to her share of the inheritance. Imām ash-Shāfiᶜī considered sexual intercourse with a woman who has been given a divorce in which the husband reserves the right to take her back (*rajᶜah*) as *ḥarām* (unlawful), but Imām Abū Ḥanīfah says that in such a case, the husband can have intercourse with her and it will amount to *rajᶜah*. It is not necessary to mention in specific words that he intends her to return back (*rajᶜah*). Imām ash-Shāfiᶜī also emphasises the need for witnesses for *rajᶜah*, but Imām Abū Ḥanīfah says that if witnesses are not easily available, there is no need for them.

Bad treatment through pre-Islamic practices

Ẓihār: Injurious comparison

The word *ẓihār* is derived from *ẓahr* meaning 'back'. An Arab, in the days of ignorance, would say to his wife, *"anti ᶜalayya: ka-ẓahri ummī"* i.e. "You are to me as the back of my mother". This was called *ẓihār*. No sooner were these words pronounced, than the relations between husband and wife would come to an end, but the woman was not at liberty to leave her husband's house and had to drag out her existence as a forsaken wife. The *Sharīᶜah* prohibits this ugly practice of *jāhiliyyah* society.

The following injunction of the Qur'ān condemns *ẓihār*:

مَّا جَعَلَ اللَّهُ لِرَجُلٍ مِّن قَلْبَيْنِ فِي جَوْفِهِ وَمَا جَعَلَ أَزْوَاجَكُمُ اللَّائِي تُظَاهِرُونَ مِنْهُنَّ أُمَّهَاتِكُمْ وَمَا جَعَلَ أَدْعِيَاءَكُمْ أَبْنَاءَكُمْ ذَٰلِكُمْ قَوْلُكُم بِأَفْوَاهِكُمْ وَاللَّهُ يَقُولُ الْحَقَّ وَهُوَ يَهْدِي السَّبِيلَ

Allah has not allotted to any man two hearts within his breast, nor has He made those of your wives you equate with your mothers your actual mothers, nor has He made your adopted sons your actual sons. These are just words coming out of your mouths. But Allah speaks the truth and He guides to the Way. (Sūrat al-Aḥzāb 33: 4)

This was an evil custom, through which the husband selfishly deprived his wife of her conjugal rights and yet kept her tied to him as a slave without her being free to remarry. Through this practice of pronouncing words implying that she was like his mother, she could not demand conjugal rights but was not yet free from his control and could not contract another marriage. Allah condemned *ẓihār* in the strongest terms and an expiation is provided for it if the husband regrets and does not in fact wish to divorce his wife. A man sometimes says such words in a fit of anger without them affecting him as such, but they degrade the position of a woman.

One of the Companions, Aws ibn aṣ-Ṣāmit, treated his wife Khawlah in this manner. Khawlah came to the Prophet ﷺ and complained of her husband's ill-treatment. The Messenger of Allah ﷺ told her that he was unable to interfere. She went back disappointed and it was then that the Prophet ﷺ received the revelation contained in Sūrat al-Mujādilah that:

> *Allah has heard the words of the woman who disputes with you about her husband and lays her complaint before Allah. Allah hears the two of you talking together. Allah is All-Hearing, All-Seeing.* (Sūrat al-Mujādilah 58: 1)

The Qur'ān further clarifies this in the following:

الَّذِينَ يُظَاهِرُونَ مِنكُم مِّن نِّسَائِهِم مَّا هُنَّ أُمَّهَاتِهِمْ إِنْ أُمَّهَاتُهُمْ إِلَّا اللَّائِي وَلَدْنَهُمْ وَإِنَّهُمْ لَيَقُولُونَ مُنكَرًا
مِّنَ الْقَوْلِ وَزُورًا وَإِنَّ اللَّهَ لَعَفُوٌّ غَفُورٌ

> *Those of you who divorce your wives by equating them with your mothers, they are not your mothers. Your mothers are only those who gave birth to you. What you are saying is wrong and a slanderous lie. But Allah is Ever-Pardoning, Ever-Forgiving.* (Sūrat al-Mujādilah 58: 2)

The immediate occasion as we have noted before was what happened to Khawlah bint Thaᶜlabah the wife of Aws ibn aṣ-Ṣāmit. Though a Muslim, he divorced her by an old pagan custom, a custom that was degrading to women. It was particularly hard on Khawlah, for she loved her husband and was pleased with her little children but had no resources to support them and under *ẓihār* her husband was not bound to support them. She presented her plea to the Prophet ﷺ and in prayer to Allah. Her plea was accepted, and it was no longer possible to retain the wife and prevent her remarrying but one had either to let her go or return to conjugal relations with her after the expiation mentioned in the following *āyāt*:

وَالَّذِينَ يُظَاهِرُونَ مِن نِّسَائِهِمْ ثُمَّ يَعُودُونَ لِمَا قَالُوا فَتَحْرِيرُ رَقَبَةٍ مِّن قَبْلِ أَن يَتَمَاسَّا ذَٰلِكُمْ تُوعَظُونَ بِهِ وَاللَّهُ بِمَا تَعْمَلُونَ خَبِيرٌ

Those who divorce their wives by equating them with their mothers, and then wish to go back on what they said, must set free a slave before the two of them may touch one another. This is what you are enjoined to do. Allah is aware of what you do. (Sūrat al-Mujādilah 58: 3)

If one does not find means to free a slave as an expiation, then he should do one of the following alternatives:

فَمَن لَّمْ يَجِدْ فَصِيَامُ شَهْرَيْنِ مُتَتَابِعَيْنِ مِن قَبْلِ أَن يَتَمَاسَّا فَمَن لَّمْ يَسْتَطِعْ فَإِطْعَامُ سِتِّينَ مِسْكِينًا ذَٰلِكَ لِتُؤْمِنُوا بِاللَّهِ وَرَسُولِهِ

Anyone who cannot find the means must fast for two consecutive months before the two of them may touch one another again. And anyone who is unable to do that must feed sixty poor people. That is to affirm your īmān in Allah and His Messenger. (Sūrat al-Mujādilah 58: 4)

Unless he performs *kaffārah* (expiation), she is owed maintenance for herself and for her children until such time as a divorce becomes final should the husband choose divorce, but her husband cannot claim his conjugal rights without expiating his *ẓihār.* If it was a hasty act and he repented of it, he cannot claim his conjugal rights until after the performance of his expiation as mentioned above. If she loved him, as in Khawlah's case, she can also herself sue for conjugal rights in the legal sense of the term and compel her husband to perform the penalty and resume marital relations.

Īlā: The Husband Swearing to Abstain from Sexual Relations with His Wife

Īlā like *ẓihār* was also an evil practice of the pre-Islamic days by which the wife was kept in a state of suspense, sometimes for the whole of her life. *Īlā* which means literally swearing, signifies technically the taking of an oath that one will not have sexual relations with one's wife. In pre-Islamic days the Arabs used to take such oaths frequently and as the period of suspension was not limited, the wife had sometimes to pass her whole life in bondage, having neither the position of a wife nor that of a divorced woman free to marry elsewhere.

After the advent of Islam, the situation was corrected through the divine revelation commanding that if a husband did not re-assert conjugal relations within the period of four month, the wife should be divorced:

لِّلَّذِينَ يُؤْلُونَ مِن نِّسَآئِهِمْ تَرَبُّصُ أَرْبَعَةِ أَشْهُرٍ فَإِنْ فَآءُو فَإِنَّ اللَّهَ غَفُورٌ رَّحِيمٌ

> *Those who swear to abstain from sexual relations with their wives can wait for a period of up to four months. If they then retract their oath, Allah is Ever-Forgiving, Most Merciful.* (Sūrat al-Baqarah 2: 226)

Īlā, in reality, was meant to make life difficult for a woman by keeping her hanging in the air. That form of the *jāhiliyyah* exists also in ordinary relations between husbands and wives when out of temper or sour relations husbands vow not to sleep with their wives.

From the words *"Those who swear to..."*, the jurists belonging to the Ḥanafī and Shāfiᶜī schools of thought conclude that this period of four month applies only to those cases of separation which are made on oath; if they remain separate for any length of time without an oath, this law would not apply to them.

On the other hand, the Mālikī jurists are of the opinion that the maximum period of four months of separation applies to all cases of deliberate abstinence from sexual intercourse if the husband intends to cause hardship. Imām Aḥmad ibn Ḥanbal also supports this opinion.

Sayyidunā ᶜAlī, Ibn ᶜAbbās and al-Ḥasan al-Baṣrī are of the opinion that this law applies only in cases of abstinence from sexual intercourse as a result of strained relations, and it does not apply to the case in which the husband and wife agree to discontinue conjugal relations with mutual consent for some common good whilst maintaing cordial relations. There are other jurists who are of the opinion that the law of *īlā* would apply to every case of separation made on oath irrespective of whether their relations remain good or bad; hence it should not go beyond the prescribed term of four months.

Some jurists interpret this to mean that if they break their oath within four months and re-establish conjugal relations, in that case there would be no expiation (*kaffārah*) for this oath, and that Allah would forgive the breach of their oath without expiation. However, the majority of the jurists are of the opinion that expiation must be made in any case. *"If they then retract their oath, Allah is Ever-Forgiving, Most Merciful"* does not mean that the expiation will be remitted. It merely means that Allah will accept the expiation and forgive the wrong done against the other during their separation.

According to the verdict of the Caliph ʿUthmān, ʿAbdullāh ibn Masʿūd, Zayd bin Thābit ﷺ and some other jurists, they can only reunite within the four months. The expiry of this term itself is a proof that the husband has decided upon *ṭalāq* (divorce). Hence after its expiry, divorce will automatically take place and the husband will forfeit the right of reunion. If, however, both of them agree, they may remarry. There is a verdict to the same effect from Sayyidunā Umar, Sayyidunā ʿAlī, ʿAbdullāh ibn ʿAbbās and ʿAbdullāh ibn ʿUmar ﷺ and the jurists of the Ḥanafī school have accepted the same.

The famous Follower, Saʿīd ibn al-Musayyab, and some others are of the opinion that after the expiry of four months, there will be an automatic single revocable divorce in which the husband will have the right to reunite within the period of *ʿiddah*, and if he does not reunite within this period, they may remarry if they still so desire.

On the other hand, ʿĀ'ishah, Abu'd-Dardā', and many other jurists of Madīnah are of the opinion that after the expiry of four months, the case should be taken to a court so that the judge may order the husband either to reunite with his wife or divorce her.

Liʿān: Imprecation by both parties

The natural outcome of marriage is procreation. Children cement the relationship between the married partners. It is through children that the lineage of a man continues. Marriage brings about legitimate children. This is the reason why Islam has forbidden adultery and marriage is made essential. Children born out of wedlock bear the name of the husband of the woman who gives birth to them as the *ḥadīth* of the Prophet ﷺ suggests:

الوَلَدُ لِلفِرَاشِ

> The child belongs to the [one on whose] bed [it is born]. (Al-Bukhārī, *bāb al-walad li al-firāsh ḥurratan kānat aw ammatan;* Muslim, *bāb al-walad li al-firāsh wa tawaqqā ashs-shubuhāt;* Ibn Jarīr in *Tahdhīb al-āthār;* ᶜAbd ar-Razzāq; Saᶜīd ibn Manṣūr in his *Sunan;* Aḥmad in his *Musnad* from ᶜĀ'ishah, Abū Umāmah al-Bāhilī and ᶜUbādah ibn aṣ-Ṣāmit; at-Tirmidhī, *bāb mā jā'a anna al-walad li al-firāsh;* an-Nasā'ī , *bāb ilḥāq al-walad bi al-firāsh idhā lam yanfihi ṣāḥib al-firāsh;* Ibn Mājah, *bāb al-walad li al-firāsh wa li al-ᶜāhir al-ḥajar;* Abū Dāwūd, *bāb al-walad li al-firāsh*)

This is because people laid claim to children through adultery, and the Prophet ﷺ gave the judgement that the child belonged to the couple to whom he was born not to the adulterer who alleged paternity.

In no circumstances should a husband intentionally deny the fatherhood of his child according to the above quoted *ḥadīth* of the Prophet ﷺ. If one merely depends on the slanderous allegations of his enemies that the child is not his own, it is still wrong on his part to disown his child. Such a drastic step could prove very harmful for the future of the child as well as the mother. However, if it is beyond any doubt in the husband's mind that his wife has been dishonest and committed adultery and a child which has been born is due to her intercourse with another man, the *Sharīᶜah,* in such cases, does not thrust the responsibility of the child on to the husband of the woman, nor does it impose the child as a responsibility on his property. In such a case in which the husband lacks four witnesses *liᶜān* or imprecation by the two parties comes into force. The process of *liᶜān* has been clearly shown in Sūrat an-Nūr of the Qur'ān:

وَالَّذِينَ يَرْمُونَ أَزْوَاجَهُمْ وَلَمْ يَكُن لَّهُمْ شُهَدَاءُ إِلَّا أَنفُسُهُمْ فَشَهَادَةُ أَحَدِهِمْ أَرْبَعُ شَهَادَاتٍ بِاللَّهِ إِنَّهُ لَمِنَ الصَّادِقِينَ ۝ وَالْخَامِسَةُ أَنَّ لَعْنَتَ اللَّهِ عَلَيْهِ إِن كَانَ مِنَ الْكَاذِبِينَ ۝ وَيَدْرَأُ عَنْهَا الْعَذَابَ أَن تَشْهَدَ أَرْبَعَ شَهَادَاتٍ بِاللَّهِ إِنَّهُ لَمِنَ الْكَاذِبِينَ ۝ وَالْخَامِسَةَ أَنَّ غَضَبَ اللَّهِ عَلَيْهَا إِن كَانَ مِنَ الصَّادِقِينَ

Those who make an accusation against their wives and have no witnesses except themselves, such people should testify four times by Allah that they are telling the truth and a fifth time that Allah's curse will be upon them if they are lying. And the punishment is removed from her if she testifies four times by Allah that he is lying and a fifth time that Allah's anger will be upon her if he is telling the truth. (Sūrat an-Nūr 24: 6-9)

The difference between unsubstantiated accusations of sexual impropriety (*qadhf*) and *liᶜān* is that the latter is restricted to the husband's accusation against his wife. In the case of *qadhf* four just witnesses[10] are required to give evidence to prove the accusation as laid down in the verse of the Qur'ān: "*But those who make accusations against chaste women and then do not produce four witnesses: flog them with eighty lashes and never again accept them as witnesses.*" (Sūrat an-Nūr 24: 5)

The person engaging in *liᶜān* has to swear four times in the name of Allah saying that he saw his wife committing adultery or that the pregnancy was not from him, and then the fifth time invoking Allah's curse (*laᶜnah*) on himself if he had accused her falsely. Likewise with the woman, if she were not guilty of adultery would also take four oaths saying that she was not guilty and that her husband had lied. The fifth time, she would also invoke Allah's curse upon herself if she was lying. This is why we never translate *liᶜān* as mutual imprecation, because that would give the false impression that the couple curse each other, whereas in reality they lay curses on themselves if they are not telling the truth.

If she confessed her guilt, she would be given the *ḥadd* punishment for adultery. If the husband hesitated and refused to take the required oaths, he would be given the *ḥadd* punishment for unsubstantiated accusations of sexual impropriety. According to Imām Abū Ḥanīfah, if he refuses to take the oaths, he must be imprisoned until he agrees to take the oath or the wife confesses her guilt, or the husband withdraws the accusation or he divorces his wife. Imām Mālik, Imām ash-Shāfiᶜī and Imām Aḥmad ibn Ḥanbal take a different view. If the husband refuses to take the required oath, he will be given the *ḥadd* punishment for *qadhf* which amounts to eighty lashes. If the wife refuses to take oaths of her innocence, she will be deemed guilty of adultery and will be given the *ḥadd* punishment accordingly. Imām Abū Ḥanīfah insists here too that she must be detained until she takes the oaths.

When the *qāḍī* hears the suit, the husband has two alternatives. He may retract or withdraw the charge before the end of the trial which will immediately bring the case to an end and there is no need to take any other action nor would there be any embarrassment for the wife. However, if he persists in his attitude and takes the oath followed by the oaths taken by the wife as to her innocence, as we have described before, the suit for *liᶜān* will be deemed complete. There will be no need for pronouncement of divorce by the *qāḍī* according to both Imām Aḥmad ibn Ḥanbal and Imām Mālik. According to Imām Abū Ḥanīfah, however, it will be essential then for the judge to pronounce divorce and dissolve the marriage. Imām ash-Shāfiᶜī, however, takes quite a different view from the other Imāms. He holds that the moment the husband finishes taking the oaths of imprecation, declaring that his wife had committed adultery and invoking the curse of Allah upon himself if he were a liar, he has given a heavy blow to the love and confidence that he had in his wife. Then *liᶜān* is complete the moment the husband finishes taking the five oaths. Once a marriage is dissolved by the *qāḍī* after the due process of *liᶜān* stipulated in the Qur'ān, it will result in irrevocable divorce according to all the schools of Islamic jurisprudence, with the exception of Imām Abū Ḥanīfah whose view was that if later the husband declares that he had lied while taking the oaths and that everything had happened in the heat of the moment and out of temper, the husband would be given the *ḥadd* punishment for *qadhf*. Thereafter they can remarry and the child will be considered his.

Notes

[1] Also *cf.* aṣ-Ṣābūnī, ᶜAbd ar-Raḥmān, *Ḥurriyyat az-zawjayni fi'ṭ-ṭalāq,* Cairo 1968, pp.85-86
[2] *Mughnī al-muḥtāj,* vol.3, p.307
[3] An-Nawawī, *Sharḥ ᶜalā Muslim,* vol.10, p.61
[4] Ad-Dardīr, *Sharḥ Mukhtaṣar Khalīl,* vol.2, p.423
[5] ᶜAbd al-Ḥakīm Muḥammad, *Aḥkām al-usrah,* p.114
[6] *Al-Fawākih al-ᶜadīdah fi fiqh al-Ḥanābilah,* vol.2, p.27
[7] *Bidāyat al-mujtahid,* vol.2, p.43
[8] These three months constitute the *ᶜiddah* period which is obligatory on wives with whom marriage has been consummated. "*Divorced women should wait by themselves for three menstrual cycles.*" Sūrat al-Baqarah 2: 228. Women who are not yet menstruating or whose menstrual cycle is over wait for three months.
[9] *Baraṣ* is sometimes called leuce, leucoderma, leukoderma or vitiligo. It is the "condition in which the pigment is lost from areas of the skin, causing whitish patches, often with no clear cause."
[10] Four witnesses are not in themselves sufficient, for they must be four 'just' witnesses, i.e. people of unimpeachable integrity.

Chapter 15

Khul^{c}

Divorce at the Request of the Wife

Definition of *khul*^{c}

KHUL^{C} IS DERIVED FROM *KHUL*^{C} *ATH-THAWB,* i.e. removing clothing from the body, because woman is the clothing of man, and vice-versa as is declared in the Qur'ān:

هُنَّ لِبَاسٌ لَّكُمْ وَأَنتُمْ لِبَاسٌ لَّهُنَّ

> *They are clothing for you and you for them.* (Sūrat al-Baqarah 2: 187)

Just as the *Sharī*^{c}*ah* provides for a husband to divorce his wife, the wife can also ask for divorce if sufficient grounds exist for it. For example, if the husband is cruel, she can ask for divorce (*khul*^{c}) and is not forced to tolerate what is intolerable to her.

Mālikī jurists define *khul*^{c} as *ṭalāq bi* ^{c}*iwaḍ* or 'divorce by giving something in return.' (*Ḥāshiyah ad-Dasūqī, dars: faṣl fī al-kalām* ^{c}*alā al-khul*^{c} *wa mā yata*^{c}*allaqu bihi min al-aḥkām*)

Ḥanafī jurists say that it is the end of a marital relationship with mutual consent either with the utterance of the word *khul*^{c} or something that means the same. (Ibn Najīm, *al-Baḥr ar-Rā'iq,* vol. 4, p. 77)

Shāfi^{c}ī jurists say that 'it is a separation sought with something given in return and with pronouncement of the word divorce or *khul*^{c}.' (*Nihāyat al-Muḥtāj,* vol. 6, p. 47) It can be achieved through the mutual agreement of the two parties or through the order of the *qāḍī* on payment by the wife to the husband of a certain amount that does not exceed what was given to her as dowry (*mahr*). (Aṣ-Ṣābūnī, *Ḥurriyyat az-zawjayni fi'ṭ-ṭalāq, Op. Cit.*, p. 495)

Guidance from Qur'ān and Sunnah on *khul*ᶜ

The Qur'ānic injunction makes it clear that a wife is entitled to ask her husband for a divorce (*khul*ᶜ) if she fears cruelty or desertion from him. Allah lays down:

وَإِنِ امْرَأَةٌ خَافَتْ مِن بَعْلِهَا نُشُوزًا أَوْ إِعْرَاضًا فَلَا جُنَاحَ عَلَيْهِمَا أَن يُصْلِحَا بَيْنَهُمَا صُلْحًا وَالصُّلْحُ خَيْرٌ وَأُحْضِرَتِ الْأَنفُسُ الشُّحَّ وَإِن تُحْسِنُوا وَتَتَّقُوا فَإِنَّ اللَّهَ كَانَ بِمَا تَعْمَلُونَ خَبِيرًا

If a woman fears cruelty or aversion on her husband's part, there is nothing wrong in the couple becoming reconciled. Reconciliation is better. But people are prone to selfish greed. If you do good and have taqwā, Allah is aware of what you do. (Sūrat an-Nisā' 4: 128)[1]

It is narrated in *Ṣaḥīḥ al-Bukhārī*:

عَنِ ابْنِ عَبَّاسٍ أَنَّ امْرَأَةَ ثَابِتِ بْنِ قَيْسٍ أَتَتِ النَّبِيَّ صَلَّى اللَّهُ عَلَيْهِ وَسَلَّمَ فَقَالَتْ ﴿يَا رَسُولَ اللَّهِ ثَابِتُ بْنُ قَيْسٍ مَا أَعْتِبُ عَلَيْهِ فِي خُلُقٍ وَلَا دِينٍ وَلَكِنِّي أَكْرَهُ الْكُفْرَ فِي الْإِسْلَامِ﴾ فَقَالَ رَسُولُ اللَّهِ صَلَّى اللَّهُ عَلَيْهِ وَسَلَّمَ ﴿أَتَرُدِّينَ عَلَيْهِ حَدِيقَتَهُ﴾ قَالَتْ ﴿نَعَمْ﴾ قَالَ رَسُولُ اللَّهِ صَلَّى اللَّهُ عَلَيْهِ وَسَلَّمَ ﴿اقْبَلِ الْحَدِيقَةَ وَطَلِّقْهَا تَطْلِيقَةً﴾

The wife of Thābit ibn Qays came to the Prophet ﷺ and said, "Messenger of Allah! Thābit ibn Qays: I do not find fault within his character or his *dīn*, but I deplore [to fall into] *kufr* in Islam." So the Messenger of Allah ﷺ said, "Do you return his orchard [which he gave as a dowry] to him?" She said, "Yes." The Messenger of Allah ﷺ said [to Thābit], "Accept the orchard and divorce her once." (Al-Bukhārī, *bāb al-khul*ᶜ *wa kayfiyyat aṭ-ṭalāq fīhi*)

The fiqh of *khul*ᶜ

The *qāḍī* Ibn Rushd wrote in his *Bidāyat al-mujtahid*:

The terms *khul*ᶜ, *fidyah* (ransom), *ṣulḥ* (conciliation) and *mubāra'ah* all refer to a single meaning, which is a woman's paying

> something in exchange for her divorce, except that the term *khul^c* refers specifically to her paying everything that he gave her [as dowry], and *ṣulḥ* refers to her paying a part of it, *fidyah* to the payment of most of it, and *mubāra'ah* to her dropping some right that she had over him, according to the claims of the *fuqahā'*. (Ibn Rushd, *Bidāyat al-mujtahid*, the book on divorce, chapter three on *khul^c*)

Thus when the wife becomes apprehensive that her husband is failing to observe the bounds prescribed by the *Sharī^{c}ah*, that is, he cannot perform the duties imposed on him by the conjugal relationship or his company is simply intolerable to her, then she can release herself from the tie, by giving up the whole of her dowry or some property in return, in consideration of which the husband is to give her *khul^c* and when they have done this, an irreversible divorce takes place by mutual consent. If the wife fails to pay the compensation however, there is yet another means to dissolve the marriage: through *mubāra'ah*,[2] according to which no complete compensation is paid, and a separation is effected by the mutual consent of the parties and her dropping her claim to some right that she is owed by her husband.[3]

Compensation (*^{c}iwaḍ*) is a matter of arrangement between the husband and wife. The wife may pay a sum less than, equal to or more than the dowry according to the Mālikī and Shāfi^{c}ī schools and other scholars, or return the whole or a portion of the dower, or she may make any other agreement for the benefit of the husband such as, for instance, that she nurse their child during its two years of suckling, or keep and maintain the child for a fixed period at her own expense after having weaned it; but this must be done in agreement with the husband.

If the wife is an unfortunate woman who is subjected to abuse and threats by a husband who in reality wants her to forfeit the whole of her dowry, she need not repay him the dowry. She can go to the *qāḍī* with a complaint against him and demand a formal separation. If her allegations are true, the *qāḍī* will call upon the husband to repudiate her. In the event that he refuses to do so, the *qāḍī* himself pronounces a divorce which will operate as a valid repudiation, and the husband will be liable for the whole of the dowry, if any has been deferred. This is called *tafrīq* or legal separation.

The first *khul*c case in Islam was quoted by Imām al-Bukhārī as we saw above.

This *ḥadīth* clearly shows that Thābit was blameless, and that the request for divorce came from the wife who feared she would not be able to observe the bounds set by Allah, and she would not be able to perform her function as a wife. The Prophet ﷺ here permitted the woman to release herself by returning the dowry to the husband as compensation.

The majority of jurists agree on the legality of *khul*c. Imām Mālik says that if by harsh treatment a husband has forced his wife to ask for *khul*c, the wife is entitled to get back the sum she has paid him for *khul*c, but the separation will still be valid under *Sharīcah*. (*Al-Mudawwanat al-kubrā*, 5, 22. Also al-Qurṭubī, *Jāmi*c *al-aḥkām*, 3, 138) The only jurist who does not agree with the legality of *khul*c is Bakr ibn cAbdullāh al-Muzanī, a famous scholar of the Followers. (*Fatḥ al-Bārī*, 9: 346) According to ash-Shawkānī, his view falls outside of the *ijmā*c or consensus (Ash-Shawkānī, *Fatḥ al-qadīr* 1: 213).

When can *khul*c be demanded

It should be noted that *khul*c must only be sought in extreme circumstances. It must not be resorted to on flimsy grounds. The following *ḥadīth* of the Prophet ﷺ gives a warning to women who ask for *khul*c without any reasonable grounds:

قَالَ رَسُولُ اللهِ ﷺ ﴿أَيُّمَا امْرَأَةٍ سَأَلَتْ زَوْجَهَا الطَّلَاقَ مِنْ غَيْرِ بَأْسٍ فَحَرَامٌ عَلَيْهَا رَائِحَةُ الْجَنَّةِ﴾

> The Messenger of Allah ﷺ said: "If any woman asks her husband for divorce without any specific harm [done her], the fragrance of the Garden will be unlawful to her." (Ash-Shawkānī, *Fatḥ al-qadīr* 1:214. Also see *al-Mughnī*, 8:174)

Al-Ḥasan al-Baṣrī also narrated a *ḥadīth* from Abū Hurayrah ؓ on the same issue:

الْمُنْتَزِعَاتُ وَالْمُخْتَلِعَاتُ هُنَّ الْمُنَافِقَاتُ

Women who ask for separation and *khul*[c] are hypocrites. (Al-Bayhaqī, *as-Sunan al-kubrā*, 7: 376)

According to Ibn Ḥajar (Shāfiʿī) *khul*[c] is disliked (*makrūh*) except when there is a fear that the limits of Allah will not be observed if release is not sought. (*Fatḥ al-Bārī*, 9:346) According to ad-Dasūqī, *khul*[c] is permissible in the best known view of Mālikī *ʿulamā'* but he acknowledges that some consider it disliked. (*Ḥāshiyat ad-Dasūqī, dars: faṣl fī al-kalām ʿalā al-khul*[c] *wa mā yataʿallaqu bihi min al-aḥkām*) The following are some of the causes for which a wife can demand a divorce by authority of the *qāḍī*. Where the wife has the right to proffer a claim of *tafrīq* through the husband's bad treatment of the wife, she will be granted a divorce without having to pay him compensation. Ibn Juzayy al-Kalbī said that one of the three stipulations on *khul*[c] is: "That the woman's *khul*[c] is by her own choice and because of her desire to separate from her husband without compulsion or harmful behaviour from him. Then if either of these two preconditions are lacking the divorce is executed but *khul*[c] is not." (*al-Qawānīn al-fiqhiyyah*) Divorce may be granted by the *qāḍī* for:

1. Habitual ill-treatment of the wife
2. Non-fulfilment of the terms of the marriage contract
3. Insanity
4. Incurable incompetency
5. Quitting the conjugal domicile without making provision for the wife
6. Any other similar causes which in the opinion of the *qāḍī* justifies a divorce

Compensation and *ʿiddah* for *khul*[c]

Once the case goes to court, the *qāḍī* will first of all try to ascertain whether the wife really dislikes the husband so much that she can no longer live with him and whether he has been the guilty party in causing her suffering. Then if the *qāḍī* is satisfied that they cannot live together happily, he will fix as compensation anything that he considers proper, and the husband will have to accept that and divorce the wife.

As soon as *khul^c* is granted, the husband forfeits the right to take her back (*raj^cah*) after divorce because it has been sought by the wife and she has given some compensation for her divorce. However, it is lawful for them to remarry in a new marriage after that with mutual consent.

According to the majority of the Muslims, the term of the *^ciddah* for the wife in case of *khul^c* is the same as for that for divorce since it is regarded as one type of divorce. But Abū Dāwūd (*bāb al-khul^c*)[4], at-Tirmidhī (*bāb mā jā'a fī al-khul^c*), and Ibn Mājah (*bāb ^ciddah al-mukhtali^cah*) have narrated *ḥadīth* to the effect that there is only one monthly course as the term for the wife after the divorce, and the Caliph ^cUthmān ☙ decided a case in accordance with this. (Ibn Kathīr, vol. 1, p. 276)

According to the Mālikī school, *khul^c* is not confined to the utterance of any particular word. Some other words like *fidyah*, *ṣulḥ* and *mubāra'ah* can also be used, as we have seen. The word *khul^c* is specially used when a woman asks for a release by returning all that was given to her as dowry, *ṣulḥ* refers to part payment, *fidyah* to payment over and above[5] and *mubāra'ah* means dropping a right that the wife had over her husband.[6] Qāḍī Abū Bakr ibn al-^cArabī has mentioned in his *Aḥkām al-Qur'ān* that Imām Mālik defined *mubāra'ah* as meaning *khul^c* (release) in consideration of payment before the consummation of marriage, while *khul^c* is effected after consummation. (Ibn al-^cArabī, *Aḥkām al-Qur'ān, sūrat al-baqarah, al-āyat as-sābi^cah wa as-sittūn, al-mas'alat as-sādisah ^cashrah*; also *see* al-Qurṭubī, *Jāmi^c al-aḥkām*, his commentary on Sūrat al-Baqarah 2: 229)

Khul^c of a terminally ill woman

If a woman sought *khul^c* during her last sickness (*maraḍ al-mawt*) and died while still in *^ciddah*, her *khul^c* is still valid and the former husband, according to the Ḥanafī school (*Al-Baḥr ar Rā'iq*, 4: 80), will receive whatever is less out of the following three options:

1. An amount agreed to be given in consideration for *khul^c*
2. One third[7] of the estate after paying her debts
3. His share of inheritance from her

Ibn Rushd, the Mālikī *qāḍī,* has narrated from Ibn Nāfi[c] from Imām Mālik that the *khul[c]* in terminal illness will be valid with all of the one-third (*thuluth*) (*Bidāyat al-mujtahid, kitābb aṭ-ṭalāq, al-bāb ath-thālith fī al-khul[c], al-faṣl ath-thānī fī shurūṭ wuqū[c]ihi, al-mas'alat ar-rābi[c]ah;* See also *Tāj al-madhhab* 2:291), i.e. her *khul[c]* is valid but as she was terminally ill and had technically thus become as if dead already, then the *khul[c]* can only be paid out of the third that is her right to bequeath, and the husband does not inherit from her. The Shāfi[c]ī school also agrees with the validity of the *khul[c]* pronounced in the throes of death, and the former husband will receive whatever is lesser of the *mahr al-mathal* (the dowry ordinarily paid to someone of her standing) or one third of the estate of the deceased. (*Op. Cit.*, vol. 2, p. 555) The Ḥanbalī view on this issue is the same as the Mālikī stand. (*Al-Mughnī* 8:215)

The *khul[c]* negotiated by anyone other than the wife, such as her father or guardian, will be null and void according to the Ẓāhirī and Ḥanbalī schools but it is valid according to the Ḥanafī, Mālikī and Shāfi[c]ī schools. It is said in the Ẓāhirī text *al-Muḥallā*[8] that in their view *khul[c]* negotiated by the father is void,[9] and that likewise, no-one is allowed to negotiate *khul[c]* on behalf of an insane or mentally deranged woman or a minor female whether he happens to be her father or the ruler or anyone else. According to the Shāfi[c]ī school, there is no difference whether *khul[c]* is negotiated on her behalf by the father or guardian of the woman or a stranger. (*Ibid.*, p. 559) The Ḥanafī school says that the father or a stranger can only negotiate *khul[c]* with the permission of the woman concerned. (*Al-Baḥr ar-rā'iq*, 4: 97)

According to the Mālikī school, *khul[c]* negotiated by a minor or an insane woman is unlawful. If the father negotiates it on behalf of his minor or insane daughter, *khul[c]* will be valid whether it is paid through the father's property or that of his daughter, and whether it is obtained with or without her permission. (*Al-Muntazi' al-Mukhtār*, 2: 435) The Ḥanafī school considers the *khul[c]* sought by an insane woman or a minor who is not a *mumayyazah,* i.e. reached the age of discernment and discrimination, as void. (*Al-Mabṣūṭ* 6:180; also *cf. al-Baḥr ar-rā'iq*, 4:80)

Can *khul*^c be given at any time?

At the outset, it would be fair to say that the conditions that apply to divorce (*ṭalāq*) will also apply in *khul*^c. There are different opinions about the *khul*^c pronounced in the period of menstruation. According to *Mukhtaṣar an-Nāfi*^c (*Mukhtaṣar an-Nāfi*^c, p. 227; see also *Jawāhir al-Kalām* 5: 360), *khul*^c can only be given in the period of purity (*ṭuhr*). The Ibadis[10] believe that it is an innovation (*bid*^c*ah*) to pronounce *khul*^c while the woman is menstruating. (*Sharḥ an-Nīl* 3:556) The Ḥanafīs consider it *makrūh* (disliked) (*Mukhtaṣar al-Qudūrī,* 2:23), but the famous scholar Ibn ^cĀbidīn said that it is not *makrūh* (*Ḥāshiyah Ibn* ^c*Ābidīn,* 2: 428), since the Messenger of Allah did not ask the wife of Thābit ibn Qays about it when *khul*^c was granted to her through the intervention of the Prophet ﷺ (*Mukhtaṣar al-Muzanī,* 4:51). Al-Kharshī, the Mālikī jurist says that when the woman has willingly obtained *khul*^c in consideration of her payment, it is her right to do so even during the period of menstruation (*Sharḥ al-Kharshī* 3:169). The Ḥanbalī jurist says that since *khul*^c comes about by mutual agreement of the two married partners, there is no harm even if it is given during menstruation (*Al-Mughnī,* 8:174).

Notes

[1] Commentators of the Qur'ān have also derived the rule in respect of *khul*ᶜ from other Qur'ānic injunctions: Sūrat an-Nisā' 4: 20, 130

[2] *Mubāra'ah* means reaching a mutually agreeable compromise in which, for example, the wife accepts the non-payment of what remained due to her of her dowry.

[3] Most matters that are agreed between two parties and are acceptable to both of them are consonant with the *Sharīᶜah*, as long as nothing *ḥarām* is committed.

[4] Abū Dāwūd commented, "The ᶜ*iddah* of the woman who has a *khul*ᶜ divorce is the same as that of a divorced woman."

[5] Ibn Rushd refers to *fidyah* as being payment of 'most of' the dowry but perhaps he meant 'more than' the dowry, and Allah knows best.

[6] *Bidāyat al-mujtahid*, 2, 40; *al-Mudawwanat al-Kubrā*, 5, 28. Here the words *mukhtaliᶜah* [the woman divorced by *khul*ᶜ] and *muftadiyah* [the woman divorced by *fidyah*] are discussed by Imām Mālik.

[7] The dying person is allowed to bequeath one third of the estate, whereas two-thirds goes to the heirs who receive fixed shares (*farā'iḍ*). The crux of the case here is to decide whether the terminally ill wife's husband is divorced and paid from the third or whether since she divorced him while dying, he should receive his ordinary share of her estate as her husband.

[8] *Ḥurriyyat az-zawjayni fi'ṭ-ṭalāq*, 2:557; see also *al-Inṣāf* 8:389

[9] Note that the Ẓāhirī *madhhab* is no longer extant and its judgements not ordinarily valid, but it is still quoted by *fuqahā'* for the sake of completeness, and because the *qāḍī* or *mujtahid* may have unusual cases in which he must resort to such judgements.

[10] The Ibadis are a remnant of the sect known as the *Khawārij* and thus

their views are only of interest in a kind of archaeological way as the sect does not and has never belonged to the People of the Sunnah and the Community.

Chapter 16

ᶜ*Iddah* – the period of waiting; guidance from Qur'ān and Sunnah

THE WORD ᶜ*IDDAH* is derived from the Arabic word ᶜ*adad* meaning 'number.' In the terminology of the *Sharīᶜah* it means the period of waiting a woman has before being capable of re-marriage after the death of a husband or separation or divorce from him. Muslim jurists have unanimously agreed that it is incumbent (*wājib*), since the injunction of the Qur'ān is quite explicit on the subject:

وَالْمُطَلَّقَاتُ يَتَرَبَّصْنَ بِأَنفُسِهِنَّ ثَلَاثَةَ قُرُوءٍ

Divorced women should wait by themselves for three menstrual cycles. (Sūrat al-Baqarah 2: 228)

The Prophet ﷺ had ordered al-Furayᶜah bint Mālik the sister of Abū Saᶜīd al-Khudrī:

امْكُثِي فِي بَيْتِكِ حَتَّى يَبْلُغَ الْكِتَابُ أَجَلَهُ.

Remain in your house until the term has reached its limit. (At-Tirmidhī, *abwāb aṭ-ṭalāq wa al-liᶜān ᶜan rasūlillāh* ﷺ, *bāb mā jā'a ayna taᶜtaddu al-mutawaffī ᶜanhā zawjuhā*)

The *Sharīᶜah* emphasises that reconciliation is a better course than divorce and gives them the opportunity to mend their relations if they have gone sour. Therefore, the Qur'ān prescribes a period of waiting after divorce has been pronounced so that a spell of temporary separation and suspension of conjugal relations may give the couple time to rethink and reconsider their own interest and that of the family and children. The ᶜ*iddah* has another important object to serve: to make it clear whether the woman is with child from her husband, so that there may be no confusion about the paternity of the child. The existence of a child may also be a factor in the couple reconsidering their separation. In the Qur'ān Allah says:

وَالْمُطَلَّقَاتُ يَتَرَبَّصْنَ بِأَنفُسِهِنَّ ثَلَاثَةَ قُرُوءٍ وَلَا يَحِلُّ لَهُنَّ أَن يَكْتُمْنَ مَا خَلَقَ اللَّهُ فِي أَرْحَامِهِنَّ إِن كُنَّ يُؤْمِنَّ بِاللَّهِ وَالْيَوْمِ الْآخِرِ وَبُعُولَتُهُنَّ أَحَقُّ بِرَدِّهِنَّ فِي ذَٰلِكَ إِنْ أَرَادُوا إِصْلَاحًا وَلَهُنَّ مِثْلُ الَّذِي عَلَيْهِنَّ بِالْمَعْرُوفِ وَلِلرِّجَالِ عَلَيْهِنَّ دَرَجَةٌ وَاللَّهُ عَزِيزٌ حَكِيمٌ

Divorced women should wait by themselves for three menstrual cycles; and it is not lawful for them to conceal what Allah has created in their wombs if they have īmān in Allah and the Last Day. Their husbands have the right to take them back within that time, if they desire to be reconciled. Women possess rights similar to those held over them to be honoured with fairness; but men have a degree above them. Allah is Almighty, All-Wise. (Sūrat al-Baqarah 2: 228)

The different kinds of *ᶜiddah*

The duration of *ᶜiddah* is prescribed in the Qur'ān as follows:

وَاللَّائِي يَئِسْنَ مِنَ الْمَحِيضِ مِن نِّسَائِكُمْ إِنِ ارْتَبْتُمْ فَعِدَّتُهُنَّ ثَلَاثَةُ أَشْهُرٍ وَاللَّائِي لَمْ يَحِضْنَ وَأُولَاتُ الْأَحْمَالِ أَجَلُهُنَّ أَن يَضَعْنَ حَمْلَهُنَّ وَمَن يَتَّقِ اللَّهَ يَجْعَل لَّهُ مِنْ أَمْرِهِ يُسْرًا

In the case of those of your wives who are past the age of menstruation, if you have any doubt, their ᶜiddah should be three months, and that also applies to those who have not yet menstruated. The time for women who are pregnant is when they give birth. Whoever has taqwā of Allah – He will make matters easy for him. (Sūrat aṭ-Ṭalāq 65: 4)

In the Qur'ān Allah lays down that there is no *ᶜiddah* for a woman whose husband divorces her before he has consummated his marriage with her. Allah says:

يَا أَيُّهَا الَّذِينَ آمَنُوا إِذَا نَكَحْتُمُ الْمُؤْمِنَاتِ ثُمَّ طَلَّقْتُمُوهُنَّ مِن قَبْلِ أَن تَمَسُّوهُنَّ فَمَا لَكُمْ عَلَيْهِنَّ مِنْ عِدَّةٍ تَعْتَدُّونَهَا فَمَتِّعُوهُنَّ وَسَرِّحُوهُنَّ سَرَاحًا جَمِيلًا

You who have īmān! when you marry believing women and then divorce them before you have touched them, there is no ᶜiddah for you to calculate for them, so give them a gift and let them go with kindness. (Sūrat al-Aḥzāb 33: 49)

However, in the case of termination of marriage due to death of the husband, the widow has an *ᶜiddah* of four months and ten days. This period corresponds to the time in which a foetus comes to completion and the spirit is blown into it. In the Qur'ān Allah says:

وَالَّذِينَ يُتَوَفَّوْنَ مِنكُمْ وَيَذَرُونَ أَزْوَاجًا يَتَرَبَّصْنَ بِأَنفُسِهِنَّ أَرْبَعَةَ أَشْهُرٍ وَعَشْرًا فَإِذَا بَلَغْنَ أَجَلَهُنَّ فَلَا
جُنَاحَ عَلَيْكُمْ فِيمَا فَعَلْنَ فِي أَنفُسِهِنَّ بِالْمَعْرُوفِ وَاللَّهُ بِمَا تَعْمَلُونَ خَبِيرٌ

Those of you who die leaving wives behind: they should wait by themselves for four months and ten nights. When their ᶜiddah comes to an end, you are not to blame for anything they do with themselves with correctness and courtesy. Allah is aware of what you do. (Sūrat al-Baqarah 2: 234)

The different kinds of *ᶜiddah* can be summed up as follows:

1. *ᶜIddah* of women who still menstruate: Three menstruations
2. *ᶜIddah* of women who have not reached or have passed the age of menstruation: Three months
3. *ᶜIddah* of widows: Four month and ten days
4. *ᶜIddah* of pregnant women whether divorced or widowed: Until they deliver.
5. There is no *ᶜiddah* for women whose marriage is not yet consummated

Some scholars like Ibn ᶜAbbās have said that since Allah has made it obligatory for women whose husbands die to wait for four months and ten days, and has specified the period of waiting for the pregnant woman to last until she has delivered, it follows that if the husband dies and the woman is pregnant she is bound by two periods concurrently, just as she would be bound to fulfil any other two duties combined together.[1]

According to Imam ash-Shāfiᶜī,[2] the Messenger of Allah said to

Subayᶜah bint al-Ḥārith, who gave birth to a child a few days after her husband's death: "You are lawful (for marriage) and you may get married." This indicates that the ᶜ*iddah*, whether in the case of being widowed or divorced, is fulfilled by (the expiration of) the required months; but if they are pregnant and they deliver their children the ᶜ*iddah* is dropped.[3]

Code of conduct for a woman in ᶜ*iddah*

The jurists have a difference of opinion about a woman in ᶜ*iddah* leaving the house. Ḥanafī jurists say that it is not lawful for a woman on whom has been declared the first and second divorce (*rajᶜah*), nor for a woman who is serving ᶜ*iddah* for a final (*bā'in*) form of *ṭalāq* to go out of the house either during the day time or at night. A widow, however, can go out during the day time or at certain times at night but must not spend the night anywhere except in the house. The difference is that in the case of divorce she has the right to be maintained from the property of her husband, and hence it is not allowed for her to leave the house of the husband; but in the case of a widow, she is not entitled to maintenance, hence she can go out in order to support herself.

According to Ḥanbalī jurists, she can go out during the day time whether she is in the ᶜ*iddah* of divorce or as a widow. Jābir has reported that his maternal aunt was divorced three times[4] (i.e. irrevocably), then she went out to cut the fruit of her date-palm. Someone met her and told her not to do so. She came to the Prophet ﷺ and reported the matter to him. The Prophet ﷺ replied:

اخْرُجِي فَجُدِّي نَخْلَكِ لَعَلَّكِ أَنْ تَصَدَّقِي وَتَفْعَلِي مَعْرُوفًا

> Go out to cut the fruits of your date palm; perhaps you may give *ṣadaqah*[5] or do something good. (Abū Dāwūd, *kitāb aṭ-ṭalāq, bāb fī al-mabtūtah takhruju fī an-nahār;* and an-Nasā'ī, *kitāb aṭ-ṭalāq, bāb khurūj al-mutawaffā ᶜanhā bi an-nahār,* the wording here being that of an-Nasā'ī.)

As a precaution she should not go out at night without any necessity because many evils happen in the dark hours of night, while during the day she can go out to fulfil her necessities and buy whatever she needs.

She must not remarry during the period of *ᶜiddah*. A *ḥadīth* gives clear instructions that widows should not wear ornaments, coloured or showy dress, nor adorn themselves with any kind of make-up during this period.

According to Imām Abū Ḥanīfah, she has the right to maintenance and a dwelling place during the period of *ᶜiddah* of irrevocable divorce, just as during the *ᶜiddah* of a divorce in which the husband may take her back, but in that case she has to spend the period of *ᶜiddah* in the matrimonial home. The maintenance is considered like a debt at the time of divorce. Imam Mālik and Imam ash-Shāfiᶜī say that she is only entitled to a dwelling place but not the maintenance except if she is pregnant. Imam Aḥmad ibn Ḥanbal, on the contrary, says that she would have neither right to maintenance nor dwelling place.

Treatment of divorced women during *ᶜiddah*

In the Qur'ān, Allah prescribes the time when divorce shall be pronounced and the treatment to be accorded to the divorced woman during *ᶜiddah*. He says:

يَا أَيُّهَا النَّبِيُّ إِذَا طَلَّقْتُمُ النِّسَاءَ فَطَلِّقُوهُنَّ لِعِدَّتِهِنَّ وَأَحْصُوا الْعِدَّةَ وَاتَّقُوا اللَّهَ رَبَّكُمْ لَا تُخْرِجُوهُنَّ
مِنْ بُيُوتِهِنَّ وَلَا يَخْرُجْنَ إِلَّا أَنْ يَأْتِينَ بِفَاحِشَةٍ مُبَيِّنَةٍ وَتِلْكَ حُدُودُ اللَّهِ

> *O Prophet! When any of you divorce women, divorce them during their period of purity and calculate their ᶜiddah carefully. And have taqwā of Allah, your Lord. Do not evict them from their homes, nor should they leave, unless they commit an outright indecency. Those are Allah's limits.* (Sūrat aṭ-Ṭalāq 65: 1)

Allah further lays down:

فَإِذَا بَلَغْنَ أَجَلَهُنَّ فَأَمْسِكُوهُنَّ بِمَعْرُوفٍ أَوْ فَارِقُوهُنَّ بِمَعْرُوفٍ وَأَشْهِدُوا ذَوَيْ عَدْلٍ مِنْكُمْ وَأَقِيمُوا
الشَّهَادَةَ لِلَّهِ

Then when they have reached the end of their ᶜiddah either retain them with correctness and courtesy or part from them with correctness and courtesy. Call two upright men from among yourselves as witnesses and carry out the witnessing for Allah. (Sūrat aṭ-Ṭalāq 65: 2)

Thus, divorced women should live in the house of the husband until she finishes the *ᶜiddah*. It is not lawful for her to leave, nor must the husband drive her away. Even if she was not present in her matrimonial home at the time of pronouncement of divorce or separation, it is essential for her to return to the house of the husband. In the Qur'ān Allah says: "*Do not evict them from their homes, nor should they leave, unless they commit an outright indecency.*" (Sūrat aṭ-Ṭalāq 65: 1)

There is, however, a difference of opinion as to whether a widow must pass the term in the house of the deceased or not. Sayyidunā ᶜUmar, Sayyidunā ᶜUthmān, ᶜAbdullāh ibn ᶜUmar, the four Imams and many other great jurists are of the opinion that she should reside in the house of the deceased husband. Sayyidah ᶜĀ'ishah, Ibn ᶜAbbās, Sayyidunā ᶜAlī and some other great jurists are of the opinion that she is free to pass the period wherever she likes.

Remarriage of widows and divorcees is encouraged in *Sharīᶜah*

Muslims sympathise with the plight of the widow and the divorcee and they are encouraged to remarry and start a new life. With respect to the widow Allah says in the Qur'ān:

وَالَّذِينَ يُتَوَفَّوْنَ مِنكُمْ وَيَذَرُونَ أَزْوَاجًا يَتَرَبَّصْنَ بِأَنفُسِهِنَّ أَرْبَعَةَ أَشْهُرٍ وَعَشْرًا فَإِذَا بَلَغْنَ أَجَلَهُنَّ فَلَا
جُنَاحَ عَلَيْكُمْ فِيمَا فَعَلْنَ فِي أَنفُسِهِنَّ بِالْمَعْرُوفِ وَاللَّهُ بِمَا تَعْمَلُونَ خَبِيرٌ

Those of you who die leaving wives behind: they should wait by themselves for four months and ten nights. When their ᶜiddah comes to an end, you are not to blame for anything they do with themselves with correctness and courtesy. Allah is aware of what you do. (Sūrat al-Baqarah 2: 234)

Similarly, He says respecting proposals of marriage to widows:

وَلَا جُنَاحَ عَلَيْكُمْ فِيمَا عَرَّضْتُم بِهِ مِنْ خِطْبَةِ النِّسَاءِ أَوْ أَكْنَنتُمْ فِي أَنفُسِكُمْ عَلِمَ اللَّهُ أَنَّكُمْ سَتَذْكُرُونَهُنَّ وَلَكِن لَّا تُوَاعِدُوهُنَّ سِرًّا إِلَّا أَن تَقُولُوا قَوْلًا مَّعْرُوفًا وَلَا تَعْزِمُوا عُقْدَةَ النِّكَاحِ حَتَّىٰ يَبْلُغَ الْكِتَابُ أَجَلَهُ وَاعْلَمُوا أَنَّ اللَّهَ يَعْلَمُ مَا فِي أَنفُسِكُمْ فَاحْذَرُوهُ وَاعْلَمُوا أَنَّ اللَّهَ غَفُورٌ حَلِيمٌ

> *Nor is there anything wrong in any allusion to marriage you make to a woman, nor for any you keep to yourself. Allah knows that you will say things to them. But do not make secret arrangements with them, rather only speak with correctness and courtesy. Do not finally decide on the marriage contract until the prescribed period has come to its end. Know that Allah knows what is in your selves, so beware of Him! And know that Allah is Ever-Forgiving, All-Forbearing.* (Sūrat al-Baqarah 2: 235)

A definite contract of remarriage with a woman during her *ᶜiddah* of widowhood is forbidden as being obviously unseemly as is also any secrecy in such matters. It would bind the woman at a time she is not fitted to exercise her fullest judgement. However, circumstances may arise when an allusion to an offer (open for future consideration but not immediately decided) may be to her interest, and this is permissible. Cherishing love in one's heart without outward show or reward is a true test of sincerity and devotion.

Notes

[1] This was the judgement of Ibn ᶜAbbās and ᶜAlī. See ash-Shawkānī, *Nayl al-awṭār,* vol. vi, pp. 306-307

[2] Ash-Shāfiᶜī, *Risālah, Op. Cit.,* p. 168. The case is also narrated by ᶜAbd ar-Razzāq in the *Muṣannaf*

[3] See Mālik, *Muwaṭṭa',* vol. ii, pp. 589-90, Abū Dāwūd, vol. ii, p. 293, ash-Shāfiᶜī, *Kitāb al-Umm,* vol. ii, pp. 205-206, ash-Shawkānī, *Nayl al-awṭār,* vol. vi, p. 305

[4] There are differences of opinion about the case of a woman divorced three times or irrevocably.

[5] *Ṣadaqah* meaning here *zakāh,* and doing good or *maᶜrūf* means optional acts of generosity and *ṣadaqah.*

Chapter 17

Maintenance, Custody and Guardianship

Nafaqah

MAINTENANCE (*NAFAQAH*) is the right of one's wives and children to food, clothing and residence, some other essential services and medicine, even if the wives happen to be wealthy. Maintenance in this form is obligatory (*wājib*) according to the Qur'ān, Sunnah and the consensus of opinion of the jurists. Where both spouses are above the age of puberty, it is the duty of the husband to supply wife and children with food, clothes and lodging on a scale commensurate with the custom and habits of the society in which they live. This last cannot be taken to be an Islamic endorsement of a consumer lifestyle, but a realistic appraisal of local custom. For example, in a previous time and in certain circumstances the provision of servants might have been taken for granted for a certain woman of standing and wealth, whereas today the same functions might be carried out by appliances such as washing machines, etc. This is clearly a tricky area fraught with dangers for those who rush to make hasty judgements.

Some jurists have given detailed instances of things to be provided as *nafaqah*[1] during the time they were writing about it. These are to be adjusted in the light of modern necessities to suit the circumstances of other countries and their living standards. For example, Ibn Juzayy al-Kalbī ⁕ wrote about the obligations of maintenace:

> 1. Food and it differs according to the standing of the husband in terms of wealth and the wife in terms of her wealth and

standing, and the circumstances of the land [in which they live]. The average for that in Andalusia is a pound and a half each day of wheat or barley or maize or pulses according to the circumstances. Ash-Shāfiᶜī said that one reckons the circumstances of the husband but not the wife so that in his view a woman of high social standing and one of humble circumstances are the same.

2. Condiments and this is according to the circumstances and the country, but there is no excuse [not to provide] water, firewood, vinegar and oil for eating, kindling, but fruit is not obligatory.

3. Maintenance of a servant, for if the wife had been someone of standing and circumstance and the husband is prosperous, then she does not have to serve in her house in any way, and he is obligated to provide her with servants. If she is not like that and the husband is poor, then she has to do the internal housework such as kneading, cooking, sweeping, spreading out bedding, drawing water [from the well] if [the well] is with her in the house. She does not have to do spinning or weaving, and if he is poor he does not have to provide servants even if she has some standing and circumstances, and she is not to be divorced from him for that reason. If the provision of servants is obligatory on him he does not have to buy [slaves] but may employ [servants]. If he wishes to change a servant with whom she is familiar he does not have the right to do that unless there is an obvious cause for doubt. Whatever woman's standing requires that she have two or more servants, then she is owed that, contrary to the two of them [ash-Shāfiᶜī and Abū Ḥanīfah].

4. Clothing according to his and her circumstances and her standing, the least of which is that which will cover the body and the hair and provide protection from heat and cold, which is of course different in winter and summer, and bedding according to the circumstances.

5. Instruments for cleaning according to the circumstances, social standing and customary usages in the country.

6. A dwelling, and he is obliged to lodge her in a dwelling which is appropriate for her, whether bought, rented or assigned [as an *ᶜariyyah* for their usage]. (Ibn Juzayy al-Kalbī, *al-Qawānīn al-fiqhiyyah, al-kitāb al-awwal fī an-nikāḥ, al-bāb at-tāsiᶜ fī an-nafaqāt)*

It is the responsibility of a father to maintain his daughters until they are married and sons until the age of puberty. Likewise, it is the duty of every Muslim to maintain his parents and grandparents, maternal as well as paternal if they are poor and if he can afford to do so. According to some, if it is possible and one has the means, one should even look after the needs of one's poor relatives. According to the Ḥanafī school every relative within the prohibited degrees is entitled to maintenance if a child and poor, infirm or blind; and if a female and she is poor she should also be maintained whether a child or adult.

If the wife is a minor, she will be maintained by her father or guardian, as we have seen before. The Messenger of Allah ﷺ made the contract to marry ᶜĀ'ishah ؓ two years before she reached the age of puberty and did not give her maintenance.

According to Qāḍī Abū Yūsuf, the Ḥanafī jurist, if the wife is a minor and the husband accepts her in his house, it is essential for him to maintain her, but if she does not come to his house, he does not have to do so. However, Imām Abū Ḥanīfah and his pupil, Imām Muḥammad, have the same view as that of the Mālikī and Shāfiᶜī schools already mentioned before.

It is not essential to provide one's wife with maintenance in the following circumstances:

1. If she has moved out of the husband's home to some other place without her husband's permission or without any specific cause
2. If she has travelled without his permission
3. If she puts on *iḥrām* for Ḥajj without his permission. But if he goes with her or she is travelling with his permission the maintenance will be given
4. If she refuses her husband sexual intercourse
5. If she is imprisoned after committing a crime
6. If her husband dies and she becomes a widow. In that case her right of inheritance supervenes. This is the very reason why the widow is not entitled to maintenance during the *ᶜiddah* for being widowed.

According to the Mālikī and Shāfiᶜī schools, if a husband has failed or neglected to provide maintenance for a period of two years, the wife is entitled to dissolution of the marriage, but in the Ḥanafī school, inability, refusal or neglect to maintain is not sufficient grounds for dissolution. If a husband intends to embark on a long journey, the wife is entitled to demand that her husband, either give her an anticipatory allowance for the whole duration of his absence, or give power of attorney to another for her maintenance. The allowance falls due at the same intervals at which the husband was in the habit of paying it.

Maintenance when the husband is poor

The husband is supposed to provide for the family. If he cannot earn enough to support the family or if his income is too little to provide for a relatively acceptable standard of living, and provided the wife is willing, she may work for gain. However:

1. The husband has the right to terminate the wife's working whenever he deems it necessary.
2. He has the right to object to any work if he feels that it would expose his wife to any harm, seduction or humiliation.
3. The wife has the right to discontinue working whenever she pleases.
4. If she works in order to help the family because of poor income then the whole purpose of her working is to help the family, therefore although the product of her work belongs to her she is not working for herself since she has started working to help the husband in his expenses. She can keep for herself whatever remains after helping the husband with what is absolutely necessary for the expenses of the household: accommodation, food and necessary clothing. She should help, for example, with the rent, the electricity and water bill, food and necessary clothes. The rest – phone bill, buying a microwave, going on holidays – is from her generosity if she does decide to help with these costs.

The key to understanding this situation is that it is a *ḍarūrah* i.e. a pressing necessity. Ordinarily the income from her work would be entirely hers alone, and she would not be compelled to share it with her family except inasmuch as she gives voluntarily. However, this case is when she works out of necessity to help her husband who is in severe need.

What needs to be remembered is that *ḍarūrah* is not a permanent condition, but a temporary exigency. The obvious example is the starving person in the desert who comes across *ḥarām* food. Because of his hardship it is obligatory for him to eat that food, and to eat sufficiently, in order for him to have the strength to get out of the desert and find the *ḥalāl* food which it is obligatory for him to seek out. He may not settle in the desert with his source of *ḥarām* food and allow it to become his way of life. Similarly, with the Muslim wife working out of necessity; it does not mean that Muslims should embrace the lifestyle of two-career, two-car families. Nor does it mean that the Muslim woman can only work out of necessity. Rather, the ordinary situation is that if she does work, she keeps all of the money for herself, except what she chooses to spend as gifts or *ṣadaqah*.

When the wife is not thus employed, the household is her first occupation as outlined. By household is meant the rearing of the children and all domestic services required for maintaining a clean and comfortable habitation. There is the traditional saying: "Cleanliness is a part of *īmān*." Motherhood is highly commended in Islam. None of this precludes her having a trade or craft with which she earns some money, as has been the way of huge numbers of Muslim women throughout history.

Maintenance after dissolution of marriage

The Noble Qur'ān points out the responsibility of maintenance in the cases of divorce in the following verse:

أَسْكِنُوهُنَّ مِنْ حَيْثُ سَكَنتُم مِّن وُجْدِكُمْ وَلَا تُضَارُّوهُنَّ لِتُضَيِّقُوا عَلَيْهِنَّ وَإِن كُنَّ أُولَاتِ حَمْلٍ
فَأَنفِقُوا عَلَيْهِنَّ حَتَّىٰ يَضَعْنَ حَمْلَهُنَّ فَإِنْ أَرْضَعْنَ لَكُمْ فَآتُوهُنَّ أُجُورَهُنَّ وَأْتَمِرُوا بَيْنَكُم بِمَعْرُوفٍ

Let them live where you live, according to your means. Do not put pressure on them, so as to harass them. If they are pregnant, maintain them until they give birth. If they are suckling for you, give them their wages and consult together with correctness and courtesy. But if you make things difficult for one another, another woman should do the suckling for you. (Sūrat aṭ-Ṭalāq 65: 6)

The responsibility of the husband for maintenance of the family is not confined to the legal duration of the marriage. It is also required in the event of divorce that the erstwhile wife receive maintenance up until the end of the *ʿiddah*, in the case of the first or second divorce, or one in which he retains the right to take her back. However, she has no maintenance in the case of a final or irrevocable divorce unless she is pregnant.

There are some people who maltreat a wife and make her life miserable after pronouncing the first divorce when she is still in *ʿiddah*. This is forbidden. She must be provided for on the same scale as before the divorce, according to the husband's status in life. There is still hope for reconciliation and, if not, the parting should still be honourable. In the event of pregnancy, the Qur'ān provides additional responsibility in that she is due maintenance until she has delivered the baby. No separation will be possible before the baby has been born and she must be properly maintained.

As for the child, its maintenance remains the duty of the father: boys until puberty and girls until they marry. If the mother's milk fails, or if such circumstances arise which bar the natural course of the mother nursing the child, then it is the father's responsibility to give the child to someone else to suckle at his expense, unless he is completely penniless. This must not induce the father to cut down reasonable maintenance for the child to which the mother is entitled.

Raḍāʿah: Suckling

The Noble Qur'ān further guides in the matter of maintenance for suckling mothers in Sūrat al-Baqarah:

وَالْوَالِدَاتُ يُرْضِعْنَ أَوْلَادَهُنَّ حَوْلَيْنِ كَامِلَيْنِ لِمَنْ أَرَادَ أَنْ يُتِمَّ الرَّضَاعَةَ وَعَلَى الْمَوْلُودِ لَهُ رِزْقُهُنَّ
وَكِسْوَتُهُنَّ بِالْمَعْرُوفِ لَا تُكَلَّفُ نَفْسٌ إِلَّا وُسْعَهَا لَا تُضَارَّ وَالِدَةٌ بِوَلَدِهَا وَلَا مَوْلُودٌ لَهُ بِوَلَدِهِ وَعَلَى

الْوَارِثِ مِثْلُ ذَلِكَ فَإِنْ أَرَادَا فِصَالاً عَن تَرَاضٍ مِّنْهُمَا وَتَشَاوُرٍ فَلَا جُنَاحَ عَلَيْهِمَا وَإِنْ أَرَدتُّمْ أَن تَسْتَرْضِعُوا أَوْلَادَكُمْ فَلَا جُنَاحَ عَلَيْكُمْ إِذَا سَلَّمْتُم مَّا آتَيْتُم بِالْمَعْرُوفِ وَاتَّقُوا اللَّهَ وَاعْلَمُوا أَنَّ اللَّهَ بِمَا تَعْمَلُونَ بَصِيرٌ

Mothers should nurse their children for two full years – those who wish to complete the full term of nursing. It is the duty of the fathers to feed and clothe them with correctness and courtesy – no self is charged with more than it can bear. No mother should be put under pressure in respect of her child nor any father in respect of his child. The same duty is incumbent on the heir. If the couple both wish weaning to take place after mutual agreement and consultation, there is nothing wrong in their doing that. If you wish to find wet-nurses for your children, there is nothing wrong in your doing that provided you hand over to them what you have agreed to give with correctness and courtesy. Have taqwā of Allah and know that Allah sees what you do. (Sūrat al-Baqarah 2: 233)

In the above injunction, the word *rizq* 'provision' is mentioned, which includes sufficient food, adequate clothing and other necessary provisions.

In order to ensure that children are properly fed, clothed and looked after, the Noble Qur'ān lays down rules in respect of *raḍāᶜah* (suckling). These rules are meant for safeguarding the interests of children both when the marriage between their parents endure and when such marriages end in divorce. If the marriage between the parents continues, it is the responsibility of both of them to look after their children and not neglect them, as they are incapable of taking care of themselves.

If the marriage ends in divorce, they can agree to some reasonable and equitable arrangement for the care of their children. Broadly speaking the husband retains the right of guardianship or *walā'*, while the wife has the right of custody or *ḥaḍānah.*

Raḍāᶜah or suckling is a duty that affects both parents and if they neglect it, they will be answerable to Allah on the Day of Judgement. The maximum period of suckling is two years. If the father of the child is afraid of the mother neglecting the child, he should arrange for a wet-nurse.

Points which become clear from the above verse are:

1. The complete period of nursing is two years.
2. The responsibility for providing maintenance to the wife or former wife or for arranging nursing for the child lies on the man. He shall bear the cost of food and clothing on equitable terms.
3. A woman who suckles her baby should not be maltreated by her husband.
4. The weaning of the child should be done by mutual agreement between the mother and the father.
5. If the man dies, his heirs will be responsible for maintenance of his widow and suckling for his child.
6. If by any chance, the mother herself cannot breast-feed and she and her husband decide to employ a foster-mother, there is no harm. But the mother should still be given her maintenance.
7. Every Muslim should know that whatever he does Allah sees him at all times, therefore he should not treat his wife or former wife and his child unfairly.

Period of nursing

Breast-feeding is to be done for a period of two years at the end of which the child should be weaned. However, the period may be extended if there are special circumstances to warrant it. In the Noble Qur'ān Allah says:

وَوَصَّيْنَا الْإِنسَانَ بِوَالِدَيْهِ حَمَلَتْهُ أُمُّهُ وَهْنًا عَلَىٰ وَهْنٍ وَفِصَالُهُ فِي عَامَيْنِ أَنِ اشْكُرْ لِي وَلِوَالِدَيْكَ إِلَيَّ الْمَصِيرُ

We have instructed man concerning his parents. Bearing him caused his mother great debility and the period of his weaning was two years: 'Give thanks to Me and to your parents. I am your final destination. (Sūrah Luqmān 31: 14)

Allah further says:

وَحَمْلُهُ وَفِصَالُهُ ثَلَاثُونَ شَهْرًا

And his bearing and weaning take thirty months. (Sūrat al-Aḥqāf 46: 15)

Commenting on the last verse, ᶜAllāmah Yūsuf ᶜAlī said: "It leaves six months as the minimum period of human gestation after which the child is known to be viable." (A Yūsuf Ali, *The Holy Qur'ān: Text, Translation and Commentary,* 1370, Beirut 1968)

Ibn Juzayy al-Kalbī said in *tafsīr* of these *āyāt*:

> Meaning that the period of his being carried [in the womb] and his sucking is thirty months, and this can only be by reducing at one of the two extremities. That is either because the period of pregnancy is six months and the period of breast-feeding is two complete years or because the period of pregnancy is nine months and the period of breast-feeding is two years less three months. From this ᶜAlī ibn Abī Ṭālib and the *ᶜulamā'* deduced that the least period of pregnancy is six months. He only expressed the period of breast-feeding by 'weaning' because it is the termination of the breast-feeding. (Al-Kalbī, Ibn Juzayy, *Kitāb at-tashīl li ᶜulūm at-tanzīl,* commentary on Sūrat al-Aḥqāf 46: 15)

The verse specifically mentioned the maintenance of the child so that no one may use the child as an excuse for driving a hard bargain on either side, whether the mother or the father.

لَا تُضَآرَّ وَالِدَةٌ بِوَلَدِهَا وَلَا مَوْلُودٌ لَّهُ بِوَلَدِهِ وَعَلَى الْوَارِثِ مِثْلُ ذَٰلِكَ

No mother should be put under pressure in respect of her child nor any father in respect of his child. The same duty is incumbent on the heir. (Sūrat al-Baqarah 2: 233)

The father and the mother must conclude all arrangements for maintenance of the child through mutual consent. They must agree to some course that is reasonable and equitable as regards the period before weaning (the maximum of which is two years), whether a wet-nurse is to be engaged or whether the child is to be fed by some other means. Further guidance on the subject is offered in the following verse:

لِيُنفِقْ ذُو سَعَةٍ مِّن سَعَتِهِ وَمَن قُدِرَ عَلَيْهِ رِزْقُهُ فَلْيُنفِقْ مِمَّا آتَاهُ اللَّهُ لَا يُكَلِّفُ اللَّهُ نَفْسًا إِلَّا مَا آتَاهَا

سَيَجْعَلُ اللَّهُ بَعْدَ عُسْرٍ يُسْرًا

He who has plenty should spend out from his plenty, but he whose provision is restricted should spend from what Allah has given him. Allah does not demand from any self more than He has given it. Allah will appoint after difficulty, ease. (Sūrat aṭ-Ṭalāq 65: 7)

As a practical life-transaction, the *Sharī^cah* of Islam does not impose burdens on either party. They must do their best in the interest of the child according to their means. If they act with integrity, Allah will provide a solution to their problems.

The necessity of providing maintenance is emphasised in the Farewell Pilgrimage address of the Prophet ﷺ (*Ḥajjat al-Wadā^c*):

> So have *taqwā* of Allah respecting women, because you have taken them as a trust of Allah and you regard sexual relations with them as permissible by the word of Allah… and they have the right over you that you provide for them and clothe them in a decent way. (Muslim, *kitāb al-ḥajj, bāb ḥajjat an-nabī* ﷺ)

In a *ḥadīth* narrated by ^cĀ'ishah ﵂:

> Hind bint ^cUtbah the wife of Abū Sufyān came to the see the Messenger of Allah ﷺ and said, "Messenger of Allah, Abū Sufyān is a miserly man. He does not give maintenance enough for me and for my children unless I take it from his property without his knowledge. Will that be held against me?" The Messenger of Allah ﷺ said, "Take from his property what is appropriate and what will suffice you and your children." (Al-Bukhārī, *kitāb an-nafaqāt, bāb idhā lam yunfiq ar-rajulu fa li al-mar'ah an ta'khudha bi ghayri ^cilmihi mā yakfīhā wa waladahā min ma^crūf*; Muslim, *kitāb al-aqḍiyah, bāb qaḍiyyah hind*)

According to Mālikī jurists, it is the duty of the husband, if he has consummated the marriage, to provide accommodation for his divorced wife during the *^ciddah*. Maintenance is due to a divorced woman, where the number of divorces is less than three. On the other hand, a pregnant woman whether repudiated once, twice or thrice, is entitled to maintenance. A woman who separated from her husband under the provision known as *khul^c*, is not entitled to maintenance except if she is pregnant, and any woman who is separated from her husband through *li^cān* cannot claim maintenance from that husband, even if she is pregnant. (Al-Qayrawānī, *ar-Risālah, Op. Cit.*, ch. 33: *Bāb fī al-^ciddah wa an-nafaqah*, pp. 98-101)

A wife, according to the Mālikī school, observing the *ᶜiddah* of mourning, is not entitled to maintenance. However, she is entitled to accommodation if the house she happens to be staying in belonged to her late husband or if the deceased had paid rent in advance. (Al-Qayrawānī, *ar-Risālah, Op. Cit.*, ch. 33: *Bāb fī al-ᶜiddah wa an-nafaqah*, pp. 98-101) This is because she will inherit property from her husband. Imām Abū Ḥanīfah said that she will be entitled to maintenance as well. A wife must not leave her house on account of divorce or the death of her husband until she has completed the *ᶜiddah* prescribed except for basic necessities if she has no one else to look after her.

In the Ḥanafī school of law, as laid down in the *Durr al-mukhtār*, the wife is treated as *aṣl* (root) and the child as *farᶜ* (branch) in establishing the priority in awarding maintenance although both are inseparable and their maintenance is *wājib* according to the jurists of all schools. The wife is not entitled to past maintenance except under the Shāfiᶜī school.

In fixing the sum by way of maintenance, the schools lay down the rule that if the *qāḍī* is called upon to adjudicate, in exercising his discretion he should consider the rank and circumstances of both the spouses, except for ash-Shāfiᶜī who considers that only the husband's circumstances are relevant. In any case the following conditions must be fulfilled:

1. It must be a valid marriage
2. She submits herself to her husband and is obedient
3. She gives him free access at all lawful times
4. She does not refuse to accompany her husband when he travels unless she strongly feels that during the journey her person and property will not be not safe, nor does she set out on a journey without his permission
5. Both parties can derive benefit from each other

If the above conditions are not fulfilled she is not entitled to maintenance. The husband's duty to provide maintenance commences when the wife attains puberty and not before.

Guardianship

Throughout history orphans, the insane and minors have sometimes been mistreated. Unscrupulous people, even close relatives, have sometimes misappropriated the funds of such unfortunates. In the period of *jāhiliyyah* prior to Islam, cases of embezzlement and misappropriation were rampant. It was a society in which might was right. Guardians appointed from among the family members of orphans, the insane and minors, often devoured their property. With the revelation of Islam special attention to the protection of the interests of the vulnerable was provided in order to minimise the risks to which the person and property of these people were generally exposed.

Under the *Sharīᶜah* there is no need of any formal appointment of a competent person to act as guardian. One should be a sane and mature person having fear of Allah (*taqwā*) and a sense of justice in order to act as a good guardian. Ordinarily it would be a close relative.

In the *Sharīᶜah* guardianship is of three kinds:

i. Guardianship of person
ii. Guardianship of property
iii. Guardianship in marriage

As far as guardianship of person and property is concerned, the following guidance is available in respect of the person and property of the orphans.

Maintenance of parents, poor relatives and the destitute in general

The Qur'ān and the *ḥadīth* abound in teachings with respect to the treatment of one's parents. In Sūrah Banī Isrā'īl we have been commanded in the following words:

وَقَضَىٰ رَبُّكَ أَلَّا تَعْبُدُوا إِلَّا إِيَّاهُ وَبِالْوَالِدَيْنِ إِحْسَانًا إِمَّا يَبْلُغَنَّ عِندَكَ الْكِبَرَ أَحَدُهُمَا أَوْ كِلَاهُمَا فَلَا تَقُل لَّهُمَا أُفٍّ وَلَا تَنْهَرْهُمَا وَقُل لَّهُمَا قَوْلًا كَرِيمًا وَاخْفِضْ لَهُمَا جَنَاحَ الذُّلِّ مِنَ الرَّحْمَةِ وَقُل رَّبِّ ارْحَمْهُمَا كَمَا رَبَّيَانِي صَغِيرًا

> *Your Lord has decreed that you should worship none but Him, and that you should show kindness to your parents. Whether one or both of them reach old age with you, do not say 'Ugh!' to them out of irritation and do not be harsh with them but speak to them with gentleness and generosity. Take them under your wing, out of mercy, with due humility and say: 'Lord, show mercy to them as they did in looking after me when I was small.'* (Sūrat al-Isrā' 17: 23-24)

These words explain in clear terms that when the parents were strong and the child helpless, parental affection was shown the child. When the child has grown up and is strong and the parents have become weak and helpless, it is his duty to bestow similar tender care on the parents and maintain them. According to the famous Ḥanafī text *al-Hidāyah* it is incumbent upon a man to provide maintenance for his father, mother and grandparents if they should happen to find themselves in necessitous circumstances. (*Al-Hidāyah*, p. 147) If the son happens to be comfortably off, he is duty-bound to maintain his poor relations. In the case of those who fall within the prohibited degrees of relationship by consanguinity, their individual maintenance is in proportion to the share that he stands to inherit upon the death of the relative in question. A wealthy person is also required as a virtuous act to help and maintain the poor and the needy living around him, without any distinction of caste, creed or colour, if he is in a position to do so.

Orphans and their guardianship

The person and property of orphans are generally exposed to many risks. Therefore, Islam gives special attention to the protection of the interests of orphans by their guardians. In the Qur'ān Allah says:

وَيَسْأَلُونَكَ عَنِ الْيَتَامَىٰ قُلْ إِصْلَاحٌ لَّهُمْ خَيْرٌ وَإِن تُخَالِطُوهُمْ فَإِخْوَانُكُمْ وَاللَّهُ يَعْلَمُ الْمُفْسِدَ مِنَ
الْمُصْلِحِ وَلَوْ شَاءَ اللَّهُ لَأَعْنَتَكُمْ إِنَّ اللَّهَ عَزِيزٌ حَكِيمٌ

> *They will ask you about the property of orphans. Say, 'Managing it in their best interests is best.' If you mix your property with theirs, they are your brothers. Allah knows a squanderer from a good manager. If*

Allah had wanted, He could have been hard on you. Allah is Almighty, All-Wise. (Sūrat al-Baqarah 2: 220)

وَآتُوا الْيَتَامَى أَمْوَالَهُمْ وَلَا تَتَبَدَّلُوا الْخَبِيثَ بِالطَّيِّبِ وَلَا تَأْكُلُوا أَمْوَالَهُمْ إِلَى أَمْوَالِكُمْ إِنَّهُ كَانَ حُوباً
كَبِيراً

Give orphans their property, and do not substitute bad things for good. Do not assimilate their property into your own. Doing that is a serious crime. (Sūrat an-Nisā' 4: 2)

وَلَا تُؤْتُوا السُّفَهَاءَ أَمْوَالَكُمُ الَّتِي جَعَلَ اللَّهُ لَكُمْ قِيَاماً وَارْزُقُوهُمْ فِيهَا وَاكْسُوهُمْ وَقُولُوا لَهُمْ قَوْلاً
مَعْرُوفاً ۝ وَابْتَلُوا الْيَتَامَى حَتَّى إِذَا بَلَغُوا النِّكَاحَ فَإِنْ آنَسْتُمْ مِنْهُمْ رُشْداً فَادْفَعُوا إِلَيْهِمْ أَمْوَالَهُمْ وَلَا
تَأْكُلُوهَا إِسْرَافاً وَبِدَاراً أَنْ يَكْبَرُوا وَمَنْ كَانَ غَنِيّاً فَلْيَسْتَعْفِفْ وَمَنْ كَانَ فَقِيراً فَلْيَأْكُلْ بِالْمَعْرُوفِ فَإِذَا
دَفَعْتُمْ إِلَيْهِمْ أَمْوَالَهُمْ فَأَشْهِدُوا عَلَيْهِمْ وَكَفَى بِاللَّهِ حَسِيباً

Do not hand over to the simple-minded any property of theirs for which Allah has made you responsible, but provide for them and clothe them out of it, and speak to them correctly and courteously. Keep a close check on orphans until they reach a marriageable age, then if you perceive that they have sound judgement hand over their property to them. Do not consume it extravagantly and precipitately before they come of age. Those who are wealthy should abstain from it altogether. Those who are poor should use it sensibly and correctly. When you hand over their property to them ensure that there are witnesses on their behalf. Allah suffices as a Reckoner. (Sūrat an-Nisā' 4: 5-6)

The words 'your property' are used in respect of an orphan's property in Sūrat al-Baqarah verse 220. All property belongs to Allah and anyone who possesses it or administers it, is merely a custodian. Ultimately all property is only held in trust by individuals. The guardians are advised as to how they administer the property of orphans: *"Those [guardians] who are wealthy should abstain from it altogether. Those who are poor should use it sensibly and correctly. When you hand over their property to them ensure that there are witnesses on their behalf. Allah suffices as a Reckoner."*

These verses are very comprehensive in meaning. They teach the Muslim community that in no case should wealth, which is so important for maintenance of life, be entrusted to such people as are feeble-minded and incapable of using or managing it properly, for they might, by its wrong use, create problems within the community for themselves and others which in the long term, if allowed to persist, could result in endemic social and economic ills. It is true that the rights of private ownership must be honoured, but at the same time they are not to be so liberally exercised as to be allowed to lead to social chaos.

As far as one's necessities of life are concerned, they must be fulfilled but none should be allowed to use these rights to the extent that it is harmful to the collective moral, cultural and economic good of the community.

One can deduce from the verse a general meaning that every owner of wealth should consider seriously before entrusting his wealth to anyone whether that person is capable of using it properly.

The Qur'ānic statement, *"Keep a close check on orphans until they reach a marriageable age,"* gives guardians an additional responsibility to keep an eye on them and on their intellectual capacity in order to ascertain to what extent they have become capable of looking after their own affairs before giving them back their property.

In other words, two conditions of puberty and sound-judgement have been laid down for the return of property to orphans. As to the application of this first condition, all jurists agree, but in regard to the second condition there is some difference of opinion. Imām Abū Ḥanīfah is of the opinion that if the orphan lacks capability when he reaches the age of puberty, his guardian may wait for a maximum period of seven years, and then he must return his property to him whether he shows signs of capability or not. But Imām Abū Yūsuf, Imām Muḥammad and Imām ash-Shāfiʿī are of the opinion that capability is a prerequisite for the return of an orphan's property. It is probable that these latter scholars were inclined to the opinion that the case of such a person should be referred to a Muslim *qāḍī*, who would himself arrange for the management of the property of the one who has not acquired the capacity for its proper management.

Guardians are further advised:

وَإِذَا حَضَرَ الْقِسْمَةَ أُولُوا الْقُرْبَى وَالْيَتَامَى وَالْمَسَاكِينُ فَارْزُقُوهُمْ مِنْهُ وَقُولُوا لَهُمْ قَوْلاً مَعْرُوفاً

> *If other relatives or orphans or poor people attend the sharing-out [of a deceased person's estate], provide for them out of it and speak to them correctly and courteously.* (Sūrat an-Nisā' 4: 8)

This verse recommending sharing with orphans and the poor at the division of a deceased person's estate was before the revelation of the specific verses on inheritance.

The cause of revelation of the verse on inheritance has been mentioned in the books of *ḥadīth*. It is narrated from Jābir ibn ᶜAbdullāh who said,

> The wife of Saᶜd ibn ar-Rabīᶜ brought her two daughters by Saᶜd to the Messenger of Allah ﷺ and said, "Messenger of Allah, these are the two daughters of Saᶜd ibn ar-Rabīᶜ; their father was killed while in your company on the day of Uḥud as a *shahīd*. And their uncle has taken their wealth and left them none, and they will not be married unless they have some wealth." He said, "Allah will give a judgement on that," and the *āyah* on inheritance was revealed, so the Messenger of Allah ﷺ sent a message to their uncle, "Give the two daughters of Saᶜd the two thirds and give their mother the eighth, and whatever remains is yours." (Aḥmad and the authors of the *Sunan* collections. The wording here is that of at-Tirmidhī, *abwāb al-farā'iḍ ᶜan rasulillāh* ﷺ, *bāb mā jā'a fī mīrāth al-banāt*)

The Qur'ān urges people to be fair and just to orphans especially when they want to marry female orphans. Allah says:

وَيَسْتَفْتُونَكَ فِي النِّسَاءِ قُلِ اللَّهُ يُفْتِيكُمْ فِيهِنَّ وَمَا يُتْلَى عَلَيْكُمْ فِي الْكِتَابِ فِي يَتَامَى النِّسَاءِ اللَّاتِي

لَا تُؤْتُونَهُنَّ مَا كُتِبَ لَهُنَّ وَتَرْغَبُونَ أَنْ تَنْكِحُوهُنَّ وَالْمُسْتَضْعَفِينَ مِنَ الْوِلْدَانِ وَأَنْ تَقُومُوا لِلْيَتَامَى

بِالْقِسْطِ وَمَا تَفْعَلُوا مِنْ خَيْرٍ فَإِنَّ اللَّهَ كَانَ بِهِ عَلِيماً

> *They will ask you for a fatwā about women. Say, 'Allah gives you a fatwā about them; and also what is recited to you in the Book about orphan girls to whom you do not give the inheritance they are owed, while at the same time desiring to marry them; and also about young children who are denied their rights: that you should act justly with respect to orphans.' Whatever good you do, Allah knows it.* (Sūrat an-Nisā' 4: 127)

Allah also says:

وَإِنْ خِفْتُمْ أَلَّا تُقْسِطُوا فِي الْيَتَامَى

> *If you are afraid of not behaving justly towards orphans,...* (Sūrat an-Nisā' 4: 3)

> Ibn Jarīr and Ibn al-Mundhir narrated from Ibn ʿAbbās ﷺ that he said, "A man in *jāhiliyyah* would have a girl orphan in his care and so he would cast his garment on her. When he did that no one was ever able to marry her. So if she was beautiful and he desired her, he would marry her and use her wealth. If she was plain he would prevent other men from ever having access to her until she died, and when she died he would inherit from her, and so Allah declared that *ḥarām* and forbade it." (As-Suyūṭī, *ad-Durr al-manthūr fī at-tafsīr bi al-ma'thūr,* in commentary on Sūrat an-Nisā' 4: 127)

Ḥaḍānah and *Wilāyah*: Custody and guardianship of minors

One must distinguish carefully between these two concepts: custody and guardianship. Custody, particularly in the case of break-up of marriage, belongs first to the wife, and then subsequently to other female relatives, and this includes actual care of the children. Guardianship belongs to the husband and this includes responsibility for them, particularly for their maintenance and, in the case of girls, deciding on the acceptability of suitors and arranging suitable terms and dowries for their marriages.

Ibn Juzayy al-Kalbī says:

> Concerning custody, about which there are two issues:

> 1. Respecting the hierarchy of custodians. Custody belongs to the mother, then the maternal grandmother, then the maternal aunt,

the paternal grandmother [and then the great grandmother] however remote, then to the sister, then the paternal aunt, the brother's daughter, and then to the best of the paternal relatives. This is the order if the first is deserving of custody, and if not then it is transferred to the next in line, and similarly, if his custody is dropped or is void.

2. Custody is dropped for four reasons: first, the custodian's travelling to a remote location, about which some say a postal stage [of twelve miles] and some say six postal stages [seventy-two miles], and some say a day's journey. Second, some infirmity in the body of the custodian such as insanity, or leprosy. Third, paucity of *dīn* and maintenance (*ṣawn*). Fourth, the marriage of the custodian and her consummation of the marriage, unless it is the grandmother of the infant married to his grandfather in which case it is not dropped contrary to Ibn Wahb. And if she marries and then is divorced, custody does not return to her in the well-known position, but some say that it does return in agreement with the two of them [Abū Ḥanīfah and ash-Shāfiᶜī].

Five derivative rulings

1. If the father or another of the guardians of the child takes up residence in a city which is not the mother's city, then he has the custody of his children and not her, and he will move them with him if he is trusted with them, unless he is contented with the person who has custody to take them with him [or her] wherever he goes.

2. Custody continues with male children until puberty in the well known position, but some say up until he loses the first teeth, and with females up until consummation of marriage. Ash-Shāfiᶜī said that when the child reaches *sinīn* he is given the choice between his parents, and whichever of them he chooses is granted custody.

3. Rent of a dwelling for the custodian and the children in care is the duty of their father in the well known position. And some say that she pays her share of the rent.

4. There is a difference of opinion as to whether custody is a right of the custodian, which is the well known position, or those being cared for, and on the basis of that whether if the one whose right it is drops it then it is dropped.

5. The one cared for is someone who is not independent such as the very young, and the mad and imbeciles even if these last two are mature. (Ibn Juzayy al-Kalbī, *al-Qawānīn al-fiqhiyyah, al-kitāb al-awwal fī an-nikāḥ, al-bāb al-ᶜāshir fī al-ḥaḍānah*)

In the absence of legal guardians, the *qāḍī* will appoint the guardian for the protection of a minor's property.

Guardianship in marriage

For guardianship in marriage see the topic: The role of guardians in valid Muslim marriages, in Chapter 10.

Notes

[1] For a complete picture see the *Mukhtaṣar* of Sidī Khalīl, which gives details of what a husband is obliged to provide for his wife.

Part IV
Crime and Punishment

Part IV
Crime and Punishment

When a group within the society denies the rights of another group, it must be taken to task, as Allah says in the Qur'ān:

وَإِن طَائِفَتَانِ مِنَ الْمُؤْمِنِينَ اقْتَتَلُوا فَأَصْلِحُوا بَيْنَهُمَا فَإِن بَغَتْ إِحْدَاهُمَا عَلَى الْأُخْرَى فَقَاتِلُوا
الَّتِي تَبْغِي حَتَّى تَفِيءَ إِلَى أَمْرِ اللَّهِ فَإِن فَاءَتْ فَأَصْلِحُوا بَيْنَهُمَا بِالْعَدْلِ وَأَقْسِطُوا إِنَّ اللَّهَ يُحِبُّ
الْمُقْسِطِينَ

> *If two parties of the mu'minūn fight, make peace between them. But if one of them attacks the other unjustly, fight the attackers until they revert to Allah's command. If they revert, make peace between them with justice, and be even-handed. Allah loves those who are even-handed.* (Sūrat al-Ḥujurāt 49: 9)

This famous *āyah,* which is about when fighting breaks out between groups of the Muslims, may have wider implications. And Allah knows best.

It is against this background that the *Sharīᶜah* does not agree with the synthetic theory or test for determining the problem of abnormality and criminality. According to this synthetic theory, "no act can be called a crime, if at the time the act was committed the doer was suffering from mental derangement or a morbid impulse of a really irresistible type that caused the loss of mental or emotional equilibrium." (Sethna, M. J., "Mental Abnormality and Crime" in *Contributions to Synthetic Jurisprudence,* edited by M. J. Sethna, Bombay 1962, p. 255)

Let us carefully examine the above view and then look at the narration in *Ṣaḥīḥ al-Bukhārī.*

> Sayyidunā ᶜAlī said, "Have you not learnt that the pen is raised from three: from the mad until he recovers, from the infant until he comes to discern, and from the sleeper until he wakes up?" (Al-Bukhārī, *bāb aṭ-ṭalāq fī al-ighlāq wa al-kurh wa as-sakrān wa al-majnūn wa amrihimā wa al-ghalaṭ wa an-nisyān*).

The *Sharīᶜah* also agrees with the view that no act can be called a crime if at the time the act was committed, the doer was suffering from some mental derangement, but does not generalise from that and consider every criminal to be mentally deranged or every criminal act merely an irresistible type of impulse. Crimes and wrong actions are often the manifestations of human selfishness, avarice, revenge, caprice and egoism, and that does not excuse them.

Benevolence is undoubtedly an ideal mode of conduct provided it does not open the way to temptation and encourage the spread of mischief in the world (*fasād fi'l-arḍ*). The crime rate would surely increase if no deterrent were provided by those responsible for social order. The twentieth century has seen crime reach plague proportions in this so called 'civilised' world of ours. Is it not a pity that one can not move freely in Allah's land? One year, I attended a conference in New York, and then began a tour of the United States of America. I was advised by friends not to carry much money with me nor go empty-pocketed. On enquiring why, I was told that if I carried plenty of money, a hooligan might assault me and take away everything that I carried, but, if he failed to find anything worth taking, he might attack me out of desperation. The cure for this unhappy situation is not to be found in dreams about "rooting out the criminality of the offending human being without destroying his humanity and the potential good within him." (Sethna, M. J., motto quoted on the first page of *Society and the Criminal, Op. Cit.*)

Dr. James Seth has said that the theories of punishment and deterrents are in no way mutually exclusive. According to him, in virtue of his manhood and personality, "the criminal must be convinced with the righteousness of the punishment." (Seth. J., *A Study of Ethical Principles*, Edinburgh 1911, pp. 322-3) But the question is: how are you going to convince the criminal who has committed a grave criminal act like homicide, armed robbery, adultery or continuous acts of theft of the rightfulness of punishment? If he was a Muslim, there was the law of Allah of which he was made aware right from his childhood in a Muslim family. The deterrent *ḥadd* punishments that he saw and heard of should have made him aware of the gravity of the crime he was committing. But if shayṭān, an open enemy to man (*ᶜaduwwun mubīn*), was more convincing to him than "the rightfulness of punishment" how can one stop others from falling into the same snare again? Can we do this through campaigns? According to eminent thinkers like Hegel, punishment in itself tends to reform the offender.[2]

The *Sharīᶜah* has provided two kinds of punishment. The first functions at one and the same time as a discouragement from re-offending as well as being an incentive for the offender to rehabilitate himself as a good and harmless member of society. This light form of punishment is called *taᶜzīr,* meaning *putting to shame* or *disgracing* the criminal for the crime he has committed against a member of the society, or against society itself; it also means to flog. The form of *taᶜzīr* is left to the discretion of a right-acting and learned judge (*qāḍī*) who may impose a public flogging, banishment or simply a stern admonition to behave well in future.

ᶜUqūbāt: Criminal law

The penal or criminal law in Islam is called *ᶜuqūbāt* (singular, *ᶜuqūbah*), literally 'consequences' but meaning punishments and detention, and covering both torts as well as criminal offences. There is very little difference between the two. The *Sharīᶜah* emphasises fulfilling the rights of all individuals as well as the public at large. A Muslim will be punished for a crime committed even if it was carried out far away from the Islamic community. Ultimately, the deed is done in the presence of Allah whether the perpetrator is in a Muslim or a non-Muslim land, and the criminal will be punished once he returns home or is brought back by the authorities if a case is brought against him and there is acceptable evidence.

The *qāḍī* or *Sharīᶜah* judge has to abide by the law prescribed in the case of *ᶜuqūbāt,* and hence is forbidden to impose a penalty other than that fixed by the Divine law in conformity with the injunctions of the Qur'ān and the Sunnah. If he does otherwise he himself becomes a wrongdoer.[3]

Ḥudūd and *taᶜzīrāt*

Ibn Juzayy al-Kalbī said in his *al-Qawānīn al-fiqhiyyah*:

> There are thirteen crimes which require punishment: killing, injury, adultery, unsubstantiated accusations of fornication or adultery, drinking wine, theft, rebellion, brigandage, reneging on Islam, heresy, cursing Allah and cursing the prophets and angels, working magic, giving up prayer and fasting.

The word *ḥudūd* is the plural of the Arabic word *ḥadd*, which means prevention, restraint or prohibition, and for this reason, it is a restrictive and preventive ordinance, or statute, of Allah concerning things lawful (*ḥalāl*) and things unlawful (*ḥarām*).

Ḥudūd of Allah are of two categories. Firstly, those statutes prescribed for mankind in respect of foods and drinks, marriages and divorce, etc., what are lawful thereof and what are unlawful; secondly, the punishments prescribed or appointed to be inflicted upon someone who does that which he has been forbidden to do. In Islamic jurisprudence, the word *ḥudūd* is limited to punishments for crimes mentioned by the Noble Qur'ān or the Sunnah of the Prophet ﷺ while other punishments are left to the discretion of the *qāḍī* or the ruler to inflict the lesser punishment of *taᶜzīr* (to disgrace the criminal).

Ḥudūd for abandonment of the obligations of Islam

Ibn Abī Zayd al-Qayrawānī said about the punishments for abandoning the obligations of Islam:

> 37.19D. Someone who refuses to pray
>
> If someone has not reneged but affirms the prayer and yet says, "I will not pray," he is given a respite until the time of the next prayer. If he does not pray, he is killed.
>
> ["I will not pray now and will pray later" or "I will not pray at all." He is still in the *ḍarūrī* time in which he can pray one *rakᶜah* without considering being at rest or balance or recitation of the Fātiḥah. This is to protect blood as much as possible. If he rises to pray, there is no problem. Otherwise he is killed with the sword immediately.]
>
> 37.19E. Refusing to pay *zakāh*

If someone refuses to pay *zakāh*, it is taken from him by force.

[Even if it leads to fighting him, and if he dies in that, his blood is of no consequence[4].]

37.19F. Refusing to go on Ḥajj

If someone does not go on Ḥajj, he is left to Allah.

[He is not threatened by death or anything else since he may not have all the preconditions for the Ḥajj, even if it seems so outwardly.] (Al-Qayrawānī, Ibn Abī Zayd, *ar-Risālah*, unpublished translation by Aisha Bewley)[5]

If someone does not pay *zakāh*, which is an act of *ṣadaqah*, i.e. worship, collected by the ruler as a tax taken from the rich and given to the poor and the other categories, the defaulter will be punished. The Prophet ﷺ appointed officials to collect *zakāh*, which was received in the *bayt al-māl* (public treasury), thus showing that its collection was a duty of the Muslim ruler. Islamic history records that when certain Arab tribes refused to pay *zakāh*, Sayyidunā Abū Bakr ؓ sent out troops against them, because the withholding of *zakāh* on the part of an entire tribe was tantamount to denial of one of the fundamental pillars of Islam, rebellion against the caliph and a violation of the rights of the poor.

Retaliation (*qiṣāṣ*)

We shall discuss in detail these crimes and their punishments, but it should be understood that in the Qur'ān a general law for retaliation against those who injure us physically is laid down in the following words:

وَجَزَاءُ سَيِّئَةٍ سَيِّئَةٌ مِثْلُهَا فَمَنْ عَفَا وَأَصْلَحَ فَأَجْرُهُ عَلَى اللَّهِ إِنَّهُ لَا يُحِبُّ الظَّالِمِينَ

The repayment of a bad action (sayyi'ah) is one (sayyi'ah) equivalent to it. But if someone pardons and puts things right, his reward is with Allah. Certainly He does not love wrongdoers. (Sūrat ash-Shūrā 42: 40)

However, when a matter which is due a *ḥadd* punishment is raised with the *amīr*, he is not permitted to pardon it. If those who are witnesses of the crime decline to raise it with the *amīr*, and pardon the wrongdoer then that is acceptable and may arguably come under the above *āyah*, and Allah knows best. It is narrated by ʿAbdullāh ibn ʿAmr ⬥ that the Messenger of Allah ﷺ said:

تَعَافُوا الْحُدُودَ فِيمَا بَيْنَكُمْ فَمَا بَلَغَنِي مِنْ حَدٍّ فَقَدْ وَجَبَ .

Pardon the [crimes which necessitate] the *ḥudūd* punishments, for whatever [crime requiring] a *ḥadd* punishment reaches me, then it is obligatory [to discharge the punishment]. (Abū Dāwūd, *awwal kitāb al-ḥudūd, bāb al-ʿafw ʿan al-ḥudūd mā lam tablugh as-sulṭān*; an-Nasāʾī, *kitāb qaṭʿ as-sāriq, bāb mā yakūn ḥirzan wa mā lā yakūn*; and al-Ḥākim from Ibn ʿUmar ⬥)

There are a number of Qurʾānic injunctions concerning retaliation against offenders:

وَإِنْ عَاقَبْتُمْ فَعَاقِبُوا بِمِثْلِ مَا عُوقِبْتُم بِهِ وَلَئِن صَبَرْتُمْ لَهُوَ خَيْرٌ لِّلصَّابِرِينَ

If you want to retaliate, retaliate to the same degree as the injury done to you. But if you are patient, it is better to be patient. (Sūrat an-Naḥl 16: 126)

ذَٰلِكَ وَمَنْ عَاقَبَ بِمِثْلِ مَا عُوقِبَ بِهِ ثُمَّ بُغِيَ عَلَيْهِ لَيَنصُرَنَّهُ اللهُ إِنَّ اللهَ لَعَفُوٌّ غَفُورٌ

That is so. And if anyone inflicts an injury the same as the one done to him and then is again oppressed, Allah will come to his aid. Allah is All-Pardoning, Ever-Forgiving. (Sūrat al-Ḥajj 22: 60)

فَمَنِ اعْتَدَىٰ عَلَيْكُمْ فَاعْتَدُوا عَلَيْهِ بِمِثْلِ مَا اعْتَدَىٰ عَلَيْكُمْ وَاتَّقُوا اللهَ وَاعْلَمُوا أَنَّ اللهَ مَعَ الْمُتَّقِينَ

So if anyone oversteps the limits against you, overstep against him the same as he did to you. But have taqwā of Allah. Know that Allah is with those who have taqwā. (Sūrat al-Baqarah 2: 194)

While in the verses quoted above and other similar verses, there is a rule laid down that the individual wronged should in the first instance try to forgive the offender, provided he makes amends. According to these verses, if retaliation should be made for wrong done to one, it should be equal to the wrong done to one and must not be greater than it. Another element comes into play in crimes that call down the *ḥadd* punishment, since they relate to acts which are done publicly and which thus set a precedent for others.

It is interesting to remember that in the Qur'ān we generally find the same word for the punishment as for the crime. Thus in Sūrah 42:40, both the crime and its punishment are called *sayyi'ah;* in Sūrah 16:126 and Sūrah 22:60, the word used is a derivative of *ᶜuqūbah* (punishment); and in Sūrah 2:194, the word used is *iᶜtidā* (aggression). The adoption of the same word 'evil' for the crime and the retaliation indicates that retaliation itself, though justified by the circumstances is, truly speaking, nothing but a necessary evil.

It is for this reason that Muslims are obliged either to forgive each other privately or reach some accommodation with each other, or go publicly through the due process of law taking the matter up to the competent *qāḍī* (judge), but never by taking law into their own hands. Otherwise they become wrongdoers (*ẓālimūn*). In private defence too, they must be just in using the amount of force necessary, but in all cases, they must not seek a compensation greater than the injury suffered by them. The most they can do is to demand equal redress, i.e. inflicting equal harm to that done to them, and no more. However, it is nobler not to seek vengeance at all but reconciliation, forgiveness and making the offender aware of the gravity of his offence, as long as the offence was not against the public and injurious to the entire society. If it was done publicly and witnessed and is likely to set a precedent, then deterrent punishment will follow.

Pardoning wrong done to one

In the Qur'ān we can read counsel in the following words:

وَلَا تَسْتَوِي الْحَسَنَةُ وَلَا السَّيِّئَةُ ادْفَعْ بِالَّتِي هِيَ أَحْسَنُ فَإِذَا الَّذِي بَيْنَكَ وَبَيْنَهُ عَدَاوَةٌ كَأَنَّهُ وَلِيٌّ حَمِيمٌ وَمَا يُلَقَّاهَا إِلَّا الَّذِينَ صَبَرُوا وَمَا يُلَقَّاهَا إِلَّا ذُو حَظٍّ عَظِيمٍ

A good action and a bad action are not the same. Repel the bad with something better and, if there is enmity between you and someone else, he will be like a bosom friend. None will obtain it but those who are truly steadfast. None will obtain it but those who have great good fortune. (Sūrah Fuṣṣilat 41: 34)

أُولَٰئِكَ يُؤْتَوْنَ أَجْرَهُم مَّرَّتَيْنِ بِمَا صَبَرُوا وَيَدْرَءُونَ بِالْحَسَنَةِ السَّيِّئَةَ وَمِمَّا رَزَقْنَاهُمْ يُنفِقُونَ

They will be given their reward twice over because they have been steadfast and because they ward off the bad with the good and give from what We have provided for them. (Sūrat al-Qaṣaṣ 28: 54)

ادْفَعْ بِالَّتِي هِيَ أَحْسَنُ السَّيِّئَةَ نَحْنُ أَعْلَمُ بِمَا يَصِفُونَ

Ward off evil with what is better. We know very well what they express. (Sūrat al-Mu'minūn 23: 96)

Muslims are thus required to be steadfast and patient (*ṣābirūn*), but they are equally asked to prevent repetition of crimes by taking steps and applying both physical and moral means. The best moral means is to turn hatred into love by forgiveness and friendship, as Allah says in the Qur'ān:

فَمَنْ عَفَا وَأَصْلَحَ فَأَجْرُهُ عَلَى اللَّهِ إِنَّهُ لَا يُحِبُّ الظَّالِمِينَ

But if someone pardons and puts things right, his reward is with Allah. Certainly He does not love wrongdoers. (Sūrat ash-Shūrā 42: 40)

Although the doctrine of offering the other cheek when one is struck by anyone occurs in Matthew and Luke,[6] it does not mean that this law was preached by the prophet Jesus ﷺ, as much of the revelation granted to him was altered after him, whether accidentally in the process of oral transmission and translation from Aramaic to Greek or deliberately we cannot say. Another possibility is that it really was his teaching, but then must be understood in the context of the law of the Tawrāh on retaliation, just as the law of pardoning in the many *āyāt* we have looked at above must also be seen in the context of the laws of *ḥadd* punishment and retaliation. Indeed, the sound position for Muslims is not to express an opinion on the authenticity or otherwise of any part of the Tawrāh or the Injīl since it is possible that in affirming it one is affirming a forgery or an interpolation, and equally that in denying it one is denying a genuine revelation to one of the earlier prophets whose interpretation we do not know.

Punishments for crime can be divided into four broad categories:

a. Physical punishments which include amputation of a hand, flogging and stoning to death
b. Restrictions of freedom which includes imprisonment or exile
c. Imposition of compensatory payments, as in the case of manslaughter and causing injury to others
d. Warnings given by a *qāḍī*

Apart from these prescribed punishments for various crimes there are other ways of making the criminal feel that he has committed a great wrong, for example, a man convicted of making unsubstantiated accusations of fornication or adultery (*qadhf*) will be deprived of the right of giving testimony (*shahādah*) and it will never be restored to him.

Prevention of *ḥadd* punishment in cases of doubt

The Prophet Muḥammad ﷺ has given the basic ruling concerning preventing the application of the *ḥadd* punishment in a *ḥadīth*:

ادرءوا الحدود بالشبهات.

> Prevent the [application of] *ḥadd* punishments because of ambivalences. (Ibn ʿAdī narrated it in a collection of *ḥadīth* from the people of Egypt and Syria via Ibn ʿAbbās)

When the benefit of doubt is resolved in favour of the accused, for example, in case of theft (*sariqah*), a lesser punishment of *taʿzīr* is given because the doubt relates to the criteria and not the conviction. In the case of adultery, if there is a doubt, no *ḥadd* punishment will be given.

In the case of theft, the accused should not be given the *ḥadd* punishment right away. In a Muslim society, every impoverished individual is entitled to receive something from the public treasury called *bayt al-māl* where funds are collected from various sources including the obligatory collection of *zakāh* if there are sufficient funds. If a citizen is driven by hunger because he could not earn his living for himself and his family due to a lack of opportunities and was not taken care of from the *bayt al-māl,* the society would be considered at fault and no *ḥadd* punishment should be executed on the accused. This is in keeping with the decision of the Caliph ᶜUmar ﷺ not to apply the *ḥadd* punishment to those accused of theft during a period of famine in Madīnah.

Even the very process of law under the *Sharīᶜah* curtails the number of *ḥadd* punishments. According to the Mālikī school of law, it is required that it be the complainant whose property is stolen who demands that the *qāḍī* consider applying the *ḥadd* punishment of amputation of the hand. In the view of the Ḥanafī *madhhab* and contrary to the view of Mālik and ash-Shāfiᶜī, if the complainant forgives the accused and forgoes the recovery of his property, the *ḥadd* punishment will not be applied, but, instead, *taᶜzīr* will be applicable.

At the most, the accused will be disgraced through the lesser punishment of lashes, fine, imprisonment or mere warning as the *qāḍī* sees fit. In the Ḥanafī school, if the person whose property is stolen asks the *qāḍī* to deem the stolen property as a donation to the accused, the *ḥadd* punishment of amputation will not be applied. The Mālikī and the Shāfiᶜī schools differ on this point and say that once the *qāḍī's* judgement is sought by the complainant to consider applying the *ḥadd* punishment, it is no longer left to the discretion of the complainant to intervene. They base their argument on a case decided by the Messenger of Allah ﷺ himself.

Another factor in awarding *ḥadd* punishment is the stipulation of two just, adult, male witnesses of high moral probity. It is not always easy to find such witnesses present at the scene of a crime. If the accused confesses the crime, the punishment will be executed. Even in this regard, Imam Abū Yūsuf of the Ḥanafī school and Imam Aḥmad ibn Ḥanbal say that two or even three sustained confessions are needed before conviction.

Apart from these measures, it must also be proved before giving the *ḥadd* punishment that in the event of theft, the accused forced open or broke into the house and actually entered it. Money, gold, silver, ornaments, diamonds, pearls and other valuables must be kept securely so as not to tempt a potential thief. If the owner failed to take enough precautions then he bears part of the blame since his own negligence is a contributory factor. In such cases where these requirements are not satisfied, but there exists sufficient ground for conviction *taᶜzīr* will be applied instead of the *ḥadd* punishment. Besides, if the stolen property is food, fruit, grass or forest wood, the *ḥadd* punishment will not be applied.

Ḥadd punishments are awarded in the following seven cases:

1. Penalties exacted for committing murder, manslaughter or bodily harm
2. Punishment for theft: the amputation of a hand
3. Punishment for fornication or adultery: stoning for a married person and one hundred lashes for an unmarried person
4. Punishment for unsubstantiated allegations of sexual impropriety: eighty lashes
5. Punishment for reneging on Islam: death
6. Punishment for inebriation: eighty lashes
7. Punishment for highway robbery (*qaṭᶜ aṭ-ṭarīq*): crucifixion, death, amputation of an alternate leg and arm, or exile, according to the seriousness of the crime and at the discretion of the *qāḍī* or *amīr*.

In other cases, *taᶜzīr* will be applied.

Taᶜzīr: Its meaning and application

Taᶜzīr means disgracing the criminal for his shameful act.

The general structure of the criminal law of the Muslims today (*as-siyāsat ash-sharᶜiyyah*) is based on the principle of *taᶜzīr*. *Taᶜzīr* is discretionary punishment for crimes whose punishment has not been fixed by law, and the *qāḍī* is allowed discretion both as to the form such punishment takes and its measure. This kind of discretionary punishment has been provided in special consideration of various factors affecting social change in human civilisation and they vary on the basis of variations in the methods of commission or the kind of criminal conduct indictable under the law.

Offences punishable by this method are those against human life, property, public peace and tranquillity.In other words, for behaviour prejudicial to one's neighbour. The punishment can take the form of lashes, imprisonment, fine, warning etc. To sum up, *taᶜzīr* can be defined as follows:

تَأْدِيبٌ عَلَى ذَنْبٍ لَا حَدَّ فِيهِ وَلَا كَفَّارَةَ

> It is a disciplinary punishment for a crime for which no specific *ḥadd* punishment is prescribed nor any form of expiation.

Ibn Juzayy al-Kalbī says in *al-Qawānīn al-fiqhiyyah*:

> In the [Mālikī] *madhhab, taᶜzīr* is permitted to the same degree as the *ḥadd* punishment, or with less or with more according to the *ijtihād* [of the *qāḍī*] but Ibn Wahb said that one does not give more than ten strokes in *taᶜzīr* because of the *ṣaḥīḥ ḥadīth* [respecting that]. Ash-Shāfiᶜī said that one does not make it amount to twenty strokes and Abū Ḥanīfah said that one does not make it amount to forty. (Al-Kalbī, Ibn Juzayy, *al-Qawānīn al-fiqhiyyah, al-kitāb as-sābi fī ad-dimā' wa al-ḥudūd, al-bāb al-khāmis fī ḥadd al-qadhf*)

Exceptions to legal responsibility

We saw above the words of ᶜAlī:

وَقَالَ عَلِيٌّ أَلَمْ تَعْلَمْ أَنَّ الْقَلَمَ رُفِعَ عَنْ ثَلَاثَةٍ عَنِ الْمَجْنُونِ حَتَّى يُفِيقَ وَعَنِ الصَّبِيِّ حَتَّى يُدْرِكَ وَعَنِ النَّائِمِ حَتَّى يَسْتَيْقِظَ

> Have you not learnt that the pen is raised from three: from the madman until he recovers, from the infant until he comes to discernment, and from the sleeper until he wakes up? (Al-Bukhārī, *bāb aṭ-ṭalāq fī al-ighlāq wa al-kurh wa as-sakrān wa al-majnūn wa amrihimā wa al-ghalaṭ wa an-nisyān*)

According to the above narration we have to consider legal liability and criminal responsibility in the *Sharīᶜah*.

The responsibility for a crime committed will be that of the criminal alone. His father, mother, brother or any other relative will not be punished for crimes committed by him as happened during the *jāhiliyyah* period before Islam. In the Noble Qur'ān Allah ﷻ says that nobody will bear the burden of another.[7]

The only collective responsibility is that of the family in respect of compensatory payments or damages resulting from a crime. In this case, the criminal as well as his relatives on his father's side will be held collectively responsible for *diyah* (compensatory payment) or damages imposed for his causing any physical injury.

Criminal liability

A child will not be given *ḥadd* punishment for a crime he commits. Since there is no legal responsibility for minors, i.e. children of any age until they reach the age of puberty, the *qāḍī* will still have the right either to admonish a juvenile delinquent or impose on him some restrictions which will help to reform him and prevent him from re-offending. According to Ibn Abī Zayd al-Qayrawānī, a Mālikī, there is no *ḥadd* punishment for minors even in respect of levelling unsubstantiated accusations of adultery (*qadhf*) or in respect of committing fornication.[8]

If a person has committed a crime in a state of insanity, he will not be punished. Imam Abū Yūsuf, said that "The *ḥadd* punishment can be imposed on the accused after his confession, unless it is made clear that he is insane, or mentally troubled. If he is free from such defects, he should then be submitted to the legal punishment." It is therefore, most essential that the *qāḍī* assures himself of the sound mind of the criminal before he pronounces his verdict.

Sleep is considered to be a lesser death. If any crime is committed while still asleep, one is not legally responsible for it provided it is ascertained that it was committed in a sleeping state. The case of Sayyidunā ᶜUmar's son ᶜUbaydullāh, who committed fornication with a sleeping woman is mentioned in some detail in the chapter on adultery. While ᶜUbaydullāh was punished the woman was acquitted.

The same principle will apply if one suffers from sleepwalking.

Although the sleepwalker looks awake, he is still sleeping and walking. If someone commits a crime in that state he will not be deemed legally responsible.

Crimes committed under duress

Crimes committed under duress come in two categories: word and deed. Words pronounced under duress are not binding, for example, if a man is coerced into divorcing his wife or pronouncing words that amount to *kufr* (although Imām Abū Ḥanīfah and his pupils held that if an *amīr* compels someone to divorce his wife, for example, the divorce would take effect). Actions done under duress, however, are not forgiven. For example, if one was compelled to murder someone or commit adultery. The following is the relevant *ḥadīth* taken from Imām an-Nawawi's collection of Forty *Ḥadīth*, followed by his own commentary.

> It is narrated from Ibn ʿAbbās 🟤 that the Messenger of Allah 🟤 said, "Allah has passed over, for my sake, my *Ummah's* mistakes and their forgetfulness and that which they are forced to do."[9]

> Imām an-Nawawī said: his 🟤 saying, "Allah has passed over, for my sake, my *Ummah's* mistakes and their forgetfulness and that which they are forced to do," i.e. He passes over the guilt of their mistakes, forgetfulness and that which they are forced to do. As for the judgement on mistakes, forgetfulness and that which they are forced to do, it is not lifted, for even if something was destroyed by mistake or something entrusted to one was lost out of forgetfulness one is bound to honour the liability [one incurred]. Being forced to commit adultery and murder are both excluded [from being passed over by Allah, exalted is He], and they are not permitted through coercion. If man pursues the thing that causes the forgetfulness, then that is excluded from [the] forgetfulness [that is forgiven], for he is guilty by doing it because of his shortcoming.[10] This *ḥadīth* contains benefits and important matters about which I have compiled a work but which this book is not capable [of containing].[11] (*Al-Arbaʿūn an-Nawawiyyah maʿa sharḥihā*, hadith 39, translated into English by Abdassamad Clarke and published as *The Complete Forty Hadith*, by Ta-Ha Publishers, London, UK, 1998)

Notes

[1] *See* Sūrat al-Aḥzāb 33: 72

[2] *Cf.* Ewing, A. C., *The Morality of Punishment*, London 1929, p. 75, Dr. Ewing has cited from *Studies in Hegelian Cosmology*, p. 133

[3] *See* Sūrat al-Mā'idah 5: 51

[4] i.e. there is no retaliation awardable against his killer nor any compensation due from him.

[5] *See* http://ourworld.compuserve.com/homepages/ABewley/RisAhkam.html. The commentary in parentheses is from *ath-Thamar ad-dānī* by ᶜAbd as-Samīᶜ al-Azharī

[6] Matthew V: 30; Luke VI: 29

[7] *See* Sūrat aṣ-Ṣaff 61: 124

[8] Al-Qayrawānī, *ar-Risālah, Op. Cit.*, ch. 33: *Bāb fi'l-aḥkām wa'l-ḥudūd*, pp. 121-130

[9] A *ḥasan ḥadīth* which Ibn Mājah, *kitāb aṭ-ṭalāq, bāb al-mukrah wa an-nāsī*, al-Bayhaqī and others narrated.

[10] It means that if one becomes involved in something that one knows is going to cause one's forgetfulness of an obligation then one is not excused because of that forgetfulness. In modern Arabic it could be construed that it refers to taking substances that cause forgetfulness, and this would equally come under this judgement.

[11] Contracts undertaken under coercion are not binding. An instance of this is that Imam Mālik held very vigorously that a divorce pronounced under compulsion is not binding. He was forbidden by the Abbasid governor of Madīnah from stating this publicly and when he continued to do so, he was humiliated and punished in public, but he refused to recant. The governor and the people of Madīnah knew that a consequence of this judgement of Mālik was that the oath of allegiance to the Abbasid Khalīfah taken under compulsion was thus not binding.

Chapter 19

Criminal law and punishment continued

IN THE *ḤĀSHIYAH* on the *Risālah* of Ibn Abī Zayd, the commentator said:

> The *ḥudūd* are deterrents to protect against loss of sanity, life, religion, honour, property, and lineage. *Qiṣāṣ* (retaliation) protects lives. Amputation for theft protects property. The *ḥadd* for illicit sex protects lineage. The *ḥadd* for drinking protects minds. The *ḥadd* for slander protects honour. Execution for apostasy protects religion. It is said that the *ḥudūd* are acts of expiation, which is sound. (Al-Qayrawānī, Ibn Abī Zayd, *ar-Risālah*, translated by Aisha Bewley, Chapter 37: Judgements on Homicide and *Ḥadd*-Punishments, unpublished translation: http://ourworld.compuserve.com/homepages/ABewley/RisAhkam.html)

A. *Qatl* (homicide)

The Qur'ānic revelation endorsed that given to the Children of Israel in this respect:

مِنْ أَجْلِ ذَلِكَ كَتَبْنَا عَلَى بَنِي إِسْرَائِيلَ أَنَّهُ مَن قَتَلَ نَفْساً بِغَيْرِ نَفْسٍ أَوْ فَسَادٍ فِي الأَرْضِ فَكَأَنَّمَا قَتَلَ النَّاسَ جَمِيعاً وَمَنْ أَحْيَاهَا فَكَأَنَّمَا أَحْيَا النَّاسَ جَمِيعاً

> *So We decreed for the tribe of Israel that if someone kills another person – unless it is in retaliation for someone else or for causing corruption in the earth – it is as if he had murdered all mankind. And if anyone gives life to another person, it is as if he had given life to all mankind.* (Sūrat al-Mā'idah 5: 32)

This is the way in which the legal injunctions of the Qur'ān have declared the sanctity of human life. In Sūrah Banī Isrā'īl, also known as Sūrat al-Isrā', Allah has said:

وَلَا تَقْتُلُوا النَّفْسَ الَّتِي حَرَّمَ اللَّهُ إِلَّا بِالْحَقِّ

> *Do not kill any person Allah has made inviolate, except with the right*[1] *to do so.* (Sūrat al-Isrā' 17: 33)

In this verse, homicide has been distinguished from capital punishment carried out in pursuit of justice. Only a competent *qāḍī* will decide whether or not an individual has forfeited his right to life by disregarding other human beings' right to life. The Prophet Muḥammad ﷺ declared homicide one of the greatest wrong actions after association [of partners with Allah]. He said:

> The greatest of great wrong actions with Allah on the Day of Rising are: association of partners with Allah, killing a believing person without right, fleeing while in the way of Allah on the day of [encountering] a host, rebelliously disobeying parents, accusing chaste women [of adultery], learning magic, consuming usury, and consuming the property of an orphan. (Abū Nuᶜaym; al-Bayhaqī in *as-Sunan al-kubrā, kitāb az-zakāh;* al-Ḥākim in *al-Mustadrak, kitāb az-zakāh*)[2]

One forfeits one's right to life in the following situations:

1. Law of retaliation (*qiṣāṣ*) applied against someone who killed someone else intentionally.
2. In *jihād* against the enemies of Islam, it is natural that some of the combatants will be killed.
3. Capital punishment for traitors who plot to overthrow or rebel against Islamic governance (*fasād fi'l-arḍ*).
4. A man or woman who having been married is given the *ḥadd* punishment for adultery (*zinā*).
5. Those who commit highway robbery (*ḥirābah*), which we will examine in more depth later, but which according to some includes crimes like breaking and entering.

The crime of committing the murder of a believer is so terrible that the criminal after getting his *ḥadd* punishment still goes to Hell and becomes an object of anger and the curse of Allah:

وَمَن يَقْتُلْ مُؤْمِنًا مُّتَعَمِّدًا فَجَزَآؤُهُ جَهَنَّمُ خَالِدًا فِيهَا وَغَضِبَ اللَّهُ عَلَيْهِ وَلَعَنَهُ وَأَعَدَّ لَهُ عَذَابًا عَظِيمًا

As for anyone who kills a mu'min deliberately, his repayment is Hell, remaining in it timelessly, for ever. Allah is angry with him and has cursed him, and has prepared for him a terrible punishment. (Sūrat an-Nisā' 4: 93)

It is not only the life of an adult that is sacrosanct; the life of a child or the unborn foetus in the womb must not be taken under any pretext whatsoever, except possibly in this latter case where the life of the mother is at stake. No amount of poverty and hunger must drive a man or woman to kill children. In the Noble Qur'ān Allah says:

وَلَا تَقْتُلُوا أَوْلَادَكُم مِّنْ إِمْلَاقٍ نَّحْنُ نَرْزُقُكُمْ وَإِيَّاهُمْ

Do not kill your children because of poverty – We will provide for you and them. (Sūrat al-Anᶜām 6: 151)

It is not only that human life is sacred, but all life. Abortion is endemic today and enormous numbers of medical practitioners are complicit. The parents of such unborn children and the doctors who perform such operations are all guilty. Allah, exalted is He, refers to an ancient practice of child killing:

وَإِذَا الْمَوْءُودَةُ سُئِلَتْ بِأَيِّ ذَنبٍ قُتِلَتْ

When the baby girl buried alive is asked for what crime she was killed. (Sūrat at-Takwīr 81: 8-9)

The question in the above *āyāt* refers to the pagan Arabs who used to commit female infanticide, sometimes due to fear of imagined poverty and sometimes because they felt ashamed to be addressed as 'father-in-law' when their daughters grew up. Hence, they used to kill some of their female children by burying them alive.

In this world, so much unjust suffering is caused through taking innocent lives without even a trace being left by which offenders can be brought to justice. For every case in which the life of the mother is genuinely at stake there are untold thousands of others with no such justification. In the spiritual world questions will be asked by Allah, and the victim who is dumb here will be able to give evidence on the Day of Rising. The proofs will be drawn from the very means used for concealment of the crime.

Not only is the killing of others forbidden under the *Sharīᶜah,* one does not have the right to take one's own life either. A great punishment awaits the suicide in the next world. In the Qur'ān Allah commands:

وَلَا تَقْتُلُوٓا۟ أَنفُسَكُمْ

And do not kill yourselves. (Sūrat an-Nisā' 4: 29)

And there are other *āyāt* and numerous *ḥadīth* which prohibit suicide for any reason whatsoever and promise Hell as its reward. Many judgements make clear that this also applies to so-called suicide bombers.

Apart from the Noble Qur'ān, the Prophet ﷺ dwelt upon the sanctity of life at length in his farewell pilgrimage (*Al-Ḥajjat al-Wadāᶜ*) address on this subject:

> Your lives and your property are sacred to each other as the sanctity of this day of yours in this month of yours in this land of yours. Everything from the affairs of the *jāhiliyyah* is under my feet and is remitted. [Retaliation for] the blood of *jāhiliyyah* is remitted. The first [retaliation for] blood which I remit is of our own blood, the blood of Rabīᶜah ibn al-Ḥārith ibn ᶜAbd al-Muṭṭalib. He was fostered among Banī Saᶜd and Hudhayl killed him. (Muslim, *kitāb al-ḥajj, bāb ḥajjat an-nabī* ﷺ; and Ibn Mājah, *kitāb al-manāsik, bāb ḥajjah rasūlillāh* ﷺ)[3]

In other words, life is so very sacred in Islam that it cannot be taken for sport or for any sacrificial or medical purposes, except possibly in exceptional circumstances of pressing necessity (*ḍarūrah*), and Allah knows best.

As far as the question of taking life in retaliation for murder or the question of punishment for spreading corruption on the earth is concerned, it can only be decided by a proper and competent *qāḍī*. If there is war with any nation or country, it can only be decided by a properly established government and certainly not by groups acting on their own initiative. In any case no human being has any right by himself to take human life in retaliation or for other causes. Therefore, it is incumbent on every human being that under no circumstances should he be guilty of taking a human life.

B. *Qiṣāṣ*: The law of retaliation

The word *qiṣāṣ* is derived from an Arabic word *qaṣṣa* meaning 'he cut' or 'he followed his track in pursuit', and it comes therefore to mean law of equitable retaliation for a murder already committed. The treatment of the murderer should be the same as his horrible act, that is, his own life should be taken just as he took the life of his fellow man. According to the Mālikīs he should also be killed in the same manner and with the same instrument or weapon as he was killed with except in the case of *qasāmah* in which case he is killed with the sword, but according to Abū Ḥanīfah he is only to be killed with a blade.

During the *jāhiliyyah* period before Islam, the Arabs were prone to take revenge even if the bad blood endured over centuries. If a member of their clan or tribe was killed by a member of another clan, the revenge was taken by killing any innocent person belonging to the enemy clan. The chain reaction that would start would not end for generations. There is a famous incident recorded in the books of history that an old man on his death-bed asked all his sons to come to his side and admonished them thus: "I am dying but I have not taken revenge from certain tribes. If you want me to achieve peace after death, take revenge on my behalf." The only love they had was for the life of their own clan. They used to demand the life of a man of the same rank from the clan of the murderer. At times blood-feuds used to start and the lives of hundreds would be lost for the life of one person. If the victim belonged to a higher rank, instead of taking the killer's life, they would insist on taking the life of a totally innocent person of higher rank from his clan.

The injunctions on *qiṣāṣ* in the Qur'ān are based on the principles of strict justice and the value of human life:

يَا أَيُّهَا الَّذِينَ آمَنُوا كُتِبَ عَلَيْكُمُ الْقِصَاصُ فِي الْقَتْلَى الْحُرُّ بِالْحُرِّ وَالْعَبْدُ بِالْعَبْدِ وَالْأُنْثَى بِالْأُنْثَى فَمَنْ عُفِيَ لَهُ مِنْ أَخِيهِ شَيْءٌ فَاتِّبَاعٌ بِالْمَعْرُوفِ وَأَدَاءٌ إِلَيْهِ بِإِحْسَانٍ ذَلِكَ تَخْفِيفٌ مِنْ رَبِّكُمْ وَرَحْمَةٌ فَمَنِ اعْتَدَى بَعْدَ ذَلِكَ فَلَهُ عَذَابٌ أَلِيمٌ

> *You who have īmān! retaliation is prescribed for you in the case of people killed: free man for free man, slave for slave, female for female. But if someone is absolved by his brother, blood-money should be claimed with correctness and paid with good will. That is an easement and a mercy from your Lord. Anyone who goes beyond the limits after this will receive a painful punishment.* (Sūrat al-Baqarah 2: 178)

In this verse, Allah, exalted is He, has mitigated the horrors of revenge and retaliation which were practised in the *jāhiliyyah* period. Equality in retaliation is prescribed with a strict sense of justice, i.e. no one may be killed but the murderer himself, but it makes a clear provision for mercy and forgiveness. The male relatives of the slain can make remission on the basis of receiving compensation.

QIṢĀṢ IN THE BOOKS OF THE PEOPLE OF THE BOOK

The law of *qiṣāṣ* was not totally new in the *Ummah* of the Prophet Muḥammad ﷺ. The followers of other religions who believed in the revealed books of Allah were also given the law of *qiṣāṣ*:

وَكَتَبْنَا عَلَيْهِمْ فِيهَا أَنَّ النَّفْسَ بِالنَّفْسِ وَالْعَيْنَ بِالْعَيْنِ وَالْأَنْفَ بِالْأَنْفِ وَالْأُذُنَ بِالْأُذُنِ وَالسِّنَّ بِالسِّنِّ وَالْجُرُوحَ قِصَاصٌ فَمَنْ تَصَدَّقَ بِهِ فَهُوَ كَفَّارَةٌ لَهُ وَمَنْ لَمْ يَحْكُمْ بِمَا أَنْزَلَ اللَّهُ فَأُولَئِكَ هُمُ الظَّالِمُونَ

> *We prescribed for them in it: a life for a life, an eye for an eye, a nose for a nose, an ear for an ear, a tooth for a tooth, and retaliation for wounds. But if anyone forgoes that as a ṣadaqah, it will act as expiation for him. Those who do not judge by what Allah has sent down, such people are wrongdoers.* (Sūrat al-Mā'idah 5: 45)

Retaliation was prescribed in three places in the Pentateuch,[4] but there is no mention of mercy or forgiveness as in the verses of the Qur'ān. In Matthew v. 38, however, the Old Law is quoted: "an eye for an eye", etc., and mention is made of forgiveness, but the Qur'ānic injunction, as the last revelation from Allah to mankind, is more universal. This appeal for forgiveness between man and man is as an act of *ṣadaqah,* which will also be an expiation for wrong actions done. Mosaic law[5] makes no mention of forgiveness; it is only found in the teachings of ᶜĪsā (Jesus) ﷺ and Muḥammad ﷺ. However, even where the injured one forgives, the *amīr* or *qāḍī* is competent to take such action as is necessary for the preservation of law and order in society, for crime has implications that go beyond the interests of the person injured since the entire community is affected by it. In particular, where the killing is clearly a premeditated crime, the *amīr* will put the killer to death no matter what the views of the victim's heirs.

Apart from homicide, there are two cases in *Sharīᶜah*: wounds or severance and destruction of limbs. In both cases if it was done deliberately there is retaliation, but if done by mistake then there is a compensatory payment (*diyah*) to be made. (Ibn Juzayy al-Kalbī, *al-Qawānīn al-fiqhiyyah, al-kitāb as-sābiᶜ fī ad-dimā' wa al-ḥudūd, al-bāb ath-thānī fī al-jirāḥāt*)

Homicide

Ibn Juzayy al-Kalbī said:

> If homicide is established, then either retaliation is due against the killer or compensatory payment due from him, and expiation and he may be due a discretionary punishment. In this chapter there are three sections:
>
> First section: on retaliation in which there are four issues.
>
> 1. The description of the homicide which can be of three types about two of which there is agreement, which are deliberate and accidental, and about one of which there is a difference of opinion, which is quasi-intentional homicide.
>
> As for intentional homicide, which is that the killer intends to kill

by striking with a sharp or blunt instrument, arson, drowning, strangulation, poisoning etc., for that retaliation is obligatory, i.e. *qiṣāṣ*. Abū Ḥanīfah said that there is no retaliation except in the case of killing with a sharp instrument.

As for unintentional homicide, which is that the person did not intend to strike nor to kill, for example if he fell upon someone else and so killed him, or shot at game but hit a human being, then there is no retaliation for that, but there is only compensatory payment due, and that is *ᶜaql*.

As for quasi-intentional homicide, that is the case when someone does intend to strike but did not mean to kill, then the best-known position (*mashhūr*) is that it is the same as intentional homicide, but some have said it is the same as unintentional homicide, and some have said that the compensatory payment is made punitive, in agreement with the judgement of ash-Shāfiᶜī. (*Ibid., al-bāb al-awwal fī al-qatl*)

In the Qur'ān Allah says:

وَمَا كَانَ لِمُؤْمِنٍ أَنْ يَقْتُلَ مُؤْمِنًا إِلَّا خَطَأً وَمَنْ قَتَلَ مُؤْمِنًا خَطَأً فَتَحْرِيرُ رَقَبَةٍ مُؤْمِنَةٍ وَدِيَةٌ مُسَلَّمَةٌ
إِلَى أَهْلِهِ إِلَّا أَنْ يَصَّدَّقُوا فَإِنْ كَانَ مِنْ قَوْمٍ عَدُوٍّ لَكُمْ وَهُوَ مُؤْمِنٌ فَتَحْرِيرُ رَقَبَةٍ مُؤْمِنَةٍ وَإِنْ كَانَ مِنْ
قَوْمٍ بَيْنَكُمْ وَبَيْنَهُمْ مِيثَاقٌ فَدِيَةٌ مُسَلَّمَةٌ إِلَى أَهْلِهِ وَتَحْرِيرُ رَقَبَةٍ مُؤْمِنَةٍ

A mu'min should never kill another mu'min unless it is by mistake. Anyone who kills a mu'min by mistake should free a mu'min slave and pay blood-money to his family unless they forgo it as a ṣadaqah. If he is from a people who are your enemies and is a mu'min, you should free a mu'min slave. (Sūrat an-Nisā' 5: 92)

In cases of homicide in which the killer's intention may have been to do violence but not to kill, as we saw, then the well known position of the Mālikī *madhhab* is that the person is killed in retaliation. However, some regard it as being the same as unintentional homicide for which *diyah* (compensatory payment) is to be paid. And where the killer could not be discovered, *diyah* is to be paid from the *bayt al-māl*.

If a group of people jointly kill one person, all of them will be killed. If a person who is drunk kills another person, he is killed.

However, if an insane person kills someone, the compensatory payment should be paid by his relatives. The deliberate injury inflicted by a minor is the same as an accidental one. It is paid by the *ᶜāqilah* if it is a third of the blood money or more. Otherwise it comes from his own property. There is no retaliation taken from a minor.[6]

A woman is killed for killing a man, and a man killed for killing a woman.[7] Likewise, whosoever is made to suffer the loss of both his hands is paid the whole *diyah* as in a case of homicide. Similarly, in respect of the loss of both legs or both eyes or both of anything which exist in the body in pairs, a complete *diyah* is to be paid. And if a man is made to suffer the loss of one of these, he is paid a half of the complete *diyah*. There is full blood money due for cutting the cartilage of the nose, causing loss of hearing, causing loss of mental understanding, breaking the back, crushing the testicles, cutting off the penis, and cutting off of the tongue or damaging it so that the victim cannot speak. There is full blood money due for destroying the breasts of a woman or for causing the loss of the eye of someone with one eye.[8]

The procedure for applying *ḥadd* punishments

It must be proved beyond any shadow of doubt that the homicide was really committed by the accused. No execution may take place in case of a homicide, except when men of integrity have given evidence, or where the murderer himself makes a confession or the relatives of the deceased swear *qasāmah* oaths to confirm it. In *qasāmah* the relatives of the deceased swear fifty times between them, after which they will be entitled to have the accused executed. The oath is to be sworn by no less than two men in a homicide case who between them swear fifty oaths. And in respect of such an oath, no more than one person is to be executed, i.e. the person who actually struck the fatal blow, even if a group of people participated in the killing. A *qasāmah* becomes necessary if the deceased declared – on being wounded – "so-and-so is responsible for my death"; or when one person having witnessed the homicide testified against the accused, or when two people testified, seeing the deceased being wounded, if he survived long enough to be able to eat and to drink and then subsequently died.

When the plaintiffs refuse to swear, the defendant is asked to swear and free himself of liability. He does that fifty times if the plaintiff was not able to get some of his kinsmen to swear fifty times. If kinsmen were suing in respect of a murdered kinsman, fifty of them must swear once each, but if there were less than fifty, the surplus oaths are re-distributed among them. A woman does not swear in a murder case. In the event of accidental homicide the heirs will swear in direct proportion to the amount they inherit of the compensatory payment (*diyah*), whether they are men or women. If the division of the oaths should present a problem by producing fractions the person with the biggest share of the compensatory payment is made to swear the extra oaths.[9]

In respect of an accidental killing, if some of the relatives of the deceased person come, while others do not show up, those present shall swear the full number of oaths in a *qasāmah*. If afterwards others turn up, they swear in direct proportion to their share of the estate.

The litigants swear standing.

Qasāmah oaths are not sworn in respect of wounds, nor for killing slaves, nor among the People of the Book where there is a claim that the deceased was killed by a Muslim, nor a person found dead between two rows of warring Muslim enemies. Nor when a dead body is found in the vicinity of some settlement.

A man can pardon in respect of his own murder, if it did not involve treachery, but in respect of accidental killing, he can only waive up to one third of the *diyah*. If one of the sons of the victim in a homicide case decided to forgive the killer, the killer cannot be executed and the person who pardoned gets nothing from the *diyah*. The remaining heirs can then have their share of the blood-money.

When in a homicide case the heirs comprise sons and daughters, the daughters are not empowered by law to waive this claim for *qiṣāṣ* or to grant pardon.

When a homicide is pardoned, he is to be given one hundred strokes of the cane and imprisoned for a year.

The compensatory payment (*diyah*) in respect of people who have camels is to consist of one hundred camels. And in respect of people who have gold, is to be one thousand dinars.[10]

Zinā: fornication and adultery

Zinā means sexual intercourse between a man and woman who are not married to each other or where the man does not own the woman as a slave. It is immaterial whether one or both parties have their own spouses or are unmarried. It is also immaterial whether it is with the consent of both parties. The word *zinā* applies to both adultery, where one or both parties are or have been married to a person or persons other than the persons involved in the sexual intercourse, and fornication in which both parties are unmarried. *Zinā* is not only a great wrong action but is also an act which opens the gate for many other shameful acts. It ruins people's reputations, has consequences in property and spreads numerous diseases, both physical and spiritual. Therefore, the Qur'ān enjoins upon people:

وَلَا تَقْرَبُوا الزِّنَى إِنَّهُ كَانَ فَاحِشَةً وَسَاءَ سَبِيلًا

> *And do not go near to fornication. It is an indecent act, an evil way.* (Sūrat al-Isrā' 17: 32)

The Prophet ﷺ declared *zinā* to be one of the greatest wrong actions after association [of partners with Allah]. He ﷺ said:

مَا ذَنْبٌ بَعْدَ الشِّرْكِ أَعْظَمَ عِنْدَ اللَّهِ مِنْ نُطْفَةٍ وَضَعَهَا رَجُلٌ فِي رَحِمٍ لَا يَحِلُّ لَهُ

> There is no wrong action after association of partners with Allah greater in the eyes of Allah than a drop [of sperm] which a man places in a womb that is not *ḥalāl* for him. (Ibn Abī'd-Dunyā)

There is another *ḥadīth* that places *zinā* next after association [of partners with Allah] and killing one's child for fear of poverty:

عَنْ عَبْدِ اللَّهِ قَالَ قُلْتُ يَا رَسُولَ اللَّهِ أَيُّ الذَّنْبِ أَعْظَمُ قَالَ أَنْ تَجْعَلَ لِلَّهِ نِدًّا وَهُوَ خَلَقَكَ قُلْتُ ثُمَّ
أَيٌّ قَالَ أَنْ تَقْتُلَ وَلَدَكَ خَشْيَةَ أَنْ يَأْكُلَ مَعَكَ قَالَ ثُمَّ أَيٌّ قَالَ أَنْ تُزَانِيَ حَلِيلَةَ جَارِكَ

> From ᶜAbdullāh ibn Masᶜūd ﷺ there is that he said, "I said, 'Messenger of Allah, which wrong action is worst?' He said, 'That you make a rival to Allah when He created you.' I said, 'Then which?' He said, 'That you kill your child for fear of him eating with you.' He said, 'Then which?' He said, 'That you commit adultery with your neighbour's wife.'" (Al-Bukhārī, *kitāb al-adab, bāb qatl al-walad khashyah an ya'kula maᶜahu*)

There are some other *ḥadīth* in which murder is considered to be a greater wrong action than adultery and other texts which indicate that usury is more serious. The Prophet ﷺ is reported to have said that if a person commits adultery, Allah will open for him in his grave eighty doors of Hell from which will emerge scorpions and snakes to trouble him until the Day of Rising.

The *Sharīᶜah* enjoins upon Muslims to keep away from all things which lead to illicit sexual liaisons. The first step towards adultery is a lustful look at a woman who is not one's wife. It is well known in the *Sharīᶜah* that if an act leads to something *ḥarām* then that act is *ḥarām*.

Other acts that lead towards adultery are prohibited. The adultery of the legs is walking with a bad intention towards a woman with whom it is unlawful to have sexual relations, the adultery of the hands is touching, patting or caressing and the adultery of the eyes is casting lustful glances.

The Punishment for *Zinā*

There are definite *ḥadd* punishments mentioned in the Qur'ān and the Sunnah for adulterers. The Qur'ānic injunctions were revealed gradually so that the new converts to Islam who were steeped in the vice of *zinā* in the Arab society of the *jāhiliyyah*, could more easily become accustomed. The first revelation spoke of the punishment as confining women guilty of sexual offences in their houses until they died. Allah said:

وَاللاَّتِي يَأْتِينَ الْفَاحِشَةَ مِن نِّسَائِكُمْ فَاسْتَشْهِدُوا عَلَيْهِنَّ أَرْبَعَةً مِّنكُمْ فَإِن شَهِدُوا فَأَمْسِكُوهُنَّ فِي
الْبُيُوتِ حَتَّى يَتَوَفَّاهُنَّ الْمَوْتُ أَوْ يَجْعَلَ اللَّهُ لَهُنَّ سَبِيلاً

If any of your women commit fornication, four of you must be witnesses against them. If they bear witness, detain them in their homes until death releases them or Allah ordains another procedure for their case. (Sūrat an-Nisā' 4: 15)

The second revelation covered both men and women and was more specific regarding punishment for *zinā*. It read:

وَاللَّذَانِ يَأْتِيَانِهَا مِنكُمْ فَآذُوهُمَا فَإِن تَابَا وَأَصْلَحَا فَأَعْرِضُوا عَنْهُمَا إِنَّ اللَّهَ كَانَ تَوَّاباً رَّحِيماً

If two men commit a like abomination, punish them. If they make tawbah and reform, leave them alone. Allah is Ever-Returning, Most Merciful. (Sūrat an-Nisā' 4: 16)

The third revelation came with a specific punishment for adultery:

الزَّانِيَةُ وَالزَّانِي فَاجْلِدُوا كُلَّ وَاحِدٍ مِّنْهُمَا مِئَةَ جَلْدَةٍ وَلاَ تَأْخُذْكُم بِهِمَا رَأْفَةٌ فِي دِينِ اللَّهِ إِن كُنتُمْ
تُؤْمِنُونَ بِاللَّهِ وَالْيَوْمِ الآخِرِ وَلْيَشْهَدْ عَذَابَهُمَا طَائِفَةٌ مِّنَ الْمُؤْمِنِينَ

A woman and a man who commit fornication: flog both of them with one hundred lashes and do not let compassion for either of them possess you where Allah's dīn is concerned, if you have īmān in Allah and the Last Day. A number of muminun should witness their punishment. (Sūrat an-Nūr 24: 2)

When this verse was revealed, it was understood that those guilty of adultery should be given one hundred lashes as a punishment.

The clinching verse is one whose recitation was abrogated but whose judgement still stands. It is in the *Muwaṭṭa'* of Imām Mālik ﷺ and in the other major *ṣaḥīḥ* collections:

وَضَرَبَ بِإِحْدَى يَدَيْهِ عَلَى الأُخْرَى، ثُمَّ قَالَ : إِيَّاكُمْ أَنْ تَهْلِكُوا عَنْ آيَةِ الرَّجْمِ، أَنْ يَقُولَ قَائِلٌ : لاَ

نَجِدُ حَدَّيْنِ فِي كِتَابِ اللَّهِ، فَقَدْ رَجَمَ رَسُولُ اللَّهِ ﷺ وَرَجَمْنَا ، وَالَّذِي نَفْسِي بِيَدِهِ، لَوْلَا أَنْ يَقُولَ النَّاسُ : زَادَ عُمَرُ بْنُ الْخَطَّابِ فِي كِتَابِ اللَّهِ تَعَالَى، لَكَتَبْتُهَا : ﴿ الشَّيْخُ وَالشَّيْخَةُ فَارْجُمُوهُمَا الْبَتَّةَ ﴾ . فَإِنَّا قَدْ قَرَأْنَاهَا .

> He [[c]Umar] struck one of his hands on the other and then said, "Take care lest you destroy the *āyah* of stoning so that one will say, 'We do not find two *ḥadd* punishments in the Book of Allah.' The Messenger of Allah ﷺ stoned, so we have stoned. By Him in Whose Hand my self is, had it not been that people would say that Umar ibn al-Khattab has added to the Book of Allah, exalted is He, we would have written it, *'The full-grown man and the full-grown woman, stone them absolutely.*" We have certainly recited that.'" (Imām Mālik ibn Anas, *al-Muwaṭṭa'*, Book 41, Number 41.1.10, translated by Aisha Bewley and Ya'qoub Johnson. Bookwork (Dec 2001))

The Prophet ﷺ clarified the injunction:

عَنْ عُبَادَةَ بْنِ الصَّامِتِ قَالَ: قَالَ رَسُولُ اللَّهِ ﷺ: ﴿ خُذُوا عَنِّي، خُذُوا عَنِّي، قَدْ جَعَلَ اللَّهُ لَهُنَّ سَبِيلاً، الْبِكْرُ بِالْبِكْرِ جَلْدُ مِائَةٍ وَنَفْيُ سَنَةٍ وَالثَّيِّبُ بِالثَّيِّبِ، جَلْدُ مِائَةٍ وَالرَّجْمُ

> From [c]Ubādah ibn aṣ-Ṣāmit who said: The Messenger of Allah ﷺ said, "Take from me! take from me! Undoubtedly Allah *'has ordained another procedure'* for them. For virgins [committing fornication] with virgins, the punishment is one hundred lashes and exile for a year. For those who have been married [committing adultery] with those who have been married, it is one hundred lashes and stoning to death." (Muslim, *kitāb al-ḥudūd, bāb ḥadd az-zinā*)

The above *ḥadīth* would appear to show that if the offender is not married, he should be given one hundred lashes and should be exiled for a period of a year. If the offender is married, he should be given one hundred lashes and stoned to death. Nevertheless, the majority of the jurists (including Abū Ḥanīfah, Mālik and ash-Shāfi[c]ī but excluding Aḥmad ibn Ḥanbal, Isḥāq and Dāwūd aẓ-Ẓāhirī) are of the view that the adult male or female who is or has been married is stoned to death, and is not flogged with a hundred lashes because the Prophet ﷺ had two Jewish adulterers stoned to death and did not punish them with lashes. This *ḥadīth* is the fulfilment of Allah's promise to *'ordain another procedure'* in the very first *āyah*.

The following conditions must be fulfilled before the *ḥadd* punishment of stoning to death is applied:

1. The offender must be sane, for the person who is insane is not responsible and may not be punished for *zinā*
2. He or she must be a Muslim, for non-Muslims cannot have the *ḥadd* punishment for adultery applied to them unless they commit *zinā* with a Muslim
3. He or she must be *muḥṣan* i.e. married or have been married and have consummated the marriage
4. He or she must have reached the age of puberty, for minors may not be stoned nor flogged for *zinā*
5. He or she must be free and not a slave, for neither male nor female slaves may be stoned to death for adultery, but are rather flogged
6. That he or she must have done it voluntarily and not have been coerced
7. That it was not done because of some ambivalence or mistaken identity, such as a man who makes love to a woman thinking that she is his wife.
8. That the person knows of the prohibition of fornication and adultery, but about this there are two opinions, some holding that he has no *ḥadd* punishment and others that the *ḥadd* is to be applied.

The method of punishment

The idea behind awarding this apparently harsh punishment may be that it should serve as a deterrent to the society, and it may be that it is a *kaffārah* expiation for the person who has done it. A very grave responsibility lies on the *qāḍī* (the judge) before he gives a verdict to stone the guilty person to death. The man or woman accused must be sane, adult, mature and *muḥṣan* i.e.

he is or has been married, for otherwise the punishment may not be carried out. This form of punishment is only accorded when it is proved beyond any doubt through the testimony of four reliable, Muslim witnesses with *taqwā* given at the same time, that they saw the guilty person actually committing the offence. The benefit of the doubt in the statement of testimony of the witnesses should be accorded the accused.

The only other proof of the guilt of the accused is a confession. A single confession suffices according to the Mālikīs, but according to Aḥmad ibn Ḥanbal it must be four confessions which such a person makes completely voluntarily in one sitting, and Abū Ḥanīfah added that it must be in four separate sittings. If the person confesses but then retracts the confession, he or she may not be stoned, to the extent that if the person retracts the confession during the actual stoning before its completion then the well-known position of the Mālikī *madhhab* is that his retraction is accepted.

It is reported that the Prophet ﷺ punished an adulterer when he bore witness against himself and confessed his wrong action. It is narrated by Jābir ibn ᶜAbdullāh al-Anṣārī ﷺ:

> From Jābir ibn ᶜAbdullāh ﷺ there is that a man of Aslam came to the Prophet ﷺ and told him that he had committed adultery, bearing witness against himself four times. So the Messenger of Allah ﷺ gave the order and he was stoned, and he had been married. They claimed that he was Māᶜiz ibn Mālik. Ibn Jurayj, "Saᶜīd told me from ᶜAbdullāh ibn Dīnār the *mawlā* of Ibn ᶜUmar that the Prophet ﷺ stood after the Aslamī [man] had been stoned and said, 'Shun this filth which Allah has forbidden, and whoever is pained with anything of it should veil himself [and not disclose his wrongdoing].'" (ᶜAbd ar-Razzāq)

Some scholars have said that because the Qur'ān is silent on stoning to death, therefore this punishment is not justifiable. This is precisely what the Caliph ᶜUmar ﷺ foresaw. Ibn ᶜAbbās ﷺ reported:

عَنْ عُمَرَ قَالَ: إِنَّ اللهَ عَزَّ وَجَلَّ بَعَثَ مُحَمَّداً صَلَّى اللّٰهُ عَلَيْهِ وَسَلَّمَ بِالْحَقِّ وَأَنْزَلَ عَلَيْهِ الْكِتَابَ

فَكَانَ فِيمَا أَنْزَلَ عَلَيْهِ آيَةُ الرَّجْمِ، فَقَرَأْنَاهَا وَوَعَيْنَاهَا وَرَجَمَ رَسُولُ اللَّهِ صَلَّى اللَّهُ عَلَيْهِ وَسَلَّمَ وَرَجَمْنَا بَعْدَهُ، فَأَخْشَى إِنْ طَالَ بِالنَّاسِ زَمَانٌ أَنْ يَقُولَ قَائِلٌ: لَا نَجِدُ آيَةَ الرَّجْمِ فِي كِتَابِ اللَّهِ فَيَضِلُّوا بِتَرْكِ فَرِيضَةٍ قَدْ أَنْزَلَهَا اللَّهُ، فَالرَّجْمُ فِي كِتَابِ اللَّهِ حَقٌّ عَلَى مَنْ زَنَى إِذَا أُحْصِنَ مِنَ الرِّجَالِ وَالنِّسَاءِ إِذَا قَامَتِ الْبَيِّنَةُ أَوِ الْحَبَلُ أَوِ الْاِعْتِرَافُ

ᶜUmar ﷺ said, "Allah ﷻ sent Muḥammad ﷺ with the Truth and sent the Book down upon him, and among that which He sent down was the *āyah* about stoning, for we have recited it and we memorised it. And the Messenger of Allah ﷺ stoned and we stoned after him. So I fear that time will become so long for people that someone will say, 'We do not find the *āyah* of stoning in the Book of Allah,' so that they go astray by abandoning an obligation which Allah had revealed. Stoning in the Book of Allah is the right against someone who commits adultery if *muḥṣan* whether men or women, if clear evidence is established or pregnancy or there is confession." (Ibn Abī Shaybah in his *Muṣannaf*; Aḥmad in his *Musnad*; al-ᶜAdanī; ad-Dārimī; al-Bukhārī, *kitāb al-muḥāribīn min ahl al-kufr wa ar-riddah, bāb al-iᶜtirāf bi az-zinā*; Muslim, *kitāb al-ḥudūd, bāb rajm ath-thayyib fī az-zinā*; also Abū Dāwūd, at-Tirmidhī, an-Nasā'ī, Ibn Mājah, Ibn al-Jārūd, Ibn Jarīr aṭ-Ṭabarī, Abū Awānah)

Islam commands purity of sex life both for men and women, at all times in their lives. Therefore, punishment for *zinā* is carried out openly so that it may be a deterrent for others in society.[11]

It should be noted here that most of the punishments carried out by the Prophet ﷺ and the four *Khulafā' ar-Rāshidūn* ﷺ were based on confession and not on accusation and proof.

Al-Liwāṭ: Sodomy

Sodomy, whether perpetrated on men or on women is an act intended to satisfy a sexual perversion, for which there is a *ḥadd* punishment when it is practised by men on men. The people of Lūṭ ﷺ (the prophet Lot), corrupted by luxury, committed sodomy on men in spite of the warnings from Lūṭ ﷺ.

The Qur'ān speaks of them in the following words:

وَلُوطاً إِذْ قَالَ لِقَوْمِهِ أَتَأْتُونَ الْفَاحِشَةَ مَا سَبَقَكُم بِهَا مِنْ أَحَدٍ مِّنَ الْعَالَمِينَ إِنَّكُمْ لَتَأْتُونَ الرِّجَالَ شَهْوَةً مِّن دُونِ النِّسَاءِ بَلْ أَنتُمْ قَوْمٌ مُّسْرِفُونَ

And Lūṭ, when he said to his people, 'Do you commit an obscenity not perpetrated before you by anyone in all the worlds? You come with lust to men instead of women. You are indeed a depraved people.' (Sūrat al-Aᶜrāf 7: 80-81)

When they did not heed the warning of their prophet, they were ruined completely through a rain of brimstone; a few remains of their buildings survive until today but the vast majority are overturned and lie underneath the lake of Lūṭ or the Dead Sea.

According to a narration of aṭ-Ṭabarānī and al-Bayhaqī, the Prophet Muḥammad ﷺ is reported to have said:

أَربعةٌ يُصبِحُونَ فِي غَضَبِ اللَّهِ، ويُمْسُونَ فِي غَضَبِ اللَّهِ: المُتَشَبِّهُونَ مِنَ الرِّجَالِ بِالنِّسَاءِ، والمُتَشَبِّهَاتُ مِنَ النِّسَاءِ بِالرِّجَالِ، والَّذِي يَأْتِي البَهِيمَةَ، والَّذِي يَأْتِي الرَّجُلَ.

Four types of people get up in the morning while under the wrath of Allah and they sleep in the night under the wrath of Allah: those men who try to resemble women and those women who try to resemble men (through dress and behaviour) and those who commit sex with animals and those men who commit sex with men. (Al-Bayhaqī, *Shuᶜab al-īmān*)

It is narrated by Abū Hurayrah that the Prophet of Allah ﷺ has also said:

إِنَّ الَّذِي يَأْتِي امْرَأَتَهُ فِي دُبُرِهَا لا يَنْظُرُ اللَّهُ إِلَيْهِ يَوْمَ القِيَامَةِ.

Whoever has anal intercourse with his wife, Allah will not look at him on the Day of Rising. (Al-Bayhaqī, *Shuᶜab al-īmān*)

If this is the case with sodomy practised on a wife, what can be said of the act when practised on men?

The Prophet ﷺ further said about sexual relationships between two men or two women:

إِذَا أَتَى الرَّجُلُ الرَّجُلَ فَهُمَا زَانِيَانِ، وَإِذَا أَتَتِ الْمَرْأَةُ الْمَرْأَةَ فَهُمَا زَانِيَتَانِ.

If a man commits an act of sex with a man, they are both adulterers and if a woman commits such an act with a woman, then both of them are adulteresses. (Al-Bayhaqī, *Shu*[c]*ab al-īmān*)

Punishment for homosexual sodomy (*liwāṭ*)

All Muslim jurists agree that sodomy is a sexual offence but differ in their punishment. According to Imām Abū Ḥanīfah, the act of sodomy does not amount to adultery and therefore there is no *ḥadd* punishment to be given to the offender but only a discretionary punishment (*ta*[c]*zīr*). According to Imām Mālik the *ḥadd* punishment will be applied whether the offender is married or not.

Ibn Juzayy al-Kalbī said:

> Whoever does the act of the people of Lūṭ, then both the active and the passive participants are stoned whether or not they are *muḥṣan*. Ash-Shāfi[c]ī[12] said that the judgement is the same as that for *zinā*: the *muḥṣan* is stoned but others are given the *ḥadd* punishment with a hundred [lashes]. Abū Ḥanīfah said he is given a discretionary punishment but not a *ḥadd* punishment. (Al-Kalbī, Ibn Juzayy, *al-Qawānīn al-fiqhiyyah, al-kitāb as-sābi*[c] *fī ad-dimā' wa al-ḥudūd, al-bāb ar-rābi*[c] *fī ḥadd az-zinā*)

As to Mālik's position:

وَحَدَّثَنِي مَالِكٌ، أَنَّهُ سَأَلَ ابْنَ شِهَابٍ عَنِ الَّذِي يَعْمَلُ عَمَلَ قَوْمِ لُوطٍ؟ فَقَالَ ابْنُ شِهَابٍ : عَلَيْهِ الرَّجْمُ، أُحْصِنَ أَوْ لَمْ يُحْصَنْ.

Mālik narrated that he asked Ibn Shihāb [az-Zuhrī] about someone who does the act of the people of Lūṭ? So Ibn Shihāb said, "He is to be stoned whether he is *muḥṣan* or not." (Mālik, *al-Muwaṭṭa'*, Book 41: The Hudud, Number 41.1.11)

An evidence for that is the following *ḥadīth*:

مَنْ وَجَدْتُمُوهُ يَعْمَلُ عَمَلَ قَوْمِ لُوطٍ فَارْجُمُوا الْأَعْلَى وَالْأَسْفَلَ جَمِيعاً

Whomever you find doing the act of the people of Lūṭ, then stone both the uppermost and the lowermost. (From Abū Hurayrah. Narrated by al-Kharā'iṭī and Ibn Jarīr aṭ-Ṭabarī.)

مَنْ وَجَدْتُمُوهُ يَعْمَلُ عَمَلَ قَوْمِ لُوطٍ ، فَاقْتُلُوا الْفَاعِلَ وَالْمَفْعُولَ بِهِ .

Whomever you find doing the act of the people of Lūṭ, then kill the one who does it and the one to whom it is done. (From Ibn 'Abbās in the *Musnad* of Aḥmad ibn Ḥanbal, ad-Dāraquṭnī, al-Ḥākim in *al-Mustadrak*, al-Bayhaqī in *Shu'ab al-īmān* and *aḍ-Ḍiyā'*; both al-Ḥākim and adh-Dhahabī said that it is *ṣaḥīḥ*)

It is also a crime to have sex with one's wife through the anus. The majority of jurists believe that in this case *ta'zīr* will apply since this is a case surrounded by doubt (*shubuhāt*) and whenever there is a doubt, the *ḥadd* punishment will not be applied.

Punishment for bestiality

There are times when human beings sink to the level of beasts and commit sexual intercourse with animals. According to Imām Mālik, Abū Ḥanīfah, and the Ẓāhirīs, only *ta'zīr* will be applied to the individual guilty of bestiality and not a *ḥadd* punishment. The flesh of the animal which was the subject of bestiality is *ḥalāl* when it is slaughtered. However, Imām Aḥmad ibn Ḥanbal and ash-Shāfi'ī hold that the *ḥadd* punishment of stoning to death should be applied to the individual and the animal which was the subject of bestiality should also be slaughtered and its flesh is unlawful (*ḥarām*). They rely on the following *ḥadīth* of the Prophet ﷺ :

مَنْ وَجَدْتُمُوهُ وَقَعَ عَلَى بَهِيمَةٍ، فَاقْتُلُوهُ وَاقْتُلُوا الْبَهِيمَةَ

Whoever you find who has had sexual relations with an animal then kill him and kill the animal. (At-Tirmidhī, *abwāb al-ḥudūd 'an rasūlillāh* ﷺ, *bāb fī mā jā'a fī man waqa'a 'alā al-bahīmah*, and al-Ḥākim in *al-Mustadrak* from Ibn 'Abbās)

Some other jurists also maintain that only a human can be punished but not an animal since it has no guilt. Ibn Juzayy said, "Nor is the animal killed and there is no harm in eating its meat, contrary to ash-Shāfi'ī." (Al-Kalbī, *Ibid.*)

Most of the *ḥadd* punishments in the first century of Islam (*al-qurūn al-ūlā*) were given on voluntary confessions made by the offenders. The person who committed adultery does not receive the *ḥadd* punishment except through such a voluntary confession or because of the evidence of pregnancy or through the testimony of adult men of integrity and *taqwā* who witnessed an action like the insertion of a *mirwad* into a *mukḥulah*.[13] These witnesses must see the action at the same time, and if one of them failed to complete the description, the three others would receive the *ḥadd* punishment for *qadhf* or unsubstantiated accusations of fornication. There is no *ḥadd* punishment for someone who has not reached maturity.[14]

Punishment for adultery in Sharīʿah, its conditions, its parity and its comparative effects: a resumé

At the conference on *Muslim Doctrine and Human Rights in Islam*[15] between Saudi Arabian scholars and European jurists, *ʿulamā'* gave the following arguments in favour of the *ḥadd* punishment for adultery:

> This penalty is prescribed only when the culprit, prior to his delict, had contracted a legal marriage, and if four witnesses known for their righteousness and their integrity, were present at the accomplishment of the sexual act, in a manner which could exclude the possibility of any doubt; it would not be sufficient namely, that they had seen the accused completely naked and stuck together....
>
> Here again, we agree with our guests on the severity of the punishment. Nevertheless, it is not imposed in Islam, unless the act, as we just said, was testified to by four objective and trustworthy witnesses. The testimony of one witness has no value before the law: in that case, the person is advised to refrain from making the denunciation, and condemned to be scourged, if he would continue in his accusation; the same thing happens, if there are only two, or even three witnesses. The primary condition required by the Verse, is the presence at the moment of the act of four witnesses who can be trusted, and have never been indicted. But if the act was accomplished in the presence of four witnesses, the judgement is that public order has been seriously offended. Whether legitimate or not, it is always improper for the sexual act

to take place in public. This is why Islam reveals the most severe attitude against offenders of public order and morality. ...

It must be noted in the matter, that the hard punishment of adultery was prescribed at the very beginning of the Islamic Message.[16] There was, at that time, an urgent necessity to bring society out of a system, where existed, in numerous walks, absolute sexual licence, and by the very fact, there was utter confusion with regard to paternity, into a new order, where procreative instinct would be regulated, and could be exercised only within the limits of legitimacy. And so, from the beginning of the Islamic predication, and during the whole life of the Prophet ﷺ, not a single case of adultery was established by evidence of four eye-witnesses. Only one case was verified, through the spontaneous confession of the culprit eager to purify himself in this life, and so to escape punishment in the other. When, coming to the Prophet ﷺ, he confessed his crime, and asked to be stoned to death, the Prophet ﷺ turned his face and refused to listen. Since the act had been accomplished in secret, and thus public order and morality did not suffer, the matter concerned only the culprit, who, in his soul and conscience, had simply to beg the Lord's forgiveness. The man, however, earnestly renewed his confession and his request, so as to prove his sincerity towards God, and to deter others from committing the same crime; again, the Prophet ﷺ turned his face. The same thing happened a third time, but when the culprit repeated his words a fourth time, the Prophet ﷺ asked him if he had become insane, or had really admitted being guilty of the crime. First by refusing to listen, then by questioning the fact, the Prophet ﷺ had long prompted him to retract, but the man so insisted, that in the end his demand had to be heard. At the moment of execution, however, he regretted his declaration and ran away; the punishment squad ran after him and killed him. The Prophet ﷺ then, pronounced his famous sentence; "Would that you had left him alive: he would have repented, and God would have been merciful to him." ...

Thus gentlemen, it was not possible to prove, by such evidence as is required, one single case of adultery at the time of the Prophet ﷺ; and yet, it was an age of transition from general sexual licence to discipline and legality on this point. Fourteen centuries have elapsed since that most severe penalty was edicted, and we can strongly affirm, that fourteen cases of stoning could hardly be numbered in all that time. In this way, punishment

> by stoning has remained what it always was, cruel in principle, but extremely rare in practice. But, through the very ruthlessness of this provision, Islam has prevented dislocation of family and confusion with respect to paternity. We surely admit that men are always men, but it remains that, under a secular legislation, where such a severe punishment, religiously motivated, is lacking, married people tend to lose the fear of God, and are more tempted to fall in this crime. Generally speaking, the state of things prevailing in non-Muslim countries has caused the dissolution of family ties, and jeopardized the conjugal happiness, which Muslim husbands and wives, faithful to one another, to their religion, and to God, enjoy.

Doctor Dawalibi made the following observations, addressed in particular to the president of the European Commission, who had, before leaving for Saudi Arabia, heard from some people hostile to Islam the remark, "So you are going to the country where they lynch women for adultery?" He said:

> If you please, Mr. President, report to these people what you have heard. You have neither heard that anyone had been stoned, nor seen any such thing in this kingdom. It would be better for a society where the fear of God is enough to prevent both crime and punishment, thus securing integrity of the family and happiness of married couples, to prescribe a strict religious penalty in this matter, rather than rely on a secular legislation, which does not provide any similar penalty, but does not instil in man any fear of God either, and which, by the same token, causes many to lose the sense of the family. There inevitably follows offences to social dignity, and encouragement to crimes of the most dreadful and varied kinds, whereas, in Muslim countries, where God is openly revered, and His law sincerely enforced, nothing comparable happens.

Qadhf

Qadhf or an unsubstantiated accusation of sexual misconduct is an offence which comes into existence when a person accuses a Muslim of fornication or doubts his paternity without the legal number of witnesses as outlined above. It is a great crime in Islam and those who commit it are called wicked transgressors in the Qur'ān:

وَالَّذِينَ يَرْمُونَ الْمُحْصَنَاتِ ثُمَّ لَمْ يَأْتُوا بِأَرْبَعَةِ شُهَدَاءَ فَاجْلِدُوهُمْ ثَمَانِينَ جَلْدَةً وَلَا تَقْبَلُوا لَهُمْ شَهَادَةً

أَبَدًا وَأُولَئِكَ هُمُ الْفَاسِقُونَ إِلَّا الَّذِينَ تَابُوا مِنْ بَعْدِ ذَلِكَ وَأَصْلَحُوا فَإِنَّ اللَّهَ غَفُورٌ رَحِيمٌ

But those who make accusations against chaste women and then do not produce four witnesses: flog them with eighty lashes and never again accept them as witnesses. Such people are deviators – except for those who after that make tawbah and put things right. Allah is Ever-Forgiving, Most Merciful. (Sūrat an-Nūr 24: 4-5)

Every Muslim is supposed to guard the honour and respect of a fellow man and not expose the hidden failings of any other Muslim. If a person accuses a Muslim of adultery and cannot prove it by producing four witnesses who have simultaneously seen the act being committed, the accuser is punished with eighty lashes, and will be considered a *fāsiq* and as such his evidence will no longer be accepted whenever he presents it.

The Prophet ﷺ also spoke of *qadhf* as a great vice and warned Muslims to avoid it:

عَنْ أَبِي هُرَيْرَةَ أَنَّ رَسُولَ اللَّهِ صلى الله عليه وسلم قَالَ: ﴿اجْتَنِبُوا السَّبْعَ الْمُوبِقَاتِ﴾ قِيلَ:

يَا رَسُولَ اللَّهِ وَمَا هُنَّ؟ قَالَ: ﴿الشِّرْكُ بِاللَّهِ، وَالسِّحْرُ، وَقَتْلُ النَّفْسِ الَّتِي حَرَّمَ اللَّهُ إِلَّا بِالْحَقِّ،

وَأَكْلُ مَالِ الْيَتِيمِ، وَأَكْلُ الرِّبَا، وَالتَّوَلِّي يَوْمَ الزَّحْفِ، وَقَذْفُ الْمُحْصَنَاتِ الْغَافِلَاتِ الْمُؤْمِنَاتِ﴾.

It is reported by Abū Hurayrah ؓ that the Prophet ﷺ said: "Keep away from seven abominable acts." He was asked, 'Messenger of Allah, and what are they?" He ﷺ replied: "Association of partners with Allah, magic, killing someone who is forbidden by Allah except when it is with due process of law, devouring the property of orphans, eating of usury, turning away on the day of the encounter of armies and the slander of the chaste but indiscreet *mu'min* women." (Muslim, *kitāb al-īmān, bāb bayān al-kabā'ir wa akbaruhā;* Abū Dāwūd; an-Nasā'ī)

At times women can be indiscreet (*ghāfilāt*). This may lead them into problems through selfish, jealous people. Such good natured women think of no evil and their innocent indiscretions may put them and those related to them in great difficulties. Such was the case of the Mother of the *mu'minūn*, ᶜĀ'ishah aṣ-Ṣiddīqah ﵂. In 5-6 AH slanderous allegations were spread about her. This put not only her but also her husband, the Prophet ﷺ himself, and her father Abū Bakr ﵁ in the most painful predicament. Fortunately, Allah exposed the falsehood of the accusation through revelation.[17] In this connection in the Qur'ān Allah says:

إِنَّ الَّذِينَ يَرْمُونَ الْمُحْصَنَاتِ الْغَافِلَاتِ الْمُؤْمِنَاتِ لُعِنُوا فِي الدُّنْيَا وَالْآخِرَةِ وَلَهُمْ عَذَابٌ عَظِيمٌ

Those who accuse women who are chaste, but who are careless and yet have īmān, are cursed both in the dunyā and the ākhirah, and they will have a terrible punishment. (Sūrat an-Nūr 24: 23)

According to Imām Mālik and Imām Aḥmad ibn Ḥanbal, even if a person accuses someone by insinuation, it is sufficient and he is punished with eighty lashes. However, according to Imām Abū Ḥanīfah and Imām ash-Shāfiᶜī, the accused should be asked about his intention in making the insinuation before punishment is sentenced against him. If he says that he did not mean to slander the woman then he will be punished with a discretionary punishment (*taᶜzīr*) only.

Repentance of the slanderer

In the Qur'ān Allah says:

وَلَا تَقْبَلُوا لَهُمْ شَهَادَةً أَبَدًا وَأُولَٰئِكَ هُمُ الْفَاسِقُونَ إِلَّا الَّذِينَ تَابُوا مِن بَعْدِ ذَٰلِكَ وَأَصْلَحُوا فَإِنَّ اللَّهَ غَفُورٌ رَّحِيمٌ

And never again accept them as witnesses. Such people are deviators – except for those who after that make tawbah and put things right. Allah is Ever-Forgiving, Most Merciful. (Sūrat an-Nūr 24: 4-5)

Therefore if the slanderer, after receiving the punishment of eighty lashes repents and assures that he would not engage in a similar activity in the future his civic right of giving evidence would be restored according to Imām Mālik. Imām Abū Ḥanīfah, however, takes a different and more serious view and considers that neither the punishment of eighty stripes nor the repudiation of his testimony is cancelled by repentance; it removes only the stigma of being regarded as a 'deviator'. Ibn Juzayy al-Kalbī said in his *tafsīr* on the *āyah*:

> It is agreed that the *'except'* refers to them being categorised as deviants and that is lifted from them by their *tawbah*, and they agree that it does not refer back to the *ḥadd* punishment which is not dropped because of *tawbah*. They differ as to whether it refers to the rejection of their testimony as witnesses or not. Mālik said, "If he makes *tawbah* then his testimony is accepted," contrary to Abū Ḥanīfah. His *tawbah* is the reform of his state in his *dīn*, but some say that it means his admission that he was lying [or wrong]. (Al-Kalbī, Ibn Juzayy, *Kitāb at-tashīl li ᶜulūm at-tanzīl*)

Slander of one spouse by the other

If a husband makes slanderous accusations against his wife, the Qur'ān lays down the following procedure:

وَالَّذِينَ يَرْمُونَ أَزْوَاجَهُمْ وَلَمْ يَكُنْ لَهُمْ شُهَدَاءُ إِلَّا أَنْفُسُهُمْ فَشَهَادَةُ أَحَدِهِمْ أَرْبَعُ شَهَادَاتٍ بِاللَّهِ إِنَّهُ لَمِنَ
الصَّادِقِينَ وَالْخَامِسَةُ أَنَّ لَعْنَتَ اللَّهِ عَلَيْهِ إِنْ كَانَ مِنَ الْكَاذِبِينَ وَيَدْرَأُ عَنْهَا الْعَذَابَ أَنْ تَشْهَدَ أَرْبَعَ
شَهَادَاتٍ بِاللَّهِ إِنَّهُ لَمِنَ الْكَاذِبِينَ وَالْخَامِسَةَ أَنَّ غَضَبَ اللَّهِ عَلَيْهَا إِنْ كَانَ مِنَ الصَّادِقِينَ

> *Those who make an accusation against their wives and have no witnesses except themselves, such people should testify four times by Allah that they are telling the truth and a fifth time that Allah's curse will be upon them if they are lying. And the punishment is removed from her if she testifies four times by Allah that he is lying and a fifth time that Allah's anger will be upon her if he is telling the truth.* (Sūrat an-Nūr 24: 6-9)

Suppose a Muslim catches his wife in an actual act of adultery, it would still be essential for him to produce four upstanding male witnesses who had seen the act, which is generally impossible.

Therefore, the husband will have to swear in the *Sharīᶜah* court four times to the fact of his wife's adultery and in addition invoke a curse on himself if he is not telling the truth, which will then be a *prima facie* proof of the wife's guilt. If the wife similarly swears her innocence four times and then invokes a curse on herself if he is telling the truth she will be acquitted of the charge. However, if she refuses to take the oaths, the charge will be deemed proved against her and she will have to face punishment. Whatever the outcome, once the oaths are taken, the marriage will be dissolved since it is quite impossible that the spouses would ever be able to live in peace and harmony after such an experience.

Miscellaneous cases

According to Ibn Abī Zayd al-Qayrawānī al-Mālikī, there is no *ḥadd* punishment of minors either for levelling an unsubstantiated accusation of unchastity (*qadhf*) or for committing fornication. Anybody who denies the paternity of another will receive the *ḥadd* punishment since this is clearly *qadhf.* Someone who makes an accusation of there being some uncertainty about paternity will always be given the *ḥadd* punishment – even if they are veiled in innuendoes. If a man says to another 'You sodomite!' he will receive the *ḥadd* punishment. If a man levels a false accusation against a group of people he will receive one *ḥadd* punishment when all of them demand it. Afterwards he is free and guiltless. (Ibn Abī Zayd al-Qayrawānī, *Risālah, Op. Cit.,* ch. 37, *Bāb fī aḥkām ad-dimā' wa'l-ḥudūd,* pp. 121-131)

If a man drinks wine repeatedly or commits adultery repeatedly he is to receive only one *ḥadd* punishment in respect of each of the offences. This rule applies in respect of someone who levels unsubstantiated accusations who is at the same time liable to be executed. The execution alone is sufficient for all that except where the *ḥadd* punishment is in respect of adultery; under such a circumstance the man must receive the *ḥadd* punishment and then be executed (*Ibid.*).

Ḥirābah: armed robbery

Ibn Juzayy al-Kalbī said:

> This (*ḥirābah*) refers to the person who unsheathes his sword, cuts off access and intends to plunder people whether or not he is in

a city or uninhabited land. Abū Ḥanīfah said that someone is not considered a *muḥārib* in a city. Similarly, someone who bears arms against people without enmity nor retaliation for murder, then such a person is a *muḥārib*. Whoever forces entry into a house at night and prevents [people] seeking help is a *muḥārib*. The person who attacks in order to rob someone is a *muḥārib*, and whoever cooperates with a *muḥārib* such as someone who gives them hiding or acts as a lookout, then the same judgement applies to them, contrary to ash-Shāfi^cī. (Al-Kalbī, Ibn Juzayy, *al-Qawānīn al-fiqhiyyah, al-kitāb as-sābi^c fī ad-dimā' wa al-ḥudūd, al-bāb ath-thāmin fī al-ḥirābah*)

Islamic teachings put a great premium on the sanctity of human life and property. The Qur'ān is a book of *hidāyah* i.e. guidance, for all mankind.[18] The Islamic way of life fosters both material well-being and spiritual upliftment.

Therefore, the guidance must to be adhered to in order to preserve the quality of human life and peaceful civilisation. As members of the *Ummah*, every Muslim has to uphold the truth of Allah and should be able to live free from fear, avarice and the taking of property or life by force of arms. As members of the *Ummah*, Muslims should strive to bring about a society based on economic and social justice. In the Qur'ān Allah, exalted is He, speaks of the economic duties enjoined upon the Muslims:

وَالَّذِينَ فِي أَمْوَالِهِمْ حَقٌّ مَعْلُومٌ لِلسَّائِلِ وَالْمَحْرُومِ

...those in whose wealth there is a known share for beggars and the destitute. (Sūrat al-Ma^cārij 70: 24-25)

However, this duty of the wealthy is not to be misunderstood to mean that poor, needy or greedy and ambitious people should be allowed to rob or steal from them.

Ḥirābah 'armed robbery' is a serious crime. It consists in a group of armed people or a single person who attack travellers or people in any other place, depriving them of their property through the use of force in circumstances when the victims are far from any immediate help. In the Qur'ān, Allah, exalted is He, refers to them as those who *'wage war on Allah and His Messenger'* and calls it an attempt to *'go about the earth corrupting it'*.

In the Qur'ān Allah, exalted is He, describes armed robbery as a grave crime and its punishment is elaborated in the verse below:

إِنَّمَا جَزَاءُ الَّذِينَ يُحَارِبُونَ اللَّهَ وَرَسُولَهُ وَيَسْعَوْنَ فِي الْأَرْضِ فَسَادًا أَنْ يُقَتَّلُوا أَوْ يُصَلَّبُوا أَوْ تُقَطَّعَ أَيْدِيهِمْ وَأَرْجُلُهُمْ مِنْ خِلَافٍ أَوْ يُنْفَوْا مِنَ الْأَرْضِ ذَٰلِكَ لَهُمْ خِزْيٌ فِي الدُّنْيَا وَلَهُمْ فِي الْآخِرَةِ عَذَابٌ عَظِيمٌ

> *The reprisal against those who wage war on Allah and His Messenger, and go about the earth corrupting it, is that they should be killed or crucified, or have their alternate hands and feet cut off, or be banished from the land. That will be their degradation in the dunyā and in the ākhirah they will have a terrible punishment.* (Sūrat al-Mā'idah 5: 33)

Giving the causes for the revelation (*asbāb an-nuzūl*) of this verse, Imām al-Bukhārī reports that some people from the tribe of ᶜUkl came to the Prophet ﷺ in Madīnah pretending that they wanted to accept Islam. Then they complained to the Prophet ﷺ that the weather in Madīnah was not favourable to them and that they suffered from ill-health. Thereupon the Prophet ﷺ ordered that they should be taken outside Madīnah to stay where the weather was better for them and drink from the milk and urine[19] of the cattle belonging to the *zakāh*.

They killed the herdsman and ran away with the cattle. When the matter was reported to the Prophet ﷺ, he ordered that they should be pursued and brought back. This verse was revealed about this incident.

Ḥirābah or armed robbery is not merely an offence against human society but, according to the above verse of the Qur'ān, it is as if one were waging war against Allah and His Messenger. To wage war against a community may result in chaos and confusion and loss of peace of mind and heart. Waging war upon the Creator and His Messenger is much more serious and amounts to a clear rebellion against the established principles of equity, justice and respect for all. So anyone who attempts to disrupt others' way of life in the manner described is an outlaw and deserves capital punishment.

Robbers or brigands are, therefore, those people who raise arms against innocent people with whom they have no previous enmity, the victims being unable find help or are prevented from crying for help. The gravity of the act of armed robbery remains the same whether it is committed in a city, village or desert.

In these circumstances it is a complete act of brigandage according to Imām Mālik but Imām Abū Ḥanīfah differed from him on the point that if such act is committed in a town, it does not amount to brigandage.[20] Brigands can be male or female but must be sane and adult for them to receive the punishment. As soon as they confess to committing the act or if two upright adult Muslim witnesses give evidence against them, even if they were the victims, the punishment is to be accorded.

The punishment for brigandage or armed robbery is spelt out in Sūrat al-Mā'idah in the verse quoted previously. In this double crime, committed against the community as well as being treason and rebellion against Allah, four alternative punishments are mentioned above, any one of which is to be applied according to the circumstances and the judgement of the *amīr* or *qāḍī*.

They include execution, i.e. cutting off the head, crucifixion, cutting off the right hand and left foot, or exile from the land (imprisonment outside the person's hometown). According to Imām Mālik if the robber kills, he should be killed or crucified and the judge has no choice in that. If the offender stole the property without killing, the judge then may use his discretion either to kill, crucify or cut off his right hand and left foot. If the offender terrorises and frightens the victims, the judge may use his discretion either to execute, crucify, maim or banish him.

In any case, sincere repentance before they are captured is recognised as grounds for mercy but they are still held responsible, so that if they have killed people there is the right of the heirs to retaliate against them, and if they have taken property they owe that property or its value to their victims, but some have said that all these matters are dropped unless they still have some of the property in their possession in which case they must return it to its rightful owners.

In the Qur'ān, Allah says:

إِلَّا الَّذِينَ تَابُوا مِن قَبْلِ أَن تَقْدِرُوا عَلَيْهِمْ فَاعْلَمُوا أَنَّ اللَّهَ غَفُورٌ رَحِيمٌ

[...in the ākhirah they will have a terrible punishment] except for those who make tawbah before you gain power over them. Know that Allah is Ever-Forgiving, Most Merciful. (Sūrat al-Mā'idah 5: 34)

What exactly constitutes highway robbery or *ḥirābah* differs from jurist to jurist. According to Imām Mālik, armed robbery committed inside the town or outside the town is *ḥirābah*. Imām Abū Ḥanīfah says that it is not *ḥirābah* if committed inside a town because the authorities are there to protect the citizens. Others say that it is the same whether committed inside or outside the town if force is used. Imām ash-Shāfiʿī says that if the authorities are weak and cannot help or protect its citizens, armed robbery committed inside the town is *ḥirābah*. The jurists have explained the act of *ḥirābah* in the following categories:

1. Robbers who only kill but don't get away with their loot
2. Who kill and take away property
3. Who take away property with the use of force without killing anyone
4. Who, even if they only frighten without the intention to rob, it still amounts to *ḥirābah*

Ibn Juzayy al-Kalbī ﷺ said:

> On the judgement on people who wage *ḥirābah* it is obligatory that they be admonished and exhorted [not to do so] first of all and made to swear an oath three times, then if they recant... but if they do then they are fought. Fighting them is *jihād*, and whoever of those who wage *ḥirābah* is killed there is to be no retaliation or compensation for his blood, and whomever they kill is a *shahīd*. If the *muḥārib* is seized before he turns in *tawbah* the *ḥadd* punishment is executed on him, and that is either capital punishment or crucifixion or having their alternate hands and feet cut off, or exile.
>
> As for capital punishment and crucifixion, they are joined together and crucifixion is done first according to [Ibn] al-Qāsim

> or it is done last according to Ashhab. As for amputation, the right hand and left foot are cut off.
>
> As for exile, that is for the free man but not for the slave and he is exiled to another land where he is imprisoned. Abū Ḥanīfah said that he is imprisoned in his own land until his *tawbah* becomes manifest. If the *muḥārib* killed someone, he must be killed whether he killed a free man, a slave or one of the People of the Book living under the dhimmah contract, and it is not permissible for the heir of the murdered person to pardon him. If he has not killed anyone then the *amīr* has the choice of executing him, amputation or exile, and he does whichever of those he thinks best on reflection, and he may not pass judgement on it out of his own whim. Ash-Shāfiᶜī said that he does not have a choice, but these punishments are dealt out according to the hierarchy of crimes, so that if he killed [then he must be killed] and if he stole property then the sentence is amputation, and if he did not kill and did not take any property, then he is exiled. (Al-Kalbī, Ibn Juzayy, *al-Qawānīn al-fiqhiyyah, al-kitāb as-sābiᶜ fī ad-dimā' wa al-ḥudūd, al-bāb ath-thāmin fī al-ḥirābah)*

Ad-Dasūqī, a great Māliki jurist, says that if a person using a weapon rapes a woman, the act is deemed *ḥirābah*.

The Qur'ānic verses (Sūrat al-Mā'idah 5: 33-34) on robbery (*qaṭᶜ at-ṭarīq*) also include the culprits who *'go about the earth corrupting it'*, and are traitors and conspire against the interest of an Islamic *dawlah*. The examples can be seen in the life history of the Prophet ﷺ and the *Khulafā' ar-Rāshidūn* ﷺ.

Treason and conspiracy

Clemency was granted to the general public of Makkah on the Opening (*Fatḥ*) of this city to Islam, but the other side of the story was that in spite of that clemency, eight persons were ordered by the Prophet himself ﷺ to be executed on charges of conspiracy and *fasād fi'l-arḍ* (going about the earth corrupting it). The Prophet ﷺ said:

> Kill them even if you find them clinging to the curtains of the Kaᶜbah. (Abū Yaᶜlā, Ibn Abī Shaybah)

This was in spite of the fact that neither before that nor since is it permitted for there to be any killing in the *ḥaram*; this exception is only for the Prophet himself ﷺ on this one occasion. The persons ordered by the Prophet Muḥammad ﷺ to be put to death were ᶜIkrimah ibn Abī Jahl, ᶜAbdullāh ibn Khaṭal and his two singing slave girls, Muqayyis ibn Ṣabābah, ᶜAbdullāh ibn Saᶜd ibn Abī Sarḥ, al-Ḥuwayrith ibn Naqīdh ibn Wahb and Sārah who was a freed slave of one of Banī ᶜAbd al-Muṭṭalib. However, only four out of the eight named persons were put to death. Thus it stands as a fact of history that even the Prophet Muḥammad ﷺ, famous for the general clemency awarded to the Makkans, and aptly known as the Mercy for all Creatures (*raḥmatan li'l-ᶜālamīn*), did not hesitate to order the said persons to be put to death for 'being conspirators and mischievous elements on the earth.' (Ibn Hishām , *Sīrah,* Vol. 2 (Arabic Edition), pp. 271-2)

When the Prophet Muḥammad ﷺ and his Companions had just returned to Madīnah after the battle of the Ditch (Khandaq), the archangel Jibrīl ﷺ appeared and commanded the Prophet ﷺ to punish the Jews of Banī Qurayẓah for their violation of their agreement and for conspiring with the enemy while the battle of the Ditch was in progress. The Jews asked that their judgement be left to Saᶜd ibn Muᶜādh of the tribe of Aws who were their allies. The Prophet ﷺ accepted their request and made Saᶜd ibn Muᶜādh the judge. Saᶜd gave judgement according to the Tawrāh that all the fighting men should be put to death, and that the women and children should become slaves of the Muslims, and the verdict was carried out. Nevertheless, each man was offered Islam, and thus life, before execution but they refused.

Stanley Lane Poole writes about the execution as follows:

> It was a harsh bloody sentence, worthy of the episcopal generals of the army against the Albigenses, or the deeds of the Augustinian age of Puritanism, but it must be remembered that the crime of these men was high treason against the state during the time of siege, and those who have read how Wellington's march could be traced by the bodies of the deserters and pillagers hanging from the trees, need not be surprised at the summary execution of a traitorous clan. (Lane, Edward, *Selections from the Qur'ān*, edited by Stanley Lane-Poole.)

The Jews of Banī Qaynuqāᶜ had been expelled from Madīnah on charges of *fasād fi'l-arḍ* and conspiracy, which are inexcusable.

When the news that Khālid ibn Sufyān al-Hudhalī was gathering people for an attack on Madīnah in Muḥarram of 4 AH, the Prophet ﷺ sent ᶜAbdullāh ibn Anīs to kill the conspirator Khālid. ᶜAbdullāh did this job quite alone and was awarded the staff (*ᶜaṣā*) of the Messenger of Allah ﷺ.

Sariqah: theft

In the year 632 CE, the Prophet Muḥammad ﷺ delivered his Farewell Address during the *Ḥajjat al-Wadāᶜ*, i.e. the Farewell Pilgrimage, on the plain of ᶜArafah. He said, "Your lives and property are forbidden to one another till you meet your Lord on the Day of Rising." Allah has thus conferred the right of security of ownership of property. In the Qur'ān Allah declares:

وَلَا تَأْكُلُوا أَمْوَالَكُم بَيْنَكُم بِالْبَاطِلِ

Do not devour one another's property by false means. (Sūrat al-Baqarah 2: 188)

Sariqah or theft is also an illegal means of acquiring another's property. A thief may be male or female and an act of theft is deemed complete by the *fuqahā'* when the following elements are present:

1. The property is taken away secretly
2. It is taken away with criminal intent
3. The property stolen was legally owned by the person from whom it was stolen
4. The stolen property was taken out of the possession of its real owner
5. The stolen thing has already come into the possession of the thief
6. The property reaches the value of the *niṣāb*[21] set for theft

In the Noble Qur'ān Allah prescribed the following for those who commit theft:

وَالسَّارِقُ وَالسَّارِقَةُ فَاقْطَعُوا أَيْدِيَهُمَا جَزَاءً بِمَا كَسَبَا نَكَالاً مِّنَ اللَّهِ وَاللَّهُ عَزِيزٌ حَكِيمٌ

As for thieves, both male and female, cut off their hands in reprisal for what they have done: an object lesson from Allah. Allah is Almighty, All-Wise. (Sūrat al-Mā'idah 5: 38)

The *asbāb an-nuzūl* or causes for the revelation of this *āyah* are mentioned in the narration of an incident of theft in the lifetime of the Prophet ﷺ. A man stole a bag of flour belonging to his neighbour and took it and dumped it in someone's house. Since the bag was leaking it was easily traced. Meanwhile, the owner complained to the Prophet ﷺ about the theft for which he suspected his neighbour, which was true. The Prophet ﷺ did not like him suspecting a neighbour of theft. When it was actually proved that the neighbour had stolen the bag, the thief ran away into the bush and died. The *āyah* above was revealed after this incident happened.

The punishment for committing theft in the times of earlier prophets was very grave. At the time of the prophet ᶜĪsā عليه السلام, anyone found guilty of committing theft under Roman law was crucified.[22]

In a *ḥadīth* of the Prophet ﷺ, a thief is not a believer at the time of committing a theft:

قَالَ أَبُو هُرَيْرَةَ رَضِيَ اللَّهُ عَنْهُ إِنَّ النَّبِيَّ صَلَّى اللَّهُ عَلَيْهِ وَسَلَّمَ قَالَ لَا يَزْنِي الزَّانِي حِينَ يَزْنِي وَهُوَ مُؤْمِنٌ وَلَا يَشْرَبُ الْخَمْرَ حِينَ يَشْرَبُهَا وَهُوَ مُؤْمِنٌ وَلَا يَسْرِقُ السَّارِقُ حِينَ يَسْرِقُ وَهُوَ مُؤْمِنٌ

Abū Hurayrah رضي الله عنه said: The Prophet ﷺ said, "The adulterer does not commit adultery when he commits adultery while being a *mu'min*, and the person who drinks wine when he drinks it does not do so while being a *mu'min*, and the thief does not steal when he steals while being a *mu'min*." (Muslim, *kitāb al-īmān, bāb bayān nuqṣān al-īmān bi al-maᶜāṣī, wa nafyuhu ᶜan al-mutalabbis bi al-maᶜṣiyah, ᶜalā irādah nafyi kamālih*)

Similarly, a thief is cursed by Allah as is mentioned in the following *ḥadīth*:

عَنْ أَبِي هُرَيْرَةَ؛ قَالَ: قَالَ رَسُولُ اللَّهِ ﷺ: ﴿لَعَنَ اللَّهُ السَّارِقَ. يَسْرِقُ الْبَيْضَةَ فَتُقْطَعُ يَدُهُ وَيَسْرِقُ الْحَبْلَ فَتُقْطَعُ يَدُهُ﴾.

Abū Hurayrah said: The Messenger of Allah ﷺ said, "Allah curses the thief who steals an egg and gets his hand cut off, and steals a rope and gets his hand cut off." (Aḥmad; an-Nasā'ī, *kitāb qaṭᶜ as-sāriq, taᶜẓīm as-sariqah;* Ibn Mājah, *kitāb al-ḥudūd, bāb ḥadd as-sāriq*)[23]

The above *ḥadīth* warns that even when a man tries to steal small things it is disgraceful and looked down upon. Ibn Ḥazm رحمه الله, who was a literalist (*ẓāhirī*), says that even for stealing an egg or a rope, the hand will be cut off, but the majority believe that the value of the item or items stolen should reach one quarter of a dīnār. The *ḥadīth* emphasises the shamefulness of the crime of theft since from small thefts, one can graduate one day to becoming a major criminal if unchecked.

Petty thefts are exempted from the punishment stipulated for theft in the *Sharīᶜah.* The general opinion of the *ᶜulamā'* based on the above injunction of the Qur'ān is that one hand should be cut off for the first theft provided that the thief is a sane adult and if it is proved beyond doubt that he has stolen the property from its proper place.

Ibn Juzayy al-Kalbī said:

The preconditions of amputation are eleven:

1. Sanity;

2. Having attained puberty, for the hand of a child or someone who is insane may not be cut off, by unanimous agreement;

3. That the person is not a slave of the person stolen from, so that a slave who steals the property of his owner does not have his hand cut off, contrary to Dāwūd [aẓ-Ẓāhirī];

4. That he [the thief] does not have a parental relation to the person stolen from, for a father's hand is not cut off for stealing the property of his son, and ash-Shāfiᶜī added the grandfather's [hand] is not to be amputated for his grandson's property, and Abū Ḥanīfah added every family member. They differ

about the husband and wife when either steals from the other's property;

5. That the thief has not been forced to steal out of hunger;

6. That the stolen item is such as can be benefited from or considered wealth and which it is permissible to sell, according to the different types of property. Abū Ḥanīfah said that there is no amputation for [the theft of] food nor for that whose origin is permissible [such as] firewood. So that there is no amputation for wine, nor for pork and the like, nor is there amputation for that which cannot be owned or considered as property except for stealing a young free person [and making him a slave], for there is amputation for it, contrary to the two of them [Abū Ḥanīfah and ash-Shāfiᶜī] and to Ibn al-Mājishūn, not with respect to [stealing an] adult free person;[24]

7. That the thief has no ownership with respect to it [the item stolen] nor any quasi-ownership, so that there is no amputation for someone who steals his own pawned item from the pawnbroker, nor his wage from his employer, nor for someone who steals something of which he owns some portion, nor for a creditor who steals from his debtor, but they differ about amputation for someone who steals from the spoils of battle before it is apportioned out if he has some share in it;

8. That the stolen property should amount to the *niṣāb* or more, contrary to al-Ḥasan al-Baṣrī, the Khawārij and the Ẓāhiriyyah. The *niṣāb* according to the two Imāms [Mālik and ash-Shāfiᶜī] is three *Sharīᶜah* dirhams of silver or a quarter of a *Sharīᶜah* dīnār of gold or whatever has the value of either of them at the time of the theft and stands for the main one of the two of them in the land. The *niṣāb* according to Abū Ḥanīfah is ten dirhams, and according to Ibn Abī Laylā five dirhams. Whoever steals a *muṣḥaf* and whoever removes a shroud from a grave are amputated if its value amounts to the *niṣāb* contrary to Abū Ḥanīfah in both cases. If a group steal something amounting to the *niṣāb* and none of their individual portions amount to the *niṣāb* they are amputated contrary to the two of them [Abū Ḥanīfah and ash-Shāfiᶜī] unless there is in the portion of each one of them a *niṣāb* in which case they are all amputated about which there is agreement;

9. That [the stolen property] should be in safekeeping, which is the place in which that stolen property was kept safe such as a house, a shop, on the back of an animal [such as a riding

beast or beast of burden], or a ship, such as is customary for people to safeguard their property in, for there is to be no amputation for someone who steals something that is not in safekeeping according to the dominant majority but contrary to the Ẓāhiriyyah. But that differs according to the different customs of people. Someone who steals the mosque's candles is not to be amputated, contrary to ash-Shāfiᶜī, and there is a difference of opinion about someone who steals from the *bayt al-māl* or someone who steals clothes hung out on a clothes-line. Nor is the guest who steals from the house which he has been given permission to enter, but there is a difference of opinion if he steals from a store in the house. And there is no amputation for trees nor for fruit which is hanging;

10. That he [the thief] brings the stolen property out of its safekeeping;

11. That he takes it in the mode of theft, which is to take it secretly not in the mode of taking it as spoils nor by snatching, which is to snatch something which is not safeguarded, contrary to Ibn Ḥanbal and the Ẓāhiriyyah, nor for forcible expropriation nor for proving treacherous over something which he is entrusted with. And Ibn Ḥanbal and the Ẓāhiriyyah said that if he borrowed something and then denied it he is amputated, contrary to the [other] three [Imāms]. (Al-Kalbī, Ibn Juzayy, *al-Qawānīn al-fiqhiyyah, al-kitāb as-sābiᶜ fī ad-dimā' wa al-ḥudūd, al-bāb as-sādis fī as-sariqah*)

Proof of theft should be established beyond doubt. There must be two reliable Muslim male witnesses whose testimony is valid. They are required to testify against the accused or the accused himself should confess the crime though he has every right to deny the charge levelled against him. The judge should be fully satisfied as to the crime and what has been stolen, from where and when it was stolen, and the value of the stolen property.

As far as the stolen property is concerned, it must be movable and legally valuable and must have been kept in its usual place of custody and should reach the *niṣāb*.

If it does not reach the *niṣāb*, there is no *ḥadd* punishment, only *taᶜzīr*.

The jurists differ in their opinion about the *niṣāb* which will merit the punishment of cutting the hand of a thief or, for a second theft, the foot up to the ankle. According to Imām Mālik, the hand of a thief will be cut off when he steals something the value of which reaches a quarter of a dīnār. He bases his opinion on the *ḥadīth* of the Prophet which is reported by ᶜĀ'ishah ﵂, the wife of the Prophet ﷺ:

لَا تُقْطَعُ يَدُ السَّارِقِ إِلَّا فِي رُبُعِ دِينَارٍ فَصَاعِداً

The hand of the thief is not amputated except for a quarter of a dīnār or more. (*Ṣaḥīḥ Muslim, kitāb al-ḥudūd, bāb ḥadd as-sariqah wa niṣābihā*)[25]

Imām Abū Ḥanīfah, on the contrary fixes the *niṣāb* for theft at ten dirhams and he bases his opinion on the tradition reported by Ibn ᶜAbbās:

عَنْ عَبْدِ اللَّه بنِ مسعودٍ رضِيَ اللّه عنه قال : لا يقطعُ يدُ السَّارقِ فِي أَقَلَّ مِنْ عَشَرَةِ دَرَاهِمَ.

From ᶜAbdullāh ibn Masᶜūd ﵁ there is that he said, "The hand of a thief is not to be cut off for less than ten dirhams." (Abū Ḥanīfah, *Kitāb al-āthār* in the narration of Muḥammad ibn al-Ḥasan ash-Shaybānī, *bāb ḥadd man qaṭaᶜa aṭ-ṭarīq aw saraq*)[26]

Similarly, Muslim jurists also differed in the case when the theft was committed collectively by many thieves. According to Imām Mālik, if the property stolen reaches the *niṣāb*, one hand of each thief should be cut off as punishment. Imām Abū Ḥanīfah says that if the stolen property is divided among them and the share received by each one of them reaches the *niṣāb*, the *ḥadd* punishment will be applied and one hand of each of the thieves will be cut off, but if the share does not reach the *niṣāb*, only *taᶜzīr* will be applied. The following *ḥadīth* of the Prophet ﷺ throws further light on *niṣāb* and would tend to support the Mālikī position:

عَنْ ابنِ عمرَ قال: قطعَ النَّبي ﷺ يدَ سَارِقٍ فِي مِجَنٍ قومٌ ثلاثةَ دراهِمَ.

From Ibn ᶜUmar ﵁ who said, "The Prophet ﷺ amputated the hand of a thief for [the theft of] a shield which was valued at three dirhams." (ᶜAbd ar-Razzāq, *al-Jāmiᶜ*; Ibn Abī Shaybah)

The *ḥadd* punishment of cutting off the hand is applied after the following conditions are fulfilled:

1. The person who has committed a theft must be sane.
2. He must be adult.
3. He must not have been compelled to commit the theft, although on this point there is a difference of opinion. Some take the position that if one is compelled to do something *ḥarām* one is still liable to punishment for that act, unlike the one who is compelled to pronounce something like divorce in which case many hold the position that the coercion invalidates the divorce, although Imām Abū Ḥanīfah ⁂ took the position that the coercion of an amīr would be valid.
4. He must not have been forced into committing theft by hunger.

There are also conditions concerning stolen property which should be met with before cutting the hand off:

1. The stolen property must reach the *niṣāb*.
2. It must be valuable.
3. It must be in safekeeping.
4. It must be owned by someone.

If the property stolen belongs to the *bayt al-māl*, according to some it will be presumed that he has a share but according to others he will be punishable. We have also seen above the conditions pertaining to a father taking a son's property, in which case he cannot have a limb amputated. Concerning a wife stealing from her husband's property or a husband from his wife's there is a difference of opinion with some regarding it as punishable when the property is clearly safeguarded in that person's private quarters. In the cases where property is not deemed to have been taken from safekeeping (*ḥirz*) and it is doubtful that it really belonged to someone, only *ta͑zīr* will apply.

Each case is to be decided taking into consideration the circumstantial evidence. The stolen property must have been lawful, i.e. stealing something which is *ḥarām* is not punishable with a *ḥadd* punishment. The item must have been removed completely from its normal custody for the *ḥadd* punishment to apply. If someone is permitted to enter a place and then steals in that place, the punishment is not then a *ḥadd* punishment. According to the Mālikī and Ẓāhirī schools, human beings cannot be stolen. Similarly, water, grass, sand and houses cannot be stolen. Other jurists say that human beings can be stolen, i.e. kidnapped or enticed by kidnappers. In this case, punishment is by *ta*ᶜ*zīr*. *Ḥadd* punishment will not be applicable in the case of a child who steals his parent's property, or parents who steals their child's property.

If a thief repents after he has committed the crime and amends his conduct, Allah turns to him in forgiveness. In the Qur'ān, He says:

فَمَن تَابَ مِن بَعْدِ ظُلْمِهِ وَأَصْلَحَ فَإِنَّ اللَّهَ يَتُوبُ عَلَيْهِ إِنَّ اللَّهَ غَفُورٌ رَّحِيمٌ

> *But if anyone makes tawbah after his wrongdoing and puts things right, Allah will turn towards him. Allah is All-Forgiving, Most Merciful.* (Sūrat al-Mā'idah 5: 39)

Once he repents after receiving his punishment, his testimony will be accepted as is mentioned by Ibn Juzayy al-Kalbī:

> As for being someone whose testimony is valid (ᶜ*adl*) this is stipulated [for witnesses] by consensus, and someone whose testimony is valid is someone who avoids major wrong actions and safeguards himself from minor wrong actions, and safeguards his manliness, so that the testimony of someone who falls into major wrong action such as fornication, drinking wine, making unsubstantiated accusations of sexual misconduct, and similarly lying, is not accepted unless he turns in *tawbah* and his reform becomes openly manifest. (Al-Kalbī, Ibn Juzayy, *al-Qawānīn al-fiqhiyyah, al-kitāb al-khāmis fī al-aqḍiyah wa ash-shahādāt wa mā yattaṣilu bi dhālik, al-bāb as-sābi*ᶜ *fī shurūṭ ash-shuhūd*)

It is important to note that any consideration of blood relationship or any other form of relationship are absolutely disallowed in matters of testimony.

عَنْ عَائِشَةَ رَضِيَ اللهُ عَنهَا أَنَّ قُرَيْشًا أَهَمَّهُمْ شَأْنُ الْمَرْأَةِ الْمَخْزُومِيَّةِ الَّتِي سَرَقَتْ فَقَالُوا وَمَنْ يُكَلِّمُ

فيها رسول الله صلى الله عليه وسلم فقالوا ومن يجترئ عليه إلا أسامة بن زيد حب رسول الله صلى الله عليه وسلم فكلمه أسامة

فقال رسول الله صلى الله عليه وسلم أتشفع في حد من حدود الله ثم قام فاختطب ثم قال إنما أهلك الذين قبلكم أنهم كانوا إذا سرق فيهم الشريف تركوه وإذا سرق فيهم الضعيف أقاموا عليه الحد وايم الله لو أن فاطمة بنت محمد سرقت لقطعت يدها

> From ᶜĀ'ishah ؓ there is that Quraysh were concerned about the affair of a Makhzūmī woman who had stolen and they said, "Who will talk on her behalf to the Messenger of Allah ﷺ." They said, "Who would dare but Usāmah ibn Zayd the beloved of the Messenger of Allah ﷺ. So Usāmah spoke to him about it and the Messenger of Allah ﷺ said, "Do you intercede respecting one of the *ḥadd* punishments of Allah?" Then he stood and delivered an address and said, "All that destroyed those who were before you was that when one of their people of high rank stole they would leave him alone, but if a weak person among them stole they established the *ḥadd* punishment on him. By Allah, even if Fāṭimah the daughter of Muḥammad stole I would cut off her hand." (Al-Bukhārī, *kitāb al-ḥudūd, karāhiyyat ash-shafāᶜah fī al-ḥadd idhā rufiᶜa ilā as-sulṭān*)

It is worth mentioning here that Imām Abū Ḥanīfah was more lenient in his interpretations in respect of giving *ḥadd* punishment in the case of theft as can be seen from the following comparative view of various schools of Islamic jurisprudence:

If a father steals a son's property, the *ḥadd* punishment of amputation of the hand will not apply according to Imām Abū Ḥanīfah and Imām Mālik. If something is stolen collectively by many people and its value reached the *niṣāb*, nobody's hand will be amputated, likewise, if either of the spouses steals the other's property, no *ḥadd* punishment will be applied according to Imām Abū Ḥanīfah, but Imām Mālik says that the punishment will be given in the first case to each of the thieves and in the latter to the spouse who steals from the other. If one's brother or uncle steals one's property, Imām ash-Shāfiʿī, Imām Aḥmad ibn Ḥanbal and Imām Mālik say that the *ḥadd* punishment will be applied to them, but Imām Abū Ḥanīfah says that there will be no *ḥadd* punishment for such near relatives. If one borrows something from someone and then refutes that he ever borrowed it, he will face *ḥadd* punishment according to the Ḥanbalī and Ẓāhirī schools, but the Mālikī, Ḥanafī and Shāfiʿī schools do not permit *ḥadd* punishments for such a defaulter. Likewise, if a man steals something and then becomes its owner by purchasing it or through gift (*hibah*), there will still be *ḥadd* punishment according to the three schools except the Ḥanafī school in the situation where the case has been brought to the attention of the *amīr*, who is duty-bound to carry out the punishment. However, all agree that if those stolen from agree restrospectively to sell the item stolen to the thief or give it to him as a gift that is acceptable. They do not have to report the matter to the *amīr*.

Non-Muslims who live under the protection of Muslim governance will not be given the *ḥadd* punishment of amputation of the hand in the event of their stealing according to Imām Abū Ḥanīfah, but the other three Imams say that *ḥadd* punishment is applied to them as well. If someone steals shrouds from the dead, there will be no *ḥadd* punishment according to Abū Ḥanīfah, but Imām ash-Shāfiʿī, Imām Mālik and Imām Aḥmad say that the *ḥadd* punishment will apply. None of the schools will give any *ḥadd* punishment for theft prompted by starvation. The Ḥanafī school will not give any *ḥadd* punishment for the theft of wood or other perishable items, but all the other schools will award a *ḥadd* punishment for such a theft if the items reach the value of *niṣāb* and if the theft fulfils the other preconditions mentioned above.

Khamr: Intoxicants

Drinking wine or alcohol and taking intoxicating drugs are forbidden (*ḥarām*) in Islam. The word for an intoxicant used in the Qur'ān is *khamr* which is derived from *khamara* meaning to cover or veil something and signifying any fermented juice of grapes, barley, dates, honey or any other thing which may make one intoxicated after consumption. It includes any liquor or thing which intoxicates. As ᶜUmar said:

الْخَمْرُ مَا خَامَرَ الْعَقْلَ

Khamr is anything that puts a curtain over one's intellect. (Al-Bukhārī, *kitāb al-ashribah, bāb mā jā'a fī anna al-khamr mā khāmara al-ᶜaql min ash-sharāb;* Ibn Abī Shaybah; Aḥmad; Ibn Abī'd-Dunyā; Abū ᶜAwānah; aṭ-Ṭaḥāwī; Ibn Abī ᶜĀṣim; al-Bayhaqī; Ibn Ḥibbān in his *Ṣaḥīḥ;* Ibn Mardawiyyah)

GRADUAL PROHIBITION INTRODUCED IN ISLAM

After the Arabs had accepted Islam and before its prohibition, they used to drink wine. They used to ask the Prophet ﷺ questions about it until the following verse was revealed:

يَسْأَلُونَكَ عَنِ الْخَمْرِ وَالْمَيْسِرِ قُلْ فِيهِمَا إِثْمٌ كَبِيرٌ وَمَنَافِعُ لِلنَّاسِ وَإِثْمُهُمَا أَكْبَرُ مِن نَّفْعِهِمَا

They will ask you about alcoholic drinks and gambling. Say, 'There is great wrong in both of them and also certain benefits for mankind. But the wrong in them is greater than the benefit.' (Sūrat al-Baqarah 2: 219)

The above verse as well as indicating its benefits pointed out the evils of wine-drinking but did not prohibit it. Later, the Divine Revelation partially forbade its use, as they were told not to pray when drunk:

يَا أَيُّهَا الَّذِينَ آمَنُوا لَا تَقْرَبُوا الصَّلَاةَ وَأَنتُمْ سُكَارَىٰ حَتَّىٰ تَعْلَمُوا مَا تَقُولُونَ

You who have īmān! do not approach the prayer when you are drunk, so that you will know what you are saying. (Sūrat an-Nisā' 4: 42)

In the last revelation drinking alcohol was entirely prohibited:

يَا أَيُّهَا الَّذِينَ آمَنُوا إِنَّمَا الْخَمْرُ وَالْمَيْسِرُ وَالْأَنصَابُ وَالْأَزْلَامُ رِجْسٌ مِّنْ عَمَلِ الشَّيْطَانِ فَاجْتَنِبُوهُ لَعَلَّكُمْ
تُفْلِحُونَ إِنَّمَا يُرِيدُ الشَّيْطَانُ أَن يُوقِعَ بَيْنَكُمُ الْعَدَاوَةَ وَالْبَغْضَاءَ فِي الْخَمْرِ وَالْمَيْسِرِ وَيَصُدَّكُمْ عَن ذِكْرِ
اللَّهِ وَعَنِ الصَّلَاةِ فَهَلْ أَنتُم مُّنتَهُونَ

You who have īmān! wine and gambling, stone altars and divining arrows are filth from the handiwork of Shaytan. Avoid them completely so that hopefully you will be successful. Shaytan wants to stir up enmity and hatred between you by means of wine and gambling, and to debar you from remembrance of Allah and from ṣalāt. Will you not then give them up? (Sūrat al-Mā'idah 5: 90-91)

According to Qatādah, the verse prohibiting wine-drinking was revealed after the battle of Aḥzāb, which took place in the fourth or fifth year of the Hijrah. Ibn Isḥāq, the famous historian, has also confirmed that it was revealed in the fourth year of the Hijrah.

The Prophet ﷺ has referred to intoxicants as the mother of all vices (*umm al-khabā'ith*). In some parts of the world, many families are destroyed because of this evil. Habitual drunkards and drug-addicts cannot live without their alcohol or drugs, and in their desperate moments are ready to commit any crime.

The Prophet ﷺ said:

الْخَمْرُ أُمُّ الْخَبَائِثِ، وَمَنْ شَرِبَهَا لَمْ يَقْبَلِ اللهُ مِنْهُ صَلاةً أَرْبَعِينَ يَوْماً، وَإِنْ مَاتَ وَهِيَ فِي بَطْنِهِ مَاتَ مِيتَةً جَاهِلِيَّةً.

Wine is the mother of all vices. Whoever drinks it, Allah will not accept his prayers (*ṣalāh*) for forty days. If he dies and there is some in his stomach, he will die the death of the *Jāhiliyyah* (the period before the advent of Islam). (Narrated by Ibn an-Najjār from Ibn ᶜUmar)

The prayer saves a man from evil thoughts and actions, as mentioned in the Qur'ān:

إِنَّ الصَّلاةَ تَنْهَى عَنِ الْفَحْشَاءِ وَالْمُنْكَرِ

Ṣalāt precludes indecency and wrongdoing. (Sūrat al-ᶜAnkabūt 29: 45)

Once wine-drinking is started it quickly becomes a habit and is difficult to be rid of. The Prophet ﷺ has also called it an embodiment of all the wrong actions.

The Prophet ﷺ said:

والخمر جماع الإثم

Wine is the embodiment of all wrong action. (Al-Bayhaqī, *Dalā'il an-nubuwwah*)[27]

Wine and *īmān* do not go together in one person and while someone drinks wine he is not a believer (*mu'min*) as mentioned in the following *ḥadīth*. The Prophet ﷺ said:

ولا يشرب الخمر حين يشربها وهو مؤمن

Nor does someone drink wine when he drinks it while being a *mu'min*. (Muslim, *kitāb al-īmān, bāb bayān nuqṣān al-īmān bi al-maᶜāṣī, wa nafyuhu ᶜan al-mutalabbis bi al-maᶜṣiyah, ᶜalā irādah nafyi kamālih;* and from Ibn ᶜAbbās and Abū Hurayrah from Aḥmad, al-Bayhaqī, an-Nasā'ī, Ibn Mājah and al-Bukhārī)

The Qur'ānic prohibition gives the Muslims a general stamp of sobriety unknown among the followers of any other religion. In Judaism, wine forms an integral part of their religious festivities and is considered a sacred drink. In Christianity, only its abuse is condemned[28] and it was never absent from the Church nor from its clergy, and it has attained enormous currency among Christians all over the world. The problems that arise from drug and alcohol abuse are too well known.

In one of the *ḥadīth* of the Prophet Muḥammad ﷺ, he says:

وإن كل مسكر حرام.

And every thing that intoxicates is prohibited (*ḥarām*). (Al-Ḥākim in *al-Mustadrak*, and al-Bayhaqī)[29]

This means that every drink or drug that intoxicates is *ḥarām* (unlawful). From the above *ḥadīth*, it is clear that hemp, hashish, marijuana,[30] opium, heroin, methadone, cocaine, ecstasy, and other drugs are equally *ḥarām*. Ḥanafī jurists call hashish smokers 'heretical innovators' (*zindīq mubtadiᶜ*).

In another *ḥadīth*, the Prophet ﷺ said:

ما أسكر كثيره فقليله حرام

That of which a great deal causes intoxication then a little of it is *ḥarām*. (At-Tirmidhī, *abwāb al-ashribah ᶜan rasūlillāh* ﷺ, *bāb mā askara kathīruhu fa qalīluhu ḥarām*)

The Prophet ﷺ said:

لعن الله الخمر وشاربها وساقيها وبائعها ومبتاعها وعاصرها ومعتصرها وحاملها والمحمولة إليه

Allah has cursed wine, the one who drinks, the one who pours it, the one who sells it, the one who purchases it, the person who extracts it,[31] or seeks for it to be extracted, the one who conveys it and the person to whom it is conveyed. (At-Tirmidhī, *abwāb al-buyūᶜ ᶜan rasūlillāh* ﷺ; *bāb mā jā'a fī bayᶜ al-khamr wa an-nahy ᶜan dhālika*; Abū Dāwūd, *kitāb al-ashribah, bāb fī al-ᶜinab yuᶜṣaru li al-khamr*. The wording is that of Abū Dāwūd)

Jurists of the four schools agree that a drunkard must be punished by flogging. Mālikī, Ḥanafī and Ḥanbalī jurists say that the *ḥadd* punishment for drinking wine is eighty lashes, but Imām ash-Shāfiᶜī said that the punishment is only forty lashes. Sayyidunā ᶜUmar ؓ also used to give punishment of eighty lashes and instructed Khālid ibn al-Walīd and Abū ᶜUbaydah to do the same in Syria in his letters to them. The punishment will be given if a person who is drunk accepts (*iqrār*) that he has drunk or on the evidence of two just witnesses.

Jurists differ as to whether the *ḥadd* punishment will be given because of having smelt the alcohol on someone's mouth. According to Imām Mālik, if the mouth smells of wine, the *ḥadd* punishment of eighty strokes will be given. Imām Abū Ḥanīfah and Imām ash-Shāfiᶜī disagreed on this point and maintained that the smell could be of something else which resembles wine. The *ḥadd* punishment will not be given to a child, or the insane or someone who was made to drink under duress.

Riddah: Reneging on Islam

Riddah means reneging on Islam in favour of another religion or of no religion, either through action or words. The act of reneging thus puts an end to one's adherence to Islam. When one rejects the fundamental principles of faith (*īmān*) such as faith in the existence of Allah or the Messengership of His Prophet Muḥammad ﷺ or of any of the prophets or messengers, as contained in the credal statement of Islam, the *shahādah,* then one has reneged on Islam. Similarly with the rejection of belief in the Qur'ān as the Book of Allah or belief in the message contained in it, or rejection of belief in any of the revealed books, or belief in the Day of Rising, or the Reward and the Punishment of Allah, will all amount to reneging on Islam.

Rejection of the obligatory practices, like *ṣalāh, zakāh, ṣiyām* (Fasting in the month of Ramadan), and Ḥajj Pilgrimage also amount to acts of *riddah*. Likewise, if one imitates the practices of non-Muslims in their religion or their prayers etc., and dresses in their clothing and attends their places of worship it is considered an act of reneging on Islam. Ibn Juzayy al-Kalbī said:

> There is no difference of opinion in declaring someone a *kāfir* who negates the Lordship or the Oneness [of Allah] or worships someone other than Him with Allah or is on the *dīn* of the Jews or the Christians or the Majūs or the Ṣābīn or said that [God] had become manifest in a form or [that he believed in] the transmigration of souls or believed that Allah is not Living or not All-Knowing or he negates any of His attributes, or said that someone other than Him created the world, or said that He was born from something, claimed to sit with Allah literally or to ascend to Him [literally] or said that the world had no beginning or had a doubt about any of that, or held that someone after Sayyidunā Muḥammad ﷺ was a prophet or held that it is conceivable for the prophets, peace be upon them, to lie, or who holds that the Message was for the Arabs in particular, or claims to have received revelation or that he enters the Garden in this world literally or he declares all of the Companions to be *kāfir* ﵁, or rejects anything of the *dīn* known to be necessarily true, or who goes to churches in the clothing and manner of Christians, or who says that some of the *awliyā'* are not obligated to do *ᶜibādah,* or who rejects a single letter or more of the Qur'ān or who adds something to it or alters it or who says that it is not a miracle or who says that reward and punishment are metaphorical (*maᶜnawī*) or who says that the Imāms are better than the prophets. (Al-Kalbī, Ibn Juzayy, *al-Qawānīn al-fiqhiyyah, al-kitāb as-sābiᶜ fī ad-dimā' wa al-ḥudūd, al-bāb al-ᶜāshir fī al-murtadd wa az-zindīq wa as-sābb wa as-sāḥir*)

The following Qur'ānic verse explains the gravity and the crime in reneging:

كَيْفَ يَهْدِي اللهُ قَوْماً كَفَرُوا بَعْدَ إِيمَانِهِمْ وَشَهِدُوا أَنَّ الرَّسُولَ حَقٌّ وَجَاءَهُمُ الْبَيِّنَاتُ وَاللهُ لاَ يَهْدِي الْقَوْمَ الظَّالِمِينَ أُولَئِكَ جَزَآؤُهُمْ أَنَّ عَلَيْهِمْ لَعْنَةَ اللهِ وَالْمَلآئِكَةِ وَالنَّاسِ أَجْمَعِينَ خَالِدِينَ فِيهَا لاَ يُخَفَّفُ عَنْهُمُ الْعَذَابُ وَلاَ هُمْ يُنظَرُونَ إِلاَّ الَّذِينَ تَابُوا مِن بَعْدِ ذَلِكَ وَأَصْلَحُوا فَإِنَّ اللهَ غَفُورٌ رَّحِيمٌ

> *How can Allah guide a people who have become kāfir after having had īmān? They bore witness that the Messenger was true and that the Clear Signs had come to them. Allah does not guide people who are wrongdoers. The repayment of such people is that Allah's curse is on them and that of the angels and of all mankind. They will be under it for ever. Their punishment will not be lightened. They will be granted no reprieve. Except for those who, after that, make tawbah and put things right. Truly Allah is Ever-Forgiving, Most Merciful.* (Sūrah Āl ᶜImrān 3: 86-89)

The *ḥadd* punishment for reneging

The punishment for reneging is prescribed in the following *ḥadīth* of the Prophet ﷺ reported by Ibn ᶜAbbās ﷺ:

مَنْ بَدَّلَ دِينَهُ فَاقْتُلُوهُ

> Whosoever changes his *dīn* [from Islam to something else], then kill him. (Al-Bukhārī, *kitāb istitābat al-murtaddīn wa al-muᶜānidīn wa qitālihim, bāb ḥukm al-murtadd wa al-murtaddah wa istitābatuhum*)[32]

The punishment by death in the case of reneging on Islam has been unanimously agreed upon by all four schools of Islamic jurisprudence. However, if someone is forced to pronounce something that amounts to *kufr*, while his heart is satisfied with *īmān* (faith), he will not be charged with reneging in those circumstances. In the Qur'ān Allah, exalted is He, says:

مَن كَفَرَ بِاللَّهِ مِن بَعْدِ إِيمَانِهِ إِلَّا مَنْ أُكْرِهَ وَقَلْبُهُ مُطْمَئِنٌّ بِالإِيمَانِ وَلَكِن مَن شَرَحَ بِالْكُفْرِ صَدْرًا فَعَلَيْهِمْ غَضَبٌ مِنَ اللَّهِ وَلَهُمْ عَذَابٌ عَظِيمٌ

Those who reject Allah after having had īmān – except for someone forced to do it whose heart remains at rest in its īmān – but as for those whose breasts become dilated with kufr, anger from Allah will come down on them. They will have a terrible punishment. (Sūrat an-Naḥl 16: 106)

In the books of *ḥadīth,* the causes of revelation (*asbāb an-nuzūl*) of this verse are mentioned referring to the case of [c]Ammār ibn Yasār. [c]Ammār's father Yāsir and his mother Sumayyah were subjected to unbearable torture for their belief in Islam and love for the Prophet ﷺ, but in spite of the tortures they never recanted. [c]Ammār was a young man. In a weak moment, while suffering great torture at the hands of the pagan Arabs and thinking of his parents' suffering he uttered something that was construed as recantation, though his heart never wavered. Abū Jahl had made iron chains and had put them around his body in those hot summer days. The chains became hot like live charcoals due to the heat of the sun. In such desperate moments he said something which was reported to the Prophet ﷺ. The Prophet ﷺ thereupon said about [c]Ammār as is narrated by Ibn [c]Abbās ﷺ:

إِنَّ عَمَّارًا مُلِئَ إِيمَانًا مِن قَرْنِهِ إِلَى قَدَمِهِ.

[c]Ammār is full of *īmān* from his crown to his feet. (Abū Nu[c]aym, *al-Ḥilyah*)

It was on this occasion that the above verse was revealed.

The other legal aspects concerning the effects of reneging on Islam on marriage, divorce and inheritance are discussed in the respective chapters dealing with them.

Al-Firār min az-zaḥf – running away from the battle-field in *jihād*

Whenever a Muslim joins the forces of *jihād* for the sake of Allah, and is on the battlefield, fighting against the enemies, his running away constitutes a great crime in the *Sharīcah*. Battle is, on the contrary, an occasion to stand firm according to the instructions of the leaders as thoughtfully planned in their strategy. It is a time to show bravery and lay down one's life, if necessary, for the sake of Allah. Running away from the battlefield could endanger the fate of others in the community. The following Qur'ānic injunction shows how grave the crime of fleeing the battlefield is.

يَا أَيُّهَا الَّذِينَ آمَنُوا إِذَا لَقِيتُمُ الَّذِينَ كَفَرُوا زَحْفًا فَلَا تُوَلُّوهُمُ الْأَدْبَارَ وَمَن يُوَلِّهِمْ يَوْمَئِذٍ دُبُرَهُ إِلَّا مُتَحَرِّفًا لِّقِتَالٍ أَوْ مُتَحَيِّزًا إِلَىٰ فِئَةٍ فَقَدْ بَاءَ بِغَضَبٍ مِّنَ اللَّهِ وَمَأْوَاهُ جَهَنَّمُ وَبِئْسَ الْمَصِيرُ

You who have īmān! when you encounter those who are kāfir advancing in massed ranks into battle, do not turn your backs on them. Anyone who turns his back on them that day, unless he is withdrawing to rejoin the fight or withdrawing to support another group, brings Allah's anger down upon himself. His refuge is Hell. What an evil destination! (Sūrat al-Anfāl 8: 15-16)

It is forbidden to flee from the enemy unless they are more than twice the Muslims either in numbers or in force and power, in which case it is permissible to flee. If someone has fled from the enemy without the excuse of the enemy's overwhelming force, he must seek the forgiveness of Allah because of the *ḥadīth* of the Messenger of Allah ﷺ:

مَنْ قَالَ أَسْتَغْفِرُ اللهَ الَّذِي لَا إِلَهَ إِلَّا هُوَ الْحَيُّ الْقَيُّومُ وَأَتُوبُ إِلَيْهِ غَفَرَ اللهُ لَهُ وَإِنْ كَانَ قَدْ فَرَّ مِنَ الزَّحْفِ

Whoever says, "I seek forgiveness of Allah, the Living, the Self Sustaining and I turn in *tawbah* to Him," Allah will forgive him even if he has fled from the massed ranks advancing in battle. (At-Tirmidhī, *aḥādīth shattā min abwāb ad-dacawāt*)[33]

The Arabic word *zaḥf* used in the verse of the Qur'ān implies meeting massed ranks of a hostile army advancing against the Muslims. The fighters obey orders and work on their own initiative when they are in combat where there is no room for second thought. He himself might die in the battle but the community will prosper through his sacrifice. His reward will be that of a warrior in the way of Allah if he survives the battle, or he will become a *shahīd* in the cause of Allah, if he dies in active service of Allah.

In modern armies, deserters and cowards are court-martialled and put to death or given harsh punishments. However, Islamic *jihād* is a nobler form based not on the coercion of fighters but on their voluntary desire to serve Allah.

The Islamic concept of *jihād,* and the circumstances in which it is obligatory or permissible are fully discussed in chapter 27 of this book.

Notes

[1] Elsewhere translated as 'due process of law.'

[2] It is reported by them in the letter that the Messenger of Allah ﷺ to the people of Yemen about *zakāh*, inheritance and many other matters, which is narrated by Abū Bakr Muḥammad ibn ᶜAmr ibn Ḥazm from his father from his grandfather.

[3] The Farewell Khuṭbah is widely reported in various fragments in all of the great works of *ḥadīth*.

[4] The Pentateuch: the first five books of the Hebrew Bible and of the Old Testament (Genesis, Exodus, Leviticus, Numbers, and Deuteronomy).

[5] Exodus XXI: 23-25; Leviticus XXIV: 18-21 and Deuteronomy XIX: 21

[6] Ibn Abī Zayd al-Qayrawānī, *Risālah*, Op. Cit., ch. 37, *Bāb fī aḥkām ad-dimā' wa'l-ḥudūd*, pp. 121-130

[7] *Ibid.*

[8] *Ibid.*

[9] Ibn Abī Zayd al-Qayrawānī, *Risālah*, Op. Cit., ch. 37, *Bāb fī aḥkām ad-dimā' wa'l-ḥudūd*, pp. 121-131

[10] Ibn Abī Zayd al-Qayrawānī, *Risālah*, Op. Cit., ch. 37, *Bāb fī aḥkām ad-dimā' wa'l-ḥudūd*, pp. 121-131

[11] The original edition of *Sharīᶜah* had the story of Abū Shaḥmah an alleged son of Sayyidunā ᶜUmar ☙, wrongly identified with ᶜUbaydullāh, another son who survived ᶜUmar and killed a number of Persians after his death believing them conspirators involved in his father's death. The story is told of how ᶜUmar had Abū Shaḥmah flogged for illicit sexual relations and he died under the flogging, and it is meant to serve as an example of the impartiality and strict

justice of Islam as exemplified by cUmar ﷺ. However, I could find no accounts of it in my references, and Ibn Ḥajar said in *al-Iṣābah* "It has been narrated in weak traditions that his father flogged him for fornication and that he died. Al-Jawdhaqānī mentioned it."

[12] This was also the position of the two Ḥanafī imāms Abū Yūsuf and Muḥammad ibn al-Ḥasan.

[13] The *mirwad* is the little stick for applying antimony to the eyelids. The *mukḥulah* is the receptacle for kohl or antimony.

[14] Ibn Abī Zayd al-Qayrawānī, *Risālah, Op. Cit.*, ch. 37, *Bāb fī aḥkām ad-dimā' wa'l-ḥudūd,* pp. 121-131

[15] Conference on *Muslim Doctrine and Human Rights in Islam,* Ministry of Justice, Riyadh, March 23rd, 1972

[16] This is mistaken. The revelation of the *ḥadd* punishment came late in the Sīrah of the Messenger of Allah ﷺ.

[17] For details of the incident see *Ṣaḥīḥ al-Bukhārī* and other works of *sīrah* and *ḥadīth.*

[18] In the Qur'ān, Allah addresses the Messenger ﷺ, the believers, the people of the Book (the Jews and the Christians), mankind, the individual human being, and those who disbelieve.

[19] Considered traditionally by the Arabs to be a healing.

[20] See *Nayl al-awṭār,* Vol. 7, p. 336; also *Ḥāshiyat ad-Dasūqī* , Vol. 4, p. 348

[21] The value such that if an item is worth less than the *niṣāb* the removal of it is not considered theft.

[22] Matthew 27:38

[23] The *ḥadīth* must be understood within the *fiqh*. There is a minimum value for which a hand may be amputated, which was held to be the value of a certain type of shield. According to Mālik and ash-Shāficī the amount for which a hand may be amputated is three dirhams of silver or a quarter of a dīnār of gold or anything of that value. Abū Ḥanīfah held that it is ten dirhams.

[24] Taking a child and enslaving him is considered theft since the child is in the safekeeping of an adult, and the property being in safekeeping (*ḥirz*) is one of the conditions for the act to be considered theft. Stealing an adult and enslaving him is not considered theft, but another judgement would apply in this case.

[25] There are numerous *ḥadīth* of the Prophet ﷺ and traditions of the Companions to the same effect.
[26] Ibn Abī Shaybah narrated it in the *Muṣannaf* Vol. 5 p. 473. Again there is a *ḥadīth* of the Messenger of Allah ﷺ and some judgements of the Companions to this effect.
[27] A great many other scholars transmit it.
[28] Judges 9:14
[29] There are many narrations of this *ḥadīth* in almost the identical wording from a number of the Companions.
[30] Hashish and marijuana refer to different parts of the same intoxicating plant: hemp or *cannabis sativa.*
[31] Literally 'presses' or 'squeezes' it.
[32] The judgement does not apply to anyone who converts from Judaism to Christianity, for example, but only to someone who abandons the *dīn* of Islam.
[33] Related by al-Qurṭubī in *Jāmi*ᶜ *al-aḥkām* his renowned *tafsīr.*

Part V
Inheritance and Disposal of Property

Chapter 20

Mīrāth: Laws of Inheritance

THE SIGNIFICANCE of the laws of inheritance is hard to overestimate. Arguably, the major factor in the very serious problems of our time, whether political, social, marital, psychological, economic or ecological, is the role of wealth and capital, and, in a word, capitalism. A number of elements have contributed to the growth of modern capitalism, in particular the promotion of paper currencies and electronic credit, the creation of credit from nothing and the fractional reserve banking system, all stemming from the destruction of the Judaeo-Christian prohibition of usury and the abrogation of the laws governing trade and commerce. However, not the least important element would have to be the practice of primogeniture whereby the first-born son laid claim to the greater portion of the inheritance, leaving other children to fend for themselves. This practice was what kept great fortunes intact over centuries and is certainly one of the reasons why we have a capitalist culture today. The laws of inheritance of Islam distribute wealth in algebraic proportions among the heirs, thus reducing capital's drive to monopoly and the economic injustices which result. Their rediscovery and re-application by the Muslims will be of the highest importance.

Inheritance in the Qur'ān

There are about thirty-five verses of the Qur'ān which refer to *mīrāth* (inheritance) or its derivatives in one form or the other. The word *mīrāth* is specifically used in the following two verses:

وَلِلّٰهِ مِيرَاثُ السَّمَاوَاتِ وَالْأَرْضِ وَاللّٰهُ بِمَا تَعْمَلُونَ خَبِيرٌ

Allah is the inheritor of the heavens and the earth and Allah is aware of what you do. (Sūrah Āl ᶜImrān 3: 180)

In Sūrat al-Ḥadīd, Allah says:

وَمَا لَكُمْ أَلَّا تُنفِقُوا فِي سَبِيلِ اللّٰهِ وَلِلّٰهِ مِيرَاثُ السَّمَاوَاتِ وَالْأَرْضِ

And how is it with you that you do not give in the Way of Allah, when the inheritance of the heavens and the earth belongs to Allah? (Sūrat al-Ḥadīd 57: 10)

Even Prophets of Allah like Zakariyā ﵇ have prayed to be given inheritors to succeed them:

وَزَكَرِيَّا إِذْ نَادَىٰ رَبَّهُ رَبِّ لَا تَذَرْنِي فَرْدًا وَأَنتَ خَيْرُ الْوَارِثِينَ

And Zakariyā when he called out to his Lord, 'My Lord, do not leave me on my own, though You are the Best of Inheritors.' (Sūrah Maryam 19: 89)

This must however be understood in the sense of a successor of the rank of prophethood since Abū Bakr ﵁ narrated that the Prophet ﷺ said about material inheritance:

لَا نُورَثُ، مَا تَرَكْنَا صَدَقَةٌ

We, the assembly of the prophets, leave no inheritance; what we leave is *ṣadaqah*. (at-Tirmidhī, *abwāb as-siyar, bāb mā jā'a fī tarikat an-nabī* ﷺ)

In legal terminology, *mīrāth* means inheritance from the property of the deceased to be divided among his heirs. The science of *mīrāth* in the *Sharīᶜah* provides rules which guide as to who inherits and who is to be inherited from, and what shares go to whom. One of the most important branches of Islamic family law is that relating to inheritance. The death of a person brings about transfer of most of his rights and obligations to persons who survive him called *wurathā'*, that is heirs and representatives, just as inheritance is called *mīrāth* in Arabic.

The transmissible rights include all rights to property as well as rights connected with property, and other contingent interests, such as debts, rights to compensation, etc. There are also the transmissible obligations which are capable of being satisfied out of the deceased's estate. What is left after the last needs of the deceased have been satisfied, namely, after the payment of funeral expenses and the discharge of his obligations and debts, is to be distributed according to the law of *mīrāth* as defined in the Qur'ānic injunctions, except that it is permissible for a Muslim to bequeath up to one third of his or her net estate to people who do not inherit fixed shares or to charitable purposes.

The rules regulating inheritance in the *Sharīcah* are based on the principle that property which belonged to the deceased should devolve on those who by reason of consanguinity or marital relations can expect to be beneficiaries of it in proportion to the strength of their claim. The deceased may, however, leave more than one person so related to or connected with him that it would be difficult to say with regard to any one of them that his claim should altogether supersede that of the others. It is laid down in the Qur'ān:

آبَاؤُكُمْ وَأَبْنَاؤُكُمْ لَا تَدْرُونَ أَيُّهُمْ أَقْرَبُ لَكُمْ نَفْعاً

> *With regard to your fathers and your sons, you do not know which of them is going to benefit you more.* (Sūrat an-Nisā' 5: 11)

The *Sharīcah* in those cases distributes the estate among the claimants in such order and proportions as are most in harmony with the natural strength of their claims. It was for this purpose and because of the proportions of the inheritance mentioned in the Qur'ān and the Sunnah that the Muslims developed their highly sophisticated science of algebra.

In the *jāhiliyyah* period, the rules of inheritance excluded both women and children from inheriting from the estate of deceased relatives, because according to them only those who could go to the battlefield in order to defend the clan were allowed to inherit. As far as a woman was concerned, she was considered to be the property of her husband's family, and she was to be included as part of his estate after the death of her husband.

When Muslims emigrated from Makkah to Madīnah, the law of succession was based on the Islamic connection. A Muslim from Madīnah could inherit from his Makkan companion by virtue of brotherhood in Islam, until the time when this verse was revealed:

وَالَّذِينَ آمَنُوا مِن بَعْدُ وَهَاجَرُوا وَجَاهَدُوا مَعَكُمْ فَأُولَٰئِكَ مِنكُمْ وَأُولُوا الْأَرْحَامِ بَعْضُهُمْ أَوْلَىٰ بِبَعْضٍ فِي كِتَابِ اللَّهِ إِنَّ اللَّهَ بِكُلِّ شَيْءٍ عَلِيمٌ

> *Those who have īmān and make hijrah later on and accompany you in doing jihād, they also are of your number. But blood relations are closer to one another in the Book of Allah. Allah has knowledge of all things.* (Sūrat al-Anfāl 8: 75)

This changed the rules from the inheritance of brotherhood in Islam to near relatives.

Essentials of Succession

The elements of inheritance are as follows:

1. The deceased person
2. Heirs
3. The estate

In most cases the estate is the most important part of the law of inheritance. But jurists differ as to what amounts to property. The Ḥanafī school says that property excludes rights and that rights are not inheritable as, for example, if somebody enters into a contract of hire, should his heirs inherit the contract also after his death? According to the Ḥanafī school the contract lapses with the death of the father, but the rest of the schools are of the opinion that rights are inheritable.

Conditions of Succession

There are three conditions of inheritance which must be satisfied:

1. The death of the subject

2. The survival of heirs at the time of death
3. A relationship between the subject and the heirs which justifies inheritance.

1. THE DEATH OF THE SUBJECT

The death of the subject must be actual and clear: either by an actual death or by the decree of the court in the case of a missing person.

2. THE SURVIVAL OF HEIRS

It has to be proved that the heir or heirs survive at the time of the death of the subject, before he or they are allowed to inherit.

In the case of an embryo that has not yet been born at the time of the death of the subject, it will not inherit unless it is subsequently born alive. Its share should be put aside pending delivery but the share which is to be kept should be the share of a male child, but according to the Mālikī school the whole estate should be saved, before distribution, pending the delivery of the child.

In the case where all the people died at the same time, and there is no way to determine who died first and who died later, then their estate should be inherited by their surviving relatives. The authority for this rule is that, after the battle of Yamāmah in which many Muslims died, Sayyidunā Abū Bakr ⚘ ordered Zayd ibn Thābit to distribute their estates, which Zayd distributed among the surviving relatives. Later he was appointed to a similar task by ʿUmar ibn al-Khaṭṭāb ⚘ as narrated by him.

قَالَ زَيد ﴿أَمَرَنِي عُمَر بِتَوْرِيثِ أَهْلِ الطَّاعُونِ وكَانَتِ الْقَبِيلَةُ تَمُوتُ بِأَسْرِها فَوَرَّثْتُ الْأَحْياءَ مِن الْأَمْواتِ ولَمْ أُوَرِّثِ الْأَمْواتِ بَعْضَهُم مِن بَعْضٍ

Zayd [Ibn Thābit] said: "ʿUmar ordered me to take charge of distributing the inheritances of people who died in the plague, and in some cases a whole tribe had died, so I made those who survived inherit from those who had died, but I did not make those who had died inherit from each other."[1]

Man's sojourn on this earth is for a limited period, and then comes his appointed time which he cannot make a minute earlier or later. He will leave behind whatever he accumulated in this world during his life, except his good actions, which go with him. The property and belongings that he leaves behind go to his heirs. The Noble Qur'ān contains rules for the disposal of his property excepting his bequest of up to a third for people who do not inherit by right or for other purposes.

In the early days of Islam, a dying man or woman, of his own free will, was to think of his parents and his next of kin, in a spirit of love and respect as those who had cherished them or whom they had cherished in this life and to make a bequest for them. This was to be done correctly and fairly (*bi'l-ma^c^rūf*):

كُتِبَ عَلَيْكُمْ إِذَا حَضَرَ أَحَدَكُمُ الْمَوْتُ إِن تَرَكَ خَيْرًا الْوَصِيَّةُ لِلْوَالِدَيْنِ وَالْأَقْرَبِينَ بِالْمَعْرُوفِ حَقًّا
عَلَى الْمُتَّقِينَ فَمَن بَدَّلَهُ بَعْدَ مَا سَمِعَهُ فَإِنَّمَا إِثْمُهُ عَلَى الَّذِينَ يُبَدِّلُونَهُ إِنَّ اللَّهَ سَمِيعٌ عَلِيمٌ

It is prescribed for you, when death approaches one of you and if he has some goods to leave, to make a will in favour of his parents and relatives, correctly and fairly: a duty for all those who have taqwā. Then if anyone alters it after hearing it, the crime is on the part of those who alter it. Allah is All-Hearing, All-Knowing. (Sūrat al-Baqarah 2: 181-2)

This was ordained long before the law of inheritance was revealed. Later the fixed shares (*farā'iḍ*) were laid down for direct heirs in Sūrat an-Nisā'. These later verses limit the powers to make bequests for named people outside the heirs or for named purposes, as we shall soon see, but they do not abrogate it. Supposing there is an orphan grandson among the kin: in the presence of surviving sons, he will not inherit according to the scheme of the *farā'iḍ* (the fixed shares) and the testator might like to provide for him under the provision of the above verses. Likewise, the injunction covers grandfathers and great grandfathers and grandmothers or great grandmothers where they are excluded from inheriting fixed shares by the presence of others, i.e. fathers and mothers.[2] However, according to a *ḥadīth*, he or she cannot dispose of more than one third of the estate.

عَنْ سَعْدِ بْنِ أَبِي وَقَّاصٍ ﷺ قَالَ: عَادَنِي رَسُولُ اللَّهِ ﷺ، فِي حَجَّةِ الْوَدَاعِ، مِنْ وَجَعٍ أَشْفَيْتُ مِنْهُ عَلَى الْمَوْتِ، فَقُلْتُ: يَا رَسُولَ اللَّهِ بَلَغَنِي مَا تَرَى مِنَ الْوَجَعِ، وَأَنَا ذُو مَالٍ، وَلَا يَرِثُنِي إِلَّا بِنْتٌ لِي وَاحِدَةٌ، أَفَأَتَصَدَّقُ بِثُلُثَيْ مَالِي؟ قَالَ ﴿لَا﴾ قَالَ قُلْتُ: أَفَأَتَصَدَّقُ بِشَطْرِهِ؟ قَالَ ﴿لَا، الثُّلُثُ، وَالثُّلُثُ كَثِيرٌ، إِنَّكَ إِنْ تَذَرْ وَرَثَتَكَ أَغْنِيَاءَ، خَيْرٌ مِنْ أَنْ تَذَرَهُمْ عَالَةً يَتَكَفَّفُونَ النَّاسَ﴾.

From Saᶜd ibn Abī Waqqāṣ ﷺ there is that he said, "The Messenger of Allah ﷺ visited me during the Ḥajjat al-Wadāᶜ because of a pain from which I was close to death, so I said, 'Messenger of Allah, the pain has reached as you see, and I am a man of some property, but no one will inherit from me but a single daughter; should I give two thirds of my property away as *ṣadaqah*?' He said, 'No.' I said, 'Then should I give a half of it away as *ṣadaqah*?' He said, 'No, a third and a third is a great deal. If you leave your heirs without need it is better than that you should leave them needy begging from people.'" (Muslim, *kitāb al-waṣiyyah, bāb al-waṣiyyah bi ath-thuluth*)

One may not be partial to one heir at the expense of the others, i.e. heirs who receive fixed shares may not receive bequests. The principle of inheritance by individual heirs of fixed shares is laid down in the following *āyah*:

لِلرِّجَالِ نَصِيبٌ مِمَّا تَرَكَ الْوَالِدَانِ وَالْأَقْرَبُونَ وَلِلنِّسَاءِ نَصِيبٌ مِمَّا تَرَكَ الْوَالِدَانِ وَالْأَقْرَبُونَ مِمَّا قَلَّ مِنْهُ أَوْ كَثُرَ نَصِيبًا مَفْرُوضًا

Men receive a share of what their parents and relatives leave and women receive a share of what their parents and relatives leave, a fixed share, no matter whether it is a little or a lot. (Sūrat an-Nisā' 4: 7)

A strict warning is given to those who are in charge of disposing and dividing an estate to have the same fear in their minds as they would have if they had left a helpless family behind. They are asked to observe the principle of justice and be kind and helpful.

وَلْيَخْشَ الَّذِينَ لَوْ تَرَكُوا مِنْ خَلْفِهِمْ ذُرِّيَّةً ضِعَافًا خَافُوا عَلَيْهِمْ فَلْيَتَّقُوا اللَّهَ وَلْيَقُولُوا قَوْلًا سَدِيدًا

People should show concern in the same way that they would fear for small children if they were to die leaving them behind. They should have taqwā of Allah and say words that are appropriate. (Sūrat an-Nisā' 4: 9)

The above verse has five legal implications:

A. The fixed shares of inheritance are not meant for men only, but women also have the right to inherit.

B. The property left behind by the deceased, however little it might be, must be distributed justly among the heirs. The *ᶜulamā'* say that even if he has left a piece of cloth, it should be cut into that number of pieces equalling the number of heirs unless one of the heirs buys the other heirs' shares.

C. The law of inheritance applies to all kinds of property, chattels or realty or of any other kind.

D. The question of inheritance only comes up when the deceased has left property.

E. The nearer relative precludes distant relatives from the inheritance, e.g. a son precludes the grandson inheriting, just as a father precludes a grandfather and a mother precludes a grandmother.

The details of the shares of each heir is given in the following verse of the Noble Qur'ān:

يُوصِيكُمُ اللَّهُ فِي أَوْلَادِكُمْ لِلذَّكَرِ مِثْلُ حَظِّ الْأُنْثَيَيْنِ فَإِنْ كُنَّ نِسَاءً فَوْقَ اثْنَتَيْنِ فَلَهُنَّ ثُلُثَا مَا تَرَكَ وَإِنْ
كَانَتْ وَاحِدَةً فَلَهَا النِّصْفُ وَلِأَبَوَيْهِ لِكُلِّ وَاحِدٍ مِنْهُمَا السُّدُسُ مِمَّا تَرَكَ إِنْ كَانَ لَهُ وَلَدٌ فَإِنْ لَمْ يَكُنْ
لَهُ وَلَدٌ وَوَرِثَهُ أَبَوَاهُ فَلِأُمِّهِ الثُّلُثُ فَإِنْ كَانَ لَهُ إِخْوَةٌ فَلِأُمِّهِ السُّدُسُ مِنْ بَعْدِ وَصِيَّةٍ يُوصِي بِهَا أَوْ دَيْنٍ
آبَاؤُكُمْ وَأَبْنَاؤُكُمْ لَا تَدْرُونَ أَيُّهُمْ أَقْرَبُ لَكُمْ نَفْعًا فَرِيضَةً مِنَ اللَّهِ إِنَّ اللَّهَ كَانَ عَلِيمًا حَكِيمًا

Allah instructs you regarding your children: A male receives the same as the share of two females. If there are more than two daughters they receive two-thirds of what you leave. If she is one on her own she receives a half. Each of your parents receives a sixth of what you leave if you have children. If you are childless and your heirs are your parents your mother receives a third. If you have brothers or sisters your mother

*receives a sixth, after any bequest you make or any debts. With regard
to your fathers and your sons, you do not know which of them is going
to benefit you more. These are obligatory shares from Allah. Allah is
All-Knowing, All-Wise.* (Sūrat an-Nisā' 4: 11)

ʿAllāmah Yūsuf ʿAlī, while explaining this verse, rightly
remarks that Muslim jurists have collected a vast amount of
learning on this subject and this body of law is enough in itself to
form the subject of life-long study. (Yusuf Ali. A,. *The Holy Qur'an.
Text. Translation and Commentary.* Beirut 1968, p. 181) This is quite
true as the *Sharīʿah* has dealt with problems of inheritance in very
minute detail. "In these provisions, we find ample attention paid
to the interest of all those whom nature places in the first rank of
our affections; and indeed it is difficult to conceive any system
containing rules more strictly just and equitable." (Macnaughten,
Principles and procedures of Mohammeden law, quoted by A. Majid
Daryabadi in *Holy Qur'an. Vol. 1,* Lahore, 1957, p. 149)

Guidance from the Sunnah on Inheritance

The *asbāb an-nuzūl* (causes of revelation) have been explained
in the *ḥadīth* of the Prophet ﷺ. It is reported in one of the most
famous collections *Ṣaḥīḥ al-Bukhārī* in the book of *tafsīr* that
this important verse on *mīrāth* "*Allah instructs you regarding your
children*" was revealed in the following circumstances:

عن محمد بن المنكدر سمع جابر بن عبد الله رضي الله عنهما يقول مرضت فعادني رسول الله
صلى الله عليه وسلم وأبو بكر وهما ماشيان فأتاني وقد أغمي علي فتوضأ رسول الله صلى
الله عليه وسلم فصب علي وضوءه فأفقت فقلت يا رسول الله كيف أصنع في مالي كيف
أقضي في مالي فلم يجبني بشيء حتى نزلت آية المواريث

From Muḥammad ibn al-Munkadir: I heard Jābir ibn ʿAbdullāh
ؓ say, "I became ill and the Messenger of Allah ﷺ and Abū Bakr
visited me and they were walking. So he came to me while I was
unconscious. The Messenger of Allah ﷺ performed *wuḍū'* and
then poured his *wuḍū'* water over me and I recovered and said,
'Messenger of Allah, what should I do with my wealth, and how

should I decide about my wealth?' But he did not answer me in anyway until the *āyāt* about inheritance (Sūrat an-Nisā' 4: 11) were revealed." (Al-Bukhārī, *kitab al-marḍā, bāb ʿiyādat al-mughmā ʿalayhi*; Muslim, *kitāb al-farā'iḍ, bāb mīrāth al-kalālah*)

The causes of the revelation of *āyah* 12 of Sūrat an-Nisā' *"You receive half of what your wives leave …"* are also mentioned in *Ṣaḥīḥ al-Bukhārī* in the *Kitāb at-tafsīr* as follows:

From Ibn ʿAbbās ⬧ there is that he said, "[In the *jāhiliyyah*] wealth belonged to the son, and bequests were made for parents, so Allah abrogated of that what He wished and He appointed the same as the inheritance of two females [daughters] for the male [son] and he appointed a sixth [if the deceased had a child] and third [if the deceased had no children] for each of the parents, and an eighth [if her husband had a child] and a quarter [if her husband had no children] for the woman and a half [if his deceased wife had no children] and a quarter [if his deceased wife had children] for the male."

There are two classes of heirs, those who have specific shares (*farḍ* pl. *farā'iḍ*) mentioned in the Qur'ān, and the *ʿaṣābah*, literally the male paternal relatives, but properly all those who are entitled to the remainder after the fixed shares.

Ibn Juzayy al-Kalbī says:

The reasons for inheritance are five: kinship, marriage, clientage due to setting a slave free, slavehood, and the *bayt al-māl*

The heirs according to Abū Bakr aṣ-Ṣiddīq, Zayd ibn Thābit, Mālik and ash-Shāfiʿī are the ones about whom there is consensus that they inherit and no others.

Of men there are fifteen:

1. The son, 2. The grandson (son's son) no matter how remote, 3. The father, 4. The grandfather no matter how remote, 5. The full brother, 6. The paternal step-brother, 7. The maternal step-brother, 8. The son of the full brother, 9. The son of the paternal step-brother, 10. The full paternal uncle (the father's brother from both his father and mother), 11. The paternal uncle who is the father's step-brother from his father, 12. The son of the full paternal uncle, 13. The son of the paternal uncle who is the father's step-brother from his father, 14. The husband, 15. And the one who frees a slave.

Of women there are ten:

1. The daughter, 2. The son's daughter no matter how remote, 3. The mother, 4. The maternal grandmother, 5. The paternal grandmother, 6. The full sister, 7. The paternal step-sister, 8. The maternal step-sister, 9. The wife, 10. And the woman who frees a slave.

ᶜAlī ibn Abī Ṭālib ﷺ, ᶜAbdullāh ibn Masᶜūd, Abū Ḥanīfah and Ibn Ḥanbal added that relations on the women's side (*arḥām*) inherit, and there are fourteen of them:

1. Daughters' children, 2. Sisters' children, 3. The brother's daughters, 4. The paternal uncle's daughters, 5. The maternal uncle, 6. And his child, 7. The paternal aunt, 8. The maternal aunt, 9 & 10. And their children, 11. The maternal grandfather, 12. The mother's paternal uncle, 13. The son of the maternal step-brother, 14. And the daughter of the paternal uncle.

They unanimously agreed that they (the *arḥām*) do not inherit if there are *ᶜaṣabah* nor if there are those who take fixed shares except for what is left over from them.

As for the types of heirs there are those who inherit fixed shares and those who inherit by their rank as *ᶜaṣabah*. Those who inherit fixed shares take their shares and nothing more, but the member of the *ᶜaṣabah*, if he is alone, takes all of the property, but if he is along with those who have fixed shares then he takes whatever is left over after them, but if there is nothing then he takes nothing.

In that respect there are four categories of heir:

The first only inherit by the fixed shares and there are six of them:

1. The mother, 2. The grandmother, 3. The husband, 4. The wife, 5. The maternal step-brother, 6. The maternal step-sister

The second only inherit as being members of the *ᶜaṣabah* and they are:

1. The son, 2. The son's son, 3. The full brother, 4. And the paternal step-brother, 5. The paternal uncle, 6. The brother's son, 7. The paternal uncle's son, 8. The male who frees a slave [he inherits from the slave], 9. The female who frees a slave [she inherits from the slave].

The third who inherit by both of the above routes and together at the same time, and there are two of them:

1. The father, 2. The grandfather.

If one of them inherits his portion, if there is anything left over after the people who have fixed shares, he takes it as a member of the *ᶜaṣabah*.

The fourth are those who inherit by both routes but not together at the same time and they are four types:

1. Of women: daughters, 2. The son's daughter, 3. The full sister, 4. And the paternal step-sister.

If there is a male of the same category along with any one of the above she inherits along with him by being members of the *ᶜaṣabah*, the male inheriting the same as two females. But if there is no male along with her, then she inherits by fixed shares as do the full sisters. And the father has the rank of *ᶜaṣabah* along with daughters. (Al-Kalbī, *al-Qawānīn al-fiqhiyyah, al-kitāb al-āshir fī al-farā'iḍ wa al-waṣāyā, al-bāb al-awwal fī adad al-wārithīn wa ṣifat al-warithah*)

Ibn Abī Zayd al-Qayrawānī says in his *Risālah:*

There are only ten male heirs:

1. The son, 2. The son's son, however remote [i.e. great grandsons through the son and grandson, etc.], 3. The father, 4. The paternal grandfather, however remote [i.e. the great grandfather of the father and grandfather], 5. The brother, 6. The son of the brother, however remote, 7. The paternal uncle, 8. The son of the paternal uncle, however remote, 9. The husband, 10. The *mawlā an-niᶜmah* the person who has freed a slave. [He inherits from the slave].

[Brothers include full brothers and stepbrothers by the father (consanguine). The same is true of paternal uncles.]

These are the only male heirs. Some of them inherit only when others do not exist, for example, a grandfather only inherits when the father is not alive.

There are only seven female heirs:

1. The daughter, 2. The daughter of the son, 3. The mother, 4. The grandmother, 5. The sister, 6. The wife, 7. The *mawlāt an-niᶜmah* the woman who has freed a slave. [She inherits from the slave].

These are the only females who are going to inherit.

Aṣḥāb al-farā'iḍ – those due fixed shares

There are four males.

1. Husband of the deceased, 2. Father of the deceased, 3. Grandfather of the deceased, 4. Uterine brothers.

Their shares are a half, a sixth, a quarter and a thirdThe females are:

1. Wife of the deceased, 2. Daughter of the deceased, 3. Daughter of the son of the deceased, 4. Mother of the deceased, 5. Grandmother of the deceased, 6. Three types of sister (full sister, uterine sister and consanguine sister).

Their shares are a quarter, an eighth, a half and two-thirds. (Translation taken from Aisha Bewley's unpublished translation available at her web-site at: http://ourworld.compuserve.com/homepages/ABewley/RisShares.html. The commentary is from ᶜAbd as-Samīᶜ al-Ābī al-Azharī's *ath-Thamar ad-dānī*.)

Table One

The male heirs among the cₐṣabah (agnates) except the husband and the mother's brother

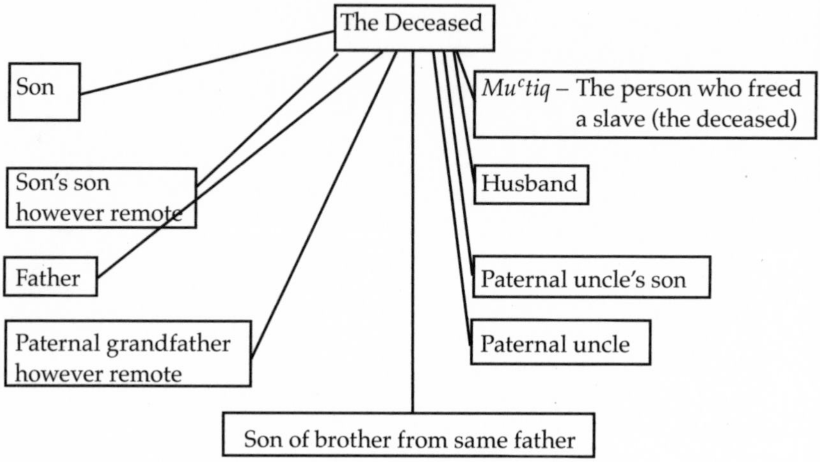

Table Two

The female heirs , who all receive fixed shares except for the woman who frees a slave [and inherits from the slave]

الوارِثات وكلّهنّ ذوات فرضٍ إلّا المعتِقة

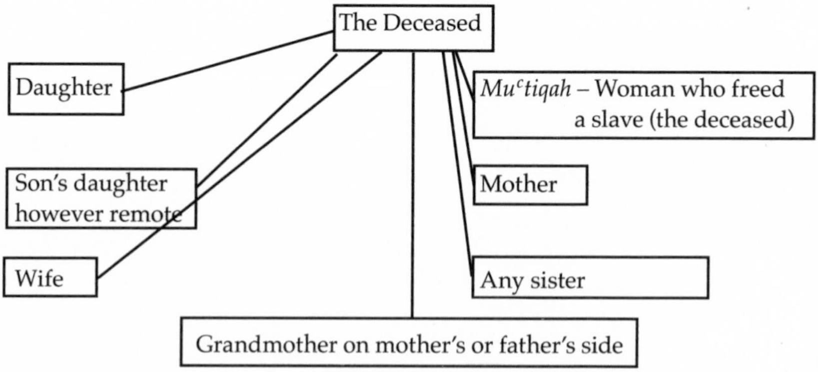

Table Three

Male and female heirs who can be co-sharers when they exist at the same time

الورثة عند اجتماع الصنفين

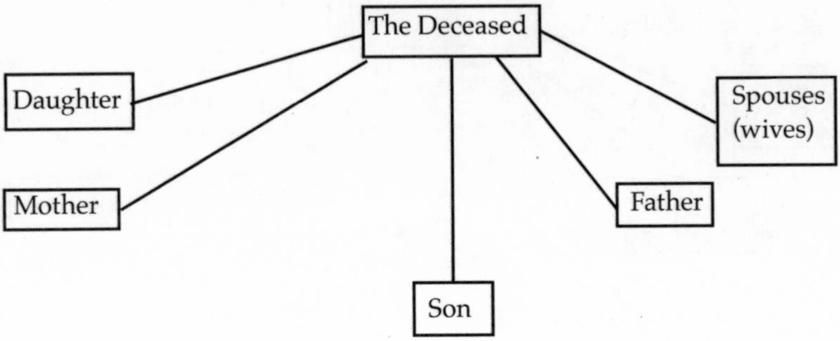

Table Four

Heirs who inherit one half when there is no male residual heir among the female heirs

ورثة النصف حيث لم يكن مع الإناث

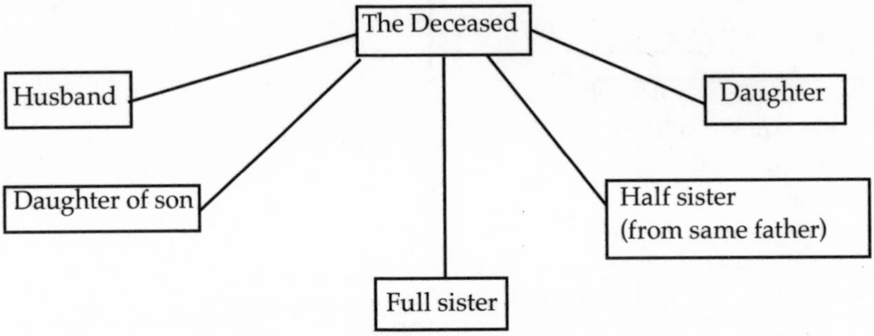

Table Five

Heirs who inherit ⅔ in the absence of male residual heirs – where there are brothers with the sisters, for example, the rule will not apply

وَرَثَةُ الثُّلُثَيْنِ

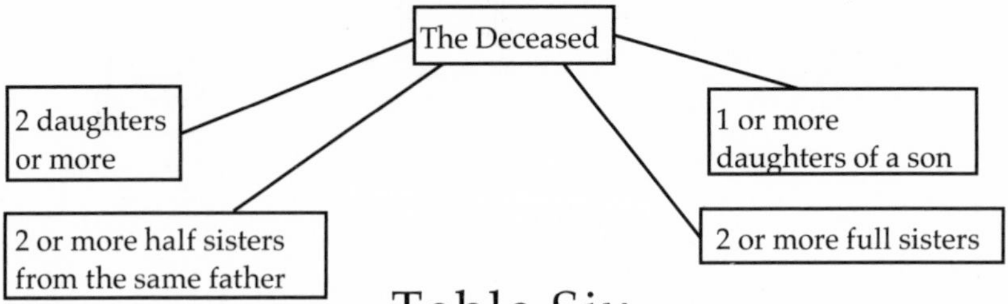

Table Six

Heirs who inherit one sixth

وَرَثَةُ السُّدُسِ

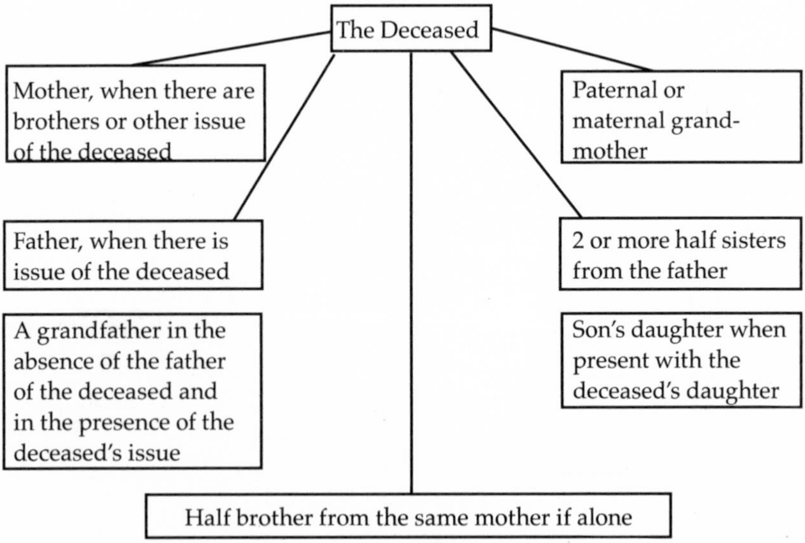

Ibn ᶜAbbās ﷺ said, "The Messenger of Allah ﷺ said, 'Make the obligatory shares of inheritance reach their people, and whatever the obligatory shares leave is for the nearest male man.'" (Al-Bukhārī, *kitāb al-farā'iḍ, bāb mīrāth al-walad min abīhi wa ummihi*; Muslim, *kitāb al-farā'iḍ, bāb alḥiqū al-farā'iḍ bi ahlihā*) Thus, when female issue is present the father takes 1/6 plus the remainder.

Table Seven

Those who are not excluded by others from inheriting

مَن لا يُحجَب

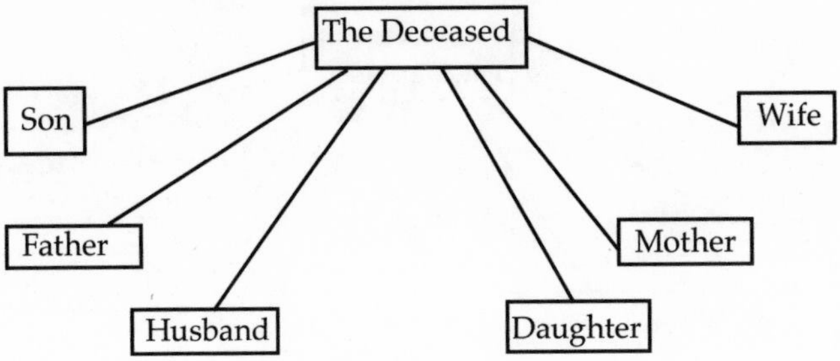

Table Eight

Those who are excluded by the deceased's son or sons

المحجوبون بالإبن أو البنين

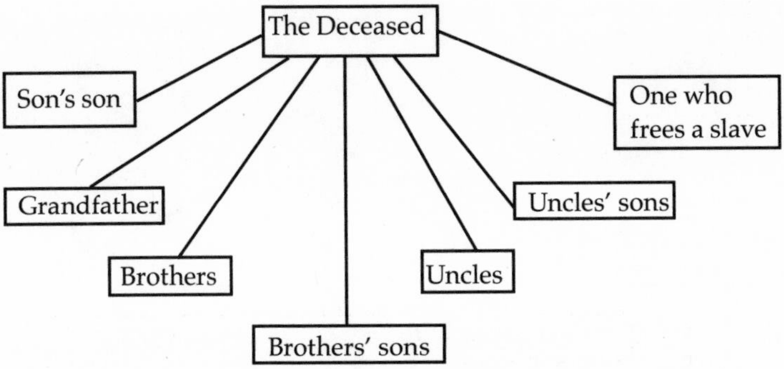

Table Nine

Those who are totally excluded by the deceased's father. They are 7.

المحجوبون بالأب

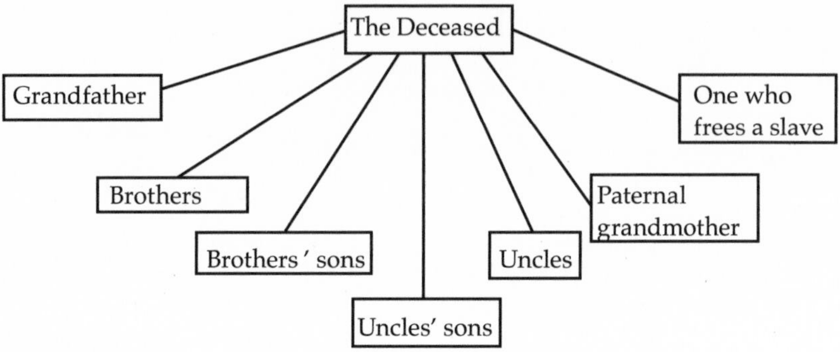

Table Ten

Those who are totally excluded by the deceased's grandfather. They are 6.

المحجوبون بالجد

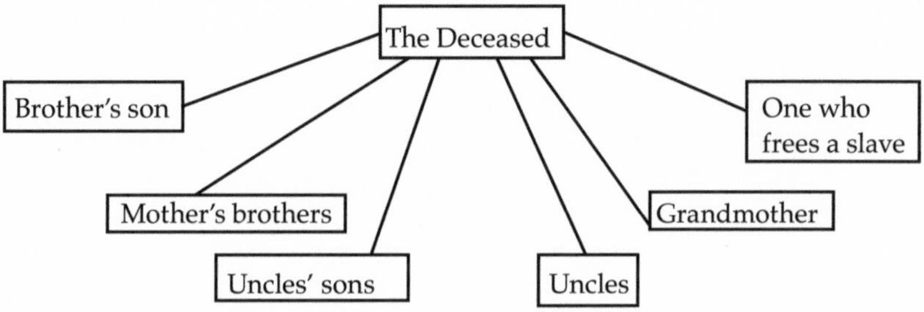

Table Eleven

Those who are totally excluded by the deceased's full brother. They are 5.

المَحْجُوبُونَ بِالأَخِ الشَّقِيقِ

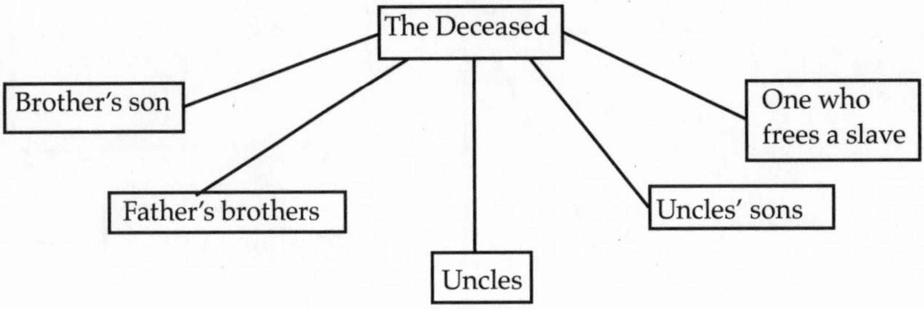

Table Twelve

Those who are totally excluded by the half-brother of the deceased through the father. They are 4.

المَحْجُوبُونَ بِالأَخِ لأَبٍ

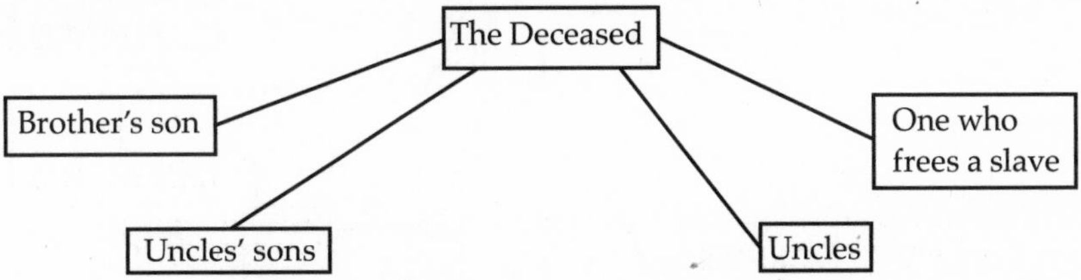

Table Thirteen

Those who are totally excluded by the paternal uncle (full brother of the deceased's father). They are 7.

الْمَحْجُوبُونَ بِالْعَمِّ الشَّقِيقِ

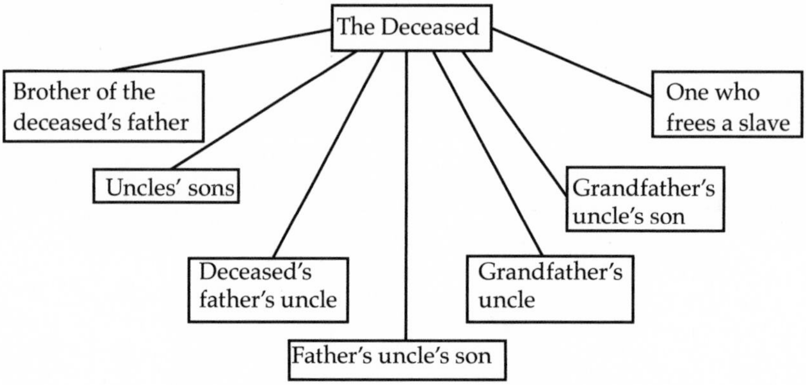

Table Fourteen

Those who are totally excluded by a consanguine brother of the father of the deceased. They are 6.

الْمَحْجُوبُونَ بِالْعَمِّ لأَبٍ

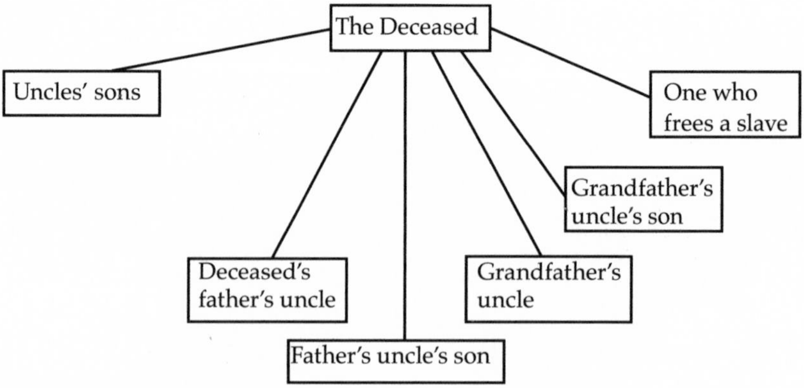

Table Fifteen

Those who are totally excluded by the deceased's uncles and uncle's sons. They are 7.

المحجوبون بالأعمام وبنيهم

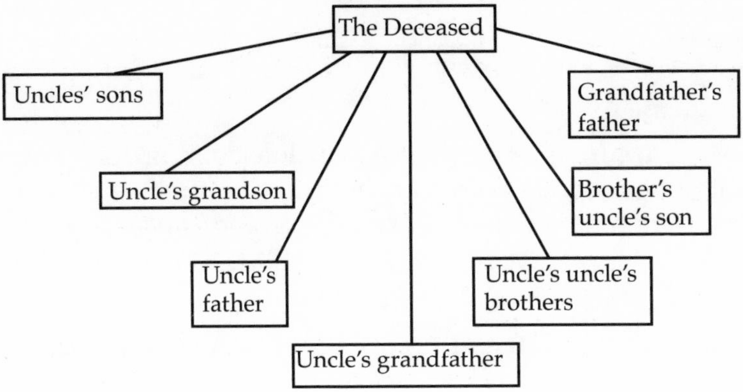

Table Sixteen

Those who are excluded by a uterine brother (a half-brother of the deceased by the mother). They are 7.

المحجوبون بالأخ لأم

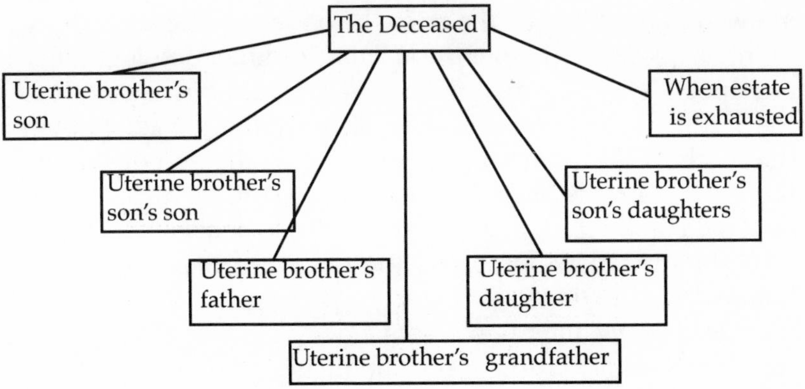

Impediments to Succession

According to some jurists the impediments to succession are six, whilst others, such as Ibn Juzayy al-Kalbī, say they are ten, but the most essential according to the majority are the following three:

1. Homicide
2. Difference of religion
3. Slavery

1. HOMICIDE (*QATL*)

All Muslim jurists agree that a murderer or someone who commits manslaughter does not inherit. The argument that they do not inherit relies on the following prophetic *ḥadīth*:

لَيْسَ لِلْقَاتِلِ شَيْءٌ ، وَإِنْ لَمْ يَكُنْ لَهُ وَارِثٌ فَوَارِثُهُ أَقْرَبُ النَّاسِ إِلَيْهِ وَلَا يَرِثُ الْقَاتِلُ شَيْئًا .

> There is nothing for the killer, and if [the deceased] has no heir then his heir is the most closely related of people, and the killer does not inherit anything. (Narrated by Abū Dāwūd, *awwal kitāb ad-diyāt, bāb diyāt al-aᶜḍā'*; al-Bayhaqī)

On the basis of this known *ḥadīth*, Sayyidunā ᶜUmar ﷺ prevented someone who had killed his own father from inheriting from him. If such people are allowed to kill and then benefit from the estate of the victims, it would encourage incidents of homicide and also it would seem as if an accused person were allowed to benefit from the crime he has committed.

On the question whether the *ḥadīth*, "the killer does not inherit anything" is also applied to bequests, Mālikī jurists say that if the victim survives for a time knowing about the act and later dies without withdrawing the bequest, we should not preclude the killer from the bequest. Imam Abū Ḥanīfah, however, said he would apply the same restriction also to bequests.

Mālikī jurists have provided the following two categories of homicide:

1. *Qatl al-ᶜamd*: intentional homicide;
2. *Qatl al-khaṭa'*: unintentional homicide.

The other three schools have added a third category of homicide called *qatl shibh al-ᶜamd*, that is a quasi-intentional homicide.

Qatl al-ᶜamd is a deliberate killing, while the act of an insane person and a minor are considered as neither intentional nor unintentional. According to Mālikī jurists it does not prevent them from inheriting while others say that it does prevent them from their right to inheritance.

The *qatl al-khaṭa'* is an unintentional killing or killing by mistake. Mālikī jurists say that it will not prevent the killer from inheriting but that he will not inherit from the compensatory payment which he pays to the victim's family.

In the following cases of homicide the right of inheritance will not be affected:

1. If it is lawful killing, as a result of executing a capital punishment or a corporal punishment resulting in death, or in war on Muslim rebels against a legitimate ruler.
2. If killing is done during a *jihād* between Muslims and non-Muslims.
3. If killing is the result of self-defence.
4. In the case of any killing that is justifiable according to the *Sharīᶜah*.
5. The act of a mad person or a minor.

As far as the Ḥanafī school is concerned, any killing whatsoever will prevent the right of inheritance whether it is intentional or unintentional with the exception of the following cases:

1. An act of a mad person or a minor.
2. The lawful killing in accordance to the verdict of a *qāḍī*
3. An indirect killing.
4. Any justifiable killing according to the *Sharīᶜah*.
5. Killing as a result of self defence.

Imām Aḥmad ibn Ḥanbal shares the same view as Imām Abū Ḥanīfah, but Imām ash-Shāfiᶜī differs from all the other schools saying that any kind of homicide whatsoever will prevent inheritance, whether it is lawful, justifiable, intentional, unintentional, direct or indirect. Even a person connected with the death in any way is not allowed to inherit.

2. Difference of Religion

Difference of religion immediately prevents inheritance subject to certain conditions. The following *ḥadīth* emphasises this point:

لَا يَرِثُ الْمُسْلِمُ الْكَافِرَ وَلَا يَرِثُ الْكَافِرُ الْمُسْلِمَ.

The *kāfir* does not inherit from the Muslim nor the Muslim from the *kāfir*. (Al-Bukhārī, *kitāb al-maghāzī, bāb ayna rakaza an-nabiyyu ﷺ ar-rāyah yawm al-fatḥ;* Muslim, *kitāb al-farā'iḍ*)

The majority of Muslim jurists take the view that a Muslim will not inherit from his deceased relative who happens to be a non-Muslim and there is consensus that a non-Muslim may not inherit from a Muslim. Supposing a Muslim husband dies leaving behind a Jewish or Christian wife, she will not inherit from him but she will be entitled to a bequest if her husband leaves it which will not be more than one-third of the net estate. Some jurists say that the share must not be more than that received by her Muslim co-wives.

Some of the Companions like Muᶜādh ibn Jabal, Muᶜāwiyah ibn Abī Ṣufyān and others were of the opinion that a Muslim is allowed to inherit from his non-Muslim relative, but a non-Muslim is not allowed to inherit from his Muslim relative. Muᶜādh had adopted his view based on the following *ḥadīth*:

الْإِسْلَامُ يَزِيدُ وَلَا يَنْقُصُ

Islam increases and does not decrease. (Aḥmad, Abū Dāwūd, *kitāb al-farā'iḍ, bāb hal yarithu al-muslim al-kāfir?;* al-Ḥākim; and al-Bayhaqī in *Shuᶜab al-īmān* from Muᶜādh)

When Muᶜāwiyah ؓ became Caliph, he introduced this rule in his courts, and it continued during the period of the Umayyad dynasty until the time of ᶜUmar ibn ᶜAbd al-ᶜAzīz who abolished the judgement after proper consultation with the Muslim jurists of that period.

As far as inheritance between the followers of different non-Islamic religions are concerned, there are different opinions of the jurists about different religions. Imam Mālik and Imam Aḥmad say that they will not inherit from each other i.e., a Jew will inherit only from a Jew, and a Christian will inherit only from a Christian and so on. They base their view on the following:

وَلَا يَتَوَارَثَانِ أَهْلُ مِلَّتَيْنِ.

> The people of two religions do not inherit from each other. (Aṭ-Ṭabarānī in *al-Kabīr* from Usāmah as cited in *Kanz al-ᶜummāl*)

But Imam Abū Ḥanīfah, Imām ash-Shāfiᶜī and Sufyān ath-Thawrī say that they will not look into the difference of their religions and will consider them as one nation. Thus a Jew will be able to inherit from a pagan and so on.

The famous Qāḍī Shurayḥ and others have divided all religions into the three following groups:

1. The *dīn* of Islam: Muslims inherit from each other;
2. Christianity, Judaism and Sabiuns: they do not inherit from each other;
3. Zoroastrians and all other religions without any Divine Book are treated as one group, and thus inherit from each other.

As far as the inheritance of an apostate is concerned, whether he is executed by *ḥadd* punishment or dies a normal death, the majority of the jurists of Hijaz, as well as Imām Mālik and Imam ash-Shāfiᶜī say that his estate will go to the public treasury, basing their authority on the *ḥadīth* quoted above.

However, the Ḥanafī jurists of Kūfa and Basra, Companions like Sayyidunā ᶜAlī and Ibn Masᶜūd, supported by Imam Abū Ḥanīfah and Sufyān ath-Thawrī say that his relatives can inherit from him. They arrive at this conclusion by analogy; since the *bayt al-māl* (Muslim Treasury) can inherit by virtue of the Islamic connection, his relatives have a stronger claim than the *bayt al-māl*, because there is a double relationship between him and his relatives, while with the public treasury he has only the one connection, which is Islam.

Imam Abū Ḥanīfah differentiates between men and women in the case of reneging on the *dīn*. He says that if a man became a renegade, his estate which he gained during the time when he was a Muslim will be inherited by his Muslim relatives, while the property he gained during the time he changed his *dīn* will go to the *bayt al-māl*. On the other hand, if a woman changes her *dīn*, all her property will go to her relatives. Other jurists do not make this kind of distinction between a man and a woman.

3. SLAVERY

All Muslim jurists agree that slavery is a bar to inheritance. They will not inherit and they will not be inherited from. If a slave dies his relatives will not inherit from him because he, as a slave, owned nothing since all that a slave owns belongs to his master and he himself is treated as property. Allah greatly rewards the freeing of slaves as a meritorious act and considers it as an expiation (*kaffārah*).

Other impediments to inheritance include:

4. LIᶜĀN DIVORCE

Where a couple engage in *liᶜān* divorce proceedings then neither of them will inherit from the other.

5. DIFFERENCE OF DOMICILE

This impediment was added by Imam Abū Ḥanīfah and it is only applicable to non-Muslims, i.e., if a non-Muslim living in a Muslim country dies, his relatives living in another part of the world will not be allowed to come and inherit the property and other rights of the deceased, unless they are citizens of the same country.

Qur'ānic Guidance on the Administration of the Estate of a Deceased Muslim

Before distributing the estate of the deceased among heirs, it is required by Qur'ānic injunction first to settle the claims of debts, other rights of Allah and of people due from the deceased, as well as the bequests that he has left behind. In the Qur'ān Allah ﷻ emphasises:

مِن بَعْدِ وَصِيَّةٍ يُوصِي بِهَا أَوْ دَيْنٍ

...after any bequest they make or any debts. (Sūrat an-Nisā' 4: 11-12.)[3]

Although in the Qur'ān Allah mentions bequests before claims, all the Companions and Muslim jurists agree on the view that the debts attached to the specific property or to a specific part of the estate like pledges and pawned items (*rahn*), the *zakāh* of crops and the *zakāh* on animals should be settled first. The Mālikī school is of the same view. Other jurists do not concern themselves with *zakāh* until the other claims on the dead person are settled.

Ibn Juzayy al-Kalbī says:

> When a person dies one takes out of his property first of all whatever is necessary to shroud and bury him, then one attends to his debts according to their priority, then the bequests are paid out of his third and then the heirs inherit what is left. (Al-Kalbī, Ibn Juzayy, *al-Qawānīn al-fiqhiyyah, kitāb al-farā'iḍ wa al-waṣāyā, muqaddimah*)

A. The settlement of debts

Normal debts means the debts that are not secured or specifically attached to the estate, i.e. loans or any other unsettled debts.

The Ḥanafī school divides debts into two groups: First, those debts which are proved by the admission of the dead person before the final illness (*maraḍ al-mawt*) either in writing or in other ways, and second, the debt to which the subject admitted while on his death bed.

According to the Ḥanafī school, the former kind of debts must be settled before the latter. It is likely that the dead person wanted to favour some of his relatives or a person who served him thus admitting the debt while on his death-bed. Other jurists do not make this distinction.

The Ḥanafī, Mālikī and Ḥanbalī schools say that the funeral expenses must first be settled before anything is taken from the estate of the deceased. However, if a person dies leaving his estate pledged in pawn (*rahn*), the majority of jurists say that the pledge must be settled first, but the Ḥanbalī school is of the view that the funeral expenses will be considered first.

The Ẓāhirīs, on the contrary, said that debts must be settled first because the funeral expenses are the responsibility of all the Muslims including the creditors.

The Shāfiᶜīs say that the debts of Allah must be settled before the debts of individuals, while Imam Mālik and Abū Ḥanīfah say that the debts of the individuals must be settled before the debts of Allah. Imam Mālik further stipulates that the *zakāh* is to be paid only if requested by the deceased before his death. (Abū Zahra, *Aḥkām at-tarakāt wa'l-mawārīth*. Cairo)

B. FUNERAL EXPENSES

Islam teaches simplicity, also when it concerns death. Everyone has a seamless shroud, so the funeral expenses should be reasonable.

According to the Mālikī school, where a wife dies leaving her husband, the husband is held responsible for her funeral expenses. If the husband dies immediately after her death, the responsibility will shift to the other surviving relatives who will inherit from him.

According to the Ḥanafī school, the husband is responsible for a wife's funeral expenses even though he himself is dead and even if the wife is rich.

Imam ash-Shaybānī of the Ḥanafī school says that if she is rich the funeral expenses will be paid out of her estate, but if she does not leave anything, the funeral expenses will be paid by her relatives because the marital relationship came to an end upon the death of her husband.

In the Shāfiᶜī school of *fiqh*, if the husband is rich, he is responsible for funeral expenses. The husband is also likely to become wealthier by inheritance from her. If she is rich, however, the funeral expenses will be paid out of her estate but excluding the share of the husband. If she is not rich, and the husband is not likely to become rich by inheriting from her, the funeral expenses will be paid from the little she has left including from the share of the husband. If she has left nothing, her relatives will bear the expense. If she has no relatives it will be paid from the *bayt al-māl*.

c. *Waṣiyyah*: bequests

After taking out the funeral expenses and debts, i.e., the debts of the right of Allah and that of individuals, the *waṣiyyah* or the bequests will be carried out. The bequests include all the gifts that are made during the final illness of the deceased, since the majority of the jurists consider them all as bequests. The bequests and gifts added together must not exceed the one-third of the estate of the deceased unless consented to by the heirs.

Notes

[1] The point here is that where a number of people die, then some of them inherit from each other, and then their heirs in turn inherit, so that it is ordinarily important to take note of the order of their deaths. Thus, when a child dies in childbirth, if it had been born alive and then died it may have inherited from its mother who died in childbirth at that moment, and then died leaving its and her property to its heirs. In this case involving the plague, because people had died together at the same time, it was not possible to work out in what order they had died, and so that was not taken into consideration.
[2] The grandfather or grandmother inherit if the deceased's father or mother predeceased him or her.
[3] It occurs three times in slightly different wordings.

Chapter 21

Shares of Each Heir

THE FOLLOWING DETAILS of the share of each sharer is given under the law of inheritance in *Sharīᶜah*. No other religious law has given such minute details as given in the *Sharīᶜah*. So much work has been done on this subject by jurists over the centuries that we are astonished to see the huge volumes left by them for posterity. Moreover, study of a work such as al-Khawarizmi's *Algebra* which transmitted that science to the west, shows that it was largely devoted to working out these difficult cases of inheritance. The encouragement to learn this came from the Prophet ﷺ. It is commonly ascribed to him that he ﷺ said that the mastery of the laws of inheritance is equal to one half of the religious knowledge as in the following *ḥadīth*:

عَنْ أَبِي هُرَيْرَةَ؛ قَالَ: قَالَ رَسُولُ اللهِ صلى الله عليه وسلم: ﴿يَاأَبَا هُرَيْرَةَ! تَعَلَّمُوا الْفَرَائِضَ وَعَلِّمُوهَا فَإِنَّهُ نِصْفُ الْعِلْمِ. وَهُوَ يُنْسَى. وَهُوَ أَوَّلُ شَيْءٍ يُنْزَعُ مِنْ أُمَّتِي﴾.

From Abū Hurayrah ﷺ there is that he said: The Messenger of Allah ﷺ said, "Abū Hurayrah! learn the *farā'iḍ* and teach it because it is a half of knowledge, and it will be forgotten, and it is the first thing to be removed from my *Ummah*."[1]

However, the *ḥadīth* suffers from some weakness, and if it is true, *farā'iḍ* is ordinarily explained not as the obligatory shares of inheritance but as the obligations of the *dīn*. Ustādh Muḥammad Fu'ād ᶜAbd al-Bāqī said:

> "Learn the *farā'iḍ*" is interpretable to mean those judgements which Allah, exalted is He, has made obligatory on His slaves. Thus, the meaning of the fact that it is half of knowledge is that it is half of the knowledge of the *Sharīᶜah,* and that the other half is knowing those things which are forbidden.[2]

It is this *ḥadīth* about *farā'iḍ* – obligations – that is commonly and mistakenly understood to refer to *farā'iḍ* – obligatory shares of inheritance. However, this is not to underestimate the importance of this science of inheritance, which is one of the key elements of the *Sharīᶜah* that prevented the rise of the rapacious capitalism that arose in Europe and which is now destroying the planet.

We shall discuss these shares in the following pages.

A. Shares Allotted to Parents

1. The rights of parents are emphasised in various chapters of the Qur'ān. As far as the shares of the parents from the property left behind by their child is concerned, each one of them will have one-sixth of that which he has left if the deceased has left behind a child. If both parents are alive and there are also children, both father and mother take a sixth each. If one of them is alive, he or she takes a sixth and the rest goes to the children.
2. If the deceased has left no children, and the parents are the only heirs, then his mother will get one-third and the father will get the remaining two-thirds.
3. If the deceased has left no children but only sisters and brothers, his mother in that case will have one-sixth and the father gets the remainder as the father excludes collaterals.
4. The same overall principle, as we have seen before, that all distribution will take place only after the legacies and debts, including funeral expenses, are first paid out of the property left behind by the deceased.
5. The Qur'ān also makes it very clear that both children and parents of the deceased always get some share if they survive, but this is determined by the number of the heirs in these categories. Both parents and children are so nearly

equally related to you, and in point of benefit whether of this world or the next, one does not know which are nearest, as emphasised in the *āyah* of the Qur'ān.

آبَاؤُكُمْ وَأَبْنَاؤُكُمْ لَا تَدْرُونَ أَيُّهُمْ أَقْرَبُ لَكُمْ نَفْعاً

With regard to your fathers and your sons, you do not know which of them is going to benefit you more. (Sūrat an-Nisā' 4: 11)

Therefore, Allah ordains fixed portions for them.

The following Qur'ānic injunction is in respect of the shares of the husband or wife of the deceased:

وَلَكُمْ نِصْفُ مَا تَرَكَ أَزْوَاجُكُمْ إِن لَّمْ يَكُن لَّهُنَّ وَلَدٌ فَإِن كَانَ لَهُنَّ وَلَدٌ فَلَكُمُ الرُّبُعُ مِمَّا تَرَكْنَ مِن بَعْدِ وَصِيَّةٍ يُوصِينَ بِهَا أَوْ دَيْنٍ وَلَهُنَّ الرُّبُعُ مِمَّا تَرَكْتُمْ إِن لَّمْ يَكُن لَّكُمْ وَلَدٌ فَإِن كَانَ لَكُمْ وَلَدٌ فَلَهُنَّ الثُّمُنُ مِمَّا تَرَكْتُم مِّن بَعْدِ وَصِيَّةٍ تُوصُونَ بِهَا أَوْ دَيْنٍ وَإِن كَانَ رَجُلٌ يُورَثُ كَلَالَةً أَوِ امْرَأَةٌ وَلَهُ أَخٌ أَوْ أُخْتٌ فَلِكُلِّ وَاحِدٍ مِّنْهُمَا السُّدُسُ فَإِن كَانُوا أَكْثَرَ مِن ذَلِكَ فَهُمْ شُرَكَاءُ فِي الثُّلُثِ مِن بَعْدِ وَصِيَّةٍ يُوصَى بِهَا أَوْ دَيْنٍ غَيْرَ مُضَارٍّ وَصِيَّةً مِّنَ اللَّهِ وَاللَّهُ عَلِيمٌ حَلِيمٌ

You receive half of what your wives leave if they are childless. If they have children you receive a quarter of what they leave after any bequest they make or any debts. They receive a quarter of what you leave if you are childless. If you have children they receive an eighth of what you leave after any bequest you make or any debts. If a man or woman has no direct heirs, but has a brother or sister, each of them receives a sixth. If there are more than that they share in a third after any bequest you make or any debts, making sure that no one's rights are prejudiced. This is an instruction from Allah. Allah is All-Knowing, All-Forbearing. (Sūrat an-Nisā' 4: 12)

Of the heirs there are some whose shares or portions have been fixed in the Qur'ān. These are called *aṣḥāb al-farā'iḍ* or "people of fixed shares" as commonly translated. They are altogether twelve in number, four males and eight females: the father, father's father however remote[3], half-brother by the mother, the husband, the wife, daughter, son's child however remote, full sister, consanguine sister, uterine sister, mother, and a true grandmother, that is, a grandmother in whose line of relationship to the deceased no false grandfather intervenes.

Their shares of the inheritance are either a half, a quarter, an eighth, two-thirds, a third or a sixth. The husband has a quarter when there is a child or son's child however remote and a half when there is no child or son's child; the wife has an eighth when there is a child or son's child and a quarter when there is not; the daughter's share is a half when there is only one and there is no son, daughters take two-thirds between them when there is one or more daughters and no son; the son's daughter takes a half if he is only one and there is no child or son's son; if there are two or more son's daughters they take two-thirds when there is no child or son's sons; and the son's daughter takes one-sixth when there is one daughter or a higher son's daughter and no son; the sister takes one-half when she is only one and there is no son or son's son. If there are two or more sisters, they take two-thirds under the same circumstances; the consanguine sister takes one half when only one and there is no son, consanguine brother or sister; if there are two or more consanguine sisters under the same circumstance they take two-thirds and the consanguine sister takes one-sixth when there is one full sister but no son, etc., or consanguine brother; the mothers share is one-sixth when there is a child or son's child or two or more brothers or sisters and one-third when not, but she takes one-third only of the remainder after deducting the wife's or the husband's share when there is a wife or husband and the father; the true grandmother has one-sixth when she is not excluded the father takes one-sixth; the grandfather's share is one-sixth when he is not excluded and the uterine brother or sister gets one-sixth when only one and no child or son's child; father or true grandfather; and if there are two or more of them they will get two-thirds in the same circumstances. Under certain circumstances some of the sharers become residuaries or take both as sharers and residuaries.

A Father's Share

In the case where there is a father along with a mother and wife or husband, he will take the remains after the share of the wife or husband and mother are given in accordance with the doctrine of *ᶜUmariyyatān*, which will be explained later.

If there is nobody to inherit with him he gets the whole of the estate. The father also inherits a sixth as a fixed share plus the remainder when there is female issue.

A Mother's Share

As is the case of a father with children, a mother will also get one-sixth as her share. Furthermore, she will be entitled to one-sixth in the presence of two or more brothers and sisters even if they are uterine, full, consanguine or mixed, but one alone will not restrict her to one-sixth.

She will get one-third of the residual share in the case where she is together with father and wife or husband.

After taking away the share of husband or wife from the rest of the estate, she will get one-third while the father will take the rest on the basis of the doctrine of *ᶜUmariyyatān*. With this discussion, it is essential for us now to understand the case of *ᶜUmariyyatān*.

The *ᶜUmariyyatān* Case

The case of *ᶜUmariyyatān* occurred during the Caliphate of Sayyidunā ᶜUmar, the second caliph, when he decided a case regarding the inheritance between father, mother and husband, and again between father, mother and wife. It is also referred to as *al-Gharrawānī II*.

The most important thing to note in this case is the share of a mother when there are:

1. Mother, father and husband,
2. Mother, father and wife.

In normal circumstances, we have seen the share of the mother is either a sixth or a third of the total estate. Where there are father, mother and husband or wife, the shares would be like this:

1.	Husband	Mother	Father
	Half	Third	Remainder
Sixths	3	2	1

2.	Wife	Mother	Father
	A quarter	Third	Remainder
Twelfths	3	4	5

When one looks carefully at the first example, one sees that the share of the mother is double the share of the father. In the normal rule where a female is together with a male, the share of a male is double the share of a female as in the case of sons and daughters or brothers and sisters; or the share is equal as in the case of father and mother in the presence of children.

In the second example also the normal rule did not apply, because the mother's share is almost equal to the father's share.

The majority of the Muslim jurists say that the ordinary rule where the mother takes her share from the total of the estate is not eminently suitable to Muslims.

So taking into consideration the case of *ᶜUmariyyatān,* it will be different with the mother. In this case, the mother will take a third of the remainder after taking away the share of the wife or the husband.

1.	Husband	Mother	Father
	Half	Third of Half	Remainder
Sixths	3	1	2

i.e. so the mother takes her share after the husband, taking a third of what he leaves, which is thus a sixth, and the father takes the remainder which is two-sixths or a third, and thus twice what the mother takes.

2.	Wife	Mother	Father
	A quarter	Third of ¾	Remainder
Twelfths	3	3	6

In this case the mother takes her third of what is left after the wife takes a quarter, and thus also takes a quarter of the total property and the father takes the remainder, i.e. a half, and thus twice what the mother takes.

Therefore the rule to be applied is that of *ᶜUmariyyatān*. If the husband or wife takes his or her share, whatever is remaining should be divided between the father and the mother by the mother first taking her third of what remains and then the father taking all of the remainder.

The jurists referred to the Qur'ānic verse which says that if the father inherits, the mother will get a third while the father will take two-thirds. This is applied only where two of them are going to inherit together. But in the case where they are together with either husband or wife, the mother will get a third of the remainder. Some Companions and jurists like Ibn ᶜAbbās, Dāwūd aẓ-Ẓāhirī, Sayyidunā ᶜAlī, Muᶜādh ibn Jabal and Qāḍī Shurayḥ, however, were of the opinion that the Qur'ānic rule must be left untouched. The Qur'ān says that in the absence of children and brothers or sisters, the mother will get a third of the total estate, therefore it must be applied as is commanded.

Ibn Sīrīn agrees with Sayyidunā ᶜUmar on the first example where the father is together with the mother and husband, but he does not accept the second formula where the father is together with the mother and wife because in that case, as he maintains, the father gets more than the mother. Therefore the rule must be amended in this case.

B. Shares Allotted to Children

1. Whatever parents leave after their death, their children and nearest of kin have the rights over their property which is shared according to the guidance of the Qur'ān.
2. As in all cases, the power of testamentary disposition, i.e. to make free-will bequests, extends to only one-third of the property; the remaining two-thirds are distributed among heirs according to this science.
3. The Qur'ānic injunctions have made it clear that there is a share for men and a share for women. This is because women and minor males were denied inheritance not only in pagan Arabia but also in the law of the Bible and

in Europe until quite recently. According to Cheyne and Black's *Encyclopaedia Biblica*:

> Women appear to have been universally and in every respect regarded as minors so far as rights of property went – only sons, not daughters, still less wives, can inherit. (Cheyne and Black, *Encyclopaedia Biblica*, 4 Vols., Black, London, cc. 2724, 2728)

Looking at the Qur'ānic injunctions it becomes clear that *"a male receives the same as the share of two females."* (Sūrat an-Nisā' 4: 11) As Sir Muhammad Iqbal remarked, this is not determined because of any inferiority inherent in her "but in view of her economic opportunities, and the place she occupies in the social structure of which she is a part and parcel." (Iqbāl, Dr. Sir Muḥammad, *Reconstruction of Religious Thought in Islam*, Lahore, pp 236-237)

He further says that while the daughter according to Muslim Law "is held to be full owner of the property given to her both by the father and the husband at the time of her marriage; while further she absolutely owns her dower money which may be prompt or deferred according to her own choice, and in the term of which she can hold possession of the whole of her husband's property till payment, the responsibility of maintaining her throughout her life is wholly thrown on the husband." (*Ibid.*) Besides, the Islamic *Sharī^cah* has put greater economic responsibility on man while a woman's role is lighter.

4. If among the offspring of the deceased, the daughters are the only heirs, and they are more than two, they will share in two-thirds of the inheritance. If there is only one, she will have a half.
5. All distribution takes place only after legacies and debts, including funeral expenses, have been paid.

C. Shares Allotted to Husband and Wives

The following shares are allotted according to the Qur'ānic injunctions in the above verse:

I. When the wife dies, the husband takes half of his deceased wife's property if she leaves no child. The residuaries get the rest of the property.

2. If the wife leaves a child, the husband gets a quarter.
3. As we have seen before, the female share is generally half of the male share. The widow, therefore, gets a quarter of her deceased husband's property, if he leaves no children.
4. If he leaves children, the widow gets only an eighth.
5. If there is more than one widow, i.e. if the husband had a number of wives, their collective share is a quarter if there are no children. But if there are children, their collective share is an eighth which they divide equally. The Bible was less kind to the widow as it does not place her among her husband's heirs. In Judaism, the Jewish widow is a charge on her children or if she has no children, she depends on her own family.[4]
6. The golden rule of inheritance still remains the same. That all distribution only takes place after legacies and debts including funeral expenses are paid.

The husband will receive a half of the estate of the deceased in the absence of sons and daughters or a daughter or son's daughters.

He will get a quarter in the presence of sons and daughters or grandsons by his sons or daughters.

The spouses will inherit from each other subject to the following two conditions: First that the contract of their marriage is valid. What is essential for the purpose of inheritance is not the consummation of the marriage but the contract of marriage. Any man or woman claiming inheritance has to prove the validity of his or her marriage in accordance with either the Māliki school or any other Sunni school. The other schools say that the marriage must have been solemnised in accordance with their own schools only.

According to the Mālikī school, if a marriage is contracted while one party is mortally ill, neither of the spouses will be allowed to inherit after the death of the other. However, some other jurists say that if the contract is with the agreement of the other inheritors, the widow or widower will be allowed to inherit.

The other condition to be satisfied is that the spouses will have to prove the death, either in fact or by law, which means that they are together or in the case of a woman she has to prove that she is divorced but is still serving her *ᶜiddah* period and that the divorce is revocable (*rajᶜī*). If the divorce is while the husband is mortally ill, she will be allowed to inherit, on presumption that perhaps the husband divorced her in order to deprive her of that right of inheritance.

The Mālikī school has taken quite a different view altogether:

39.18A. A woman finally divorced in the final illness

A woman who has been trebly divorced in the final illness of her husband inherits from her husband, but if she dies first, he does not inherit from her. The same ruling applies if the divorce was a single one and he dies of that illness after her *ᶜiddah* has finished. [She inherits from him because the Prophet ﷺ forbade excluding an heir by doing that. ᶜUthmān judged that the wife of ᶜAbd ar-Raḥmān ibn ᶜAwf inherit from him after her *ᶜiddah* was over. He had divorced her absolutely when he was ill and he died of that illness. The man does not inherit from her because she is unrelated to him by virtue of the divorce. Even if her *ᶜiddah* is over, she still inherits if he dies of that illness.]

39.18B. Divorce while he is in good health

If someone in good health pronounces a single divorce against his wife, they still inherit from one another as long as she is still in her *ᶜiddah*. If the *ᶜiddah* has finished, they do not inherit from one another. [There is no suspicion about divorce when the person is healthy.] (Ibn Abī Zayd al-Qayrawānī, *ar-Risālah,* unpublished translation by Aisha Bewley. http://ourworld.compuserve.com/homepages/ABewley/RisShares.html. The commentary in parentheses is from *ath-Thamar ad-dānī* by ᶜAbd as-Samīᶜ al-Azharī)

The husband will not inherit from the wife if she died in such condition. According to the Ẓāhirī school, if the divorce is final she will not be allowed to inherit, even if it is proved that the husband divorced her intentionally to prevent her from her right of inheritance.

The Shāfiᶜī school partly agrees with the Ẓāhirī school and partly with the Ḥanafīs on this issue. The Ḥanafī view is that she will be entitled to inherit from the husband if she is still serving her *ᶜiddah* period.

The Ḥanafī school holds that she will inherit even if she has finished her *ᶜiddah* provided that she has not remarried.

If the divorce has resulted due to the woman's request (*khulᶜ*) or due to compulsion, then one cannot be accused of preventing her from inheriting. It is interesting to note that ᶜUthmān gave inheritance to the wife of ᶜAbd ar-Raḥmān ibn ᶜAwf and ᶜAlī in turn later gave inheritance to the wife of ᶜUthmān ☙.

The following examples help to further elucidate the shares:

1. When a wife dies leaving her husband and other heirs the inheritance will be divided as follows:

Husband	Daughter's son	Daughter's daughter	Father	Total
Half	Nothing	Nothing	Remainder	
3	0	0	3	6

2. When a wife dies leaving a husband and a son

Husband	Son	Total
Quarter	Remainder	Unity
1	3	4

3. When a husband dies without issue leaving a wife, then the inheritance will be divided as follows:

Wife		Total
A quarter	No-one inherits remainder	¾ remains
1	0	4 quarters

Three quarters remain unallocated[5]

4. Suppose the husband leaves a son the inheritance will be divided as follows:

Wife	Son	Total
Eighth	Remainder	Unity
1	7	8

Because the wife inherits an eighth in this case then the property is considered to consist of eight portions, one of which she inherits and seven of which the son inherits as the remainder.

5. Suppose there is no issue and there is more than one widow, the inheritance will be divided as follows:

4 wives	No child	Total is 16 portions
Quarter	Nothing	Unity
4	0	12 portions remain[6]

Each wife must share in a quarter of the estate, which is initially considered as four portions for that reason. But since there are four wives, then the logical step is to divide the estate into sixteen portions, and this is called the *taṣḥīḥ,* and the quarter that belongs to the wives is then four portions, with each wife taking one.

Suppose there is issue, e.g. a son. It will look like this:

4 Wives	Son	Total
Eighth	Remainder	Unity
1	7	8 portions

The wives share an eighth, so in the case of four wives, they together take an eighth of the total and the son takes the remainder, i.e. if the estate is considered to consist of eight portions. The *taṣḥīḥ* is then to multiply the eight by four so that the estate is considered to consist of thirty-two portions, with each wife taking one portion, and the son taking the remaining twenty-eight.

D. Shares Allotted to Daughters

In the absence of a son inheriting from the father, a daughter receives a half if she is the only daughter, but if there are two or more daughters, they share in two-thirds in the absence of a son. When a daughter is present along with a son or sons, each son inherits double the share of a daughter.

E. Shares Allotted to Daughters of Sons

Daughters of a son of the deceased will inherit in the absence of an actual son or daughter, or a son of the son who is in the same generation as them or any son from the generation above them. However, if the son is from a generation below them (i.e. a great-grandson), he will not affect them, and they will inherit from the two-thirds inherited by two or more daughters in the absence of sons, sons of sons, etc. If there is a single daughter, the daughter will inherit a half and the son's daughter a sixth in order to bring the share of the daughters up to two-thirds in all.

If there is a single granddaughter she will receive a sixth if there are one or more daughters in the presence of one proper daughter, or any daughter in the generation above her. Here the daughter of the son will take a sixth after the proper daughter has taken her half to complete the share of females which is two-thirds.

EXAMPLES

1. The deceased has no son[6] but a daughter; she inherits half. There is no son of the son but five daughters (of the son) who together inherit a sixth. They inherit a sixth in order to complete the two-thirds allotted to daughters in general, since a sixth and a half, which is three-sixths, add up to four-sixths or two-thirds. In order not to deal with fractions one applies *taṣḥīḥ* and considers the estate to consist of thirty parts. The daugher inherits fifteen parts and the granddaughters one part each.

Here there is no son and no grandson. The great grandson, i.e. the son of the son of the son, is excluded.

2. Then there is the case where the deceased leaves no son or daughter, his son and his son's son having predeceased him. His son's daughter takes a half. Then where there is a daughter of the son of the son, she takes a sixth to complete, along with the granddaughter's half, the two-thirds that goes to daughters.

There are no sons or grandsons to exclude her from inheriting. There is no son, grandson or son of the son's son.

3. In the case where there is no son, or son of the son, both having predeceased the deceased, and there is a daughter of the son but there is no son or daughter of the son of the son of the son, then the daughter of the son of the son of the son takes a sixth in order, along with the half of the daughter of the son, to make up the two-thirds going to daughters.

As a member of the *ᶜaṣabah* she inherits together with her class, either from her class or from the lower class. They inherit on the principle of, *"The males receive the share of two females."* (Sūrat an-Nisā' 4: 11)

a. If there is son of the son of the same class they will inherit on the above principle.

If there is a son of a son and a daughter of a son and no one else, then he inherits two-thirds and she one-third.

If there is a son of a son and two daughters of a son and no one else, then he inherits a half and the two daughters inherit a quarter each, thus sharing the other half between them.

b. When she is supported by a male from a lower class e.g., there is no son, but there are two daughters, in which case two-thirds is allocated to females. Since there are a daughter of the son and a son of the son of the son, the daughter of the son would ordinarily get nothing and the son of the son of the son would receive the share of *ᶜaṣabah*.

Jurists, however, are of the opinion that the daughter of the son is closer than the son of the son of the son, and that it would be an injustice to exclude her and give the share to someone else from a lower class. Therefore, according to them, he will support her and they will inherit on the principle of *"the males receive the share of two females"*.[7] The daughter of the son is excluded totally in the presence of a son or any male child from the upper class, i.e., any male coming from the upper class will exclude all the other lower classes, whether they are male or female.

Let us see the following examples to elucidate our point:

Zayd died and left behind:

c. A son who takes a half, and his son's daughter who takes a sixth along with the son's son's[8] son who inherits a third as *ᶜaṣabah,* i.e. double the son's daughter's share. Considering the sum as six shares, the son takes three, the son's daughter one and the son's son's son, two shares.

d. A daughter who takes a half and a son's daughter who takes a sixth and a son's[9] son who takes a third as *ᶜaṣabah*.

4. *A* died leaving:

A husband, mother, father, daughter, a son's[10] daughter and son's son.

The husband gets a quarter, the mother a sixth, the father a sixth, the daughter a half and the son's children take the remainder as *ᶜaṣabah,* the male getting twice the portion of the female. Considering the inheritance as twelve shares, the husband gets three, the mother and father two each, the daughter six, leaving one share.

Thus for *taṣḥīḥ* one has to consider the inheritance as thirty-six shares, the husband getting nine, the mother and father six each, the daughter eighteen and the son's daughter one share and the son's son two shares.

5. Zayd died leaving:

A wife, two daughters, two daughters of a son, a daughter of the son of the son and a son of the son of the son.[11]

The wife inherits an eighth, the two daughters inherit two-thirds between them, and the rest inherit the remainder as *ᶜaṣabah*, the male taking the portion of two females. In this case the great grandson's presence means that the great grand-daughter and the granddaughter will both inherit, although they would not otherwise have done so.

Because of the eighth and the thirds, we will consider the inheritance to consist of twenty-four shares, the wife inheriting three, the daughters each inheriting eight, thus leaving thirteen for the *ᶜaṣabah*. They comprise two daughters of the son and a daughter of the son of the son, and the son of the son of the son, i.e. three women and one man, he taking twice the portion of a woman, making a total of five. Because it is inelegant to divide thirteen into five, it is better to consider the entire inheritance as being 120 shares, the wife getting fifteen, each daughter getting forty, leaving twenty-five shares for the *ᶜaṣabah*, the two granddaughters and the great granddaughter each getting five shares, and the great grandson getting ten.

A male child will support females who happen to be in the same generation with him and also those who are in the generation above him, causing them to inherit.

F. Shares Allotted to Uterine[12] Brothers and Sisters

Kalālah are those who die leaving neither male ascendants nor descendants. The word *kalālah,* according to Sayyidunā ᶜUmar, the second caliph, was difficult to define since it was not defined in the lifetime of the Prophet ﷺ. The caliph ᶜUmar wished that the Prophet had defined three terms: one concerning the *khilāfah*, the second concerning *ribā* (usury) and the third *kalālah*.

It is concerned with the inheritance of a person who has left no descendant or ascendants however distant, but only collaterals with or without a widow or a widower. If there is a widow or widower surviving, she or he takes the share as already defined, before the collaterals come in.

Full or consanguine brothers and sisters as heirs of someone who dies without leaving children or a father inherit according to:

يَسْتَفْتُونَكَ قُلِ اللَّهُ يُفْتِيكُمْ فِي الْكَلَالَةِ إِنِ امْرُؤٌ هَلَكَ لَيْسَ لَهُ وَلَدٌ وَلَهُ أُخْتٌ فَلَهَا نِصْفُ مَا تَرَكَ وَهُوَ يَرِثُهَا إِنْ لَمْ يَكُنْ لَهَا وَلَدٌ فَإِنْ كَانَتَا اثْنَتَيْنِ فَلَهُمَا الثُّلُثَانِ مِمَّا تَرَكَ وَإِنْ كَانُوا إِخْوَةً رِجَالًا وَنِسَاءً فَلِلذَّكَرِ مِثْلُ حَظِّ الْأُنْثَيَيْنِ

They will ask you for a fatwā. Say: 'Allah gives you a fatwā about people who die without direct heirs: If a man dies childless but has a sister she receives half of what he leaves, and he is her heir if she dies childless. If there are two sisters they receive two-thirds of what he leaves. If there are brothers and sisters the males receive the share of two females. (Sūrat an-Nisā' 4: 176)

Ibn Juzayy al-Kalbī said:

> What is meant by sister and brother here are full brothers and sisters and consanguine brothers and sisters if there are no full brothers and sisters. (Al-Kalbī, Ibn Juzayy, *Kitāb at-tashīl li ᶜulūm at-tanzīl*)

Uterine brothers and sisters inherit according to:

وَإِنْ كَانَ رَجُلٌ يُورَثُ كَلَالَةً أَوِ امْرَأَةٌ وَلَهُ أَخٌ أَوْ أُخْتٌ فَلِكُلِّ وَاحِدٍ مِنْهُمَا السُّدُسُ فَإِنْ كَانُوا أَكْثَرَ مِنْ ذَلِكَ فَهُمْ شُرَكَاءُ فِي الثُّلُثِ

If a man or woman has no direct heirs, but has a brother or sister, each of them receives a sixth. If there are more than that they share in a third. (Sūrat an-Nisā' 4: 12)

Ibn Juzayy al-Kalbī said:

> What is meant here is the uterine brother and uterine sister by consensus (*ijmāᶜ*). (Al-Kalbī, Ibn Juzayy, *Kitāb at-tashīl li ᶜulūm at-tanzīl*)

Unusually in this latter case, brothers and sisters share equally by unanimous agreement.

The uterine brother or sister, if he or she is only one, will receive a sixth in the absence of any child, whether son or daughter or son of a son or daughter of a son. If there are any children, whether male or female, they exclude him or her.

Similarly, they inherit with the ascendants of the deceased. If they are two or more mixed, they will share equally from a third. Sometimes they share the third with full brothers or full sisters or with full brothers and sisters as in the following cases:

X died leaving behind:

a. A mother, two full brothers, and three uterine sisters.

The mother receives a sixth, and the three uterine sisters share a third, and the two full brothers take the remainder as *ᶜaṣabah*. If we consider the inheritance to consist of thirty-six shares, then the mother takes six, the three uterine sisters take four shares each, and the two full brothers take nine each.

b. A husband, mother, two uterine sisters, a uterine brother, and three full brothers.

The husband takes a half, the mother a sixth, the uterine brothers and sisters share a third, and the full brothers share the remainder. However, considering the estate in terms of sixths, the husband takes three shares, the mother one and the uterine brother and two sisters share two, leaving nothing. So the full brothers would ordinarily receive nothing. However, the full brothers and sisters have more right than uterine brothers and sisters, in addition to which they are the *ᶜaṣabah*. Thus, in this case they must share with uterine brothers and sisters in their third, i.e. in two shares.

If we apply *taṣḥīḥ*, then we will consider the estate to consist of 18 shares, the husband receiving nine, the mother three, and the six brothers and sisters sharing six. Uterine brothers and sisters do not inherit in the proportion such that the male receives twice the portion of the female, and when the full brothers and sisters are added to them, the same applies to them, so each of them receives one share.

c. A wife, mother, uterine sister and brother and full brother. The wife takes a quarter, the mother a sixth, and the uterine brother and sister share a third, and the full brother takes the remainder. If we consider the estate to consist of twelve shares, then the wife takes three shares, the mother two, and the uterine brother and sister share four, i.e. two shares each, and the full brother the remainder, i.e. three shares.

d. A husband, mother, two uterine brothers, two uterine sisters, two full brothers and two full sisters. The husband takes a half, the mother a sixth, and the uterine brothers and sisters take a third. However, this would leave nothing for the full brothers and sisters, who would ordinarily have precedence as *ᶜaṣabah*. Thus, in this case all the brothers and sisters share in the third of the uterine brothers and sisters and they share equally. If we consider the estate as consisting of six parts, then the husband takes three, the mother two and the eight brothers and sisters share in two parts. Thus, applying *taṣḥīḥ*, we consider the estate to consist of twenty-four shares, the husband taking twelve of them, the mother taking four, and each of the brothers and sisters each taking one share. This is called 'mixed' or *mushtarakah*.

e. A husband, mother, two uterine brothers and a full brother. The husband takes a half, the mother a sixth, and the two uterine brothers and the full brother share a third equally. So that if the estate is in sixths, the husband takes three shares, the mother one, and the two uterine brothers and the full brother share two. Applying *taṣḥīḥ*, we make the estate eighteen shares, the husband taking nine shares, the mother three, and the three brothers take two shares each.

f. A husband, mother, two uterine brothers, two uterine sisters, and two full sisters. The husband takes a half, the mother a sixth, the two uterine brothers and two uterine sisters would share a third because of *āyah* 12 of Sūrat an-Nisā', and the two full sisters would take two thirds because of *āyah* 176 of the same sūrah. Whenever a husband, a mother, two uterine brothers, or a uterine sister, or a uterine brother or two uterine brothers are present with a full brother and a full sister then the brothers and sisters will all share the third equally. This again is called the *mushtarakah* or the 'mixed' case.

In those cases where there is one of the *ᶜaṣabah* who takes the remainder, but there is no remainder because the possessors of fixed shares (*farā'iḍ*) have taken the entire estate, then the jurists are of the view that it is unfair to give those who are related to the deceased only from the mother's side but prevent those receiving a share who are related to the deceased from both the mother's and the father's sides. This case is known as *al-Ḥimāriyyah, Hajariyyah* or *Yammiyyah*.

Where there is a father or daughter of the son they will exclude both full and uterine brothers and sisters. The granddaughter will also exclude the uterine brothers and sisters.

If there is only one uterine brother present together with the full brother and sister, then it will be a straightforward case, since the uterine brother will receive a sixth and the rest will go to the full brother and sister who take it as *ᶜaṣabah*. The jurists of Madīnah and Kūfa differed in their views on this issue. Sayyidunā ᶜUmar and Zayd ibn Thābit ﷺ, the two Companions, followed by Imām Mālik and Imām ash-Shāfiᶜī, adopted the rule that when the uterine brother or sister is present with full brothers and sisters, they share the third. They argued: how can the more remote brothers descended only from the mother inherit, and prevent from inheriting those who are nearer in relationship to the deceased, being descended from both the father and mother?

Other Companions of the Prophet ﷺ such as Sayyidunā ᶜAlī and ᶜAbdullāh ibn Masᶜūd ﷺ, followed by Imām Abū Ḥanīfah, Imām Aḥmad, Dāwūd aẓ-Ẓāhirī, Sufyān ath-Thawrī and others, opposed the above view and said that the rule must be left as it is in the Qur'ān. Allah, exalted is He, has said in the Qur'ān that the uterine brother and sister are to receive a third. They said that whatever remains will go to the full brothers as the remainder which they will take as the *ᶜaṣabah* and that no one should try to change this injunction.

For example, in this case, where someone dies leaving:

A husband, mother, uterine brother, ten full brothers and ten sisters. In this case, the husband takes a half, the mother a sixth, the uterine brother a sixth, and the ten sisters and ten full brothers sharing the remainder, i.e. a sixth, as ʿaṣabah.

All the Muslim jurists adopted the above case. The Ḥanafīs asked why the first group, i.e. the Madinans, also adopted the same position without applying qiyās, whereas in this case one uterine brother receives the same share as that of 20 brothers and sisters?

The other jurists replied that they did not wish to interfere in such cases because sometimes the full brother gets more and sometimes he gets less.

According to Ibn ʿAbbās ♦, however, they will share according to the principle *"the males receive the share of two females"*, while others took the position that they share equally because the verse of Qurʾān in this regard begins with equality, *"each of them receives a sixth"* and we should not end up with inequality in *"they share in a third"*:

$$ \text{وإن كان رجل يورث كلالة أو امرأة وله أخ أو أخت فلكل واحد منهما السدس فإن كانوا أكثر} $$

$$ \text{من ذلك فهم شركاء في الثلث} $$

If a man or woman has no direct heirs, but has a brother or sister, each of them receives a sixth. If there are more than that they share in a third.
(Sūrat an-Nisāʾ 4: 12)

SOME OTHER CASES:

Someone dies leaving a husband, a mother, a uterine brother and a full brother. The husband takes a half, the mother a sixth, the uterine brother a sixth and the full brother the remainder, as ʿaṣabah, which is a sixth. Thus if the estate is considered to consist of six shares, the husband takes three, the mother one, the uterine brother one, and the full brother one share.

Someone dies leaving a wife, ten uterine brothers, and a full brother. The wife inherits a quarter, the uterine brothers share a third, and the full brother takes the remainder. Thus if we consider the estate to consist of twelve shares, the wife takes three, the ten uterine brothers share four shares, and the full brother takes the remainder which is five shares. Applying *taṣḥīḥ* we now consider the estate to consist of sixty shares, the wife taking fifteen, the ten uterine brothers taking twenty, i.e. two shares each, and the full brother taking the remainder, which is twenty-five shares.

G. Shares allotted to full brothers and full sisters

1. If there is only one full sister, she will inherit a half in the absence of children who are heirs, a father or grandfather or a full brother.
2. If there are two or more full sisters, they share two-thirds in the absence of children who are heirs, a father or grandfather or a full brother.
3. They inherit as *ᶜaṣabah* in the presence of full brothers and divide according to the principle of *"the males receive the share of two females"*.
4. In the case where a full sister is present with a daughter or daughters of the deceased or daughters of the son of the deceased, she will inherit as one of the *ᶜaṣabah* after they receive their shares. This is treated as exceptional.

a. Someone dies leaving a daughter and a full sister. The daughter takes a half of the estate and the full sister takes the remaining half as *ᶜaṣabah*. If the estate consists of two shares, they each take one share.

b. Someone dies leaving a daughter and two full sisters. The daughter takes a quarter and the two full sisters take the remainder, which is three quarters. If the estate consists of four shares, the daughter takes one share, and the two sisters share three shares. Therefore, by *taṣḥīḥ*, we consider the estate to consist of eight shares, the daughter taking two, and the two sisters sharing six shares, i.e. taking three shares each.

c. Someone dies leaving two daughters and two full sisters. The two daughters share two-thirds of the estate, and the two full sisters share the remainder, which is a third. If we consider the estate to consist of three shares, then the two daughters share two shares, and the two sisters share one. If we apply *taṣḥīḥ*, then we will consider the estate to consist of six shares, the two daughters taking four shares, i.e. two shares each, and the two full sisters sharing the remainder, i.e. two shares, thus taking a share each.

If one daughter or more are present with a full brother and also with uterine sisters, they will share the third equally in a joint group *mas'alah mushtarakah*:

Someone dies leaving a husband, mother, uterine brother, full sister and full brother. The husband takes a half, the mother a sixth, and the brothers and sisters share the remainder, which is a third, equally. Thus if the inheritance is six shares, the husband takes three, the mother one, and the brothers and sisters share two. Thus, applying *taṣḥīḥ*, we consider the estate to consist of eighteen shares, the husband taking nine, the mother taking three, and the brothers and sisters sharing six shares equally, thus taking two shares each.

In the case where she is present with a grandfather, he will make her part of the *ᶜaṣabah* as the full brother does.

The authority for giving the sister the remains if is she is present with daughters is that of the *ḥadīth* which is narrated from ᶜAbdullāh ibn Masᶜūd ﷺ. He said that the Prophet ﷺ decided a case in which there was a daughter and the daugher of a son, to whom he gave two-thirds, giving the remains of the estate, one third to the full sister.

جَاءَ رَجُلٌ إِلَى أَبِي مُوسَى الْأَشْعَرِيِّ وَسَلْمَانَ بْنِ رَبِيعَةَ الْبَاهِلِيِّ فَسَأَلَهُمَا عَنْ رَجُلٍ تَرَكَ ابْنَتَهُ وَابْنَةَ ابْنِهِ فَقَالَا: ﴿ لِلْإِبْنَةِ النِّصْفُ، وَلَيْسَ لِابْنَةِ الْابْنِ شَيْءٌ، وَائْتِ ابْنَ مَسْعُودٍ! فَإِنَّهُ سَيُتَابِعُنَا ﴾، قَالَ: فَجَاءَ الرَّجُلُ إِلَى عَبْدِ اللَّهِ بْنِ مَسْعُودٍ فَأَخْبَرَهُ بِمَا قَالَا، قَالَ: ﴿ قَدْ ضَلَلْتُ إِذًا وَمَا أَنَا مِنَ الْمُهْتَدِينَ وَلَكِنْ سَأَقْضِي فِيهَا بِقَضَاءِ رَسُولِ اللَّهِ ﷺ، قَضَى رَسُولُ اللَّهِ ﷺ فِي رَجُلٍ تَرَكَ ابْنَتَهُ

وابنة ابنه وأخته فجعل للإبنة النصف، ولابنة الابن السدس وما بقي للأخت ﴾. (أخرجه البيهقي في السنن الكبرى كتاب الفرائض باب فرض ابنة الابن

> A man came to Abū Mūsā al-Ash^c^arī ☙ [who was the governor of Kūfa] and Salmān ibn Rabī^c^ah and asked them about [the inheritance in the case] where a man left a daughter and daughter of his son. They both said, "The daughter has a half and the son's daughter has nothing. Go to Ibn Mas^c^ūd, because he will confirm us." …The man went to ^c^Abdullāh ibn Mas^c^ūd and told him what they had said. He said, "I had certainly gone astray then and I would not have been of one of those who are guided. But I will pass judgement on it with the judgement of the Messenger of Allah ﷺ, for the Messenger of Allah ﷺ passed judgement concerning a man who left his daughter and his son's daughter and his sister, and he appointed for the daughter a half, for the daughter of his son a sixth, and what remained for the sister." (Al-Bayhaqī, *as-Sunan al-kubrā, kitāb al-farā'iḍ, bāb farḍ ibnat al-ibn,* 6: 230)

When they went and informed Abū Mūsā what ^c^Abdullāh ibn Mas^c^ūd had said, Abū Mūsā told them not to ask him anything as long as that learned man (^c^Ibn Mas^c^ūd) was alive among them.

Mu^c^ādh ibn Jabal ☙ also decided a similar case during the lifetime of the Prophet ﷺ in which there was a daughter and a full sister, among others. He gave one third to the daughter, and the remainder, which was a quarter, to the sister.

^c^Abdullāh ibn ^c^Abbās ☙ differed with the other jurists in the case of the inheritance of a full sister. He said that in the case where the full sister was present with the daughter, she will not get anything neither as one of those due obligatory shares (*aṣḥāb al-farā'iḍ*) nor as *^c^aṣabah*. He cited Qur'ānic authority that the *^c^aṣabah* will only inherit in the absence of children, but that in this case there is already a child. As far as the *^c^aṣabah* are concerned they must be either male or include a male with the females. He would not allow a female on her own to act as *^c^aṣabah* because it would then be contrary to the Qur'ān. He once decided a case in which the deceased left a daughter and a full sister, giving the daughter a half and excluding the full sister. When told that Sayyidunā ᶜUmar ﷺ had decided such a case and had given the daughter a half and the full sister a half (the remainder), Ibn ᶜAbbās ﷺ said that the decision of ᶜUmar ﷺ was not binding on him, since the authority of the Qur'ān was higher.[13]

H. Shares allotted to a consanguine sister

1. In the absence of children, father, full brother or sister and a consanguine brother, the consanguine sister receives a half.
2. If there are two or more, they receive two-thirds, provided they are not excluded, in which case they get nothing, or added into the *ᶜaṣabah*, in which case they share in the remainder.
3. In the presence of one full sister, the consanguine sister receives a sixth.
4. If the consanguine sister is included among the *ᶜaṣabah* by a consanguine brother, she will share as one of the *ᶜaṣabah*.

She is excluded by a son, son of a son, father, full brother, one full sister if she is acting as *ᶜaṣabah*, a daughter or daughter of a son, and also if they are not included among the *ᶜaṣabah* because of a consanguine brother or grandfather.

She will be included among the *ᶜaṣabah* if she is present with a consanguine brother or a grandfather, or with a daughter or a son's daughter in the absence of a full sister.

a. Someone dies leaving two daughers and a full sister. The two daughters share two-thirds and the full sister inherits a third.
b. Someone dies leaving two daughters and a consanguine sister. The two daughters share two-thirds and the consanguine sister takes the remainder, i.e. a third.
c. Someone dies leaving two daughters, a full sister and a consanguine sister. The two daughters share two-thirds, the full sister takes the remainder, which is a third, and the consanguine sister is excluded by the full sister and receives nothing.

d. A man dies leaving a full sister, and ten consanguine sisters. The full sister inherits a half, and the ten consanguine sisters share a sixth, because the sixth together with the half of the full sister make two-thirds, which is the total amount sisters may inherit.

5. She inherits as *ᶜaṣabah* when she is present along with a grandfather. The grandfather has the effect of including her in the *ᶜaṣabah*, but only if she is already going to get something.

I. Share allotted to the Grandmother

The grandmother will inherit a sixth of the total estate, but their number must not exceed four. Great grandmothers are included among grandmothers. They may be paternal or maternal grandmothers, i.e. the mother of the mother and her mother, and the mother of the father and her mother. This definition of the grandmother is according to the Mālikī school. The Ḥanafī school limits the category of grandmothers who will inherit to the mother of the father, the mother of the mother, and the mother of the paternal grandfather, i.e. the father's father.

According to Imām Mālik there cannot be more than two grandmothers, and where there are two of them they will share a sixth. The Ḥanafī school says that there may be three grandmothers who will still share a sixth, e.g. the mother of the mother's mother, the mother of the father's mother and the mother of the father's father.

The Mālikī school excludes the mother of the father's father but agrees with the Ḥanafī school on the mother of the mother's mother. They say that this is in agreement with the Sunnah of the Prophet ﷺ. About the father's maternal grandmother, Imām Mālik agreed with the *ijtihād* of ᶜUmar ﷛ who allowed her and the father's maternal grandmother to share a sixth, but he said that the father's paternal grandmother does not inherit because there is no authority for this.

Ibn Juzayy said:

Only four grandmothers inherit: the mother's mother and her

mothers, the father's mother and her mothers. The grandfather's mother does not inherit according to Mālik but contrary to Zayd, ᶜAlī, Ibn ᶜAbbās and Abū Ḥanīfah ﷺ. According to the *madhhab* only two grandmothers and no more may be united in inheritance, but for other matters three may be united. (Al-Kalbī, Ibn Juzayy, *al-Qawānīn al-fiqhiyyah, al-kitāb al-ᶜāshir fī al-farā'iḍ wa al-waṣāyā, al-bāb ath-thānī fī al-ḥajb wa as-sihām*)

Those who can exclude the grandmother are:

1. The mother will exclude the mother's mother and the father's mother and their mothers.
2. The father will exclude only the father's mother and her mothers, but will not exclude the mother's mother and her mothers.
3. The nearer from the mother's side, i.e. the mother's mother and her mother will exclude those who are remote from the mother's side and also from the father's side.

According to the Ḥanafī school, the nearer relation will exclude all those who are remote from any other side although the Māliki school takes quite a different view. This argument is based on the degree of relationship.

The Mālikī school, on the contrary, says that the person inheriting through the process of *ijtihād* cannot exclude someone who is inheriting in accordance with the Sunnah, i.e., the father's mother's mother will inherit according to *ijtihād* while the mother's mother's mother will inherit according to the Sunnah of the Prophet ﷺ.

J. Share allotted to the paternal grandfather

1. If the paternal grandfather is the sole survivor, he will get the whole of the estate.
2. If the paternal grandfather is present with other male issue, e.g., a son, or son of son, he will inherit a sixth of the net estate.
3. If he is present with female issue, e.g., a daughter, daughter of a son, he will be entitled to a sixth plus the remainder as *ᶜaṣabah*.
4. If he is present with brothers, whether full or con-

sanguine, and/or sisters, he will have to choose whether to take a third of the entire estate or be treated as a brother. For example if he chooses to be counted as a brother:

a. The deceased leaves a paternal grandfather and a full brother. Each takes a half.
b. The deceased leaves a brother's son, who inherits as the brother would have done, i.e. a half, and a paternal grandfather, who again takes a half.
c. The deceased leaves two full sisters and a paternal grandfather. He inherits a half on the basis of *"the males receive the share of two females"*, and takes a half of the estate, with the sisters sharing a half between them.

In the above examples he is treated as a brother since it is more advantageous for him to be treated in that way.

If he is present with two full or consanguine brothers, or four full or consanguine sisters, it will be the same whether he chooses to be a brother or to take a third as his share. But in the case where he is present with more than two full or consanguine brothers, or more than four full or consanguine sisters, he is going to be given the share that suits him the most, i.e. the third.

5. Supposing he is present together with a group of both full brothers and consanguine brothers, he will either take a third of the entire estate or be counted as a brother, but here although the consanguine brother will not inherit because he is excluded by the full brother, still the full brother will count him in in order to prevent the grandfather from getting more than a third. As for example where the grandfather is present with both a full brother and a consanguine brother, each takes a third.

If he is counted as a brother, when they share equally, the full brother will return and receive the share of the consanguine brother because the consanguine brother will not inherit in the presence of the full brother, i.e. the grandfather will take a third, and the full brother will take two-thirds, one third his own third, and the other third that of the consanguine brother, who may not inherit in the presence of a full brother.

Another example is the presence of a full sister along with the paternal grandfather and a consanguine brother.

The grandfather in this case inherits two-fifths, the sister a fifth, and the consanguine brother two-fifths, on the basis of *"the males receive the share of two females"*.

In this case, after every one of them has got his share, the full sister will go back and insist that she must get her specific share as specified in the Qur'ān, *"If a man dies childless but has a sister she receives half of what he leaves"* (Sūrat an-Nisā' 4: 176). Thus she will reduce the share of the consanguine brother to make her own share a half, and the consanguine brother will be left with a tenth as the remainder. The case will then be like this:

The grandfather still receives two-fifths, the full sister receives a half of the estate and the consanguine brother receives the remainder of the estate which is a tenth. If we consider the estate as consisting of ten shares, then the grandfather receives four shares, the full sister five shares, and there remains one share for the consanguine brother, i.e. a tenth.

6. If the paternal grandfather is present with other Qur'ānic heirs he is entitled to the best of one of three alternatives:

a. One sixth of the total estate;
b. A third of the remains of the estate after the people who have fixed shares by Qur'ānic edict inherit; or
c. He will be counted as a brother and share with them.

Thus, for example, the deceased leaves a grandfather, a full brother and a wife.

i. The grandfather takes a sixth, the wife a quarter, and the full brother the remainder. If we consider the estate to consist of twelve shares, then the grandfather receives two shares, the wife three shares, and the full brother seven shares.

ii. The wife takes a quarter of the estate, and the grandfather receives a third of the remainder, with the brother taking the rest. Thus if we consider the estate to consist of four shares, the wife takes one share, leaving three shares, of which the grandfather takes a third, i.e. one share, and the full brother the remaining two shares.

iii. The wife receives a quarter, and the full brother and grandfather share the three-quarters, the grandfather acting as a brother. Thus if we consider the inheritance to consist of eighths, the wife will receive two shares, and the full brother and grandfather each receive three shares.

iv. In another case, the deceased leaves a grandfather, full brother, mother, and wife. If the grandfather is treated as a brother, then the mother gets a third, the wife a quarter and he and the full brother share the remainder. Therefore, we consider the estate as consisting of twelve shares, the mother getting four shares, the wife three, and the full brother and paternal grandfather sharing the remainder, i.e. five shares. Applying *taṣḥīḥ*, so that we do not have fractions, then we consister the estate as consisting of twenty-four shares, the mother getting eight shares, the wife six, and the full brother and grandfather five each.

In these two cases, it is better for him to be treated as a brother.

v. The deceased leaves a grandfather, full brother, mother and husband. The grandfather takes a sixth, the mother a third, the husband a half, and the full brother the remainder. If we consider the estate as consisting of six shares, then the grandfather takes one share, the mother two, and the husband three, and there is nothing left as remainder, so that the full brother receives nothing. If the grandfather had decided to be treated as a brother, he would have shared the remainder and received nothing, so that accepting the sixth is better in this case for him.

The deceased leaves two daughters, a full brother and a grandfather.

vi.a. The two daughters share two-thirds of the estate, the grandfather takes a sixth and the full brother takes the remainder. Thus, if we consider the estate as consisting of six shares, the daughters each receive two shares, the grandfather one share, and the full brother the remainder, i.e. one share.

vi.b. If in the same situation, the grandfather is treated as a brother and shares the remainder after the two-thirds inherited by the two sisters, then again, they will take one share each.

All these examples are according to the decisions of Zayd ibn Thābit and Mālik ibn Anas.

vii. In the case where the deceased leaves a mother, a full sister and a grandfather, the mother receiving a third of the estate, and the grandfather and full sister take the remainder, i.e. two-thirds of the estate, the grandfather being treated like a brother, and on the basis of *"the males receive the share of two females"* taking twice the full sister's share, i.e. four-ninths. Then if we consider the estate to consist of nine shares, the mother takes three, the grandfather four and the full sister two.

In the case where a grandfather is present with full sisters or consanguine sisters, the shares will be as follows:

1. The deceased leaves a mother, grandfather and full or consanguine sister. The mother takes a third, and the grandfather and full or consanguine sister share the remainder. But see the detailed working out of this case known as *al-Gharrā'* below. This is according to Imam Mālik and Zayd ibn Thābit.
2. But according to Abū Bakr and ᶜAbdullāh ibn ᶜAbbās ﷺ the mother takes a third, the grandfather takes the remainder, i.e. two-thirds, excluding the full or consanguine sister.
3. According to Sayyidunā ᶜAlī the mother inherits a third, the sister a half and the grandfather takes the remainder. So that if the estate is six shares, the mother inherits two shares, the sister three, and the grandfather one.

Al-Gharrā' or *al-Akdariyyah*

Imam Mālik was of the view that when a sister is present with a grandfather, she will not inherit as *ṣāḥib al-farḍ* (possessor of a fixed share), but she will be agnatised, i.e. included in the *ᶜaṣabah* by the grandfather, as in the following example:

The deceased leaves a husband, mother, grandfather and full sister. The husband takes a half, the mother a third, and the grandfather and full sister share the remainder, in this case a sixth, and *"the males receive the share of two females"*.

As far as the Mālikī school is concerned, the grandfather does not get less than a sixth and in the above case the remainder is a sixth. In this case because the grandfather shares the remainder with the full sister he will in reality get less than that. Imām Mālik says that she will be given her specific share and the grandfather will be given his own share which is a sixth. They bring their shares together and add them and then divide according to the principle of *"males receive the share of two females"*.

Thus the husband takes a half, the mother a third, the grandfather a sixth and the full sister a half. If we consider the estate to consist of six shares, then the full sister would take three shares and the grandfather one, making four in total, but there is in fact only one share to divide between them. This is called *ᶜawl* (excess), i.e. the shares 'exceed' the total estate, which we will treat in detail later. We have already seen that it has to be divided according to *"the males receive the share of two females"*.

The way the case is treated is that there are six shares, the husband taking three, the mother two, and the grandfather one. Then the sister's half of the inheritance is included so that she should also get an additional three shares, making the total of shares nine. Then the sister's three shares are added to the grandfather's one, making four, but it is not possible to divide four shares according to *"the males receive the share of two females"*, so they are to be multiplied by three, and thus the whole estate is multiplied by three to give twenty-seven shares, the husband taking nine, the mother six, and the grandfather and full sister sharing the remaining twelve, she taking four shares, and he taking eight. This is the case known in Mālikī *fiqh* as *al-Gharrā'* or *al-Akdariyyah.*[14] This is an example of *ᶜawl* when the number of shares owed the heirs exceeds the total of the estate.

According to Sayyidunā ᶜUmar where there is a husband, mother, grandfather and full sister, the husband gets a half, the mother a third, the grandfather a sixth and the full sister a half, and so this is a case of *ᶜawl,* i.e. considering the estate as three shares, then the husband gets three shares, the mother two, the grandfather one, and the full sister three, giving a total of nine shares. Thus each must have their share reduced proportionately by considering the estate to consist of nine shares and giving each heir the number of shares mentioned above.

When the deceased leaves a husband, mother, grandfather and two full sisters. The husband takes a half of the estate, the mother now takes a sixth, the grandfather a sixth, and the two full sisters share a sixth. So applying *taṣḥīḥ* we consider the estate to consist of twelve shares, the husband taking six, the mother two, the grandfather two, and the full sisters taking one each.

If the grandfather is present with a full brother, the case is treated differently than when he is present with a full sister. In this case the husband takes a half of the estate, the mother a third, the grandfather a sixth, and the full brother takes the remainder, but in fact there is nothing remaining and so he receives nothing.

In this case the grandfather must be given his sixth which will not be shared with the full brother. Since there is nothing remaining, the full brother will get nothing.

> "And if there is in place of her" i.e. the sister in the *Akdariyyah,* "a consanguine brother and along with him uterine brothers" two or more, then the consanguine brother "is omitted" because [it is as if the] grandfather says to him 'If you had been there without my existing you would not have inherited anything, because the remaining third after the husband the mother is taking by the children of the mother, but I prevent the inheritance of every uterine relation,' so the grandfather alone takes the third entirely. And this case is known as the *Mālikiyyah* and he is increased with the consanguine brother's sixth. And it is said that Mālik did not differ from Zayd [ibn Thābit] in any other case but this one. (*Ash-Sharḥ al-kabīr ᶜalā Ḥāshiyah ad-Dasūqī*)

In the case where there is a husband, mother, grandfather, consanguine brother and one uterine brother, the view of Imām Mālik, known as *shubh al-Mālikiyyah* (similar to the *Mālikiyyah*), was that the husband receives a half, the mother a third and the grandfather a sixth and that the grandfather excludes both the consanguine and the uterine brothers. In this view Imām Mālik differed from Zayd ibn Thābit who said that the husband takes a half, the mother a sixth, the grandfather a sixth, the consanguine brother taking the remainder, which is a sixth, and excluding the uterine brother.

The Concept of *ᶜAwl*

ᶜAwl was neither known nor practised during the time of the Prophet ﷺ or during the caliphate of Abū Bakr, the first caliph. A case arose during the time of ᶜUmar, the second caliph, who decided it after consultation with and the agreement of the *Ṣaḥābah* (the Companions of the Prophet ﷺ). The first case that came to Sayyidunā ᶜUmar concerned the inheritance when there were two full sisters, and a husband. Ordinarily the husband receives a half and the two full sisters share two-thirds, thus giving a total greater than the entire estate. ᶜUmar ؓ said:

> By Allah, I do not know which of you Allah has put first and which comes next.

Sayyidunā ᶜUmar then invited the Companions of the Prophet ﷺ and asked their advice on this case, saying that if he gave the two sisters their specified share, the husband would not get his specified share, but if he gave the husband his share, the sisters would not get their share.

What should he do? There are differences of opinion as to who suggested how to treat *ᶜawl*. Some say that it was ᶜAbbās, while others said it was ᶜAlī and others that it was Zayd ibn Thābit ؓ.

This *ᶜawl* first appeared in the time of ᶜUmar and people agreed with him except for Ibn ᶜAbbās, who expressed his disagreement after the death of ᶜUmar, but did not deliver a verdict on it [during the life of ᶜUmar]. Then later the *Ummah* reached consensus on it, and no one took the verdict of Ibn ᶜAbbās ؓ except for people who are not to be reckoned with. (*Ash-Sharḥ al-kabīr ᶜalā Ḥāshiyah ad-Dasūqī*)

The case of how to treat *ᶜawl* is suggested in a hypothetical proposition that if a man died leaving six dirhams, and there were two people claiming their debt from the estate, one of them claiming three dirhams and the other claiming four dirhams, we have to adopt the rule of bankruptcy and divide it proportionally. Sayyidunā ᶜUmar agreed to this proposition. Then ᶜAbbās said:

"This is then the rule to be applied here". If the husband is to get a half and the two full sisters to get two-thirds, then if we consider the estate as consisting of six shares, the husband should get three shares, and the two sisters four shares, making a total of seven shares. Thus, we now consider the estate to consist of seven shares, the husband getting three of them and each of the two sisters getting two of them, thus reducing all the shares proportionately from sixths of the estate to sevenths.

Some said the first case of *ᶜawl* was that of the deceased leaving a husband who took a half of the estate, a full sister who took a half, and a uterine sister who took a sixth, in which if we consider the estate as consisting of six parts, the husband took three parts, the full sister three parts, and the uterine sister two parts, making a total of eight. Thus the estate is considered to consist of eight parts, with each heir taking the same number of parts, as eighths rather than sixths.

Others said the first case was that of the deceased who left a husband who took a half, a full sister who took a half, and a mother who took a third. Thus, if the estate consists of six shares, the husband takes three, the sister takes three, and the mother takes two shares, again making eight shares in total, the same procedure being followed as above in considering the estate to consist of eight shares and the heirs taking eighths rather than sixths.

All the Companions agreed with the case except Ibn ᶜAbbās, who expressed his disagreement after the death of Sayyidunā ᶜUmar and after the consensus had been achieved, his disagreement thus not being reckoned with.[15]

> Then Ibn ᶜAbbās said, "By Allah, if only he had advanced those whom Allah had advanced, and put back those whom Allah had put back then the obligatory shares would not have exceeded [the estate]." So Zufar said to him, "So which of them did He advance and which did He put back." He said, "Every obligatory share which only declines to another obligatory share,[16] then that is the one which Allah advanced, and they are: the share of the husband who receives a half but if it declines then to a quarter without being decreased from that, and the wife who receives a quarter but if it decreases from that then it becomes an eighth

not decreasing beyond that. The sisters who share two-thirds and the single sister who receives a half, but who if daughters are included with them then they have what remains, then these are the ones who are put back. So if he had given those whom Allah had advanced the complete obligatory share and had then shared what remained among those whom Allah had put back, proportionately then the obligatory shares would not have exceeded [the estate]." Zufar said to him, "So what prevented you counselling ᶜUmar with this view?" He said, "I was in awe of him, by Allah!" Az-Zuhrī said, "By Allah! If it had not been that the Imām of guidance [ᶜUmar] had preceded him, whose affair was scrupulous,[17] no two of the people of knowledge would have disagreed with Ibn ᶜAbbās." (Abū ash-Shaykh, *al-Farā'iḍ;* al-Bayhaqī, *as-Sunan al-kubrā, kitāb al-farā'iḍ, bāb al-ᶜawl fī al-farā'iḍ,* as cited in *Kanz al-ᶜummāl*)

Radd (return) is the rule where the obligatory shares are less than the estate, and the excess is redistributed or 'returned' to the *bayt al-māl* according to Mālikīs and Shāfiᶜīs or to possessors of fixed shares or the *ᶜaṣabah* according to Ḥanafīs and Ḥanbalīs.

In the case where the total shares are more than the *aṣl* (original estate), this is a case of *ᶜawl*. The total shares are then used as a new *aṣl*, e.g.:

1. Where there are two full sisters and a husband, they inheriting two-thirds and the husband a half, the *aṣl* is six shares because the only way to work with a half and thirds is by treating them as sixths, but the new *aṣl* being seven shares because the husband has three shares and the two sisters four.
2. Where there is a husband who takes a half, i.e. three sixths, two full sisters who take two thirds, i.e. four sixths, a mother who takes one sixth and a uterine sister who takes one sixth, making nine sixths in all. So the original *aṣl* is six shares, and new *aṣl* is nine shares.
3. Where there is a husband who takes a half, i.e. three sixths, two full sisters who take two thirds, i.e. four sixths, a mother who takes one sixth, and two uterine sisters who take two sixths, making ten sixths in all. So the original *aṣl* is six shares, and the new *aṣl* is ten shares.

4. Jurists observed that out of seven *aṣl*, *ᶜawl* is only in six, twelve, and twenty-four; that is where *ᶜawl* will occur. Where there is a wife, two full sisters, two uterine sisters and a mother, this is known as *"ash-Shurayḥiyyah"* because it was decided by Qāḍī Shurayḥ.
5. Where there is a wife who takes an eighth, two daughters who take two-thirds, a mother and father who each take a sixth. Thus the estate is considered to consist of twenty-four shares, the wife taking three shares, the two daughters taking 16 shares and the mother and father each taking four shares, making twenty-seven shares in all. So the original *aṣl* is twenty-four and the new *aṣl* is twenty-seven.

This case is known as *"al-Minbariyyah"* because it was decided by Sayyidunā ᶜAlī spontaneously on the Minbar, and Ibn ᶜAbbās is reported to have considered this the very first instance of *ᶜawl*.[18]

The following provides a good example of *radd*:

The deceased leaves a daughter who inherits a half, a son's daughter who inherits a sixth, a wife who inherits an eighth and a mother who inherits a sixth. Thus considering the estate to consist of twenty-four shares (because two, six, and eight are all factors of twenty-four), then the daughter inherits twelve shares, the son's daughter inherits four, the wife three and the mother four, making a total of twenty-three shares out of an *aṣl* of twenty-four shares. This is a case of *radd* because the total shares of the heirs are less than the entire estate. We will cover how the extra amount is shared among the other heirs according to the Ḥanafī *madhhab* in the section on *radd.*

Examples of *taᶜṣīb* (i.e. giving the status of *ᶜaṣabah* to someone):

1. There is a wife who takes one eighth, a daughter who takes a half, i.e. four eighths, and two full sisters who take the remainder, i.e. three eighths by being *ᶜaṣabah*. The *aṣl* here is to consider the estate to consist of eight shares, but because that forces us to divide three shares between two

sisters, we multiply the *aṣl* by two to make the new *aṣl* of sixteen shares, the wife taking two shares, the daughter eight, and each full sister three shares.

2. There are eight daughters of a son who inherit together two-thirds, a mother, who inherits a sixth, and father who inherits a sixth as his fixed share and the remainder as *ᶜaṣabah*. We consider the estate to consist of six shares because three and six are factors of it. Thus the daughters inherit four shares, and the mother and father each inherit one share. There is no remainder to go to the father as *ᶜaṣabah* and so he inherits a sixth like the mother. However, the eight granddaughters are to divide four shares between them, and therefore it is better to consider the *aṣl* of six shares being multiplied by two to give a new *aṣl* of twelve share, the eight daughters of the son taking a share each, and the mother and father taking two shares each.
3. There is a husband who inherits a half, and five full sisters who inherit two-thirds between them. We consider the *aṣl* as six shares, since two and three are both factors of six. Thus the five sisters will inherit four shares and the husband three. Thus this is a case of *ᶜawl*, there being seven shares, and so this is the new *aṣl*. However, the five sisters are sharing four shares, so the *aṣl* is multiplied by five to give a new *aṣl* of thirty-five, with each sister taking four shares, the husband fifteen shares.
4. There are three daughters of a son who together inherit two-thirds, three grandmothers who together inherit a sixth and three full sisters who take the remainder. Therefore we consider the *aṣl* to consist of six shares, since three and six are both factors of six, the three daughters of the son taking four shares, the three grandmothers sharing one share and the three full sisters sharing one share. In order to avoid fractions we multiply the *aṣl* by three to make a new *aṣl* of eighteen, the three daughters of the son now sharing twelve shares and taking four

shares each, and the three grandmothers taking a share each and the three full sisters taking a share each.

5. There are six daughters of a son, three grandmothers, and three full sisters, the granddaughters sharing two-thirds, the grandmothers sharing a sixth, and the sisters taking the remainder, a sixth, as *ᶜaṣabah*. Thus the *aṣl* is six shares since three and six are both factors of it. The six granddaughters share four shares, the three grandmothers share one, and the three full sisters share the remainder which is one share. Thus we multiply the original *aṣl* of six by three to get a new *aṣl* of eighteen shares, the six granddaughters of the son sharing twelve shares and thus taking two shares each, the three grandmothers sharing three shares and thus taking one share each, and similarly the three full sisters sharing three shares and thus taking one share each.
6. There are four wives who inherit a quarter, three grandmothers who share a sixth, and four full sisters and four full brothers who inherit the remainder. Thus we consider the estate to consist of an *aṣl* of twelve shares, since three and six are both factors of twelve, the wives inheriting three shares, the three grandmothers sharing two shares, and the four brothers and four sisters sharing the remainder, which is seven shares, on the basis of "*the males receive the share of two females*".
   We multiply the original *aṣl* of twelve by twelve to give a new *aṣl* of 144 shares, the four wives getting thirty-six shares, each receiving nine shares, the three grandmothers getting twenty-four shares, each one getting eight shares, the brothers and sisters sharing the remainder of eighty-four "*the males receive the share of two females*". Two-thirds of eighty-four is fifty-six, which goes to the brothers leaving twenty-eight which goes to the sisters. Thus the four full brothers get fourteen shares each and the four full sisters seven shares each.
7. There are three grandmothers who share a sixth, four

wives who share a quarter, two uterine brothers who share a third, and five consanguine brothers who take the remainder as *ᶜaṣabah*. Considering the *aṣl* to consist of twelve shares, because six, four, and three are factors of twelve, the three grandmothers receive two shares, the four wives share three shares, the two uterine brothers share four shares, and the five consanguine brothers share the remainder which is three shares. The *aṣl* of twelve is multiplied by 5 X 4 X 3 i.e. sixty to give a new *aṣl* of 720 shares, the three grandmothers sharing 120 shares and getting forty shares each, the four wives sharing 180 shares and thus getting forty-five shares each, the two uterine brothers sharing 240 shares and thus getting 120 each, and the five consanguine brothers sharing 180 shares and thus getting thirty-six shares each.

Rules of Exclusion from Inheritance

According to the principles of the *Sharīᶜah* exclusion is based on three main principles:

1. The nearer in degree excludes someone who is remoter. (e.g., a son excludes a son's son, and a father excludes a grandfather).
2. A person who is related to the deceased through another is excluded by the presence of the latter, (e.g., a father excludes a brother.) There is, however, one exception to this rule: a mother does not exclude a brother or sister.
3. Full blood excludes half blood, (e.g., a full sister excludes a consanguine sister.) The exception to this rule is that the uterine relations are not excluded on this ground.

Total exclusions under the *Sharīᶜah* are enforced on the following grounds:

a. Difference of Religion: According to the *Sharīᶜah* a non-Muslim cannot inherit from a Muslim nor a Muslim from a non-Muslim, but non-Muslims of different religions may inherit from each other. If a Muslim changes his or her religion, he or she is excluded from inheritance.

b. If someone causes the death of another whether intentionally or unintentionally, he cannot inherit from the deceased. There is a difference between the Ḥanafī and Mālikī legal systems. The Ḥanafīs say that if an infant or insane person commits an act that causes the death of another person, this does not exclude such an infant or insane person from inheritance.

Moreover, the act causing the death should be of a direct nature. For example, when a person digs a well into which another falls or places a stone on the road against which another stumbles and is killed in consequence, then these are are not sufficient causes for his exclusion.

Māliki jurists say that someone who intentionally kills or causes the death of another, directly or indirectly, will be precluded from any right to inherit from him, while someone who kills another by accident, even by a direct act, such as shooting a pistol or flinging a bomb, will not suffer any such deprivation.

c. Slavery: the status of slavehood is a bar to inheritance.
d. Illegitimacy: a bastard, in Ḥanafī Law, cannot inherit from the father; he can inherit from the side of the mother.

According to the *madhhabs*, the child by fornication and the child of parents who are divorced because they have engaged in the form of divorce known as *liᶜān*,[19] are both regarded as illegitimate, and only inherit from the mother's side. Likewise, the son of a uterine brother does not inherit.

> A full brother excludes a consanguine brother, but a consanguine brother takes precedence over the son of a full brother. The son of a full brother takes precedence over the son of a consanguine brother. A son of a consanguine brother excludes a full paternal uncle. A full paternal uncle excludes a consanguine paternal uncle. A consanguine paternal uncle excludes the son of a full paternal uncle. The son of a full paternal uncle excludes the son of a consanguine paternal uncle. So the nearer relative always has the greater entitlement.
>
> Those who do not inherit include the children of sisters of whatever sort, the sons of daughters, the daughters of a brother of whatever sort, the daughters of a paternal uncle, the maternal

grandfather, and a uterine paternal uncle. (Al-Qayrawānī, Ibn Abī Zayd, *ar-Risālah, bāb al-farā'iḍ*)

A slave does not inherit, nor does a slave who is in the process of being freed. [This includes the *umm walad* and *mudabbar*.]

A Muslim does not inherit from an unbeliever nor an unbeliever from a Muslim. [The majority position is that a Muslim does not inherit from an unbeliever and there is consensus that an unbeliever does not inherit from a Muslim.]

Others who do not inherit are: the son of a uterine brother, the maternal grandfather and the mother of the maternal grandfather.

Nor does the mother of the paternal grandfather inherit along with her son, the father of the deceased. [She, in fact, does not inherit at all.]

Uterine brothers do not inherit with the paternal grandfather, nor with the sons or daughters or grandchildren through a son. Siblings of any sort do not inherit with the father.

A paternal uncle does not inherit with the paternal grandfather nor the son of a brother with the paternal grandfather. [Because the level of the grandfather is that of the brother, and the brother excludes his son and those in his rank.]

The murderer does not inherit either the estate or blood money. Someone guilty of accidental homicide does not inherit any of the blood money, but does inherit from the estate. [This is about the person who kills the deceased. As for someone who kills deliberately without transgression, like the ruler executing someone from whom he inherits for a *ḥadd* punishment obliged on him, or like someone killing his father who is a bandit, they do inherit. In the case of accidental homicide, he is excluded in one place and not in another. For example, there are two brothers and one of them kills the other, then the mother inherits a sixth from the brother and the rest is for the two brothers together, because the brother excludes her from a third to a sixth and she inherits a third of the blood money because the killer does not inherit blood money and so he does not exclude her.]

Anyone who does not inherit for some reason cannot then exclude another heir. [Except in the five cases mentioned in the *uṣūl*.]

A woman who has been trebly divorced in the final illness of her husband inherits from her husband, but if she dies first, he does not inherit from her. The same ruling applies if the divorce was a single one and he dies of that illness after her *ᶜiddah* has finished. [She inherits from him because the Prophet ﷺ forbade excluding an heir by doing that. ᶜUthmān judged that the wife of ᶜAbd ar-Raḥmān ibn ᶜAwf inherit from him after her *ᶜiddah* was over. He had divorced her absolutely when he was ill and he died of that illness. The man does not inherit from her because she is unrelated to him by virtue of the divorce. Even if her *ᶜiddah* is over, she still inherits if he dies of that illness.]

If someone in good health pronounces a single divorce against his wife, they still inherit from one another as long as she is still in her *ᶜiddah*. If the *ᶜiddah* has finished, they do not inherit from one another. [There is no suspicion about divorce when the person is healthy.]

If a man marries in his illness, they do not inherit from one another. [Because the marriage is invalid.]

A maternal grandmother inherits a sixth as does a paternal grandmother. [Absolutely because it is established that the Prophet ﷺ gave her a sixth. (*Muwaṭṭa'*)]

If there are both of them, then the sixth is shared between them, unless the maternal grandmother is a degree closer, in which case she is more entitled to it because there is a text about her. If it is the paternal grandmother which is closer, then the sixth is shared between them. [The other inherits by way of analogy with the maternal grandmother. The sixth is equally divided unless there is a generational difference. If, however, it is the paternal one which is closer, they share in the sixth because her position is based on analogy, not text.] According to Mālik, only two grandmothers inherit: the father's mother and the mother's mother or their respective mothers. Zayd ibn Thābit is reported to have allowed three grandmothers to inherit: one on the mother's side and two on the father's side: the father's mother and the mother of the father's father. None of the Khalīfahs is reported to have allowed more than two grandmothers to inherit. [They take their place in their absence since the nearer excludes the further as we stated.] (*Ibid.* Commentary in parenthesis, ᶜAbd as-Samīᶜ al-Ābī al-Azharī, *al-Fawākih ad-dānī*)

Al-Ḥajb wa'l-Ḥaram – Prevention from Inheritance

Ḥajb means prevention. In *Sharīcah,* the term is used where a person is prevented from inheriting because of some impediments. One who comes under this category will either be totally or partially excluded. The total exclusion is called "*ḥajb ḥarmānī*" and the partial exclusion is termed "*ḥajb nafsānī*". According to Muslim Jurists, the total exclusion does not apply to sons' and daughter's father and mother, and husband and wife. But the others will be subject to total exclusion, e.g., the daughter of the son in the presence of a son or two daughters; brothers on the father's side or the grandfather's side and so on. It is also the view of jurists that if an heir is excluded on the ground of impediment, he will be considered as if he does not exist at all. His physical presence will not affect others. For example, if there is a mother and two Christian brothers, they will not prevent the mother from getting a third, but if the brothers are Muslims they are only prevented partially by the presence of the father. They reduce her from the range of a third to the range of a sixth.

cAbdullāh ibn Mascūd said that the presence of someone who is either prevented totally or partially would affect the other, e.g., a son who had murdered someone, would affect the others. In a case where there are son, mother and father, the presence of the son who has killed will have the effect of reducing them to the range of one sixth.

The Scheme of *Radd* (Return)

After giving away the shares of the heirs, if there is any residue left and there is no residuary heir, the remainder reverts to the *bayt al-māl* or to the sharers in proportion to their shares. In the *Sharīcah* this is called *radd*.

The jurists have differences of opinion on the question of *radd*. Some of them are of the view that the residue will go to the public treasury (*bayt al-māl*) in the case of *radd,* while others say that it will be divided among the Qur'ānic heirs.

Zayd ibn Thābit was of the opinion that where *radd* is applied the remainder will go to the *bayt al-māl*. Imām Mālik adopted this view as did Imām ash-Shāfiᶜī and Ibn Ḥazm. They said that in the Qur'ān Allah has provided for the specific share of every heir. If we add anything to it, we are exceeding the laws of Allah.

Imām ash-Shāfiᶜī said that in the verses of the Qur'ān, Allah has mentioned the sister and has given her a maximum of a half if she is alone. If she is given the total share by applying *radd*, we are in fact acting completely against the clear rule of the Qur'ān.

Other Companions of the Prophet ﷺ, various Followers, Imām Abū Ḥanīfah and Imām Aḥmad ibn Ḥanbal adopted the principle of *radd*, i.e. distributing what remains among the heirs.

Jurists who adopted this position said that the remainder will go to Qur'ānic heirs excluding spouses. Recent Ḥanafī jurists took the view that if if there is no *bayt al-māl* or the *bayt al-māl* is corrupt and if there are no relatives other than the spouse then, only in this case, the spouse will inherit the rest of the wealth.

Sayyidunā ᶜUthmān ibn ᶜAffān and Jābir ibn Zayd were of the opinion that we should apply *radd* to all the Qur'ānic heirs including spouses.

ᶜAbdullāh ibn Masᶜūd said that we should apply *radd* but should exclude spouses, daughters of the son in the presence of a proper daughter, uterine sisters and brothers in the presence of the mother, and consanguine sisters in the presence of full sisters and the grandmother.

ᶜAbdullāh ibn ᶜAbbās, on the contrary, excluded spouses and the grandmother.

However, let us not allow the differences of the Companions to confuse us, for then we will make a simple situation unnecessarily complicated.

THE DIFFERENCES OF THE COMPANIONS

Qāḍī ᶜIyāḍ said:

> There was among them a degree of difference of opinion in some of the things which they discussed which could keep the *muqallid* in a perpetual state of confusion, and require of him the kind of reflection and review for which he is not yet prepared. And indeed the full elaboration of questions, resolving of problems, and setting-out the discussions, only came about in response to

those matters, the appearance of which had been anticipated, after the Companions were gone.

Consequently, the *Tābiᶜūn*, the Followers, came and reflected on the differences of opinions of the Companions, and built on the foundations which they had laid down. Then after them came the *ᶜulamā'* from among the Followers of the Followers. By that time, the occurrences which had happened had already become many and the problematic events had already occurred, while *fatwas* regarding all of this had branched out into many details. Therefore they gathered together the opinions of them all, and they committed their *fiqh* to memory.

They sought out the differences of opinion of the earlier generations as well as their areas of agreement, but they were cautious about the matter of this disagreement spreading and of its getting out of control. Therefore they did *ijtihād* regarding all these parts of the Sunnah, and of the precise articulation of fundamental principles. They asked questions and they got answers. They built up the foundations of the basic precepts and they made accessible the basic principles. Upon them they delineated the solutions to problems and events and they put them down in writing for the people, and organised them. Each of them worked on the basis of the inspiration he was given and the accomplishment to which Allah had guided them. So they became the ultimate in the science of *uṣūl* and of the specific details of the *Sharīᶜah* in the matters of agreement and disagreement. And on the basis of this knowledge which had come to them, they made *qiyās*, analogy, according to the indications, and the similarities that they had got. May Allah be pleased with all of them and may He give them the full extent of the reward of their *ijtihād*.

Therefore it is an individual obligation that falls on the ordinary *muqallid* and the student of knowledge in his beginning stages, to take recourse in his *taqlīd* to these great men, or the explicit texts regarding the problems and events that befall him. Recourse must be had to them regarding all of these matters which are problematic because of the fact that they were immersed in knowledge of *Sharīᶜah* and it literally revolved around them.

They alone have precise understanding of the schools, of who had gone before, and the earlier generations, and that knowledge is enough for all who have come after them in later generations.

Nevertheless, it is simply not possible that all of these earlier *fuqahā'* can be simultaneous objects of *taqlīd* regarding the most difficult problems and the majority of questions, because of their differences among themselves caused by conflicting opinions about the fundamental principles upon which they built. Moreover, it is not valid for the *muqallid* to do *taqlīd* of any among them merely on the basis of personal whim or chance that he has come upon a decision on the basis of what he happened to find the people of his region doing, or his family doing.

The portion of *ijtihād* that falls to his lot in this case, is that he seek to discuss by reflection which of them was the most knowledgeable and come to know which of them is most worthy of being an object of *taqlīd* from among all of them so that in his practice and his *fatwas*, the ordinary man can trust him and rely on him and trust that in his acts of worship, he had taken on himself only what that *mujtahid* had and discerned as correct. The ordinary man therefore must give to the most knowledgeable among the adherents to the schools of these earlier *fuqahā'*, the status which by right, he deserves. It is not permissible for him that he go beyond them in his seekings of *fatwas* to one who does not follow the opinion of this school. For as some of the Shaykhs have said, "The Imām is, with regard to one who adheres to his school, like the Prophet ﷺ is with regard to his *Ummah*." This has been expressed quite correctly, and the correct way will become clear to those who have insight, and eyes with which to see, on the basis of what we have elaborated and the stipulations we have laid down.

(Qāḍī ᶜIyāḍ, *Tartīb al-madārik, bāb tarjīḥ madhhab Mālik wa al-ḥujjah fī wujūb taqlīdihi wa taqdīmihi ᶜalā ghayrihi min al-a'immah*, as cited by: as-Sufi, Shaykh Abdalqadir, *Root Islamic Education*)

What the Qāḍī is saying is that we are utterly reliant on the Imāms of the *madhhabs* for discriminating between the positions adopted by and the verdicts issued by the Companions and the earliest generations, and if we do not take their understanding we will simply be utterly confused. Moreover, we are bound to work out which of the Imāms was the most discerning and most knowledgeable, and not to emulate an Imām simply because he was the traditional Imām of our culture or of our family.

Thus, in essence most *fiqh* differences that matter can be reduced to the differences between the four *madhhabs*. In this case Imām Mālik and ash-Shāfiʿī agreed on returning the residue to the *bayt al-māl* after the heirs have inherited, and Abū Ḥanīfah and Aḥmad ibn Ḥanbal agreed on redistributing it among the heirs, although differing on some points in how that is to be done. Therefore the examples below are of how *radd* is performed in the Ḥanafī *madhhab*. It is necessarily somewhat complex involving as it does more of the same mathematics of fractions that we have already seen.

Examples of *Radd* according to the Ḥanafī *Madhhab*

The scenarios in which there is *radd* are of four types;

1. There is no husband or wife (*man la yuradd*) and only one type of those who receive obligatory shares (*man yuradd ʿalayhim*)

2. There is no husband or wife and more than one type of those who receive obligatory shares

3. There is a husband or wife and only one type of those who receive obligatory shares

4. There is no husband or wife and more than one type of those who receive obligatory shares

Hence there are four rules for *radd* as follows:

1. If there is no husband or wife and only one type of those who receive obligatory shares then the *mas'alah* (denominator) will be according to the number of heads, e.g. if there are two daughters, then the denominator will be two and they will get a half each, and if there are three they will get a third each.

2. If there is no husband or wife and there is more than one type of those who receive obligatory shares then the denominator will be according to the total number of shares, e.g. a daughter and a mother. The daughter should inherit a half i.e. three-sixths and the mother should get a sixth as their obligatory shares. The total number of shares is thus four (3+1=4) so the daughter will be given three-quarters and the mother a quarter of the remainder.

3. If there is a husband or wife and only one type of those who receive obligatory shares then give the husband or wife their

share from the lowest possible denominator and the remaining portion will be dealt with as follows:

a. If the remaining shares can be distributed amongst the number of heads of those who receive obligatory shares equally then they should be distributed accordingly, e.g. a husband and three daughters. The husband gets a quarter as his obligatory share and the three daughters share two-thirds as obligatory shares. The husband will take a quarter of the remainder, because the denominator will be four (lowest possible denominator for the husband) due to his inheriting a quarter as an obligatory share, and there are three-quarters of the remainder remaining which can easily be distributed amongst the three daughters.

Thus, because in the obligatory shares the husband takes a quarter and the three daughters share two-thirds, then we consider the estate to consist of twelve shares, since four and three are both factors of twelve. Thus, the husband takes three shares, and the three daughters share two-thirds of twelve, i.e. eight shares and there is one share left. It is better then to consider the *aṣl* to be 36 shares, the husband taking nine shares, and the three daughters sharing twenty-four, thus taking eight shares each, with a remainder of three shares.

Now for the remainder, it is divided into four because of the husband's quarter, he taking one share, and the three daughters taking one each. But these would be fractions, and so it is better to go back to the beginning and revise our *aṣl* to 144 shares, i.e. 36 X 4. The husband takes thirty-six shares as obligatory, the three daughters sharing ninety-six and thus taking thirty-two shares each, leaving twelve shares as a remainder, the husband taking three, and the daughters each taking three.

b. If the remaining shares cannot be distributed amongst those who receive obligatory shares equally then the number of heads of those who receive obligatory shares should be multiplied by the denominator of the husband or wife and the result will be the *taṣḥīḥ*, e.g. a husband and five daughters.

The husband gets a quarter as his obligatory share so the denominator will be four.

The remainder cannot be distributed amongst the five daughters so five (the number of heads) will be multiplied by four (the *mas'alah*). The resulting twenty will be the *taṣḥīḥ*. The husband will get a quarter of twenty, which is five, and the remaining fifteen will be distributed amongst the five daughters giving them three each.

Note: If there is a relationship between the number of heads and the denominator such that one is a factor of the other, the *wifq*[1] of the number of heads will be multiplied by the *mas'alah*, e.g. a husband and six daughters.

The husband is given a quarter and a remainder of three needs to be distributed among the six daughters. However rather than multiplying three by six we can find a number which goes into both which is three. Three goes into three once and into six twice so the *wifq* of six is two. Two will be multiplied by four so the *taṣḥīḥ* is eight. The husband gets two eighths, and the six daughters get an eighth share each.

4. If there is a husband or wife and more than one type of those who receive obligatory shares, give the husband or wife his/her share as you did in rule No. 3. Then make a separate *mas'alah* for those who receive obligatory shares as you did in rule No. 2.

If the share remaining from the *mas'alah* of the husband or wife can be divided by the *mas'alah* of those who receive obligatory shares then there is no need for further *taṣḥīḥ*, the *mas'alah* of the husband or wife will be the *mas'alah* for both groups, e.g. a husband, two maternal brothers and a mother.

The *mas'alah* of the husband is four. A separate *mas'alah* will be made for those who receive obligatory shares, the mother receiving a sixth and the brothers a third or two-sixths, i.e. one sixth each.

Therefore the *mas'alah* will be six which will be changed to the number of shares, three (as in rule No. 2). The share remaining from the *mas'alah* of the husband or wife is three and the *mas'alah* of those who receive obligatory shares is also three so the final *mas'alah* will be four with the husband getting a quarter and the mother and brothers also receiving a quarter each.

If the remaining shares cannot be divided by the *mas'alah* of those who receive obligatory shares then the *mas'alah* of those who receive obligatory shares will be multiplied by the remainder from the *mas'alah* of the husband or wife, and the result will be the *taṣḥīḥ*.

Finally, to give each inheritor their share you should multiply the shares of each person in the first group by the *mas'alah* of the second group and then multiply the shares of each person in the second group by the remainder of the first *mas'alah*. Each result will be that inheritor's share, e.g. a husband, a daughter and a mother.

Firstly, the husband will be given a quarter and a separate *mas'alah* will be made for those who receive obligatory shares which will be four (the daughter taking three and the mother one).

The two fours will be multiplied to give a result of 16 which will be the final *mas'alah*.

The husband will receive a quarter which is four.

The daughter will receive nine (three multiplied by the remainder of the first *mas'alah* which is also three)

The mother will receive three (1 X 3=3) (Ajmeri, Mawlānā Maḥmūd Ḥasan, *Muᶜīn al-farā'iḍ*, translated by Nuᶜmān ᶜAbd ar-Raḥīm)

Dhawū al-arḥām – Uterine Relations

The *dhawū al-arḥām* or uterine heirs are those who are neither Qur'ānic sharers nor the residuary (agnatic) heirs or *ᶜaṣabah*. *Dhawū al-arḥām* literally means kindred who are female agnates and cognates, whether male or female. The *dhawū al-arḥām* form a vast and complicated class of heirs.

Ibn Juzayy al-Kalbī enumerated the *dhawū al-arḥām* thus:

> ᶜAlī ibn Abī Ṭālib, ᶜAbdullāh ibn Masᶜūd, Abū Ḥanīfah and Ibn Ḥanbal added that relations on the women's side inherit, and there are fourteen of them: the daughters' children, sisters' children, the brother's daughters, the paternal uncle's daughters, the maternal uncle and his child, the paternal aunt and the maternal aunt and their children, the maternal grandfather, and the mother's paternal uncle, and the son of the mother's brother, and the daughter of the paternal uncle.
>
> They unanimously agreed that they do not inherit if there are *ᶜaṣabah* nor if there are those who take fixed shares except for what is left over from them. (Al-Kalbī, Ibn Juzayy, *al-Qawānīn al-*

fiqhiyyah, al-kitāb al-ᶜāshir fī al-farā'iḍ wa al-waṣāyā, al-bāb al-awwal fī ᶜadad al-wārithīn wa ṣifat al-warathah)

Famous learned Companions of the Prophet ﷺ like Zayd ibn Thābit as well as jurists such as Imām Mālik, ash-Shāfiᶜī and the Ẓāhirīs are of the opinion that these *dhawū al-arḥām* have no place in the Islamic scheme of inheritance. Hence, they do not inherit in any circumstances. Others of the Companions, the jurists of Kūfa and Baṣra, including Imam Abū Ḥanīfah, say that on the contrary, *dhawū al-arḥām* do inherit. Imām Mālik, Imām ash-Shāfiᶜī and other jurists' opinions are that the question of shares of inheritance cannot be settled by the use of *qiyās* – analogical deduction, but must be based on the Qur'ān, the Sunnah and *ijmāᶜ* – the consensus of opinion of the *ᶜulamā'*. Ḥanafī jurists also base their argument on the Qur'ān the Sunnah and *ijmāᶜ*. They maintain that in the Qur'ān, the following verse speaks of the rights of *dhawū al-arḥām*:

وَأُولُوا الْأَرْحَامِ بَعْضُهُمْ أَوْلَىٰ بِبَعْضٍ فِي كِتَابِ اللَّهِ

But blood relations are closer to one another in the Book of Allah. (Sūrat at-Tawbah 9: 75)

Ibn Juzayy al-Kalbī said;

Some said that this abrogates inheritance between the Emigrants and the Helpers [who are mentioned in the same *āyah*: *"Those who have īmān and make hijrah later on and accompany you in doing jihād, they also are of your number."*] Mālik said, "It is not about inheritance." Abū Ḥanīfah said, "It is about inheritance," and because of it he regarded it as obligatory for the maternal uncle and aunt and others of *dhawū al-arḥām* to inherit. (Al-Kalbī, Ibn Juzayy, *Kitāb at-tashīl li ᶜulūm at-tanzīl*)

A Missing Person's (*mafqūd*) Right of Inheritance

When someone is missing and his whereabouts cannot be traced what will happen to his property?

The Muslim jurists say that according to the concept *istiṣḥāb* (legal presumption of continuance of conditions) we presume that the person is still alive until the contrary is proved. According to rules governing inheritance, no one is to be inherited from until he is definitely proved dead, and no one will be allowed to inherit until it is proved that he was still alive when the propositus died. Therefore according to *istiṣḥāb* the person is not to be inherited from until his death is declared either by evidence or by a decree of a court.

Ibn Juzayy said:

> Fourth section, concerning the missing person, and this is the person who is absent so that all trace of him is lost and no news is known of him. There are four types: those who are in Muslim lands, those in enemy lands, those lost in fighting between the Muslims and the *kuffār*, and those lost in fighting in civil war.
>
> As for those missing in Muslim lands, if his wife raises the matter to the *qāḍī*, he charges her with proving the validity of their marriage and of his absence, and then he seeks news about him, for that purpose writing to the different lands. Then if he comes upon news about him, he is not a missing person, and he writes to him that either he must return or declare divorce. If he continues in this injurious behaviour [the *qāḍī*] will declare the divorce. If [the *qāḍī*] does not come upon any news of him, and neither his life nor death is known, then a term is set for him, four years for a free man and two years for a slave, from the day on which she raised the matter. Then when the term expires she perfoms the *ᶜiddah* of the widow [of four months and ten days], and then she may remarry if she wishes. Abū Ḥanīfah and ash-Shāfiᶜī said that the wife of a missing person does not become free to marry until his death is reliably established. …
>
> As for his property, a stop is put on it and it is not inherited until it is known that he is dead, or a term is set such that no one would ordinarily live that long, but people differed about that, the well known position being seventy years, but some said eighty, ninety or a hundred and Abū Ḥanīfah said a hundred and twenty. All of that is reckoned from the beginning of his life, so if he goes missing when he is seventy years old, one waits ten years after that according to the best known position.
>
> (Al-Kalbī, Ibn Juzayy, *al-Qawānīn al-fiqhiyyah, al-qism ath-thānī min al-qawānīn al-fiqhiyyah fī al-muᶜāmlāt, al-kitāb al-awwal fī an-nikāḥ, al-bāb as-sābiᶜ fī asbāb al-khiyār*)

About the missing person, Imām Mālik and Imām Abū Ḥanīfah

say that if his relative dies after he is declared missing but before he is declared dead, the relative has no entitlement to inherit,[20] but the missing person will inherit from those of his relatives who died before he was declared missing. As far as his own estate is concerned, it is to be kept until he is declared dead. It is after a judicial declaration of his death that his relatives will inherit.

According to Imām ash-Shāfiʿī and Imām Aḥmad ibn Ḥanbal, the missing person will be entitled to inherit from all his relatives who have passed away after him, his share is to be added to his original property until the time when the court declares him dead. Imām Mālik and Imām Abū Ḥanīfah say that the evidence of *istiṣḥāb* is considered only as a shield to protect his estate, but will not entitle him to inherit others, i.e. his estate will be kept entire until he is legally declared dead, but he will not inherit from anyone during that period; but Imām ash-Shāfiʿī and Imām Aḥmad ibn Ḥanbal say it helps to protect his estate as well as giving him the right to inherit others and will be both a shield as well as a sword. If such a case arises, it can be solved in two ways. If we assume that the missing person is either alive or dead, and his daughter dies leaving husband, mother, full sister and the father, who is missing, then apart from the fact of the father being missing, this case has other considerations that are better to clarify first. Allah, exalted is He, said:

يُوصِيكُمُ اللَّهُ فِي أَوْلَادِكُمْ لِلذَّكَرِ مِثْلُ حَظِّ الْأُنثَيَيْنِ فَإِن كُنَّ نِسَاءً فَوْقَ اثْنَتَيْنِ فَلَهُنَّ ثُلُثَا مَا تَرَكَ وَإِن
كَانَتْ وَاحِدَةً فَلَهَا النِّصْفُ وَلِأَبَوَيْهِ لِكُلِّ وَاحِدٍ مِّنْهُمَا السُّدُسُ مِمَّا تَرَكَ إِن كَانَ لَهُ وَلَدٌ فَإِن لَّمْ يَكُن
لَّهُ وَلَدٌ وَوَرِثَهُ أَبَوَاهُ فَلِأُمِّهِ الثُّلُثُ فَإِن كَانَ لَهُ إِخْوَةٌ فَلِأُمِّهِ السُّدُسُ مِن بَعْدِ وَصِيَّةٍ يُوصِي بِهَا أَوْ دَيْنٍ
آبَاؤُكُمْ وَأَبْنَاؤُكُمْ لَا تَدْرُونَ أَيُّهُمْ أَقْرَبُ لَكُمْ نَفْعاً فَرِيضَةً مِّنَ اللَّهِ إِنَّ اللَّهَ كَانَ عَلِيماً حَكِيماً وَلَكُمْ
نِصْفُ مَا تَرَكَ أَزْوَاجُكُمْ إِن لَّمْ يَكُن لَّهُنَّ وَلَدٌ فَإِن كَانَ لَهُنَّ وَلَدٌ فَلَكُمُ الرُّبُعُ مِمَّا تَرَكْنَ مِن بَعْدِ وَصِيَّةٍ
يُوصِينَ بِهَا أَوْ دَيْنٍ وَلَهُنَّ الرُّبُعُ مِمَّا تَرَكْتُمْ إِن لَّمْ يَكُن لَّكُمْ وَلَدٌ فَإِن كَانَ لَكُمْ وَلَدٌ فَلَهُنَّ الثُّمُنُ مِمَّا تَرَكْتُم

مِّن بَعْدِ وَصِيَّةٍ تُوصُونَ بِهَا أَوْ دَيْنٍ وَإِن كَانَ رَجُلٌ يُورَثُ كَلالَةً أَو امْرَأَةٌ وَلَهُ أَخٌ أَوْ أُخْتٌ فَلِكُلِّ وَاحِدٍ مِّنْهُمَا السُّدُسُ فَإِن كَانُوٓاْ أَكْثَرَ مِن ذَلِكَ فَهُمْ شُرَكَاءُ فِي الثُّلُثِ مِن بَعْدِ وَصِيَّةٍ يُوصَى بِهَا أَوْ دَيْنٍ غَيْرَ مُضَآرٍّ وَصِيَّةً مِّنَ اللَّهِ وَاللَّهُ عَلِيمٌ حَلِيمٌ

Allah instructs you regarding your children: A male receives the same as the share of two females. If there are more than two daughters they receive two-thirds of what you leave. If she is one on her own she receives a half. Each of your parents receives a sixth of what you leave if you have children. If you are childless and your heirs are your parents your mother receives a third. If you have brothers or sisters your mother receives a sixth, after any bequest you make or any debts. With regard to your fathers and your sons, you do not know which of them is going to benefit you more. These are obligatory shares from Allah. Allah is All-Knowing, All-Wise.

You receive half of what your wives leave if they are childless. If they have children you receive a quarter of what they leave after any bequest they make or any debts. They receive a quarter of what you leave if you are childless. If you have children they receive an eighth of what you leave after any bequest you make or any debts. If a man or woman has no direct heirs, but has a brother or sister, each of them receives a sixth. If there are more than that they share in a third after any bequest you make or any debts, making sure that no one's rights are prejudiced. This is an instruction from Allah. Allah is All-Knowing, All-Forbearing. (Sūrat an-Nisā' 4: 10-11)

Ibn Juzayy al-Kalbī said in commentary on these *āyāt*:

"*...And [if] your heirs are your parents your mother receives a third*". Allah only appointed a third for the mother on two conditions, first that there are no children, and the second, that the parents take the entire inheritance. For that reason the letter *waw* comes in to conjoin one condition to the other. He was silent about the father's share because it is understood since nothing remains after the third but two-thirds, and there is no other heir but the parents, so that necessarily requires that the father takes the remains of the property, i.e. two-thirds. "*If you have brothers or sisters your mother receives a sixth*" The *ᶜulamā'* agree unanimously that three siblings make the mother return to inheriting a sixth, and they differed as to whether two siblings do, the majority taking the position that two of them do return her to taking a sixth, but the *madhhab* of Ibn ᶜAbbās is that they do not, but that two are like a single brother. His argument is that the word *ikhwah* – "*brothers or sisters*" – is not used for two because it is a plural and not a dual and the least amount of a plural is three. Others said that the plural form of words may be used for two such as in His words, "*We were Witness to their*[21] *judgement,*" (Sūrat al-Anbiyā' 21: 78) and "*How they*[22] *climbed up to the Upper Room,*" (Sūrah Ṣād 38: 21) and "*and at both*[23] *ends of the day*" (Sūrat al-Anbiyā' 21: 130) and they argued by his words ﷺ, "Two and more are a group (*jamāᶜah*)." (Ibn Mājah, *kitāb iqāmat aṣ-ṣalāh wa as-sunnah fīhā, bāb al-ithnayn jamāᶜah,* and Ibn ᶜAdī from Abū Mūsā; Aḥmad and aṭ-Ṭabarānī in *al-Kabīr* from Abū Umāmah; ad-Dāraquṭnī in *as-Sunan* from ᶜAmr; Ibn Saᶜd, al-Baghawī and al-Bāwardī from al-Ḥakam ibn ᶜUmayr) and Mālik said, "The Sunnah is already existent that '*brothers or sisters*' are two and more," and his *madhhab* is that the least amount of the plural is two. So on this basis, the parents are blocked from receiving a third and instead take a sixth whether the two are full siblings or consanguine or uterine or mixed, whether they are two males, two females or a male and a female. Then if there is a father with them, he inherits the remainder of the property [as *ᶜaṣabah*] and the siblings get nothing according to the dominant majority, so that they both prevent the father from inheriting [a fixed share] and they themselves do not inherit. Some people[24] said that they take the sixth which they prevented the mother inheriting. And if there is no father, then they inherit. (Al-Kalbī, Ibn Juzayy, *Kitāb at-tashīl li ᶜulūm at-tanzīl*)

Thus one of the following two cases will take place when, for example, a daughter dies while her father is missing:

1. Presumed dead

His daughter dies leaving a husband who takes a half, her mother who takes a third, her father's sister, who is excluded by the father, and the missing father who takes the remainder of the remainder.

Thus, we consider the estate to consist of six shares, because two and three are factors of six, then the husband takes three shares, the mother takes one share, since this is a third of the remaining three shares, the father's sister gets nothing as she is excluded, and the father takes the remaining two shares of the remainder. However, the father is missing, presumed dead, and so he is excluded. Thus, the husband takes a half, i.e. three shares, the mother a third or two shares and the father's sister a half or three shares. This would result in an inheritance of eight sixths thus exceeding the total estate. So we must apply *ᶜawl* and consider the estate to consist of eighths, with the husband taking three shares, the mother two and the father's sister three. To consider the *aṣl* as twenty-four shares, we multiply by three, the husband taking nine shares, the mother six and the father's sister nine.

2. PRESUMED ALIVE

In the case where the father is missing presumed alive, the husband takes a half or three shares, the mother a third of the remainder or one share, the father's sister is blocked by the father, and the father takes the remainder of the remainder two shares. To make the *aṣl* twenty-four shares, we multiply by four, with the husband taking twelve shares, the mother four and the father eight.

In the above case we presume that the missing person is alive and his share is to be reserved until he is declared dead. The husband will get nine as his minimum share, the mother will get four as her minimum share and the full sister will be excluded by the father.

Notes

[1] Ibn Mājah, *Sunan,* edition prepared by Muḥammad Fu'ād ᶜAbd al-Bāqī, Dar Ihya at-Turath al-Arabi.
[2] Ibid
[3] i.e. great grandfather etc.
[4] Letournean, *Evolution of Marriage,* pp. 259-269
[5] See then the later adjustment for the use to which these three uncollected portions are put.
[6] i.e. the son has died before his daughter.
[7] Sūrat an-Nisā' 4: 11
[8] The grandson having died.
[9] The son having died.
[10] The son having died.
[11] Both the son and son's son having died.
[12] Uterine brothers and sisters share the same mother but not the same father.
[13] The differences of the Companions ❁ is one of the major reasons that it is obligatory to follow the *madhhab* of a *mujtahid* who is capable of reaching a decision about those matters about which they differed, and the *Ummah* are unanimously agreed that there are only four such *madhhabs* remaining: those of Mālik, Abū Ḥanīfah, ash-Shāfiᶜī and Aḥmad ibn Ḥanbal, may Allah have mercy on them.
[14] This case is taken in detail from *al-Fawākih ad-dānī* which is a *sharḥ* by ᶜAbd as-Samīᶜ al-Ābī al-Azharī on the *Risālah* of Ibn Abī Zayd al-Qayrawānī. The name *al-Akdariyyah* is mentioned in the *Ḥāshiyah* of ad-Dasūqī.
[15] An *ijmāᶜ* that has been achieved, particularly that of the Companions, cannot be overturned by a later dissenting voice, no matter

how persuasive. Thus, the later *'ijtihād'* decisions of people like Muḥammad ᶜAbduh and those who adhered to his view are not able to overturn clearly established decisions about which consensus was achieved in earlier generations. Thus a great deal of modernist Islam is simply invalid.

[16] Both the obligatory shares being stipulated by clear texts.

[17] Apart from the great authority and integrity of Sayyidunā ᶜUmar ﷺ, the real significance of many of his decisions is the fact that they were achieved while the great majority of the Companions were still alive and thus represent their consensus (*ijmāᶜ*), if they expressed no opposition to him.

[18] As in the *ḥadīth* from Abū ash-Shaykh, *al-Farā'iḍ*; al-Bayhaqī, *as-Sunan al-kubrā, kitāb al-farā'iḍ, bāb al-ᶜawl fī al-farā'iḍ*, as cited in *Kanz al-ᶜummāl*.

[19] See Chapter 12 on Divorce.

[20] If the relative had inherited before himself dying, then his heirs would inherit from the missing person when his death was declared.

[21] The pronoun *'their'* refers to Dāwūd and Sulaymān, peace be upon both of them, but is not in the dual but the plural form.

[22] The pronoun *'they'* refers to the two litigants who went to see Dāwūd ﷺ, but the plural form is used and not the dual.

[23] The word *'both ends'* (*aṭrāf*) is in the plural form rather than the dual.

[24] 'Some people' in the technical usage Ibn Juzayy employs in the *al-Qawānīn al-fiqhiyyah* means 'outside of the four *madhhabs*,' such as the Ẓāhirī school, for example.

[25] *Tawāfuq* is a mathematical rule. *Tawāfuq* between two numbers is when there is a common factor by which both the numbers can be divided. The amount of times that number goes into the numbers is called their *wifq*. This method is used to keep the numbers shorter.

Chapter 22

Disposal of Property

A. *Waṣiyyah*: Bequest

IN THE *JĀHILIYYAH* PERIOD BEFORE ISLAM, Arabs disposed of their property as they liked because no law concerning bequests or inheritance existed to guide them. They could make a bequest in favour of anyone, depriving their own parents, children and wives. At times the bequest was made in favour of rich and influential members of the clan.

Waṣiyyah 'bequest' comes from its Arabic root *waṣā* which means 'he conveyed.' In other words *waṣiyyah* means a gift of property by its owner to another, contingent on the giver's death. The legal Qur'ānic injunctions in respect of bequests or a will was revealed in Sūrat al-Baqarah in which Allah, exalted is He, says that it is the responsibility of the right-acting God-fearing persons to leave a *waṣiyyah* behind.

كُتِبَ عَلَيْكُمْ إِذَا حَضَرَ أَحَدَكُمُ الْمَوْتُ إِن تَرَكَ خَيْرًا الْوَصِيَّةُ لِلْوَالِدَيْنِ وَالْأَقْرَبِينَ بِالْمَعْرُوفِ حَقًّا
عَلَى الْمُتَّقِينَ فَمَن بَدَّلَهُ بَعْدَ مَا سَمِعَهُ فَإِنَّمَا إِثْمُهُ عَلَى الَّذِينَ يُبَدِّلُونَهُ إِنَّ اللَّهَ سَمِيعٌ عَلِيمٌ فَمَنْ خَافَ
مِن مُّوصٍ جَنَفًا أَوْ إِثْمًا فَأَصْلَحَ بَيْنَهُمْ فَلَا إِثْمَ عَلَيْهِ إِنَّ اللَّهَ غَفُورٌ رَّحِيمٌ

It is prescribed for you, when death approaches one of you and if he has some goods to leave, to make a will in favour of his parents and relatives, correctly and fairly: a duty for all those who have taqwā. Then if anyone alters it after hearing it, the crime is on the part of those who alter it. Allah is All-Hearing, All-Knowing. But if someone fears bias or wrongdoing on the part of the person making the will, and puts things right between the people involved, in that case he has not committed any crime. Allah is Ever-Forgiving, Most Merciful. (Sūrat al-Baqarah 2: 180-2)

These verses were revealed when no law was yet fixed in the matter of inheritance. Later in Sūrat an-Nisā' complete guidance was given to Muslims concerning inheritance and fixed portions for each heir. The Islamic law in respect of inheritances and the will is further clarified by the Prophet ﷺ in the following manner:

عَنْ سَعْدِ بْنِ أَبِي وَقَّاصٍ رَضِيَ اللَّهُ عَنْهُ قَالَ جَاءَ النَّبِيُّ صَلَّى اللَّهُ عَلَيْهِ وَسَلَّمَ يَعُودُنِي وَأَنَا بِمَكَّةَ
وَهُوَ يَكْرَهُ أَنْ يَمُوتَ بِالْأَرْضِ الَّتِي هَاجَرَ مِنْهَا . . .قُلْتُ يَا رَسُولَ اللَّهِ أُوصِي بِمَالِي كُلِّهِ قَالَ لَا
قُلْتُ فَالشَّطْرُ قَالَ لَا قُلْتُ الثُّلُثُ قَالَ فَالثُّلُثُ وَالثُّلُثُ كَثِيرٌ إِنَّكَ أَنْ تَدَعَ وَرَثَتَكَ أَغْنِيَاءَ خَيْرٌ مِنْ أَنْ
تَدَعَهُمْ عَالَةً يَتَكَفَّفُونَ النَّاسَ فِي أَيْدِيهِمْ وَإِنَّكَ مَهْمَا أَنْفَقْتَ مِنْ نَفَقَةٍ فَإِنَّهَا صَدَقَةٌ حَتَّى اللُّقْمَةُ الَّتِي
تَرْفَعُهَا إِلَى فِي امْرَأَتِكَ وَعَسَى اللَّهُ أَنْ يَرْفَعَكَ فَيَنْتَفِعَ بِكَ نَاسٌ وَيُضَرَّ بِكَ آخَرُونَ وَلَمْ يَكُنْ لَهُ يَوْمَئِذٍ
إِلَّا ابْنَةٌ

From Saᶜd ibn Abī Waqqāṣ ؓ there is that he said, "The Prophet ﷺ came to visit me [when I was sick] while I was in Makkah" – and he disliked for him to die in the land from which he had emigrated – "…I said, 'Messenger of Allah, should I bequeath all of my wealth?' He said, 'No.' I said, 'Then a half?' He said, 'No.' I said, 'A third.' He said, 'Then a third, and a third is a great deal. That you should leave your heirs free of need is better than that you should leave them needy begging from people with their hands. And whatever you spend of maintenance it is a *ṣadaqah* even until the morsel which you raise to your wife's mouth. And perhaps Allah will raise you up so that some people will benefit from you and others will be harmed by you.'" And he only had one daughter at that time. (Al-Bukhārī, *kitāb al-waṣāyā, bāb an yatruka warathatahu aghniyā' khayrun min an yatakaffafuna an-nās*)

The Islamic Law in respect of inheritances and bequests is further clarified:

1. The bequest (*waṣiyyah*) can be made only for a third of the entire property and no more.
2. No one can make a bequest in respect of any of those relatives whose portions are fixed in the Qur'ān; one cannot bequeath them any increase or decrease through bequests, nor can one deprive a legal heir through a bequest to someone else. However, if someone does that with the permission of the heirs it is acceptable.

Ibn Juzayy al-Kalbī ﷺ said:

The essential elements of a bequest are three:

1. The testator, and that is every free, owner [of property] who possesses discrimination, so that it is not valid for slaves, nor for the insane except during the state of recovery, nor children who do not possess discrimination, but it is valid from children who do possess discrimination if they grasp that it is an act of worship (*qurbah*), contrary to the position of Abū Ḥanīfah, and from someone retarded, and from a *kāfir* except if he bequeaths wine or pigs to a Muslim.

2. The person who is the object of the bequest, and that is every person for whom it is conceivable that he own property whether older or younger, free or slave, whether he is alive or expected to be alive such as an unborn person but excluding heirs for it is unanimously agreed that it is not valid for them, but if all the rest of the heirs permit it then it is permissible according to the Four [Imāms] but contrary to the Ẓāhiriyyah. If the person who is the recipient of the bequest dies before the testator then the bequest is invalidated. It is stipulated that the person who is the recipient of the bequest should accept it if he is competent to receive it, just as with gifts, contrary to ash-Shāfiʿī.

Derivative ruling: whoever makes a bequest in favour of someone who is dead thinking him alive then the bequest is invalid by unanimous agreement, but if he bequeaths him after knowing of his death, then it is valid and is for the heirs of the recipient of the bequest, contrary to the two of them [Abū Ḥanīfah and ash-Shāfiʿī].

3. That which is bequeathed, and this is of five types:

a. That which is obligatory on the heirs to execute and this is a testament to discharge an obligatory act of worship such as *zakāh*, acts of expiation, or a recommended act such as *ṣadaqah*, freeing a slave and the best of which is making a bequest for close relatives.

b. That about which there is a difference of opinion as to whether it is obligatory to execute it or not, such as leaving a testament to buy or sell something.

c. That which if the heirs wish they may execute it or reject it, and it is of two sorts: making a bequest for an heir, and making a bequest for more than a third.

d. That which it is not permissible to execute, and this is a testament demanding something unacceptable such as exaggerated mourning etc.

e. That the execution of which is disliked, such as bequeathing something which is *makrūh*. (Al-Kalbī, Ibn Juzayy, *al-Qawānīn al-fiqhiyyah, al-kitāb al-ᶜāshir fī al-farā'iḍ wa al-waṣāyā, al-bāb al-ᶜāshir fī al-waṣāyā*)

In spite of the clear guidance in respect of shares of inheritance in the Qur'ān and the Sunnah, *waṣiyyah* still remains an operative injunction up to the maximum of one-third of one's property but should be done with a strict sense of justice and equity. This provision can be used to leave something for those who are helpless but are not recipients of Qur'ānic shares like the children of those sons or daughters who have already died during the lifetime of their grandfathers. Similarly, there may be some really needy persons outside the family circle whom one wishes to help through bequests, or one would like to spend money for public welfare purposes which one fears the heirs would not willingly support after his death if he did not make adequate provision through his bequests. The most cherished matter is to leave some property as a *waqf* or endowment, whose income or use is dedicated to some charitable end, since the reward of such a thing accrues to the dead person as long as the *waqf* endures.

In the verses of injunctions concerning inheritance it is made clear that the obligatory shares will be distributed only after the debt left behind by the deceased is paid and the bequest is carried out. There is a consensus of the *ᶜulamā'* that although the bequest is mentioned before the debt, the debt should be paid first and then the bequest, and then the distribution of the shares to the heirs will follow. The point that has been emphasised in verse 12 of Sūrat an-Nisā' is that the man paying a debt or making a bequest should remember that Allah is watching him and knows all his intentions. He is not borrowing money or making bequests in order to deprive the Qur'ānic beneficiaries of their legitimate shares after his death.

The temptation to do so becomes greater in respect of the collaterals when the deceased dies leaving neither children nor parents (*kalālah*) and the property is to be given to distant relatives. He might think that rather than property going to collaterals, it is better that he give it away through bequests or through the pretext of debt. This will be against the letter and the spirit of the law of inheritance.

A Muslim who owns property is given permission to bequeath his property for a charitable object or to anyone excepting a legal heir. This is called *waṣiyyah*. The making of a will is specially recommended. The Noble Qur'ān speaks of the making of a will as a duty incumbent upon a Muslim when he leaves sufficient property for his heirs. The Prophet ﷺ is reported to have said:

عَنْ عَبْدِ اللَّهِ بْنِ عُمَرَ، أَنَّ رَسُولَ اللَّهِ ﷺ قَالَ : مَا حَقُّ امْرِئٍ مُسْلِمٍ لَهُ شَيْءٌ يُوصِي فِيهِ، يَبِيتُ لَيْلَتَيْنِ، إِلَّا وَوَصِيَّتُهُ عِنْدَهُ مَكْتُوبَةٌ

> It is narrated from ᶜAbdullāh ibn ᶜUmar ﷺ that the Messenger of Allah ﷺ said: "It is the duty of a Muslim man who has something to be given as a bequest not to spend two nights without writing a will about it." (Imām Mālik, *al-Muwaṭṭa'*, Book 37: Wills and Testaments Section 1: Command to Write Testaments)

However, this duty, or right, is subject to certain limitations. In the first place, not more than one-third of the property can be disposed of by will. Secondly, no will can be made in favour of an heir, but as expressly stated in the Noble Qur'ān, the making of a will is incumbent only on well-to-do people.

The reason for limiting the bequest to one-third is clearly stated in the aforementioned *ḥadīth* of the Prophet ﷺ: "That you should leave your heirs free of need is better than that you should leave them needy begging from people with their hands." And the reason for excluding the heirs is that no injustice may be done to certain heirs at the expense of others. A *waṣiyyah* which is against these principles would be illegal and invalid to that extent. It may be added that if a property in respect of which a bequest is made is encumbered with debt, the debt is payable before the will is executed. If the amount of the *waṣiyyah* exceeds one-third, it will not be executed except where the heirs give their consent.

Someone who makes *waṣiyyah* is called *mūṣī* in Arabic. It should be noted that the *waṣiyyah* takes effect only after the death of the *mūṣī*. For a valid *waṣiyyah*, he must be *mumayyiz*, i.e. someone who can discriminate between what is good or bad, who should know that he is really doing good and not depriving anyone of his due rights and that he is not disobeying Allah. This condition is specified by the Mālikī school. The Ḥanafī school on the contrary, rejected the *waṣiyyah* made by children who are *mumayyiz* equating it with a free-will worldly contract. Imām Mālik says that we prevent the child who is *mumayyiz* from making free-will worldly contracts only to protect his property upon which he will one day depend. Since the *waṣiyyah* will only take place after his death, there is no need to prevent him from bequeathing. The same rule will apply in the case of a person who is retarded (*safīh*) but not someone who is insane or mentally deranged.

The person in favour of whom the *waṣiyyah* is made, must be capable of ownership whether he exists or is capable of existing (i.e. an unborn child), whether insane or sane, adult or minor. If he is not capable of accepting it, like minors or insane persons, it can be accepted by his guardian on his behalf. The only essential condition is that he must not be among the heirs, unless with the agreement of the other heirs. The Mālikī jurists have based their judgement on the known *^c^amal* of Madīnah and the *ḥadīth* of the Prophet ﷺ:

عَنْ أَبِي أُمَامَةَ الْبَاهِلِيِّ قَالَ: سَمِعْتُ رَسُولَ اللَّهِ ﷺ يَقُولُ فِي خُطْبَتِهِ عَامَ حَجَّةِ الْوَدَاعِ: «إِنَّ اللَّهَ تَبَارَكَ وَتَعَالَى قَدْ أَعْطَى لِكُلِّ ذِي حَقٍّ حَقَّهُ فَلَا وَصِيَّةَ لِوَارِثٍ.

From Abū Umāmah al-Bāhilī who said: I heard the Messenger of Allah ﷺ saying in his *khuṭbah* the year of the Farewell Pilgrimage, "Allah, blessed is He and exalted, has already given to everyone possessing a right his right, so there is no bequest to be made in favour of an heir." (At-Tirmidhī, *abwāb al-waṣāyā ᶜan rasūlillāh* ﷺ, *bāb mā jā'a anna an-nabiyya lam yūṣi*)

The Mālikī school also allows a *waṣiyyah* in favour of a dead person if the person doing so knows that the person is actually dead. The *waṣiyyah* in fact is intended to go to his heirs. *Waṣiyyah* can also be made in favour of a mosque for its maintenance by bequeathing property that yields an income for that purpose, in which case it will be a *waqf* for the mosque for all time to come. The *waṣiyyah* can be made in favour of an animal although the animal is not capable of owning anything. It will really mean that the *waṣiyyah* is made over to the person taking care of the animal to feed and look after it. *Waṣiyyah* can also be made to the heir to give *zakāh* if it is due out of the estate, but if the *waṣiyyah* for the payment of *zakāh* is for past years, it will be to the proportion of one-third of the *waṣiyyah*.

Imām Muḥammad ibn Idrīs ash-Shāfiᶜī discussed the following two verses of the Noble Qur'ān as showing an example of abrogating (*nāsikh*) and abrogated (*mansūkh*) verses and the role of Sunnah and *ijmāᶜ* in deciding the rule of law on *waṣiyyah*:

128. [Shāfiᶜī said] God, Blessed and Most High, said:

كُتِبَ عَلَيْكُمْ إِذَا حَضَرَ أَحَدَكُمُ الْمَوْتُ إِن تَرَكَ خَيْرًا الْوَصِيَّةُ لِلْوَالِدَيْنِ وَالْأَقْرَبِينَ بِالْمَعْرُوفِ حَقًّا عَلَى الْمُتَّقِينَ

It is prescribed for you, when death approaches one of you and if he has some goods to leave, to make a will in favour of his parents and relatives, correctly and fairly: a duty for all those who have taqwā. (Sūrat al-Baqarah 2: 180)

Allah, exalted is He, also said:

وَالَّذِينَ يُتَوَفَّوْنَ مِنكُمْ وَيَذَرُونَ أَزْوَاجاً وَصِيَّةً لِّأَزْوَاجِهِم مَّتَاعاً إِلَى الْحَوْلِ غَيْرَ إِخْرَاجٍ فَإِنْ خَرَجْنَ فَلاَ جُنَاحَ عَلَيْكُمْ فِي مَا فَعَلْنَ فِي أَنفُسِهِنَّ مِن مَّعْرُوفٍ وَاللَّهُ عَزِيزٌ حَكِيمٌ

Those of you who die leaving wives behind should make a bequest to their wives of maintenance for a year without them having to leave their homes. But if they do leave you are not to blame for anything they do with themselves with correctness and courtesy. Allah is Almighty, All-Wise. (Sūrat al-Baqarah 2: 240)

Ash-Shāfi^cī ؓ said:

Thus God provided [legislation] for the inheritance of parents as well as for near relatives whether together with them or as successors, and for the inheritance of the husband from his wife and the wife from her husband.

The two [foregoing] verses may be interpreted either to confirm bequests for the parents and the near relatives, bequest for the wife, and inheritance together with bequests, so that inheritance and bequest are lawful; or that [the legislation concerning] inheritance abrogates [that concerning] bequests.[1]

Since both interpretations are possible, as we pointed out, it is obligatory upon the learned to find an evidence in the Book of God [as to which of the two is valid]; if nothing is found in the text of the Book of God they should try the Sunnah of the Apostle. If such an evidence is found, it should be accepted as if accepted from the Apostle, as [if] accepted from God by virtue of His command to obey His [Apostle].

We have found that those learned in legal interpretation and the authorities in the campaigns [of the Prophet] - whether from [the tribe of] Quraysh or other [tribes] - are agreed that in the year of the capture [of Makkah (8 AH/630 CE)] the Prophet said:

"No bequest to a successor [is valid], nor shall a believer be slain for [the blood of] an unbeliever." (Abū Dāwūd, Vol. III, p. 113; ash-Shawkānī, *Nayl al-Awṭār*. Vol. VI, p. 43; ash-Shāfi^cī, *Kitāb al-Umm*, Vol. IV, pp. 27, 36, 40)

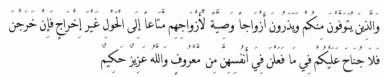

This tradition has been transmitted from those who have heard it from the authorities on the [Prophet's] campaigns. So this is a transmission by the public from the public[2] and is therefore of greater authority than the transmission of one (individual) from another. Further, we have found that the scholars are agreed [on the acceptance of this tradition].[3] . . .

We have concluded that the Prophet's ﷺ ruling: "No bequest for a successor [is valid]," as I have stated, [means] that [the legislation on] inheritance has abrogated that on bequests for the parents and the wife, on the strength of the information related by those learned in matters concerning the Prophet's ﷺ campaigns, interrupted traditions from the Prophet ﷺ, and the agreement of the public.[4]

A great number of jurists also have held that [the legislation concerning] bequests for relatives was abrogated and is no longer obligatory; for whenever they are entitled to inherit, they are so by virtue of the [law of] inheritance; but when they are not entitled to inherit, it is not obligatory that they should inherit by a bequest.

Ṭāwūs [ibn Kaysān] and a few other [authorities], however, held that the [legislation concerning] bequests for parents has been abrogated, though it was confirmed for relatives not entitled to inherit. So it is not permissible for him who bequeaths to do so [to persons] other than relatives.

It also indicates that the bequest of the deceased cannot exceed one third of his estate.

Bequests to parents are no longer valid, since their right to inheritance as successors is confirmed. A bequest made by a deceased to anyone – if he is not an heir – is valid. It is commendable if the deceased leaves a bequest to his relatives.

Opinions differ as to whether the provision of a year's maintenance with residence for a widow is abrogated by the share which the widow gets (one-eighth or one-fourth) as an heir. As Allah, exalted is He, said:

وَالَّذِينَ يُتَوَفَّوْنَ مِنكُمْ وَيَذَرُونَ أَزْوَاجًا وَصِيَّةً لِّأَزْوَاجِهِم مَّتَاعًا إِلَى الْحَوْلِ غَيْرَ إِخْرَاجٍ

Those of you who die leaving wives behind should make a bequest to their wives of maintenance for a year without them having to leave their homes. (Sūrat al-Baqarah 2: 240)

Ibn Juzayy al-Kalbī says in *tafsīr* of the *āyah* in *Kitāb at-tashīl li ᶜulūm at-tanzīl*:

> This *āyah* is abrogated, and its meaning is that when a man dies his wife has the right to reside in his house for a year during which he [i.e. his heirs] spends upon her from his wealth, which is a bequest to her. Then later her residence for a year was abrogated by the four months and ten days, and the expenditure was abrogated by the quarter or the eighth which she has from the inheritance as is mentioned in Sūrat an-Nisā'.[5]

Thus, as we have seen, *waṣiyyah* offers to the testator a complementary means of enabling some of the poor relatives who are excluded from inheritance to obtain a share in his property according to the law of succession. The will or bequest also offers an opportunity to the testator to recognise the services rendered to him by a total stranger whom he wants to reward, although such power given to the testator must not be exercised to the detriment of the lawful heirs. Hence, the testator cannot exceed while making his will the limit of a third of his property.

It is unfortunate that some western scholars, as well as Muslim scholars such as Fyzee[6] and Ameer Ali[7] influenced by these western scholars, try to explain the Qur'ānic restriction about the limit of one third conjecturing that the restriction was influenced by Roman law.

Any Muslim who is sane, has attained majority and has some property, can make a will. Any will or bequest that exceeds a third of the estate or is made during *maraḍ al-mawt,* the final sickness, is not valid. Likewise, a person who has taken poison or has tried to commit suicide by some other means and makes a bequest, it will not be considered valid. The will can be made either orally or in writing. It is desirable, however, that it should be rendered in writing. If the bequest is in writing it is permissible for it not to be signed and if it is signed it is permissible for it not to be attested. What is really important is that the intention of the testator must be very clear. Even a dumb person can make a valid bequest through gestures. Bequests can be made in favour of a male or female, Muslim or non-Muslim as long as they are capable of holding property. Even an unborn child, who cannot be a legatee (i.e. does not inherit a fixed share as he is in the womb), if born within six months from the date of making the bequest can validly receive a bequest made in his favour. The jurists of all schools of Islamic jurisprudence except the Shāfiʿīs are of the opinion that the bequest made by Muslims to non-Muslims is valid. A renegade from Islam cannot be a legatee.

It is permissible to make a valid bequest in favour of educational, charitable and religious institutions. Once the bequest or *waṣiyyah* is made, it can be revoked by the testator either by a subsequent will or through express or implied statement made orally or in writing. The implied revocation of a bequest is made when the testator subsequently acts in such a way that the revocation can be inferred. As for example, he makes a bequest in respect of a plot of land and subsequently he builds a dwelling place on it. In this case, by implication he has revoked the bequest.

If the testator has made a bequest and then subsequently makes another on the same property in favour of another person, the previous bequest becomes null and void.

In conclusion it can be added that *waṣiyyah* is optional both on the part of the testator as well as the beneficiary. The testator may or may not make the bequest as he pleases, while the beneficiary is free either to accept it or reject it.

Every will or bequest made by a person during his lifetime is valid and only becomes executable after his death.

B. *Hibah*: Gift

Hibah means a gift from one living person to another without usurping or neglecting the rights of his descendants and near relatives and must be an immediate and unqualified transfer of the corpus of the property without any return (*ʿiwaḍ*).

In other words, it is a transfer of a determinate property free of consideration with a definite offer on the part of the person who gives the gift and acceptance on the part of the person to whom the gift is given. Valid *hibah* under Islamic law must pay attention to three main elements:

1. There must be a declaration of the gift by the person who wants to give it away, using some form of words that makes clear that it is a gift or a present.
2. The person to whom the gift is given must accept it either by himself or through an agent.
3. Ownership of the gift should be transferred by the donor to the person receiving it.

The law governing *hibah* does not specify that it must only be given to a destitute or poor person; a gift can also be made in favour of a rich man. The poor, in reality, are more deserving, and it is encouraged that they also should be made recipients of gifts.

The Prophet ﷺ emphasised making a habit of exchanging gifts since it is beneficial in strengthening relationships and it fosters love and affection and takes away rancour. The Prophet ﷺ is reported to have said:

تَهَادُوا تَحَابُّوا

Give each other gifts and you will love each other. (Narrated by Abū Yaᶜlā from Abū Hurayrah)

There are some other *ḥadīth* on showing the wisdom of *hibah* and the benefits to be obtained from it. The Prophet ﷺ has said:

وتَهَادُوا فإِنَّ الهَدِيَّةَ تذْهِبُ الغِلَّ.

Give gifts to one another, because a gift removes grudges. (Narrated by Ibn ᶜAsākir from Ibn ᶜUmar)

He further says:

عَنْ ابْنِ عَبَّاسٍ رضي الله عنهما قَالَ: قَالَ النَّبِيُّ ﷺ ﴿العَائِدُ فِي هِبَتِهِ كَالْكَلْبِ يَعُودُ فِي قَيْئِهِ لَيْسَ لَنَا مَثَلُ السَّوْءِ﴾

From Ibn ᶜAbbās ؓ there is that he said: The Prophet ﷺ said,

"Someone who seeks to take back a gift is like a dog who returns to its vomit. An evil likeness does not befit us [Muslims]." (Al-Bukhārī, *kitāb al-ḥiyal, bāb fī al-hibah wa ash-shufᶜah*)

Ibn Juzayy al-Kalbī said:

Concerning the different types of gifts, which are of two sorts: the gift of ownership [of a thing] and the gift which of a benefit. The gift of a benefit is such things as *ᶜariyyah* (the benefit that derives from an orchard or a specific tree such as a date palm) and *ᶜumrā* (a man's assigning to a person the use of a house for his *ᶜumr* i.e. 'lifetime'). The gift entailing ownership is of three types:

1. For the sake of the Face of Allah, exalted is He, and it is named *ṣadaqah*, and there is basically no way to take it back, and it is not right for the giver to try and get it back by renting it or in any other way. If it is a tree, he should not eat any of its fruit, and if it is a riding animal, he should not mount it, unless it returns to him by inheritance.

2. A gift from affection and love, which it is not possible for the giver to take back, except in the case of that which the father gives to his child whether minor or major, for he may take it for himself, and that is by taking it back even if the child has taken possession of it. Taking it for oneself is only valid under five conditions:

a. That the child has not married after the gift;

b. That it has not become a debt for a stipulated period;

c. That the gift has not changed from its [original] condition;

d. That the person who was given it has not introduced something new into it;

e. That neither the giver of the gift nor its recipient has become [seriously] ill, for if any of those things has occurred then the opportunity to take the gift back has passed.

3. A gift for a recompense on the basis that the person given the gift must give [the giver] an equivalent gift, which is permissible, contrary to ash-Shāfiᶜī, and the person given the gift has the choice of accepting it or rejecting it. (Al-Kalbī, Ibn Juzayy, *al-Qawānīn al-fiqhiyyah, al-kitāb ath-thāmin fī al-hibāt wa al-aḥbās wa mā shākalahā, al-bāb al-awwal fī al-hibah*)

Any free-will transfer of property which is made with the intention of obtaining its reward in the next world is called *ṣadaqah,* but if something is given to someone to show one's respect and affection for them, it is *hibah,* a present or a gift. *Hibah,* therefore, is an immediate and unqualified transfer of ownership of a determinate object which is done in the lifetime of the person who transfers it without obtaining a *quid pro quo.*[8] In other words, it is the transfer of the right of property (*tamlīk al-ᶜayn*) by one person to another without any consideration or equivalent (*ᶜiwaḍ*). Note that as Ibn Juzayy said, the Mālikīs consider giving a gift for some compensation also to be a valid form of *hibah.*

The giving and accepting of gifts is recommended by the Prophet ﷺ very strongly. One must not despise even the smallest gift.[9] *Hibah* is allowed in favour of a child, but it is recommended that similar gifts should be made in favour of other children and that there should be an equal treatment of all one's children.[10] A husband can make a gift to his wife, and a wife can give a gift to her husband, or someone other than her husband.[11] Gifts can be accepted from and given to non-Muslims.[12]

A gift can be compensated.[13] *Hibah bi-sharṭ al-ᶜiwaḍ* i.e. a gift made on the condition that the receiver will give to the donor some definite thing in return for the gift, is also allowed. The *hibah* is complete when the receiver has accepted it and taken possession of the gift. It is not allowed for a person to revoke the *hibah* when it has been accepted by the receiver[14] because it has already become the other person's property. Whereas a bequest is allowed only to the extent of one-third of the property, no such limitation exists on *hibah,* because in this case the owner divests himself of all rights in the property immediately, while in the case of a will (*waṣiyyah*) it is not the owner but the heirs who are deprived.

It should be noted that a gift, a *ṣadaqah,* or any endowment (*waqf*) is incomplete unless they are received by those to whom they are given. If the benefactor should die before such acceptance is effected, they will be treated as part of the legacy except where they are received while the deceased is sick. Under such circumstances they can be executed so long as they do not exceed one-third of the legacy and the beneficiaries are not heirs.

Is Gift a Charity?

A gift to a relative or a poor person is like a *ṣadaqah* and cannot be withdrawn. If a person gives a *ṣadaqah* to his child, he cannot take it back. He is permitted to take back a gift given to a minor or adult child, as long as the donee has not become married nor used the property to become married or given the money on loan, nor converted the object of the gift into something else, or become seriously ill. A mother can withdraw a gift to her child as long as the father remains alive, but if the father dies, she cannot then take back the gift since her child has in essence become an orphan. Likewise, a gift made to an orphan cannot be withdrawn.[15] According to some, in the case of a gift made to a child who has attained majority, the father may not take possession of the article already gifted, but according to the Mālikīs, he may.

Once something is given as a *ṣadaqah*, it cannot be withdrawn nor can it revert back to him, except through inheritance (*mīrāth*). There is no harm in a person taking back a cow, sheep or goat he has given as *ṣadaqah* for someone to drink its milk, but he cannot buy back things he has given as *ṣadaqah*. When a gift is given on the condition that the giver receives something in return, the donee has the option of either giving the donor some article of equal value or he may return the gift immediately.

If a gift is made which is not received by the person for whom it was intended and the donor subsequently becomes seriously ill or is declared bankrupt, it becomes unlawful for the intended recipient to accept the gift. However, in the case when the person to whom the gift was made dies, his heirs can claim it from the donor of the gift unless he has been declared bankrupt.[16]

It is reprehensible for a father to give some of his children all his property. However, he is permitted to give some of them some of it. A man is permitted to give away the whole of his property to poor people or to anyone he likes.

When the donor and the recipient reside in the same house the process of the gift is complete even without the physical transfer of the object of the gift, like a gift from a husband to his wife, a father to his child, a mother to her son and a guardian to his ward.

WHO CAN MAKE A GIFT?

Every Muslim who has reached the age of maturity and is sane is capable of making a gift. The gift should be made without exercise of force or being under duress. It is essential for the donor to be aware of the implications of his act. A person on his deathbed in the last minutes of his life cannot make a valid gift because, in reality, it is neither *hibah* nor *waṣiyyah*. If a gift is made during the *maraḍ al-mawt*, the final illness, it is considered at the time of sharing out the inheritance, but in any circumstances may not exceed a third of the estate after the payment of funeral expenses and debts as required by the injunctions of the Qur'ān. This is so because the property of a person on his deathbed actually becomes the property of the heirs and he only retains the right to dispose of a third of it. While making a gift, one must be just and must not deprive any of the heirs of their legitimate rights.

Gifts can be made in favour of any living person who is capable of holding property. Gifts can also be made in favour of a child in the womb of his mother, a mosque building, a school or any charitable institution. Gifts can also be made to non-Muslims. Imām Abū Ḥanīfah says that a gift of *mushāᶜ* property[17] which means joint and undivided property subject to the right of more than one individual, is invalid if it is done by one of the co-sharers. However, his disciples Imām Abū Yūsuf and Imām Muḥammad ibn al-Ḥasan ash-Shaybānī and the Mālikīs hold that it is valid.

Imām Abū Ḥanīfah's point of view was that when several persons jointly own a property no one is in a position to say that his interest is attached to any specific part of it. Therefore, *hibah* or gift by one of the co-sharers in such a property is likely to create some confusion in its enjoyment by the co-sharers.[18] This is somewhat akin to partnership in business in which in Mālikī *fiqh* any one of the partners can dispose of the entire partnership and commit the entire partnership to contracts without consulting the others.

In the case when gifts are made to two or more persons jointly or if the gift is made by two persons jointly to one person, Ḥanafī jurists hold that it is still valid. As we have seen above, Imām Abū Ḥanīfah does not hold that such a gift is valid in the former case. Gifts of *mushāᶜ* property are not encouraged simply because without proper division of the divisible things, disputes and complications would affect the enjoyment of the objects of such gifts. Therefore, it is essential in the case of *hibah* that its entity should be a known property. If the specification is not given, it is bound to give rise to confusion.

According to the Mālikī school, a gift made in favour of a near relative or a poor person will be considered a *ṣadaqah*. Hence, such gifts will be irrevocable. The person giving an ordinary gift to his child may take it back if he so wishes, but if the gift is made the basis of his or her marriage it becomes irrevocable. Similarly, a mother can revoke a gift given to her child as long as the father of the child is alive, but if the father dies, the gift becomes irrevocable since any gift given to an orphan cannot be revoked.[19] According to the Shāfiᶜī school of jurisprudence, once the gift is validly made nobody can retract it except the father. According to Ḥanafī jurists, any revocation of a gift is considered abominable in any circumstance whatsoever. However, if the transfer of possession of the gift has not been effected, it can still be revoked. Once the transfer of possession of the gift is done, its revocation will not be possible unless a decree has been issued by the *qāḍī* or if the recipient has consented to it.[20]

C. *Waqf* or *ḥubus*

In Islamic legal terminology, *waqf* pl. *awqāf* means "tying up a property in perpetuity" so as to prevent it from becoming the property of a third party. The *waqf* property thus belongs to Allah, and no human being can alienate it for his own purpose.[21]

Ibn Juzayy al-Kalbī said:

On the *Waqf* – and it is the *Ḥubus* – concerning which there are
six issues:

1. On the judgement on making a *ḥubus* (*waqf*), which is that
it is permissible according to the two Imāms and others and
contrary to Abū Ḥanīfah, but his pupil Abū Yūsuf recanted
that when Mālik exchanged views with him and [Mālik] proved
his case with the *aḥbās* of the Messenger of Allah ﷺ and of the
Companions and the Followers ◈. So later Ḥanafīs came to deny
the Imām's prohibition of it and they would say, "His *madhhab*
is that it is permissible but that it is not obligatory." (Al-Kalbī,
Ibn Juzayy, *al-Qawānīn al-fiqhiyyah, al-kitāb ath-thāmin fī al-hibāt
wa al-aḥbās wa mā shākalahā, al-bāb ath-thānī fī al-waqf wa huwa
al-ḥubus*)

In Islam it is incumbent upon every Muslim to give *ṣadaqah* out
of one's property. While the payment of *zakāh* of $2\,^1/_2\%$ of held
wealth over the legal minimum (*niṣāb*) is obligatory and becomes
the right of the poor and the needy and is to be paid from one's
savings on which a year has passed, *ṣadaqah* is to be given at any
time from one's property, but voluntarily. The establishment
of *waqf* property came into existence in order to organise and
institutionalise the voluntary charities. Although there are no
Qur'ānic verses specifically mentioning *waqf* or the establishment
of *waqf* property, the provision is covered in a large number of
verses scattered throughout the Noble Qur'ān on the theme of
infāq fī sabīlillāh meaning, "spending in the way of Allah."

The history of the establishment of *awqāf* started right in the time
of the Prophet Muḥammad ﷺ when he built the first mosque in
Madīnah, *the* city par excellence, in the first year of the Hijrah.
The Prophetic Mosque, or *al-Masjid an-Nabawī* as it is called, was
built on a plot of land belonging to two orphans.

In spite of the Prophet's wish to pay for the land, the orphans
insisted that they would not accept the price from the Prophet ﷺ
but would take it from Allah in the next world. The establishment
of *awqāf* continued when ʿUthmān ◈, who later became the
third caliph, bought a well and made it a trust property for the
charitable use of all and sundry in order to relieve Muslims of

the difficulties imposed by some of the Jews who had banned Muslims drawing water from another well.

The Messenger of Allah ﷺ is narrated to have said:

عَنْ أَبِي هُرَيْرَةَ أَنَّ رَسُولَ اللَّهِ ﷺ قَالَ: ﴿إِذَا مَاتَ الإِنْسَانُ انْقَطَعَ عَمَلُهُ إِلاَّ مِنْ ثَلاَثٍ: صَدَقَةٍ جَارِيَةٍ، أَوْ عِلْمٍ يُنْتَفَعُ بِهِ، أَوْ وَلَدٍ صَالِحٍ يَدْعُو لَهُ﴾.

> From Abū Hurayrah ﷺ there is that the Messenger of Allah ﷺ said, "When a person dies his action is cut off except for three: an enduring *ṣadaqah*, or knowledge by which benefit is obtained, or a right-acting child who supplicates for him." (Muslims, *kitāb al-waṣiyyah, bāb mā yalḥaqu al-insān min ath-thawāb ba*c*da wafātihi*)

This tradition mentions the three things that a person can leave behind that will benefit him after his death which we can expand in this manner: the establishment of welfare institutions like digging a well, canal or building of a hospital, or erecting an educational institution, orchards whose proceeds go to feed specified groups of people, land whose income sustains specific groups, a scholar whose teaching or writing of a book benefits people even after his death and right-acting progeny who will pray for the parents after their death.

This *ḥadīth* encouraged the companions of the Prophet to 'tie up' part of their property for people's welfare. Hence cUmar ibn al-Khaṭṭāb ﷺ bought land in the area of Khaybar. He went to the Prophet ﷺ and asked his guidance in order to make the best use of it. The Prophet ﷺ replied:

عَنِ ابْنِ عُمَرَ رَضِيَ اللَّهُ عَنْهُمَا أَنَّ عُمَرَ بْنَ الْخَطَّابِ أَصَابَ أَرْضًا بِخَيْبَرَ فَأَتَى النَّبِيَّ صَلَّى اللَّهُ عَلَيْهِ وَسَلَّمَ يَسْتَأْمِرُهُ فِيهَا فَقَالَ يَا رَسُولَ اللَّهِ إِنِّي أَصَبْتُ أَرْضًا بِخَيْبَرَ لَمْ أُصِبْ مَالاً قَطُّ أَنْفَسَ عِنْدِي مِنْهُ فَمَا تَأْمُرُ بِهِ قَالَ إِنْ شِئْتَ حَبَسْتَ أَصْلَهَا وَتَصَدَّقْتَ بِهَا قَالَ فَتَصَدَّقَ بِهَا عُمَرُ أَنَّهُ لاَ يُبَاعُ وَلاَ يُوهَبُ وَلاَ يُورَثُ وَتَصَدَّقَ بِهَا فِي الْفُقَرَاءِ وَفِي الْقُرْبَى وَفِي الرِّقَابِ وَفِي سَبِيلِ اللَّهِ وَابْنِ السَّبِيلِ وَالضَّيْفِ لاَ جُنَاحَ عَلَى مَنْ وَلِيَهَا أَنْ يَأْكُلَ مِنْهَا بِالْمَعْرُوفِ وَيُطْعِمَ غَيْرَ مُتَمَوِّلٍ

From Ibn ᶜUmar ﷺ there is that "ᶜUmar ibn al-Khaṭṭāb acquired some land in Khaybar and so he came to the Prophet ﷺ asking him to tell him what to do about it. He said, 'Messenger of Allah, I have acquired some land in Khaybar, and I have never acquired property more precious to me than it, so what do you tell me to do with it?' He said, 'If you wish, tie up the original property and give *ṣadaqah* from it.'" He said, "So ᶜUmar gave it as *ṣadaqah* on the basis that it was not be sold nor given as a gift nor inherited, and *ṣadaqah* was to be given from it to the poor, close relatives, slaves, in the way of Allah, and on travellers, and the guest; there being no wrongdoing on the part of the person who administers it if he eats from it moderately and feeds [others] without taking property from it." (Al-Bukhārī, *kitāb al-waṣāyā, bāb al-waqf kayfa yuktabu;* at-Tirmidhī, *abwāb al-aḥkām ᶜan rasūlillāh* ﷺ, *bāb mā jā'a fī al-waqf.* The wording is that of al-Bukhārī)

Imām al-Bukhārī, the famous compiler of *Ṣaḥīḥ al-Bukhārī*, has full chapters on the institution of *waqf.* Abū Ṭalḥah gave his choicest piece of land, known as the orchard of Bayruḥā' in Madīnah, to the Prophet ﷺ. The Prophet ﷺ gave it back to him advising him that he should make it an endowment for his relatives. Abū Ṭalḥah thereupon gave the orchard as a *ṣadaqah* to Ubayy and Hasan. (*See* al-Bukhārī, *kitāb al-waṣāyā*)

The specific Prophetic directive in respect of *waqf* is contained in the following words which sum up the definition of *waqf.*

إِنْ شِئْتَ حَبَسْتَ أَصْلَهَا وَتَصَدَّقْتَ بِهَا

If you wish, tie up the original property[22] and give *ṣadaqah* from it. (*Ibid.*)

Ibn Juzayy al-Kalbī said:

2. On its elements which are four:

i. The one who endows the *ḥubus,*

ii. That which is made into a *ḥubus,*

iii. The one for whom the *ḥubus* is dedicated,

iv. And the form in which it is carried out.

As for the one who endows the *ḥubus* then he is like the giver of a gift (see the previous section on *hibah*). (Al-Kalbī, Ibn Juzayy,

> *al-Qawānīn al-fiqhiyyah, al-kitāb ath-thāmin fī al-hibāt wa al-aḥbās wa mā shākalahā, al-bāb ath-thānī fī al-waqf wa huwa al-ḥubus*)

Every wealthy Muslim who is not a minor or insane has the right to endow a *waqf* provided he is the owner of the property he is dedicating. He should not do so under duress nor should he be defrauded into creating a *waqf*.

Any *waqf* created during a person's final illness (*maraḍ al-mawt*) is not valid because by then the property has almost passed into the hands of his heirs. In this case the *wāqif*, that is the person who creates the *waqf* in his will, must not dedicate more than one-third of his estate as *waqf* property unless his heirs give their consent to it.

The objective for which the *waqf* is set up must not be against the principles of Islam. In other words, a Muslim must not create a *waqf* in favour of idol worshippers or a temple or a deity since this will conflict with the fundamental principle of *tawḥīd*, nor must it be dedicated to any other *ḥarām* usage. Again from Ibn Juzayy:

> 1. As for the one for whom the *ḥubus* is dedicated it is sound for it to be a person, or something else such as mosques and madrasahs, and it is sound that it be for someone who is alive and present and for someone not yet born, for someone specific and for someone unknown (possibly a category such as 'the poor'), for the Muslim and for the *dhimmī* (member of the people of the Book living under Islamic governance and paying the *jizyah*), for a near relative or for a non-relative. (*Ibid.*)

There exist slight differences of opinion among the jurists about the type of property that can be dedicated as a *waqf*. Imām Abū Ḥanīfah says that only immovable property can be made *waqf*. His eminent student Imām Abū Yūsuf also agreed with his master but made an exception when he said that beasts of burden and weapons of war can also be dedicated as *waqf*. The view of another eminent student of Imām Abū Ḥanīfah, namely Imām Muḥammad, is quite different from the view of his master and his colleague. He agreed with other imams and famous jurists and held that all articles or movables that can be subject to the dealings and transactions of man can be made *waqf*.

Ibn Juzayy al-Kalbī said:

> ii. As for that which is made into a *ḥubus* (*waqf*), then it is permissible to make a *ḥubus* of property such as lands, houses, shops, gardens, mosques, wells, canals, graveyards, pathways, etc. It is not permitted to make a *ḥubus* of food because its benefit lies in its consumption. There are two differing narrations about [the permissibility of] making a *ḥubus* of goods, slaves and beasts [in general] since making a *ḥubus* of horses in the way of Allah is a well known matter. (*Ibid.*)

The jurists, particularly Imām Abū Ḥanīfah, say that to establish *waqf* is recommended (*mustaḥabb*) but not obligatory (*wājib*).

Waqf literally means detention (*ḥubus*), but its legal meaning is the dedication of a property for a good purpose whether educational or charitable. Actually, it is the detention of a specific thing from the property of the proprietor, and devoting or dedicating its profits or charity for the poor or for other good purposes. According to Imām Muḥammad ibn Idrīs ash-Shāfiᶜī. Imām Mālik and the two disciples of Imām Abū Ḥanīfah, Abū Yūsuf and Imām Muḥammad (the *Ṣāḥibayn*), *waqf* signifies the extinction of the proprietor's ownership of the thing dedicated and the dedication of the thing to the ownership of Allah (*ᶜalā ḥukm milki'llāh*) in such a manner that its profit should be made use of for the good of mankind from the beginning to the end.

The establishment of *waqf*, in other words, extinguishes the right of the *wāqif* (endower) and transfers its ownership to Allah. On its establishment, Ibn Juzayy al-Kalbī said:

> iii. As to the form of dedicating the property it is with the word *ḥubus*, *waqf* and *ṣadaqah*, and every phrase which would require the same meaning, such as saying, 'It is sacrosanct (*muḥarram*), it may not be sold and may not be given away,' and actions such as the *adhān* for [calling] people to the prayer in a place which he built as a mosque. It is not stipulated that the one for whom the *ḥubus* is dedicated should accept it unless it is a specific person who is responsible for his own affairs. (*Ibid.*)

When such a *waqf* is created, a right-acting person or a group of people are appointed as managers of the *waqf*. In some places, such a person is called *mutawallī* but the property of the *waqf* does not vest in the managers. Once a *waqf* is created, it will always remain *waqf* property and cannot change its character. Since it is created for an unselfish object, the *waqf* property is not to be sold or given to someone as an inheritance or a gift. Since *waqf* is created for general welfare, it is of two kinds.[23]

A. *Waqf ahlī*: Family *waqf*

B. *Waqf khayrī*: Welfare *waqf*

Waqf ahlī is created for the security of the welfare of near relatives of the endower (*wāqif*) and his family and their descendants to ensure that they get their needs from it throughout their lives, and then reverts to the welfare of the poor people after their deaths and the extinction of the line. It can be made of both moveable and immovable property.

Ibn Juzayy al-Kalbī said:

> iv. As for the word 'child' or children', if he said, 'I have dedicated this *ḥubus* to my child (*walad*)' or 'to my children (*awlād*)', then it encompasses his own children, the male and female, and the children of the males since they inherit, and it does not encompass the children of the females contrary to the view of Abū ᶜUmar ibn ᶜAbd al-Barr. If he said, 'I dedicate this *ḥubus* (*waqf*) to my children and to their children,' then there is also disagreement as to whether the children of the daughters are covered. If he said, 'My children, male and female,' whether he named them or not and then later he said, 'and their descendants,' or 'their children' then in that case it covers the children of the daughters. As for the wording *ᶜaqb* ('children' also) its ruling is the same as the ruling of the word children (*awlād*) in everything which we have mentioned and similarly the word *banīn* (literally 'sons' but it may mean 'children') although it may particularly mean 'sons' unless he says 'the male and female of them'. As for the word *dhurriyyah* 'offspring' and *nasl* 'progeny', the children of the daughters enter into both of them according to the most sound view. As for the wording *āl* and *ahl* 'family' it covers the males of the children and the daughters, brothers, sisters, paternal uncles and aunts, and there is a disagreement as to whether maternal uncles and aunts are included. As to the wording *qarābah* 'near relatives' it is more general and compasses all kin both men and women, whether they are of the degrees which it is forbidden to marry or of the degrees that are eligible for marriage (cousins, etc.), according to the soundest view. (*Ibid.*)

Waqf khayrī is created to cater for the needs of orphans, the destitute, the blind and the handicapped, and the type of *awqāf* that yield income can be created for maintaining mosques, schools, hospitals, graveyards and other places of public welfare, etc., but these buildings themselves can also themselves be *awqāf* and are ordinarily so.

In conclusion, it should be noted that the establishment of a philanthropic *waqf* is voluntary and not an obligation like the payment of *zakāh* but since they encapsulate *ṣadaqah jāriyah* or enduring charity whose benefits go to the endower as long as the *ṣadaqah* continues then to establish *waqf* endowments was highly desired by Muslims, so much so that in Ottoman society 60% of property and more was owned by *waqf* endowments.

The following must be satisfied in the creation of a *waqf*:

1. The object of a *waqf* must belong to the *wāqif* (endower) at the time of his dedicating it. Ibn Juzayy al-Kalbī said:

> On its precondition, which is possession as we have mentioned in [the section] on gifts. If the one who dedicates the *ḥubus* dies or becomes [terminally] sick or bankrupt before [the one to whom the *ḥubus* is dedicated] takes possession then the endowment of the *ḥubus* is invalidated. Similarly if he resides in a dwelling before the completion of a year or takes the revenues of a land for himself then the *ḥubus* is invalidated. It is permissible that someone else may take possession on behalf of an adult even though he is present, as distinct from the case of a gift. The father takes possession for his small son, and the legal guardian takes possession on behalf of his charge. The one responsible for the *awqāf* takes possession of that which has been dedicated as a *ḥubus* for the mosques and dwellings and the like of it. There must be clear supervision of taking possession if the one for whom the *ḥubus* is dedicated is in somewhere else than in the administrative district of the one who endows the *ḥubus* or if he is in his administrative district and the *ḥubus* is in a house of his dwelling or in which he has placed his goods for trade, then it is not sound unless he vacates the place and there is supervision [of that]. Whenever the one for whom the *ḥubus* is dedicated, or the one who has been given, contracts to rent out the property of that which has been made *ḥubus* or has been given as a gift or he alights to live there, then that is [considered to be] taking possession. (*Ibid.*)

2. The person dedicating a *waqf* must not be a minor or a person of unsound mind.
3. A *waqf* of *mushā*ᶜ or "undivided shared" property may form the subject of a *waqf* but for the purpose of a mosque or a burial ground, it is not valid.
4. The purpose for which the *waqf* is created must be one recognised by the *Sharīᶜah*.
5. The object of *waqf* must be shown with reasonable certainty.
6. Any *waqf* made by a will or during someone's final illness, cannot operate on more than one-third of the net assets without the consent of the heirs.
7. A *waqf* created by a will in which there is a clause that the *waqf* shall not operate if a child is born to the *wāqif* is not invalid, since a will can be revoked or modified at any time before death. The same applies to a *waqf* which is created by a will.

The institution of *waqf* assumed a very definite legal form in the second century of the Hijrah. The large *awqāf* which were established during the Umayyad period were supervised by the *qāḍīs*. It was during this period that *Dīwān an-Naẓr fī al-Maẓālim*, a bureau to investigate grievances, was established which apart from looking at miscarriages of justice was entrusted with the responsibility of supervising *waqf* property and its administration.[24] During the Abbasid caliphate *qāḍīs* continued to supervise *awqāf*.[25] In most Muslim countries today, *mutawallīs* are appointed to supervise *awqāf*.

Hundreds of *awqāf* dating from the Umayyad and Abbasid period of Islamic history have come down to us. In most parts of the Muslim world, a number of schools, colleges, hospitals, orphanages, mosque buildings and scholarship funds are run through the help of *waqf* properties. It is really surprising that in some West African countries like Nigeria, Ghana, Chad, Niger and other neighbouring countries such *awqāf* foundations are not yet established. Looking at the successful public welfare activities carried out through *awqāf*, it is strongly recommended that Muslims in these countries should work towards the establishment of *awqāf.* At present, a large number of *awqāf* exist throughout the Muslim world. In India alone there are more than 100,000 Muslim *awqāf* valued at more than a billion Indian rupees.[26] In Ottoman society,[27] *awqāf* properties "comprised such a huge range and reached to such an extent that according to some, two thirds of the city of Istanbul was *waqf* property."[28]

D. *Shufᶜah*: The Right of Pre-emption

The word *shufᶜah* in Arabic means 'coupling or adjoining' since it refers to property sold which is joined to the property of the *shāfiᶜ* or the pre-emptor, i.e. the person claiming the right of pre-emption. In *Ṣaḥīḥ al-Bukhārī* there is:

عَنْ جَابِرِ بْنِ عَبْدِ اللَّهِ رَضِيَ اللَّهُ عَنْهُمَا قَالَ قَضَى رَسُولُ اللَّهِ صَلَّى اللَّهُ عَلَيْهِ وَسَلَّمَ بِالشُّفْعَةِ فِي كُلِّ مَا لَمْ يُقْسَمْ فَإِذَا وَقَعَتِ الْحُدُودُ وَصُرِّفَتِ الطُّرُقُ فَلَا شُفْعَةَ

> From Jābir ibn ᶜAbdullāh ﵁ who said, "The Messenger of Allah ﷺ gave the judgement that there is pre-emption in all that has not been divided up, but when the limits have been set and pathways have been made distinct, then there is no pre-emption."(Al-Bukhārī, *kitāb ash-sharikah, bāb idhā iqtasama ash-shurakā' ad-dawr aw ghayrahā fa laysa lahum rujūᶜ wa lā shuᶜfah*)

This is the basic *ḥadīth* on the matter showing that it pertains to *mushāᶜ* property owned by partners, whether family or not, which has not been divided up. When property is divided up and become distinct separate properties, then there is no *shufᶜah.* Ibn Ḥajar defines it as the transference of a share of property from one partner to another, which would have been transferred to an outsider, for the same price named.

In Islamic legal terminology it means becoming an owner of property sold for the price at which the purchaser has bought it even if he does not consent to it.[29] In the *Ṣaḥīḥ* of Imām Muslim, a prophetic tradition is narrated as follows:

عَنْ جَابِرٍ قَالَ: قَالَ رَسُولُ اللّٰهِ ﷺ : ﴿مَنْ كَانَ لَهُ شَرِيكٌ فِي رَبْعَةٍ أَوْ نَخْلٍ، فَلَيْسَ لَهُ أَنْ يَبِيعَ

حَتَّى يُؤْذِنَ شَرِيكَهُ، فَإِنْ رَضِيَ أَخَذَ، وإِنْ كَرِهَ تَرَكَ ۞ .

Anyone who has a partner in a house or date-palm grove should not sell till his partner gives permission; then if [the partner] is willing he takes it, but if he does not wish he should leave it. (Muslim, *kitāb al-musāqāh, bāb ash-shufʿah*)

Imām al-Bukhārī has also reported a *ḥadīth* of the Prophet ﷺ on the same theme in his *Ṣaḥīḥ* in the following words:

عَنْ عَائِشَة رَضِيَ اللَّه عَنْها قُلْتُ يا رَسُولَ اللَّه إِنَّ لِي جَارَيْنِ فَإِلَى أَيِّهِمَا أُهْدِي قَالَ إِلَى أَقْرَبِهِما

مِنْكِ بَابًا

There is from ʿĀ'ishah ﵂, "I asked the Prophet ﷺ: 'Messenger of Allah, I have two neighbours. Which one of the two shall I give a gift." He replied, "To the one whose door is nearer to yours." (Al-Bukhārī, *kitāb ash-shufʿah, bāb ayyu al-jiwār aqrab*)[30]

This last *ḥadīth* has been adduced in support of the position taken by Abū Ḥanīfah, contrary to the other Imāms, that neighbours have a right of pre-emption. Ibn Baṭṭāl said, "There is no proof in this *ḥadīth* for those who hold that it is incumbent for neighbours to have the right of pre-emption, because ʿĀ'ishah only asked about which neighbour she should begin with when giving gifts and so he told her that the closer one would be more appropriate." However, Ibn Ḥajar saw that when in his view pre-emption has been granted to neighbours by another *ḥadīth* then this *ḥadīth* logically establishes by analogical reasoning which neighbour has first priority over it.

Ibn Juzayy al-Kalbī said:

Shufʿah is incumbent with five preconditions:

1. That it relates to properties such as dwellings, land, orchards and wells, and there is a difference of opinion in the [Mālikī] *madhhab* concerning trees and fruits, and there are two [differing] narrations related from Mālik. Ash-Shāfiʿī and Abū Ḥanīfah said that it is prohibited. There is also a difference of opinion concerning those properties that have not been divided up such as public baths and the like, and about debt and rent. According

to the dominant majority there is no pre-emption with respect to animals and goods.

2. That it should be in *mushāᶜ* property that has not been divided up. If it has been divided up, there is no pre-emption.

3. That the pre-emptor must be a partner, for there is no pre-emption for a neighbour, contrary to Abū Ḥanīfah.[31]

4. That nothing appears from the pre-emptor which would show the waiving of the [right to] pre-emption whether words, deeds, or silence for a period of a year or more along with his knowing about it and his being present, but if he is absent and did not know then by unanimous agreement his [right to] pre-emption is not waived. If he knew but he was absent, then [his right to] pre-emption is not waived, contrary to some people. Some people said that [his right to] pre-emption is waived after his remaining silent for three days. And pre-emption is waived if he waives it after the purchase and it is not waived if he waived it before the purchase. Similarly, it is waived if the purchaser haggled over the share or rented it from him and he was silent until he introduced the planting of a tree or built on it.

5. That the portion for which pre-emption is being made had become the property of the person being pre-empted by some form of exchange such as purchase, as a dowry, from a *khulᶜ* [divorce settlement], as a compensatory payment for injury or homicide. If it had become his through inheritance then there is unanimous agreement that there is no pre-emption for it. And if it became his through gift, then there are two positions with respect to that: some said that pre-emption is incumbent and some said that it is not. Abū Ḥanīfah confined it to purchase. If the pre-emption becomes incumbent for a partner and he undertakes it, then he takes the portion being pre-empted at the price which the person being pre-empted paid for it, and if it had been paid immediately to the person being pre-empted then it is paid immediately to the pre-emptor, and if it was being paid at a certain date to the person being pre-empted then that date is set for the pre-emptor. If the person being pre-empted did not take it for a definite price such as his paying for a dowry or as a compensatory payment, then the pre-emptor takes it for its value.

The underlying principle behind *shufᶜah* is practicality and the desire to prevent the introduction of a stranger among partners

– and neighbours in a certain locality in the view of Abū Ḥanīfah – who is likely to cause inconvenience or vexation. If the law of *shufcah* is not applied it is likely to damage the comfort of the partners and their privacy in their enjoyment of their property rights. The right of *shufcah*, therefore, does not exist with respect to any movable property but it only exists with respect to land and what is naturally included in it e.g. buildings, trees, fruits etc. Ibn Abī Zayd al-Qayrawānī said:

36.1A The right of pre-emption

Pre-emption is allowed in something which is jointly owned.

[*Shufcah* is derived from *shafc* (even), the opposite of odd, because the pre-emptor (*shāfic*) adds the share which he takes to his share and so his share becomes two shares. Ibn al-Ḥājib defined it as the partner taking his share from his partner by compulsory purchase.

Then he moves to the relationship of the neighbour. Our position is that he has no pre-emption. What is taken by force can be a voluntary sale. It is an allowance which is allowed to avert harm to the partner. Jābir said, "The Messenger of Allah ﷺ judged that there was pre-emption in all un-demarcated property. When there are clear boundaries and roads are clear, then there is no pre-emption." (Al-Bukhārī, *kitāb al-ḥiyal, bāb fī al-hibah wa ash-shufcah;* and others,) There are two rulings based on this *ḥadīth*: the obligation of pre-emption is for the partner rather than the neighbour because the ruling in the *ḥadīth* is that there is no pre-emption after demarcation, and so a neighbour cannot pre-empt his neighbour. The second is that the obligation concerns real estate rather than goods, and this is what he indicates by mentioning joint ownership (*mushāc*). He means that the right concerns land, buildings and trees attached to it. Al-Fākihānī said that the wisdom in affirmation of pre-emption is the removal of annoyance to the partner and it is particular to real estate because annoyance occurs most frequently in it. They agree that there is no pre-emption in animals, clothes, utensils and all moveables. A precondition for pre-emption is that it is something in which division is feasible, thus excluding things which cannot be divided without being rendered unsound, like a bath-house.] (Al-Qayrawānī, Ibn Abī Zayd, *Risālah, 36. Property Rights, 36.1 Pre-emption in property (shufcah)*

The right of pre-emption, according to Ḥanafī jurists, can only be exercised by an owner who has an undivided share in the property sold. This right cannot be exercised by a tenant no matter how long he stays in the premises. Shāfi^cī jurists are of the opinion that the right of *shuf^cah* can only be exercised with respect to a sale which means an immediate transfer for a definite price including, however, a pledge by conditional sale whenever it becomes absolute.

Mālikī jurists have set a time limit about exercising the right of pre-emption. They say that the pre-emptor must sue within one year of the sale but Shāfi^cī jurists are of the opinion that the pre-emptor must sue with all reasonable speed. Ḥanafī jurists say that the pre-emptor must make three specific demands for his right of pre-emption.

The right of *shuf^cah*, it should be noted, has not been mentioned in the text of the Noble Qur'ān, but the prophetic guidance contained in the *ḥadīth* make reference to this right. In reality this is the right of good partnership in which case a partner tries to save his partner an embarrassment and the problems which may otherwise be caused because of the nearness of the house or property or land situated to each other. As we have seen, it simply amounts to the right which the owner of an immovable property possesses to acquire by purchase another immovable property which has been sold to another person. The partner must be consulted before such sale is executed since he has the first right either to purchase that property or to have reasonably good people as owners of property in this shared property.

As we have noted, in Ḥanafī *fiqh* the neighbour has a right to pre-emption but this is not the case in the other three *madhhabs*. This is from the *Risālah* of Ibn Abī Zayd al-Qayrawānī and its commentary:

36.1B When there is no right to pre-emption

There is no pre-emption in what has been divided, nor is there pre-emption with respect to a neighbour, a road, the courtyard of a house whose rooms have been divided, a male palm tree or a well when the palm trees or the land has been divided. There is only pre-emption in land and the buildings and trees on it.

[Pre-emption was prescribed either to avoid harm in the division or harm to a partner. That does not exist in demarcated property which is why there is no pre-emption in it. Three of the Imāms agree that the neighbour has no pre-emption while Abū Ḥanīfah disagrees and affirms pre-emption for the neighbour, but in his view the partner takes precedence over the neighbour. There is no pre-emption for a private road shared between partners in a house or a garden. As for public roads, it is not permitted to sell them. As for a yard when the house is divided, there is no pre-emption, but if the estate is not divided and then is sold and one of the partners has his share of the estate and the road, then there is agreement that there is pre-emption in both the estate and the road.] (*Ibid.*)

Categories of Pre-emptors

In the *Majallah,* an Ottoman manual of the *fiqh* of *muᶜāmalāt* (ordinary transactions), there is this outline:

SECTION 1. DEGREES OF PRE-EMPTION.

1008. There are three causes of pre-emption.

1. Where a person is the joint owner of the property sold. As where two persons jointly own an undivided share of real property.

This is termed *ash-shāfiᶜ ash-sharīk*. Whenever the right of pre-emption is in respect of a partner in the property or real estate that is sold it is commonly called pre-emption by a partner. This right is derived from previously quoted prophetic *ḥadīth* and a large number of others which, in different wordings, establish that partners in un-demarcated land or property have the right to pre-emption.

2. Where a person is part of a servitude in the thing sold. As where a person shares in a private right of taking water or in a private road. (See 3rd at the end of Examples)

Examples:

A. One of several gardens each having shares in a private right of taking water is sold. Each of the owners of the other gardens obtains a right of pre-emption, whether they are adjoining neighbours or not.

B. A house opening on to a private road is sold. Each of the owners of the other houses giving on to the private road obtains a right of pre-emption, whether they are adjoining neighbours or not.

But if a house taking water from a river which is open to the use of the public or the doors of which give on to a public road is sold, the owners of the other houses taking water from such river, or which give on to the public road, do not possess any right of pre-emption.

This is termed *ash-shāfic al-khalīṭ*. Whenever this right is in respect of a partner in the amenities and appendages of the property (such as the right to access to private shared water and roads, or common (public) facilities access).

3. Where a person is an adjoining neighbour to the thing sold.

This is *ash-shāfic al-jār*. This right is derived from the prophetic *ḥadīth* which says:

جَارُ الدَّارِ أَحَقُّ بِدَارِ الْجَارِ

The neighbour of the house has more right to the neighbour's house. (Abū Dāwūd, *kitāb al-ijārah, bāb fī ash-shufcah*, at-Tirmidhī, *abwāb al-aḥkām can rasūlillāh ﷺ, bāb mā jā'a fī ash-shufcah*)

There are a number of *ḥadīth* in this same sense, pertaining to property and to land. Again from the *Majallah*.

1009. The right of pre-emption belongs:

First, to the person who is a joint owner of the thing sold.

Second, to the person who is a joint owner of the servitude[32] over the thing sold.

Third, to the adjoining neighbour.

If the first person claims his right of pre-emption, the others lose theirs. If the second person claims his right of pre-emption, the third person loses his. (*The Mejelle; being an English translation of Majallah el-aḥkām-i-cadliya and a complete code on Islamic civil law* by Charles Robert Tyser, Sir; D G Demtriades; Ismail, Efendi; Turkey. Published widely on the Internet, for example at: http://www.iiu.edu.my/deed/lawbase/al_majalle)

So clearly the neighbour is the last person in the chain of people who may have pre-emption according to the Ḥanafī *madhhab*.

The following conditions are strictly to be adhered to while claiming or awarding the right of *shuf*ᶜ*ah*:

1. If there are a number of pre-emptors claiming the right of *shuf*ᶜ*ah*, a partner in property would be preferred to a partner in amenities and a partner in amenities is preferred to a neighbour. If the first relinquishes his right the second becomes entitled to it. When the second one gives up his right then the third, that is the neighbour, is entitled to pre-empt the property. This can be illustrated in a case when a large building is situated in a cul-de-sac and is jointly owned by two persons. When one of them sells the share the right of *shuf*ᶜ*ah* will logically be claimed by the partner in the building. Supposing the partner relinquishes his right, the people living in that street will claim the right without any distinction since they share the amenity, i.e. the passage leading to that building. If they all give up their rights then the right will automatically devolve on to the neighbour who lives right behind the building.
2. If a non-Muslim buys a house from another non-Muslim not paying in cash but in something *ḥarām*, and if the right of *shuf*ᶜ*ah* was claimed by another non-Muslim there is no harm in his substituting himself for the previous buyer by paying with the same *ḥarām* commodity. However, if the right of *shuf*ᶜ*ah* is claimed by a Muslim he cannot, from the point of view of *Sharī*ᶜ*ah*, pay in terms of something *ḥarām*. He can only pay in cash. (*Cf. Fatāwā* ᶜ*Ālamgīrī*. vol. 5, p. 383)
3. There does not exist any right of pre-emption in *awqāf*, charitable endowments and establishments. In this case

neither the person or persons managing the *waqf* property (*mutawallī*) nor any beneficiary can claim this right.[33]

4. There is no right of *shufᶜah* in agricultural lands belonging to the *bayt al-māl*, that is, the public treasury.

The right of *shufᶜah*, it should be emphasised, exists only at the time of executing the sale and only in *ᶜaqār*, i.e. real estate. This right is awarded on demand (*ṭalab*). A decree is obtained from the *qāḍī* or judge as regards the ownership of the property only after a valid sale and after a cessation of the seller's ownership of the property sold is established. If the sale is invalid the right of pre-emption does not exist. Similarly, there is no right of pre-emption when the property is acquired by inheritance or gift or the property is given as dower or on hire. The right of *shufᶜah* can be claimed by Muslims and non-Muslims alike, although this was not the position of Aḥmad ibn Ḥanbal, male or female, adult or minor. For a minor the father or guardian would claim the right.

The demand or *ṭalab* made by the person who is claiming the right of pre-emption is divided in the following three categories:

1. *Aṭ-Ṭalab al-Muwāthabah*: This means that the demand is made immediately. As for example, the moment that the person who is claiming the right of *shufᶜah* comes to know about the sale of the property, he must claim his right immediately without losing any time. Supposing he remains silent without making a *ṭalab* or claim to his right, the right would lapse. Imām Muḥammad ibn al-Ḥasan ash-Shaybānī, the Ḥanafī jurist, was of the view that there is no harm if the demand is made at any time during the meeting in which the news of the sale is received. There is no special formula in which the demand is expressed. It will be quite appropriate if the words or sentences clearly show the intention to exercise the right of pre-emption.
2. *Ṭalab al-Ishhād*: This means that the demand is made with the invocation of witnesses. In this case the person claiming the right of *shufᶜah* calls witnesses to attest his

demand which will provide him with proof in case the seller denies that the demand was ever made. The pre-emptor then can call his witnesses to testify that he did make the demand in the presence of witnesses as soon as he heard of the sale. Thus, he did not abandon his right when he heard of the news of the sale before he rose from the meeting in which the news of the sale of the property reached him.

3. *Ṭalab al-Khaṣūmah*: This is a claim of the right of *shufᶜah* by litigation. In this case, a person claiming the right of pre-emption petitions the judge to order the purchaser of the property to surrender it to him. This mode of claim is also known as *ṭalab at-tamalluk* whose actual sense means obtaining the decree of the *qāḍī*. The right of pre-emption will not be annulled if the pre-emptor is not in a position to litigate the matter due to illness or imprisonment. As far as possible he should appoint an agent but if he is unable to do so the right of pre-emption will still exist and he can claim it later.

The right of *shufᶜah* becomes null and void when it is abandoned voluntarily (*ikhtiyārī*). Once the sale has taken place, the pre-emptor says in no uncertain terms that he has made his right of pre-emption void or that he has waived the right of pre-emption. The right is rendered null and void necessarily (*ḍarūrī*) when the pre-emptor dies after making the demand and before taking possession of the property. In this case, the Ḥanafī jurists are of the view that the claimant's right is extinguished by his death. However, if the seller of the property dies, the pre-emptor can still demand his right from the heirs of the owner of the property. If the seller of the property gives the property as a gift to the buyer, and brings witnesses while doing so, the right of pre-emption is invalidated.

Likewise, when the owner of the property gives the property as *ṣadaqah* to someone the right of pre-emption is invalidated.

The right of *shufᶜah* is not exercised or claimed by many people in some Muslim countries (like West Africa) simply because they are unaware of such right. It is, therefore, the duty of the *ᶜulamā'* and the jurists to educate the people so that the right of *shufᶜah* may be properly claimed.

Notes

[1] *Cf.* aṭ-Ṭabarī, *Tafsīr,* Vol. III, pp. 384-96; V, pp. 250-62.
[2] i.e. The generality of the *fuqahā'* transmitting to the generality of the *fuqahā'*. Ed.
[3] Ash-Shāfiᶜī, *Risālah,* translated by Majid Khadduri, *Op. Cit.* pp. 141-2.
[4] The generality of the *fuqahā'*. Ed.
[5] Ordinarily the practice of Ibn Juzayy al-Kalbī in his *tafsīr* and in his *al-Qawānīn al-fiqhiyyah* is to note the differences of the *madhhabs* where they exist, so that his silence on the matter indicates a general agreement.
[6] Fyzee, A. A. A., *Mohammedan Law,* p. 348
[7] Ameer Ali, *Muslim Law,* 1938, p. 366
[8] For further definition of *hibah cf.* Ibn ᶜĀṣim, *Tuḥfat al-ḥukkām,* rule 1191: *al-Hidāyah,* Vol. 3, p. 291
[9] Al-Bukhārī 51: 1
[10] Al-Bukhārī 51:12
[11] Al-Bukhārī 51:14-15
[12] Al-Bukhārī 51:28-29
[13] Al-Bukhārī 51:11
[14] Al-Bukhārī 51:30
[15] Al-Qayrawānī, *Risālah, Op. Cit.,* ch. 36: *Bāb fī ash-shufᶜah wa al-hibah* pp. 116-120
[16] Al-Qayrawānī, *Risālah, Op. Cit.,* ch. 36: *Bāb fī ash-shufᶜah wa al-hibah,* pp. 116-120
[17] *Mushāᶜ* property is that which is undivided and shared in common by a group of people.
[18] *Fatāwā ᶜĀlamgīrī* Vol. 4, p. 526

[19] Ibn ᶜĀṣim, *Tuḥfat al-ḥukkām*, No. 1212 and 1213.
[20] *Fatāwā ᶜĀlamgīrī*, Vol. 4, p. 537; *Durr al-Mukhtār*. Vol. 3, p. 499.
[21] For detailed study of *waqf*, see Shalabi (Dr.) Muḥammad Muṣṭafā, *Muḥāḍarāt fī al-waṣiyyah*, Cairo 1956, p. 9.
[22] Literally make a *ḥubus* of it.
[23] Al-Ilī, ᶜAbd al-Ḥakīm Ḥasan, *Al-Ḥurriyyat al-ᶜammah*, Cairo 1974, pp. 505-506
[24] Von Kremer, *The Orient under the Caliphs*, translated by Khuda Buksh, University of Calcutta, 1920, P. 285: also cf. Khālid Rashīd, *Op. Cit.*, p. xix
[25] Ameer Ali, *A Short History of the Saracens*, London, 1951. P. 422
[26] Khālid Rashīd, *Muslim Law*, Lucknow, 1979, P. 140. This statement is quoted on the authority of Professor Humayun Kabir at one time Minister of Scientific Research and Cultural Affairs and Awqaf in India.
[27] A recommended general work on Ottoman history is Maksudoglu, Mehmet, *Osmanli History*. 1999. ISBN 983-9727-05-2. Research Centre IIUM: Kuala Lumpur.
[28] As-Sufi, Shaykh Dr. Abdalqadir, *Sultaniyya*, Chapter 3, *Waqf*, by Prof. Mehmet Maksudoglu, p. 57. In this chapter by Prof. Maksudoglu he gives a great deal of detail on the workings of Osmanli *awqāf*.
[29] For a Ḥanafī definition of *shufᶜah* see *Durr al-Mukhtār* vol. 4 p. 126; *al-Hidāyah* vol. 3, p. 561 and *Fatāwā ᶜĀlamgīr*, chapter 7.
[30] For further details of *ḥadīth* on the same subject see *Muwaṭṭa'* of Imām Mālik p. 371 and *Musnad* of Imām Abū Ḥanīfah, p. 308
[31] A matter of disagreement among the *ᶜulamā'* with the three other Imāms agreeing that the neighbour has no right to pre-emption.
[32] This term used by the translator was already explained: "As where a person shares in a private right of taking water or in a private road."
[33] This example is difficult to understand as a *waqf* may not be sold.

Part VI
The Economic Way

Chapter 23

Tijārah: Trade and Commerce

Guidance from the Qur'ān and Sunnah on the Islamic Way of Transacting Commerce

THERE ARE A NUMBER of Qur'ānic injunctions which have encouraged Muslims to engage themselves in lawful trade and in a wide range of commercial activities. Some of the injunctions mention trade as seeking the *"faḍl* of Allah", the bounty of Allah. There are a number of *ḥadīth* of the Prophet ﷺ which also support the Qur'ānic injunctions. In order to do successful trade, Muslims have been asked to undertake travel.

عَلِمَ أَن سَيَكُونُ مِنكُم مَّرْضَىٰ وَآخَرُونَ يَضْرِبُونَ فِي الْأَرْضِ يَبْتَغُونَ مِن فَضْلِ اللَّهِ وَآخَرُونَ يُقَاتِلُونَ فِي سَبِيلِ اللَّهِ

> *He knows that some of you are ill and that others are travelling in the land seeking Allah's bounty, and that others are fighting in the Way of Allah.* (Sūrat al-Muzzammil 73: 20)

Ibn Juzayy al-Kalbī said about this *āyah* in *Kitāb at-tashīl li ᶜulūm at-tanzīl*:

> Then He made exceptions from this obligation [to stand in prayer at night][1] for three categories:
>
> First, the sick since their sickness is a valid excuse. Lastly, the *mujāhidūn* because of the importance of *jihād*. In between these two categories there is a third, who are the traders whom He refers to as *"travelling in the land seeking Allah's bounty."*

The noted scholar aṣ-Ṣāwī said in his gloss on the *tafsīr* of the *Jalālayn*:

> Allah, exalted is He, in this *āyah* regarded as equal: *mujāhidūn* and those earning *ḥalāl* livelihoods in order to spend it on themselves and their dependants, indicating that earning wealth is of the same rank as *jihād*, because of that which is transmitted in the *ḥadīth*, "Whoever conveys food from one city to another and sells it at its price on that day will have the rank of the martyrs with Allah."
>
> Ibn Masᶜūd said, "Whatever man conveys anything from one of the cities of Islam patiently anticipating [a reward from Allah] and sells it at its price on that day, has a rank with Allah like that of the martyrs," and then he recited, *"others travelling in the land seeking Allah's bounty."* (Aṣ-Ṣāwī, *al-Ḥāshiyah ᶜalā al-Jalālayn*)

There are so many bounties of Allah mentioned in the Qur'ān, and one of them is the use of the seas, oceans and rivers for help in internal and external trade and movements of goods and commodities.

وَتَرَى الْفُلْكَ مَوَاخِرَ فِيهِ وَلِتَبْتَغُوا مِنْ فَضْلِهِ وَلَعَلَّكُمْ تَشْكُرُونَ

> *And you see the ships cleaving through it so that you can seek His bounty, and so that hopefully you will show thanks.* (Sūrat an-Naḥl 16: 14)

Allah has also helped in sending the wind for sailors to sail the sea for wayfarers seeking the bounties of Allah through trade:

وَمِنْ آيَاتِهِ أَنْ يُرْسِلَ الرِّيَاحَ مُبَشِّرَاتٍ وَلِيُذِيقَكُمْ مِنْ رَحْمَتِهِ وَلِتَجْرِيَ الْفُلْكُ بِأَمْرِهِ وَلِتَبْتَغُوا مِنْ فَضْلِهِ
وَلَعَلَّكُمْ تَشْكُرُونَ

> *Among His Signs is that He sends the winds bearing good news, to give you a taste of His mercy, and to make the ships run by His command, and to enable you to seek His bounty so that hopefully you will be thankful.* (Sūrat ar-Rūm 30: 46)

Analogous to the wind for the age of sailing ships is the bounty of Allah in creating the oil that drives contemporary forms of transport.

In Sūrat al-Jumuᶜah, however, we have been warned that engagement in trade must not make us negligent of our duties to Allah. As soon as the call for Friday's prayer is given, and likewise the call for other prayers, we are asked to close our business and answer the call earnestly and loyally and submit to Allah:

يَا أَيُّهَا الَّذِينَ آمَنُوا إِذَا نُودِيَ لِلصَّلاَةِ مِن يَوْمِ الْجُمُعَةِ فَاسْعَوْا إِلَى ذِكْرِ اللَّهِ وَذَرُوا الْبَيْعَ ذَلِكُمْ خَيْرٌ لَّكُمْ إِن كُنتُمْ تَعْلَمُونَ

You who have īmān! when you are called to ṣalāh on the Day of Jumuᶜah, hasten to the remembrance of Allah and abandon trade. That is better for you if you only knew. (Sūrat al-Jumuᶜah 62: 9)

Apart from prayers, the Mosque provides for believers a meeting place, a place of consultation where contacts are also established. Brothers in Islam become closer, and thus it helps in cementing relationships even outside the Mosque. After the prayers, we are asked to disperse in the land of Allah and continue our trade and transactions and earn our livelihood in *ḥalāl* ways:

فَإِذَا قُضِيَتِ الصَّلاَةُ فَانتَشِرُوا فِي الْأَرْضِ وَابْتَغُوا مِن فَضْلِ اللَّهِ وَاذْكُرُوا اللَّهَ كَثِيراً لَّعَلَّكُمْ تُفْلِحُونَ

Then when the ṣalāh is finished spread through the earth and seek Allah's bounty and remember Allah much so that hopefully you will be successful. (Sūrat al-Jumuᶜah 62: 10)

We are reminded, however, that the business and trade must not make us forget our responsibility towards Allah and His Messenger ﷺ. During the time of the Prophet ﷺ, once he was delivering a sermon and people heard the voices of a caravan of traders arriving. Some people rushed away without listening to the *khuṭbah* (sermon) of the Prophet ﷺ in order to do business with the caravan that was arriving. Therefore, the following verse was revealed as a reproach:

وَإِذَا رَأَوْا تِجَارَةً أَوْ لَهْواً انفَضُّوا إِلَيْهَا وَتَرَكُوكَ قَائِماً قُلْ مَا عِندَ اللَّهِ خَيْرٌ مِّنَ اللَّهْوِ وَمِنَ التِّجَارَةِ وَاللَّهُ خَيْرُ الرَّازِقِينَ

But when they see a chance of trade or entertainment they scatter off to it and leave you standing there. Say: 'What is with Allah is better than trade or entertainment. Allah is the Best of Providers.' (Sūrat al-Jumuᶜah 62: 11)

The Messenger of Allah ﷺ engaged in trade as an agent of his wife Sayyidatunā Khadījah. He once said:

التَّاجِرُ الأَمِينُ الصَّدُوقُ المُسْلِمُ مَعَ الشُّهَدَاءِ يَوْمَ القِيَامَةِ

The trustworthy, honest Muslim trader is with the martyrs on the Day of Rising. (Ibn Mājah, *kitāb at-tijārāt, bāb al-ḥathth ᶜalā al-makāsib*)

In yet another *ḥadīth*, he ﷺ said:

التَّاجِرُ الصَّدُوقُ الأَمِينُ، مَعَ النَّبِيِّينَ وَالصِّدِّيقِينَ وَالشُّهَدَاءِ

The trustworthy honest trader is with the prophets, the utterly truthful (*ṣiddīqūn*), and the martyrs. (Al-Ḥākim, *al-Mustadrak*)

These words of the Prophet ﷺ have given honest trading such a high status that those engaged in it are likened to the martyrs who fight and give their lives in *jihād fī sabīlillāh* (war in the path of Allah). That an honest trader will rise up with the martyrs also means that if he continues his trade without deceiving people and without practising usury and adheres to other rulings of lawful trade, then it will be construed as if he has passed his life waging 'economic *jihād*.'

How should trade and business be carried out

The following code of conduct for Muslim traders is given in the Generous Qur'ān:

يَا أَيُّهَا الَّذِينَ آمَنُوا لاَ تَأْكُلُوا أَمْوَالَكُمْ بَيْنَكُمْ بِالْبَاطِلِ إِلاَّ أَنْ تَكُونَ تِجَارَةً عَنْ تَرَاضٍ مِنْكُمْ وَلاَ تَقْتُلُوا أَنْفُسَكُمْ إِنَّ اللهَ كَانَ بِكُمْ رَحِيماً

You who have īmān! do not consume one another's property by false means, but only by means of mutually agreed trade. And do not kill yourselves. Allah is Most Merciful to you. (Sūrat an-Nisā' 4: 29)

The above verse of the Noble Qur'ān has set down an important principle concerning trade (*tijārah*). Every Muslim should live his life knowing that he is always in the presence of Allah.

We have to think that we hold all property as a trust from Allah, whether the property is in our own name or in someone else's name or belongs to the entire community. The Qur'ānic words "false means (*bi'l-bāṭil*)" refer to those practices which are against the *Sharīʿah* and are thus unlawful. The trade should be such that in the process there is an exchange of benefits as profit without exercising any unlawful pressure or fraud on either party. There should be no bribery or usury in the trade.

The Qur'ānic verse emphasises mutual agreement in the trade which means that there should be no dissatisfaction or disagreement between the parties in a commercial transaction. People often think that there is no harm in practising bribery or usury, if there is the full agreement of both parties. In reality, even this agreement has come about by force of circumstances. There is still a great deal of concealed 'pressure' to enter into such agreements, just as in gambling there is seemingly an agreement between the parties to a bet, but in reality, that sort of tacit agreement has come about as a result of false hopes in their minds that they are going to win. One does not participate in gambling in the hope of losing. Likewise, in fraudulent practices in trade there also seems to be an agreement between parties but it is not such that the loser in the fraud is aware of the actual fraud. Had he known about it, he would certainly have refrained from it.

In Sūrat al-Baqarah, believers are asked not to use their property to corrupt judges or those in authority with the intention of wrongfully and knowingly consuming other people's property.

وَلَا تَأْكُلُوا أَمْوَالَكُم بَيْنَكُم بِالْبَاطِلِ وَتُدْلُوا بِهَا إِلَى الْحُكَّامِ لِتَأْكُلُوا فَرِيقًا مِّنْ أَمْوَالِ النَّاسِ بِالْإِثْمِ وَأَنتُمْ
تَعْلَمُونَ

Do not devour one another's property by false means nor offer it to the judges as a bribe, trying through crime to knowingly usurp a portion of other people's property. (Sūrat al-Baqarah 2: 188)

Although the above verse speaks of bribing judges and other authorities in acquiring someone's property, many such cases arise out of contractual trade agreements between two parties that end up in the law courts where one of the parties, through the influence of bribes, wins the case wrongfully and thus acquires someone else's property.

The Qur'ānic injunction puts a stop to such practices. Even though the court may order in favour of the wrong party, it will not become lawful (*ḥalāl*) for him as the *ḥadīth* of the Prophet ﷺ testifies:

إِنَّمَا أَنَا بَشَرٌ، وَإِنَّكُمْ تَخْتَصِمُونَ إِلَيَّ، فَلَعَلَّ بَعْضَكُمْ أَنْ يَكُونَ أَلْحَنَ بِحُجَّتِهِ مِنْ بَعْضٍ، فَأَقْضِى لَهُ
عَلَى نَحْوِ مَا أَسْمَعُ مِنْهُ، فَمَنْ قَضَيْتُ لَهُ بِشَيْءٍ مِنْ حَقِّ أَخِيهِ فَلَا يَأْخُذَنَّ مِنْهُ شَيْئًا، فَإِنَّمَا أَقْطَعُ
لَهُ قِطْعَةً مِنَ النَّارِ

> I am but a man to whom you bring your disputes. Perhaps one of you is more eloquent in his proof than the other, so I give judgement according to what I have heard from him. Whatever I decide for him which is part of the right of his brother, he must not take any of it, for I am granting him a portion of the Fire. (Mālik in the *Muwaṭṭa'*, Book 36: Judgements, Section 1: Stimulation of Desire to Judge Correctly, Number 36.1.1, Aḥmad, al-Bukhārī, *kitāb al-maẓālim, bāb ithm man khāṣama fī bāṭil wa huwa ya^clamuhu;* Muslim, *kitāb al-aqḍiyah, bāb al-ḥukm bi aẓ-ẓāhir wa al-laḥn bi al-ḥujjah;* and the four authors of the *sunan* collections, from Umm Salamah)

As they are human weaknesses, greed and temptations overpower man, particularly greed for wealth and property.

According to a tradition, man ages and two things become younger in him: the desire to accumulate more wealth and the desire to live longer. Ordinarily, honest men and true believers in Allah are content with whatever they get. In their trade and business they are straightforward and they establish right with justice as commanded by Allah:

وَأَقِيمُوا الْوَزْنَ بِالْقِسْطِ وَلَا تُخْسِرُوا الْمِيزَانَ

Give just weight – do not skimp in the balance. (Sūrat ar-Raḥmān 55: 9)

Every Muslim must be honest in every matter, such as weighing out things when he is selling and in all other dealings with people. He must not cheat by displaying specimens of a good quality and then selling inferior stuff, or giving less weight than agreed upon.

Every Muslim is ordered to earn his livelihood in a lawful manner. If one acquires property through unlawful means and then gives out charity (*ṣadaqah*) and *zakāh* to the poor and needy, it will not be acceptable to Allah. On the contrary, he will be deemed to have committed a wrong action.

مَنْ جَمَعَ مَالاً حَرَاماً ثُمَّ تَصَدَّقَ بِهِ لَمْ يَكُنْ لَهُ فِيهِ أَجْرٌ ، وَكَانَ إِصْرُهُ عَلَيْهِ

Whosoever acquires unlawful wealth and then gives it away as *ṣadaqah* will have no reward, and he will have to bear the burden [of his wrongdoing]. (Ibn Khuzaymah, Ibn Ḥibbān and al-Ḥākim from Abū Hurayrah, as cited in *Kanz al-ᶜummāl*)

Any property earned in an unlawful manner and through *ḥarām* means, has no blessing from Allah, and whatever property such a person leaves behind for his progeny, also becomes a source of greater problems in this world and the next world. Allah, our Creator, does not wipe out evil with evil or dirt with dirt. Any property earned with evil means continues its evil effect for generations to come. Lawful property acquired with lawful means will have its blessings which will become perceptible even among one's progeny.

The Messenger of Allah has said:

وَلَا يَكْسِبُ عَبْدٌ مَالاً مِنْ حَرَامٍ فَيُنْفِقُ مِنْهُ فَيُبَارَكُ لَهُ فِيهِ ، وَلَا يَتَصَدَّقُ بِهِ فَيُقْبَلُ مِنْهُ ، وَلَا يَتْرُكُهُ خَلْفَ ظَهْرِهِ إِلَّا كَانَ زَادَهُ إِلَى النَّارِ ، إِنَّ اللهَ لَا يَمْحُو السَّيِّئَ بِالسَّيِّئِ وَلَكِنْ يَمْحُو السَّيِّئَ بِالْحَسَنِ ، إِنَّ الْخَبِيثَ لَا يَمْحُو الْخَبِيثَ .

When a slave of Allah earns property in a *ḥarām* manner and then spends from it, he will have no blessing from it and if he gives *ṣadaqah* from it, it will not be accepted of him. If he leaves it behind [to be inherited] it becomes his provision for the Fire. Allah does not erase evil by means of evil, but He erases evil by means of good. Dirt does not erase dirt. (Aḥmad, al-Ḥākim in *al-Mustadrak*, and al-Bayhaqī in *Shuᶜab al-īmān* from Ibn Masᶜūd, as cited in *Kanz al-ᶜummāl*)

When we try to understand the Divine injunctions and the further explanations given by the Prophet ﷺ, it becomes clear that the Divine laws strike at the very root of modern capitalism. They enjoin moral rules upon man in his earning and spending and hold him responsible for the wellbeing of his fellow man. Hoarding is thus condemned,[2] usury forbidden,[3] extravagance denounced[4] and moderation enjoined.[5] Wealth is not to be devoured in vanity[6] but is to be developed by fair means and through generosity and trade so that it is used for the welfare of the community, hence there will be no need for inventions such as socialism.

The Qur'ān thus enjoins the cardinal values of equity, justice, mutual co-operation and self-sacrifice for organising the socio-economic fabric of Islamic society. It is narrated that the Prophet ﷺ said:

مَنْ وَلِيَ شَيْئاً مِنْ أُمُورِ الْمُسْلِمِينَ لَمْ يَنْظُرِ اللَّهُ فِي حَاجَتِهِ حَتَّى يَنْظُرَ فِي حَوائِجِهِمْ.

Whoever is put in charge of any of the affairs of the Muslims, Allah will not look into his needs until he looks into their needs. (Aṭ-Ṭabarānī in *al-Kabīr* from Ibn ᶜUmar)

He has further said, speaking about public office:

وَإِنَّهَا أَمَانَةٌ. وَإِنَّهَا ، يَوْمَ الْقِيَامَةِ، خِزْيٌ وَنَدَامَةٌ. إِلَّا مَنْ أَخَذَهَا بِحَقِّهَا وَأَدَّى الَّذِي عَلَيْهِ فِيهَا

It [public office] is a trust, and it will be on the Day of Rising a humiliation and a cause for regret except for those who take it according to its right and discharge what is due from them in it. (Muslim, *kitāb al-imārah, bāb kirāhat al-imārah bi ghayri ḍarūrah*)

Again:

مَا آمَنَ بِي مَنْ بَاتَ شَبْعَانَ وَجَارُهُ جَائِعٌ إِلَى جَنْبِهِ وَهُوَ يَعْلَمُ بِهِ.

Whoever knowingly passes the night satiated while his close neighbour is hungry does not believe in me. (Al-Bazzār, aṭ-Ṭabarānī from Anas)

It was for this reason that the Caliph ʿUmar ※ declared: "ʿUmar ibn al-Khaṭṭāb would be answerable to Allah if a camel starved to death along the Euphrates."

A study of the teachings of the Qur'ān and the Prophet's sayings suggests the objective of setting up a just economic order which stops exploitation and sets up a contented, satisfied society. Islamic society is genuinely devoted to human welfare. It would need a voluminous book to detail what the early Islamic governments did to achieve this objective.

Directions for Sale Transactions

Men and women are allowed to engage in lawful trade in the *Sharīʿah*. In the *ḥadīth* literature, men and women are mentioned as selling to and buying from one another.[7]

All are equally entitled to trade, hence while a transaction is being carried on with one man and agreement has been reached, another should not intervene because of the words of the Messenger of Allah ※: "Do not let any of you bid against each other." (*Al-Muwaṭṭa'*, Book 31, Number 31.44.96) The *Sharīʿah* allows an auction, because, although it is forbidden to bid on top of someone else's bid, this is only in the case when the seller and purchaser have reached agreement. Before that it is permissible to bid.

Traders should not go out to meet the caravans that come for trade because of the *ḥadīth* of the Messenger of Allah ※: "Do not go out to meet the caravans for trade." (*Al-Muwaṭṭa'*, Book 31, Number 31.44.97) This malpractice is known in English as 'forestalling', and it was by way of its proliferation that key modalities of modern trade have become prevalent. It is, however, forbidden in the *Sharīʿah* as it was forbidden in Common Law, which is the basis of both US and UK law.

Hoarding food is unlawful.[8] It is through this inhuman practice that society suffers, while the hoarder raises the price. The cattle seller is prohibited from leaving them unmilked for some days before selling so that they might fetch a higher price.[9] This is simply deception. Fruits or crops must not be sold before they are in a fit condition because it is not guaranteed that they will reach maturity.[10] The fruits on trees can only be sold if they are properly estimated.[11] Someone who buys some fruit, fresh or dry, should not resell it until he gets full possession of it.[12] Frivolously making oaths in sale transactions is also expressly forbidden. This practice is rampant in many Muslim countries where traders keep on taking oaths to describe their merchandise and their prices.

The Noble Qur'ān, as we have seen before, lays stress on honest and straightforward dealing in the very earliest revelations:

وَيْلٌ لِّلْمُطَفِّفِينَ الَّذِينَ إِذَا اكْتَالُوا عَلَى النَّاسِ يَسْتَوْفُونَ وَإِذَا كَالُوهُمْ أَو وَّزَنُوهُمْ يُخْسِرُونَ

Woe to the stinters! Those who, when they take a measure from people, exact full measure, but when they give them a measure or weight, hand over less than is due. (Sūrat al-Muṭaffifīn 83: 1-3)

وَأَوْفُوا الْكَيْلَ إِذَا كِلْتُمْ وَزِنُوا بِالْقِسْطَاسِ الْمُسْتَقِيمِ ذَٰلِكَ خَيْرٌ وَأَحْسَنُ تَأْوِيلًا

Give full measure when you measure and weigh with a level balance. That is better and gives the best result. (Sūrat al-Isrā' 17: 35)

أَوْفُوا الْكَيْلَ وَلَا تَكُونُوا مِنَ الْمُخْسِرِينَ وَزِنُوا بِالْقِسْطَاسِ الْمُسْتَقِيمِ وَلَا تَبْخَسُوا النَّاسَ أَشْيَاءَهُمْ وَلَا تَعْثَوْا فِي الْأَرْضِ مُفْسِدِينَ

Give full measure. Do not skimp. Weigh with a level balance. Do not diminish people's goods and do not go about the earth, corrupting it. (Sūrat ash-Shuᶜarā' 26: 180-2)

ᶜUqbah ibn ᶜĀmir said, "It is not *ḥalāl* for a man to sell goods knowing that there is a defect in them without making it known." (Al-Bukhārī, *kitāb al-buyūᶜ, bāb idhā bayyana al-bayyiᶜāni wa lam yaktumā wa naṣaḥā*)

It is mentioned that al-ᶜAdā' ibn Khālid said, "The Prophet ﷺ wrote to me: 'This is what Muḥammad the Messenger of Allah ﷺ has bought from al-ᶜAdā' ibn Khālid, the sale from a Muslim to a Muslim, there being no defect in it, nor anything *ḥarām*, and no deception." (*Ibid.*)

According to another *ḥadīth* from Ḥakīm ibn Ḥizām ؓ from the Prophet ﷺ there is that he said:

> Then if the two of them are truthful and make [things] clear, they will be blessed in their sale, but if they conceal [things] and they lie, the blessing of their sale is obliterated. (Al-Bukhārī, *kitāb al-buyū^{c}, bāb mā yamḥaqu al-kadhiba wa al-kitmān fī al-bay^{c}*)

Trade in all forms must be clean and honest. If one carries it out according to the guidance of the Qur'ān and the Sunnah, one will see Allah's blessings even though he may not be able to amass fabulous wealth. After all, as the Messenger of Allah ﷺ has said:

> Nine tenths of provision is in trade, and a tenth in cattle. (Sa^{c}īd ibn al-Manṣūr narrated it)

Trade was encouraged by the Messenger of Allah ﷺ so much that when the *Muhājirūn* (emigrants) fled to Madīnah due to the unbearable persecution of the Makkan pagans, the *Anṣār* (Helpers) became their brothers in *īmān*, and not only gave them shelter but some of them also divided their belongings in half and shared them with their brothers of the *Muhājirūn*. Sa^{c}d ibn ar-Rabī^{c} al-Anṣārī divided all his property into two parts and decided to give one part to ^{c}Abd ar-Raḥmān ibn ^{c}Awf but he said: "May Allah bless you in your family and your property; show me the way to the market." (Al-Bukhārī, *kitāb an-nikāḥ, bāb qawl ar-rajul li akhīhi unẓur ayya zawjatayya shi'ta ḥattā anzila laka ^{c}anhā*) Sa^{c}d informed him that there Banī Qaynuqā^{c} had a big market. Next day, ^{c}Abd ar-Raḥmān ibn ^{c}Awf went to the market with cheese and butter, and made a profit. Later he became a very successful businessman and used his property for the cause of Islam. ^{c}Abd ar-Raḥmān ibn ^{c}Awf was simply following the examples of the Prophet ﷺ, Abū Bakr, ^{c}Umar, and other companions who were engaged in lawful trade at one time or the other in their lives.

As long as there is no coercion, deceit, hoarding, undercutting, usury, uncertain transactions involving *gharar,* two sales in one transaction, every Muslim is encouraged to do trade and business. The only trade that is declared unlawful is that of dealing in usury, wine and other intoxicants, pigs and idols.

It is unlawful, as al-Qayrawānī says, in trading to swindle, cheat or lie in respect of the price, or to deceive. Nor is it lawful to hide defects; nor is it lawful to mix a commodity of poor quality with one of good quality. Furthermore, it is not lawful for a seller to conceal some aspect of his commodity, mention of which could discourage the buyer from buying it, or to hide a defect the mention of which could lower the price.[13]

Here let me point out that Allah is the real owner of all things and man only a legal owner, more appropriately, a trustee with usufructuary rights. Private property is, indeed, a trust in possession and one has to deal with it as is expected of a trustee, and should remember the definition of *īmān* as being true to the trust placed in one by Allah.

Law of Contract

The Arabic word for contract is *ᶜaqd,* which literally means an obligation or a tie. It is an act of 'putting a tie to a bargain.' When two parties enter into contract, it is called *inᶜiqād,* that is joining or tying the offer and the acceptance together. The obligations thus arising out of contracts are called *ᶜuqūd*. We are ordered through Qur'ānic injunction to fulfil all our obligations:

يَا أَيُّهَا الَّذِينَ آمَنُوا أَوْفُوا بِالْعُقُودِ

You who have īmān! fulfil your contracts. (Sūrat al-Mā'idah 5: 1)

The word *ᶜuqūd* used in the Qur'ān is very meaningful and comprehensive. All human beings are required to fulfil the *ḥuqūq Allāh,* the rights of Allah, by establishing the *ṣalāh* (prayers), *ṣawm* (fasting), *zakāh* (poor-due) and Ḥajj (pilgrimage) and to fulfil the *ḥuqūq al-ᶜibād,* the rights of the slaves of Allah, such as repaying debts, honouring contracts, neighbourliness, kindness and mercy to all human beings (and animals). Thus the term *ᶜuqūd* has a much wider connotation compared to the term "contract" in common law.

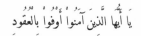

Milk or ownership in Islamic law refers to a relationship between a man and his property, which is under his control to the exclusion of other claimants. One may have physical possession of the property (*milk al-yad*) or right of disposal of the property (*milk at-taṣarruf*) or may have proprietary rights (*milk ar-raghābah*).

The Law of Contract centres round property (*māl*)

Māl is something that exists and can be held in use and be beneficial at the time of need. Air and water cannot be secured and hence, cannot constitute *māl*. Likewise grass and wild trees would not be considered as *māl*. The usufruct of the property will also be included in *māl*, as for example, the rent to be collected by the landlord from his tenant in respect of a house let to him.

Consideration

In the *Sharīᶜah*, a contract is made only when one party offers something to another party for some consideration and the other party accepts the offer. The offer and acceptance must be made in a free manner. The consideration must be lawful. The parties must also agree upon their rights and duties.[14]

Offer

An offer is the first stage of making a contract. The offer can be made in a number of ways:

1. It can be made verbally (*bi'l-kalām*). This kind of offer is to be made in the same meeting.
2. It can be made in writing (*bi'l-kitābah*). This form of offer becomes effective as soon as the letter leaves the person offering and will remain valid until received by the recipient. The offer must be replied to immediately.
3. It can be made through a message sent with some person, a messenger (*rasūl*) whose honesty is not doubted and if the offer is accepted, it will be a good acceptance. Mālikī, Shāfiᶜī and Ḥanbalī jurists are of the opinion that the offer must be made by the owner of the property in return for

a due consideration, but the Ḥanafī jurists say that it can come from either party.

4. It can be made through signs and gestures, particularly in those cases where the person offering is deaf or dumb or when the recipient does not understand the language of the person offering. The Mālikī school regards as valid the well-known signs made by a person without any impediments, since the main idea is that the person offering should communicate the offer. Most jurists believe that the known signs of dumb persons made to constitute an offer are valid, but there are some jurists who consider signs and gestures invalid as modes of making an offer.
5. It can be made by conduct (*fiᶜl*). An offer made through the delivery of goods is valid according to the Mālikī school.

However, an offer cannot be made through silence. If the contracting person keeps silent while he is expected to express himself, it will be deemed an invalid contract.

WITHDRAWAL OF AN OFFER

The time between the making of an offer and its acceptance is called *majlis al-ᶜaqd* (the sitting for the contract). Ḥanafī and Ḥanbalī jurists say that the person offering has the option to withdraw his offer before it has been accepted. Since the person who is to receive has been given the chance to make up his mind whether to accept or reject the offer, it seems equitable that the person offering should also have the right to withdraw his offer before acceptance is made. It is likely that the person offering might have made some mistake or forgotten to include something in his offer, therefore he can quickly withdraw his offer while the other party is still busy in making up his mind whether or not to accept it. But the Mālikī school takes a different view and says that once the offer is communicated to the recipient the person offering has no right to withdraw the offer because he ought to have made up his mind before making an offer, and will not be permitted to change it later on.

Consideration (price)

Consideration is an essential ingredient of a valid contract. Anything that is impossible to attain cannot form a valid consideration.[15]

The consideration must be lawful. Therefore, wine, pork etc., which are not lawful in Islam cannot be offered as a consideration. A contract by a Muslim to sell grapes or dates for preparing wine, will be invalid according to the Mālikī and the Ḥanbalī schools. Likewise, the sale of weapons to robbers or rebels is void.

Competency of parties

The parties who want to enter into a contract must be legally competent to do so. A minor (someone who has not reached the age of puberty), or a slave, or an insolvent person or someone of unsound mind, or an intoxicated person cannot enter into a contract.

Likewise, a person who is terminally ill (*maraḍ al-mawt*) cannot make a valid contract.[16]

Termination of contract

The contract can be terminated by the mutual consent of the parties according to the terms stipulated in their contract, or on the basis of the nature of the contract. Some contracts are terminated unilaterally, while there are others which would need the agreement of both parties. If the consent of one of the parties has been obtained to the contract in a manner which means that it is not a free contract due to coercion, undue influence, fraud, misrepresentation or a mistake then such party may void the contract at his option; but the other party cannot do so.

The contract of sale *ᶜaqd al-bayᶜ*

The contact of sale (*bayᶜ*) means the delivery of a definite object which possesses legal value in exchange for something equivalent in value (called the price). The concept of sale also includes barter (i.e. exchange of one thing for another of equivalent value) although there are a number of limitations on this. Price may be paid immediately on delivery of goods sold, or it may be paid after delivery of the goods bought has been made, or goods may be delivered immediately and the price may be paid later. It is possible to postpone the payment of the price as well as the delivery of the goods.

The purchaser (*mushtarī*) and the seller (*bā'iᶜ*) are each referred to by one generic name *ᶜāqid*. The *ᶜāqid* must possess the following qualifications:

1. He must be *mumayyiz,* a discriminating person, i.e. he must be able to understand the implications of the contract of sale. Thus an insane person or a minor who does not understand the implications of the contract of sale will not be a *mumayyiz*. However, according to all the schools of Islamic Jurisprudence (except ash-Shāfiᶜī) if a minor is *mumayyiz* the contract is valid.
2. He must be capable of disposing of his property.
3. He must be free to use his own discretion (*mukhtār*) i.e. he must not be working under coercion, undue influence, misrepresentation, fraud or a misapprehension.

THE OBJECT FOR SALE

1. It must be owned by the seller or his agent.
2. It must be in a position to be delivered. The sale of a bird in the air or fish in the sea is void.
3. It must be lawful (*ḥalāl*) and wholesome (*ṭāhir*). The sale of unwholesome things like wine, pig and dead animals (except fish) is void.

Ḥawālah: Transfer of Debts

Some contracts are transferrable. As for example, if A lends some money to B, A may, by contracting with B and C, transfer the claim to C, i.e. arrange that B repay the money to C rather than to A. This is called *ḥawālah*[17] (i.e. assignment, transfer or referral). Imām Mālik approves of such transfer but other jurists of the Shāfiᶜī and Ḥanbalī schools oppose it, while the Ḥanafīs allow it in exceptional cases. However, all jurists permit A to sell his claim against B to anyone A wishes or to make a gift of it to any person other than the debtor B. The following are the conditions requisite for a valid *ḥawālah*:

1. The debt which is the subject matter of the contract must be a lawfully subsisting obligation.
2. The original creditor A and debtor B must mutually agree that the assignee debt that constitutes the object of the transfer, should be paid by B to C.
3. The debt must have fallen due, even though it consists of the price to be paid by a slave for his freedom; but it is not necessary that the debt owed to the transferrer C should have fallen due.
4. Both debts must consist in objects of the same kind, equal in quantity and quality; there are several opinions however, as to the varying fineness of coins.[18]
5. The two debts must not consist of foodstuffs which have been purchased.

The uncertain sale (*bay^c^ al-gharar*)

The *gharar*[19] sale is a kind of sale in which uncertainty is involved, such as the sale of fish in the sea or birds in the air before they are caught, and thus it encompasses futures transactions in modern finance. The Messenger of Allah ﷺ has forbidden the *gharar* sale, e.g. the sale of dry dates for unripe dates on the tree except in the case of *^c^arāyā* (pl. of *^c^ariyyah,*[20] see below). Where two or more distinct articles are the objects of a single sale, the price of each should be individually known and determined, otherwise the transaction is void because of uncertainty (*gharar*) and two sales in one sale is forbidden. The *gharar* sale, in other words, involves speculative risks in the contract.

نَهى رَسُولُ اللهِ ﷺ عَنْ بَيْعِ الْحَصَاةِ، وَعَنْ بَيْعِ الْغَرَرِ

The Messenger of Allah ﷺ forbade sale through [casting] pebbles[21] or the *gharar* sale. (Muslim, *kitāb al-buyū^c^, bāb buṭlān bay^c^ al-ḥaṣāh wa al-bay^c^ alladhī fīhi gharar*; Aḥmad)

The *gharar* sale resembles the present sale of future goods recognised by the Sale of Goods Acts in Common Law[22] countries.

Muzābanah and *ᶜAriyyah* Sales: A Misunderstanding Removed

The *ḥadīth* in the *Muwaṭṭa'* of Imām Mālik on the subject of *muzābanah* sale are as follows:

حَدَّثَنِي يَحْيَى، عَنْ مَالِك، عَنْ نَافِعٍ، عَنْ عَبْدِ اللَّهِ بْنِ عُمَرَ : أَنَّ رَسُولَ اللَّهِ ﷺ نَهَى عَنِ الْمُزَابَنَةِ. وَالْمُزَابَنَةُ بَيْعُ الثَّمَرِ بِالتَّمْرِ كَيْلاً، وَبَيْعُ الْكَرْمِ بِالزَّبِيبِ كَيْلاً

> Yaḥyā related to me from Mālik from Nāfiᶜ from ᶜAbdullāh ibn ᶜUmar that the Messenger of Allah ﷺ forbade *muzābanah*. *Muzābanah* is selling fresh dates for dried dates by measure, and selling grapes for raisins by measure. (*Al-Muwaṭṭa'*, Book 31, Number 31.13.23)

In another *ḥadīth*, *muzābanah* sale is defined as:

وَالْمُزَابَنَةُ اشْتِرَاءُ الثَّمَرِ بِالتَّمْرِ فِي رُؤُوسِ النَّخْلِ

> *Muzābanah* is selling fresh dates for dried dates while they are still on the trees. (*Al-Muwaṭṭa'*, Book 31, Number 31.13.24)

Muzābanah is a general rule while *ᶜariyyah* is an exception in the principles of contract of sale, because it is a charitable act to grant the produce of a date-palm or a vine to someone. *Muzābanah* in date-palms and grape-vines, when applied to wheat, is sometimes called *muḥāqalah*. In the above *ḥadīth* narrated by Saᶜīd ibn al-Musayyab he said, "*Muḥāqalah* was buying unharvested wheat in exchange for threshed wheat and renting land in exchange for wheat[23]." Mālik said explaining the practice current in Madīnah at his time:

> Mālik said, "The Messenger of Allah ﷺ forbade *muzābanah*. The explanation of *muzābanah* is that it is buying something whose number, weight and measure is not known with something whose number, weight or measure is known, for instance, if a man has a stack of food whose measure is not known, either

> of wheat, dates, or whatever food, or the man has goods of wheat, date kernels, herbs, safflower, cotton, flax, silk, and does not know its measure or weight or number and then a buyer approaches him and proposes that he weigh or measure or count the goods, but, before he does, he specifies a certain weight, or measure, or number and guarantees to pay the price for that amount, agreeing that whatever falls short of that amount is a loss against him and whatever is in excess of that amount is a gain for him. That is not a sale. It is taking risks and it is an uncertain transaction. It falls into the category of gambling because he is not buying something from him for something definite which he pays. Everything which resembles this is also forbidden." (*Al-Muwaṭṭa'*, Book 31, Number 31.13.25)

Dry fruits cannot be bartered for fresh or unripe fruits on the tree, because it becomes *muzābanah*.

The *ḥadīth* on *ʿariyyah* sale mentioned in the *Muwaṭṭa'* is as follows:

حَدَّثَنِي يَحْيَى، عَنْ مَالِكٍ، عَنْ نَافِعٍ، عَنْ عَبْدِ اللَّهِ بْنِ عُمَرَ، عَنْ زَيْدِ بْنِ ثَابِتٍ: أَنَّ رَسُولَ اللَّهِ
ﷺ أَرْخَصَ لِصَاحِبِ الْعَرِيَّةِ، أَنْ يَبِيعَهَا بِخَرْصِهَا

> Yaḥyā related to me from Mālik from Nāfiʿ from ʿAbdullāh ibn ʿUmar from Zayd ibn Thābit that the Messenger of Allah ﷺ allowed the holder of an *ʿariyyah* to barter the dates on the palm for the amount of dried dates it was estimated that the palms would produce. (*Al-Muwaṭṭa'*, Book 31, Number 31.9.14)

Ibn Juzayy al-Kalbī said in *al-Qawānīn al-fiqhiyyah*:

> As for the *ʿariyyah* it is that someone gives to him [a poor person] the dates of a date-palm or the fruits of a tree but not their original [tree]. It is permissible for the person giving the *ʿariyyah* to buy them from him [the poor person] with their amount estimated in dried dates, under four conditions, which are:
>
> 1. That their ripeness has appeared;
>
> 2. That they are five *wasq* measures or less;
>
> 3. That the amount paid should be of the same type as the *ʿariyyah;*
>
> 4. And that he gives him the fruit at the time of the cutting of

> the fruit from the palm-tree, not as a cash payment, and that is an exception from *muzābanah.* (Al-Kalbī, Ibn Juzayy, *kitāb al-ᶜuqūd, al-bāb ath-thālith fī al-ᶜumrā wa ar-ruqbā wa al-minḥah wa al-ᶜariyyah*)

Ash-Shāfiᶜī permitted its purchase by the donor of the *ᶜariyyah* and from someone else,[24] but only permitted it in dates or grapes.

ᶜAbd ar-Raḥmān ibn al-Qāsim said in the *Mudawwanah*:

> Mālik said, "*ᶜAriyyah* is in date-palms and in all fruits such as are dried and stored such as grapes, figs, acorns (*jawz* possibly walnuts), almonds and the like of those things that are dried and stored." (Ṣaḥnūn, *al-Mudawwanah al-kubrā, Kitāb al-ᶜarāyā*)

ᶜAriyyah is a special permission given in the case when a rich person wants to give the produce of a certain date-palm or a certain fruit tree to a poor person as a *ṣadaqah* but the poor man may need the dried fruit urgently hence the rich person can give him dried fruit in exchange for the fresh fruit estimating the measure of fresh fruit on the tree, so as to save him the trouble. Imām Aḥmad ibn Ḥanbal reports from Sufyān ibn Ḥusayn:

العَرَايَا نَخْلٌ كَانَتْ تُوهَبُ لِلْمَسَاكِينِ فَلَا يَسْتَطِيعُونَ أَنْ يَنْتَظِرُوا بِهَا فَيَبِيعُونَهَا بِمَا شَاؤُوا مِنْ ثَمَرِهِ.

> *ᶜArāyā* are date-palms which would be given to bereft people, so they would not be able to wait for them and so they would sell them for whatever they wished of their fruits. (Aḥmad ibn Ḥanbal, *Musnad)*

Imām Mālik said that during famine, the Arabs used to give the fruit of some trees full of dates as *ṣadaqah* to poor people just as owners of herds of camels and goats used to dedicate one or two of them to some poor people to drink their milk.[25] Imām Mālik restricted the purchase of the fresh fruit of the *ᶜariyyah* in exchange for dried fruit to the donor of the use of the tree, but Imām ash-Shāfiᶜī and Imām Aḥmad ibn Ḥanbal said that anyone can buy the fresh fruit with dried fruit.[26]

Imām Mālik further says that *ᶜariyyah* are those fruits which are in someone else's orchard. The owner of land may not like frequent visits by the owner of one or two trees, so the landowner with the majority of the trees can give dried dates to the estimated measure of the fruits on the tree. This is also permissible.[27] Imām Mālik's view is based on the principle of *taḍarrur*, because one may not interfere in someone else's property. According to Imām Mālik:

العرية أن يعري الرجل نخلة، ثم يتأذى بدخوله عليه فرخص له أن يشتريها منه

> The *ᶜariyyah* is that a man grants a date-palm [or several], and then he is bothered by [the poor person's] entering upon him, so that then he is granted a concession to buy them from him.

It will be clear from these examples, therefore, that to regard the *muzābanah* sale and the *ᶜariyyah* as the same is to misunderstand completely their provisions and significance as stipulated in the *ḥadīth* on the two types of sale. After discussing *muzābanah* and *ᶜariyyah* contracts, Professor Coulson says in his book *A History of Islamic Law*:

> The *Muwaṭṭa'* here simply reflects the stage of a rough and uneasy compromise between the comparatively liberal and practical outlook of the earliest scholars and the rigid approach of the doctrinaire group. (Coulson, *A History of Islamic Law*, Edinburgh 1971, p. 44)

One is at a loss to find 'an uneasy and rough compromise' in such a simple and straightforward Prophetic solution and special dispensation in the matter of *ᶜariyyah*. For a Muslim scholar, it is difficult to see such watertight compartments as the imaginary 'doctrinaire group' and 'earliest scholars' for they did not exist during that period. To us they were all *as-salaf aṣ-ṣāliḥūn* the right-acting earliest generations who, we believe, were sincere and who carefully followed in the footsteps of the Messenger of Allah ﷺ and depended solely on the Book of Allah and Sunnah of His Messenger ﷺ.

The Doctrine of *Khiyār al-Majlis*

The Prophet ﷺ is reported by Abū Barzah al-Aslamī ؓ to have said:

عَنْ أَبِي بَرْزَةَ الأَسْلَمِيِّ قَالَ قَالَ رَسُولُ اللَّهِ ﷺ ﴿ البَيِّعَانِ بِالْخِيَارِ مَالَمْ يَتَفَرَّقَا ﴾

> Each of the parties to a contract of sale has the option against the other party as long as they have not separated. (Aḥmad; Abū Dāwūd, *awwal kitāb al-ijārah, bāb fī khiyār al-mutabāyiᶜayn;* and Ibn Mājah, *kitāb at-tijārāt, bāb al-bayyiᶜān bi al-khiyār mā lam yaftariqā;* from Abū Barzah. Ibn Mājah and al-Ḥākim, in *al-Mustadrak,* also narrated it from Samurah)

This *ḥadīth* of the Prophet ﷺ expresses the doctrine known as *khiyār al-majlis,* which gives the parties to a contract, duly completed by offer and acceptance, the right to repudiate the agreement during the session (*majlis*) of the bargain.

Imām Mālik comments on this *ḥadīth* in the following words:

وَلَيْسَ لِهَذَا عِنْدَنَا حَدٌّ مَعْرُوفٌ، وَلَا أَمْرٌ مَعْمُولٌ بِهِ فِيهِ.

> With us [the People of Madīnah] there is no well known definition in this case nor any matter which is acted upon. (*Muwaṭṭa',* Book 31, Number 31.37.80)

He meant there is no definition of what constitutes their separating and no established practice with respect to that. Professor Coulson remarks on the point of view of Imām Mālik in the following words:

> This is one of the many occasions on which the law expressed in the reported precedents of the Prophet or later authorities was rejected by the early Medinan scholars when it ran counter to their currently accepted doctrine. (Coulson, *A History of Islamic Law,* Edinburgh 1971, p. 46)

He erroneously brands the *ḥadīth* of the Prophet ﷺ quoted above as merely "the alleged statement of the Prophet." (*Ibid.*)

Professor Coulson falls into the error of assuming that Imām Mālik was in the habit of rejecting Prophetic traditions and the authority of the precepts of the Prophet ﷺ expressing Islamic Law. The *Muwaṭṭa',* on the contrary, shows that Imām Mālik always quotes a *ḥadīth* or a precedent of the *Khulafā' ar-Rāshidūn* ؓ or very prominent Companions. Many Muslim scholars of the past have considered the *Muwaṭṭa'* as a book that has rendered a great service to the cause of collection of *ḥadīth* long before Imām al-Bukhārī and Imām Muslim and other scholars of *ḥadīth* began to produce their systematic compilations of *ḥadīth*. As we have seen before, great scholars like Imām ash-Shāfiʿī have rated the *Muwaṭṭaʾ* as 'the most authentic book after the Book of Allah.'

The misunderstanding in the above example of this detached academic arises out of the statement of Imām Mālik in the *Muwaṭṭaʾ* in the matter of *khiyār al-majlis* which does not in the least disregard or reject the most authentic *ḥadīth* the Prophet ﷺ quoted at the beginning of chapter 38 (*bāb bayʿ al-khiyār*). Imām Mālik has only stated the fact as to what operated in his time in Madīnah. It should be pointed out that it is typical of the Mālikī school that the *ʿamal ahl al-Madīnah* (the practice of the People of Madīnah) is very much relied upon. The practice of the People of Madīnah, which Imām Mālik mentioned here, was based on the Sunnah of the Prophet ﷺ. It was the learned and right-acting Imām's view that Madīnah was the birthplace of Islam and the place to which the Prophet ﷺ emigrated; the nerve centre of the *Ummah*, the centre where important legal verdicts were given by the Prophet ﷺ and the *Khulafāʾ ar-Rāshidūn* ؓ, the place where the Companions and their Followers lived and taught according to the Book of Allah and the Sunnah of the Messenger of Allah ﷺ. Hence, the practice of the people of Madīnah could not be contrary to the Sunnah of the Prophet ﷺ especially during the early period in which Imām Mālik lived and taught.

As far as *khiyār al-majlis* is concerned, other schools of law have contested its validity. There were scholars like Ibn Ḥajar who were of the opinion that the doctrine does not contradict the *ʿamal* of the People of Madīnah because it had been the view of Ibn ʿUmar, Saʿīd ibn al-Musayyab, az-Zuhrī and Ibn Abī Dhiʾb who were eminent leaders in their eras in Madīnah.[28]

Forbidden Contracts of Sale

The following contracts of sale are forbidden in the Sunnah of the Prophet ﷺ. They are self explanatory:

1. TWO TRANSACTIONS IN ONE SALE

عَنْ أَبِي هُرَيْرَةَ، قَالَ: ﴿ نَهَى رَسُولُ اللَّهِ ﷺ عَنْ بَيْعَتَيْنِ فِي بَيْعَةٍ ﴾ .

There is from Abū Hurayrah ﵁, "The Messenger of Allah ﷺ forbade making two transactions of sale into one contract of sale." (At-Tirmidhī, *abwāb al-buyūᶜ ᶜan rasūlillāh ﷺ, bāb mā jā'a fī an-nahy ᶜan bayᶜatayni fī bayᶜah*; an-Nasā'ī, *kitāb al-buyūᶜ, bāb at-tijārah; Muwaṭṭa'*, Book 31, Number 31.33.72)

Many modern transactions use this practice, for example, all the offers to buy a product and get something extra for free. Mālik gives many examples in the *Muwaṭṭa'*, including having a different price for a product if it is bought with cash or on credit.

2. EXTRA CONDITION ATTACHED TO A SALE

أَنَّ النَّبِيَّ ﷺ نَهَى عَنْ بَيْعٍ وَشَرْطٍ

The Prophet ﷺ forbade a contract with a stipulation. (Narrated by al-Haytamī from Imām Abū Ḥanīfah in *Majmaᶜ az-zawā'id* in which he attributed it to aṭ-Ṭabarānī in *al-Awsaṭ)*

The contract must not he combined with an extra condition.

3. SALE OF WHAT ONE DOES NOT OWN

عَنْ حَكِيمِ بنِ حِزَامٍ قَالَ ﴿ نَهَانِي رَسُولُ اللَّهِ ﷺ أَنْ أَبِيعَ مَا لَيْسَ عِنْدِي ﴾ .

From Ḥakīm ibn Ḥizām there is that he said, "The Messenger of Allah forbade me to sell a thing which I don't have." (At-Tirmidhī, *abwāb al-buyūᶜ ᶜan rasūlillāh ﷺ, bāb mā jā'a fī karāhiyyah bayᶜ mā laysa ᶜindahu*)

4. *MULĀMASAH* AND *MUNĀBADHAH* SALES

نَهَى النَّبِيُّ ﷺ عَنْ الْمُلَامَسَةِ وَالْمُنَابَذَةِ

The Prophet ﷺ forbade *mulāmasah* and *munābadhah*. (Al-Bukhārī, *kitāb al-buyūᶜ, bāb bayᶜ al-munābadhah;* Muslim, *kitāb fī al-buyūᶜ, bāb*

> *ibṭāl bay al-mulāmasah wa al-munābadhah;* Aḥmad, Abū Dāwūd, an-Nasā'ī and Ibn Mājah also transmitted it)

Mālik explained these two sales in the *Muwaṭṭa'*:

> *Mulāmasah* is when a man can feel a garment but is not allowed to unfold it or examine what is in it, or he buys by night and does not know what is in it. *Munābadhah* is that a man throws his garment to another, and the other throws his garment without either of them making any inspection. Each of them says, "this is for this." This is what is forbidden of *mulāmasah* and *munābadhah*. (*Al-Muwaṭṭa'*, Book 31, Number 31.35.76)

5. Bidding in order to raise the price (*najash*) is forbidden

نَهَى عَنِ النَّجَشِ.

> [The Messenger of Allah] ﷺ has forbidden bidding up the price [dishonestly, not intending to purchase]. (Al-Bukhārī, *kitāb al-buyū*ᶜ, *bāb an-najash wa man qāla lā yajūzu dhālika al-bay*ᶜ; and Muslim, *kitāb al-buyū*ᶜ, *bāb taḥrīm bay*ᶜ *ar-rajul alā bay*ᶜ *akhīhi;* Ibn Mājah and an-Nasā'ī also transmitted it)

This is the practice of dishonestly entering a bid for something, not intending to buy it, but merely in order to raise the price.

6. Forestalling (*talāqī rukbān*)

عَنْ ابْنِ عَبَّاسٍ رَضِيَ اللهُ عَنْهُمَا قَالَ: قَالَ رَسُولُ اللهِ صَلَّى اللهُ عَلَيْهِ وَسَلَّمَ لَا تَلَقَّوْا الرُّكْبَانَ...

> Ibn ᶜAbbās ؓ said, "The Messenger of Allah ﷺ said, "Do not go out to meet the caravan [in order to buy from them or sell to them]…." (Al-Bukhārī, *kitāb al-buyū*ᶜ, *bāb an-nahy li al-bā'i*ᶜ *an lā yaḥfila al-ibil wa al-baqar wa al-ghanam wa kulla maḥfalah*)

This sort of trade can lead to fraudulent practices such as buying things at a very cheap rate in order to sell at an exorbitant price since the people of the town would not be able to discover the actual price, or buying up and hoarding in order to be able to dictate the price. It might also be to deceive the caravan traders by offering them a low price before they come to the town and discover that they have been cheated.

Similarly, during famine, the traders might go out to caravans to buy foodstuffs from them at a nominal price without telling them the current market price in the town.

Unfortunately, this prohibition has long since been subverted in the East and the West, and this practice has become a standard of modern commercial life.

7. THE SALE OF A CITY DWELLER FOR A COUNTRY DWELLER (*BAYᶜ ḤĀḌIR LI BĀD*)

عَنْ ابنِ عَبَّاسٍ رَضِيَ اللّٰهُ عَنْهُمَا قَالَ: قَالَ رَسُولُ اللّٰهِ ﷺ . . . وَلَا يَبِعْ حَاضِرٌ لِبَادٍ

> Ibn ᶜAbbās ﷛ said, "The Messenger of Allah ﷺ said, '...And someone who is resident must not sell or buy[29] on behalf of a country dweller.'"[30]

That is, he should not act as a broker for him. This was what Ibn ᶜAbbās ﷛ explained it as in the two *ṣaḥīḥ* books.[31]

Country-dweller here means first of all nomads and people who live in rural areas and then secondarily village dwellers if they are not familiar with the markets of the city and the prices there.

This *ḥadīth* refers to two types of transactions: a city dweller has a lot of merchandise in the city which he could easily sell, but, in order to gain large profits he takes the commodity to sell in the villages although the city-dwellers are in need of those things. Secondly, he tries to stop direct trade between villagers and city-dwellers, and becomes a self-imposed agent on behalf of the villagers and buys or sells commodities on their behalf at artificial prices ensuring himself an extra large profit.

Acceptable contracts

1. *SHIRKAH*: PARTNERSHIP

The words sharing and partnership occur several times in the Qur'ān: Mūsā ﵇ prays to Allah to make Hārūn ﵇, his brother, his partner in his mission to Pharaoh:

وَاجْعَل لِّي وَزِيرًا مِّنْ أَهْلِي هَارُونَ أَخِي اشْدُدْ بِهِ أَزْرِي وَأَشْرِكْهُ فِي أَمْرِي

Assign me a helper from my family, my brother Hārūn. Strengthen my back by him and let him share in my task. (Sūrah Ṭā Hā 20: 29-32)

Sharing the estate in inheritance is mentioned here:

فَإِن كَانُوا أَكْثَرَ مِن ذَٰلِكَ فَهُمْ شُرَكَاءُ فِي الثُّلُثِ

If there are more than that they share in a third. (Sūrat an-Nisā' 4: 12)

Shirkah,[32] or partnership contract, signifies the conjunction of two or more persons to carry on a business sharing profits accruing from joint investment or joint labour. In the widest sense of the term *shirkah,* the partnership exists where property is held in common between two or more co-proprietors. A person thus alienates an undivided share of his property, in return for an undivided share of the property of another each having the right to administer the whole.

> Linguistically it means "to mix", and in *Sharīᶜah,* the compiler [ad-Dardīr] said, "Partnership is the permission" from each one of the two, or of them,[33] to the other "to transact" i.e. for him to transact in property "belonging to the two of them" i.e. to the two granted permission together. (Ibn ᶜArfah ad-Dasūqī, *ash-Sharḥ al-kabīr ᶜalā Ḥāshiyat ad-Dardīr ᶜalā Mukhtaṣar Khalīl, bāb fī bayān ash-shirkah wa aḥkāmihā wa aqsāmihā*)

The *shirkah* may be effected in a specified amount of capital or in labour on contribution of labour and skill or in credit where no capital is contributed and the partners buy and sell on credit on understanding that they shall share the profits. There may be a *shirkah* of mixed characters in cases of capital and labour, agricultural farms and labour and so on and so forth. The *madhhabs* take different views on the permissibility of each form, and we will examine that below.[34]

Ibn Juzayy al-Kalbī said:

> There are two types of partnership in property: *ᶜinān* partnership and *mufāwaḍah* partnership. (Al-Kalbī, Ibn Juzayy, *al-Qawānīn al-fiqhiyyah, al-kitāb ar-rābiᶜ min al-qism ath-thānī fī al-ᶜuqūd al-mushākalah li al-buyūᶜ, al-bāb al-khāmis fī ash-shirkah*)

Shirkat al-ᶜInān: Limited Partnership

Shirkat al-ᶜInān is a limited partnership in which a partner is not allowed to do anything without his partner. Ibn Juzayy said:

> *ᶜInān*[35] partnership is that each of the two partners puts wealth and then they mix it or put it into a single box and both trade from it together and neither of them acts independently of the other in transacting. (*Ibid.*)

Shirkat al-Mufāwaḍah: Unlimited Partnership

Ibn Juzayy said:

> *Mufāwaḍah* partnership is that each of the two delegates transacts on behalf of the other [partner] both when he is present and when he is absent and he is bound by everything which his partner does. Ash-Shāfiᶜī forbade *mufāwaḍah* partnership and Abū Ḥanīfah stipulated equality of capital investments. (*Ibid.*)

Ibn Juzayy says further about partnership in property:

> It is incumbent in partnership in property that the profit be divided between them in the proportion to the share of each of the two of them from the property, and it is not permissible that either of them stipulate for himself more of the profit than his share of the wealth, contrary to Abū Ḥanīfah.
>
> And that kindness which either of the two partners does is taken from his share in particular unless it is such as whose benefit is hoped for in respect of trade, such as giving hospitality to traders and the like of that. (*Ibid.*)

Shirkat al-Abdān: Partnership in Labour

Islamic Law allows two or more persons to associate themselves for the exercise of a profession or a handicraft. The profits will be practically equal for the partners with a view to lending mutual assistance even though the associates work separately. Imām Mālik is cited by Ṣaḥnūn in *al-Mudawwanah al-kubrā* as saying that the stock of tools may be provided by each partner in such labour associations, but the other jurists say that the tools will be owned by the association or hired by the association at common expense. In this kind of *shirkah*, any payment received or engagement entered upon by one of the associates for some work done or to be done binds the other, and the payment remains at their risk even after the dissolution of the partnership. It will be illegal for one of the associates to hold a greatly predominant share in the stock of tools. Ibn Juzayy al-Kalbī said:

> As for partnership in labour, that is in manufacture and work, it is permissible, contrary to ash-Shāfiᶜī, but it is only permissible under two conditions:
>
> 1. That it is in the same manufacture such as two tailors, and two blacksmiths. It is not valid with differing trades such as a tailor and a carpenter.
>
> 2. That it takes place in the same venue in which they both work, and if they are in two different places it is not valid, contrary to Abū Ḥanīfah in respect to both conditions. If one of the two has more tools than the other, then if it is worthless he renders it ineffectual, and if they have a significance he leases his share of them. (*Ibid.*)

Shirkat al-Wujūh: Partnership in Liabilities

Ibn Juzayy al-Kalbī said:

> As for *wujūh* partnership, it is that they both share not in wealth nor in work, and it is partnership in liabilities such that if the two of them buy something it is their joint liability and if they sell it they divide its profits between them, but this is not valid, contrary to Abū Ḥanīfah. (*Ibid.*)

Summary by Ibn Juzayy al-Kalbī

> Mālik declared *ᶜinān, mufāwaḍah* and partnership in labour valid but declared *wujūh* partnership invalid, whereas Abū Ḥanīfah permitted all four, and ash-Shāfiᶜī permitted *ᶜinān* in particular. (*Ibid.*)

This summary here is intended to clarify the distinct position of each of the *madhhabs,* since it is one of the features of our age that the science of Islamic commercial transactions is being rebuilt in our time on the shaky foundations of *multi-madhhabism,* with the result that usury all to easily enters into equation.

2. *Qirāḍ* or *Muḍārabah*: Dormant Partnership

Qirāḍ agreement is a contract by which a person entrusts funds to a trader (*ᶜāmil*) in order that he trade with them, subject to the lender having a share in the profit. Ibn Juzayy al-Kalbī said:

> The Iraqis call it *muḍārabah* and its nature is that a man pays wealth to another for him to trade with and the extra will be shared between them according to that which they agree upon: a half or a third or a quarter etc., after repayment of the capital sum. *Qirāḍ* is permissible and is excepted from being an uncertain transaction or an unknown return. (Al-Kalbī, Ibn Juzayy, *al-Qawānīn al-fiqhiyyah, al-kitāb ar-rābiᶜ min al-qism ath-thānī fī al-ᶜuqūd al-mushākalah li al-buyūᶜ, al-bāb ar-rābi fī al-qirāḍ*)

Thus, in *qirāḍ*, the capital is handed over to an agent to trade with, and the contract comes into force when the agent starts his trading journey. *Qirāḍ* was encouraged by the Prophet himself ﷺ, and it was a common form of trading in the early days of Islam. Commercial enterprises in the time of the Prophet ﷺ used to be organised under the charge of a caravan leader commissioned by one or more rich persons of the community. The caravan continued to be a major factor in commerce until the contravention of the laws forbidding forestalling became widespread.

In the contract of *qirāḍ*, a certain capital is handed over to the agent on condition that the person entrusting it shall participate in the profits in a pre-agreed proportion. The dormant partner remains the owner of the capital. The agent is only in possession by virtue of the trust reposed in him. He is only held responsible for negligence or breaking the rules of the contract.

Capital in Qirāḍ Partnership

Ibn Juzayy al-Kalbī said:

> First, that the capital should be dinars or dirhams, for it is not acceptable with goods and other things, but there is a difference of opinion concerning unminted gold and silver and nuggets of gold and silver, and *fulūs*.[36] If he is owed money by a man it is not valid for him to pay it to him as a *qirāḍ* according to the dominant majority. It is the same if he owes another person money and tells [the agent] to take possession of it so that he can give it to him as a *qirāḍ*. (*Ibid.*)

In the dormant partnership, the capital should not consist of a debt owed by a debtor to his creditor nor should it consist of a pledge or of a security. That is, the debtor or the holder of the pledge should not be the agent and the creditor should not be the dormant partner. Capital should not consist of debased coins nor of goods which the agent has taken upon himself to realise because in these cases the value of the capital cannot be strictly determined. In *qirāḍ* partnership, the risk for the enterprise should not be thrown exclusively upon the agent, otherwise the contract will become invalid. It is prohibited that the shares of the profit be ambiguous or fake, otherwise, it will create confusion later on; the parties must be clearly agreed upon them before the enterprise begins. The agent will be required to perform his duties in good faith taking into consideration the good of the entrepreneur. He should take the same amount of care as he would do if the concern were solely his own.

Difference between Ordinary Partnership and the Qirāḍ Partnership

Ordinary partnership has its existence where the partners live and work. All the partners play an active part in the concern and each contributes his share of the capital.

In the *qirāḍ* or dormant partnership, on the other hand, an investor furnishes the funds but the active agent operates the concern almost without control. The agent can be far from the place where the contract was entered into. In the *qirāḍ* partnership the capital must consist as a general rule in cash, specifically gold and/or silver, but in the ordinary form of partnership it is not so.

Qirāḍ is also called *muḍārabah* which may be from the phrase *ḍarb fi'l-arḍ* or "moving about in the land of Allah seeking for trade or work" which is mentioned in al-Baqarah.[37] Perhaps, the word *muḍārabah* is derived from this Qur'ānic phrase.

3. *Wakālah*: Agency

The word *wakīl* appears about twenty-four times in the Noble Qur'ān. In the following verse in Sūrat al-Anᶜām, it is used to convey the meaning 'a person responsible for arranging one's affair' or a 'guardian':

وَكَذَّبَ بِهِ قَوْمُكَ وَهُوَ الْحَقُّ قُل لَّسْتُ عَلَيْكُم بِوَكِيلٍ

Your people deny it and yet it is the Truth. Say: "I am not here as your guardian." (Sūrat al-Anᶜām 6: 66)

The same word is further repeated in verse 107 of the same sūrah to convey the same meaning:

وَمَا أَنتَ عَلَيْهِم بِوَكِيلٍ

And you are not set over them as their guardian. (Sūrat al-Anᶜām 6: 107)

In Islamic law, *wakālah* or agency arises where one person authorises another to replace him in the exercise of his civil rights. The person thus authorised is called *wakīl*. A *wakīl* can be entrusted with all acts which can be done by a representative, such as concluding or rescinding a contract, collecting a sum due, assigning a debt or discharging a debtor, even though the amount of the debt be unknown to all three. Once one appoints a *wakīl*, the latter should not act unless he has full powers. The principal cannot delegate his *wakīl* to take an oath on his behalf, nor can he appoint an agent to commit an illegal act. A general agent can be appointed to deal with all matters on behalf of the principal except the principal's divorce, or for giving consent to the marriage of the principal's virgin daughter or to sell the principal's house. If he is a special agent, his powers will be limited according to the instructions given by the principal.

Ibn Juzayy al-Kalbī said:

> Concerning agency (*wakālah*) about which there are six issues.
>
> 1. Concerning the person who authorises and the agent. The agency of a person who is absent and a woman and a sick person are permissible by unanimous agreement as is the agency of a healthy person who is present, but contrary to Abū Ḥanīfah. As for the agent, every person for whom it is permissible to transact on his own behalf in any matter, then it is permissible for him to

deputise in it for someone else except that it is not permissible to charge an enemy as agent nor a *kāfir* in buying and selling or paying advance deposits in case they do something *ḥarām*, nor is it permissible to charge them with taking possession of something from Muslims in case they raise themselves up over them.

2. Concerning that in which agency is valid and invalid. Agency is valid in every thing in which it is valid to deputise someone of financial matters and other things and in acts of *ᶜibādah* and worship except for those related to physical activity such as prayer and fasting for which it is not valid to deputise someone, although it is valid to deputise in acts of worship connected with property such as *zakāh*, but they differ about it in the Ḥajj. (Al-Kalbī, Ibn Juzayy, *al-Qawānīn al-fiqhiyyah, al-kitāb as-sādis fī al-abwāb al-mushākalah li al-aqḍiyah li taᶜalluqihā bi al-aḥkām, al-bāb ath-thāmin fī al-wakālah*)

Obligations of a Wakīl

A *wakīl* will be responsible to sell or buy for a price, and should declare clearly to the third party: "I am sent by my principal so-and-so in order that you may sell to him this and that." He will be responsible for any breach of warranty in the thing already sold, unless the buyer has been informed that the vendor was acting simply as an agent for so-and-so.

He must accept only *sharīᶜah* legal tender, i.e. gold and silver, as payment, or if the principal has authorised, he may accept barter in a *ḥalāl* manner. He must, however, conform to the current market price, otherwise the principal is not bound to ratify his transactions.

It is essential for the *wakīl* to comply with the instructions given by his principal, otherwise the latter may refuse to accept the purchase or part with the merchandise. Likewise, if the thing is bought at a reduced price or has some defect. He should also comply with his principal's instructions as to the time and place of the purchase or sale, nor should he raise or reduce the price of the commodity for which limits are agreed and fixed although fluctuations up to five percent (5%) will be tolerated. If the *wakīl* exchanges foodstuff for foodstuff or has exchanged gold for gold, the principal may rescind the sale, as that can be usury. The principal is bound to ratify a sale or purchase made by his *wakīl* under more favourable but lawful terms.

The *wakīl* cannot sell the wares which are given to him for sale to himself, nor can he sell them to one of his wards under his guardianship although he is allowed to sell to his wife since, in Islamic Law, it is only the person of the spouses that are in common, not their personalities. A Muslim must not appoint a Jew, a Christian or an enemy of his debtor as his agent in the transactions of sale and purchase although there are differences of opinion on this subject given the complex nature of modern society.

If the principal and his *wakīl* have, independently of each other, sold the same goods, the first sale in point of time shall be considered valid provided the subsequent sale was not followed by immediate delivery. The *wakīl* must obtain a receipt for the payment of the principal's debt, otherwise, in case of complaints, the *wakīl* will be held liable. The principal will remain the vendor's debtor so long as the vendor has not received his purchase price.

4. *ḌAMĀN*: GUARANTEE AND LIABILITY

Ḍamān, liability or guarantee, is a form of contract by which a third person constitutes himself liable for the debt of another.

He is called *ḍāmin* and is also known as *ḥamīl, kafīl* and *zaᶜīm* 'claimant.' According to Islamic law, a person who becomes *ḍāmin* or surety must enjoy full civil rights.

A married woman can become a guarantor. A sick person can be a guarantor to the extent of responsibility for the value of the disposal of the third of his or her estate. Such a surety (*ḍāmin*) may be given for a debt which is not yet due and may be paid at once provided it is one which can be legally extinguished before it has fallen due. An extension of the period may be sought by the *ḍāmin* provided the debtor is solvent. If he has the means to discharge the debt, it will be considered illegal to ask for such an extension through surety. A *ḍāmin* or a surety can withdraw so long as the loan has not been made, but he cannot withdraw prior to the creditor taking an oath as to the existence of the debt. The debt in question must be such that it can be discharged by the surety.

The *ḍāmin* has his remedies if his principal proves to be a defaulter. He can sue him in the court of the *qāḍī* for what he has paid either in money or in kind but he will have to prove that such payment was made. Everything that discharges the obligation of the principal debtor also discharges the obligation of the *ḍāmin*. If the surety dies, the payment of the debt that he has guaranteed is to be made chargeable upon his estate. A surety can be sued as long as the debtor is present and solvent. In the case where several persons constitute themselves as sureties for one debtor and for one and the same debt, the creditor can only claim from each co-surety the amount each has given guarantee for unless they have constituted themselves jointly and severally liable.

5. Ijārah: Hire

The contract of hire in Islamic law is called *ijārah* (also known as *kirā'*) which is derived from an Arabic word *ajr* meaning remuneration or reward.

There are three cases:

1. The hire of human beings, which is called *ijārah*.
2. The hire of animals, properties or land which is called *kirā'*.
3. The hire of things such as ships which are conditional, i.e. there is no guarantee that a ship will complete its voyage and return, so that the payment of the wage *juᶜl* is not made until the completion of the voyage.

Ibn Juzayy al-Kalbī said:

> The noun *ijārah* is used in particular for [hiring] humans and the noun *kirā'* is used for [hiring] animals,[38] houses and land.

He also said:

> Second section, concerning the *juᶜl* (wage), which is *ijārah* for a benefit the obtainment of which is stood surety for, and it is permissible, contrary to Abū Ḥanīfah. The difference between it and *ijārah* has three aspects:

1. That the benefit is not obtained by the person paying the wage until the work is completed such as the return of a slave or a fugitive that has fled, contrary to *ijārah* because he obtains the benefit according to the amount of the work that has been done, and so for that reason when an employee has done a part of the work for which he is being paid, then he gets the wage according to the measure of what he has done. But he does not obtain any of the *juᶜl* until the work has been done, and renting ships is an example of *juᶜl*, so that the wage is not obliged except by fulfilment, contrary to Ibn Nāfiᶜ.

2. That the work done for a *juᶜl* may be known or it may be unknown, such as digging a well until water emerges from it, and it may be close or far, contrary to *ijārah*, for which it is necessary that the work for it should be known. There is some doubt between *juᶜl* and *ijārah* concerning stipulating for a doctor the recovery of a sick person, and concerning a teacher being employed to teach the Qur'ān.

3. That it is not permissible to stipulate advance payment of the wages for *juᶜl* contrary to the case with *ijārah*. (Al-Kalbī, Ibn Juzayy, *al-Qawānīn al-fiqhiyyah, al-kitāb ar-rābiᶜ min al-qism ath-thānī fī al-ᶜuqūd al-mushākalah li al-buyūᶜ, al-bāb al-awwal fī al-ijārah wa al-juᶜl wa al-kirā'*)

The price in these cases should be in proportion to the temporary benefit sold. The famous Mālikī scholar and jurist ad-Dardīr says that the words *ijārah* and *ajr* are synonymous.

Ijārah is referred to in the Qur'ān in respect of hiring the services of Mūsā ﷺ by a figure, said to be Shuᶜayb ﷺ, on the recommendation of his daughter after Mūsā ﷺ had helped them in watering their flocks:

قَالَتْ إِحْدَاهُمَا يَا أَبَتِ اسْتَأْجِرْهُ إِنَّ خَيْرَ مَنِ اسْتَأْجَرْتَ الْقَوِيُّ الْأَمِينُ قَالَ إِنِّي أُرِيدُ أَنْ أُنكِحَكَ
إِحْدَى ابْنَتَيَّ هَاتَيْنِ عَلَىٰ أَن تَأْجُرَنِي ثَمَانِيَ حِجَجٍ فَإِنْ أَتْمَمْتَ عَشْرًا فَمِنْ عِندِكَ

One of them said, "Hire him, father. The best person to hire is someone strong and trustworthy." He said, "I would like to marry you to one of these two daughters of mine on condition that you work for me for eight full years. If you complete ten, that is up to you." (Sūrat al-Qaṣaṣ 28:26-27)

Ships are excluded from the above definition of *ijārah* because transport by sea can only form the object of a conditional contract which is termed *miyārah*, the chartering of a ship.

For *ijārah* to be valid, the ingredients essential are the hireling (the person to be hired) and the lessee, the price or remuneration for the hire and the consent of the person hired. The contracting parties must be legally capable to enter into the *ijārah* contract and there must be proper stipulation of price or remuneration. Ibn Juzayy al-Kalbī said:

> First section, concerning *ijārah* and it is permissible according to the dominant majority, and its principle elements are four:
>
> 1. The lessee.
>
> 2. The hireling, and with respect to both of them the same is stipulated as is stipulated for two parties to a sale. It is abhorrent for a Muslim to hire himself to a *kāfir.*
>
> 3. The wage.
>
> 4. The benefit, about which it is stipulated the same as is stipulated in general concerning the price and the thing priced. (Al-Kalbī, Ibn Juzayy, *al-Qawānīn al-fiqhiyyah, al-kitāb ar-rābi^c min al-qism ath-thānī fī al-^{c}uqūd al-mushākalah li al-buyū^c, al-bāb al-awwal fī al-ijārah wa al-ju^{c}l wa al-kirā'*)

The remuneration for hire is to be paid day by day but in the following cases, it is to be paid in advance:

1. If it consists of a definite object.
2. If there has been a stipulation to that effect.
3. If it is a local custom to do so.
4. If it is for hire of any animal for some definite journey which is not yet commenced.

The same value will presumably apply in cases of modern means of transport.

The *ijārah* contract will be void if it is combined with a conditional agreement, e.g. a person agrees to grind corn subject to his receiving the barn, or that he agrees to weave cloth in return for a proportional share of the cloth. The contract will be null and void if in a letting agreement of land, the rent is given in the form of foodstuff. The remuneration or salary in an *ijārah* contract may be fixed in proportion to the work to be done. An employer may hire from his employee the things he has let. A master who takes an apprentice may stipulate that the apprentice shall engage himself for one year.

Hired servants, workmen or persons hiring moveables will be considered as simple bailees, and hence, the risk will not be at their charge as long as there has been no negligence on their part. The caretaker of houses or workmen working for their employer or brokers or agents shown to be honest persons or sailors whose ship has been lost due to an act of Allah will not be deemed responsible for the loss or damage.

An agreement in respect of *ijārah* can be rescinded if the hirer or lessee is evicted or if a workshop is closed by order of the government authorities or if a hired wet-nurse becomes pregnant or falls ill and is unable to nurse the child. The *ijārah* agreement ceases on the death of the workmen engaged, but does not cease on the death of an employer.

Likewise, the *kirā'* agreement ceases if the thing hired out is lost but not on the death of a person who has hired it.

Where disputes arise in respect of a verbal letting agreement of land or houses, and neither side can prove their allegations, each party is called upon to swear an oath and the contract will be annulled.

6. *TAḤKĪM*: ARBITRATION CONTRACT

Taḥkīm or arbitration contract is that form of contract in which it is agreed that in case of any dispute or disagreement in the terms of the contractual agreement, it will be settled through the appointment of a *ḥakam* or arbitrator.[39]

Notes

[1] The *āyāt* at the beginning of Sūrat al-Muzzammil are held to have made standing in prayer at night obligatory at the beginning of Islam.

[2] Sūrat al-Humazah 104: 2

[3] Sūrat al-Baqarah 2: 275

[4] Sūrat al-Isrā' 17: 26

[5] Sūrat al-Isrā' 17: 29

[6] Sūrat an-Nisā' 4: 2

[7] Al-Bukhārī 34, *ḥadīth* 67

[8] *Al-Muwaṭṭa'*, Book 31, Number 31.24.56 which is a *ḥadīth* of cUmar.

[9] *Al-Muwaṭṭa'*, Book 31, Number 31.44.97

[10] *Al-Muwaṭṭa'*, Book 31, Number 31.8.10

[11] Al-Bukhārī 34, *ḥadīth* 75, 82, 83

[12] *Al-Muwaṭṭa'*, Book 31, Number 31.15.27

[13] Al-Qayrawānī, *Risālah, Op. Cit.*, See chapter: *Bāb fī al-buyūc wa mā shākala al-buyūc*, pp. 102-112

[14] *Cf.* Ṣaḥnūn, *al-Mudawwanah al-kubrā*. 15:197: ash-Shāṭibī, *al-Muwāfaqāt fī uṣūl ash-sharīcah*, vol. 2, pp. 248-264; al-Kāshānī, *Badā'ic aṣ-ṣanā'ic*, 7, 171.

[15] Al-Jawzī, Ibn Qayyim, *al-Iclām*, vol. 3, p. 96; also see ash-Shāṭibī, *al-Muwāfaqāt, Op. Cit.*, vol. 2, p. 327

[16] Ash-Shāfiʿī, *Kitāb al-umm*, vol. 3., p. 194; *al-Mughnī*: vol. 4, p. 525: al-Kāshānī, *Badā'ic aṣ-ṣanā'ic*, cit., vol. 1, p. 170

[17] *Al-Minhaj*, p. 174; *Durr al-mukhtār*, vol. 3, p. 201

[18] Coins may be differing qualities of gold and silver.

[19] *Gharar* sale comprises a large number of sales of unknown or uncertain products, many of which are catalogued in the *ḥadīth* and

in the books of *fiqh* separately but are in fact examples of *gharar*, such as *munābadhah* and *mulāmasah*.

[20] *ᶜAriyyah* is to assign, for example, a date palm and its produce to a person for their use. In this case, it is permissible for the person to sell the ripe dates on the tree, whose value has been estimated, for a consignment of dry dates.

[21] There are various forms that this can take, such as selling whatever a thrown pebble lands on.

[22] Common Law is the basis of law in the UK and the US. However, futures transactions are now conducted globally.

[23] This transaction was the basis of what is called sharecropping. It was the contract by which the newly 'freed' slaves in the southern states of America were permanently indebted. See Oliver, Paul, *The Story of the Blues*. Chilton Book Co. (Jan. 1982)

[24] But the other *madhhabs* only permit the original donor of the *ᶜariyyah* to purchase the dates.

[25] ash-Shawkānī, *Nayl al-awṭār*, Cairo (undated), vol. 5, p. 226

[26] *Ibid.*

[27] aṭ-Ṭaḥāwī reports from Imām Mālik, cf. ash-Shawkānī, *Nayl al-awṭār*, *Op. Cit.*, p. 226

[28] Also see Ibn Ḥajar, *Fatḥ al-Bārī sharḥ Ṣaḥīḥ al-Bukhārī*, vol. 4, pp. 276-277

[29] The verb can have the sense of selling to a person and buying on his behalf.

[30] *Ibid.* The second half of the previous *ḥadīth* from *Ṣaḥīḥ al-Bukhārī*. There are a number of *ḥadīth* in the same sense.

[31] az-Zurqānī from his commentary on the *Muwaṭṭa'*.

[32] "*Shirkah*, *sharkah* and *sharikah*, but the first is the more chaste." Ad-Dasūqī in his *Ḥāshiyah*.

[33] Mostly authors refer to partnerships of two people, but the author here seems to refer to the permissibility of two or more partners.

[34] For details, see *Al-Mughnī*, vol. 5, p. 111; *Minhāj*, p. 179; *Durr al-mukhtār*, vol. 2, p 546

[35] *shirkah ᶜinān* is *the co-partnership of two persons in one particular thing, exclusive of the rest of the articles of property of either.* Lane's *Arabic-English Lexicon*.

[36] *Fulūs* sing. *fals,* is coinage of non-precious metals, which were used for small transactions. Their value does not exceed that of half of a dirham. According to all the Imāms except for Abū Ḥanīfah they are not included in *zakāh* assessment except by traders.

[37] Sūrat al-Baqarah 2: 273

[38] Such as mounts or beasts of burden.

[39] *al-Minhāj* p. 181; *Sharḥ al-Wiqāyah,* vol. 3, p. 740

Chapter 24

Ill-gotten Wealth

Money or property which is acquired through unjust means is definitely unclean and unlawful, and anyone who makes use of it or spends it on his or his family's needs does himself and them great harm. As the Prophet ﷺ has warned, such a person's prayers will not find acceptance with Allah, his supplications will not be answered, his petitions will not be granted, and if he does good deeds they will avail him nothing. In the Next world, there will be no share for him in the special favours of Allah, exalted is He, unless Allah forgives him.

The Prophet ﷺ said:

عَنْ أَبِي هريرة قال: قال رسول الله ﷺ: ﴿أيها النّاس إن الله طيب لا يقبل إلاّ طيباً. وإن الله أمر المؤمنين بما أمر به المرسلين. فقال: ﴿يا أيها الرسل كلوا من الطيبات واعملوا صالحاً إني بما تعملون عليم﴾ وقال: ﴿يا أيها الذين آمنوا كلوا من طيبات ما رزقناكم﴾. ثم ذكر الرجل يطيل السفر. أشعث أغبر. يمد يديه إلى السماء. يا رب يا رب ومطعمه حرام، ومشربه حرام، وملبسه حرام، وغذي بالحرام. فأنى يستجاب لذلك؟﴾.

From Abū Hurayrah ﷺ there is that he said: The Messenger of Allah ﷺ said, "Allah, exalted is He, is pure[1] and only accepts that which is pure. Allah ordered the believers with that with which he ordered the Messengers, and He said, exalted is He, *'Messengers, eat of the good things and act rightly'* (Sūrat al-Mu'minūn 23: 52) and He said, exalted is He, *'You who have īmān! eat of the good things We have provided for you'* (Sūrat al-Baqarah 2: 171)," and then he mentioned a dishevelled dusty man lengthening his journey and stretching out his hands to the sky, 'Lord, Lord!' and his food is *ḥarām*, his drink *ḥarām*, his clothing *ḥarām*, he has been fed on the *ḥarām*, so how can he be answered? (Muslim, *kitāb az-zakāh, bāb qabūl aṣ-ṣadaqah min al-kasb aṭ-ṭayyib wa tarbiyatihā*)

The above *ḥadīth* amply demonstrates that when a person draws his livelihood from impure means his prayers are no longer worthy of being answered. Another *ḥadīth* of the Prophet ﷺ reads:

مَنِ اشْتَرَى ثَوْباً بِعَشَرَةِ دَرَاهِمَ وَفِيهِ دِرْهَمٌ حَرَامٌ لَمْ يَقْبَلِ اللهُ لَهُ صَلَاةً مَا دَامَ عَلَيْهِ مِنْهُ شَيْءٌ.

Whoever buys a garment for ten dirhams of which one dirham is *ḥarām*, Allah will not accept a *ṣalāh* of his as long as any of it remains on him. (Aḥmad narrated it from Ibn ᶜUmar ﷺ in his *Musnad*)

In another *ḥadīth*, he says, "All flesh which grows from the *ḥarām*[2] deserves to be thrown into the Fire [of hell]." (Ad-Daylamī narrated it from Ibn Masᶜūd ﷺ)

On the basis of these principles of Islamic economy outlined here and in the previous chapter, it is not lawful for one to liquidate one debt with another. When one sells a commodity at a price to be paid later, one must not buy it back at a lower price either with cash or to be paid at a date earlier than that date fixed first; nor buy it back at a higher price to be paid at a date later than the date fixed for the first agreement.[3] However, it is permissible to buy back the property for a price to be paid on the date fixed first.[4]

There is no harm in buying commodities in a sack when the contents are described and made known, but it is not lawful to buy garments that cannot be unfolded or described, or at night in the darkness where people cannot look at them or recognise the sack's contents. Similarly, it is unlawful to sell an animal at night in the darkness. One must not outbid the bid of his brother

Muslim, but that is when the contracting parties have reached an agreement, nor at the beginning of making an offer.[5] It is also unlawful to sell fish while they are still at large in rivers or pools. Nor is it permissible to sell a foetus, whether of a slave or of an animal, while still in its mother's womb. It is not lawful to buy in advance the offspring of what the foetus of a she-camel will bear, nor to sell the semen of male camels that will produce young when they fertilise female ones.

It is equally unlawful to exchange ripe dates for dried ones or raisins for grapes. In this respect neither greater nor equal amounts can be received in exchange; there is to be no exchange of ripe juicy ones for dried fruits of the same type. This is prohibited because it involves selling or exchanging a known thing in return for something which is unknown.[6] The trader must not exploit the buyer nor vice-versa. The government in later centuries on the basis of the practice of the Prophet ﷺ and of the *Khulafā' ar-Rāshidūn* ❁ took interest in market conditions and developed the institution of the *ḥisbah,* the inspectorate that was responsible for stopping usurious practices, adulteration, under-weighing, over-work by employers, employment in risky jobs, encroachment on the thoroughfares, unhealthy trades, unlawful professions and cruelty to animals.

Such inspectorates were headed by a *muḥtasib.* There are numerous instances to suggest that the government intervened if the rules of justice and fair trade were violated. The Prophet's ﷺ treaties with Thaqīf, Hawāzin and the people of Najrān stipulated a ban on transactions involving uncertainty. The Prophet ﷺ not only appointed an inspector to ensure that the unlawful transactions were avoided but he also visited the marketplaces advising the traders to observe the *Sharīcah* in trade. His successors, the *Khulafā' ar-Rāshidūn* ❁, were also active in eliminating malpractices in trade and commerce. Serious actions were taken against adulteration of any kind. Minting of coins was regulated so as to prevent debasement and dishonesty and save the general public from being defrauded. Most of the later rulers and caliphs in Islamic history were vigilant about prices in the different markets, and initiated various institutions to control the harm ensuing from the actions of selfish and greedy traders and trade companies.

A Warning to selfish and dishonest traders

The following traditions of the Prophet ﷺ speak of the punishment for selfish and dishonest traders. Wāthilah ibn al-Asqaᶜ said that once the Messenger of Allah ﷺ came to them and said:

يَا مَعْشَرَ التُّجَّارِ إِيَّاكُمْ وَالْكَذِبَ.

> Traders! Beware of telling lies. (Aṭ-Ṭabarānī narrated it in *al-Kabīr* from Wāthilah)

Some traders are habituated to swearing in the name of Allah while selling their commodities. The Prophet ﷺ has said about them:

> There are three at whom Allah will not look on the morrow: an adulterous older man, and a man who takes oaths as a merchandise swearing for every true and false matter and a fraudulent boastful and proud poor man. (Aṭ-Ṭabarānī narrated it in *al-Kabīr* from ᶜIṣmah ibn Mālik)

The following narration is in respect of a bedouin who sold goods but used to swear in the name of Allah:

مَرَّ أَعْرَابِيٌّ بِشَاةٍ فَقُلْتُ : تَبِيعُنِيهَا بِثَلَاثَةِ دَرَاهِمَ؟ فَقَالَ لَا وَاللَّهِ! ثُمَّ بَاعَنِيهَا ، فَذَكَرْتُ ذَلِكَ لِرَسُولِ اللَّهِ ﷺ فَقَالَ ﴿ بَاعَ ءَاخِرَتَهُ بِدُنْيَاهُ ﴾

> A bedouin Arab passed by with a sheep, so I said, "Will you sell it to me for three dirhams?" So he said, "No, by Allah!" Then later he sold it to me. I mentioned that to the Messenger of Allah ﷺ and he said, "He sold his *ākhirah* for his *dunyā*." (Ibn Ḥibbān narrated it in his *Ṣaḥīḥ* from Abū Saᶜīd al-Khudrī)

Ribā: Usury

One such wrong way of acquiring wealth that is condemned in the Generous Qur'ān in no uncertain terms is *ribā* – usury, a practice prevalent in the *jāhiliyyah* period (the pre-Islamic era), and much more prevalent in the modern age. In order to satisfy their lust for ever more wealth, some people say, as Allah, exalted is He, quoted them as saying:

ذَٰلِكَ بِأَنَّهُمْ قَالُوا إِنَّمَا الْبَيْعُ مِثْلُ الرِّبَا

That is because they say, "Trade is the same as ribā." (Sūrat al-Baqarah 2: 275)

They see no difference between the two, but the former is permitted in Islam and the latter forbidden completely, as Allah said:

وَأَحَلَّ اللَّهُ الْبَيْعَ وَحَرَّمَ الرِّبَا

But Allah has permitted trade and He has forbidden ribā. (Ibid.)

With this introduction, we shall examine the Qur'ānic injunctions forbidding usury and the guidance from the Sunnah of the Prophet Muḥammad ﷺ on the same subject.

The Qur'ānic injunction contained in Sūrat al-Baqarah says:

الَّذِينَ يَأْكُلُونَ الرِّبَا لَا يَقُومُونَ إِلَّا كَمَا يَقُومُ الَّذِي يَتَخَبَّطُهُ الشَّيْطَانُ مِنَ الْمَسِّ ذَٰلِكَ بِأَنَّهُمْ قَالُوا إِنَّمَا الْبَيْعُ مِثْلُ الرِّبَا وَأَحَلَّ اللَّهُ الْبَيْعَ وَحَرَّمَ الرِّبَا فَمَنْ جَاءَهُ مَوْعِظَةٌ مِنْ رَبِّهِ فَانْتَهَىٰ فَلَهُ مَا سَلَفَ وَأَمْرُهُ إِلَى اللَّهِ وَمَنْ عَادَ فَأُولَٰئِكَ أَصْحَابُ النَّارِ هُمْ فِيهَا خَالِدُونَ

Those who practise ribā will not rise from the grave except as someone driven mad by Shaytan's touch. That is because they say, 'Trade is the same as ribā.' But Allah has permitted trade and He has forbidden ribā. Whoever is given a warning by his Lord and then desists, can keep what he received in the past and his affair is Allah's concern. But all who return to it will be the Companions of the Fire, remaining in it timelessly, for ever. (Sūrat al-Baqarah 2: 275)

Furthermore:

يَمْحَقُ اللَّهُ الرِّبَا وَيُرْبِي الصَّدَقَاتِ وَاللَّهُ لَا يُحِبُّ كُلَّ كَفَّارٍ أَثِيمٍ

Allah obliterates ribā but makes ṣadaqah grow in value! Allah does not love any persistently ungrateful wrongdoer. (Sūrat al-Baqarah 2: 276)

The *mu'minūn* must give up the practice of usury immediately:

يَا أَيُّهَا الَّذِينَ آمَنُوا اتَّقُوا اللَّهَ وَذَرُوا مَا بَقِيَ مِنَ الرِّبَا إِنْ كُنْتُمْ مُؤْمِنِينَ

You who have īmān! have taqwā of Allah and forgo any remaining ribā if you are mu'minūn. (Sūrat al-Baqarah 2: 277)

If someone does not stop the practice of usury, he is given notice of war from Allah and His Messenger:

إِنْ لَمْ تَفْعَلُوا فَأْذَنُوا بِحَرْبٍ مِنَ اللَّهِ وَرَسُولِهِ وَإِنْ تُبْتُمْ فَلَكُمْ رُؤُوسُ أَمْوَالِكُمْ لَا تَظْلِمُونَ وَلَا تُظْلَمُونَ

If you do not [forgo ribā], know that it means war from Allah and His Messenger. But if you make tawbah you may have your capital, without wronging and without being wronged. (Sūrat al-Baqarah 2: 278)

The promise of prosperity in this and the Next World is given to those who stop this practice:

يَا أَيُّهَا الَّذِينَ آمَنُوا لَا تَأْكُلُوا الرِّبَا أَضْعَافًا مُضَاعَفَةً وَاتَّقُوا اللَّهَ لَعَلَّكُمْ تُفْلِحُونَ

You who have īmān! do not feed on ribā, multiplied and then remultiplied. Have taqwā of Allah so that hopefully you will be successful. (Sūrah Āl ʿImrān 3: 130)

Those who devour usury are the rejectors of faith:

وَأَخْذِهِمُ الرِّبَا وَقَدْ نُهُوا عَنْهُ وَأَكْلِهِمْ أَمْوَالَ النَّاسِ بِالْبَاطِلِ وَأَعْتَدْنَا لِلْكَافِرِينَ مِنْهُمْ عَذَابًا أَلِيمًا

And because of their practising ribā when they were forbidden to do it, and because of their consuming people's wealth by wrongful means, We have prepared for the kāfirūn among them a painful punishment. (Sūrat an-Nisā' 4: 160)

Wealth does not increase by practising usury but decreases in the long run:

وَمَا آتَيْتُم مِّن رِّبًا لِّيَرْبُوَ فِي أَمْوَالِ النَّاسِ فَلَا يَرْبُو عِندَ اللَّهِ وَمَا آتَيْتُم مِّن زَكَاةٍ تُرِيدُونَ وَجْهَ اللَّهِ فَأُولَٰئِكَ هُمُ الْمُضْعِفُونَ

What you give with usurious intent, aiming to get back a greater amount from people's wealth, does not become greater with Allah. But anything you give as zakāh, seeking the Face of Allah – all who do that will get back twice as much. (Sūrat ar-Rūm 30: 39)

There are a number of *ḥadīth* of the Prophet ﷺ which condemn usury among them one in which he ﷺ pronounced a curse on those involved in the practice of usury:

عَنْ جَابِرٍ قَالَ: لَعَنَ رَسُولُ اللَّهِ ﷺ آكِلَ الرِّبَا وَمُوكِلَهُ وَشَاهِدَيْهِ وَكَاتِبَهُ، وَقَالَ هُمْ سَوَاءٌ .

There is from Jābir that he said: The Messenger of Allah ﷺ cursed the person who consumed usury, the person who gives it, the two witnesses to it and its scribe, and he said, "They are all the same." (Ibn Jarīr aṭ-Ṭabarī narrated it in *Tahdhīb al-āthār*)

The following *ḥadīth* explains non-usurious transactions:

عَنْ أَبِي سَعِيدٍ الْخُدْرِيِّ قَالَ: قَالَ رَسُولُ اللَّهِ ﷺ: ﴿ الذَّهَبُ بِالذَّهَبِ، وَالْفِضَّةُ بِالْفِضَّةِ، وَالْبُرُّ بِالْبُرِّ، وَالشَّعِيرُ بِالشَّعِيرِ، وَالتَّمْرُ بِالتَّمْرِ، وَالْمِلْحُ بِالْمِلْحِ، مِثْلًا بِمِثْلٍ، يَدًا بِيَدٍ، فَمَنْ زَادَ أَوِ اسْتَزَادَ فَقَدْ أَرْبَى، الآخِذُ وَالْمُعْطِي فِيهِ سَوَاءٌ ﴾ .

There is from Abū Saᶜīd al-Khudrī that he said: The Messenger of Allah ﷺ said: "Gold for gold, silver for silver, wheat for wheat, barley for barley, dates for dates, and salt for salt, must be like for like, hand to hand. If anyone gives more or asks for more, he has dealt in usury. The receiver and giver are equally guilty." (Muslim, *kitāb al-musāqāh, bāb aṣ-ṣarf wa bayᶜ adh-dhahab bi al-wariq naqdan*)

Even receiving a gift after giving a loan amounts to usury:

قَالَ أَنَسُ بْنُ مَالِكٍ: قَالَ رَسُولُ اللَّهِ ﷺ : ﴿ إِذَا أَقْرَضَ أَحَدُكُمْ قَرْضًا فَأَهْدَى لَهُ، أَوْ حَمَلَهُ عَلَى الدَّابَّةِ، فَلَا يَرْكَبْهَا وَلَا يَقْبَلْهُ، إِلَّا أَنْ يَكُونَ جَرَى بَيْنَهُ وَ بَيْنَهُ قَبْلَ ذَلِكَ ﴾ .

Anas ibn Mālik said: The Messenger of Allah ﷺ said, "If any of you gives a loan and [the recipient] gives him a gift or conveys him on a mount he should not mount it nor accept it, unless it was something that had happened ordinarily between them beforehand." (Ibn Mājah, *kitāb aṣ-ṣadaqāt, bāb al-qarḍ*)

One dirham of usury is a far greater crime than adultery:

عَنْ عَبدِ اللهِ بنِ حنظَلَةَ قال: قال رَسولُ اللهِ ﷺ: ﴿ درهمٌ رِباً يأكُلُه الرَّجلُ وهو يعلمُ أشدُّ عِندَ اللهِ من ستَّةٍ وثلاثين زينةً ﴾.

ᶜAbdullāh ibn Ḥanẓalah said: The Messenger of Allah ﷺ said, "A dirham of usury which a man consumes knowingly is worse in Allah's view than thirty-six acts of adultery." (Aṭ-Ṭabarānī narrated it in *al-Kabīr,* and Aḥmad in the *Musnad*)

The least act of usury is equivalent to incest:

الرِّبا اثْنانِ وسَبْعون باباً أَدْناها مِثْلُ إتيانِ الرَّجُلِ أُمَّه

Usury is seventy-two gates the least of which is like a man having sexual relations with his mother. (ᶜAbd ar-Razzāq narrated it in *al-Jāmiᶜ*)

Ultimately usury leads to poverty:

إنَّ الرِّبا وإنْ كَثُرَ فإنَّ عاقبتَه تصيرُ إلى قُلٍّ.

Ibn Masᶜūd narrated that the Messenger of Allah ﷺ said: "Even though usury be much it leads in the end to penury." (Aḥmad narrated it in the *Musnad,* and aṭ-Ṭabarānī in *al-Kabīr)*

The Prophet ﷺ foretold what was to happen:

عَنْ أَبي هُريرةَ؛ قال: قالَ رَسولُ اللهِ ﷺ: ﴿ ليأْتِيَنَّ على النَّاسِ زمانٌ لا يبقَى مِنهُمْ أحدٌ إلاَّ آكِلُ الرِّبا. فمَنْ لم يأْكُلْ، أصابهُ مِنْ غُبارِه ﴾.

It is narrated that Abū Hurayrah said: The Messenger of Allah ﷺ said, "There will certainly come to people a time in which not one of them but he will consume usury, and whoever does not consume it will be struck by its dust." (Ibn Mājah, *kitāb at-tijārāt, bāb at-taghlīẓ fī ar-ribā*; Abū Dāwūd, *kitāb al-bujūᶜ*, *bāb fī ijtināb ash-shubuhāt*; al-Ḥākim in *al-Mustadrak* and others)

Usury was not new to Arabia

Even before the advent of Islam, the system of usury prevailed in the Arabian Peninsula, and much of the trade economy was based on it. Let no one imagine that it was simply a question of isolated transactions between individuals. Quraysh undertook considerable trade with Syria in the summer and with the Yemen in the winter. The capital of Quraysh was invested in this trade. Let us not forget that the caravan of Abū Sufyān, which the Muslims ambushed at the battle of Badr and which then evaded them to be replaced by Allah with something better for them, contained a thousand camels loaded with goods. If usury had simply been practised in restricted individual dealings, and had not been a comprehensive system of economic life, it would not have deserved the repeated and scorching attack made on it by Allah, exalted is He, in the Qur'ān, and the pursuance of that attack by the Prophet ﷺ. This capital, this commercial activity and this economy were all based on the system of usury. Moreover, the *Sharīᶜah* has been revealed for every community until the end of time, and so the prohibition of usury is particularly relevant to us today, since it is now difficult to have an ordinary transaction that does not involve usury.

Shortly before the coming of the Prophet ﷺ, the economies of various countries came to be gathered into this system, as for example in Madīnah, where the economy was dominated by Jews who held usury as the basis of their transactions with non-Jews.

This was the economic 'reality' on which the life of the land was based. Then Islam came, denying and rejecting this unjust and criminal system, and setting forth in its stead a new basis: that of *zakāh*, of the goodwill loan, of co-operation and mutual solidarity and of the many profit-sharing transactions, partnership and agency contracts available for people in commercial life.

The thoroughness of the Prophetic condemnation of usury which was made after the dawn of Islam, leaves no room for any part for it, however indirect, in our transactions. The Messenger of Allah ﷺ cursed the receiver (literally, the eater) of interest, and the clerk who writes the bond, and the two witnesses thereof, and declared them all equally culpable.

The Prophet ﷺ forbade the barter of a heap of dates of unknown weight for a specified quantity. Similarly, Muslims are forbidden to sell fruit upon the trees before it is ripe, even when both parties are willing to partake in the risk.

Thus the Book of Allah and the Sunnah have prohibited all of those transactions that militate against the realisation of equity and the prevention of injustice, whether light or grave. Those aspects forbidden according to Ibn Taymiyyah, include: "appropriation of the property of others unjustly, or by usury and gambling." Certain aspects of usury and gambling, in particular, which the Prophet ﷺ has forbidden are, for example:

1. Selling commodities or land not possessed by the seller.
2. Selling animals still unborn.
3. Selling birds and fish not yet caught.
4. Selling a ewe which has not been milked for a long time to impress on the buyer falsely that its milk is always abundant.
5. Selling commodities the defects of which have been disguised.
6. Selling commodities while allowing the buyer to touch them only, without seeing (or examining) them.
7. Selling a piece of cloth (or a garment) without exposing it adequately to the buyer.
8. Selling commodities haphazardly without weighing or measuring.
9. Selling agricultural produce that is not yet ripe.
10. Prearranging with a man to bid a high price for a commodity, so as to induce others to buy it at a higher price.
11. Selling fruits before they show any sign of ripening.

Added to all these are also prohibited all kinds of invalid partnerships, such as partnerships in cultivating a tract of land in return for the products of a certain piece of it.[7]

Besides, as al-Qayrawānī has mentioned in his *Risālah* and as is found in all the works of *fiqh* and collections of *ḥadīth*, selling silver for silver in a direct exchange in which one of the parties gives more than he receives, is also usurious, as we saw above. It is also usury, to sell gold for gold, one of the parties giving more than he receives. It is not lawful to exchange silver for silver or exchange gold for gold except in equal quantities in direct and immediate exchange. The exchange of silver for gold is usury, except when done with immediate effect. In respect of foodstuffs such as cereals, legumes and similar things, which can be stored, all kinds of foodstuffs and condiments, it is unlawful to exchange those of the same type, except by giving equal quantities and with immediate effect. It is not lawful for one party to delay compliance with these rules. It is not lawful to exchange foodstuff for foodstuff, whether of the same type or not and whether of the type that can be stored or not, when one or both parties are permitted to delay compliance with meeting their obligation.

There is no harm in exchanging fruits and vegetables and other things that cannot be stored, while one party gives more than the other even if they are of the same type, through direct exchange. It is not lawful for one party to give more than the other in respect of commodities of the same type which can be stored, such as dried fruits and other condiments, foodstuffs and drinks, except water alone.

As for commodities of different types of grain, fruits and foodstuffs, there is no harm in one party giving more than the other, in direct immediate exchange.

In exchanging commodities of one type it is not lawful for one party to give more than he receives except in respect of vegetables and fruits.[8]

Wheat, barley and huskless barley are considered one category in respect of lawfulness and unlawfulness. Raisins of all types are considered another category. Similarly, dried dates are all considered a single category. Legumes are considered to consist of many categories in respect of trading. Imām Mālik, however, held a different view on this. Imam Mālik considered legumes to consist of one category for the purpose of *zakāh*. The flesh of quadrupeds whether tame or wild is considered to be of the same category. Further, the flesh of all birds is considered to consist of one category. Again, the flesh of all aquatic animals is considered to be of the same category. Any fat extracted from the flesh of animals regarded as one category is considered, like the flesh, to be of one category. The milk of that category mentioned as well as the cheese and ghee from it are all considered one category.

Whoever buys foodstuffs, it is not lawful for him to sell them off before he takes possession of them, if the purchase is done through weighing, measuring or counting. However, he is permitted to do that if he bought the foodstuff en bloc. The same rule applies to all foodstuffs, condiments and drinks, with the exception of water alone.

Now, if the commodity to be sold happens to be drugs or legumes from which oil cannot be extracted, then it will not be unlawful to be sold before it is received after purchase. In trading such legumes one party can give more than he receives of that same commodity.

There is no harm for foodstuffs bought on credit to be sold before they are taken possession of.

Every sale or hire or rental contract which involves some hazard or uncertainty in respect of price or the object of sale, or uncertainty in the time payment is due, is not lawful.

It is not lawful for a sale to involve uncertainty nor is it lawful to sell an unknown commodity. Besides, it is not lawful to sell a commodity payment of which shall be due at an unknown time.

Here it may be mentioned that the *Sharī^{c}ah* does not tolerate any fixed profit which is stipulated at the time of the contract (i.e. predetermined profit) because apart from being *ribā* it is risky in that it may not all be realised, or even if realised, it may be less than the stipulated amount. The *Sharī^{c}ah* does permit a stipulation in the case of *qirāḍ* or *muḍārabah* of a percentage of the profit.

Distribution of Income and Wealth

The Islamic policy of distribution of wealth through inheritance (*mīrāth*), *zakāh*, *ṣadaqah* etc., significantly discourages the accumulation of wealth and its concentration in a few hands. It assures that in the process of distribution none of the factors of production exploit the other. Landowners, labourers and the owners of capital jointly share in their productivity.

As a practical religion and way of life, it compulsorily retains a portion of this produced wealth for those who are unavoidably prevented from making a full productive contribution due to social, physical or economic handicap.

The Prophet ﷺ and the *Khulafā' ar-Rāshidūn* ؓ achieved this goal through prohibiting a very large number of exploitative and unjust techniques in trade and commerce. A study of the *ḥadīth* literature is suggestive of those measures, which include disciplinary restrictions on the landlord and the farmer, the employer and the employee and the producer and the trader. Our study on the prohibition of *ribā* has explained some of these measures.

Al-Amānah: The Trust

The law of Allah categorically declared:

وَلَا تَأْكُلُوٓا أَمْوَٰلَكُم بَيْنَكُم بِٱلْبَٰطِلِ

Do not devour one another's property by false means. (Sūrat al-Baqarah 2: 188)

If someone deposits his property as a trust with a trustworthy person, he is duty bound to look after this property just as he would look after and protect his own.

A man who keeps someone's property in trust is an *amīn*, a trustworthy person. Because of his integrity, honesty, sincerity and faith in Allah, he does not devour another's wealth by false or illegal means, nor does he exchange someone else's superior quality thing for something inferior. The life of the Prophet ﷺ offers us the best model as he was given the honorific title *al-*

Amīn even by people who had not accepted Islam, because of his qualities of character as a trustworthy person. Even on the day of *hijrah* from Makkah to Madīnah while his enemies had laid a plot to murder him, he made sure to hand over to his cousin, ʿAlī ibn Abī Ṭālib, all the property he held in trust, for him to return to their rightful owners.

The Noble Qur'ān speaks about *amānah* (trust) in the following words:

إِنَّ اللَّهَ يَأْمُرُكُمْ أَن تُؤَدُّوا الْأَمَانَاتِ إِلَىٰ أَهْلِهَا وَإِذَا حَكَمْتُم بَيْنَ النَّاسِ أَن تَحْكُمُوا بِالْعَدْلِ إِنَّ اللَّهَ نِعِمَّا يَعِظُكُم بِهِ إِنَّ اللَّهَ كَانَ سَمِيعًا بَصِيرًا

> *Allah commands you to return to their owners the things you hold on trust and, when you judge between people, to judge with justice. How excellent is what Allah exhorts you to do! Allah is All-Hearing, All-Seeing.* (Sūrat an-Nisā' 4: 58)

The trustee is charged with a great responsibility in Islam. His duty is to guard the interests of the person on whose behalf he holds the trust and to render back the property and accounts when required according to the terms of the trust. This duty of keeping trust is linked with the sanction of the religion of Islam which requires a higher standard even than that stipulated by common law. In the Qur'ān Allah says:

فَإِنْ أَمِنَ بَعْضُكُم بَعْضًا فَلْيُؤَدِّ الَّذِي اؤْتُمِنَ أَمَانَتَهُ وَلْيَتَّقِ اللَّهَ رَبَّهُ

> *If you leave things on trust with one another the one who is trusted must deliver up his trust and have taqwā of Allah his Lord.* (Sūrat al-Baqarah 2: 283)

The Islamic concept of life is such that all our mortal life in this world must be lived as if in the presence of Allah Who sees all our actions, and knows fully our thoughts and intentions. Any breach of trust or bad intentions will be accounted for, if not in this world, on the day of Judgement. A *ḥadīth* of the Prophet ﷺ enumerates the signs of the hypocrite, one of which is a man who becomes dishonest in the matter of a trust deposited with him:

عَنْ أَبِي هُرَيْرَةَ رَضِيَ اللَّهُ عَنْهُ أَنَّ رَسُولَ اللَّهِ ﷺ قَالَ ﴿آيَةُ الْمُنَافِقِ ثَلَاثٌ إِذَا حَدَّثَ كَذَبَ وَإِذَا اؤْتُمِنَ خَانَ وَإِذَا وَعَدَ أَخْلَفَ﴾

Abū Hurayrah ؓ narrated that the Messenger of Allah ﷺ said, "The sign of the hypocrite is threefold: when he speaks he lies, and when he is entrusted he is treacherous, and when he promises he breaks the promise." (Al-Bukhārī, *kitāb ash-shahādāt, bāb man amara bi injāz al-wa^cd wa fa^calahu al-ḥasanu*; Muslim, *kitāb al-īmān, bāb bayān khiṣāl al-munāfiq*; an-Nasā'ī and at-Tirmidhī also transmitted it)

The Qur'ānic injunction further emphasises keeping the trust in the following words:

يَا أَيُّهَا الَّذِينَ آمَنُوا لَا تَخُونُوا اللَّهَ وَالرَّسُولَ وَتَخُونُوا أَمَانَاتِكُمْ وَأَنْتُمْ تَعْلَمُونَ

You who have īmān! do not betray Allah and His Messenger, and do not knowingly betray your trusts. (Sūrat al-Anfāl 8: 27)

The trust referred to in this verse may be of various kinds:

1. Property, goods, credit, etc., and in the case of property, goods, money etc., it is often called *wadī^cah* or deposit.
2. Plans, confidences, secrets, etc.;
3. Knowledge, talents, opportunities, etc., which we are expected to make use of on behalf of our fellow men.

Men betray the trust of Allah and His Messenger ﷺ by misusing property, or abusing the confidence reposed in them or the knowledge or talents given to them.

Dayn: Debt

In life, there are ups and downs. There are periods of trials from Allah as He says in the Qur'ān:

وَلَنَبْلُوَنَّكُمْ بِشَيْءٍ مِّنَ الْخَوْفِ وَالْجُوعِ وَنَقْصٍ مِّنَ الْأَمْوَالِ وَالْأَنْفُسِ وَالثَّمَرَاتِ وَبَشِّرِ الصَّابِرِينَ

We will test you with a certain amount of fear and hunger and loss of wealth and life and fruits. But give good news to the steadfast. (Sūrat al-Baqarah 2: 155)

In such circumstances, we are asked to remain steadfast. When one has a family to look after and some sudden need arises to borrow money, one is required to go to friends, neighbours, relatives or philanthropic people to ask for a loan. The Generous Qur'ān has laid down principles concerning the repayment of loans and debts. It is important to bear in mind that another example of debt is when business people purchase things on credit, i.e. with a promise to pay later. A great deal of commercial life relies on credit.

The guidance from the Sunnah also supports the Qur'ānic teachings on this subject. We shall first consider the Qur'ānic injunctions:

إِنَّ اللَّهَ يَأْمُرُكُمْ أَن تُؤَدُّوا الْأَمَانَاتِ إِلَىٰ أَهْلِهَا

Allah commands you to return to their owners the things you hold on trust. (Sūrat an-Nisā' 4: 57)

In Islam debt is also a trust which should be returned to its owner. Imam al-Bukhārī has used this verse as the caption for a chapter (Al-Bukhārī, *kitāb fī al-istiqrāḍ wa adā' ad-duyūn wa al-ḥajr wa at-taflīs, bāb adā' ad-duyūn*) concerning repayment of debt.

The Noble Qur'ān has guided Muslims in respect of lending and borrowing in Sūrat al-Baqarah in the following manner:

يَا أَيُّهَا الَّذِينَ آمَنُوا إِذَا تَدَايَنتُم بِدَيْنٍ إِلَىٰ أَجَلٍ مُّسَمًّى فَاكْتُبُوهُ وَلْيَكْتُب بَّيْنَكُمْ كَاتِبٌ بِالْعَدْلِ وَلَا
يَأْبَ كَاتِبٌ أَن يَكْتُبَ كَمَا عَلَّمَهُ اللَّهُ فَلْيَكْتُبْ وَلْيُمْلِلِ الَّذِي عَلَيْهِ الْحَقُّ وَلْيَتَّقِ اللَّهَ رَبَّهُ وَلَا يَبْخَسْ
مِنْهُ شَيْئًا فَإِن كَانَ الَّذِي عَلَيْهِ الْحَقُّ سَفِيهًا أَوْ ضَعِيفًا أَوْ لَا يَسْتَطِيعُ أَن يُمِلَّ هُوَ فَلْيُمْلِلْ وَلِيُّهُ بِالْعَدْلِ
وَاسْتَشْهِدُوا شَهِيدَيْنِ مِن رِّجَالِكُمْ فَإِن لَّمْ يَكُونَا رَجُلَيْنِ فَرَجُلٌ وَامْرَأَتَانِ مِمَّن تَرْضَوْنَ مِنَ الشُّهَدَاءِ
أَن تَضِلَّ إِحْدَاهُمَا فَتُذَكِّرَ إِحْدَاهُمَا الْأُخْرَىٰ وَلَا يَأْبَ الشُّهَدَاءُ إِذَا مَا دُعُوا وَلَا تَسْأَمُوا أَن تَكْتُبُوهُ
صَغِيرًا أَوْ كَبِيرًا إِلَىٰ أَجَلِهِ ذَٰلِكُمْ أَقْسَطُ عِندَ اللَّهِ وَأَقْوَمُ لِلشَّهَادَةِ وَأَدْنَىٰ أَلَّا تَرْتَابُوا إِلَّا أَن تَكُونَ
تِجَارَةً حَاضِرَةً تُدِيرُونَهَا بَيْنَكُمْ فَلَيْسَ عَلَيْكُمْ جُنَاحٌ أَلَّا تَكْتُبُوهَا وَأَشْهِدُوا إِذَا تَبَايَعْتُمْ وَلَا يُضَارَّ

كَاتِبٌ وَلَا شَهِيدٌ وَإِن تَفْعَلُوا فَإِنَّهُ فُسُوقٌ بِكُمْ وَاتَّقُوا اللَّهَ وَيُعَلِّمُكُمُ اللَّهُ وَاللَّهُ بِكُلِّ شَيْءٍ عَلِيمٌ

You who have īmān! when you take on a debt for a specified period, write it down. A writer should write it down between you justly. No writer should refuse to write; as Allah has taught him, so he should write. The one incurring the debt should dictate and should have taqwā of Allah his Lord and not reduce it in any way. If the person incurring the debt is incompetent or weak or unable to dictate, then his guardian should dictate for him justly. Two men among you should act as witnesses. But if there are not two men, then a man and two women with whom you are satisfied as witnesses; then if one of them forgets, the other can remind her. Witnesses should not refuse when they are called upon. Do not think it too trivial to write down, whether small or large, with the date that it falls due. Doing that is more just in Allah's sight and more helpful when bearing witness and more likely to eliminate any doubt – unless it is an immediate transaction hand to hand, taken and given without delay. There is nothing wrong in your not writing that down. Call witnesses when you trade. Neither writer nor witness should be put under pressure. If you do that, it is deviancy on your part. Have taqwā of Allah and Allah will give you knowledge. Allah has knowledge of all things. (Sūrat al-Baqarah 2: 282)

The verse on debt and its repayment is among the detailed verses of commandments (*āyāt al-aḥkām al-mufaṣṣalah*). The *fiqh* of the above is:

1. When money or something else is lent for a specific term, it should be written down in a document.
2. The scribe who is called upon to write should not refuse since Allah has gifted him with the art of writing. He should write exactly what is dictated.
3. The person taking the debt should dictate.
4. Supposing such a person is ignorant of the ordinances, or if he does not know what dictation is or cannot dictate well, or he is of an immature age or senile or a foreigner who is ignorant of the language of the land, then his guardian or agent should dictate justly.
5. Two Muslim witnesses should be called to witness the deed. They must be adult, of unimpaired reason, free men and of good character. Disputes, if any, are to be

decided on the testimony of these witnesses, and not on the strength of the written document, the role of which is only secondary or subsidiary.

6. If two male witnesses are not available, then one Muslim man and two Muslim women should be asked to witness. When we compare this with the Jewish code where the testimony of a woman is inadmissable,[9] we realise the practical view Islam has taken about witnesses.[10]
7. In the entire affair, the parties concerned should fear Allah and do justice.

The Guidance from the Sunnah

1. Intention in taking on a debt

عَنْ أَبِي هُرَيْرَةَ رَضِيَ اللّٰهُ عَنْهُ عَنِ النَّبِيِّ صَلَّى اللّٰهُ عَلَيْهِ وَسَلَّمَ قَالَ مَنْ أَخَذَ أَمْوَالَ النَّاسِ يُرِيدُ أَدَاءَهَا أَدَّى اللّٰهُ عَنْهُ وَمَنْ أَخَذَ يُرِيدُ إِتْلَافَهَا أَتْلَفَهُ اللّٰهُ

Abū Hurayrah ﷺ said: The Messenger of Allah ﷺ said, "If someone takes people's property intending to repay it, Allah will repay it for him, and if someone takes it intending to waste it, Allah will destroy him." (Al-Bukhārī, *kitāb fī al-istiqrāḍ wa adā' ad-duyūn wa al-ḥajr wa at-taflīs, bāb man akhadha amwāl an-nās yurīdu adā'ahā aw itlāfahā*; and Ibn Mājah, *kitāb aṣ-ṣadaqāt, bāb man addāna daynan lam yanwi qaḍā'ahu*)

2. Re-payment of a debt is essential

قَالَ أَبُو هُرَيْرَةَ رَضِيَ اللّٰهُ عَنْهُ قَالَ رَسُولُ اللّٰهِ صَلَّى اللّٰهُ عَلَيْهِ وَسَلَّمَ لَوْ كَانَ لِي مِثْلُ أُحُدٍ ذَهَبًا مَا يَسُرُّنِي أَنْ لَا يَمُرَّ عَلَيَّ ثَلَاثٌ وَعِنْدِي مِنْهُ شَيْءٌ إِلَّا شَيْءٌ أُرْصِدُهُ لِدَيْنٍ

Abū Hurayrah ﷺ said: The Messenger of Allah ﷺ said, "Even if I had the like of Uḥud in gold it would not please me that three [days] would pass me by and I still had anything of it except for some I set aside for a debt." (Al-Bukhārī, *kitāb fī al-istiqrāḍ wa adā' ad-duyūn wa al-ḥajr wa at-taflīs, bāb adā' ad-duyūn*)

3. DEBT MAY LEAD TO WRONGDOING

عَنْ عُرْوَةَ أَنَّ عَائِشَةَ رَضِيَ اللَّهُ عَنْهَا أَخْبَرَتْهُ أَنَّ رَسُولَ اللَّهِ صَلَّى اللَّهُ عَلَيْهِ وَسَلَّمَ كَانَ يَدْعُو فِي الصَّلَاةِ وَيَقُولُ اللَّهُمَّ إِنِّي أَعُوذُ بِكَ مِنَ الْمَأْثَمِ وَالْمَغْرَمِ فَقَالَ لَهُ قَائِلٌ مَا أَكْثَرَ مَا تَسْتَعِيذُ يَا رَسُولَ اللَّهِ مِنَ الْمَغْرَمِ قَالَ إِنَّ الرَّجُلَ إِذَا غَرِمَ حَدَّثَ فَكَذَبَ وَوَعَدَ فَأَخْلَفَ

It is narrated from ʿUrwah that ʿĀ'ishah ؓ informed him that the Messenger of Allah ﷺ used to supplicate in the *ṣalāh* and say, "O Allah I seek refuge with You from wrongdoing and debt." So someone said to him, "How often you seek refuge, Messenger of Allah, from debt!" He said, "When a man becomes indebted, he speaks and lies, and he promises and breaks his promise." (Al-Bukhārī, *kitāb fī al-istiqrāḍ wa adā' ad-duyūn wa al-ḥajr wa at-taflīs, bāb man istaʿādha min ad-dayn*)

4. REPAYMENT OF DEBTS BY A WEALTHY PERSON

Abū Hurayrah ؓ narrated:

قَالَ رَسُولُ اللَّهِ صَلَّى اللَّهُ عَلَيْهِ وَسَلَّمَ مَطْلُ الْغَنِيِّ ظُلْمٌ

Procrastination in repaying debts by a wealthy person is injustice. (Al-Bukhārī, *kitāb al-ḥawālāt, bāb fī al-ḥawālah, wa hal yarjiu fī al-ḥawālah*; Muslim, *fī al-musāqāh, bāb taḥrīm maṭl al-ghanī wa ṣiḥḥat al-ḥawālah*)

5. ENCOURAGEMENT

عَنْ عَبْدِ اللَّهِ بْنِ جَعْفَرٍ ؛ قَالَ : قَالَ رَسُولُ اللَّهِ ﷺ : ﴿كَانَ اللَّهُ مَعَ الدَّائِنِ حَتَّى يَقْضِيَ دَيْنَهُ . مَا لَمْ يَكُنْ فِيمَا يَكْرَهُ اللَّهُ﴾ . قَالَ ، فَكَانَ عَبْدُ اللَّهِ بْنُ جَعْفَرٍ يَقُولُ لِخَازِنِهِ : اذْهَبْ فَخُذْ لِي بِدَيْنٍ . فَإِنِّي أَكْرَهُ أَنْ أَبِيتَ لَيْلَةً إِلَّا وَاللَّهُ مَعِي . بَعْدَ الَّذِي سَمِعْتُ مِنْ رَسُولِ اللَّهِ ﷺ

ʿAbdullāh ibn Jaʿfar ؓ said: The Messenger of Allah ﷺ said, "Allah is with the debtor until he settles his debt as long as it is not for something which Allah dislikes." ʿAbdullāh ibn Jaʿfar used to say to his treasurer, "Go and contract a debt for me. I dislike to spend a night without Allah being with me." (Ibn Mājah, *kitāb aṣ-ṣadaqāt, bāb man addāna daynan lam yanwi qaḍā'ahu*, with a *ḥasan isnād*. Al-Ḥākim says it is *ṣaḥīḥ*.)

Rahn: Pledging or pawning

Rahn literally means a proof or something that has been held in pledge. The word *rahīnah* occurs in the Noble Qur'ān in the following verse:

كُلُّ نَفْسٍ بِمَا كَسَبَتْ رَهِينَةٌ إِلَّا أَصْحَابَ الْيَمِينِ

> *Every self is held in pledge against what it earned, except for the companions of the Right.* (Sūrat al-Muddaththir 74: 38-39)

In the *Sharīah*, it means holding something that has a value as a pledge while giving something on loan. The Qur'ān has laid down this condition in the following verse:

وَإِن كُنتُمْ عَلَى سَفَرٍ وَلَمْ تَجِدُوا كَاتِبًا فَرِهَانٌ مَقْبُوضَةٌ فَإِنْ أَمِنَ بَعْضُكُم بَعْضًا فَلْيُؤَدِّ الَّذِي اؤْتُمِنَ
أَمَانَتَهُ وَلْيَتَّقِ اللَّهَ رَبَّهُ وَلَا تَكْتُمُوا الشَّهَادَةَ وَمَن يَكْتُمْهَا فَإِنَّهُ آثِمٌ قَلْبُهُ وَاللَّهُ بِمَا تَعْمَلُونَ عَلِيمٌ

> *If you are on a journey and cannot find a writer, something can be left as a security (rihān). If you leave things on trust with one another the one who is trusted must deliver up his trust and have taqwā of Allah his Lord. Do not conceal testimony. If someone does conceal it, his heart commits a crime. Allah knows what you do.* (Sūrat al-Baqarah 2: 283)

Where parties do not trust each other, something should be deposited as security, a convenient form of closing the bargain as mentioned in the above verse.

Depositing something as a security for something bought on credit is allowed in the *Sharīᶜah* as is shown by the action of the Prophet ﷺ:

عَنْ عَائِشَةَ رَضِيَ اللهُ عَنْهَا أَنَّ النَّبِيَّ صَلَّى اللهُ عَلَيْهِ وَسَلَّمَ اشْتَرَى طَعَامًا مِنْ يَهُودِيٍّ إِلَى أَجَلٍ
وَرَهَنَهُ دِرْعًا مِنْ حَدِيدٍ

It is narrated from ᶜĀ'ishah that the Prophet bought food from a Jew on credit and deposited a shield made of iron as security with him. (Al-Bukhārī, *kitāb fī al-istiqrāḍ wa adā' ad-duyūn wa al-ḥajr wa at-taflīs, bāb man ishtarā bi ad-dayn wa laysa indahu thamanuhu aw laysa by ḥaḍratihi*)

The thing pawned must possess value. If the time stipulated while undertaking a debt on the basis of the item placed as security expires, the debt can be recovered from the mortgaged property.

A valid pledge must satisfy the following three conditions:

1. Both the pledger and the pledgee must have the legal capacity to possess and dispose of the property. Therefore, the pledge of an insane person or a minor will not be valid.
2. While making the agreement, the terms of the pledge must be expressed, e.g. "I loan you a certain amount for a certain period in lieu of this pledge."
3. The debt as well as the pledged property should not be unlawful commodities transacting in which is forbidden under the *Sharīᶜah*, like wine, pigs, etc.

Ibn Juzayy al-Kalbī said:

Concerning the pledge, it is permissible to pledge everything which it is valid to own of goods, animals and real estate, and it is permissible to pledge undivided, shared (*mushāᶜ*) property, contrary to Abū Ḥanīfah, and it is permissible to pledge dinars if they are printed on, and it is permissible to pledge a debt, contrary to ash-Shāfiᶜī, and to pledge fruit before its ripeness has appeared, and it is permissible to pledge before the right falls due, contrary to ash-Shāfiᶜī, and after it falls due, by unanimous agreement. The pledge is retained because of the debt as long as there remains even a dirham of it, and some of it is not released by the payment of some of the debt. (Al-Kalbī, Ibn Juzayy, *al-Qawānīn al-fiqhiyyah, kitāb as-sādis fī al-abwāb al-mushākalah li al-aqḍiyah li taᶜalluqihā bi al-aḥkām, al-bāb al-khāmis fī ar-ruhūn*)

Ibn Abī Zayd al-Qayrawānī said:

If the pledged things are fowl, the eggs belong to the pledger. Likewise, if bees in a hive are pledged or a house, then the honey as well as the rent belong to the pledger. But the foetus, wool and hair of an animal all remain with the pledgee. When a horse is given as a security, the pledgee is allowed to use it for riding as a compensation for feeding it. Similarly a milch-animal's milk will be allowed to the pledgee when he feeds the animal. Hence, we might deduce that it is evident that when agricultural land or a house is pledged, the pledgee can also derive benefit from it if he pays land-revenue or house-tax, or spends money on the upkeep of the property.

The pledge agreement will be considered incomplete until the article pledged is taken possession of. In this regard a witness [to the verbal agreement] is of no consequence as long as the witness failed to see the transfer of the article pledged. Responsibility for damage or loss of the article pledged shall be borne by the pledgee. But the pledgee only makes good what is lost while in his possession. He does not make good what is lost while in possession of others. (Ibn Abī Zayd al-Qayrawānī, *ar-Risālah*, op.cit., ch. 36)

Bayt al-māl: The Centre of the Financial Organisation of the *Ummah*

Bayt in Arabic means house, and *māl* means property. *Bayt al-māl*, therefore, means the public treasury. The very basis of the *bayt al-māl* is the concept of trust: the wealth of *bayt al-māl* is to be treated as the Muslims' wealth, as against the imperial treasury that was known in medieval times. This concept implies that wealth paid into the treasury is Allah's trust and that the *khalīfah* or ruler is in the position of a trustee whose duty it is to spend it on the common concerns of all Muslims while allowing himself nothing more than a fixed stipend.

The concept of Islamic governance and the establishment of the *bayt al-māl* are inseparable. The phrase *bayt al-māl* does not occur in the Qur'ān as such, but many of the sources from which the funds flow into the *bayt al-māl* are mentioned in the Generous Qur'ān. The institution is mentioned frequently in the *ḥadīth* of the Prophet ﷺ. The *bayt al-māl* came into being in the lifetime of the Prophet ﷺ, immediately after the coming into existence of the polity of the Islamic city of Madīnah. It developed fully in the time of the *Khulafā' ar-Rāshidūn* ☙, particularly the second Caliph 'Umar ibn al-Khaṭṭāb.

The sources from which funds are collected in the *bayt al-māl* are:

1. ZAKĀH

One of the pillars of Islam which demands that 2 $1/2$% or $1/40$ of our held monetary wealth should be given to the poor and needy. These funds were collected and managed in the *bayt al-māl* of the Muslims for the welfare of the *Ummah*. The *zakāh* is only payable by Muslim subjects from their held wealth in terms of cash, gold and silver, trade merchandise, certain crops and herds of cattle and flocks of sheep and goats. Non-Muslims are exempted from the payment of *zakāh*. *Zakāh*, however, is not stored in the *bayt al-māl* except for the very brief period between its collection and disbursement which ought to be as immediate as possible.

Being one of the five pillars of Islam there occur a good number of verses containing injunctions on *zakāh* in the Qur'ān:

$$\text{وَأَقِيمُوا الصَّلَاةَ وَآتُوا الزَّكَاةَ}$$

a. *Establish ṣalāh and pay zakāh* (Sūrat al-Baqarah 2: 43)

$$\text{وَوَيْلٌ لِلْمُشْرِكِينَ الَّذِينَ لَا يُؤْتُونَ الزَّكَاةَ وَهُم بِالْآخِرَةِ هُمْ كَافِرُونَ}$$

b. *Woe to those who associate others with Him: those who do not pay zakāh and reject the ākhirah.* (Sūrah Fuṣṣilat 41: 6-7)

$$\text{وَرَحْمَتِي وَسِعَتْ كُلَّ شَيْءٍ فَسَأَكْتُبُهَا لِلَّذِينَ يَتَّقُونَ وَيُؤْتُونَ الزَّكَاةَ وَالَّذِينَ هُم بِآيَاتِنَا يُؤْمِنُونَ}$$

c. *My mercy extends to all things but I will prescribe it for those who have taqwā and pay zakāh and those who believe in Our Signs.* (Sūrat al-A'rāf 7: 156)

$$\text{وَمَا آتَيْتُم مِّن زَكَاةٍ تُرِيدُونَ وَجْهَ اللَّهِ فَأُولَٰئِكَ هُمُ الْمُضْعِفُونَ}$$

d. *But anything you give as zakāh, seeking the Face of Allah – all who do that will get back twice as much.* (Sūrat ar-Rūm 30: 39)

2. Ṣadaqah or Infāq fī Sabīli'llāh

Ṣadaqah, although denoting *zakāh* as well as voluntary generosity to the poor in the language of the Qur'ān and the usage of the *ᶜulamā',* is ordinarily used for a voluntary donation, over and above the payment of compulsory *zakāh,* given by individuals for the sake of Allah to relieve the problems and sufferings of fellow human beings. According to the *ḥadīth, ṣadaqah* must be given in such a way that even the left hand of the donor does not know what the right hand gives. The words *ṣadaqah* and *infāq fī sabīli'llāh* occur numerous times in the Noble Qur'ān:

وَفِي أَمْوَالِهِمْ حَقٌّ لِّلسَّائِلِ وَالْمَحْرُومِ

a. *And beggars and the destitute received a due share of their wealth.* (Sūrat adh-Dhāriyāt 51: 19)

وَأَنفِقُوا فِي سَبِيلِ اللَّهِ وَلَا تُلْقُوا بِأَيْدِيكُمْ إِلَى التَّهْلُكَةِ

b. *Spend in the Way of Allah. Do not cast yourselves into destruction.* (Sūrat al-Baqarah 2:195)

يَا أَيُّهَا الَّذِينَ آمَنُوا أَنفِقُوا مِن طَيِّبَاتِ مَا كَسَبْتُمْ

c. *You who have īmān! give away some of the good things you have earned.* (Sūrat al-Baqarah 2: 267)

فَآتِ ذَا الْقُرْبَىٰ حَقَّهُ وَالْمِسْكِينَ وَابْنَ السَّبِيلِ

d. *Give relatives their due, and the poor and travellers.* (Sūrat ar-Rūm 30: 38)

يَا أَيُّهَا الَّذِينَ آمَنُوا أَنفِقُوا مِمَّا رَزَقْنَاكُم

5. *You who have īmān! give away some of what We have provided for you.* (Sūrat al-Baqarah 2: 254)

3. Jizyah

The *jizyah* is an annual poll tax levied on non-Muslims

living under Islamic governance. Just as the Muslims pay the compulsory *zakāh*, the non-Muslims pay the *jizyah*. In return, it is the duty of the Muslim rulers to protect their lives and property. The payment of *jizyah* thus exempts them from military service. The Muslims in spite of their payment of *zakāh*, ᶜ*ushr* and *ṣadaqah* are still required to take up arms in *jihād* and in *ribāṭ* (manning the frontiers prepared to fight). The *jizyah* collected goes to the *bayt al-māl*. The Qur'ānic injunction in respect of *jizyah* is as follows:

قَاتِلُوا الَّذِينَ لَا يُؤْمِنُونَ بِاللَّهِ وَلَا بِالْيَوْمِ الْآخِرِ وَلَا يُحَرِّمُونَ مَا حَرَّمَ اللَّهُ وَرَسُولُهُ وَلَا يَدِينُونَ دِينَ
الْحَقِّ مِنَ الَّذِينَ أُوتُوا الْكِتَابَ حَتَّى يُعْطُوا الْجِزْيَةَ عَنْ يَدٍ وَهُمْ صَاغِرُونَ

> *Fight those of the people who were given the Book who do not have īmān in Allah and the Last Day and do not make ḥarām what Allah and His Messenger have made ḥarām and do not take as their dīn the dīn of Truth, until they pay the jizyah with their own hands in a state of complete abasement.* (Sūrat at-Tawbah 9: 29)

4. *KHARĀJ*

Kharāj is a tax levied on the produce of landed property owned by non-Muslims living under Islamic governance. Just as the Muslims pay ᶜ*ushr* (ten or twenty percent of certain crops), non-Muslims are supposed to pay *kharāj* to the *bayt al-māl*. According to Imam Abū Yūsuf *kharāj* is a kind of *fay'*.[11] (Abū Yūsuf, *Kitāb al-kharāj*, p. 23) Ibn Juzayy al-Kalbī said:

> As for wealth, it is in four divisions: first, that which belongs purely to Allah, and it is the *jizyah*, the *kharāj*, and the ᶜ*ushr* of the people of the *dhimmah*[12] and the people under treaty, and whatever is taken without fighting, and all of that is *fay'*, and so the imām [ruler] does with that whatever he thinks best and no fifth is taken from it, contrary to ash-Shāfiᶜī. (Al-Kalbī, Ibn Juzayy, *al-Qawānīn al-fiqhiyyah, al-kitāb as-sābi*ᶜ *fī al-jihād, al-bāb ath-thālith fī al-maghānim*)

5. *FAY'*

Fay' is property captured from the enemy without fighting any battles with them. Such property, if acquired, goes to categories mentioned in the *āyah* of Sūrat al-Ḥashr above, and will probably be stored in the *bayt al-māl* in the interim.

The Qur'ānic injunction on *fay'* is as follows:

مَا أَفَاءَ اللَّهُ عَلَى رَسُولِهِ مِنْ أَهْلِ الْقُرَى فَلِلَّهِ وَلِلرَّسُولِ وَلِذِي الْقُرْبَى وَالْيَتَامَى وَالْمَسَاكِينِ وَابْنِ السَّبِيلِ كَيْ لَا يَكُونَ دُولَةً بَيْنَ الْأَغْنِيَاءِ مِنْكُمْ

Whatever booty Allah gives to His Messenger from city dwellers belongs to Allah and to the Messenger and to near relatives and orphans and the very poor and travellers, so that it does not become something which merely revolves between the rich among you. (Sūrat al-Ḥashr 59: 6)

6. ᶜUSHR (ZAKĀH) – A TENTH ON CROPS

The taxation, which is a part of *zakāh*, to be paid on the produce of the landed property of the Muslims at the rate of ten per cent if it is through natural rainfall, watering by springs and rivers and is called *ᶜushr* i.e. a "tenth." If water has been supplied through irrigation, it will be at half that rate i.e. a twentieth. (Abū Yūsuf, *Kitāb al-kharāj*, p. 23) This amount may be be stored in the *bayt al-māl* from which those responsible distribute it among the categories who may receive *zakāh*. The Qur'ānic injunction in respect of *ᶜushr* is as follows:

وَآتُوا حَقَّهُ يَوْمَ حَصَادِهِ

...and pay their due on the day of their harvest. (Sūrat al-Anᶜām 6: 141)

One does not wait for a year to pass to collect this type of *zakāh*, but it is collected at the time of harvest.

7. ᶜUSHR – A TENTH ON TRADE OF THE PEOPLE OF THE BOOK

ᶜUshr constitutes revenue collected from the proceeds of the trade and business carried out by the People of the Book when they go outside of the land in which they reside and in which they have made the agreement called the *dhimmah*. This revenue goes to the *bayt al-māl*. Mālik clarified it thus:

> As long as they are in the country they have agreed to live in, they do not have to pay anything on their property except the *jizyah*. If, however, they trade in Muslim countries, coming and going in them, a tenth is taken from what they invest in such trade. …
>
> If in any one year they frequently come and go in muslim countries then they have to pay a tenth every time they do so, since that is outside what they have agreed upon, and not one of the conditions stipulated for them. (Mālik, *Muwaṭṭa'* 17.24.46)

8. *KHUMS* – A FIFTH

A fifth of whatever a Muslim army obtains as booty (*ghanīmah*) through fighting war with enemies and gaining the victory is retained, after the distribution of the rest among the fighting men, and is called *khums* (a fifth). Such proceeds go to the *bayt al-māl* and are used for the welfare of the nation. The injunction of the Noble Qur'ān in respect of *khums* is as follows:

وَاعْلَمُوا أَنَّمَا غَنِمْتُم مِّن شَيْءٍ فَأَنَّ لِلَّهِ خُمُسَهُ وَلِلرَّسُولِ وَلِذِي الْقُرْبَى وَالْيَتَامَى وَالْمَسَاكِينِ وَابْنِ السَّبِيلِ

> *Know that when you take any booty a fifth of it belongs to Allah, and to the Messenger, and to close relatives, orphans, the very poor and travellers…* (Sūrat al-Anfāl 8: 41)

Likewise, a certain percentage of the income from natural resources, mines, petroleum and other natural hidden treasures owned by individuals is also called *khums* according to some.

This is the narration from the *Muwaṭṭa'*:

> Yaḥyā related to me from Mālik from Ibn Shihāb from Saᶜīd ibn al-Musayyab and from Abū Salamah ibn ᶜAbd ar-Raḥmān from Abū Hurayrah that the Messenger of Allah ﷺ said, "There is a tax of a fifth (*khums*) on buried treasure (*rikāz*)."
>
> Mālik said, "The position which we are agreed upon, and which I have heard the people of knowledge mentioning, is that *rikāz*

refers to treasure which has been found which was buried during the *jāhiliyyah,* as long as neither capital is required, nor expense, great labour or inconvenience incurred in recovering it. If capital is required or great labour is incurred, or on one occasion the mark is hit and on another it is missed, then it is not *rikāz.*" (Mālik, *Muwaṭṭa'* 17.4.9)

Here is an overview from Ibn Juzayy al-Kalbī:

Concerning buried treasure (*rikāz*) and minerals from mines (*ma*ᶜ*dan*)

As for buried treasure (*rikāz*), and they are those buried in the earth, then the ruling on them differs according to the different lands in which they are found, and they are of four types:

1. That they are found in smooth deserts and are of those things buried in the *jāhiliyyah,* in which case they belong to the person who finds them, and a fifth is due on them if they are gold or silver, but if they are anything else nothing is due, but it has been said that a fifth is due.

2. That they are found in land that is owned, so some say that they belong to whoever finds them, and some have said they belong to the owner of the land.

3. That they are found in land that has been conquered by force, and so some say that they belong to whoever finds them, and some say to those who conquered the land.

4. That they are found in land conquered by treaty, and so some say they belong to whoever finds them, and some say to the people who made the treaty. All of this is as long as they are not under the stamp (*ṭābi*ᶜ) of the Muslims, but if they are under the stamp of the Muslims then they have the same ruling as lost property.

As for mined minerals they are those which comes out of the earth of gold or silver, which is worked and purified, and concerning it there are two issues:

1. Concerning its ownership, and that divides into three categories:

a. That it is in land which is unowned, in which case it is for the *imām* [ruler].

b. That it is in land which is owned by a specific person, in which case it belongs to [the land's] owner, but some say to the *imām.*

c. That it is in land owned but not by a specific person, such as land that has been conquered by force, so some say that it belongs to those who conquered it, and some say to the *imām*.

2. What is obligatory on mined minerals is *zakāh,* and that is a fortieth if it reaches the *niṣāb*. If it is less than the *niṣāb,* there is nothing due on it unless after that the completion of the *niṣāb* is produced from its attainment (*nayl*), and then *zakāh* is given from what comes out after that whether it is a little or much as long as the attainment continues. If it is interrupted and then comes out it is said to be another and what comes out of it is not adjoined to the first, and the second has its own judgement. There is no year in *zakāh* of minerals from mines, but on the contrary *zakāh* is taken right away just as in the case with crops, contrary to ash-Shāfiᶜī. Abū Ḥanīfah said that minerals from mines have a fifth [taken from them] and in his view they are like buried treasure when they are gold, silver or something else. (Al-Kalbī, Ibn Juzayy, *al-Qawānīn al-fiqhiyyah, al-kitāb ar-rābiᶜ fī az-zakāh, al-bāb ar-rābiᶜ fī ar-rakā'iz wa al-maᶜādin*)

9. *ḌARĀ'IB* – TAXES

There are no taxes due from Muslims other than the *zakāh*. When the bedouin asked the Messenger of Allah ﷺ about what taxation was due from him, he ﷺ told him that only the *zakāh* and nothing else is due from him unless he voluntarily wished to give it:

عَنْ طَلْحَةَ بنِ عُبَيْدِاللَّهِ: جَاءَ رَجُلٌ إِلَى رَسُولِ اللَّهِ ﷺ مِنْ أَهْلِ نَجْدٍ ثَائِرَ الرَّأْسِ يُسْمَعُ دَوِيُّ صَوْتِهِ وَلَا يُفْقَهُ مَا يَقُولُ حَتَّى دَنَا فَإِذَا هُوَ يَسْأَلُ عَنِ الْإِسْلَامِ . . . وَذَكَرَ لَهُ رَسُولُ اللَّهِ ﷺ الصَّدَقَةَ.

قَالَ: ﴿فَهَلْ عَلَيَّ غَيْرُهَا؟﴾ قَالَ: ﴿إِلَّا أَنْ تَطَوَّعَ﴾

From Ṭalḥah ibn ᶜUbaydullāh: Once one of the people of Najd came to the Messenger of Allah ﷺ. He had dishevelled hair and although his voice could be heard we could not make out what he was saying until he drew nearer and then we found he was asking about Islam. …The Messenger of Allah ﷺ mentioned *zakāh*. The man said, "Is there anything else that I have to do?" He said,

"No, except what you do of your own accord." (Al-Bukhārī, *kitāb al-ḥiyal, bāb fī az-zakāh wa an lā yufarraqa bayna mujtamaᶜin wa lā yujmaᶜa bayna mutafarraqin khashyat aṣ-ṣadaqah*; Muslim, *kitāb al-īmān, bāb bayān aṣ-ṣalawāt allatī hiya arkān al-islām*; Abū Dāwūd also narrated it)

So this *ḥadīth* is the proof that the Muslim is not obliged with the payment of any other tax than the *zakāh*, unless he voluntarily chooses to do so.

Ḍarā'ib are levies which the ruler asks for in the event of an emergency. This is acceptable based on the episode in Madīnah in which the Messenger of Allah ﷺ called on the People of Madīnah to give towards the relief of a tribe who had been struck by misfortune. The proceeds may rest in the *bayt al-māl* if there is need for storage for a period. The following text clarifies that:

> *Ḍarā'ib* imposed on the citizenry for their own benefit, whether that is for *jihād* or for something else. They are only imposed on them if there is not enough in the *bayt al-māl* for that and if it is for an overwhelming necessity. Otherwise it is a non-*Sharīᶜah* source of revenue. (*Al-Mawsūᶜah al-fiqhiyyah, al-juz' ath-thāmin, mawārid bayt al-māl*)

The following are thought to include sanction for such taxes:

فَآتِ ذَا الْقُرْبَى حَقَّهُ وَالْمِسْكِينَ وَابْنَ السَّبِيلِ

> *Give relatives their due, and the poor and travellers.* (Sūrat ar-Rūm 30: 38)

ᶜAbdullāh ibn ᶜUmar is reported to have said:

> In your property, there are other rights than *zakāh*. (Ibn Ḥazm, *al-Muḥallā*, vol. 6, p.158)

This cannot, however, be equated with modern taxation by the state.

10. The estate left by someone who has no heirs

If a Muslim dies and leaves behind an estate but no heirs to inherit the property or does not leave any will behind or any other claimant, the property will go to the *bayt al-māl*.

Ibn Ḥazm aẓ-Ẓāhirī, the celebrated author of *al-Muḥallā* has said: "If the income of the *bayt al-māl* falls short of the needs of the poor, the Amīr or ruler can compel the rich to provide the poor with the indispensable food and the necessary clothing to protect them against the heat of the summer and the cold of winter and a shelter to save them from rain, heat and storm." (Ibn Ḥazm, *al-Muḥallā,* vol. 6, p. 156) According to the Caliph ᶜUmar each and every individual Muslim has a right on the property of the *bayt al-māl* whether he exercises it or not. (Abū ᶜUbayd, *al-Amwāl,* p.304) This is how the well-being of the poor is looked after in Islam.

Again, on the authority of Abū Saᶜīd al-Khudrī, the Prophet ﷺ is reported to have said:

> He who has extra means of transport, let him pass it on to him who has none; he who has surplus food, let him give it to him who has no food." The Prophet continued enumerating different kinds of property to such an extent that Abū Saᶜīd thought he had no right to own whatever is surplus. (Ibn Ḥazm, *al-Muḥallā, Op. Cit.*, vol. 6, pp. 157-158)

It is reported by Muḥammad, the son of the Caliph ᶜAlī, that his father (ᶜAlī) said:

> Allah had charged the rich with the duty to satisfy the needs of the poor and if they are left hungry and naked due to the negligence of the rich, then the rich shall be severely punished by Allah. (*Ibid.*, p. 158)

The Caliph ᶜUmar is reported to have said:

> Had I known what I came to to know later, I would have taken all the surplus (wealth) from the rich to distribute it among the poor and the immigrants. (*Ibid.*)

In truth, the above categories of wealth, which are said to go to the *bayt al-māl* are all different categories, which are distributed to different groups of people, it often being *ḥarām,* as in the case of *zakāh,* for them to go to any other categories. In the case of *zakāh* too, its immediate disbursement is preferable to its being lodged for any period of time.

The Right of the Poor and the Handicapped
As promised in the Qur'ān:

يَمحَق اللهُ الرِّبا ويُربِي الصَّدَقات

Allah obliterates ribā but makes ṣadaqah grow in value! (Sūrat al-Baqarah 2: 275)

Thus, Islam lays great stress on the relief of poverty by the rich:

وفِي أَموالِهم حَقٌّ للسائِلِ والمحروم

And beggars and the destitute received a due share of their[13] *wealth.* (Sūrat adh-Dhāriyāt 51: 19).

It is not considered to be a favour by the rich if they help the poor; but it is a duty of the rich and the prosperous to take part in the economic upliftment of the poor. The Qur'ān condemns all those who go on accumulating wealth but do not spend it for charitable purposes:

والَّذينَ يَكنِزونَ الذَّهبَ والفِضَّةَ ولا يُنفِقونَها في سَبيلِ اللهِ فبشِّرهُم بعذابٍ أَليم

As for those who hoard up gold and silver and do not spend it in the Way of Allah, give them the news of a painful punishment. (Sūrat at-Tawbah 9: 34)

It must be noted, however, that the pivot of all charitable spending is the *zakāh* and it is the only obligatory tax on a Muslim's wealth. The above *āyah* created a controversy among the Companions themselves ☙, but they reached unanimity on the fact that it refers to those who do not pay the *zakāh*. It is clear that in this time, the *zakāh* simply does not exist in any recognisable form. Thus, the first imperative for the Muslims today is its restoration.

The Noble Qur'ān reminds us that in the past many nations were destroyed because the rich and well-to-do among them did nothing to better the condition of the poor, and hence kept them in a state of poverty and treated them with great disrespect and indignity. The prophet Shuᶜayb ﷺ, when he began to remind the rich people of his people of their duties towards the poor, he was told by the well-to-do classes:

قَالُوا يَا شُعَيْبُ أَصَلَاتُكَ تَأْمُرُكَ أَن نَّتْرُكَ مَا يَعْبُدُ آبَاؤُنَا أَوْ أَن نَّفْعَلَ فِي أَمْوَالِنَا مَا نَشَاءُ

They said, "Shu'ayb, do your prayers instruct you that we should abandon what our fathers worshipped or stop doing whatever we want to with our wealth?" (Sūrah Hūd 11: 87)

This shows that in all ages the prophets of Allah taught that men are not free to use and spend their wealth as they like, but that the poorer sections of the people have a right to their wealth and possessions. The Prophet ﷺ was a great friend of the poor and treated them with respect and kindness. He not only instituted the system of *zakāh* as ordained by Allah to relieve poverty, but also stressed the fact that if a man has paid his *zakāh,* his duty towards the unfortunate members of the community has not ended. He is still required to help the poor and the needy, but this requirement is no longer that of legal obligation but a recommendation. Allah, exalted is He, and His Messenger ﷺ urge us to go further than the simple requirements of what is legally obligatory, but without making it an obligation. A *ḥadīth* of the Prophet ﷺ says:

عَنْ سَهْلٍ قَالَ رَسُولُ اللَّهِ صَلَّى اللَّهُ عَلَيْهِ وَسَلَّمَ وَأَنَا وَكَافِلُ الْيَتِيمِ فِي الْجَنَّةِ هَكَذَا وَأَشَارَ بِالسَّبَّابَةِ وَالْوُسْطَى وَفَرَّجَ بَيْنَهُمَا شَيْئًا

From Sahl there is that the Messenger of Allah ﷺ said, "And I and the one who cares for an orphan will be thus in the Garden," and he indicated with his index and middle fingers and separated them slightly. (Al-Bukhārī, *kitāb aṭ-ṭalāq, bāb al-liᶜān*)

In another *ḥadīth,* ᶜĀ'ishah ﷺ narrated that the Prophet ﷺ said:

وَالسَّاعِي عَلَى الْيَتِيمِ وَالْأَرْمَلَةِ وَالْمِسْكِينِ كَالْمُجَاهِدِ فِي سَبِيلِ اللَّهِ وَالصَّائِمِ الْقَائِمِ لَا يَفْتُرُ.

And the person who exerts himself on behalf of the orphan and the widow and the bereft is like the person who wages *jihād* in

> the way of Allah and the person who fasts [in the day] and who stands in prayer [at night] without breaking his fast. (Abū Yaʿlā and aṭ-Ṭabarānī in *al-Awsaṭ*)

The Prophet ﷺ has made no distinction in these traditions between a Muslim and a non-Muslim. In fact, he used to help Jews in Madīnah out of the funds which were collected from the Muslims. Similarly, the Caliph ʿUmar was of the opinion that the word *miskīn* used in the Qur'ān for the poor, means the non-Muslim poor, while *fuqarā'* means poor Muslims. So both should be helped. In the treaty of Hira, Khālid ibn al-Walīd made an express promise to the Christians that if there was an old man or woman among them, or a disabled person or a blind man, the Muslim governors would grant him or her a pension for life from the *bayt al-māl*. This is because Muslims stand for the good and happiness of all mankind, Muslims and non-Muslims alike. The Muslims have been ordered to work for the upliftment of all mankind and to show by their conduct that their minds and hearts are free from partisan or religious hatred.

While Muslims ought not to live an extravagant life, those who are blessed with the bounties of Allah are not expected to live in rags, for the Prophet ﷺ has said that Allah likes to see traces of His bounty on His slaves.

يُحِبُّ أَنْ يَرَى أَثَرَ نِعْمَتِهِ عَلَى عَبْدِهِ

> He loves that the trace of His blessing should be seen upon His slave. (Narrated by a large number of Companions such as ʿImrān ibn Ḥuṣayn, Abū Saʿīd al-Khudrī, Ibn ʿAmr, Alil ibn Zayd ibn Jadʿān, Ibn ʿUmar, Zuhayr ibn Abī ʿAlqamah, in differing narrations from aṭ-Ṭabarānī, al-Bayhaqī, Ibn Abi'd-Dunyā, at-Tirmidhī, al-Ḥākim, Ibn ʿAsākir, Abū Yaʿlā, and Aḥmad)

Miserliness condemned in the Sharīʿah

Miserliness is consisered to be a wrong action in Islam. Muslims do not believe in merely hoarding up property and living a miserly life. A generous man is considered to be a friend of Allah according to the teachings of the Prophet ﷺ. He is close to Allah, beloved of men and is closer to the Garden. The message of the Qur'ān is quite clear in respect of wealth and wealthy men:

وَآتِ ذَا الْقُرْبَى حَقَّهُ وَالْمِسْكِينَ وَابْنَ السَّبِيلِ وَلَا تُبَذِّرْ تَبْذِيرًا

Give your relatives their due, and the very poor and travellers but do not squander what you have. (Sūrat al-Isrā' 17: 26)

With Muslims, the worship of Allah is linked up with kindness - to parents, kindred, those in want, those who are far from their homes though they may be total strangers to us. The mention of kindness is not merely verbal. They have certain rights which must be fulfilled.

The Qur'ān further says about misers:

إِنَّ الْمُبَذِّرِينَ كَانُوا إِخْوَانَ الشَّيَاطِينِ وَكَانَ الشَّيْطَانُ لِرَبِّهِ كَفُورًا

Squanderers are brothers to the shaytans, and Shaytan was ungrateful to his Lord. (Sūrat al-Isrā' 17: 27)

Asking for *ṣadaqah*

Muslims are asked to work to earn a lawful livelihood, and not merely depend on charity.

وَالْيَدُ الْعُلْيَا خَيْرٌ مِنَ الْيَدِ السُّفْلَى

The upper hand [that gives] is better than the lower [that takes]. (Narrated by Abū Nuᶜaym in *al-Ḥilyah* from Ibn Masᶜūd)

Indeed, the above *ḥadīth* refers to the nobility of being a person who gives generously in *ṣadaqah* and gifts to others, and that this is a better station than simply receiving the generosity and *ṣadaqah* of others. This is something to which Muslims aspire. However, there do come times in most people's lives in which the economic pressures are severe and they may look to others to help them. This section is about the correct courtesy of such situations. The first thing that is negated is the possibility of it being acceptable for a Muslim to be passive in the affair of his economic well-being and dependent on the good will and generosity of others.

Hence a Muslim is required not to sit idle or live in a secluded corner of a forest or a monastery shunning his responsibility towards his wives and children. As the Noble Qur'ān says:

وَأَن لَّيْسَ لِلْإِنسَانِ إِلَّا مَا سَعَىٰ وَأَنَّ سَعْيَهُ سَوْفَ يُرَىٰ

... and that man will have nothing but what he strives for; that his striving will most certainly be seen. (Sūrat an-Najm 53: 39-40)

One should not use trust in Allah as an excuse to shun working to gain a lawful livelihood. Indeed, the real work is not for livelihood, but to ensure that it is *ḥalāl*. The ignorant think that there is some difficulty in finding provision, but the difficulty is in making sure that one earns and consumes what is *ḥalāl*.

In the Qur'ān Allah says:

هُوَ الَّذِي جَعَلَ لَكُمُ الْأَرْضَ ذَلُولًا فَامْشُوا فِي مَنَاكِبِهَا وَكُلُوا مِن رِّزْقِهِ

It is He who made the earth submissive to you, so walk its broad trails and eat what He provides. (Sūrat al-Mulk 67: 15)

It is clear that the earth is made by Allah and we are merely asked to get the benefit out of it from our efforts by tilling, ploughing and harvesting, and likewise, utilising mineral resources for our benefit, and engaging in useful activities, but all these need effort on our part. Sitting down without making an effort will bring forth neither harvest nor the rich mineral wealth of the earth. Although one should not depend on charity one can turn to it as the last resort when unable, in spite of one's efforts, to get the necessities of life.

The context of many of the *ḥadīth* concerning *su'āl*, a term that means asking, rather than literally 'begging' and indeed can mean simply asking a question as much as asking for money, often indicate that it means asking the ruler or *amīr* for something from the *zakāh* or from other funds for which he is responsible. What is deplored about asking in these circumstances is that it is possible the asker has no right in the *Sharīʿah* to those funds, and that an injustice would be done if his request were granted.

The Messenger of Allah ﷺ is also narrated to have said:

عن حُبْشِيّ بن جُنَادَة السَّلُولِيّ . قال : سَمِعْتُ رسولَ الله ﷺ يقول في حَجّة الوداعِ وهو واقفٌ بعرفةَ ﴿إنّ المسْألَةَ لا تَحِلّ لغَنِيّ ولا لذي مِرّةٍ سَوِيّ إلّا لذي فَقْرٍ مُدْقِعٍ أو غُرْمٍ مُفْظِعٍ ، ومَنْ سألَ النّاسَ لِيُثْرِيَ به مالَه كان خُمُوشاً في وجهه يومَ القِيَامة ورَضْفاً يأكُلُه مِن جهنم ، ومَنْ شاءَ فليُقِلّ ومَنْ شاءَ فليُكْثِرْ﴾ .

From Ḥubshī ibn Junādah as-Salūlī who said: I heard the Messenger of Allah ﷺ saying on the Farewell Ḥajj while he was standing on ᶜArafah, "*Ṣadaqah*[14] is not *ḥalāl* for a person in no need[15] nor for a strong able-bodied person, but only for someone degradingly poor or shockingly indebted. Whoever asks from people in order to enlarge his wealth, then it will be scratches on his face on the Day of Rising and heated stones that he will eat from *Jahannam;* and whoever wishes then let him take little and whoever wishes let him take much." (At-Tirmidhī, *abwāb az-zakāh ᶜan rasūlillāh* ﷺ, *bāb mā jā'a fī man lā taḥillu lahu aṣ-ṣadaqah*)

The Prophet ﷺ asked a man to endure a little hardship and collect wood from the forest and sell it to earn a living rather than asking him for help.

The only time asking for *ṣadaqah* is permitted is when a man is sorely pressed and has no other way to survive than asking for help. Truly speaking, it is the responsibility of the Muslims to look after the have-nots and the destitutes living in their localities. One of the side-benefits of the five-times daily prayers in Islam is that the Muslims meet each other and understand the needs of their neighbours. One may realise that they are handicapped in some way and not in a position to look after their family, and so should provide for their needs before they resort to asking others for help.

A Muslim is his brother's keeper. The exceptional circumstances in which a man is permitted to ask for help are recorded in *ḥadīth* quoted by Imam Muslim:

From Qabīṣah ibn Mukhāriq al-Hilālī who said: I undertook a debt,[16] and so I came to the Messenger of Allah ﷺ asking him for something for it, and he said, "Stand until the *ṣadaqah* comes to us, and we will command some of it for you." Then he said, "Qabīṣah, asking is not *ḥalāl* for any but one of three: a man who undertakes a debt, for whom asking is *ḥalāl* until he obtains it at which point he refrains; and a man whose property is destroyed by a calamity for whom asking is *ḥalāl* until he obtains the livelihood to discharge his necessities and a person whom poverty strikes so much so that three intelligent members of his people say, 'So-and-so has certainly been struck by poverty,' so asking is *ḥalāl* for him until he obtains the livelihood to discharge his necessities. Every other type of asking, Qabīṣah, is *ḥarām*, the person who does it eats it as something *ḥarām*." (Muslim, *kitāb az-zakāh, bāb man taḥillu lahu aṣ-ṣadaqah*)

Rishwah: Bribery

Rishwah or bribery is that which is offered or promised to someone in order to influence him or persuade him to do something wrong in favour of the giver. Thus, bribery is given to deprive someone else of their right or to bring undue pressure on him or to tyrannise someone or to free a criminal or to get his punishment reduced or to pervert justice in some other form.

Bribery is a dishonest practice in order to usurp the rights of people. The Prophet ﷺ therefore has said as narrated by Thawbān:

لَعَنَ اللّٰهُ الرَّاشِي وَالْمُرْتَشِي وَالرَّائِشَ الَّذِي يَمْشِي بَيْنَهُمَا

Allah has cursed the person who bribes and the person who is bribed and the person who goes between them. (Aḥmad in the *Musnad* and al-Ḥākim in *al-Mustadrak*)

It is essential for the administrators and civil servants who are employed in the collection of *ṣadaqah, zakāh, jizyah* and other forms of annual taxes gathered by the government not to accept any gift from people because it amounts to accepting a bribe in order to give relief either from full payment of the tax or to get under-assessed or to gain time for the payment. The Prophet ﷺ sent a man to collect the *zakāh* from the tribe of Banī Sulaym.

عَنْ أَبِي حُمَيْدٍ السَّاعِدِيِّ رَضِيَ اللهُ عَنْهُ قَالَ اسْتَعْمَلَ النَّبِيُّ صَلَّى اللهُ عَلَيْهِ وَسَلَّمَ رَجُلًا مِنَ الأَزْدِ يُقَالُ لَهُ ابْنُ الأُتْبِيَّةِ عَلَى الصَّدَقَةِ فَلَمَّا قَدِمَ قَالَ هَذَا لَكُمْ وَهَذَا أُهْدِيَ لِي قَالَ فَهَلَّا جَلَسَ فِي بَيْتِ أَبِيهِ أَوْ بَيْتِ أُمِّهِ فَيَنْظُرُ يُهْدَى لَهُ

From Abū Ḥumayd as-Sāᶜidī ﷺ who said: The Prophet ﷺ employed a man from Azd called Ibn al-Utbiyyah to collect *ṣadaqah* (*zakāh*). When he came he said, "This is for you, and this was given to me as a gift." He said, "If he had sat in his father's house or his mother's house, then let him see if he would be given gifts." (Al-Bukhārī, *kitāb al-aḥkām, bāb hadāyā al-ᶜummāl*; Muslim, *kitāb al-imārah, bāb taḥrīm hadāyā al-ᶜummāl*)

Such gifts are not to be accepted and if they are given, they should be paid into public treasury (*bayt al-māl*).

A *mu'min* will neither give bribes nor accept gifts during his tenure of office as an administrator. In the caliphate of Abū Bakr, Khālid ibn al-Walīd imposed the annual *jizyah* tax on the people of Hirah in Syria. The inhabitants of Hirah were so impressed by the justice of the Muslims and their cordial relationship and good behaviour that they insisted on sending gifts to Abū Bakr. It was very difficult for Khālid to persuade them not to do so, and so he accepted the gifts and later counted it as a part of the compulsory tax and reduced the actual amount of payment and sent it to the *bayt al-māl*.

The Caliph ᶜUmar sent all his governors the following message:

إِيَّاكُمْ وَالْهَدَايَا فَإِنَّهَا مِنَ الرِّشَى

Beware of gifts because they are of the nature of bribes.

ᶜUmar's statement is correct when we think of the point of view of our modern society where 'commissions', kick-backs and other mechanisms are so rampant - given and taken in the name of gifts. The right-acting Caliph ᶜUmar ibn ᶜAbd al-ᶜAzīz flatly rejected gifts. Someone said to him that the Messenger of Allah ﷺ used to receive gifts, he replied:

كَانَتْ لَهُ هَدِيَّةً وَلَنَا رِشْوَةً لِأَنَّهُ كَانَ يُتَقَرَّبُ إِلَيْهِ لِنُبُوَّتِهِ لَا لِوِلَايَتِهِ وَنَحْنُ يُتَقَرَّبُ إِلَيْنَا لِلْوِلَايَةِ

> It was a gift for him but for us it is actually a bribe, since people wanted to come closer to him because of his prophethood and not because of his rulership while they wish to come closer to us because of our rulership.

In other words, the Prophet ﷺ used to accept gifts, and often gave them away to the poor. Those who brought gifts to him did not have any ulterior motive. While in the case of rulers in later days the intention of giving gifts was to secure undue and unjust favours.

This does not prohibit the mutual exchange of gifts among friends and relatives. According to the prophetic traditions, gifts help to remove rancour and increase love and affection. The Messenger of Allah ﷺ has also said:

تَهَادُوا تَحَابُّوا

> Exchange gifts, and you will love each other. (Ibn ʿAsākir and Abū Yaʿlā from Abū Hurayrah)

The taking of gifts by government officers and administrators in the process of discharging their duties is thus forbidden under the *Sharīʿah*.

Usury in history

The idea of usury is quite evident in the concept of modern bank interest. The rate of interest as defined by modern economists is the price of money, the price at which money can be borrowed and it is determined like other prices by the interaction of the forces of supply and demand.[17]

Originally, usury meant any premium whatsoever paid for the use of money. *The Oxford Dictionary of English Etymology* has preserved the original meaning of the word, as understood until recently - "Usury: lending money at interest" i.e. not merely *extortionate* or *exorbitant* interest as in dictionaries of current usage. Nowadays, it means the practice of demanding an exorbitant premium of interest. Attempts were made, particularly by the Romans, to provide maximums for the rates of interest, but they were unsuccessful. Later, while being condemned by the Christian Church, usury was for a short period allowed to fall into the hands of the Jews, but was soon taken back into 'Christian' hands, in spite of the Catholic Church's condemnation of usury as a mortal wrong action, with the emergence of the Italian banking houses, most famously the Medicis, and the German Fuggers. Indeed, so two-faced was the Church about it that the Medicis were not only tolerated but became the Pope's bankers and themselves supplied a pope. Borrowing with interest is now a worldwide phenomenon.[18]

Thomas Erskine writing in 1809 CE said:

> The crime of usury before the Reformation (i.e the 16th Century) consisted in the taking of any interest for the use of money and now in taking a higher rate of interest than is authorised by law.

Since then, all modern banks function on the basis of interest. Every business man in need of loans is driven by force of circumstances to borrow from the banks, which charge high rates of interest.

It is a consensus of the *ᶜulamā'* that the interest given by the banks on the deposit account is *ribā*, and likewise one who receives loans from the banks and pays interest also gives *ribā* to the banks, both transactions being forbidden.

Coulson in *A History of Islamic Law* and some Muslim 'orientalists' confuse trade and *ribā*, which have been differentiated in the Noble Qur'ān. He gives the following definition:

> *Ribā*: Basically, interest on a capital loan. In classical doctrine, however, the term covers many forms of gain or profit which accrue as the result of a transaction and which were not precisely calculable at the time of the transaction being concluded. (Coulson, *A History of Islamic Law, Op. Cit.* p.239)

The correct and clear definition would be: Any amount of interest on capital, or an unfair gain in a transaction.

Muslims were the first to lay down the foundations of proper trade and even some of the acceptable elements of banking in modern civilisation. Hence, present day banking terminology is permeated with Arabic words and expressions. The very word cheque is originally Arabic. Its etymology is from *ṣakk* (pl. *ṣukūk*).

Indeed, cheques go back to the time of Caliph ᶜUmar ibn al-Khaṭṭāb. He was the first to draw a cheque (634-644 CE). Al-Yaᶜqūbī, an eminent Muslim historian who died in 897 CE mentions in his History:

إِنَّ عُمَرَ بْنَ الْخَطَّابِ كَانَ أَوَّلَ مَنْ صَكَّ وَخَتَمَ أَسْفَلَ الصِّكَاكِ

ᶜUmar ibn al-Khaṭṭāb was the first to draw cheques and put his stamp underneath them. (Yaᶜqūbī, *at-Tārīkh*, vol. II, pp.132-133)

Al-Jahashiyari, who died in 942 CE, makes similar statements with regard to Hārūn ar-Rashīd:

سَأَلَهُ الْفَضْلُ أَنْ يَصُكَّ بِهَذَا الْمَبْلَغِ بِخَطِّهِ

Al-Faḍl asked him (i.e., ar-Rashīd) to draw a cheque in his own hand with regard to this sum of money (which was a million dirhams).

Ibn Miskawayh (d. 1030 CE) in his *Tajārīb al-umam* mentions that the salaries of the army were paid by cheques. One of the charges made against Muḥammad ibn Dāwūd is that he paid the army in cash and not in cheques. From that time onwards the custom of using cheques by the people, as a whole, became quite familiar. We bear in mind, however, that it is not *ḥalāl* to trade with such cheques.

Centres of money exchange were established by Muslim merchants in different parts of the Muslim world. This precludes using the cheques themselves as a currency. Muslim dynasties inherited well established money transfer systems, but never engaged in the practice of *ribā* without which modern banks, as the general impression is given to all of us, cannot work.[19]

The interest-free commercial transactions of medieval Muslim society seem to have baffled and surprised many Western scholars, who believe that it is simply unworkable in modern times. The following from Sabory explains our point:

> In the important area of commercial law, the Shariah was hampered by what at first sight appears to be an unsurmountable handicap. I refer, of course, to the Qur'ānic prohibition, which is quite specific, on the taking of interest (*ribā*). Such a prohibition would appear to be totally divorced from the realities of trade and commerce in a free society. Yet the classical theory of Islamic law, as developed by the jurists, far from affording any relaxation, of this ban, made it even more rigid.
>
> The jurists evolved the doctrine that any speculative transaction, any transaction which resulted in the 'unjustified enrichment' of one party, was forbidden. If a profit were made, it should be given to the poor. This doctrine was derived from Qur'ānic phrase 'God will abolish interest and cause charity to increase.' In the case of barter deals there are two principles involved, according to the jurists: first, the two amounts to be traded must be equal in weight or quantity; second, there must be no time lag in the completion of the transaction, because during the interval the value of one commodity might fluctuate, and this would permit one party or the other to make a speculative gain.
>
> Since the whole principle of usury was so expressly prohibited in the Qur'ān, people were naturally reluctant openly to act in defiance of the Qur'ānic injunction. On the other hand, trade was vitally important to the medieval Islamic world, and so the jurists developed a whole series of complicated 'stratagems' or 'devices' known as *ḥiyal* (for example, partnerships etc.) to enable people to get around the law. (Sabory, R.M. *Introduction to Islamic Civilizations*, p. 59)

It is really not true to say partnerships, etc., were devices to get around the law. In that case, we might classify even free trading as a 'stratagem' to get around *ribā*. There is a point at which *ribā* and 'profiteering' and 'speculation' stop and lawful profit starts. However, even in trade, Muslim jurists have limited the amount of profit made to a reasonable percentage.

The Devastating Effects of the Modern Economic System

One has to be realistic in one's approach to human life on this planet. Yet, while it is true that man has various economic needs in life, it is not necessary to exaggerate their importance to the extent that they are reckoned as the only matter of importance in life. Man does not live by bread alone. Therefore, it is a blunder to shape our lives, our ethical and moral values, our culture and society on economic foundations. A Muslim sage remarked that man does not live to eat but eats to live.

If we attempt to build our society only on economic foundations, it would really mean that man's position is reduced to that of a grazing animal. In a purely materialistic society, as we can see in our world today in both East and West, the selfish appear to thrive. However, the application of profit motives and commercial ideas to social conduct has reduced man's role to that of an economic animal.

As a result, we forget that we are merely custodians of our property and not its masters and that wealth is to be acquired by lawful means and not through dishonesty and treachery. The wealthy, forgetting the human's role as caliph of Allah on earth, have as their motto: money, money, money. We have multiplied our desires over and above our real needs. This has created artificial requirements and we struggle hard all our lives for their fulfilment. 'Necessities' have grown so much that people have devised methods of increasing wealth through hoarding, giving short weight and measure, supplying inferior commodities, cut-throat competition, usury, selling human organs, pornography and prostitution etc.

There is ample evidence that the most significant factor in recent history has been the emergence and growth of banking. From the time of the Italian Medicis and the German Fuggers up until the French Revolution – the watershed in European history when bankers arguably came to dominate the state itself – bankers and financiers have moved to a previously unimaginable position of wealth and control.

Due to financiers, society has experienced the disappearance of actual wealth, such as gold, silver, land and property, into the hands of a decreasingly small number of fabulously wealthy individuals who are veiled from us by the anonymity of the stock market. Traditional societies in which the poor had little actual wealth but no debt whatsoever, have been replaced by those in which the wealthy are impossibly indebted yet dominate extraordinary realms of wealth and power, and the poor live in an inescapable squalor and poverty that was unthinkable before our age. The ravages of this iniquitous class, the financiers, are experienced right across the planet as the world is transformed into a high volume debt-driven marketplace.

One factor in their emergence is the transformation of currency into a grossly inflatable matter, so that in a few decades British house prices between the late twentieth century and the beginning of the twenty-first, rose from a few thousand pounds to prices of the order of a million in some cities or in the hundreds of thousands of pounds throughout the British Isles, while the general population happily accepted the myth that this was an increase in wealth rather than an inflationary collapse in the value of currency, inflation being the bankers' tax on the people of the world by means of which they syphon off their wealth. This process is of course not unique to Britain.

Those things that contribute to hardship in the economy first take their toll on the family, for the family is extraordinarily susceptible to economic pressure. Investigation of divorce rates would almost certainly show that finance usually figures prominently in marital breakdown. With marital breakdown there is a concomitant availing of sexual pleasures elsewhere, whether through prostitution, casual sex, or homosexuality. Modern people are accustomed, to an almost unbelievable degree, to serial relationships, series of 'partners', 'girlfriends' or 'boyfriends'. The effects that this has on the young – who are terribly maligned today when in fact they ought to be congratulated for surviving at all – are to perpetuate and amplify this trend.

Money and the effects of the stock exchange have transformed the work place from a secure setting for the creation of wealth into a piranha-like feeding frenzy from which nothing creative, useful, benign or beautiful emerges, but rather the multiplication of meaningless tasks which largely mean the destruction of something in the natural world, all in the name of living in 'the real world', that reality being defined by a predatorial class who are making what is left of the world and its peoples over in their own image.

Money

The question that is no longer asked, and which must be reasserted is: What is the nature of money?

Modern money, i.e. paper money, enters history as the record of a debt. The paper note was originated as a record of the deposit of gold or silver with the goldsmith, such records themselves quickly becoming used in trade. And, it is precisely trading with such records of debts that is clearly seen as usury in the first community of Madīnah.

عَنْ مَالِكٍ، أَنَّهُ بَلَغَهُ : أَنَّ صُكُوكاً خَرَجَتْ لِلنَّاسِ فِي زَمَانِ مَرْوَانَ بْنِ الْحَكَمِ مِنْ طَعَامِ الْجَارِ،

فَتَبَايَعَ النَّاسُ تِلْكَ الصُّكُوكَ بَيْنَهُمْ، قَبْلَ أَنْ يَسْتَوْفُوهَا، فَدَخَلَ زَيْدُ بْنُ ثَابِتٍ، وَرَجُلٌ مِنْ أَصْحَابِ

رَسُولِ اللَّهِ ﷺ عَلَى مَرْوَانَ بْنِ الْحَكَمِ، فَقَالَا : أَتُحِلُّ بَيْعَ الرِّبَا يَا مَرْوَانُ ؟ فَقَالَ : أَعُوذُ بِاللَّهِ، وَمَا

ذَاكَ ؟ فَقَالَا : هَذِهِ الصُّكُوكُ تَبَايَعَهَا النَّاسُ، ثُمَّ بَاعُوهَا قَبْلَ أَنْ يَسْتَوْفُوهَا، فَبَعَثَ مَرْوَانُ الْحَرَسَ،

يَتْبَعُونَهَا يَنْزِعُونَهَا مِنْ أَيْدِي النَّاسِ، وَيَرُدُّونَهَا إِلَى أَهْلِهَا

From Mālik there is that he had heard that receipts were given to people in the time of Marwān ibn al-Ḥakam for the produce of the market at al-Jār. People bought and sold the receipts among themselves before they took delivery of the goods. Zayd ibn Thābit and one of the Companions of the Messenger of Allah ﷺ went to Marwān ibn al-Ḥakam and said, "Marwān! Do you make usury *ḥalāl*?" He said, "I seek refuge with Allah! What is that?" He said, "These receipts which people buy and sell before they take delivery of the goods." Marwān therefore sent a guard to follow them and to take them from people's hands and return them to their owners. (Mālik ibn Anas, *al-Muwaṭṭa'*, 31.19.44)

However, this only relates to notes when they were redeemable in real value. How much more serious it became, first at Bretton

Woods[20] and then finally in the time of Richard Nixon, when the possibility of redemption of these receipts was completely abolished, i.e. the person could no longer go to the bank and ask for his gold back. Thus, we have a situation in which the words "I promise to pay the bearer on demand the sum of ..." written on the face of British paper money is largely a puzzle and a joke for modern man.

But the situation is even worse than that, for with Fractional Reserve Banking, each bank deposit becomes the basis for the creation of multiples in new bank loans which themselves, when deposited, become the basis for fresh loans, resulting in a currency whose inflation is spiralling out of control, while the impression is created that this represents the increase of wealth.

The modern banking system and interest-free Muslim banks

Unfortunately, the Muslim world has by and large until fairly recently failed in its response to this catastrophic situation, and we are competing mistakenly, in my view, in imposing the same transformation on our own societies, a transformation that is almost complete. Indeed, it appears mainly to be people who come from within the very citadels of high finance, the great Western nations, who are critical of this process, since the peoples of the so-called Third and Developing Worlds are too busy rushing after illusory debt-based wealth.

Among the worst mistakes the Muslims in this scenario are making is their adoption of the 'Islamic State' and the 'Islamic bank', which are in essence the assimilation into the *Sharīᶜah* of two very powerful elements of *kufr* itself.

THE FALSITY OF THE ISLAMIC STATE

The modern concept of the state emerged in tandem with the worldview of men such as Galileo and Descartes who articulated their vision of the world, and implicitly also the human being and society, as a machine. This naturally led to the recasting of natural social modalities as mechanical-industrial processes. Schooling, for example, emerged recreated as the processing of children by an industrial assembly line process on which they were programmed to take their places as consumers in the technical world, and the state itself became a giant heartless machine for processing citizens from birth to death as bearers of debt and taxation.

Now the modern state is ultimately a mechanism for borrowing from banks and then taxing the citizens to service the loan on the debt. Everything else is window-dressing. So the role of the bank must be confronted. In history it emerges in the form of the goldsmith's safe in which the citizens stored their gold, taking away receipts for their deposits which soon came to be used as a currency and then to evolve to become our banknotes. Rapidly the bank transformed to become the institution that was licensed by the state to manufacture money, for which privilege it charged the state interest.

The purpose of the Islamic *dawlah* is to implement the *dīn* with particular emphasis on the *zakāh*.

The falsity of the Islamic Bank

As for the idea of an Islamic bank, it necessarily rests on a blindness to the falsity of a paper money and electronic credit money currency, thus reducing the Muslims' very real horror of usury to a focus on the simple operation of interest charges.

The legitimation of paper money has come from the assertion that it is *ᶜurf*, i.e. it is customary, and thus may serve as currency. This view is mistaken since we have already seen the text in which two of the Companions regarded the use of receipts of this nature as usurious, and *ᶜurf* may not be utilised if it contradicts a *naṣṣ*, a clear textual statement.

The fact that every 'Islamic' bank and financial institution is fully plugged into the greater banking system, and that the least whiff of financial danger will bring them tumbling down with the other banks, seems not to have occurred to its votaries. Thankfully, many thoughtful and articulate Muslims have now seen through the empty promises of Islamic banking, and there is finally the possibility of the emergence of a genuine Islamic alternative, because it is properly only in the *Sharī˓ah* of Islam that there is any genuine alternative.

THE GENUINE ISLAMIC ALTERNATIVE

There are a number of ways that this alternative will appear, and they will of course be in harmony with the original *salafī* practice of the Muslims that endured throughout more than a thousand years until the colonial era and our disastrous flirtation with modernism.

The first matter of importance will be the reclamation by the Muslims of the concept of *fuqahā'*. The lifeblood of Islamic society was the trader, and scratch the trader and one found a *faqīh* underneath. As Sayyidunā ˓Umar ✿ said:

رُوِيَ عَنْ عُمَرَ بْنِ الْخَطَّابِ ﴿ أَنَّهُ قَالَ : ﴿ لَا يَتَّجِرْ فِي سُوقِنَا إِلَّا مَنْ فَقِهَ وَإِلَّا أَكَلَ الرِّبَا ﴾

Let no one trade in our market except for those who know the *fiqh* [of trade], for if not they will consume usury. (Narrated in the introduction by Abū Salmān Muḥammad al-Amrāwī as-Sijilmāsī to *Aḥkām as-sūq* by Abū Zakariyyā Yaḥyā ibn ˓Umar ibn Yūsuf al-Kinānī al-Andalūsī)

قَالَ عُمَرُ بْنُ الْخَطَّابِ ﴿ : ﴿ لَا يَبِعْ فِي سُوقِنَا إِلَّا مَنْ (قَدْ) تَفَقَّهَ فِي الدِّينِ ﴾ .

˓Umar ibn al-Khaṭṭāb ✿ said, "Let only those sell in our market who have already gained knowledge of the *fiqh* of the *dīn*." (At-Tirmidhī, *abwāb aṣ-ṣalāh, bāb mā jā'a fī faḍl aṣ-ṣalāh ˓alā an-nabī* ﷺ)

Az-Zurqānī said in his commentary on the *Muwaṭṭa'* that ˓Umar ✿ used to eject people from the marketplace who did not know the judgements on trade.

The ordinary trader must know the *fiqh* of trade just as the ordinary Muslim knows the *fiqh* of prayer, *wuḍū'* and fasting, etc. There is no disagreement among the *˓ulamā'* that the Muslim who buys and sells or enters the commercial world must know enough *fiqh* to be sure of avoiding usury.

> And some [knowledge] is *farḍ ᶜayn* and some *farḍ kifāyah.* The *farḍ ᶜayn* is that which is obligatory on the person charged with responsibility, of knowledge of the sources of the *dīn* and its derivative rulings. So that when he reaches adulthood it is obligatory on him first of all to know purification and prayer, and then when Ramaḍān enters it is obligatory on him to know how to fast, and if he has wealth it is incumbent on him to know the *zakāh,* and if he sells and buys it is incumbent on him to know sales, and it is similar with all the other chapters of *fiqh.* (Al-Kalbī, Ibn Juzayy, *al-Qawānīn al-fiqhiyyah, kitāb al-jāmiᶜ, al-bāb ath-thālith fī al-ᶜilm)*

The whole practice of the right-acting first generations, with men such as Abū Ḥanīfah ﷺ who was a trader throughout his life, is our evidence for this. We also adduce in evidence illuminated cities such as Timbuktu, which at the height of its culture was peopled by trader-*fuqahā'* who through their trade were thus independent of the ruler and free to counsel the *amīr* honestly and fearlessly.

The reference of first resort which we would recommend for all the matters concerning ordinary transactions, most importantly buying and selling, are the chapters from the *Muwaṭṭa'* on *buyūᶜ* or sales. Here we have the transmission of the key *ḥadīth* on trade and the description of the first community's diligent avoidance of usury and the *ḥarām,* and their implementation of the *ḥalāl* entrepreneurial practices of partnership, *qirāḍ* or *muḍārabah,* etc., which were the motor behind a dynamic Islamic trade for more than a millennium.

This material is underlined by the *ṣaḥīḥ* works of *ḥadīth* which confirm the basic material we have already seen.

The next reference is *al-Mudawwanah al-kubrā* in which Saḥnūn records in more than three quarters of the book the transmission of Mālik and others of the *ḥadīth* and the practice of the People of Madīnah on the matters of everyday transactions such as trade. We take this book not because it is a book of the Mālikī *madhhab* but because of its recording the trade practices of the early community.

Two other books, from the Ḥanafī tradition, are spoken of in high regard in this respect: the *Majallah,* that great Osmanli work on the *Sharīᶜah,* and the *Fatāwā ᶜĀlamgīrī* compiled at the command of Aurangzeb towards the end of the Mughal era. These are our references because they were written before the advent of the colonial era and before the proliferation of a *fiqh* that is bank-friendly and thus fatally compromised.

Now every single classical work on Islam, whether it be the major *ḥadīth* collections or the works on *fiqh* and *Sharīᶜah,* assumes in the realm of trade the use of gold and silver coinage alongside barter. It has been the mistake of those claming to speak for 'Islamic economics', that they have elected to replace the dīnār and dirham in their thinking with paper money. However, using a paper and/or electronic currency based on debt and riddled with inflation is to import a Trojan horse right into the innermost sanctum of the *Sharīᶜah.* Thus, the first thing that needs to be grasped is that one may not automatically assume the equivalence of paper and gold.

There are a number of initiatives that are important in this arena:

THE ISLAMIC GOLD DINAR

The gold Islamic dīnār whose minting according to the weights and measures of ᶜUmar ibn al-Khaṭṭāb[21] was re-initiated by ᶜUmar Ibrāhīm Vadillo,[22] perhaps the leading contemporary *faqīh* and activist in this domain. This was taken up by Dr Erbakan, then prime minister of Turkey, and by Dr Mahathir Mohamad, then prime minister of Malaysia, who instituted the minting of gold dinars and silver dirhams by the Malaysian Royal Mint, and worked indefatigably for the use both of the dīnār as a unit of currency and for the use of gold as a means of exchange by governments for the settlement of debt between them.

The greatest significance for the dīnār and the dirham is their use in the payment of the *zakāh* on *ᶜayn* or cash holdings. Once it is understood that the *zakāh* is an act of *ᶜibādah* just like the prayer, with which it is paired repeatedly in the Noble Qur'ān, and it is understood that it is not merely an act of social welfare, even though it undoubtedly has enormous implications socially, then the Muslims will quickly move to restore *zakāh* to its pristine condition, collected by *zakāh* collectors under the instruction of Muslim leaders, and collected in gold and silver coins and not in paper money. It is this simple obedience to the *salafī* imperatives of the *dīn* that will almost by-the-way restore gold and silver coinage as world currencies.

Gold and silver: non-inflationary currencies

There is much evidence that gold and silver have suffered almost no inflation. Let us take a closer look at the *ḥadīth* from *Ṣaḥīḥ al-Bukhārī* which states:

عَنْ عُرْوَةَ أَنَّ النَّبِيَّ صَلَّى اللَّهُ عَلَيْهِ وَسَلَّمَ أَعْطَاهُ دِينَارًا يَشْتَرِي لَهُ بِهِ شَاةً فَاشْتَرَى لَهُ بِهِ شَاتَيْنِ فَبَاعَ إِحْدَاهُمَا بِدِينَارٍ وَجَاءَهُ بِدِينَارٍ وَشَاةٍ فَدَعَا لَهُ بِالْبَرَكَةِ فِي بَيْعِهِ وَكَانَ لَوْ اشْتَرَى التُّرَابَ لَرَبِحَ فِيهِ

> From ᶜUrwah [al-Bāriqī] there is that the Prophet ﷺ gave him a dīnār with which to buy a ewe for him, but he bought two ewes with it for him, then he sold one of them for a dīnār and brought him a dīnār and a ewe. So he [the Prophet ﷺ] supplicated for *barakah* for him in his buying and selling, and he was such that even if he had bought dust he would have made a profit with it. (Al-Bukhārī, *kitāb al-manāqib, bāb su'āl al-mushrikīn an yuriyahum an-nabiyyu* ﷺ *āyah, fa arāhum inshiqāq al-qamar*)

At the time of writing [2008] the value of the dīnār is such that one can buy one sheep, sometimes even two, with one dīnār. This is not only true in the UK, but in widely differing societies such as Chad and Afghanistan. Thus, the dīnār by this perfectly ordinary measure has suffered no inflation in almost a millennium and a half.

Open markets

The nature of the Muslim market is its complete openness. It is widely reported that the market of Madīnah was established by the Messenger of Allah ﷺ himself and that he stipulated that it was not to be reduced nor any tax levied on its trade:

عَنْ عَطَاءِ بْنِ يَسَارٍ قَالَ: لَمَّا أَرَادَ رَسُولُ اللَّهِ ﷺ أَنْ يَجْعَلَ لِلْمَدِينَةِ سُوقًا أَتَى سُوقَ بَنِي

قَيْنُقَاعَ، ثُمَّ جَاءَ سُوقَ الْمَدِينَةِ فَضَرَبَهُ بِرِجْلِهِ وَقَالَ: ﴿ هَذَا سُوقُكُمْ، فَلَا يُضَيَّقْ، وَلَا يُؤْخَذْ فِيهِ

خَرَاجٌ ﴾ .

From 'Aṭā' ibn Yasār 🙵 there is that he said: When the Messenger of Allah 🙵 intended to appoint a market for Madīnah he went to the market of Banī Qaynuqā' and then came to the market of Madīnah, and struck it with his foot and said, "This is your market, so let it not be reduced and let no tax (kharāj) be levied on it." (Ibn Shabbah, Tārīkh Madīnah)[23]

The following is from 'Alī ibn Abī Ṭālib 🙵 when he was the Caliph in Kūfa:

عَنِ الْأَصْبَغِ بْنِ نَبَاتَةَ : قَالَ عَلِيُّ بْنُ أَبِي طَالِبٍ ﴿ سُوقُ الْمُسْلِمِينَ كَمُصَلَّى الْمُصَلِّينَ، مَنْ سَبَقَ إِلَى

شَيْءٍ فَهُوَ لَهُ يَوْمَهُ حَتَّى يَدَعَهُ ﴾ .

From al-Aṣbagh ibn Nabātah who said: 'Alī ibn Abī Ṭālib 🙵 said, "The Muslims' market is like the mosque for those who pray;[24] whoever gets first to any of it then it is his for that day of his until he leaves it." (Abū 'Ubayd in al-Amwāl)[25]

And as to the takeover of the free and open market space by shops and supermarkets, then this is not permitted.[26] From the caliphate of 'Umar it is widely reported that:

دَخَلَ عُمَرُ بْنُ الْخَطَّابِ السُّوقَ وَهُوَ رَاكِبٌ فَرَأَى دُكَّانًا قَدْ أُحْدِثَ فِي السُّوقِ فَكَسَرَهُ .

'Umar ibn al-Khaṭṭāb 🙵 entered the market mounted, and saw a shop that had been introduced into the market, and so he demolished it. (Al-Hindī, Kanz al-'ummāl, citing from al-Bayhaqī in his Sunan)

The Muslims must move to protect those existing free open markets, in which traders may come and trade without reserving a place, and without paying rent or being taxed, for this is the true foundation of free and open trade, in this case trade that is free for the poor and for all sections of society, rather than free for the hyper-wealthy but closed to everyone else.

Where such markets do not exist, whether in Muslim countries or elsewhere, it is one of the first duties of Muslim leaders and their communities to bring them about, for Muslims and non-Muslims, a duty that stands beside the creation of mosques just as for the Messenger of Allah ﷺ his creation of the market of Madīnah stood beside his institution of the mosque of Madīnah.

These are two of the key elements of Islamic trade that ought to be preserved where they still exist and brought into existence again where they have ceased to exist.

Conclusion

The raison d'etre of Islamic trade is the act of worship that is known as *zakāh* and *ṣadaqah*. Man was created to worship Allah, and one mode of such worship is expressed through wealth. However, in order for that to be acceptable it must come from acceptable wealth, for as we know from the *ḥadīth* narrated by Abū Hurayrah:

عَنْ أَبِي هُرَيْرَةَ قَالَ: قَالَ رَسُولُ اللهِ ﷺ : ﴿أَيُّهَا النَّاسُ إِنَّ اللهَ طَيِّبٌ لَا يَقْبَلُ إِلَّا طَيِّبًا﴾ .

> People, Allah is pure and He only accepts the pure. (Muslim, *kitāb az-zakāh, bāb qabūl aṣ-ṣadaqah min al-kasb aṭ-ṭayyib wa tarbiyatuhā*)

So that *zakāh* and *ṣadaqah* are not acceptable from trade that is permeated with usury. For *zakāh* to be restored, and thus Islam itself, trade must be cleansed of usury. It is thus fitting that the first step in that should be the restoration of gold and silver currency.

Notes

[1] *Ṭayyib* 'pure, wholesome, sweet, fragrant' derives from the same root as '*ṭīb*' which is a perfume, so that *ṭayyib* has the sense of 'fragrant' a meaning which is reinforced by its opposition in the Qur'ān to *khabīth* which means 'foul', 'malodorous' or 'stinking' and is translated variously as 'bad', etc.

[2] The *ḥarām* that is 'eaten' constitutes both foodstuffs and earnings from illegal sources such as usury, the earnings of prostitution and theft etc.

[3] These transactions are concealed ways of lending something and charging for the loan.

[4] Ibn Abī Zayd al-Qayrawānī, *Risālah, Op. Cit.* ch. 34: *Bāb fi'l-buyū^c wa māshākala al-buyū^c* pp 102-112

[5] *Ibid.*

[6] *Ibid.*

[7] Cf. *Ibn Taimiyyah on Public and Private Law in Islam or Public Policy in Islamic Jurisprudence.* Translated from Arabic by Omar Farrukh, Beirut, 1966, pp. 179-180.

[8] Ibn Abī Zayd al-Qayrawānī, *ar-Risālah*, op.cit., See ch. 34: *Bāb fi'l-buyū^c wa mā shākala al-buyū^c*, pp. 102.112

[9] *Cf.* Cohen's *Everyman's Talmud* (Dent. London), p.326. It says "The witnesses must be men, not women or minors." See also *Jewish Encyclopaedi*a (Frank and Wagnallel, New York,) vol. v, p. 177

[10] It is not in every case that two Muslim women witnesses are required. In some cases one woman is sufficient.

[11] *Fay'* is whatever is taken in *jihād* without fighting.

[12] The *dhimmah* is the treaty of protection under which non-Muslims of the People of the Book may live under Muslim governance.

[13] Referring to the people of *taqwā*.

[14] *Ṣadaqah* means *zakāh* as well as voluntary giving.

[15] *Ghanī* is someone without need, and thus by extension, 'rich'.

[16] Such a debt as is undertaken on behalf of another party or parties to put things right between a group of people, or for some other such worthy cause, e.g. undertaking to pay the compensatory payments for people killed in order to bring reconciliation between the feuding parties.

[17] Hanson, J. L. *Monetary Theory and Practice*, London, 1974, p. 180

[18] Alington, C. A., *The New Standard Encyclopaedia*, 1932. p. 1254. (see article on *Usury*)

[19] Ibn Maskawayh, *Tajārīb al-umam*, vol. 3, p. 45

[20] The 1944 United Nations Monetary and Financial Conference, more commonly known as the 'Bretton Woods Conference,' that took place at the Mount Washington Hotel resort in Bretton Woods, NH, resulting in the Bretton Woods Agreement that established the international Bretton Woods system and hence the World Bank, IMF, and international gold standard.

[21] Dīnār - Weight: 4.3 grammes, Alloy: 22 carats (0.916) Gold, Diameter: 23 millimetres. Dirham - Weight: 3.0 grammes, Alloy: Sterling. 925 Silver, Diameter: 25 millimetres. (The World Islamic Trading Organisation, following the standard of ᶜUmar ibn al-Khaṭṭāb)

[22] ᶜUmar Ibrāhīm Vadillo, *The Return of the Gold Dinar, Study of Money in Islamic Law*, Bookwork, 1996.

[23] *Tārīkh Madīnah* is one of the earliest and most reliable histories of Madīnah, which aṭ-Ṭabarī relied upon for his more famous history.

[24] No one may reserve a place in the mosque, and thus no one may reserve a place in the market.

[25] Someone like Sayyidunā ᶜAlī ⬥ would not say something like this as his own opinion, and it has also been narrated as a *hadīth* of the Prophet ⬥.

[26] Shops are not permitted in the free market space, but they are permitted elsewhere and for other categories of products than the basic necessities ordinarily sold in the free market.

PART VII
EXTERNAL AND OTHER RELATIONS

Chapter 25

Siyar: Military Campaigns and International Relations

IN ANCIENT TIMES, there was nothing like international law as such. Whatever elements of international law existed in their legal system, there was nothing international nor legal about it. It was considered as a part of politics and solely depended on the manoeuvres and machinations of statesmen. Even the native American tribe, the Iroquois had some notion of international law as they sent and received envoys, and they knew very well the rights of war and peace but still continued eating their prisoners.[1] In other words, we cannot consider the ancient system as international law since it was not based on principles. The rules of international law worked out by ancient peoples applied only to a limited number of states or city-states inhabited by people of the same race or following the same religion, or speaking the same language, for example, the Greeks, in spite of some Phoenician cultural influence, were so very narrow-minded that their international law could only be applied between the city-states of the Greek Peninsula.

According to their law, non-Greeks were considered barbarians. As Aristotle once said: "nature intended barbarians to be slaves of the Greeks." (Aristotle, *Politics*, book 1, ch. 7)

Plato had advised his countrymen to be more lenient in their mutual treatment, but he could not tolerate that non-Greeks be treated mildly. The Greek city states had formed a kind of league of nations and were instructed not to destroy any town or cut running water in the time of war or peace, but this principle was to be applied strictly amongst the city-states.

Later, the Romans also evolved their own legal system. The new system was as advanced as the Greek system but did not go far enough. As far as the life and property of a citizen of a state which had not a treaty of friendship with Rome was concerned, the inhabitants of that city could be made slaves and their properties could be seized. Roman martial law remained very much the same, recognising no right for the enemy combatant. As for the non-Roman enemy, they were entirely at the mercy of Roman whim. The only people who were treated honourably were ambassadors.[2] Even the *jāhiliyyah* Arabs, before the advent of Islam, had some form of international law. The Arab chiefs used to visit foreign rulers and sent and received ambassadors.[3] The Yemenis sent envoys to Madyan to ask for Persian help against the Abyssinians. These Yemenis used to receive the ambassadors of several foreign rulers including the Byzantine empire.[4]

The *jāhiliyyah* Arabs too sent envoys to solicit the return of the Muslim refugees at the court of the Negus of Abyssinia in the year 612 CE.[5] In spite of these rules of international relations, applied only whenever they served their purpose, they proved to be very cruel in the treatment meted out to other people with whom they had no such relations.

After the advent of Islam, the Muslims were the first to accord a dignified place to international relations in the *Sharīᶜah*. Thus there came into being both rights and obligations in international relations that developed as a branch of study into an independent science known as *as-siyar*. It made no discrimination between foreigners and dealt equitably with non-Muslim states all over the world.[6]

The *Sharīᶜah* has enshrined within itself the principles of Islamic International Law right from its inception and as early as 150 years after the Hijrah it regulated the conduct and behaviour of the Muslim world in war, peace and neutrality. The general concept of international law restricts its jurisdictional application to nations only but the concepts of Islamic international law in the *Sharīʿah* regulated not only the conduct of the Muslim world with other nations, but also the relationship of non-Muslim states and non-Muslim individuals living under Muslim rule.

The object was to enlarge the concepts of international Islamic law to encompass all public functions conducted by the ruler or his subjects in any intercourse not necessarily subject to private regulations in the performance of public needs or functions. As Dr. Ḥamīdullāh puts it, "When Islam came and founded a state of its own, the earliest name given by Muslim writers to the special branch of law dealing with war, peace and neutrality seems to have been *siyar,* the plural form of *sīrah,* meaning conduct and behaviour." (Ḥamīdullāh, Mohammad, *Muslim conduct of State,* Lahore, 1973, p. 10)

Muslim jurists are of the opinion that the term *as-siyar* to connote international law was first used by Imam Abū Ḥanīfah (d. 150 AH), the founder of the Ḥanafī School, while delivering a series of discourses on the theme of international law. Imam Muḥammad ibn al-Ḥasan ash-Shaybānī (d. 188 AH), the famous pupil of Imam Abū Ḥanīfah and a noted scholar attached to the Abbasid caliphate, rendered the great service of editing and recording these discourses in his famous books *Kitāb as-siyar aṣ-ṣaghīr* and *Kitāb as-siyar al-kabīr.* These books of *as-siyar* discuss, among other things, the behaviour of Muslims in dealing with non-Muslims, the covenanted people (*ahl ad-dhimmah*), resident aliens, apostates, rebels, and so on and so forth.[7]

The unqualified use of the word *sīrah* means the conduct of the Prophet ﷺ, and more specifically, in his wars.[8] Later it came to be used for the conduct of Muslim rulers in international affairs.[9] In the works of European jurists of the middle ages like Grotious, Puffendorf and others, one notices that they intentionally excluded the Muslims and the science of *as-siyar* from all commonality of interest with the Christian nations of Europe. Their law originated in the necessity of governing the relations of the new sovereign states which arose because of the urgent need of the temporal unity of Christendom. Later European jurists, out of necessity, thought that their international law was limited to Christendom only, and then enunciated broad principles to include others as well. Some Muslim scholars hold to the view that, "these European principles were just echoes of the time. Moreover, their human modifications for civilization came only after they intensively borrowed Islamic principles by the impact of Muslim Spain, the Crusades and earlier Ottomans." (Qadrī, Anwar Aḥmad, *Islamic Jurisprudence in the Modern World*, Lahore, 1973, pp. 277-278)

The impact of *as-siyar*, Muslim international law, can be properly assessed from the fact that the earliest European writers on international law like Pierre Bellow, Ayala, Victoria, Gentiles and others, all hailed from Spain or its neighbour Italy, and were influenced by Islam and Muslims during the Renaissance, which had come about because of the impact of Islam on Christendom. The famous author Grotins was born in Holland but he had also read and was influenced by Muslim International Law as can be seen from his discovery that postilimium was known to Muslim Law.[10]

Fundamental Human Rights under *Siyar*

The fundamental human rights of man in the *Sharīᶜah* rest on the premise that man is the Caliph of Allah on earth and hence the centre of the universe.

'Human rights' as ordinarily understood are an expression of the mathematical way that forms the basis of all modern thinking since Galileo, Descartes and Newton. It is not mathematical in the sense of using numbers but in the sense of proceeding as did Euclid, in this manner:

1. The definition of terms
2. The formulation of axioms or 'self-evident truths'
3. The advancing of hypotheses
4. Their proofs
5. The theorems that result when hypotheses are proved

This way emerged as an alternative to the old Christian doctrines which demanded faith in the unseen. Descartes *et al* hoped to arrive at certainty by this method, and to make a way that would create a body of certain knowledge, and this is the fundamental drive behind science. It is a sub-conscious drive to create a new religion. That is quite understandable given the contradictory dogmas Christians are required to believe. It has now penetrated all types of thinking. With the American Declaration of Independence it entered the political realm: "We hold these truths to be self-evident..." i.e. the authors meant that they were axioms. So the statements of human rights and constitutional government are part of the attempt to forge a new religion.

This process, however, is fundamentally flawed on many levels, something recognised among philosophers and historians of science. Firstly, the definition of terms which while moderately possible in mathematics, nevertheless along with mathematics' dependence on axioms, led to a crisis in mathematical thinking that has never seriously been resolved and it is a great deal simpler in mathematics to define one's terms and to formulate axioms in a rigorous fashion than in other disciplines. If it cannot work in mathematics, it must certainly fail in the zone of philosophy. The greatest of the philosophers recognised this centuries ago. Unfortunately, lesser minds press on with this programme in the political realm, with terrible results.[11]

The Declaration of Human Rights adopted by the United Nations General Assembly is mere words binding on no state or country. One of the purposes of the United Nations, according to Article 1 of its Charter, is to provide and encourage respect for human rights. Later the General Assembly adopted two agreements,[12] which are known as the 'Covenant on Civil and Political Rights' and the 'Covenant on Economic, Social and Cultural Rights.' The former covenant includes the following rights:

1. The right to life and liberty and security of person
2. The right to privacy
3. The right to marry and found a family
4. The right to education

5. Freedom of thought, conscience and belief
6. Freedom of expression of opinion
7. Freedom of movement
8. Right to peaceful assembly and association
9. The right to fair trial and equality before law
10. The right to be free from arbitrary arrest and detention.

States which voluntarily sign the covenant would be legally obliged to abide by its provisions. In recent times, we have seen states which have signed the covenant but have not implemented all of its provisions.

The paradoxical reality is that the culture that proclaimed these seemingly admirable rights has in their name set up prison camps across the earth, re-introduced torture, which few in their wildest fantasies had ever thought to see again, abandoned habeas corpus which was for centuries the defence of ordinary people against arbitrary arrest and detainment, and initiated a global control order of horrendous dimensions. However, we should have known because it was to the cry of Liberté, Egalité and Fraternité that the French revolutionaries butchered extraordinary numbers of men, women and children, very few of whom were their hated aristocratic enemies.

Since we have discussed the characteristics of the *Sharīcah*, we should bear in mind that individual freedom is important within the limits imposed by the *Sharīcah*, and it is considered so as long as it does not conflict with the larger social interest or as long as the individual does not transgress the rights of others.[13]

Treaty Relations in the *Sharīcah*

The Prophet ﷺ was the ruler of his community and he respected treaties and pledges, and he held that it was important to strictly observe the terms of treaties entered into by Muslims. Sometimes in observing the terms of treaties, he had to forego the advantage of his little Commonwealth of Islam which functioned on the principles of the *Sharīcah*.

Ḥudhayfah ibn al-Yamān could not migrate to Madīnah with the Prophet. He entered into a contract with the Quraysh that he would not fight against them, and in consideration thereof he remained free from molestation in Makkah. Subsequently, at the Battle of Badr, he joined the Prophet ﷺ to fight against the Quraysh. The Prophet ﷺ was informed of the solemn contract between Ḥudhayfah and the Quraysh and ordered him to refrain from attacking the Quraysh, in fulfilment of his contract.

Once the Quraysh sent Abū Rāfiᶜ as their ambassador to the Prophet ﷺ. When he came to Madīnah he was greatly influenced by the intrinsic merit of Islam and expressed his willingness to accept it. The Prophet ﷺ could not accept his declaration at that time, as the detaining of an ambassador on any ground whatsoever is a breach of his ambassadorial functions.

The importance of observing the terms of treaties, pledges and pacts with non-Muslims under the *Sharīᶜah* is sanctified in the conduct of the Messenger of Allah ﷺ and stands above all other considerations. For example, non-Muslims are entitled to *diyah* (compensatory payments for injuries and homicide) if they happen to be in treaty relations with Muslims, while there is no provision of *diyah* to the relatives of a Muslim who belongs to a people with no treaty relations with the Muslims.

The best example of this can be seen in Ḥudaybiyyah when the Prophet ﷺ entered into a treaty relation with non-Muslims even though the terms of the treaty were unfavourable to the Muslims. A man called Suhayl negotiated the terms of the treaty with the Prophet ﷺ on behalf of Quraysh while his son, Abū Jandal, who had accepted Islam and was persecuted by Quraysh for having done so, managed to escape the hands of the enemies. It was verbally agreed between Suhayl and the Prophet ﷺ (and not yet written down or sealed) that if a Muslim emigrated from Makkah during the terms of treaty the Muslims would return him to Quraysh, but that if any of the Muslims in Madīnah should renege on Islam and return to Makkah, Quraysh would not return them to Madīnah. In the *Sharīᶜah* a verbal agreement is binding, and the witnessing and recording of it in writing are simply to keep a record in case differences arise. In the Qur'ān Allah says:

وَالَّذِينَ آمَنُوا وَلَمْ يُهَاجِرُوا مَا لَكُم مِّن وَلَايَتِهِم مِّن شَيْءٍ حَتَّىٰ يُهَاجِرُوا وَإِنِ اسْتَنصَرُوكُمْ فِي الدِّينِ فَعَلَيْكُمُ النَّصْرُ إِلَّا عَلَىٰ قَوْمٍ بَيْنَكُمْ وَبَيْنَهُم مِّيثَاقٌ وَاللَّهُ بِمَا تَعْمَلُونَ بَصِيرٌ

But as for those who have īmān but have not made hijrah, you are not in any way responsible for their protection until they make hijrah. But if they ask you for help in respect of the dīn, it is your duty to help them, except against people you have a treaty with. Allah sees what you do. (Sūrat al-Anfāl 8: 73)

While the treaty was still in the process of negotiation, but the Prophet ﷺ had agreed to the terms, Abū Jandal fled the non-Muslim Makkans and came for refuge to the Muslims. The moment Suhayl saw his son, he declared: "Muḥammad, the matter between you and myself has already been settled." To this the Prophet ﷺ replied: "You speak the truth." When Abū Jandal heard this, he said: "Muslims, am I to be returned to the idolaters to be deprived of my *dīn*?" But Abū Jandal was returned to the non-Muslims according to the terms of the treaty although many Companions ﷺ raised objections.

The practice of dealing correctly with non-Muslims continued during the period of Muslim rule in most countries, and any case of injustice should be considered a deviation and a sign of weakness on the part of the individual ruler. Imam Abū Yūsuf, an eminent jurist and the famous disciple of Imām Abū Ḥanīfah says about the treaty rights of the non-Muslims: "We shall take from them only what was mutually fixed at the time of peace-making. All terms of the treaty shall be strictly adhered to and no additions permitted." (Abū Yūsuf, *Kitāb al-kharāj,* Cairo, p. 35)

Notes

[1] Montesquieu, *De L'esprit des Lois*; Paris 1860, liver ch. 3, p. 7
[2] *Cf.* Oppenheim, *International Law*, 4th Edn., vol. 1. pp. 59-61
[3] Aṭ-Ṭabarī, *Tārīkh* vol. 1, p. 1537, also see Masᶜūdī, *Murūj adh-dhahab*, vol. 4, p. 250
[4] Nadvi, Sulaiman, *Arḍ al-Qur'ān*, vol. 1, p. 319
[5] Ibn Hishām, *Kitāb al-maghāzī*, pp. 217-221
[6] Ḥamīdullāh, Mohammad, *Introduction to Islam*, I.I.F.S.O. Publication, Kuwait 1970, p. 188-189
[7] As-Sarakhṣī, *al-Mabṣūṭ*, vol. 10, p. 2
[8] As-Sarakhṣī, *al-Muḥīṭ*. vol. 1. fol. 567 a, b. (MS. Waliud Dīn, Istanbul, No. 1356)
[9] Ḥamīdullāh, *Op. Cit.* p. 21
[10] De Jure Belli, X, 3, v. quoted by Dr. Ḥamīdullāh in *Muslim Conduct of State*, Lahore 1937, p. 72
[11] See my essay, *Rigorous mathematics and Deductive Reasoning*, at: http://www.bogvaerker.dk/axioms.html
[12] See critical analysis given on this topic by, Anwer, Beg, *Civil and Political Rights in Islam*, No. 1-2, vol. 14 *Al-lttiḥād*, January-April 1977, p. 41
[13] For further details on this subject, see Doi, A. Raḥmān I., *Non-Muslims under Sharīᶜah*, Maryland, 1980.

Chapter 26

Non-Muslims and the *Sharīᶜah*

NON-MUSLIMS who live under Islamic governance and enjoy the rights enshrined in the contract they make under the *Sharīᶜah* are called *Ahl adh-dhimmah* or *dhimmis*, 'covenanted people.' *Dhimmis* living under Islamic governance are guaranteed the protection of their life, property and honour as are Muslims. It becomes every Muslim's duty to protect the life, property and honour of a non-Muslim *dhimmī* since it forms a part and parcel of faith (*īmān*).

The word *dhimmah* literally means pledged (*ᶜahd*), guarantee (*ḍamān*) and safety (*amān*).

Non-Muslims are called *dhimmis* because they have the pledge of Allah, the pledge of the Messenger of Allah and the pledge of the Muslim community so that they can live under the protection of Islam. In other words, they are under the protection of Muslims and have their guarantee. The pledge of security and guarantee given to non-Muslims is equivalent in some senses to the citizenship granted in modern times on the basis of which people acquire all their rights as the nationals of a certain country together with its attendant duties and responsibilities. The *dhimmis* from this point of view are 'people of the abode of Islam' (*ahl dār al-Islām*).[1]

Non-Muslims under the jurisdiction of Muslim governance

Muslim jurists have classified non-Muslim citizens under different categories. The most prevalent view is that there are three kinds of non-Muslims who may be found in any Islamic polity:

1. Those who have not fought but have negotiated a treaty in which is mention of their *jizyah* and the *kharāj* payment on their lands. The Muslim ruler is duty bound to observe all the conditions of their treaty.
2. Those who have been fought and conquered, and are compelled to pay the *jizyah*.
3. People who are passing through, for example as traders.

Ibn Juzayy al-Kalbī said:

> Taking the *jizyah* from the people of the *dhimmah*, concerning which there are three issues:
>
> 1. Concerning the one making the contract and the one with whom the contract is made. No one makes the contract of the *dhimmah* except the Imām (the ruler) and it is not made with anyone except for an adult male *kāfir* who is able to pay the *jizyah*, whose confirmation of his debt is valid, who is not insane or overwhelmed in his intellect, nor a monk who is secluded in his dwelling. As for women, slaves and children, they are followers and there is no *jizyah* due from them. It is similar with the poor and those incapable of earning. When the child reaches puberty then the *jizyah* is taken from him. Ibn al-Mājishūn said there is no *dhimmah* contract except for the People of the Book, and ash-Shāfiᶜī said it is for the People of the Book and the Majūs and for no other *kuffār*.
>
> 2. Concerning that which is due to us from them:
>
> a. Paying the *jizyah* directly themselves in a state of humbleness, and it is four dinars[2] per annum from every person of those whose [currency is] gold and forty dirhams[3] from people whose [currency is] silver, and it is not to be increased above that because of someone's strength nor decreased because of his weakness. Ash-Shāfiᶜī said that the *jizyah* is a dīnār from every person, and if they were given a treaty on the basis of more than that it is valid. Abū Ḥanīfah and Aḥmad ibn Ḥanbal said that the *jizyah* is twelve dirhams from the poor, twenty-four dirhams from middle [income] people and forty-eight dirhams from the prosperous. When the *dhimmī* accepts Islam, the *jizyah* is no longer obligatory from him even if it is one day before the end of the year.

b. A tenth of their trade outside of their own lands in which they reside. That is because the *jizyah* is of three types: the *jizyah* of a tenth, and it is this one, and *jizyah* due to conquest and it is the aforementioned, and *jizyah* by treaty, and there is no definition [or limit] of it nor of those from whom it is taken except for whatever the terms of the treaty are.

c. That they do not build a church nor leave one built in a township which the Muslims have built or conquered by force. If they have opened up the town by treaty and they stipulate that it has to remain then that is valid, but there are two views about their stipulating the building of it. ...

3. What is due to them from us, which is abiding by their residing in our lands apart from the Arabian Peninsula, which comprises the Ḥijāz and the Yemen, and that one desists from [harming] them and that we protect them with the guarantee in their persons and in their property, and that we do not lay a hand on their churches, their wine, their pigs as long as they do not make a public display of them. (Al-Kalbī, Ibn Juzayy, *al-Qawānīn al-fiqhiyyah, al-kitāb as-sābi^c^ fī al-jihād, al-bāb at-tāsi^c^ fī akhdh al-jizyah min ahl adh-dhimmah*)

It is essential to remove some misconceptions about these distinctions in the *Sharī^c^ah* between Muslims, *dhimmis* and non-Muslims. Some scholars tend to give a misleading analogy of this distinction and compare it with the Roman concept of jurisdiction in the *Jus Civile* or the *Pax Romana*. It should be remembered that non-Muslims are not outside the jurisdiction as is the case with *Jus Civile*. Likewise, Muslims are not to consider themselves as 'Lords of the population of the globe' as they are simply 'Slaves of Allah' (*^c^ibād* Allah) and even as rulers, merely the custodians of Allah's property and not absolute owners because Muslims know that everything in the heavens and the earth belongs to Allah. Non-Muslims are to receive just treatment under the law in every aspect. The distinction in the terms of 'Muslims' and 'non-Muslims' remains one of political administration and not of human rights.

Since the *dhimmis* are under *dhimmat-Allah*, the protection of Allah, they enjoy religious, administrative and political autonomy – a right guaranteed to them in return for their loyalty and the payment of the tax called *jizyah* which is utilised in the defence and administration of the commonweal.[4]

Muslims and non-Muslims: Guidelines from the Qur'ān

It is a wrong presumption that since an Islamic polity is based on a definite adherence to Islam, it will annihilate non-Islamic elements within its fold. There are guidelines in the Qur'ān and the Sunnah which speak of strengthening and cementing the relationship between Muslims and non-Muslims. The basic foundation of this relationship is referred to in the Qur'ān in the following words:

لَا يَنْهَاكُمُ اللَّهُ عَنِ الَّذِينَ لَمْ يُقَاتِلُوكُمْ فِي الدِّينِ وَلَمْ يُخْرِجُوكُمْ مِنْ دِيَارِكُمْ أَنْ تَبَرُّوهُمْ وَتُقْسِطُوا
إِلَيْهِمْ إِنَّ اللَّهَ يُحِبُّ الْمُقْسِطِينَ ۝ إِنَّمَا يَنْهَاكُمُ اللَّهُ عَنِ الَّذِينَ قَاتَلُوكُمْ فِي الدِّينِ وَأَخْرَجُوكُمْ مِنْ دِيَارِكُمْ
وَظَاهَرُوا عَلَى إِخْرَاجِكُمْ أَنْ تَوَلَّوْهُمْ وَمَنْ يَتَوَلَّهُمْ فَأُولَٰئِكَ هُمُ الظَّالِمُونَ

> *Allah does not forbid you from being good to those who have not fought you in the dīn or driven you from your homes, or from being just towards them. Allah loves those who are just. Allah merely forbids you from taking as friends those who have fought you in the dīn and driven you from your homes and who supported your expulsion. Any who take them as friends are wrongdoers.* (Sūrat al-Mumtaḥanah 60: 7-9)

According to the above verses of Sūrat al-Mumtaḥanah, Muslims are not forbidden to deal with unbelievers kindly and justly unless they are out to destroy Muslims and their *dīn* as was shown by the example of the Prophet Muḥammad ﷺ in the treaties of Ḥudaybiyyah and the prior treaty made in Madīnah with the Jews who agreed to live under Islamic governance.

The best example of such treatment can be seen in the life of the Prophet ﷺ. In the early days of Islam, Muslims had to migrate from their place of birth because of persecution at the hands of pagan Makkans. Qutaylah bint ^c^Abd al-^c^Uzzā, the mother of Asmā' bint Abī Bakr and the wife of Abū Bakr, did not migrate from Makkah to Madīnah in 622 CE nor did she accept the *dīn* of Islam. After the treaty of Ḥudaybiyyah, when Makkans visited Madīnah, Qutaylah came to Madīnah to see her daughter. ᶜAbdullāh ibn az-Zubayr, the illustrious son of Asmā', narrates that Asmā' first refused to see her non-Muslim mother. When she asked the Prophet ﷺ whether or not she could see her, the Prophet ﷺ told her to see her and treat her well.[5]

From the above incident, jurists have deduced that it is essential for every Muslim to treat their parents, brothers, sisters and other relatives with respect no matter what their faith or lack thereof. They should also try to help them in their hour of need, provided they do not profess open enmity towards Islam.[6]

As far as the people of the Book are concerned, that is Jews and Christians, they have been given a special position in the Qur'ān since their religions were originally based on the Heavenly Scriptures, like the Tawrāh and Injīl. In the Qur'ān, Allah says in respect of the People of the Book:

وَلَا تُجَادِلُوا أَهْلَ الْكِتَابِ إِلَّا بِالَّتِي هِيَ أَحْسَنُ إِلَّا الَّذِينَ ظَلَمُوا مِنْهُمْ وَقُولُوا آمَنَّا بِالَّذِي أُنزِلَ إِلَيْنَا وَأُنزِلَ إِلَيْكُمْ وَإِلَٰهُنَا وَإِلَٰهُكُمْ وَاحِدٌ وَنَحْنُ لَهُ مُسْلِمُونَ

> *Only argue with the People of the Book in the kindest way – except in the case of those of them who do wrong – saying, 'We have īmān in what has been sent down to us and what was sent down to you. Our God and your God are one and we submit to Him.'* (Sūrat al-ᶜAnkabūt 29: 46)

In order to achieve their purpose as standard bearers of Allah, Muslims are required to find true common ground of belief, as stated in the latter part of the above verse, and also to show their kindness, sincerity, truth and genuine anxiety for the good of others, that they are not cranks or merely self-seeking. However, those who are deliberately trying to wrong or injure others will have to be treated firmly, as we are guardians of each other. With them there is little question of finding common ground or showing patience, until the injury is prevented or stopped.

Fundamental Rights of Non-Muslims

The fundamental rights of non-Muslims in an Islamic polity are of two kinds:

1. Their protection from all external threats.
2. Their protection from all internal tyranny and persecution.

The first kind of protection is the same as in the case of Muslims. The ruler and those in authority are bound to look after the interests of all subjects using all the resources at their command. The famous Mālikī Scholar Imām al- Qarāfī, quotes the statement of Ibn Ḥazm from his book *Marātib al-ijmāʿ*:

> If enemies at war come to our country aiming at a certain *dhimmī*, it is essential for us that we come out to fight them with all our might and weapons since he is under the protection of Allah and His Messenger. If we did anything less than this, it means we have failed in our agreement for protection.[8]

This principle of the *Sharīʿah* was amply demonstrated by the famous Shaykh Ibn Taymiyyah when the Tartars invaded Syria. The Shaykh went to see Qatlushah to get him to spare the sufferings of people and he agreed to do so for the Muslims but refused to treat non-Muslims in the same way as Muslims. The Shaykh said that would not please the Muslims since the Jewish and Christian families were under their protection.

The more important protection is to accord non-Muslims and Muslims protection from internal high-handedness, persecution, tyranny and injustice. The Muslims are duty bound to withhold their hands and tongues from hurting non-Muslim subjects. They must not harbour enmity or hatred against them, since Allah does not like tyrants but gives them a quick punishment in this world or gives them a greater punishment in the next. There are a number of verses of the Noble Qur'ān warning wrongdoers, and the following saying of the Prophet ﷺ warns Muslims against any high handedness towards non-Muslim subjects.

عَنْ عِدَّةٍ مِنْ أَبْنَاءِ أَصْحَابِ رَسُولِ اللَّهِ ﷺ عَنْ آبَائِهِمْ دِنْيَةً عَنْ رَسُولِ اللَّهِ ﷺ قَالَ: ﴿أَلَا مَنْ

ظلم معاهداً أو انتقصه أو كلفه فوق طاقته أو أخذ منه شيئاً بغير طيب نفس فأنا ﷺ حجيجه يوم القيامة ﴾.

From a number of sons of the Companions of the Messenger of Allah ﷺ narrating from their fathers from the Messenger of Allah ﷺ who said, "Certainly, whoever wrongs someone with a covenant or causes him a shortfall [in his rights] or imposes on him more than is his ability or takes anything from him against his will, then I will dispute with him on the Day of Rising." (Abū Dāwūd, *kitāb al-kharāj, bāb fī taᶜshīr ahl adh-dhimmah idhā ikhtalafū bi at-tijārāt*)

The Prophet ﷺ also said:

عن ابن مسعود رضي الله عنه أن النبي قال ﴿ من آذى ذمياً فأنا خصمه، ومن كنت خصمه خصمته يوم القيامة ﴾.

Ibn Masᶜūd narrated that the Prophet ﷺ said, "Whoever hurts a *dhimmī*, I shall be his adversary, and for whosoever I am an adversary, I shall altercate with him on the Day of Rising." (Al-Khaṭīb, *at-Tārīkh*)

The Prophet ﷺ also said:

من آذى ذمياً فقد آذاني ومن آذاني فقد آذى الله

Whoever hurts a *dhimmī*, hurts me; and whoever hurts me, hurts Allah. (Al-Bayhaqī, *as-Sunan al-Kubrā*, vol. 5, p. 205. Narrated by al-Khaṭīb with an authentic *isnād*)

Some Muslim jurists like Ibn ᶜĀbidīn (d. 1836 CE) have argued that since Muslims are given the responsibility of protecting the blood and property of non-Muslims and since the persecution of weak persons at the hands of the strong is considered one of the greatest crimes, the persecution of non-Muslims in an Islamic polity is considered a greater crime than the persecution of Muslims by non-Muslims.[9]

Muslim – non-Muslim Relations at the time of the Prophet ﷺ

When Muḥammad ﷺ started to teach *tawḥīd* openly, i.e. that there is only One Lord for the whole universe, Allah, and that none has the right to be worshipped, but Allah and that Allah is absolute Oneness, the pagan aristocracy of Makkah turned against him and his followers. They did accept that Allah is the supreme God, but insisted that their idols of wood and stone, Lāt, Manāt, ᶜUzzā and Hubal, were intermediary gods and were thus their source of happiness and sorrow, reward and punishment.

Nonetheless, a good number of eminent Qurayshīs rallied round the Prophet ﷺ and then the inveterate enemies of *tawḥīd* started inflicting torture and injury upon the Prophet ﷺ and his followers so that others would not dare to join them. Nevertheless, the number of the Prophet's followers grew, which was an indication to them of a serious movement undermining their mode of worship, unjust ways of life and their very existence as the custodians of the Kaᶜbah.

To save their own institutions from destruction, the Quraysh persecuted the Muslims; it was then that the Prophet ﷺ advised his followers to seek refuge in the nearby Christian Kingdom of the Ḥabashah (Abyssinia; today's Ethiopia).

He told his followers:

لَوْ خَرَجْتُمْ إِلَى أَرْضِ الْحَبَشَةِ فَإِنَّ بِهَا مَلِكاً لا يُظْلَمُ عِنْدَهُ أَحَدٌ ، وَهِيَ أَرْضُ صِدْقٍ ، حَتَّى يَجْعَلَ اللّٰهُ لَكُمْ فَرَجاً مِمَّا أَنْتُمْ فِيهِ

> If you were to go to the land of the Ḥabash (Ethiopians), for there is a king there under whom none is wronged, and it is a land of truthfulness, until Allah makes a deliverance from that which you are in. (Ibn Hishām, *Sīrah, fitnat al-muslimīn*)

Consequently, in 615 CE, a small group of eleven men and four women including ᶜUthmān ibn ᶜAffān and his wife Ruqayyah the daughter of the Prophet ﷺ, ᶜAbd ar-Raḥmān ibn ᶜAwf, and az-Zubayr ibn al-ᶜAwwām crossed the Red Sea and reached the hospitable land of Ethiopia. They were followed by another batch of eighty-three men and eighteen women under the leadership of Jaᶜfar ibn Abī Ṭālib, the cousin of the Prophet ﷺ and brother of Sayyidunā ᶜAlī.

This emigration is referred to as the first *hijrah* in the history of Islam.

The news that these Muslims were kindly received and lived under the protection of the Najāshī (Negus), the King of the Ḥabashah, filled the Quraysh with dismay and subsequently they deputed ᶜAbdullāh ibn Abī Rabīᶜah and ᶜAmr ibn al-ᶜĀṣ ibn Wā'il with precious gifts to the king to request that the fugitives be returned. The Quraysh were well acquainted with Abyssinia through trading relations. The king of Abyssinia granted an audience to those deputed by Quraysh and told them he would himself question the refugees. The Quraysh expected their prospects for the morrow to be excellent. The king summoned the refugees in the presence of the Christian bishops and asked: "What is the religion for which you have abandoned your people and yet have neither adopted mine nor any other known religion?"

Jaᶜfar ibn Abī Ṭālib answered in words that reflect Arab life before the birth of the Prophet Muḥammad ﷺ and the early stages of Islam:

> O King, we were a barbarous nation, worshipping idols, eating carrion, disregarding every feeling of humanity, committing shameful deeds, killing our blood relations, forgetting our duty towards our neighbours, the strong men among us devouring the weak, we knew no law save that of the jungle. Such was our state until Allah sent us an Apostle, from amongst ourselves, with whose lineage, integrity, trustworthiness, excellence of character and purity of life we were fully aware.
>
> He summoned us to Allah, to believe in His unity, to worship Him and abandon the stones and idols which we and our fathers worshipped in His stead. He commanded us to speak the truth, to be faithful in our trusts, to observe our duties to our kinsfolk and neighbours, to refrain from forbidden things and bloodshed, from committing immoralities and deceits, from consuming the property of orphans and from slandering virtuous women. He ordered us to worship Allah and associate no other with Him,

to offer prayer, give alms, and observe the fast. So we trusted in His word and followed the teaching he brought us from Allah. (This is our fault), and for this reason our countrymen turned against us and persecuted us to try and seduce us from our faith, that we might abandon the worship of our God and return to the worship of idols.

The Negus asked Jaᶜfar, "Do you have anything that he brought from Allah?" Jaᶜfar recited from the Qur'ān the beginning of Sūrah Maryam. (This sūrah was revealed before the first Muslim hijrah to Ethiopia). On hearing this the Negus and all his bishops wept, and the Negus said, "This and that which ᶜĪsā brought issue from the same niche." (Ibn Hishām, *as-Sīrat an-nabawiyyah, al-ḥuwār alladhī dāra bayna al-muhājirīn wa an-najāshī*)

The next day ᶜAmr tried to set the Christians against the Muslims by alleging that Muslims said something bad about ᶜĪsā ﷺ. Jaᶜfar was summoned and asked about this and he said,

"We say about him what our Prophet ﷺ brought us. He says: he is the slave of Allah and His messenger and His spirit and His word which He cast to the Virgin Maryam." The Negus affirmed everything they said and said, "Go for you are safe in my land." … He added, "I would not want to have a mountain of gold if I harmed one man from among you." Then he said to his people, "Return their gifts to them [the two emissaries of Quraysh] for I have no need of them." (*Ibid.*)

The Quraysh ambassadors returned empty-handed, and the Prophet ﷺ held the Ḥabashah (Abyssinians) in considerable affection. He blessed the king and his progeny. He is reported to have said, "Leave the Ḥabashah alone as long as they leave you alone." (Abū Dāwūd, *awwal kitāb al-malāḥim, bāb ab-nahy ᶜan tahyīj al-ḥabashah*; and al-Ḥākim in *al-Mustadrak* narrated it from Ibn ᶜAmr)

Afterwards, Muḥammad ﷺ wrote a letter to the king about his mission, which was the Prophet's first letter about Islam to any non-Muslim king. That letter was brought to Ethiopia by ᶜAmr ibn Umayyah.

The king received the letter with reverence and "the Najāshī declared his belief in the Prophet's mission." (Ibn Hishām. *Sīrah*, Cairo, 1937, p. 343)

The Muslims who had taken refuge in Ethiopia lived in peace under the protection of the king. Some of the emigrants returned to Makkah when conditions appeared to have improved at home, for some of the Quraysh had joined the Prophet ﷺ in his mission, but the news had been misleading and the Muslims were forced to emigrate again, but this time to Madīnah.

With respect to friend and foe, Muslim and non-Muslim, the Prophet ﷺ followed the Qur'ānic injunctions:

وَلَا يَجْرِمَنَّكُمْ شَنَآنُ قَوْمٍ عَلَىٰ أَلَّا تَعْدِلُوا اعْدِلُوا هُوَ أَقْرَبُ لِلتَّقْوَىٰ

Do not let hatred for a people incite you into not being just. Be just. That is closer to taqwā. (Sūrat al-Mā'idah 5: 8)

إِنَّ اللَّهَ يَأْمُرُ بِالْعَدْلِ وَالْإِحْسَانِ وَإِيتَاءِ ذِي الْقُرْبَىٰ

Allah commands justice and doing good and giving to relatives. (Sūrat an-Naḥl 16: 90)

يَا أَيُّهَا الَّذِينَ آمَنُوا كُونُوا قَوَّامِينَ بِالْقِسْطِ شُهَدَاءَ لِلَّهِ وَلَوْ عَلَىٰ أَنْفُسِكُمْ أَوِ الْوَالِدَيْنِ وَالْأَقْرَبِينَ

You who have īmān! be upholders of justice, bearing witness for Allah alone, even against yourselves or your parents and relatives. (Sūrat an-Nisā' 4: 135)

In the Qur'ān Allah, exalted is He, again says:

وَإِذَا قُلْتُمْ فَاعْدِلُوا وَلَوْ كَانَ ذَا قُرْبَىٰ

...that you are equitable when you speak – even if a near relative is concerned. (Sūrat al-Ancām 6: 152)

Once, a Muslim woman who was from an important family and who had stolen, was brought to the Messenger of Allah ﷺ. After the evidence was produced, he ordered her hand to be cut off. His Companions considered it a very severe sentence particularly because the woman was someone of good standing. The Prophet ﷺ said:

وَالَّذِي نَفْسِي بِيَدِهِ لَوْ كَانَتْ فَاطِمَةُ بِنْتُ مُحَمَّدٍ لَقَطَعْتُ يَدَهَا

> Had she been Fāṭimah the daughter of Muḥammad I would certainly have cut off her hand. (Muslim, *kitāb al-ḥudūd, bāb qaṭᶜ as-sāriq*; al-Bukhārī, *kitāb al-anbiyā', bāb am ḥasibta anna aṣḥāb al-kahf wa arraqīm*; Abū Dāwūd, *awwal kitāb al-ḥudūd, bāb fī al-ḥadd yushaffaᶜ*; Ibn Mājah and others also narrated it)

Once, in a trial between a Muslim and a Jew, he gave a decision in favour of the Jew who at once exclaimed: "By Allah, you have decided with truth." He did not fear that by this act he would alienate the sympathy of the clan to which the Muslim belonged.

Once, a ruffian of Banī Thaᶜlabah killed an Anṣārī. The heirs of the murdered Anṣārī demanded the surrender of his son and his death in revenge for the murder. The Prophet ﷺ prohibited it and said: "A son is not guilty for the crime of his father."

When the whole of Arabia came under the sway of Islam, one of his Companions was found murdered in the Jewish city of Khaybar. The Prophet ﷺ could not find out who the culprit was. Consequently, he paid compensation of one hundred camels to the heirs of the murdered person from the *bayt al-māl* since the case was not proven against any of the Jews.[10]

The Prophet ﷺ used to pass judgement according to the law to which the complainant belonged. Once a man of Banī Qurayẓah was killed by a man of Banī Naḍīr. When the complaint was laid before the Prophet ﷺ, he enforced the law of the Tawrāh: a life for a life. In disputes between Jews, Muslims and other tribes, the Prophet ﷺ was the final court of appeal.

The Caliphs' treatment of Non-Muslims

Non-Muslim subjects must be treated with leniency and must not be oppressed by the ruler, must not be taxed beyond their capacity and nothing should be taken from them except for what is obligatorily due from them. The prophetic tradition we saw earlier emphasises this point: "Whoever hurts a *dhimmī*, I shall be his adversary, and for whosoever I am an adversary, I shall altercate with him on the Day of Rising." (Al-Khaṭīb) The second caliph of Islam, Sayyidunā ᶜUmar ibn al-Khaṭṭāb ؓ is reported to have said in the last moments of his life:

> I exhort my successor regarding the treatment to be meted out to the covenanted people by the Messenger of Allah ﷺ. They should receive fulfilment of their covenant, and their life and property should be defended even if it requires going to war (with oppressors), and they should not be taxed beyond their capacity.

The *Khulafā' ar-Rāshidūn* (the Caliphs who took the right way) used to enquire about non-Muslims whenever people came to see them from the neighbouring countries or provinces. Whenever any complaint came from non-Muslims, they used to give their urgent attention to it in order to ensure that justice was done to them. It is narrated by aṭ-Ṭabarī in his famous historical work, that Caliph Umar used to question delegates concerning the condition of non-Muslims and used to ask if any Muslim had hurt non-Muslims in their countries. Once he asked some delegates to narrate the treatment of non-Muslims at the hand of Muslims in their home towns. They replied:

مَا نَعْلَمُ إِلَّا الْوَفَاءَ

> We do not know anything except [fair treatment by] fulfilling their pledge.

The *dīn* of Islam and the *Sharīᶜah* have so emphasised the rights of non-Muslims under Muslim governance that any Muslim who violates any of their rights is deemed to have committed a grave wrong action.

In Islam we reject all these man-made distinctions even if they are given religious colouring. The only unifying factor in Islam is the identity of *īmān* and *taqwā* which solely depend on the choice of man and not upon the accidents and hazards of birth, race, colour and geographical location. All men have their legal rights in Islam, and even if one does not choose to follow the *dīn* of Islam, he has every right to live in peace and tranquillity in a Muslim polity or in Muslim majority areas as an honoured subject with all rights and privileges. Neither the *dīn* of Islam nor the *Sharīᶜah* can be forced on anyone against his will according to the teachings of the Qur'ān and the Sunnah of the Prophet ﷺ.

This is the much misunderstood *āyah* of Qur'ān:

لاَ إِكْرَاهَ فِي الدِّينِ قَد تَّبَيَّنَ الرُّشْدُ مِنَ الْغَيِّ

> *There is no coercion into the dīn. Right guidance has become clearly distinct from error.* (Sūrat al-Baqarah 2: 255)

Ibn Juzayy al-Kalbī said:

> *"There is no coercion into the dīn"* means that the *dīn* of Islam is at the furthest limit of clarity with the most obvious proofs of its authenticity, such that there is no need to coerce anyone to enter into it, but on the contrary every person possessing a sound intellect will enter into it voluntarily without coercion, and this is shown by His saying, *"Right guidance has become clearly distinct from error,"* i.e. it has become clear that Islam is right guidance and *kufr* is error so that after this clarity there is no need for coercion. (Al-Kalbī, Ibn Juzayy, *Kitāb at-tashīl li ᶜulūm at-tanzīl* in commentary on Sūrat al-Baqarah 2: 255)

The main emphasis of the *Sharīᶜah* is on the sanctity of the concept of due process to guarantee the life, liberty, property and honour of every human being. Therefore, Muslim law justly regulates the conduct of the faithful in this world and in the world hereafter. *Mutatis mutandis,* the Muslim laws of *siyar* aim at the fair regulation of the Muslim polity in its external relations. The *Sharīᶜah* is the unified source of moral precepts and law, and so it prevents double standards in internal versus external affairs because in Islam what sanctions the individual's private conduct also sanctions the society's public conduct.

Ash-Shāṭibī in his *Muwāfaqāt* elaborated an understanding of the purposes (*maqāṣid*) of the *Sharīᶜah* as preserving *dīn,* life, property, lineage, sanity, and some add, honour. This preservation is naturally extended to all who live under Islamic governance, as can be seen from the treaties made by the People of the Book throughout history.

According to the *Sharīᶜah,* all mankind is one entity, all are the people of Muḥammad ﷺ, but divided into those who accept him and those who reject him, and yet Muslims should think of the well-being of all human beings. All the provisions granted by the

Sharīᶜah – are meant for the welfare of the world. These provisions of the *Sharīᶜah* were revealed 1,400 years ago.

When one looks at articles 1-30 of the Universal Declaration of Human Rights, it seems as if they are reflections of the aims and objectives of the *Sharīᶜah,* and yet paradoxically they are having the reverse effect of that intended by their authors, for the world slides further away from justice with each day. That is because they are conceived as a new secular religion which by its nature does not partake of the divine mercy, but is the subject of human whims and passions.

The individual is viewed by Muslims both as a single and unique unit and also as a part and parcel of a composite unit, i.e., the *Ummah*. It has historically been the nature of the Muslim polity that it contained substantial communities of the People of the Book, who were granted a serious measure of autonomy under Muslim rule. Thus it was that for the Jews the high point of their culture is still considered to be Islamic Andalusia. When Andalusia fell to the Christians, who then broke their treaties and instituted the Spanish Inquisition to hunt out Muslims and Jews and coerce them into Christianity, many Jews fled with the Muslims to North Africa, and many others made the long journey east to Istanbul to the protection of the Ottoman sultanate.

It is also a lesson for us that under Islamic rule, al-Quds (Jerusalem) was always maintained as a place of pilgrimage and a sanctuary for all faiths, contrary to its recent bloody history.

Notes

[1] As-Sarakhsī, *Sharḥ as-Siyar al-kabīr*, vol. 1, p. 140; Ibn Qudāmah, *Al-Mughnī*, vol. 5, p. 516; al-Kāshānī, *Al-Badā'i^c wa'ṣ-ṣanā'i^c*, vol. 5, p. 281.

[2] The dīnār is a gold coin whose dimensions and weight we have given earlier and whose value is determined by the weight of gold it contains. At present values (June 2007) a dīnār is approximately £45, giving a *jizyah* of £180 per year.

[3] The dirham is a silver coin whose dimensions and weight were given earlier in the book. Ordinarily, the exchange rate between gold and silver was that ten dirhams were equal to one dīnār, but at the time of writing silver is greatly undervalued and the dirham is less than the value of a £1.

[4] Abū Zahrah, Muḥammad, *Al-Jarīmah wa'l-^cuqūbah fī fiqh al-Islām*, Dar al-Fikr al-Arabi, undated, p. 189 (footnote)

[5] This incident is recorded in *Musnad* Aḥmad, al-Bukhārī and Muslim.

[6] Al-Jaṣṣāṣ, *Aḥkām al-Qur'ān*: also *Rūḥ al-ma^cānī*

[8] Imām al-Qarāfī, Shihāb ad-Dīn, Abu'l-^cAbbās Aḥmad ibn Idrīs al-Mālikī, *Al-Furuq*, Cairo 1346, vol. 3, pp. 14-15

[9] Ibn ^cĀbidīn, Muḥammad Amīn, *Radd al-muḥtār ^calā durr al-mukhtār*, Cairo 1327 AH

[10] Al-Bukhārī, *kitāb al-adab, bāb ikrām al-kabīr wa yabda'u al-akbar bi al-kalām wa as-su'āl*; Muslim, *kitāb al-qasāmah wa al-muḥāribīn wa al-qiṣāṣ wa ad-diyāt, bāb al-qasāmah*; and others narrated it.

Chapter 27

∞

Jihād

IT IS SURELY IN THE REALM OF WAR that the *Sharīʿah* is meaningful
in this age in which the devastation of civilian populations
in the name of total war has reached even into the heart of
the Muslim community itself, resulting in conflicts ostensibly in
the name of Allah in which both sides compete in barbarities.
War has rules in the *Sharīʿah*.

The Messenger of Allah ﷺ is narrated to have defined *jihād* in
the way of Allah in the following way:

عَنْ أَبِي مُوسَى رَضِيَ اللَّهُ عَنْهُ قَالَ جَاءَ رَجُلٌ إِلَى النَّبِيِّ صَلَّى اللَّهُ عَلَيْهِ وسلم فَقَالَ... ﴿فَمَنْ

فِي سَبِيلِ اللَّهِ؟﴾ قَالَ ﴿مَنْ قَاتَلَ لِتَكُونَ كَلِمَةُ اللَّهِ هِيَ الْعُلْيَا فَهُوَ فِي سَبِيلِ اللَّهِ﴾

From Abū Mūsā al-Ashʿarī ؓ there is that he said: A man came to
the Prophet ﷺ and said, "So who is in the way of Allah?" He said,
"Whoever fights so that the Word of Allah may be uppermost
then he is in the way of Allah." (Aḥmad in his *Musnad*; al-
Bukhārī, *kitāb al-jihād wa as-siyar, bāb man qātala li takūna kalimat
Allāh hiya al-ʿulyā*, Muslim, *kitāb fī al-imārah, bāb man qātala li
takūna kalimat Allāh hiya al-ʿulyā*; and Abū Dāwūd, at-Tirmidhī,
an-Nasāʾī and Ibn Mājah also transmitted it)

In this pivotal sentence, the stress may be laid quite differently,
for example: "Whoever *fights* so that the Word of Allah may be
uppermost," or "Whoever fights *so that the Word of Allah may
be uppermost.*" Undoubtedly both elements must be present to
preserve the full sense of being 'in the way of Allah' but it makes
quite a difference on which term one lays the stress. If we take the

latter alternative first, then we must explicate what the Word of Allah is, and of course by it we mean the Qur'ān. The Qur'ān is held to contain three elements: *tawḥīd* or the teaching of the divine unity, *aḥkām* or rulings of the *Sharīᶜah*, and stories. Leaving aside this latter for the moment, there is a clear sense and meaning to fighting so that the *tawḥīd* of Allah may be uppermost, but given the nature of our book let us then consider for our purposes the sense of the *aḥkām* rulings being uppermost. In the very deepest sense of the word 'law' the only law that exists is the divine law. Other laws are no more profound than the rules that children devise for games or adults for their sports: a set of artificial rules that permit a game to be carried on. The *Sharīᶜah* is from the very core of existence, from the same source as the laws of physics and nature, and is revealed for the purpose of allowing humans to create just and merciful societies. There is no other decent reason to fight. To fight for that reason, and then to resort to the barbarities that have characterised modern warfare would be the ultimate betrayal. It would be the ends justifying the means.

Jihād is derived from the Arabic word *jahd* meaning struggle or striving, and the word *jāhada* means 'he struggled or exerted himself'. *Jihād* does not necessarily mean resorting to the use of weapons and shedding blood. The word *jihād*, therefore, is so comprehensive that it is also includes striving, undergoing hardship and forbearance in great difficulties, while standing firm against one's enemies. The actual words for war and fighting in Arabic are *ḥarb* and *qitāl*.

The initial permission to wage *jihād* was revealed thus:

أُذِنَ لِلَّذِينَ يُقَاتَلُونَ بِأَنَّهُمْ ظُلِمُوا وَإِنَّ اللَّهَ عَلَى نَصْرِهِمْ لَقَدِيرٌ الَّذِينَ أُخْرِجُوا مِنْ دِيَارِهِمْ بِغَيْرِ
حَقٍّ إِلَّا أَنْ يَقُولُوا رَبُّنَا اللَّهُ وَلَوْلَا دَفْعُ اللَّهِ النَّاسَ بَعْضَهُمْ بِبَعْضٍ لَهُدِّمَتْ صَوَامِعُ وَبِيَعٌ وَصَلَوَاتٌ
وَمَسَاجِدُ يُذْكَرُ فِيهَا اسْمُ اللَّهِ كَثِيرًا وَلَيَنْصُرَنَّ اللَّهُ مَنْ يَنْصُرُهُ إِنَّ اللَّهَ لَقَوِيٌّ عَزِيزٌ

Permission to fight is given to those who are fought against because they have been wronged – truly Allah has the power to come to their support – those who were expelled from their homes without any right, merely for saying, 'Our Lord is Allah' (if Allah had not driven some people back by means of others, monasteries, churches, synagogues and mosques, where Allah's name is mentioned much, would have been pulled down and destroyed. Allah will certainly help those who help Him – Allah is All-Strong, Almighty). (Sūrat al-Ḥajj 22: 39-40)

And some of the *āyāt* regulating *jihād* are:

وَقَاتِلُوا فِي سَبِيلِ اللَّهِ الَّذِينَ يُقَاتِلُونَكُمْ وَلَا تَعْتَدُوا إِنَّ اللَّهَ لَا يُحِبُّ الْمُعْتَدِينَ

Fight in the Way of Allah against those who fight you, but do not go beyond the limits. Allah does not love those who go beyond the limits. (Sūrat al-Baqarah 2: 190)

وَقَاتِلُوهُمْ حَتَّى لَا تَكُونَ فِتْنَةٌ وَيَكُونَ الدِّينُ لِلَّهِ فَإِنِ انْتَهَوْا فَلَا عُدْوَانَ إِلَّا عَلَى الظَّالِمِينَ

Fight them until there is no more fitnah and the dīn belongs to Allah alone. If they cease, there should be no enmity towards any but wrongdoers. (Sūrat al-Baqarah 2: 193)

The Prophet ﷺ was asked in the Qur'ān to:

ادْعُ إِلَى سَبِيلِ رَبِّكَ بِالْحِكْمَةِ وَالْمَوْعِظَةِ الْحَسَنَةِ وَجَادِلْهُمْ بِالَّتِي هِيَ أَحْسَنُ

Call to the way of your Lord with wisdom and fair admonition, and argue with them in the kindest way. (Sūrat an-Naḥl 16: 125)

His mission in Makkah was to invite people to Allah, acting on Allah's command while undergoing persecution at the hands of the idolaters. His companions, the early Muslims, also endured untold hardships because of their profession of and dedication to the *dīn* of Islam.

وَاصْبِرْ لِحُكْمِ رَبِّكَ فَإِنَّكَ بِأَعْيُنِنَا

So wait steadfastly for the judgement of your Lord – you are certainly before Our eyes. (Sūrat aṭ-Ṭūr 52: 48)

The man of Allah must strive his utmost to proclaim the message of Allah. As far as the result is concerned, it is not in his hands or at his command. He has to wait patiently in the knowledge and with the conviction that he has not been forgotten by Allah, and knowing that he is constantly under the eyes of Allah, under His loving care and protection. He must continue in his good work undaunted.

The Qur'ān further says:

فَاصْفَحْ عَنْهُمْ وَقُلْ سَلَامٌ فَسَوْفَ يَعْلَمُونَ

Turn from them and say, 'Peace! They will soon come to know.' (Sūrat az-Zukhruf 43: 89)

Quraysh persecuted the Muslims so much that the Prophet ﷺ was counselled in the above verse to turn away from them, and was assured by Allah that the truth would prevail soon. The Prophet ﷺ was asked to console his followers in those first extremely difficult days thus:

قُل لِّلَّذِينَ آمَنُوا يَغْفِرُوا لِلَّذِينَ لَا يَرْجُونَ أَيَّامَ اللَّهِ

Tell those who have īmān that they should forgive those who feel no fear about the Days of Allah. (Sūrat al-Jāthiyah 45: 14)

Ibn Juzayy al-Kalbī explains the '*Days of Allah*' as:

> His punishments to the previous nations, and some said His blessings to Banī Isrā'īl, and the wording encompasses blessings and afflictions. He expressed it as 'days' because it happened over days. (Al-Kalbī, Ibn Juzayy, *Kitāb at-tashīl li ᶜulūm at-tanzīl*)

The Prophet ﷺ was not commanded to do away with evil by using another evil or to get rid of torture by using torture nor initially to fight those who were opposing his call and invitation to the way of Allah or to fight those who were persecuting the believing men and women. In such almost unbearable circumstances, in the Qur'ān Allah initially instructed them:

ادْفَعْ بِالَّتِي هِيَ أَحْسَنُ السَّيِّئَةَ نَحْنُ أَعْلَمُ بِمَا يَصِفُونَ

Ward off evil with what is better. We know very well what they express. (Sūrat al-Mu'minūn 23: 96)

When the situation got out of control the Prophet ﷺ was asked to emigrate with his companions and followers to a peaceful place,

Madīnah, some distance away from Makkah. It was in Madīnah the verses of *jihād* were revealed to the Prophet ﷺ because the enemies of Islam did not want to leave them in peace in Madīnah in spite of the fact that the Prophet ﷺ and his followers were far away from them. It was imperative in such circumstances to defend the cause of the *dīn*, the new Islamic society, and the newly found locus of the Islamic polity.

Permission for *Jihād* only given after the *Hijrah*

Permission for *Jihād* was given for the following three reasons:

1. The innocent Muslims were persecuted in the early days of the Prophet's mission for no other fault of theirs except their saying that Allah is One, and for establishing a way of life quite different from the pagan system of Arabia.
2. If permission for *jihād* had not been given, the enemies would have destroyed the mosque of the Prophet ﷺ, the place of worship in which the name of Allah was pronounced and remembered. The *kāfirūn* would have persisted in their tyranny in order to force people to give up their belief in Allah and the Last Day.
3. Permission for *jihād* was granted at that time so that the order of Allah could be established firmly on earth, which could already be seen in the institutions of the prayer (*ṣalāh*) and the poor-rate (*zakāh*). The idolators wanted to destroy these newly found institutions. The enemy stood not only for an order that was idolatrous, but one that oppressed the poor and downtrodden.

If permission for *jihād* had not been given, the Makkans would have forcibly stopped the work of *da[c]wah*, i.e. of inviting people to the right path and discouraging them from following the wrong path (*al-amr bi'l-ma[c]rūf wa'n-nahy [c]an al-munkar*). Therefore, it was in the second year of the Hijrah that *jihād* was made obligatory:

كُتِبَ عَلَيْكُمُ الْقِتَالُ وَهُوَ كُرْهٌ لَّكُمْ وَعَسَىٰ أَن تَكْرَهُوا شَيْئًا وَهُوَ خَيْرٌ لَّكُمْ وَعَسَىٰ أَن تُحِبُّوا شَيْئًا
وَهُوَ شَرٌّ لَّكُمْ وَاللَّهُ يَعْلَمُ وَأَنتُمْ لَا تَعْلَمُونَ

Fighting is prescribed for you even if it is hateful to you. It may be that you hate something when it is good for you and it may be that you love something when it is bad for you. Allah knows and you do not know. (Sūrat al-Baqarah 2: 216)

Jihād is *farḍ kifāyah* which means that it is obligatory on all of the Muslims such that if some of them discharge it the others are absolved of their responsibilities, i.e. not every Muslim need be engaged in it on every occasion.

The other obligations like *īmān* (faith), *ṭahārah* (purification), *ṣalāh* (prayers), *zakāh* (poor-rate), *ṣiyām* (fasting) are *farḍ ᶜayn*, meaning that every individual is duty-bound to fulfil these obligations at all times. The following injunctions of the Qur'ān makes the above point more clear:

وَمَا كَانَ الْمُؤْمِنُونَ لِيَنفِرُوا كَافَّةً فَلَوْلَا نَفَرَ مِن كُلِّ فِرْقَةٍ مِّنْهُمْ طَائِفَةٌ لِّيَتَفَقَّهُوا فِي الدِّينِ وَلِيُنذِرُوا قَوْمَهُمْ إِذَا رَجَعُوا إِلَيْهِمْ لَعَلَّهُمْ يَحْذَرُونَ

It is not necessary for the muminun to go out all together. If a party from each group of them were to go out so they could increase their knowledge of the dīn they would be able to notify their people when they returned to them so that hopefully they would take warning! (Sūrat at-Tawbah 9: 122)

This *āyah* is understood particularly to stress the importance of learning knowledge of the *dīn*, an importance so great that it can absolve the student of the obligation of *jihād*, although many of the great *ᶜulamā'* nevertheless would continue to go on *jihād*, such as Ibn Juzayy al-Kalbī, who died in *jihād* in the battle of Tareefah (741 AH/1340 CE), similarly to many of the right-acting first generations.

In the Qur'ān Allah further says:

يَا أَيُّهَا الَّذِينَ آمَنُوا خُذُوا حِذْرَكُمْ فَانفِرُوا ثُبَاتٍ أَوِ انفِرُوا جَمِيعاً

You who have īmān! take all necessary precautions, then go out to fight in separate groups or go out as one body. (Sūrat an-Nisā' 4: 171)

In a *ḥadīth* narrated by Muslim there is:

عَنْ أَبِي سَعِيدٍ الْخُدْرِيِّ أَنَّ رَسُولَ اللَّهِ صلى الله عليه وسلم بَعَثَ بَعْثاً إِلَى بَنِي لِحْيَانَ، مِنْ هُذَيْلٍ. فَقَالَ: ﴿ لِيَنْبَعِثْ مِنْ كُلِّ رَجُلَيْنِ أَحَدُهُمَا . وَالأَجْرُ بَيْنَهُمَا ﴾ .

From Abū Saᶜīd al-Khudrī ﵁ that the Messenger of Allah ﷺ sent a party against Banī Liḥyān of Hudhayl and said, "One of every two men must hasten to go forth and the reward will be between them." (Muslim, *kitāb al-imārah, bāb faḍl iānat al-ghāzī fī sabīl Allāh bi markūb wa ghayrihi wa khilāfatihi fī ahlihi bi khayr*)

If it had been compulsory that each one of them should go for *jihād* the other necessary social and worldly matters would have suffered. That is why only some were asked to fulfil the obligation. Those who stayed behind and supported the fighters and their families while they were away shared in the reward. People took their turns in the fighting and in staying behind.

In the following circumstances, *jihād* becomes *farḍ ᶜayn*:

1. If a man goes for *jihād* and is stationed on the battlefield, it is obligatory for him to continue fighting. Otherwise he will create confusion and the whole strategy will fall apart. In the Qur'ān Allah says:

يَا أَيُّهَا الَّذِينَ آمَنُوا إِذَا لَقِيتُمْ فِئَةً فَاثْبُتُوا وَاذْكُرُوا اللَّهَ كَثِيراً لَعَلَّكُمْ تُفْلِحُونَ

You who have īmān! when you meet a troop, stand firm and remember Allah repeatedly so that hopefully you will be successful. (Sūrat al-Anfāl 8: 45)

From this we see that even in the middle of the battle, matters hinge on the *dhikr* or remembrance of Allah. Indeed, running away at this point is one of the major wrong actions, if the enemy are not more than twice the strength of the Muslims. If the enemy are more than twice the Muslims' strength, then it is permissible for the fighters to retreat in order to fight again i.e. one is *'withdrawing to rejoin the fight or withdrawing to support another group'*. Allah, exalted is He, further says:

يا أيها الذين آمنوا إذا لقيتم الذين كفروا زحفا فلا تولوهم الأدبار ومن يولهم يومئذ دبره إلا متحرفا لقتال أو متحيزا إلى فئة فقد باء بغضب من الله ومأواه جهنم وبئس المصير

You who have īmān! when you encounter those who are kāfir advancing in massed ranks into battle, do not turn your backs on them. Anyone who turns his back on them that day, unless he is withdrawing to rejoin the fight or withdrawing to support another group, brings Allah's anger down upon himself. His refuge is Hell. What an evil destination! (Sūrat al-Anfāl 8: 14-15)

2. If enemies attack an enclave of Muslims, it is obligatory for every resident of that place to come out and repel the enemy. Otherwise, the enemy will wipe them out and ruin their villages and cities and Allah will no longer be worshipped.
3. When the Muslim ruler, whether just or unjust, orders someone to join the forces of *jihād* , it will be obligatory for him to join without hesitation. The following *ḥadīth* is narrated by Ibn ᶜAbbās:

عن ابن عباس قال: قال رسول الله ﷺ يوم الفتح، فتح مكة ﴿لا هجرة. ولكن جهاد ونية. وإذا استنفرتم فانفروا﴾.

From Ibn ᶜAbbās there is that he said: The Messenger of Allah ﷺ said on the day of the Opening, the Opening of Makkah [to Islam], "There is no hijrah, but there is *jihād* and intention, and when you are asked to go out on an expedition then go out." (Muslim, *kitāb al-imārah, bāb al-mubāyaᶜah baᶜd fatḥ Makkah ᶜalā al-islām wa al-jihād wa al-khayr, wa bayān maᶜnā (lā hijrah baᶜd al-fatḥ)*)

In other words, the obligation to make *hijrah* for the Muslims of that time had been abrogated by this *ḥadīth* since Makkah had accepted Islam, but still *hijrah* from the 'abode of war' (*dār al-ḥarb*) to the 'abode of security' (*dār al-amān*) is not abrogated. It is obligatory for someone to emigrate when they fear that their *dīn* is not safe by continuing to live in a hostile place. Similarly, when a leader, whether or not he is just, demands that one should go out for *jihād*, one must not refuse. In the Qur'ān Allah ﷻ says:

يَا أَيُّهَا الَّذِينَ آمَنُوا مَا لَكُمْ إِذَا قِيلَ لَكُمُ انفِرُوا فِي سَبِيلِ اللَّهِ اثَّاقَلْتُمْ إِلَى الْأَرْضِ أَرَضِيتُم بِالْحَيَاةِ الدُّنْيَا مِنَ الْآخِرَةِ فَمَا مَتَاعُ الْحَيَاةِ الدُّنْيَا فِي الْآخِرَةِ إِلَّا قَلِيلٌ

You who have īmān! what is the matter with you that when you are told, 'Go out and fight in the way of Allah,' you sink down heavily to the earth? Are you happier with the dunyā than the ākhirah? Yet the enjoyment of the dunyā is very small compared to that of the ākhirah. (Sūrat at-Tawbah 9: 38)

Ibn Juzayy al-Kalbī said:

> It is not permitted to rise up against the people in authority even if they are tyrannical, unless they openly display clear disbelief. It is obligatory to obey them in whatever a man loves and dislikes, unless they order disobedience [to Allah] for there is no obedience due to a creature if it involves disobedience to the Creator. (Al-Kalbī, Ibn Juzayy, *al-Qawānīn al-fiqhiyyah, al-fātiḥah fī mā yajibu fī al-iᶜtiqādāt min uṣūl ad-diyānāt, al-bāb ath-thāmin fī al-imāmah*)

He also says:

> There is no harm in waging *jihād* along with unjust tyrannical rulers. (*Ibid.*)

Ibn Abī Zayd al-Qayrawānī said in the *Risālah*:

> The enemy are to be fought whether the commander of the Muslims is right-acting or not. [It is obligatory for those for whom *jihād* is obligatory to fight the enemy. The Prophet said, "Allah will support his *dīn* by the impious man." Perhaps if one does not fight along with him, there might be harm for the Muslims.] (Al-Qayrawānī, Ibn Abī Zayd, *ar-Risālah*, 30.2g. Fighting under any commander, from Aisha Bewley's unpublished translation on her website at: http://ourworld.compuserve.com/homepages/ABewley/Page49.html.)

On whom *jihād* is obligatory

Jihād is obligatory on someone who is:

1. Muslim; 2. Male; 3. Sane; 4. Who has reached the age of puberty; 5. Who has sufficient means to maintain his family until he returns from *jihād*.

In other words, it is not obligatory for a non-Muslim, a woman, a child, a blind man, or an old man and a sick person. In the Qur'ān Allah ﷻ says:

لَّيْسَ عَلَى الضُّعَفَاءِ وَلَا عَلَى الْمَرْضَى وَلَا عَلَى الَّذِينَ لَا يَجِدُونَ مَا يُنفِقُونَ حَرَجٌ إِذَا نَصَحُوا لِلَّهِ وَرَسُولِهِ مَا عَلَى الْمُحْسِنِينَ مِن سَبِيلٍ وَاللَّهُ غَفُورٌ رَّحِيمٌ

Nothing is held against the weak and sick nor against those who find nothing to spend, provided they are true to Allah and His Messenger – there is no way open against good-doers, Allah is Ever-Forgiving, Most Merciful. (Sūrat at-Tawbah 9: 93)

He ﷻ further says in Sūrat al-Fatḥ:

لَّيْسَ عَلَى الْأَعْمَى حَرَجٌ وَلَا عَلَى الْأَعْرَجِ حَرَجٌ وَلَا عَلَى الْمَرِيضِ حَرَجٌ وَمَن يُطِعِ اللَّهَ وَرَسُولَهُ يُدْخِلْهُ جَنَّاتٍ تَجْرِي مِن تَحْتِهَا الْأَنْهَارُ وَمَن يَتَوَلَّ يُعَذِّبْهُ عَذَابًا أَلِيمًا

There is no constraint on the blind, nor on the lame, nor on the sick. We will admit all who obey Allah and His Messenger into Gardens with rivers flowing under them. But We will punish with a painful punishment anyone who turns his back. (Sūrat al-Fatḥ 48: 18)

There is from ᶜAbdullāh ibn ᶜUmar ؓ that:

أَنَّ رَسُولَ اللَّهِ ﷺ عَرَضَهُ يَوْمَ أُحُدٍ وَهُوَ ابْنُ أَرْبَعَ عَشْرَةَ سَنَةً فَلَمْ يُجِزْنِي ثُمَّ عَرَضَنِي يَوْمَ الْخَنْدَقِ وَأَنَا ابْنُ خَمْسَ عَشْرَةَ سَنَةً فَأَجَازَنِي

The Messenger of Allah ﷺ reviewed him on the day of Uḥud when he was fourteen years old, "and he did not permit me [to fight], and then he reviewed me on the Day of the Trench (Khandaq) when I was fifteen years old and he permitted me." (Al-Bukhārī, *kitāb ash-shahādāt, bāb bulūgh aṣ-ṣibyān wa shahādatuhum*; Muslim, *kitāb fi al-imārah, bayān sinn al-bulūgh*)

Likewise ᶜĀ'ishah ؓ asked the Prophet ﷺ:

عَنْ عَائِشَةَ؛ قَالَتْ: قُلْتُ يَا رَسُولَ اللَّهِ عَلَى النِّسَاءِ جِهَادٌ؟ قَالَ ﴿نَعَمْ. عَلَيْهِنَّ جِهَادٌ لَا قِتَالَ فِيهِ: الْحَجُّ وَالْعُمْرَةُ﴾.

From ᶜĀ'ishah ﷺ that she said: I said, "Messenger of Allah is there any *jihād* due on women?" He said, "Yes, there is *jihād* due on them in which there is no fighting: Ḥajj and ᶜUmrah." (Ibn Mājah, *kitāb al-manāsik, bāb al-ḥajj jihād an-nisā'*)

Women can also render service in *jihād* by giving water to the warriors and bandaging and nursing the wounded. One of the traditions of the Prophet ﷺ discusses the priority of the actions (*ᶜamal*). The Prophet ﷺ was asked about the actions dearest to Allah:

عَنْ عَبْدِ اللَّهِ بْنِ مَسْعُودٍ قَالَ: سَأَلْتُ رَسُولَ اللَّهِ ﷺ أَيُّ الْعَمَلِ أَفْضَلُ؟ قَالَ: ﴿الصَّلَاةُ لِوَقْتِهَا﴾ قَالَ قُلْتُ: ثُمَّ أَيٌّ؟ قَالَ: ﴿بِرُّ الْوَالِدَيْنِ﴾ قَالَ قُلْتُ: ثُمَّ أَيٌّ؟ قَالَ: ﴿الْجِهَادُ فِي سَبِيلِ اللَّهِ﴾ فَمَا تَرَكْتُ أَسْتَزِيدُهُ إِلَّا إِرْعَاءً عَلَيْهِ.

From ᶜAbdullāh ibn Masᶜūd there is that he said: I asked the Messenger of Allah ﷺ, "Which action is best?" He said, "The prayer at its time." He said: I said, "Then what?" He said, "Good treatment of parents." He said: I said, "Then what?" He said, *Jihād* in the way of Allah." And I gave up asking him for more, out of mercy for him. (Al-Bukhārī, *kitāb mawāqīt aṣ-ṣalāh, faḍl aṣ-ṣalāh li waqtihā*; Muslim, *kitāb fī al-īmān, bāb kawn al-īmān billāh taᶜālā afḍalu al-aᶜmāl*)

In other words, prayer at its time is the best action. If parents are old and need the services of their son, it is better that he attends to them rather than going to participate in *jihād*.

There are differences of opinion among jurists whether hypocrites, drunkards and non-Muslims will be allowed to participate in *jihād*. We have evidence that ᶜAbdullāh ibn Ubayy and his hypocrite companions went out on *jihād* with the Prophet ﷺ. Likewise there was a well-known drunkard who still fought in the later *jihād* against Persia. The jurists differed particularly about the participation of non-Muslims. Imām Mālik and Imām Aḥmad ibn Ḥanbal say that they absolutely should not join the *jihād*. Imām Mālik said that if non-Muslims happen to be servants in the houses of Muslims, they will be allowed. Imām Abū Ḥanīfah said that non-Muslims can also help in *jihād*, but they will have to follow the orders of the Muslim commandant. Imām ash-Shāfiᶜī says that their participation will be allowed but he stipulated some conditions.

Other matters that are considered *jihād*

Jihād is not limited to the use of force. There can also be a *jihād* through speech and writing particularly when the wrongdoer is the established authority. In the following *ḥadīth* it is mentioned that to speak up for the truth is the best *jihād*.

عَنْ أَبِي سَعِيدٍ الْخُدْرِيِّ؛ قَالَ: قَالَ رَسُولُ اللَّهِ ﷺ: ﴿أَفْضَلُ الْجِهَادِ، كَلِمَةُ عَدْلٍ عِنْدَ سُلْطَانٍ جَائِرٍ﴾.

From Abū Saᶜīd al-Khudrī there is that he said: The Messenger of Allah ﷺ said, "The best *jihād* is a word of justice[25] in the presence of an unjust *sulṭān*." (Ibn Mājah, *kitāb al-fitan, bāb al-amr bi'l-maᶜrūf wa an-nahy ᶜan al-munkar*)

It must be remembered that this is governed by the imperative to maintain good manners, and use good language courteously and respectfully. When Allah, exalted is He, sent His prophets Mūsā and Hārūn, peace be upon both of them, to Firᶜawn, He ordered him thus:

فَقُولَا لَهُ قَوْلًا لَّيِّنًا لَّعَلَّهُ يَتَذَكَّرُ أَوْ يَخْشَىٰ

But speak to him with gentle words so that hopefully he will pay heed or show some fear. (Sūrah Ṭā Hā 20: 43)

The intelligent person will deduce from this that no person who warns a tyrant is as noble in the sight of Allah as these two messengers, and that no tyrant is ever likely to be as hateful to Him as Firᶜawn who claimed to be a god, so that every warner is advised to treat every tyrant with the same courtesy as is commanded in this *āyah*. Moreover, the modes of 'commanding the right and forbidding the wrong' are very well known to the people of knowledge and do not include abrasive and ugly behaviour.

It is reported that once the Prophet ﷺ was returning from the jihād to Madīnah and he said to his Companions on the way:

﴿رَجَعْنَا مِنَ الْجِهَادِ الْأَصْغَرِ إِلَى الْجِهَادِ الْأَكْبَرِ﴾ قَالُوا ﴿وَمَا الْجِهَادُ الْأَكْبَرُ﴾ قَالَ ﴿جِهَادُ الْقَلْبِ﴾ .

"We have returned from the lesser jihād to the greater jihād." They said, "And what is the greater jihād?" He said, "The jihād of the heart."[2]

The Companions were surprised to hear this because they were in fact returning from active fighting and now they were going to Madīnah, a peaceful place. The Prophet ﷺ here meant that actual fighting is a smaller jihād but fighting against one's selfish whims and desires[3] is the greater jihād.

We should bear in mind that once tawḥīd and right action appears, opposition appears from those who have vested interests or whose world picture is threatened, for tawḥīd is about the reality of Allah and the unreality of the human self and its projects. They resent the people of tawḥīd and use all means at their disposal to crush the new movement. This is the reason why the dīn of Islam in those early days had to face great opposition in Makkah, its birthplace. Similar situations arise at all times, since the battle between reality and unreality is not merely confined to a particular time or geographical region or a nation. Islam allows great latitude to its opponents to understand and respond to its teachings.

With this in mind Muslims go through a stage of tolerance and endurance but they are not encouraged to suffer kufr indefinitely or fall prey to their opponents. The period of perseverance thus becomes one of training to enable them to confront kufr. Whenever the truth arises the falsehood disappears. Muslims are asked to follow strictly the covenants and treaties entered into by their leaders even though sometimes their terms go against them, just as happened in the case of the treaty of Ḥudaybiyyah between the Prophet ﷺ and the Makkans. However, if the enemy does not adhere to the terms stipulated in the treaty, jihād will be fought. Thus the military actions taken by Muslims will establish peace through *jihād* like a tailor who cuts a piece of cloth into smaller pieces only to design it and shape it into a beautiful garment.

When one looks at the conquests of Napoleon, Hitler or the British, Dutch, French and German colonialists, one sees that they were all meant for the purpose of depriving free nations of their innate freedom, and more significantly their commerce, wealth, resources and trade. *Jihād* in Islam is not fought for mere territorial gain and colonialism. If there is any desire on the part of genuine *mujāhidūn* it is to spread what they consider to be the truth, particularly where they were invited by the rulers or by oppressed people of distant lands.

Many non-Muslim biographers of the Prophet ﷺ have tried to paint an ugly picture of the Prophet ﷺ, of a man with a sword in one hand and the Qur'ān in the other. When one really studies the events which led to the battles of the Prophet ﷺ in the ten years of military activities in the Madīnan period the total loss of life incurred was 255 Muslims and 759 enemies of Islam. With this small number of casualties Islam had spread over all of Arabia, an area of around a million square miles, and the people entered into Islam in totality.

It is interesting to note that the total number of prisoners taken in all the *jihāds* of the Prophet ﷺ was 6,564 prisoners of war, of whom two were executed for definite crimes, while 6,347 were released. The remaining 215 prisoners probably accepted Islam right away and became one with the Muslim *Ummah*, most of the rest accepting Islam later.

Code of conduct for *mujāhidūn* in *jihād*

Jihād can be fought with one's property and with one's life as is specified in the Qur'ān :

إِنَّ الَّذِينَ آمَنُوا وَهَاجَرُوا وَجَاهَدُوا بِأَمْوَالِهِمْ وَأَنفُسِهِمْ فِي سَبِيلِ اللَّهِ

Those who have īmān and have made hijrah and done jihād with their wealth and themselves in the Way of Allah… (Sūrat al-Anfāl 8: 72)

The following *ḥadīth* further stresses the point:

عَنْ أَبِي سَعِيدٍ الْخُدْرِيِّ؛ أَنَّ رَجُلاً أَتَى النَّبِيَّ ﷺ فَقَالَ: أَيُّ النَّاسِ أَفْضَلُ؟ قَالَ: ﴿ رَجُلٌ

مُجَاهِدٌ فِي سَبِيلِ اللهِ بِنَفْسِهِ وَمَالِهِ ﴾.

From Abū Sa'īd al-Khudrī there is that a man came to the Prophet ﷺ and said, "Who are the best people?" He said, "A man who wages *jihād* in the way of Allah with his life (*nafs*) and his property." (Ibn Mājah, *kitāb al-fitan, bāb al-'uzlah*)

Spending one's property means to ensure the needs of those who join the forces of *jihād* (*mujāhidūn*) and their dependants by providing clothing, food, weapons, means of transport and medical supplies.

عَنْ عُمَرَ ابْنِ الْخَطَّابِ؛ قَالَ: سَمِعْتُ رَسُولَ اللَّهِ ﷺ يَقُولُ: ﴿ مَنْ جَهَّزَ غَازِياً فِي سَبِيلِ اللَّهِ حَتَّى

يَسْتَقِلَّ كَانَ لَهُ مِثْلُ أَجْرِهِ، حَتَّى يَمُوتَ أَوْ يَرْجِعَ ﴾.

From 'Umar ibn al-Khaṭṭāb there is that he said: I heard the Messenger of Allah ﷺ saying, "Whoever equips a warrior in the way of Allah until he is independent [of need for support] will have the same reward as him until he dies or returns." (Ibn Mājah, *kitāb al-jihād, bāb man jahhaza ghāziyan*)

It is essential that the commander of the forces of *jihād* is chosen by the Islamic ruler carefully. He should be a Muslim with *taqwā*, a wise, mature, well disciplined and brave man who commands the respect of his soldiers and who takes decisions with some foresight in planning strategy against the enemy. He does not have to be an older man, as one of the last actions of the Messenger of Allah ﷺ was to appoint Usāmah ibn Zayd to lead an army against the Byzantines when he was still in his teens.

The Muslim forces must summon the enemy to accept Islam. If they refuse they are offered to live under Muslim governance and to pay the *jizyah*. If they refuse that they are to be fought. This is because of the *āyah*:

قَاتِلُوا الَّذِينَ لَا يُؤْمِنُونَ بِاللَّهِ وَلَا بِالْيَوْمِ الْآخِرِ وَلَا يُحَرِّمُونَ مَا حَرَّمَ اللَّهُ وَرَسُولُهُ وَلَا يَدِينُونَ دِينَ
الْحَقِّ مِنَ الَّذِينَ أُوتُوا الْكِتَابَ حَتَّى يُعْطُوا الْجِزْيَةَ عَنْ يَدٍ وَهُمْ صَاغِرُونَ

Fight those of the people who were given the Book who do not have
īmān in Allah and the Last Day and do not make ḥarām what Allah
and His Messenger have made ḥarām and do not take as their dīn the
dīn of Truth, until they pay the jizyah with their own hands in a state
of complete abasement. (Sūrat at-Tawbah 9: 29)

Once the enemy inclines towards peace, Muslims should at once
agree to it as the Qur'ān says:

وَإِنْ جَنَحُوا لِلسَّلْمِ فَاجْنَحْ لَهَا وَتَوَكَّلْ عَلَى اللَّهِ إِنَّهُ هُوَ السَّمِيعُ الْعَلِيمُ

If they incline to peace, you too incline to it, and put your trust in Allah.
He is the All-Hearing, the All-Knowing. (Sūrat al-Anfāl 8: 61)

Muslims engaged in *jihād* must make sure that the civilians
of the area where they are waging war are protected in all
circumstances. Their lives, property and freedom must be
protected. There should be no cases of high handedness on the
part of any *mujāhid*. There should be no devastation of houses and
crops through burning and laying waste. Old people, invalids,
women and children must not be killed under any circumstances,
unless they actively engage in fighting. No places of worship
should be demolished, nor their priests and monks killed. The
following advice of Sayyidunā Abū Bakr, the first caliph, to
Yazīd ibn Abū Sufyān while the latter was engaged in *jihād* on
the coasts of Syria, provides us with the strict code of conduct
Muslim armies followed in the past:

إِذَا سِرْتَ فَلَا تَعْنِفْ أَصْحَابَكَ فِي السَّيْرِ، وَلَا تَغْضَبْ قَوْمَكَ، وَشَاوِرْهُمْ فِي الْأَمْرِ، وَاسْتَعْمِلْ
الْعَدْلَ وَبَاعِدْ عَنْكَ الظُّلْمَ وَالْجَوْرَ، فَإِنَّهُ مَا أَفْلَحَ قَوْمٌ ظَلَمُوا، وَلَا نُصِرُوا عَلَى عَدُوِّهِمْ، وَإِذَا
انْتَصَرْتُمْ عَلَى عَدُوِّكُمْ فَلَا تَقْتُلُوا وَلِيدًا، وَلَا شَيْخًا وَلَا امْرَأَةً، وَلَا طِفْلًا، وَلَا تَقْرَبُوا نَخْلًا، وَلَا
تُحْرِقُوا زَرْعًا، وَلَا تَقْطَعُوا شَجَرًا مُثْمِرًا، وَلَا تَغْدِرُوا إِذَا عَاهَدْتُمْ، وَلَا تَنْقُضُوا إِذَا صَالَحْتُمْ.

وستمرون بأقوامٍ في الصوامع رهبانٍ ترهبوا لله، فدعوهم وما انفردوا إليه، وارتضوه لأنفسهم، فلا تهدموا صوامعهم، ولا تقتلوهم، والسلام

When you travel, do not drive your companions so much that they get tired on the journey. Do not be angry at your people, but consult them in affairs. Do justice and keep away from tyranny and oppression, because a community that engages in tyranny, does not prosper, nor do they win victory over their enemies. When you become victorious over your enemies, do not kill their children, old people and women. Do not even approach their date-palms, nor burn their harvest, nor cut the fruit-bearing trees. Do not break a promise once you have made it, and do not break the terms of treaty, once you have entered into it. You will meet on your way people in the monasteries, who have become monks for the sake of Allah; leave them alone with that to which they have dedicated themselves and with which they are content for themselves, and do not destroy their monasteries, and do not kill them. May the peace of Allah he upon you. (Al-ᶜAjūz, *Manāhij ash-sharīᶜah al-islāmiyyah, Op. Cit.*, Vol. 1. p. 345)

Prisoners of war and their treatment

The *Sharīᶜah* stipulates that the Imām (the ruler) has five choices with respect to *kāfir* male prisoners of war captured in battle: he may kill them, ransom them, enslave them, set them free or take the *jizyah* from them, depending on the circumstances of how they fought and for what reason and his own judgement of the case. In the Qur'ān Allah says:

فَإِذا لَقِيتُمُ الَّذِينَ كَفَرُوا فَضَرْبَ الرِّقابِ حَتَّى إِذا أَثْخَنْتُمُوهُمْ فَشُدُّوا الْوَثاقَ فَإِمَّا مَنًّا بَعْدُ وَإِمَّا فِداءً حَتَّى تَضَعَ الْحَرْبُ أَوْزارَها

Therefore when you meet those who are kāfir strike their necks. Then when you have decimated them, tie their bonds tightly and set them free or ransom them, until the war is finally over. (Sūrah Muḥammad 47: 4)

They must not be tortured or punished. They deserve kindness and good care whilst in captivity to Muslims. Provision must be made for their nourishment and necessary clothing. Islam has made the giving of food to the prisoners a virtuous deed for the believers just as the Qur'ān declares:

وَيُطْعِمُونَ الطَّعَامَ عَلَى حُبِّهِ مِسْكِيناً وَيَتِيماً وَأَسِيراً

They give food, despite their love for it, to the poor and orphans and captives. (Sūrat al-Insān 76: 8)

Ibn Juzayy al-Kalbī said in *Kitāb at-tashīl li ᶜulūm at-tanzīl* in commentary on this *āyah*:

> We had already mentioned the poor and the orphan, and as for the captive there are five statements about him, first, that it refers to the *kāfir* captive among the Muslims, for there is a reward for feeding him since for everything that possesses a moist liver there is a reward. Some have said that that is abrogated by the [*āyah* of the] sword. Second, that it is the Muslim captive when he goes out of the *dār al-ḥarb* seeking a ransom. Third, is that it is the slave [who is metaphorically a captive]. Fourth, that it is the person in prison. Fifth, that it is woman because of his words ﷺ, "Accept counsel that you treat women well because they are captives with you," but this is unlikely, and the first is the weightiest because it is narrated of the Prophet ﷺ that he used to be brought an idolater as a captive and he would pass him over to one of the Muslims and say, "Treat him well."[4]

The Prophet ﷺ and the Muslims are further instructed:

مَا كَانَ لِنَبِيٍّ أَنْ يَكُونَ لَهُ أَسْرَى حَتَّى يُثْخِنَ فِي الْأَرْضِ تُرِيدُونَ عَرَضَ الدُّنْيَا وَاللَّهُ يُرِيدُ الْآخِرَةَ وَاللَّهُ عَزِيزٌ حَكِيمٌ

It is not fitting for a prophet to take captives until he has let much blood in the land. You desire the goods of the dunyā, whereas Allah desires the ākhirah. Allah is Almighty, All-Wise. (Sūrat al-Anfāl 8: 68)

This *āyah* was revealed after the Prophet ﷺ had spared the prisoners of Badr in spite of the opposition of some Companions to such clemency.

An ordinary war may be for territory or trade-routes, or to capture prisoners of war, for revenge or military glory or for 'temporal goods of this world'. Such a war is condemned in the

Sharīᶜah. But *jihād* is fought under strict conditions, under a leader, purely for the sake of Allah and to raise His word uppermost. All baser motives, therefore, are strictly excluded. The greed for gain in the shape of ransom from captives has no place in the *jihād*, so this is left to the decision of the ruler which is taken with a view to the realities of the situation and to strengthen the *dīn* and the Muslims and weaken the *kuffār*.

Seventy prisoners of war were taken in the Battle of Badr, the first serious battle in Islam. They were soon freed, and in some cases those who were literate were asked to teach in lieu of a ransom. Among the prisoners taken were the Prophet's uncle ᶜAbbās and Sayyidunā ᶜAlī's brother ᶜAqīl, who afterwards became Muslims.

ᶜAbbās was the ancestor of the founder of the Abbasid dynasty which played such a notable part in Islamic history. In the case of all prisoners, if there was any good in their hearts, their very fight against Islam and their capture led to their being blessed with Islam. Thus Allah's plan works in a marvellous way, and produces good out of what is seemingly evil. In the Qur'ān Allah says:

يَا أَيُّهَا النَّبِيُّ قُل لِّمَن فِي أَيْدِيكُم مِّنَ الْأَسْرَىٰ إِن يَعْلَمِ اللَّهُ فِي قُلُوبِكُمْ خَيْرًا يُؤْتِكُمْ خَيْرًا مِّمَّا أُخِذَ مِنكُمْ وَيَغْفِرْ لَكُمْ وَاللَّهُ غَفُورٌ رَّحِيمٌ

O Prophet! say to those you are holding prisoner, 'If Allah knows of any good in your hearts, He will give you something better than what has been taken from you and forgive you.' Allah is Ever-Forgiving, Most Merciful. (Sūrat al-Anfāl 8: 70)

This verse gives a consolation to prisoners of war that in spite of their *kufr*, and their previous hostility, Allah in His mercy will forgive them if there is any good in their hearts, and confer upon them a far higher gift than anything they have ever lost. This gift in its highest sense is the blessing of Islam.

Kindness may be shown to prisoners of war, but one must not do so if one suspects that by showing kindness to them, and releasing them, they will again create problems for the *Ummah*.

وَإِن يُرِيدُوا خِيَانَتَكَ فَقَدْ خَانُوا اللَّهَ مِن قَبْلُ فَأَمْكَنَ مِنْهُمْ وَاللَّهُ عَلِيمٌ حَكِيمٌ

But if they mean to betray you, they have already previously betrayed Allah, so He has given you power over them. Allah is All-Knowing, All-Wise. (Sūrat al-Anfāl 8: 71)

Spoils of battle

عَنْ أَبِي هُرَيْرَةَ أَنَّ رَسُولَ اللَّهِ ﷺ قَالَ: «فُضِّلْتُ عَلَى الْأَنْبِيَاءِ بِسِتٍّ: أُعْطِيتُ جَوَامِعَ الْكَلِمِ. وَنُصِرْتُ بِالرُّعْبِ. وَأُحِلَّتْ لِيَ الْغَنَائِمُ. وَجُعِلَتْ لِيَ الْأَرْضُ طَهُوراً وَمَسْجِداً. وَأُرْسِلْتُ إِلَى الْخَلْقِ كَافَّةً. وَخُتِمَ بِيَ النَّبِيُّونَ».

From Abū Hurayrah there is that the Messenger of Allah ﷺ said: "I have been preferred over the prophets with six things: I have been given concise comprehensive speech, I have been helped by terror, the spoils were made *ḥalāl* for me, the earth has been made a means of purification for me and a place for prostration, I have been sent to all creation, and the prophets are concluded by me." (Muslim, *kitāb aṣ-ṣalāh, bāb aṣalāh fī thawb wāḥid wa ṣifah labsihā*)

A distinctive feature of Muslim warfare is that the Muslims gather the spoils of battle, and then the *amīr* takes a fifth and the other four-fifths are divided among the fighters. This was not permitted to the earlier peoples.

Terrorism

The *ḥadīth* above also makes a reference to the way that the Prophet ﷺ was helped by Allah by His casting terror into his enemies' hearts. This is, however, fundamentally, different from terrorism. The former is a distinctive feature of the prophethood of Muḥammad ﷺ because Allah, exalted is He, cast terror miraculously into his enemies' hearts, whereas terrorism derives from the French Revolution. The practices of total war, of slaughtering innocent bystanders, of murdering civilians, and of the total destruction of all habitation and property are completely unacceptable in the *Sharī^cah*. Moreover, the innovation of suicide bombing, whether in Israel or elsewhere, is completely *ḥarām* and for that there are numerous proofs, and every single evidence that has been adduced in favour of suicide bombing has been shown to be empty and false.[5]

Caliphate, Amirate, Sultanate, etc.

Allah, exalted is He, says about obedience and its three dimensions:

يَا أَيُّهَا الَّذِينَ آمَنُوا أَطِيعُوا اللَّهَ وَأَطِيعُوا الرَّسُولَ وَأُولِي الْأَمْرِ مِنكُمْ فَإِن تَنَازَعْتُمْ فِي شَيْءٍ فَرُدُّوهُ
إِلَى اللَّهِ وَالرَّسُولِ إِن كُنتُمْ تُؤْمِنُونَ بِاللَّهِ وَالْيَوْمِ الْآخِرِ ذَٰلِكَ خَيْرٌ وَأَحْسَنُ تَأْوِيلًا

> *You who have īmān! obey Allah and obey the Messenger and those in command among you. If you have a dispute about something, refer it back to Allah and the Messenger, if you have īmān in Allah and the Last Day. That is the best thing to do and gives the best result.* (Sūrat an-Nisā' 4: 59)

Al-Qurṭubī explains the above *āyah* thus:

> Since in the previous *āyah*[6] He turned to rulers and began with them and ordered them to restore things held on trust and to judge between people with justice, then in this *āyah* He turned to the subjects and first of all ordered obedience to Himself ﷻ, which is to obey His commands and to avoid His prohibitions, and then secondly obedience to His Messenger in that which he ordered and prohibited, and then thirdly obedience to *amīrs* according to the position of the dominant majority, Abū Hurayrah, Ibn ^cAbbās and others.[7]

He continues:

> Sahl ibn ^cAbdullāh at-Tustarī said, "Obey the *sulṭān*[8] in seven things: minting dirhams and dinars, measures and weights, judgements, Ḥajj, Jumu^cah, the two *^cĪds* and *jihād*."
>
> Sahl said, "When the *sulṭān* prohibits the *^cālim* from giving *fatwā* then he may not give *fatwā*, and if he does give *fatwā* then he is disobedient even if the *amīr* is a tyrant."
>
> Ibn Khuwayz Mandād said, "As for obedience to the *sulṭān*, it is

obligatory in respect of that in which he is due obedience, and it is not due to him in that in which there is disobedience to Allah. For that reason we say: it is not permissible to obey the rulers of our age nor to cooperate with them nor to honour them, but it is obligatory to go on military expeditions with them whenever they do so, and judgement comes from their verdicts, as does the appointment of *imāms* and the *ḥisbah*,[9] and that is all established according to the *Sharīᶜah*. If they lead us in prayer, and they are corrupt deviants in terms of acts of disobedience then prayer with them is acceptable, but if they are innovators prayer is not valid along with them unless one is afraid and prays with them in order to safeguard oneself, in which case the prayer is to be repeated."

Ibn Juzayy al-Kalbī said:

> [*Jihād's*] obligations are six: intention, obedience to the *imām* (ruler), not misappropriating the spoils, fulfilling one's treaties and safe conduct, remaining firm at the encounter of the two hosts, avoiding working corruption, and there is no harm in waging *jihād* along with tyrannical unjust rulers. (Al-Kalbī, Ibn Juzayy, *al-Qawānīn al-fiqhiyyah, al-kitāb as-sābi fī al-jihād, al-bāb al-awwal fī al-muqaddimāt*)

It is clear from all of the above that the *sulṭān* of the Muslims is not only someone who leads them in war, but someone upon whom devolves responsibility for many matters of the *dīn*, such as the minting of coins, etc. Thus, there is no room in our picture of the *dīn* for guerrilla warfare without the basis of an established community and leader working to bring the *Sharīᶜah* into effect, and there is certainly no basis for terrorist cells.

As we have shown, *jihād* is no less than the extra work required to bring about the practice of the *dīn* in its fullness, i.e. to put into effect the contents of this book.

Notes

[1] In another narration it is 'a word of truth'.

[2] "Ibn Ḥajar said in *Tasdīd al-qaws*, 'It is famously repeated on people's tongues, but it is from the words of Ibrāhīm ibn ᶜAylah.' I [al-ᶜAjalūnī] say that the *ḥadīth* is in the *Iḥyā'*. Al-ᶜIrāqī said, 'He narrated it with a weak *isnād* from Jābir, and al-Khaṭīb narrated it in his *Tārīkh* from Jābir with the words, "The Prophet ﷺ came back from an expedition and said ﷺ, 'You have returned in the best way, and you have returned from the lesser *jihād* to the greater *jihād*.' They said, 'What is the greater *jihād*?' He said, 'The slave's struggle with his whims and passions (*hawā*).'" (*Kashf al-khafā*, Imām al-ᶜAjalūnī)

[3] *Hawā* pl. *ahwā'* is often translated as whims and desires, whereas *shahawāt* are appetites.

[4] It is well to remember that this text is from an epoch when the Muslims were strong and unapologetic and were not trying to impress non-Muslims about how pleasant they were, so that it is an accurate reflection of practice in times of war, just as undoubtedly on some occasions male prisoners of war were executed, ransomed, enslaved, or made to pay the *jizyah*.

[5] Clarke, Abdassamad, *Examination of an article claiming to legitimise suicide bombings*: http://www.bogvaerker.dk/suicide.html.

[6] *Allah commands you to return to their owners the things you hold on trust and, when you judge between people, to judge with justice.* Sūrat an-Nisā' 4: 58

[7] Another less well held view is that this *āyah* commands obedience to the *ᶜulamā'*.

[8] The *sulṭān* is the person in authority among the Muslims.

[9] The *ḥisbah* is the institution which inspects markets, in particular

ensuring that weights and measures are correct and that there is no usury, etc.

Chapter 28

Sharīᶜah and the Future

THE ARABS HAVE A SAYING:

فَاقِدُ الشَّيْءِ لاَ يُعْطِيهِ

The person who lacks something can't give it.

For example, someone who doesn't have the *dīn* of Islam cannot give it to you.

We suggest that there is no more productive matter in this time than learning the *dīn* properly, not necesarily becoming *ᶜulamā'*, but learning precisely what is needed for this unusual age, and for the circumstances that actually face us whether individually or collectively. The trader must know the *fiqh* of trade, and each one needs to know precisely enough about monetary transactions to avoid the fatal mistake of usury and the other *ḥarām* transactions, just as the person who enters Islam needs to understand the unitary teaching (*tawḥīd*) and then must know enough of the prayer to be able to perform it correctly in its time.

A group needs to know more than that, if only to teach the rest the above matters. They will be recognised by their conforming to Imām Mālik's famous statement, which is narrated in various wordings:

الْعِلْمُ نُورٌ يَجْعَلُهُ اللهُ حَيْثُ يَشَاءُ ، لَيْسَ بِكَثْرَةِ الرِّوَايَةِ

Knowledge is a light which Allah places wherever He wishes; it is not a great deal of narration. (As-Suyūṭī, Jalāl ad-Dīn, *Manāqib Mālik*, citing al-Aṣbahānī, Abū Nuᶜaym, *Ḥilyat al-awliyā'* 6:319)

There are probably few things more barren than the cult of orthodoxy for its own sake, for its product is like the man who has the very best bred Arabian horse but doesn't ride it, or has a beautiful calligraphic copy of the Qur'ān but doesn't recite it, or a wonderful sword of the finest steel, but hangs it on his wall as a decoration, or, in the Qur'ānic simile, like a donkey loaded with books.[1]

We need scholars who are aware of the nature of the society that we actually live in, whether in the east or the west, who know its history, and the real nature of its beliefs, and its economics, but they are unlikely to learn that in any of the academic institutions of the age, since they have by and large been taken over by the state, the military, the intelligence services, finance and commerce. Few are the voices calling to the truth in that arena, except for the rare celebrity commentators who are token honest voices, whose very honesty sanctions the general dishonesty.

For the restoration of knowledge, the uneasy truth is that there is nothing that can be done, in the sense of being done by governments and the like. The matter that has been lost is the pivotal relationship that ought to exist between rulership and knowledge, which is founded entirely on the independence of the people of knowledge from the ruler, and his dependence upon them, for the ruler is only there to put the law into effect and he cannot do that without people of knowledge and integrity. Once the *ᶜālim* takes up residence in the palace (or for that matter in the committee rooms of the houses of parliament), the whole matter has been subverted, just as it has when he is made the starting point for civil war, insurrection or terrorism.

The history of the modern state, both in the east and in the west, has been its taking control of the institutions of knowledge and teaching, with disastrous consequences. British educational systems are in chaos simply because the state has seized control of them, and sidelined the people who actually teach. We may well grant that it is understandable that state functionaries should want to cling to control when, in an age they do not fully comprehend, they feel alarmed at it slipping from their grasp. Nevertheless, it has resulted in a deterioration in knowledge and teaching, and a flowering of nihilism in previously unrecognised shapes and forms, not least the suicide bomber.

In the realm of the *dīn*, the seizure by the state of the *awqāf* endowment properties which sustained students and teachers and guaranteed their independence, and the political appointment by the state of the directors of institutions of education such as the Azhar, have been a disaster which has discredited knowledge and the *ᶜulamā'* in the eyes of the increasingly radicalised young and the poor. This has contributed to the harvest of despair that we are reaping today.

The state must undo this in two ways, trusting in the benign nature of this *dīn* and its knowledgeable people: first by releasing the *awqāf* and restoring them to their original purposes, and second by leaving the *ᶜulamā'* alone, however uncomfortable what they have to say is. In this they would do well to follow the wise example of King Ḥasan II of Morocco ﷺ among whose last acts was the restoration of teaching in the Qayrawiyyin mosque, after the period of time in which it took place on a campus outside of Fez. However partial, incomplete and imperfect, it was an utterly definite step in the right direction.

The same must happen with the Azhar. The dismemberment of the Azhar by Gamāl ᶜAbd an-Nāṣir, and its being rehoused in concrete tower blocks some distance from the Azhar mosque, resulted in an institution which is the joke of the Muslim world, and from which *fatwās* issue that have no bearing on the lives of people and for which the great masses of people have little respect.

However, more serious than the condition of the once noble Azhar is the dreadful state of Madīnah University, widely misunderstood as a *salafī* institution, but in fact, a cycnically 'objective' and 'scientific' body cultivating a generation of intellectually detached and uncommitted *ᶜulamā'* whose 'objectivity' and 'detachment' are nowhere in evidence when it comes to their entrenched opposition to and undermining of the traditional practice and study of the *dīn*. The sad truth is that if nothing is done to restore the honour due to traditional *ᶜulamā'* and teachers, this institution will, in harmony with its ethos which is derived from the French Revolution, be the source of even greater trials.

The connection between *ᶜibādah* and the study of knowledge is fundamental, for even in the west the great centres of learning such as Oxford and Cambridge were always centred around places of worship.

We have, alhamdulillah, seen the first seeds of a new impulse: a generation of young people from Europe and the West have gone to Cairo, Damascus, Fez, the Sous, and the Yemen for instruction in the *dīn* and in the Arabic language, a flow that received much less publicity than the comparatively trivial numbers who went to terrorist training camps in the hills of Afghanistan. Given the disarray of the institutions and the societies they encounter, some of them are nevertheless going to be a new leadership for Islam in the west, but only if they observe certain conditions:

They must bring back the tri-fold Islam to which the *ḥadīth* of Jibril refers: Islam, Iman, and Ihsan. There is simply no more room for sterile and heart-deadening literalist Islam, which has inarguably fostered a generation of nihilists, in fulfilment of the words so widely quoted by *ᶜulamā'* from Imām Mālik:

مَنْ تَفَقَّهَ وَلَمْ يَتَصَوَّفْ فَقَدْ تَفَسَّقَ وَمَنْ تَصَوَّفَ وَلَمْ يَتَفَقَّهْ فَقَدْ تَزَنْدَقَ وَمَنْ جَمَعَ بَيْنَهُمَا فَقَدْ تَحَقَّقَ

> Whoever learns *fiqh* but does not take on *taṣawwuf* has become a deviant, and whoever takes on *taṣawwuf* and does not learn *fiqh* has become a heretic, and whoever unites the two has realisation. (*Ḥāshiyah* of al-ᶜAllāmah al-ᶜAdawī on the *Sharḥ* of az-Zurqānī on *al-ᶜIzziyyah fi'l-fiqh al-Mālikī*, but widely narrated by scholars in numerous other transmissions)

Let it not be said, however, that we are in any way encouraging the woolly new-age cult that is being called Sufism in our time. For that may well become heretical without the balance of the *Sharīᶜah*, and since the *Sharīᶜah* almost nowhere exists, the mark of the genuine Ṣūfī will be his immersion in the world in the service of the restoration of the *dīn*.

In particular, our advice to the Muslims in general, and to young students of knowledge in particular, is to come to know the *muᶜāmalāt* and in particular those pertaining to trade and commerce. There is a body of the people of knowlege who are becoming very wealthy from putting such knowledge at the service of the false discipline of Islamic banking, but for the rest this is the royal road to the recovery of the *dīn* in our time. Since the real preservation of knowledge lies in action and not only in memorisation and scholarship, then the real *fuqahā'* will be those who have a place in the world and in the marketplace, which they will have to bring about in the first place, since it can no longer be meaningfully said to exist.

The second element necessary is the relinquishment of the idea of codification of the *Sharīᶜah*. The state in its relentless growth and in its subjugating everything to its own ends, must needs codify and create uniformity in its laws. This is a part of the process of the technique culture that sees world, state and the human being each as differing types of machine, and it is this disastrous vision that lies at the heart of the very nihilism whose various manifestations are causing so much havoc in our time.

The essence of *Sharīᶜah* is the personal act of the *qāḍī* sitting to reach a decision, with all his human frailty, but drawing on the light in his heart, his *taqwā* of Allah, his yearning to meet Him with a clean record sheet and his sense of compassion for the Muslims. It is only such a being who can act out of mercy, compassion and a desire for the justice of Allah and His Messenger ﷺ, something of which the machine and mechanical people are incapable. It is Allah alone Who grants success.

Notes

[1] Sūrat al-Jumu'ah 62: 5

Conclusion

In our traversing this topic we have been accompanied throughout by the Book of Allah, the opening words of which, after the Fātiḥah, show that we can have no access to it, and thus to the *Sharīᶜah*, without being people of *taqwā*:

ذَٰلِكَ الْكِتَابُ لَا رَيْبَ فِيهِ هُدًى لِّلْمُتَّقِينَ الَّذِينَ يُؤْمِنُونَ بِالْغَيْبِ وَيُقِيمُونَ الصَّلَاةَ وَمِمَّا رَزَقْنَاهُمْ يُنفِقُونَ

That is the Book, without any doubt. It contains guidance for those who have taqwā: those who have īmān in the Unseen and establish ṣalāh and give of what We have provided for them. (Sūrat al-Baqarah 2: 2-3)

As much as this defines personal conduct, it is even more the outline of a community or society, the society of Islam. The implicit assumption of our entire book is not only the solitary individual or family striving to perfect their conduct but the existence of a community. Indeed, the *Sharīᶜah* cannot be brought into effect without the restoration of community, whether by setting out to find it, or by bringing it about oneself wherever one is.

In our setting out, it is well to be clear about the goal of our journey, lest we make the means our end. *Sharīᶜah,* as we saw, in its root meanings refers to a road leading to drinking water.

As our beginning is determined by the beginning of the Book, so our goal is determined by its end, just prior to the two sūrahs which seal it, by Sūrat al-Ikhlāṣ, the most trenchant statement of the Divine Unity, knowledge of which is the goal of our journey for Allah, exalted is He, said:

$$وَمَا خَلَقْتُ الْجِنَّ وَالْإِنْسَ إِلَّا لِيَعْبُدُونِ$$

I only created jinn and man to worship Me. (Sūrat adh-Dhāriyāt 51: 56)

The great Follower Mujāhid said about the meaning of the words *"to worship Me"* that they mean, *"To know Me (li yaʿrifūnī)."* (Al-Qurṭubī, *al-Jāmi li aḥkām al-Qur'ān*). Thus, man is created for knowledge of Allah.

Ibn Juzayy ☙ who has also accompanied us throughout our journey, both in his *tafsīr* of the Book and in his *fiqh*, deals must luminously with this matter of the Divine Unity in his commentary on the words in Sūrat al-Baqarah:

$$وَإِلَٰهُكُمْ إِلَٰهٌ وَاحِدٌ$$

Your God is One God. (Sūrat al-Baqarah 2: 162)

Know that people's *tawḥīd* of Allah has three degrees:

1. The *tawḥīd* of the generality of the Muslims which is that which preserves the person from destruction in the world and saves them from abiding in the Fire in the next life, and it is the refutation of partners and equals (أَنْدَاد), of a female partner and children, and of [other] beings who resemble [Allah], and of opposites.

2. The *tawḥīd* of the elect which is that [the person of this degree] sees all actions issuing from Allah alone, witnessing that by means of unveiling (مُكَاشَفَة), not by means of the reasoning which every Muslim attains. But the station of the elect in *tawḥīd* enriches the heart with an imperative knowledge which doesn't need proof. The fruit of this knowledge is the full devotion of attention to Allah, dependence on Him alone, and rejection of people so that he doesn't hope for any but Allah, and fears no-one other than Him, since he sees no doer but Him, and he sees all people in the grasp of overwhelming power, and that none of the matter is in their hands. So he rejects secondary causes and discards [other] lords.

3. [The person] does not see in existence any but Allah alone, so that he withdraws from looking at people until it is as if they were non-existent for him. This is what the Sufis call the station of annihilation (فَنَاء), which means becoming absent from people until he has become annihilated from his own self and from his *tawḥīd*, i.e. he withdraws from that with his absorption in witnessing Allah. (Al-Kalbī, Ibn Juzayy, *Kitāb at-tashīl li ᶜulūm at-tanzīl*)

In one way, this goal of the journey is also a beginning, a conundrum which can only be resolved in metaphor, for when the reciter finishes his recitation of the Qur'ān, he immediately begins afresh.

The book is finished on the 12th Dhi'l-Ḥijjah 1428 AH/23th December 2007 CE, and praise and thanks belong to Allah.

The Authors

Abdur Rahman I. Doi

The late Professor Abdur Rahman I. Doi, born in an Islamic environment in Himmatnagar (India) started his early education in *madrasah*. He secured his BA (Hon.) first class from the University of Bombay and was awarded a gold-medal. He passed his MA examination first-class from the same University and was awarded a gold-medal. The University of Bombay then awarded him a merit scholarship to join the University of Cambridge as a research scholar. In England he had enormous opportunities to work on Arabic and Islamic manuscripts deposited in various libraries. He obtained his PhD degree in 1964. He revived the Muslim Students' Association at the University of Cambridge which had lain dormant for many years after Sir Muhammad Iqbal's departure.

In 1965, he took up his appointment at the University of Nigeria, Nsukka, where he designed, introduced and taught the courses in Islamic studies. In 1967 he moved to the University of Ife as a research scholar in the Institute of African Studies. Later on he became Head, Department of Religious Studies and Philosophy at Ife. When the department was split into two he became the Head, Department of Religious Studies. In 1977 he was appointed Professor and Director, Centre for Islamic Legal Studies, Ahmadu Bello University, Zaria.

Professor Doi served on many Committees and Boards concerned with Islamic studies and the *Sharīʿah*. He was for a period the Editor-in-Chief of the Nigerian Journal of Islam. He was

Chairman, Editorial Board of *Sharīᶜah* Law Reports and Editorial Board Journal of Islamic and Comparative Law. He was a member of the Editorial Boards of various journals abroad including The Search: Journal on Arabic Islamic Studies, Miami (USA). He was Vice-President of the Nigerian Association for study of Religion. He was a founder member of the Colleges of Islamic Legal Studies in the various states of Nigeria. He contributed at least 100 articles to well known periodicals in Islamic studies. His books include: *Women in Sharīᶜah; Non-Muslims in Sharīᶜah; Sharīᶜah in the 15th Century Hijrah; Islam in Nigeria; Introduction to the Qur'ān; Introduction to the Hadith; The Cardinal Principles of Islam;* and *Prayers from Qur'ān and Sunnah.*

He attended a number of international conferences on Islam including The First World Conference on Muslim Education, Conference on Islamic Social Science, Riyadh.

He later lived and taught in South Africa.

Professor Abdur Rahman's academic career took him to Nigeria, Malaysia and South Africa where latterly he held a position at Rand Afrikaans University, Johannesburg. He also held the position of honorary professor at Universitas Islamica, Italy, and visiting professor to the University of Bayreuth, Germany and University of Bordeaux, France. He died in Madras in India of liver ailment, may Allah have mercy on him.

Abdassamad Clarke

Abdassamad Clarke is from Ulster and was formally educated in Mathematics and Physics in Edinburgh. He accepted Islam at the hands of Shaykh Dr. Abdalqadir as-Sufi in 1973 and later studied Arabic, *tajwīd* and other Islamic sciences in Cairo. In the 1980s he was secretary to the imam of the Dublin Mosque, and in the early 1990s *imām khaṭīb* of the Norwich Mosque, where he is currently an imām and teacher.

He has lived in Ireland, Scotland, England, Egypt, the Outer Hebrides and Denmark, and has travelled widely, particularly in Morocco and Arabic countries.

He has translated, jointly with Muḥammad ᶜAbdarraḥmān, the

Muwaṭṭa' of Imām Muḥammad by Imām Muḥammad ibn al-Ḥasan ash-Shaybānī, which was published by Turath Publishing at the end of July 2004 and a number of other works from Arabic:

al-Qawl al-muᶜtamad fī mashrūᶜiyyat adh-dhikr bi'l-ism al-mufrad by Shaykh al-ᶜAlawī on the standing in *Sharīᶜah* of using the divine name in dhikr, which was published by Diwan Press as first part of *The Two Invocations* and since republished by Madinah Press;

The *History of the Khalifahs* (the chapters on the *Khulafā' ar-Rāshidūn* from as-Suyūṭī's *Tārīkh al-Khulafā'*);

The Complete Forty Hadith (translation of Imām an-Nawawī's *Forty Hadith* along with the Imam's explanation of their *fiqh* and linquistic usages);

Kitāb al-Jāmiᶜ by Ibn Abī Zayd al-Qayrawānī (published as *A Madinan View*);

Rijāl – narrators of the Muwaṭṭa of Imām Muḥammad, all published by Ta-Ha Publishers of London;

Kitāb al-āthār by Imām Abū Ḥanīfah and transmitted by Imām Muḥammad ibn al-Ḥasan ash-Shaybānī (Turath Publishing 2006);

The Compendium of Knowledge and Wisdom (a translation of *Jāmiᶜ al-ᶜulūm wa'l-ḥikam* by Ibn Rajab al-Hanbali, published by Turath Publishing, July, 2007).

Along with Jakob Werdelin and Suád Østergaard he has completed a volume of a translation of the Qur'ān into Danish, comprising Sūrat al-Fātiḥah, Sūrat al-Baqarah and Sūrah Āl ᶜImrān, which was recently published as *Den gavmilde Qur'an: en fremlægning of de tre første suraer* by Havens Forlag of Copenhagen.

Translations yet to be published include *Traditions of the Sunnah* (*Āthār as-sunan*) by Shaykh Muḥammad ibn ᶜAlī an-Nīmawī (jointly with Maẉlānā Inᶜāmuddīn) to be published by Turath Publishing Ltd.

Among his unpublished translations are the *Sciences of Tafsir* comprising portions of Ibn Juzayy al-Kalbī's Qur'ānic commentary *at-Tashīl li ᶜulūm at-tanzīl,* in particular his introductory sections on the essential elements of the sciences necessary for *tafsīr*.

He is author of a small number of children's books, *The Year of the Elephant*, *The Great Victory* and *The Last Battle* all of which are on the *sīrah* of the Messenger of Allah ﷺ, as well as *The Story of Stories* about the Prophet Yusuf ﷺ in which he drew a great deal on the commentary of Ibn Juzayy ﷺ.

He has a poem *God is Dead* published in the Minaret journal of Stockholm, Sweden, and which has been translated into Danish, Spanish and Catalan.

He teaches both adults and children Qur'ān recitation (*tajwīd*) and meanings, Arabic language and the *dīn* in general. Most recently he has organised and taken part in a conference under the auspices of Islamic Events of London on the History of the Islamic Khalifate, and given discourses in London, Edinburgh, Dublin and the Midlands.

Bibliography

Abū Dāwūd, Sulaymān ibn al-Ash[c]ath, *as-Sunan*, edited by Kamāl Yūsuf al-Ḥūt.

Abū Ḥanīfah, *Kitāb al-āthār*, in the narration of Muḥammad ibn al-Ḥasan ash-Shaybānī, edited with a commentary by al-Multānī, Ḥāfiẓ Riyāḍ Aḥmad, Maktabah Imdadiyyah, Multan, Pakistan. Translated into English by Abdassamad Clarke and published by Turath Publishing Ltd., London, UK, 1428 AH/2007 CE.

al-[c]Asqalānī, Ibn Ḥajar, *Fatḥ al-Bārī sharḥ Ṣaḥīḥ al-Bukhārī*, edited by Muḥammad Fu'ād [c]Abd al-Bāqī, al-Maktabah as-Salafiyyah. Dar al-Hadith, Damascus, Syria.

al-[c]Aẓīmābādī, Abū aṭ-Ṭayyib, Muḥammad Shams al-Ḥaqq, *[c]Awn al-ma[c]būd sharḥ Sunan Abī Dāwūd*, Dar al-Hadith, Damascus, Syria.

al-Bukhārī, Abū [c]Abdullāh Muḥammad ibn Ismā[c]īl, *Ṣaḥīḥ al-Bukhārī*, edited by Muṣṭafā Dīb al-Baghā, digital edition from Dar al-Hadith, Damascus, Syria.

al-Jarrāḥī, Ismā[c]īl al-[c]Ajalūnī, *Kashf al-khafā*, Dar Ihya at-Turath al-Arabi, Beirut, 1351 AH. Dar al-Hadith, Damascus, Syria.

al-Juwaynī, *al-Waraqāt fī uṣūl al-fiqh*.

al-Kalbī, Muḥammad ibn Aḥmad Ibn Juzayy, *Kitāb at-tashīl li [c]ulūm at-tanzīl*, Dar al-Kitab al-Arabi, Beirut, Lebanon, 1393 AH/1973 CE.

al-Kalbī, Muḥammad ibn Aḥmad Ibn Juzayy, *al-Qawānīn al-fiqhiyyah*, Dar al-Kitab al-Arabi, Beirut, Lebanon, 1409 AH/1989 CE.

al-Kalbī, Muḥammad ibn Aḥmad Ibn Juzayy, *Taqrīb al-wuṣūl ilā [c]ilm al-uṣūl*, edition prepared by Jalāl [c]Alī al-Jihānī al-Laknawī, ᶜAbd al-Ḥayy, *at-Taᶜlīq al-mumajjad li Muwaṭṭa' al-Imām Muḥammad* edited by Dr. Taqī ad-Dīn an-Nadwī, Dār al-Qalam, Damascus, first edition 1413 AH/1991 CE. Use was also made of the text from Dar al-Hadith, Damascus, Syria.

al-Mubārakfūrī, Muḥammad ibn ᶜAbd ar-Raḥmān, *Tuḥfat al-aḥwadhī sharḥ Jāmiᶜ at-Tirmidhī.*

al-Muttaqī al-Hindī, *Kanz al-ᶜummāl,* Mu'assasah ar-Risalah, 1989 CE.

al-Mālikī al-Ḥasanī, Muḥammad ibn ᶜAlawī, *Anwār al-masālik ilā riwāyāt Muwaṭṭa' Mālik,* Doha, Qatar, Muḥarram 1400 AH.

al-Qayrawānī, Ibn Abī Zayd, *ar-Risālah* (with commentary from *ath-Thamar ad-Dānī* translated by Aisha Bewley see http://ourworld.compuserve.com/homepages/ABewley/Page17.html).

al-Qurṭubī, Muḥammad ibn Aḥmad ibn Abī Bakr Abū ᶜAbdullāh al-Anṣārī, *al-Jāmiᶜ li aḥkām al-Qur'ān,* Dar Ihya at-Turath al-Arabi, Beirut, Lebanon, 1405 AH/1985 CE.

an-Nasā'ī, Abū ᶜAbd ar-Raḥmān Aḥmad, *as-Sunan.*

an-Nawawī, *al-Arbaᶜūn an-Nawawiyyah bi sharḥihā,* (published in translation as the *Complete Forty Hadith,* translated by Abdassamad Clarke, Ta-Ha Publishers Ltd., London, UK).

an-Nawawī, Ibn Sharaf, *Ṣaḥīḥ Muslim bi sharḥ an-Nawawī,* Dar al-Hadith, Damascus, Syria.

ar-Ruᶜaynī, Muḥammad ibn Muḥammad, *Qurrat al-ᶜayn li sharḥ Waraqāt Imām al-Ḥaramayn,* edition prepared by Jalāl ᶜAlī al-Jihānī.

aṣ-Ṣāwī, Aḥmad ibn Muḥammad aṣ-Ṣāwī al-Miṣrī al-Khalwatī al-Mālikī, *al-Ḥāshiyah ᶜalā tafsīr al-Jalālayn,* Dar al-Fikr, Beirut, Lebanon 1419 AH/1998 CE

ash-Shaybānī, Muḥammad ibn al-Ḥasan, *The Muwaṭṭa' of Imām Muḥammad,* translated by Abdassamad Clarke and Muhammad 'Abd ar-Rahman, Turath Publishing Ltd., London, UK

as-Sindī, *Ḥāshiyat as-Sindī ᶜalā an-Nasā'ī,* Dar al-Hadith, Damascus, Syria.

as-Sufi, Shaykh Dr. Abdalqadir, *Root Islamic Education,* Madīnah Press, 2nd revised edition, 1993.

as-Suyūṭī, Jalāl ad-Dīn, *al-Jāmi^c aṣ-ṣaghīr,* Dar al-Hadith, Damascus, Syria.

as-Suyūṭī, Jalāl ad-Dīn, *Is^{c}āf al-Mubaṭṭa' bi rijāl al-Muwaṭṭa'*, Dār Iḥyā' al-Kutub al-^{c}Arabiyyah, Egypt.

as-Suyūṭī, Jalāl ad-Dīn, *Ziyādah al-Jāmi^c aṣ-ṣaghīr,* Dar al-Kutub al-Arabiyyah al-Kubra, Egypt.

at-Tirmidhī, *al-Jāmi^c aṣ-ṣaḥīḥ.*

Bewley, Abdalhaqq and Aisha, *The Noble Qur'an, a new rendering of its meanings in English,* Bookwork, Norwich UK, 1420 AH/1999 CE.

Bewley, Aisha, *A Glossary of Islamic Terms,* Ta-Ha, London, UK.

Dutton, Yasin, *The Origins of Islamic Law: The Qur'ān, the Muwaṭṭa', and Madīnan ^{c}Amal,* Curzon Press, Surrey, 1999.

Ibn al-Athīr, Imām Majd ad-Dīn, *an-Nihāyah fī gharīb al-ḥadīth wa'l-athar,* Cairo 1965. Text from Dar al-Hadith, Damascus, Syria.

Ibn Mājah, Abū ^{c}Abdullāh Muḥammad ibn Yazīd al-Qazwīnī, *as-Sunan,* edited by Muḥammad Fu'ād ^{c}Abd al-Bāqī, Dar Ihya at-Turath al-Arabi, Beirut, 1395 AH/1975 CE.

al-Yaḥṣubī, Qāḍī ^{c}Iyāḍ ibn Mūsā, *Tartīb al-madārik wa taqrīb al-masālik li ma^{c}rifah a^{c}lām madhhab Mālik*

Lane, E.W., *Arabic-English Lexicon,* The Islamic Texts Society, Cambridge, England, 1984.

Muslim, Abū al-Ḥusayn Muslim ibn al-Ḥajjāj, *Ṣaḥīḥ Muslim,* edited by Muḥammad Fu'ād ^{c}Abd al-Bāqī, Dar Ihya at-Turath al-Arabi, 1412 AH/1991 CE.

Mālik ibn Anas, Imām, *al-Muwaṭṭa'* in the narration of Yaḥyā ibn Yaḥyā al-Laythī, edition prepared by Muḥammad Fu'ād Abd al-Bāqī, Dar Ihya at-Turath al-Arabi, Cairo, Egypt. Translated by Aisha Bewley and Ya'qub Johnson, Madinah Press, Norwich, 1982.

Mālik ibn Anas, Imām, *bi riwāyah* al-Imām Saḥnūn ibn Sa^{c}īd at-Tanūkhī *^{c}an* al-Imām ^{c}Abd ar-Raḥmān ibn al-Qāsim, *al-Mudawwanat al-kubrā,* Dar al-Fikr, Beirut, Lebanon, 1398 AH/1978 CE

Vadillo, Umar Ibrahim, *The Esoteric Deviation in Islam,* Madinah Press, Cape Town, South Africa, 2003.